6d

D1578031

CITYGUIDE
CHICAGO

FODOR'S TRAVEL PUBLICATIONS, INC.

NEW YORK • TORONTO • LONDON • SYDNEY • AUCKLAND

WWW.FODORS.COM

1

STREETFINDER

Lake Michigan

Glencoe
Winnetka
Kenilworth
Wilmette
Evanston
Skokie

CHICAGO
Midway
Airport

N

0   4 miles
0   6 km

COUNTY

Blue
Island
Dolton
Whiting
East
Chicago
Oak
Forest
South
Holland
Calumet
City
Markham
Hammond
Gary
Hazel
Crest
Thornton
Lansing
Glenwood
Munster
Lake
Station
Flossmoor
Lynwood
Highland
PORTER
COUNTY
Matteson
Chicago
Heights
Sauk
Village
Dyer
LAKE COUNTY
Griffith
Hobart
South Chicago
Heights
New Elliott
Richton
Park
Steger
Crete
Schererville
Merrillville
ILLINOIS
INDIANA

E   F   G   H

1

2

3

4

5

6

7

8

GREATER CHICAGO

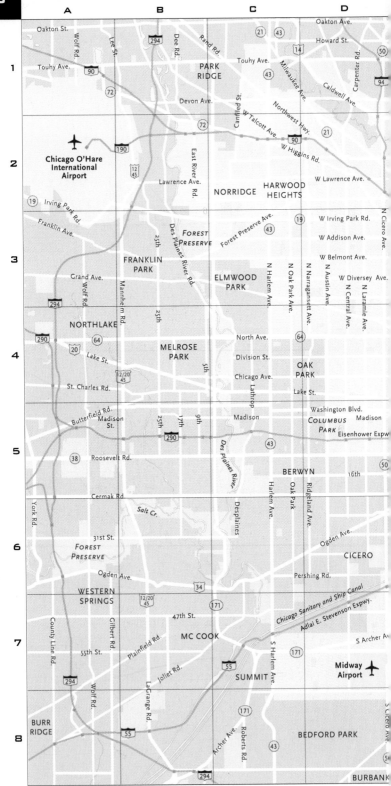

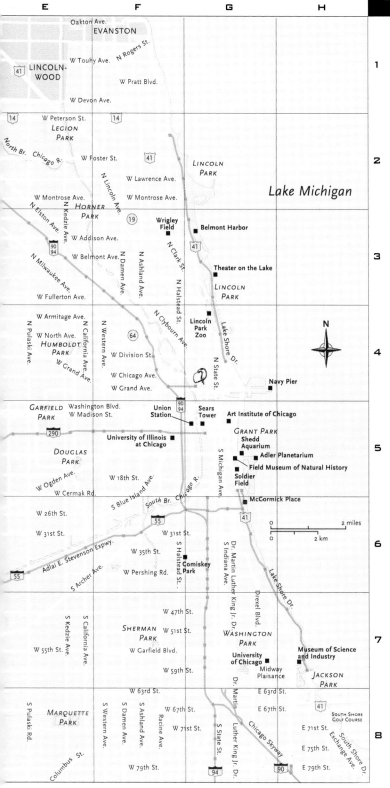

E   F   G   H

Oakton Ave.
EVANSTON

W Touhy Ave.   N Rogers St.

1

LINCOLN-
WOOD   41

W Pratt Blvd.

W Devon Ave.

14   W Peterson St.   14

LEGION
PARK

North Br. Chicago R.   W Foster St.   41

LINCOLN
PARK

2

Lake Michigan

W Lawrence Ave.
W Montrose Ave.   W Montrose Ave.

N Elston Ave.   N Kedzie Ave.   HORNER   19   Wrigley
N Milwaukee Ave.   PARK   N Lincoln Ave.   Field   Belmont Harbor

W Addison Ave.   41

90
94   W Belmont Ave.   N Damen Ave.   N Ashland Ave.   N Clark St.   3

Theater on the Lake

W Fullerton Ave.   N Halstead St.   LINCOLN
PARK

W Armitage Ave.   N Clybourn Ave.   Lincoln
N Pulaski Ave.   N California Ave.   N Western Ave.   Park
W North Ave.   HUMBOLDT   Zoo   4
PARK   64
W Grand Ave.   W Division St.   N State St.   Lake Shore Dr.

W Chicago Ave.   Navy Pier
W Grand Ave.

90
94
GARFIELD   Washington Blvd.   Union   Sears   Art Institute of Chicago
PARK   W Madison St.   Station   Tower
GRANT PARK
290   Shedd
University of Illinois   Aquarium   5
DOUGLAS   at Chicago   Adler Planetarium
PARK   S Michigan Ave.   Field Museum of Natural History
W Ogden Ave.   W 18th St.   Soldier
W Cermak Rd.   S Blue Island Ave.   Field

South Br. Chicago R.   McCormick Place
W 26th St.
55
W 31st St.   W 31st St.   41   0   2 miles
0   2 km   6
Adlai E. Stevenson Expwy.   W 35th St.   S Halstead St.   S Indiana Ave.   Dr. Martin Luther King Jr. Dr.   Lake Shore Dr.
55   S Archer Ave.   W Pershing Rd.   Comiskey
Park

W 47th St.   Drexel Blvd.
S Kedzie Ave.   S California Ave.   SHERMAN   W 51st St.   WASHINGTON
PARK   W Garfield Blvd.   PARK   Museum of Science   7
W 55th St.   University   and Industry
of Chicago
W 59th St.   Midway   JACKSON
Plaisance   PARK

Dr. Martin
W 63rd St.   E 63rd St.
S Pulaski Rd.   MARQUETTE   S Western Ave.   S Damen Ave.   S Ashland Ave.   Racine Ave.   W 67th St.   E 67th St.   41
PARK   Luther King Jr. Dr.   Chicago Skyway   SOUTH SHORE   8
W 71st St.   GOLF COURSE
S State St.   E 71st St.   S Exchange Ave.   S Shore Dr.
Columbus St.   W 79th St.   94   E 75th St.
90   E 79th St.

3

A   B   C   D

MONTROSE CEMETERY

BOHEMIAN CEMETERY

4000 W

Bernard Ave.

Catalpa Ave.

3200 W

Balmoral Ave.

1

Berwyn Ave.

N. Branch Chicago R.

ST. LUCAS CEMETERY

5200N   Foster Ave.

Foster Ave.

Pulaski Rd.

EUGENE FIELD PARK

GOMPERS PARK

Carmen Ave.

3600 W

Kimball Ave.

Kedzie Ave.

Carmen Ave.

Carmen Ave.

N. Br. Chicago R.

KIWANIS PARK

2

Kostner Ave.
Lowell Ave.
Kildare Ave.
Tripp Ave.
Keeler Ave.
Kedvale Ave.

Argyle St.

Ridgeway Ave.

Ainslie St.

ALBANY PARK

4800N

Lawrence Ave.

Leland Ave.

Karlov Ave.
Keystone Ave.
Pulaski Rd.
Harding Ave.
Springfield Ave.
Avers Ave.
Hamlin Ave.
Lawndale Ave.
Monticello Ave.
Central Park Ave.
Drake Ave.
St. Louis Ave.

Kimball Ave.

3

Elston Ave.

Kelso Ave.

Kasson Ave.

Wilson Ave.

Kostner Ave.

Keokuk Ave.

Sunnyside Ave.

Bernard Ave.

4

4400N

Lowell Ave.
Kildare Ave.
Tripp Ave.
Keeler Ave.
Kedvale Ave.

Montrose Ave.

Cullom Ave.

Elston Ave.

Berteau Ave.

90
94

Belle Plaine Ave.

5

4000N

Avondale Ave.

Irving Park Rd.

INDEPENDENCE PARK

19

Kedzie Ave.
Sawyer Ave.
Spaulding Ave.
Christiana Ave.
Kimball Ave.
Bernard Ave.

Byron St.

Byron St.

Grace St.

Kedvale Ave.

Grace St.

6

Waveland Ave.

Waveland Ave.

Elston Ave.

3600N

Addison St.

Eddy St.

Cornelia Ave.

AVON

Kostner Ave.
Lowell Ave.
Kildare Ave.
Tripp Ave.
Keeler Ave.

Karlov Ave.

Milwaukee Ave.

Roscoe St.

School St.

Hamlin Ave.
Ridgeway Ave.
Lawndale Ave.
Monticello Ave.
Central Park Ave.
Drake Ave.

Kedzie Ave.

7

3200N

Tripp Ave.

Karlov Ave.

Pulaski Rd.

Belmont Ave.

Milwaukee Ave.

Kimball Ave.

Barry Ave.

8

Kostner Ave.
Lowell Ave.

Kearsarge Ave.

Wellington Ave.

4000 W

Daylin Ct.
Haussen Ct.

Ridgeway Ave.

3600 W

0   1200 FEET

0   400 METERS

3200 W

STREETFINDER

E   F   G   H

Catalpa Ave.

2800W

Campbell Ave.

2400W

ROSEHILL CEMETERY

2000W

Virginia Ave.

Balmoral Ave.

Bowmanville Ave.

LEGION PARK

1

Summerdale Ave.

Berwyn Ave.

Berwyn Ave.

Farragut Ave.   41

Farragut Ave.

Foster Ave.

5200N

WEST RIVER PARK

EAST RIVER PARK

Washtenaw Ave.

Rockwell St.

Western Ave.

Claremont Ave.

Oakley Ave.

Leavitt St.

WINNEMAC PARK

2

RONAN PARK

California Ave.

Argyle St.

Hoyne Ave.

Damen Ave.

Winchester Ave.

Ainslie St.

Ainslie St.

Gunnison St.

Lawrence Ave.

4800N

Virginia Ave.

Leland Ave.

Leland Ave.

3

Manor Ave.

RAVENSWOOD

Wilson Ave.

Wilson Ave.

Sunnyside Ave.

Sunnyside Ave.

WELLES PARK

Montrose Ave.

Montrose Ave.

4400N

IRVING

Pensacola Ave.

4

HORNER PARK

Cullom Ave.

Cullom Ave.

PARK

Lincoln Ave.

Berteau Ave.

Maplewood Ave.

Rockwell St.

Campbell Ave.

Western Ave.

Berteau Ave.

Belle Plaine Ave.

Belle Plaine Ave.

5

Tro St.

Albany Ave.

Whipple St.

Sacramento Ave.

Richmond St.

Francisco Ave.

Mozart St.

California Ave.

Irving Park Rd.

4000N

REVERE PARK

CALIFORNIA PARK

Byron St.

NORTH

Grace St.

N

6

CENTER

Bradley Pl.

Waveland Ave.

Addison St.

3600N

Rockwell St.

Western Ave.

Hamilton Ave.

Hoyne Ave.

Seeley Ave.

Damen Ave.

Wolcott Ave.

DALE

7

Cornelia Ave.

Oakley Ave.

Bell Ave.

Claremont Ave.

Leavitt St.

Roscoe Ave.

Roscoe Ave.

Henderson St.

BRANDS PARK

School St.

Campbell Ave.

School St.

Melrose St.

Belmont Ave.

Washtenaw Ave.

Elston Ave.

Rockwell St.

Belmont Ave.

3200N

Fletcher St.

Fletcher St.

Barry Ave.

Barry Ave.

Nelson St.

HAMLIN PARK

8

2800W

Wellington Ave.

2400W

Clybourn Ave.

Wellington Ave.

Wellington Ave.

Wellington Ave.

	A	B	C	D

1

Wolcott Ave.
Catalpa Ave.
Rascher Ave.
Balmoral Ave.
Summerdale Ave.
Berwyn Ave.
Farragut Ave.
1600W
Glenwood Ave.
Wayne Ave.
Lakewood Ave.
Magnolia Ave.
1200W
Broadway
Winthrop Ave.
Kenmore Ave.
Sheridan Ave.

FOSTER AVE. BEACH
41

5200N 41 Foster Ave. 41

2

Winona St.
Carmen Ave.
Winnemac Ave.
Argyle St.
Winona St.
Argyle St.
Ainslie St.
Carmen Ave.
Margate Ter.
Castlewood Ter.
Marine Dr.
41
Ravenswood Ave.
Hermitage Ave.
Paulina St.
Ashland Ave.
Clark St.

ST. BONIFACE CEMETERY
14

Gunnison St.

3

4800N
Lawrence Ave.
CHASE PARK
Leland Ave.
Lakeside Pl.
Leland Ave.
Lawrence Dr.
Lake Shore Dr.

UPTOWN
RAVENSWOOD
Clark St.
Wilson Ave.
Wilson Ave.
Windsor Ave.
Broadway
800W
Clarendon St.
CLARENDON PARK
Sunnyside Ave.
Sunnyside Ave.
Agatite Ave.

4

4400N
Montrose Ave.
Montrose Ave.
Pensacola Ave.
Cullom Ave.
Cullom
Hazel
Hutchinson St.
Clark St.
Hutchinson St.

GRACELAND CEMETERY
Kenmore Ave.
Sheridan Ave.
Buena Ave.

Berteau Ave.
Warner Ave.
Gordon Ter.
Belle Plaine Ave.
Belle Plaine Ave.

5

Cuyler Ave.
Cuyler Ave.
Bittersweet Pl.
4000N
Irving Park Rd.
19
Dakin St.
Sheridan Rd.
Byron St.

6

Ravenswood Ave.
Hermitage Ave.
Paulina St.
Marshfield Ave.
Grace St.
Bosworth Ave.
Greenview Ave.
Janssen Ave.
Southport Ave.
Wayne Ave.
Lakewood Ave.
Magnolia Ave.
Racine Ave.
Clifton Ave.
Kenmore Ave.
Sheffield Ave.
Wilton Ave.
Fremont St.
Grace St.
Pine Grove Ave.
Broadway
Waveland Ave.
Waveland Ave.
Wrigley Field
Addison St.
3600N
Reta Ave.
Halsted Ave.

7

Eddy St.
Cornelia Ave.
Newport Ave.
Clark St.
LAKEVIEW
Roscoe Ave.
Roscoe St.
Buckingham Pl.
Ravenswood Ave.
Paulina St.
Ashland Ave.
Henderson St.
School St.
Melrose St.
Lakewood Ave.
Racine Ave.
Clifton Ave.
Seminary Ave.
Kenmore Ave.
Sheffield Ave.
Aldine Ave.
Broadway

8

3200N
Belmont Ave.
Belmont Ave.
Fletcher St.
Barry Ave.
Nelson St.
Wellington Ave.
Greenview Ave.
Southport Ave.
1600W
1200W
800W
Fletcher St.
Barry Ave.
Nelson St.
Wellington Ave.
Oakdale Ave.
Oakdale Ave.
Briar Pl.
Waterloo Ct.

STREETFINDER

E   F   G   H

1

*Lake
Michigan*

2

LINCOLN
PARK

3

Simonds Dr.

Wilson
Dr.

MONTROSE-WILSON
BEACH

Montrose Dr.

*Montrose
Harbor*

4

WAVELAND AVE.
GOLF COURSE

5

6

Sheridan Rd.

Belmont Harbor Dr.

Cornelia
Ave.
Stratford
Pl.

Hawthorne
Pl.

Roscoe St. [41]

N

7

Aldine Ave.

Melrose St.

*Belmont
Harbor*

Sheridan Rd.

Lake Shore Dr.

Briar Pl.

Barry Ave.

8

Pine
Grove
Ave.

400W

0   1200 FEET
0   400 METERS

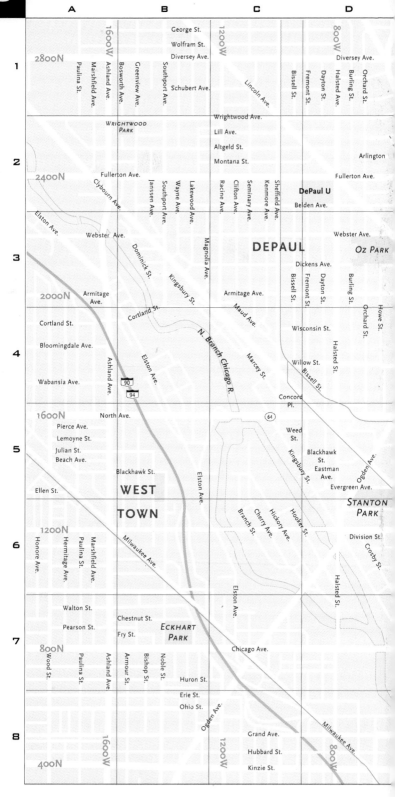

5

	A	**B**	**C**	**D**

1 2800N

George St.
Wolfram St.
Diversey Ave.

1600 W
Paulina St.
Marshfield Ave.
Ashland Ave.
Bosworth Ave.
Greenview Ave.
Southport Ave.

Schubert Ave.

1200 W

Lincoln Ave.

Bissell St.
Fremont St.
Dayton St.
Halsted St.

800 W
Burling St.
Orchard St.

Diversey Ave.

WRIGHTWOOD PARK

Wrightwood Ave.
Lill Ave.
Altgeld St.
Montana St.

Arlington

2 2400N

Fullerton Ave.

Clybourn Ave.
Janssen Ave.
Southport Ave.
Wayne Ave.
Lakewood Ave.
Racine Ave.
Clifton Ave.
Seminary Ave.
Kenmore Ave.
Sheffield Ave.

Fullerton Ave.

DePaul U
Belden Ave.

Elston Ave.

Webster Ave.

Dominick St.

Magnolia Ave.

Kingsbury St.

DEPAUL

Webster Ave.

Oz Park

3 2000N

Armitage Ave.

Dickens Ave.

Armitage Ave.

Bissell St.
Fremont St.
Dayton St.
Burling St.
Orchard St.
Howe St.

Cortland St.

Cortland St.

Maud Ave.

Wisconsin St.

4 Bloomingdale Ave.

Ashland Ave.

Elston Ave.

N. Branch Chicago R.

Marcey St.

Willow St.

Halsted St.

Bissell St.

Wabansia Ave.

90
94

Concord Pl.

5 1600N

Pierce Ave.
Lemoyne St.
Julian St.
Beach Ave.

North Ave.

64

Weed St.

Blackhawk St.

Kingsbury St.

Blackhawk St.
Eastman Ave.

Ogden Ave.

Ellen St.

Elston Ave.

Evergreen Ave.

WEST

STANTON PARK

TOWN

Branch St.
Cherry Ave.
Hickory Ave.
Hooker St.

6 1200N

Honore Ave.
Hermitage Ave.
Paulina St.
Marshfield Ave.
Paulina St.

Milwaukee Ave.

Elston Ave.

Division St.

Crosby St.

Halsted St.

7 800N

Walton St.
Pearson St.

Chestnut St.
Fry St.

ECKHART PARK

Chicago Ave.

Wood St.
Paulina St.
Ashland Ave.
Armour St.
Bishop St.
Noble St.

Huron St.

Erie St.
Ohio St.

Ogden Ave.

8 400N

1600 W

1200 W

Grand Ave.
Hubbard St.
Kinzie St.

Milwaukee Ave.

800 W

STREETFINDER

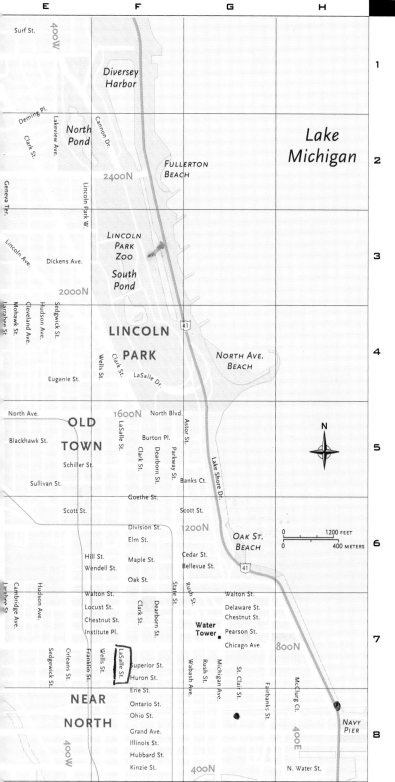

	E	F	G	H	

Surf St.

400W

Diversey
Harbor

1

Deming Pl.

Lakeview Ave.

Clark St.

North
Pond

Cannon Dr.

FULLERTON
BEACH

Lake
Michigan

2

2400N

Geneva Ter.

Lincoln Park W.

Lincoln Ave.

Dickens Ave.

LINCOLN
PARK
ZOO

South
Pond

3

2000N

Larrabee St.

Mohawk St.

Cleveland Ave.

Hudson Ave.

Sedgwick St.

Wells St.

Clark St.

LaSalle Dr.

41

LINCOLN

PARK

NORTH AVE.
BEACH

4

Eugenie St.

North Ave.

Blackhawk St.

OLD

TOWN

Schiller St.

Sullivan St.

1600N

LaSalle St.

Clark St.

Dearborn St.

Parkway St.

North Blvd.

Burton Pl.

Banks Ct.

Astor St.

Lake Shore Dr.

N

5

Scott St.

Goethe St.

Scott St.

1200N

OAK ST.
BEACH

0   1200 FEET
0   400 METERS

6

Hill St.

Wendell St.

Hudson Ave.

Cambridge Ave.

Larrabee St.

Maple St.

Oak St.

Division St.

Elm St.

Clark St.

Dearborn St.

State St.

Rush St.

Cedar St.

Bellevue St.

41

Walton St.

Locust St.

Chestnut St.

Institute Pl.

Walton St.

Delaware St.

Chestnut St.

Pearson St.

Chicago Ave.

800N

**Water
Tower**

Michigan Ave.

St. Clair St.

Fairbanks St.

McClurg Ct.

7

Sedgewick St.

Orleans St.

Franklin St.

Wells St.

LaSalle St.

Superior St.

Huron St.

Erie St.

Dearborn St.

Wabash Ave.

Rush St.

NEAR

NORTH

400W

Ontario St.

Ohio St.

Grand Ave.

Illinois St.

Hubbard St.

Kinzie St.

400N

400E

NAVY
PIER

N. Water St.

8

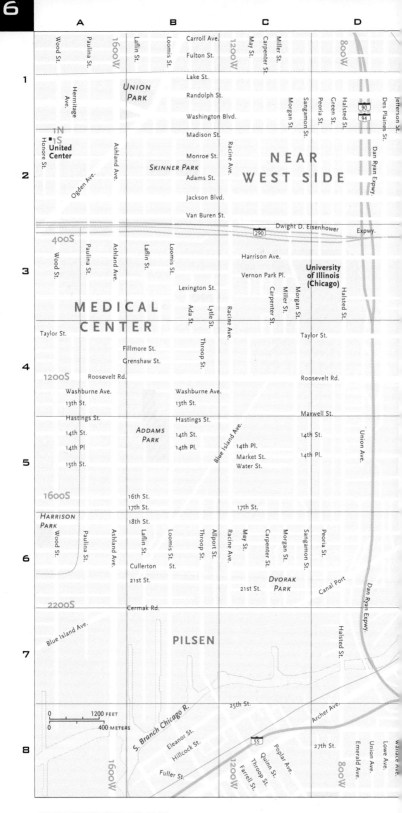

	A	B	C	D

Wood St. · Paulina St. · **1600W** · Laflin St. · Loomis St. · Carroll Ave. · Fulton St. · **1200W** · May St. · Carpenter St. · Miller St. · **800W**

Jefferson St. · Des Plaines St.

1

Hermitage Ave. · **UNION PARK** · Lake St. · Randolph St. · Washington Blvd. · Morgan St. · Sangamon St. · Peoria St. · Green St. · Halsted St. · 90 94 · Dan Ryan Expwy.

1N 1S · Honore St. · **United Center** · Ashland Ave. · Madison St. · Monroe St. · **SKINNER PARK** · Adams St. · Jackson Blvd. · Van Buren St. · Racine Ave.

N E A R W E S T S I D E

2

Ogden Ave.

Dwight D. Eisenhower Expwy. · 290

400S

Wood St. · Paulina St. · Ashland Ave. · Laflin St. · Loomis St. · Harrison Ave. · Vernon Park Pl. · Lexington St. · Carpenter St. · Miller St. · Morgan St. · Halsted St.

University of Illinois (Chicago)

3

M E D I C A L C E N T E R

Ada St. · Lytle St. · Throop St. · Racine Ave.

Taylor St. · Fillmore St. · Grenshaw St. · Taylor St.

4

1200S · Roosevelt Rd. · Roosevelt Rd.

Washburne Ave. · 13th St. · Washburne Ave. · 13th St. · Maxwell St.

Hastings St. · Hastings St. · Union Ave.

14th St. · **ADDAMS PARK** · 14th St. · 14th St.

14th Pl · 14th Pl. · 14th Pl. · 14th Pl.

Blue Island Ave. · Market St. · Water St.

5

15th St.

1600S · 16th St. · 17th St. · 17th St.

HARRISON PARK · 18th St.

Wood St. · Paulina St. · Ashland Ave. · Laflin St. · Loomis St. · Throop St. · Allport St. · Racine Ave. · May St. · Carpenter St. · Morgan St. · Sangamon St. · Peoria St.

Cullerton St.

6

21st St. · **DVORAK PARK** · 21st St. · Canal Port · Dan Ryan Expwy.

2200S · Cermak Rd.

Blue Island Ave. · Halsted St.

P I L S E N

7

25th St. · Archer Ave.

0 ____ 1200 FEET
0 ____ 400 METERS

S. Branch Chicago R. · Eleanor St. · 55 · Poplar Ave. · 27th St. · Wallace Ave. · Lowe Ave. · Union Ave. · Emerald Ave.

Hillcock St. · Quinn St. · Throop St.

8

Fuller St. · **1600W** · **1200W** · Farrell St. · **800W**

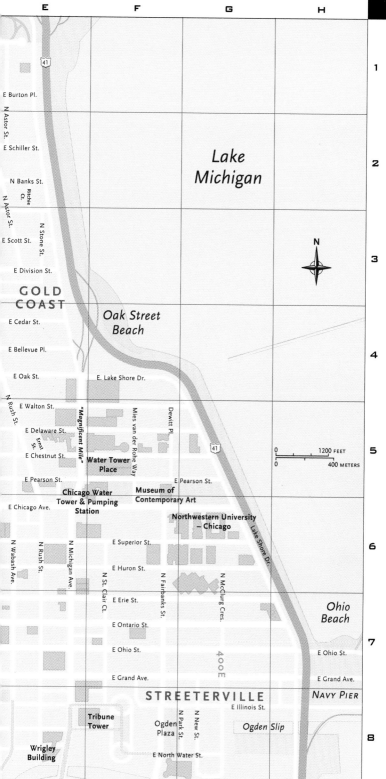

E
F
G
H

1

2

E Burton Pl.

N Astor St.

E Schiller St.

N Banks St.

Ritchie Ct.

N Astor St.

N Stone St.

E Scott St.

3

E Division St.

GOLD COAST

Lake Michigan

N

E Cedar St.

Oak Street Beach

E Bellevue Pl.

4

E Oak St.

E. Lake Shore Dr.

N Rush St.

E Walton St.

"Magnificent Mile"

Mies van der Rohe Way

Dewitt Pl.

E Delaware St.

Ernst Ct.

E Chestnut St.

Water Tower Place

41

5

0   1200 FEET
0   400 METERS

E Pearson St.

E Pearson St.

Chicago Water Tower & Pumping Station

Museum of Contemporary Art

E Chicago Ave.

Northwestern University – Chicago

N Wabash Ave.

N Rush St.

N Michigan Ave.

N St. Clair Ct.

E Superior St.

N Fairbanks St.

N McClurg Cres.

6

E Huron St.

E Erie St.

Ohio Beach

E Ontario St.

7

E Ohio St.

400 E

E Ohio St.

E Grand Ave.

E Grand Ave.

STREETERVILLE

NAVY PIER

E Illinois St.

Tribune Tower

N Park St.

N New St.

Ogden Plaza

Ogden Slip

8

Wrigley Building

E North Water St.

Lake Shore Dr.

NEAR NORTH

A B C D

1

Chicago River

W. Wacker Dr.

N Clinton St.

N Canal St.

400 W

N Post Pl.

W Haddock Pl.

W Lake St.

Thompson
State of
Illinois
Center

W Couch Pl.

W Couch
Pl.

1 E

2

Ogilvie
Transportation
Center

N Wacker Dr.

W Randolph St.

W Court
Pl.

W Court Pl.

N Clark St.

Daley
Plaza

City
Hall

N Dearborn St.

N State St.

W Washington Blvd.

Picasso
Sculpture

W Calhoun Pl.

W Calhoun Pl.

1 N
1 S

W Madison St.

W Arcade Pl.

LOOP

3

Clinton St.

Canal St.

S Wacker Dr.

S Franklin St.

S Wells St.

S LaSalle St.

W Monroe St.

W Adams St.

Union
Station

Sears
Tower

W Quincy St.

Chicago
Board of Trade

W Jackson Blvd.

4

400 S

W Van Buren St.

Harold
Washington
Library
Center

290 Dwight D. Eisenhower Expwy.

LaSalle
Street
Station

Congress Pkwy.

5

U.S. Post
Office

S. Br. Chicago River

S Wells St.

S Sherman St.

S LaSalle St.

S Clark St.

S Federal St.

S Dearborn St.

S Plymouth St.

W Harrison Ave.

W Polk St.

W Polk St.

S State St.

6

W Cabrini
St.

Dearborn
Station

W 9th St.

7

W DeKoven
St.

W Taylor St.

S 11th Pl.

1 E
1 W

W Grenshaw
St.

1200 S

W Roosevelt Rd.

W Roosevelt Rd.

8

S Clark St.

*DEARBORN
PARK II*

W Maxwell St.

STREETFINDER

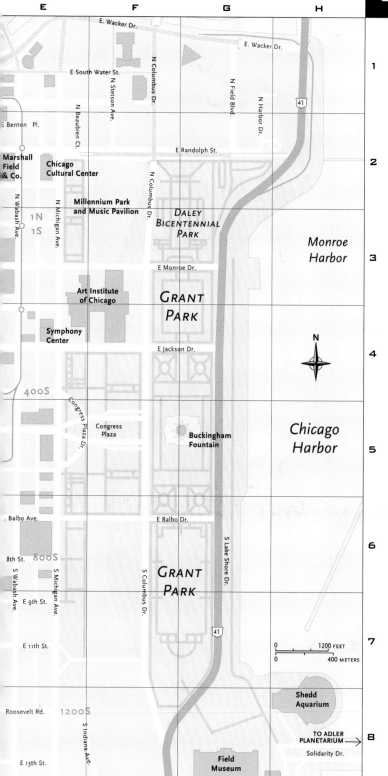

E   F   G   H

E. Wacker Dr.

E. Wacker Dr.

1

E South Water St.

N Columbus Dr.

N Stetson Ave.

N Field Blvd.

N Harbor Dr.

41

E Benton Pl.

N Beaubien Ct.

E Randolph St.

2

Marshall
Field
& Co.

Chicago
Cultural Center

Millennium Park
and Music Pavilion

N Columbus Dr.

DALEY
BICENTENNIAL
PARK

Monroe
Harbor

3

N Wabash Ave.

N Michigan Ave.

1N
1S

E Monroe Dr.

GRANT
PARK

Art Institute
of Chicago

N

4

Symphony
Center

E Jackson Dr.

400S

Congress Plaza Dr.

Congress
Plaza

Buckingham
Fountain

Chicago
Harbor

5

E Balbo Ave.

E Balbo Dr.

6

8th St.

800S

S Lake Shore Dr.

S Wabash Ave.

S Michigan Ave.

E 9th St.

S Columbus Dr.

GRANT
PARK

7

E 11th St.

41

0   1200 FEET
0   400 METERS

Shedd
Aquarium

Roosevelt Rd.

1200S

S Indiana Ave.

TO ADLER
PLANETARIUM →

8

E 13th St.

Solidarity Dr.

Field
Museum

LOOP AND GRANT PARK

BUSES

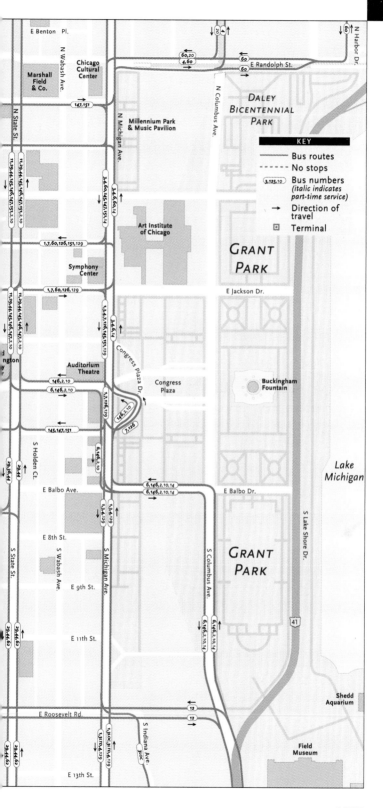

E Benton Pl.

N Wabash Ave.

Marshall Field & Co.

Chicago Cultural Center

147,151

N Michigan Ave.

Millennium Park & Music Pavilion

N Columbus Ave.

60,20
4,60

60
60

E Randolph St.

N Harbor Dr.

DALEY BICENTENNIAL PARK

KEY

— Bus routes

---- No stops

3,125,10 Bus numbers
(italic indicates part-time service)

→ Direction of travel

▣ Terminal

N State St.

11,29,44,145,146,147,151,2,10

3,4,60,145,147,151,14

Art Institute of Chicago

GRANT PARK

1,7,60,126,151,129

Symphony Center

1,7,60,126,129

E Jackson Dr.

11,29,44,145,146,147,2,10

3,4,7,126,145,146,151,129

3,4,6,14

Congress Plaza Dr.

Congress Plaza

Buckingham Fountain

Auditorium Theatre

146,2,10

6,146,2,10

146,2,10

7,126

145,147,151

6,146,2,10

29,36,44

39,44

Lake Michigan

E Balbo Ave.

6,146,2,10,14
6,146,2,10,14

E Balbo Dr.

3,4,129

E 8th St.

S Wabash Ave.

S Michigan Ave.

S State St.

E 9th St.

S Columbus Ave.

GRANT PARK

S Lake Shore Dr.

39,44,62

E 11th St.

6,146,2,10,14
6,146,2,10,14

41

Shedd Aquarium

12

E Roosevelt Rd.

12

S Indiana Ave.

39,44,62

1,3,130,4,129

130K

Field Museum

E 13th St.

BUSES

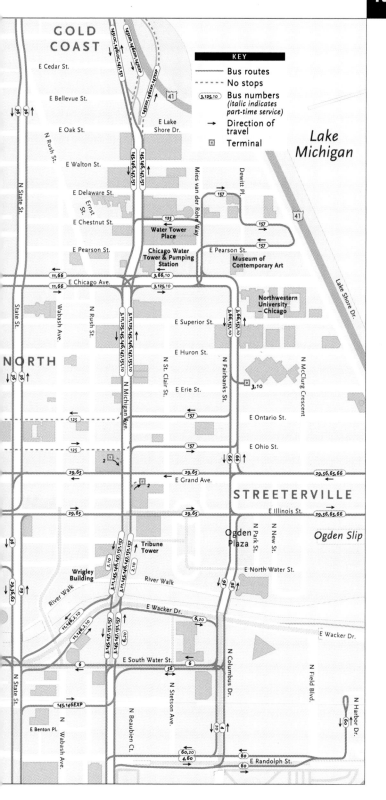

KEY

- —— Bus routes
- ----- No stops
- (3,125,10) Bus numbers (*italic indicates part-time service*)
- → Direction of travel
- ▣ Terminal

GOLD COAST

E Cedar St.

E Bellevue St.

E Oak St.

E Walton St.

E Delaware St.

E Chestnut St.

E Pearson St.

N Rush St.

Ernst St.

N State St.

E Lake Shore Dr.

Mies van der Rohe Way

Dewitt Pl.

Lake Michigan

41

157

157

157

145,146,147,151

Water Tower Place

Chicago Water Tower & Pumping Station

E Pearson St.

Museum of Contemporary Art

11,66

11,66 E Chicago Ave.

3,66,10

3,125,10

NORTH

State St.

Wabash Ave.

N Rush St.

N St. Clair St.

N Michigan Ave.

N Fairbanks St.

E Superior St.

E Huron St.

E Erie St.

Northwestern University – Chicago

N McClurg Crescent

Lake Shore Dr.

3,66,157,10

3,10

125

157

E Ontario St.

125

157

E Ohio St.

66

99

29,65

29,65

E Grand Ave.

STREETERVILLE

29,56,65,66

29,65

E Illinois St.

29,56,65,66

Ogden Plaza

N Park St.

N New St.

Ogden Slip

36

2,10

145,146,147,151,157

Tribune Tower

Wrigley Building

River Walk

E North Water St.

56

29,36,62

River Walk

11,146,2,10

E Wacker Dr.

6,20

E Wacker Dr.

145,147,151,157

E South Water St.

6

56

N Columbus Dr.

N Field Blvd.

N Stetson Ave.

N Beaubien Ct.

6

145,146 EXP

N Wabash Ave.

E Benton Pl.

20

60,20

4,60

60

N Harbor Dr.

60

E Randolph St.

60

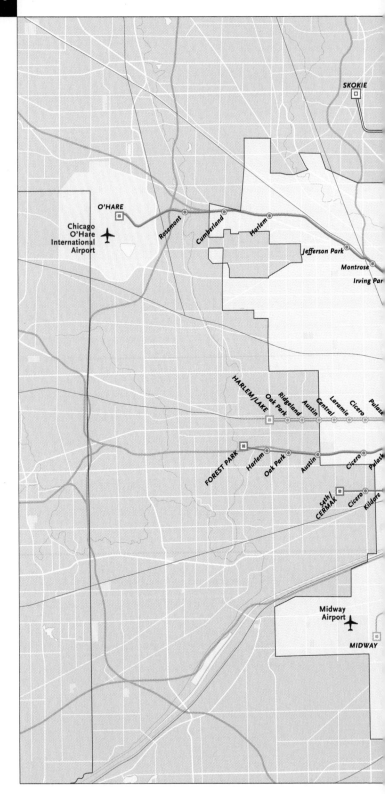

SKOKIE

O'HARE

Chicago
O'Hare
International
Airport

Rosemont

Cumberland

Harlem

Jefferson Park

Montrose

Irving Par

HARLEM/LAKE

Oak Park

Ridgeland

Austin

Central

Laramie

Cicero

Pulask

FOREST PARK

Harlem

Oak Park

Austin

Cicero

Pulask

54th/
CERMAK

Cicero

Kildre

Midway
Airport

MIDWAY

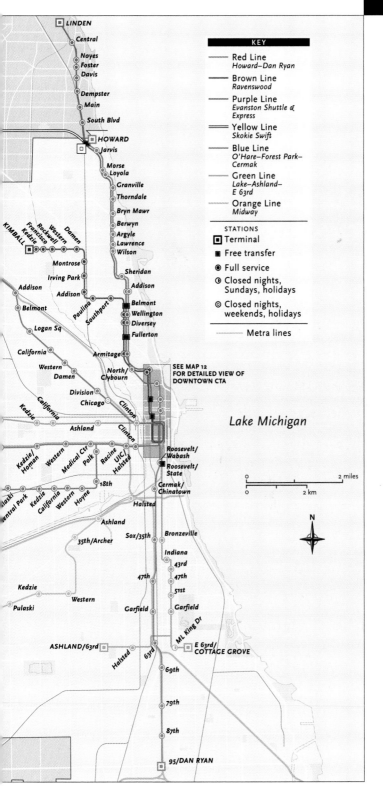

KEY	
——	Red Line *Howard–Dan Ryan*
┈┈	Brown Line *Ravenswood*
——	Purple Line *Evanston Shuttle & Express*
══	Yellow Line *Skokie Swift*
——	Blue Line *O'Hare–Forest Park–Cermak*
——	Green Line *Lake–Ashland–E 63rd*
┅┅	Orange Line *Midway*

STATIONS

▣	Terminal
■	Free transfer
◉	Full service
◑	Closed nights, Sundays, holidays
◎	Closed nights, weekends, holidays
┈┈┈	Metra lines

SEE MAP 12
FOR DETAILED VIEW OF
DOWNTOWN CTA

Lake Michigan

0 ————— 2 miles
0 ————— 2 km

N

OLD TOWN

KEY

CTA STATIONS (MULT-LINE)
Free transfer
Closed nights, Sundays, holidays
Closed nights, weekends, holidays

CTA STATIONS (SINGLE LINE)
Full service
Closed nights, Sundays, holidays
Closed nights, weekends, holidays

Metra lines

Sedgwick

N Cleveland St.
N Hudson St.
N Sedgwick St.
N Orleans St.
N Park St.
N Wieland St.
N Wells St.

W Schiller St.

W Sullivan St.

W Evergreen St.

Goethe St.

W Goethe St.

W Scott St.

N LaSalle St.

N Parkway St.

W Division St.

W Division St.

Clark/ Division

SEWARD PARK

W Elm St.

W Maple St.

W Hill St.

W Wendell St.

N Hudson Ave.

N Wells St.

W Oak St.

W Walton St.

W Locust St.

W Chestnut St.

W Institute Pl.

Newberry Library

WASHINGTON SQUARE

W Delaware St.

W Delaware St.

W Chestnut St.

Chicago

Chicago

N State St.

W Chicago Ave.

N Hudson Ave.
N Sedgwick St.
N Orleans St.
N Franklin St.

W Chicago Ave.

N LaSalle St.

Clark St.

Dearborn St.

State St.

W Superior St.

W Huron St.

RIVER NORTH

W Erie St.

N

W Ontario St.

W Ohio St.

600 feet

200 meters

Grand

N Kingsbury St.

W Grand Ave.

W Illinois St.

METRA

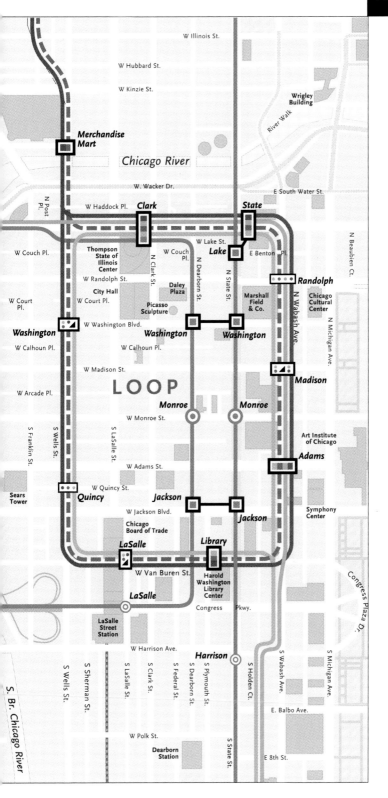

W Illinois St.

W Hubbard St.

W Kinzie St.

Wrigley
Building

Merchandise
Mart

Chicago River

River Walk

W. Wacker Dr.

E South Water St.

N Post
Pl.

W Haddock Pl.

Clark

State

W Lake St.

W Couch Pl.

Thompson
State of
Illinois
Center

W Couch
Pl.

Lake

E Benton Pl.

N Beaubien Ct.

W Randolph St.

City Hall

Daley
Plaza

Randolph

Chicago
Cultural
Center

W Court
Pl.

W Court Pl.

Picasso
Sculpture

Marshall
Field
& Co.

N Michigan Ave.

Washington

W Washington Blvd.

Washington

Washington

W Calhoun Pl.

W Calhoun Pl.

Madison

W Madison St.

LOOP

W Arcade Pl.

Monroe

Monroe

W Monroe St.

S Franklin St.

S Wells St.

S LaSalle St.

N Clark St.

N Dearborn St.

N State St.

N Wabash Ave.

Art Institute
of Chicago

Adams

W Adams St.

Quincy

W Quincy St.

Sears
Tower

Jackson

Jackson

W Jackson Blvd.

Symphony
Center

Chicago
Board of Trade

LaSalle

Library

W Van Buren St.

Harold
Washington
Library
Center

LaSalle

Congress Plaza Dr.

Congress Pkwy.

LaSalle
Street
Station

W Harrison Ave.

Harrison

S Sherman St.

S Wells St.

S LaSalle St.

S Clark St.

S Federal St.

S Plymouth St.

S Dearborn St.

S Holden Ct.

S Wabash Ave.

S Michigan Ave.

E. Balbo Ave.

W Polk St.

Dearborn
Station

S State St.

E 8th St.

S. Br. Chicago River

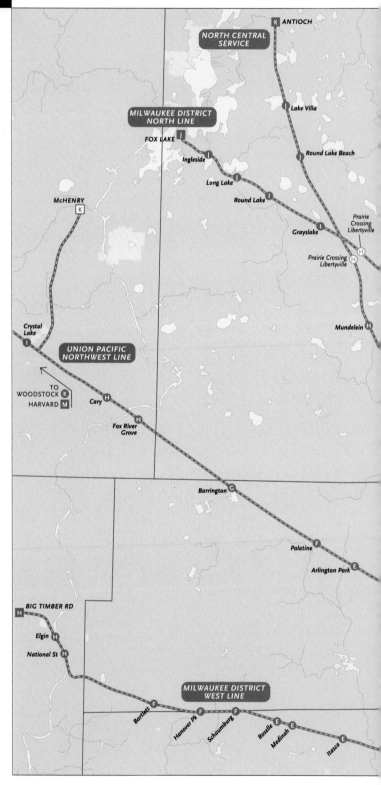

NORTH CENTRAL SERVICE

K ANTIOCH

Lake Villa

MILWAUKEE DISTRICT NORTH LINE

FOX LAKE J

Round Lake Beach

Ingleside J

Long Lake J

Round Lake J

Prairie Crossing Libertyville

McHENRY K

Grayslake J

Prairie Crossing Libertyville H

Crystal Lake J

Mundelein H

UNION PACIFIC NORTHWEST LINE

TO
WOODSTOCK K
HARVARD M

Cary H

Fox River Grove H

Barrington G

Palatine F

Arlington Park E

BIG TIMBER RD H

Elgin H

National St H

MILWAUKEE DISTRICT WEST LINE

Bartlett F

Hanover Pk F

Schaumburg F

Roselle E

Medinah E

Itasca E

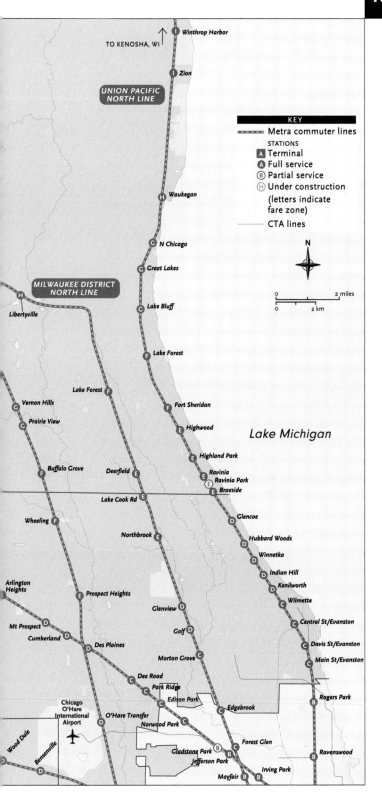

TO KENOSHA, WI

Ⓗ Winthrop Harbor

Ⓘ Zion

UNION PACIFIC NORTH LINE

KEY
Metra commuter lines
STATIONS
Ⓐ Terminal
Ⓐ Full service
Ⓑ Partial service
Ⓗ Under construction
(letters indicate
fare zone)
CTA lines

N

Ⓗ Waukegan

Ⓖ N Chicago

Ⓖ Great Lakes

MILWAUKEE DISTRICT NORTH LINE

Ⓗ Libertyville

Ⓖ Lake Bluff

0   2 miles
0   2 km

Ⓕ Lake Forest

Ⓕ Lake Forest

Ⓒ Vernon Hills

Ⓖ Prairie View

Ⓕ Fort Sheridan

Ⓔ Highwood

Lake Michigan

Ⓔ Highland Park

Ⓕ Buffalo Grove

Ⓔ Deerfield

Ⓔ Ravinia
Ⓔ Ravinia Park
Ⓔ Braeside

Lake Cook Rd

Ⓔ

Ⓓ Glencoe

Ⓕ Wheeling

Ⓔ Northbrook

Ⓓ Hubbard Woods

Ⓓ Winnetka

Ⓓ Indian Hill

Ⓓ Kenilworth

Arlington Heights

Ⓔ Prospect Heights

Ⓒ Wilmette

Ⓓ Glenview

Ⓒ Central St/Evanston

Ⓓ Mt Prospect

Ⓓ Golf

Ⓒ Davis St/Evanston

Ⓓ Cumberland

Ⓓ Des Plaines

Ⓒ Morton Grove

Ⓒ Main St/Evanston

Ⓓ Dee Road

Ⓒ Park Ridge

Chicago O'Hare International Airport

Ⓒ Edison Park

Ⓑ Rogers Park

Ⓓ O'Hare Transfer

Ⓒ Edgebrook

Ⓒ Norwood Park

Ⓓ Wood Dale

Ⓒ Forest Glen

Bensenville

Ⓑ Gladstone Park
Ⓒ

Ⓑ Ravenswood

Ⓓ

Ⓑ Jefferson Park

Ⓑ Mayfair

Ⓑ Irving Park

NORTHERN SUBURBS

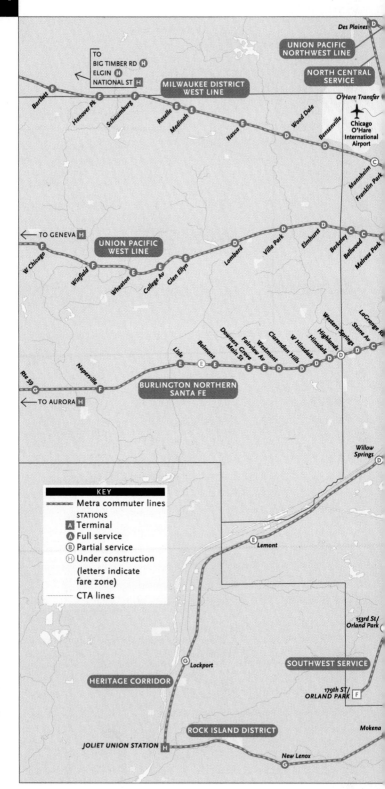

METRA

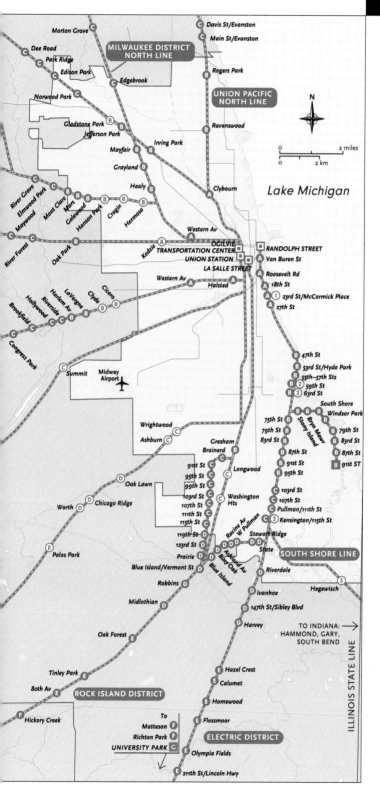

Morton Grove

Dee Road
Park Ridge
Edison Park

MILWAUKEE DISTRICT
NORTH LINE

Edgebrook

Norwood Park

Davis St/Evanston
Main St/Evanston

Rogers Park

UNION PACIFIC
NORTH LINE

N

Gladstone Park
Jefferson Park

Ravenswood

River Grove
Elmwood Park
Mont Clare
Maywood
Galewood
Hanson Park

Mayfair
Grayland

Irving Park

Healy

Cragin
Hermosa

River Forest
Oak Park

Western Av

Kedzie

Clybourn

2 miles
2 km

Lake Michigan

OGILVIE
TRANSPORTATION CENTER
UNION STATION
LA SALLE STREET

RANDOLPH STREET
Van Buren St
Roosevelt Rd

Western Av

LaVergne
Clyde
Cicero

Hollywood
Harlem Av
Riverside
Brookfield

Western Av
Halsted

18th St
23rd St/McCormick Place
27th St

Congress Park

Summit

Midway
Airport

47th St
53rd St/Hyde Park
55th–57th Sts
59th St
63rd St

South Shore
Windsor Park

Wrightwood
Ashburn

Gresham
Brainerd

75th St
79th St
83rd St

Bryn Mawr
Stony Island

79th St
83rd St

87th St

87th St

91st St
95th St

91st ST

91st St
95th St
99th St
103rd St
107th St
111th St
115th St

Longwood

Washington
Hts

103rd St
107th St
Pullman/111th St
Kensington/115th St

Oak Lawn

Worth
Chicago Ridge

Racine Av
W Pullman
Stewart Ridge

SOUTH SHORE LINE

Palos Park

119th St
123rd St
Prairie

Ashland Av
Blue Oak
Blue Island

State

Blue Island/Vermont St

Riverdale

Robbins

Midlothian

Hegewisch

Ivanhoe

TO INDIANA:
HAMMOND, GARY,
SOUTH BEND

Oak Forest

147th St/Sibley Blvd

Harvey

Tinley Park

80th Av

ROCK ISLAND DISTRICT

Hazel Crest

Calumet

Homewood

Hickory Creek

Flossmoor

To
Matteson
Richton Park
UNIVERSITY PARK

ELECTRIC DISTRICT

Olympia Fields

211th St/Lincoln Hwy

ILLINOIS STATE LINE

DRIVING AND PARKING

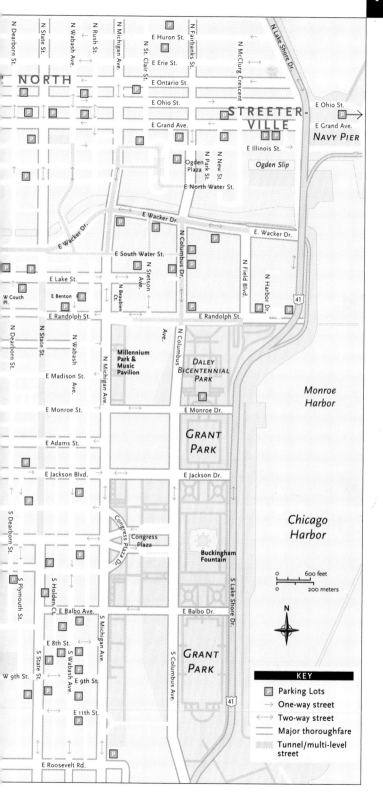

The Sourcebook
for Your
Hometown

MANY MAPS • WHERE & HOW

FIND IT ALL • NIGHT & DAY

ANTIQUES TO ZIPPERS

BARGAINS & BAUBLES

ELEGANT EDIBLES • ETHNIC EATS

STEAK HOUSES • BISTROS

DELIS • TRATTORIAS

CLASSICAL • JAZZ • COMEDY

THEATER • DANCE • CLUBS

COCKTAIL LOUNGES

COUNTRY & WESTERN • ROCK

COOL TOURS

HOUSECLEANING • CATERING

GET A LAWYER • GET A DENTIST

GET A NEW PET • GET A VET

MUSEUMS • GALLERIES

PARKS • GARDENS • POOLS

BASEBALL TO ROCK CLIMBING

FESTIVALS • EVENTS

DAY SPAS • DAY TRIPS

HOTELS • HOT LINES

GET A LAWYER • GET A DENTIST

PASSPORT PIX • TRAVEL INFO

HELICOPTER TOURS

DINERS • DELIS • PIZZERIAS

BRASSERIES • TAQUERÍAS

BOOTS • BOOKS • BUTTONS

BICYCLES • SKATES

SUITS • SHOES • HATS

RENT A TUX • RENT A COSTUME

BAKERIES • SPICE SHOPS

SOUP TO NUTS

Fodor's

CITYGUIDE
CHICAGO

FODOR'S TRAVEL PUBLICATIONS
NEW YORK • TORONTO • LONDON • SYDNEY • AUCKLAND
WWW.FODORS.COM

FODOR'S CITYGUIDE CHICAGO

EDITOR
Lauren A. Myers

EDITORIAL CONTRIBUTORS
Nuha Ansari, Suzanne Carmel, Elaine Glusac, Steve Knopper, Robin Kurzer,
Joe Pixler, Polina Shklyanoy, Lisa Skolnik, Judy Sutton Taylor

EDITORIAL PRODUCTION
Stacey Kulig

MAPS
David Lindroth Inc., *cartographer*; Bob Blake, *map editor*

DESIGN
Fabrizio La Rocca, *creative director*; Allison Saltzman, *text design*; Tigist Getachew,
cover design; Jolie Novak, *senior photo editor*; Melanie Marin, *photo editor*

PRODUCTION/MANUFACTURING
Yexenia M. Markland

COVER PHOTOGRAPH
©1996 Dominik Obertreis/Bilderberg/Aurora

COPYRIGHT

Second Edition

ISBN 0-679-00784-9

ISSN 1534-1348

SPECIAL SALES

CONTENTS

METROPOLITAN LIFE

On a bad day in a big city, the little things that go with living shoulder-to-shoulder with a few million people wear us all down. But the special pleasures of urban life have a way of keeping us around town—and thankful, even, for every second of stress. The field of daffodils in the park on a fine spring day. The perfect little black dress that you find for half price. The markets—so fabulously well stocked that you can cook any recipe without resorting to mail-order catalogs. The way you can sometimes turn a corner and discover a whole new world, so foreign you can hardly believe you're only a few miles from home. The never-ending wealth of possibilities and opportunities.

If you know where to find it all, the city cannot defeat you. With knowledge comes power. That's why Fodor's prepared this book. It will put phone numbers at your fingertips. It'll take you to new places and remind you of those you've forgotten. It's the ultimate urban companion—and, we hope, your **new best friend in the city.**

It's the **citywise shopaholic,** who always knows where to find something, no matter how obscure. We've made a concerted effort to bring hundreds of great shops to your attention, so that you'll never be at a loss, whether you need a special birthday present for a great friend or some obscure craft items to make Halloween costumes for your kids.

It's the **restaurant know-it-all,** who's full of ideas for every occasion—you know, the one who would never send you to Café de la Snub, because she knows it's always overbooked, the food is boring, and the staff is rude. In this book we'll steer you around the corner, to a perfect little place with five tables, a fireplace, and a chef on his way up.

It's a **hip barfly buddy,** who can give you advice when you need a charming nook, not too noisy, to take a friend after work. Among the dozens of bars and nightspots in this book, you're bound to find something that fits your mood.

It's the **sagest arts maven you know,** the one who always has the scoop on what's worthwhile on any given night. In these pages, you'll find dozens of concert venues and arts organizations.

It's also the **city whiz,** who knows how to get you where you're going, wherever you are.

It's the **best map guide** on the shelves, and it puts **all the city in your briefcase** or on your bookshelf.

Stick with us. We lay out all the options for your leisure time—and gently nudge you away from the duds—so that you can truly enjoy metropolitan living.

YOUR GUIDES

No one person can know it all. To help get you on track around the city, we've hand-picked a stellar group of local experts to share their wisdom.

Hotel chapter updater **Suzanne Carmel** travels all over the world while freelancing for print and Internet publications. Her articles have appeared in *Travel America*, *Zoom* (the Vanguard Airlines magazine), *DoubleDown* and *Interval* magazines, and many others. Despite the travel lure, she loves to unpack her bags in Chicago and explore her much-loved native city.

Author of the bulk of the Restaurants chapter, **Elaine Glusac** writes about food and travel for the *International Herald Tribune*, *Travel & Leisure*, *American Way*, *Southwest Spirit*, *Endless Travel*, and *Shape*. Her Chicago dining reviews appear in both the print and electronic editions of the *Chicago Tribune*.

Steve Knopper, who updated the Places to Explore and Arts, Entertainment & Nightlife chapters, met his wife in Grant Park, married her in Old Town, and lives with her in Lincoln Park. He has written for *Rolling Stone*, *Spin*, *George*, *Chicago*, and the *Chicago Tribune*. A strange fascination with mobsters notwithstanding, his specialty is pop music.

In a previous life, **Robin Kurzer** played quarterback, center, and goalie on various sports teams. In this life, she updated the Parks, Gardens & Sports chapter. In her spare time, she moonlights as an advertising copywriter and travel writer.

Joe Pixler, who revised the City Sources chapter, wrote and edited articles aimed at tourists as well as local fun-seekers while a senior contributing editor of the metromix online guide to Chicago. Currently, he's managing editor at Red Rover Digital and a freelance writer for the *Chicago Tribune* and other publications.

Polina Shklyanoy, who contributed to the Restaurants chapter, loves the food in Chicago so much, she eats every single meal there. As a Chicago native, she's got a natural feel for where to dine in the Windy City, letting the secret out as a writer for several local publications.

Shopping chapter updater **Lisa Skolnik** was born and bred in Chicago. While growing up, her weekends were spent exploring bargain basements with one of her grandmothers and scouring antiques shops with the other. She still pursues these activities, and she contributes regularly to the *Chicago Tribune*, in addition to *Metropolitan Home*, *Good Housekeeping*, and other national magazines. She has also written several books on home design.

Shopping chapter updater **Judy Sutton Taylor** is a Chicago-based freelance writer who contributes to local and national publications on retail trends. She's always on the lookout for cool new shops in the Windy City.

HOW TO USE THIS BOOK

The first thing you need to know is that everything in this book is **arranged by category and by alphabetical order** within category.

Now, before you go any further, check out the **city maps** at the front of the book. Each map has a number, in a black box at the top of the page, and grid coordinates along the top and side margins. On the text pages, nearly every listing in the book is keyed to one of these maps. Look for the map number in a small black box preceding each establishment name. The grid code follows in italics. For establishments with more than one location, additional map numbers and grid codes appear at the end of the listing. To locate a museum that's identified in the text as **7** *e-6*, turn to Map 7 and locate the address within the e-6 grid square. To locate restaurants that are nearby, simply skim the text in the restaurant chapter for listings identified as being on Map 7.

Where appropriate throughout the guide, we name the neighborhood or town in which each sight, restaurant, shop, or other destination is located. We also give you complete opening hours and admission fees for sights, and reservations, credit-card, closing hours, and price information for restaurants.

At the end of the book, in addition to an **alphabetical index,** you'll find **directories of shops and restaurants by neighborhood.**

Chapter 7, City Sources, lists essential information, such as entertainment hot lines (for those times when you can't lay your hands on a newspaper), and resources for residents—everything from vet and lawyer-referral services to caterers worth calling.

We've worked hard to make sure that all of the information we give you is accurate at press time. Still, time brings changes, so always confirm information when it matters—especially if you're making a detour.

Feel free to drop us a line. Were the restaurants we recommended as described? Did you find a wonderful shop you'd like to share? If you have complaints, we'll look into them and revise our entries in the next edition when the facts warrant. So send us your feedback. Either e-mail us at editors@fodors.com (specifying *Fodor's CITYGUIDE Chicago* on the subject line), or write to the *Fodor's CITYGUIDE Chicago* editor at Fodor's, 280 Park Ave., New York, NY 10017. We look forward to hearing from you.

Karen Cure

Karen Cure
Editorial Director

chapter 1

RESTAURANTS

E ver since Carl Sandburg called Chicago "Hog Butcher for the World," the City of Big Shoulders has shouldered a meat-and-potatoes reputation. The kernel of truth in the stereotype is that Chicago supports umpteen more steak houses than vegan cafés. And several wheat-stacker (a phrase from Sandburg's poem "Chicago") worthy dishes were developed here, including deep-dish pizza and grilled hot dogs.

But since 1916, when Sandburg wrote his apt, epic ode to the city, a new wave of immigrants has supplanted the Irish, Swedes, and Germans of old. A patchwork of ethnic neighborhoods in Chicago creates a crazy quilt of cuisines, including homeland-hearty Polish along Milwaukee Avenue, fiery Mexican that spices up 18th Street, aromatic Indian that perfumes Devon Avenue, and a Chinese–Korean–Middle Eastern stew that simmers on Lawrence Avenue. Chicago eats along historic boundaries, too: Scandinavian and German on the North Side, soul on the South. And right in the center—in the Loop, in River North, in the Gold Coast—is a sophisticated streak, supporting award-winning upscale ethnics, from bodegas to brasseries, and contemporary kitchens that excel at leavening regional American recipes or expanding our worldview by reaching out to Asia.

The meaty rap, it seems, has gone the way of the stockyards.

general information

RESERVATIONS

On weekends and for hot restaurants downtown, reservations are a must. Reviews here note when they are essential or not accepted. Fortunately for the plan-averse, reservations can often be secured the day before and sometimes the same day, though the trendier the restaurant, the more in advance the better. Early walk-ins are usually seated; many restaurants only reserve half their tables, leaving a good portion open to walk-ins. Neighborhood eateries require a lot less strategy to secure a table, though there, too, you may be required to wait on weekends.

TIPPING

Standard tipping ranges from 15% at most restaurants up to 20% in the high-price establishments. Doubling the tax—8.5% in most parts of town—is good shorthand for roughly figuring the amount.

PRICE CATEGORIES

Restaurant price categories are based on the average cost of a dinner that includes appetizer, entrée, and dessert.

CATEGORY	COST*
$$$$	over $45
$$$	$30–$45
$$	$18–$30
$	under $18

*per person, excluding drinks, service, and sales tax (8.5%)

restaurants by cuisine

AFRICAN

4 d-5

OFIE

The West African decorations and batik paintings point to the restaurateurs' heritage, as does the restaurant's name, the African word for "home." Akara (fried black-eyed peas) and kelwele (fried plantains) are a good start. Most of the entrées can be eaten with the hands, especially the signature fufu dishes; fufu looks like mashed potatoes, but it's made from yams or plantains and is usually mashed up to form a spoon for eating fish, meat, or oxtail stews. You can order any degree of spiciness, and if you overextend yourself, a little palm wine made from palm trees is a good way to cool down. *3911 N. Sheridan Rd., near Irving Park Rd., Wrigleyville, 773/ 248–6490. AE, D, DC, MC, V. Closed Sun. No lunch. $$*

AMERICAN

5 *d-5*

GOOSE ISLAND

Chicago's first and arguably its best microbrewer—certainly its most successful—serves suds in a warren of woody rooms. Stick to simple sandwiches and burgers. The free homemade potato chips warrant a second beer, if not a special trip. *1800 N. Clybourn Ave., near North Ave., Lincoln Park, 312/915–0071. AE, D, DC, MC, V. $$–$$$*

4 *c-6*

3535 Clark St., at Addison St., Wrigleyville, 773/832–9040.

6 *d-1*

GRACE

A Randolph Street trendy, Grace distinguishes itself from its too-cool neighbors by not attempting to intimidate. The warmly lit, brick-walled restaurant showcases chef Ted Cizma's love affair with wildlife. The game-heavy menu touts all manner of beast from blackberry-stuffed venison to herb-crusted boar, though fish and salads satisfy tamer tastes. As at Cizma, the vibe is stylish but friendly. *623 W. Randolph St., between Jefferson and DesPlaines Sts., West Loop, 312/928– 9200. AE, D, DC, MC, V. Closed Sun. No lunch Sat. $$–$$$*

7 *c-7*

HUDSON CLUB

The traders and office escapees who crowd three deep at the bar come more for cocktails than cuisine. The city's best purveyor of wines by the glass, Hudson Club pours 100. The visually entertaining, Jordan Moser–designed cavernous dining room takes off on the theme of streamlined airplanes, providing a respite from the singles scene. Dine on pork tenderloin or lamb loin and you won't miss your seat at the bar. *504 N. Wells St., at Grand Ave., River North, 312/467–1947. AE, D, DC, MC, V. Closed Sun. No lunch. $$–$$$*

2 *h-7*

VALOIS

A cross-section of Chicagoans—from aldermen to garbagemen to student spendthrifts—crowds around the orange Formica tables. Following the slogan "See Your Food," cafeteria diners view the stick-to-your-ribs fare—such as spaghetti, New York strip, or Florida grouper, plus numerous sides like macaroni and cheese and mashed potatoes— before choosing it with the aid of cheerful cooks. This Chicago institution is worth its pennies in people-watching. *1518 E. 53rd St., at Lake Park Ave., Hyde Park, 773/667–0647. No credit cards. $*

2 *f-4*

ZOOM KITCHEN

A contemporary cafeteria, it does American staples in an arty interior. Jocular servers dish up field greens, homemade soups, and carved sandwiches of turkey and roast beef slathered with nouveau relishes à la chipotle mayonnaise and cilantro pesto. Heartier appetites will appreciate the meat loaf or sirloin steak accompanied by sides like rye bread stuffing or spicy mac and cheese. Zoom caters to area shopkeepers and pantry-poor commuters. *1646 N. Damen Ave., near North Ave., Bucktown, 773/278– 7000. AE, MC, V. BYOB. $*

4 *d-8*

620 W. Belmont Ave., near Broadway, Lakeview, 773/325–1400.

7 *e-5*

923 N. Rush St., near Walton St., Magnificent Mile, 312/440–3500.

AMERICAN/CASUAL

7 *e-6*

AMERICAN GIRL PLACE CAFÉ

If hordes of little girls with look-a-like dolls don't scare you, make reservations months in advance for the prix-fixe tasting menu. Mothers and daughters fight for spots near the window overlooking Chicago Avenue during the lunch, tea, and dinner seatings. There are kid classics like "Tic Tac Toe" pizza with pepperoni "O" and green-pepper "X," plus sweets named after characters from the American Girl books, such as Addy's Peanut Butter and Preserves Stars or Samantha's Petite Fours. A harpist plays at teatime. Menu offerings change monthly, so call in advance. *111 E. Chicago Ave., near Rush St., Magnificent Mile, 877/247–5223. Reservations essential. AE, D, DC, MC, V. $*

8 *d-2*
ATWOOD CAFÉ
It caters to everyone, and everyone comes here in droves. Without reservations, pre- and post-theatergoers are out of luck: the 80-seat eatery fills up quickly, and the nine-table lounge is always buzzing. Good old American comfort foods are the staples here—pork chops, burgers, and potpies, but with an updated twist. There's a formal tea every afternoon, including a host of decadent desserts. *Hotel Burnham, 1 W. Washington St., near State St., Loop, 312/ 368–1900. Reservations essential. AE, D, DC, MC, V. $$$*

7 *e-7*
BANDERA
Start with a raspberry lemonade and look through the wall of windows at the shoppers down below. Then get ready to order. The fare includes a grilled steak sandwich with arugula served with mashed potatoes, and the signature spit-roasted chicken or lamb. The homemade ice cream sandwich makes a perfect ending. *535 N. Michigan Ave., near Ohio St., Magnificent Mile, 312/644–3524. AE, DC, V. $$*

7 *b-6*
BAR LOUIE
Bar Louie's formula—a casual joint with better-than-average bar food and muraled and mosaic-tiled looks—proved so successful in its original River North location that duplicates have proliferated across town. Reasonably priced Italian sandwiches, calamari, and generous martinis draw legions of twentysomethings to Louie for both food and flirtation. *226 W. Chicago Ave., at Franklin St., River North, 312/337–3313. AE, D, DC, MC, V. $*

2 *f-4*
1704 N. Damen Ave., near North Ave., Bucktown, 773/645–7500.

4 *c-7*
3545 N. Clark St., near Addison St., Wrigleyville, 773/296–2500.

6 *d-1*
123 N. Halsted St., near Randolph St., West Loop, 312/207–0500.

5 *e-4*
1800 N. Lincoln Ave., at Wells St., Lincoln Park, 312/337–9800.

7 *e-8*
BILLY GOAT TAVERN
Years after John Belushi made them famous on *Saturday Night Live*, the Goat's short-order cooks still chirp, "No Coke! Pepsi!" and "No fries! Chips!" The city's favorite hole-in-the-wall, a lower Michigan Avenue bar and "cheezboiger" joint, is big with reporters from both the *Trib* and *Sun-Times* as well as assorted desk jockeys and tourists. Grab an Old Style and "Butt in any time," as they say at the tavern, for some great late-night goofing. *430 N. Michigan Ave., lower level, at Illinois St., Magnificent Mile, 312/ 222–1525. Reservations not accepted. No credit cards. $*

2 *f-4*
BITE CAFÉ
A slacker's delight, this place serves the same set that patronizes the fringe-hip music club Empty Bottle next door. Sandwiches and pastas are cheap, cheap, cheap, and daily dinner specials rarely top $10. Though you don't go for the decor, funky fellow diners create a lively tableau all their own. *1039 N. Western Ave., between Thomas and Cortez Sts., Bucktown, 773/395–2483. MC, V. $*

5 *d-4*
BLACK DUCK TAVERN & GRILLE
This handsome corner bar-restaurant has American staples like Ritz crackers and cheese, steak, and giant martinis and a largely yuppie Lincoln Park clientele. Golf clubs and rowing oars on the walls speak to a country clubber's version of the outdoors. Proximity to Steppenwolf Theater makes this a nice nosh spot before curtain. *1800 N. Halsted St., at Willow St. north of North Ave., Lincoln Park, 312/664–1801. AE, D, DC, MC, V. No lunch. $$*

7 *f-7*
BOSTON BLACKIE'S
As soon as you enter this Cheers-with-food, dark-wood pub, you feel like everybody knows your name. Sip from frosted mugs of ice-cold beer, watch the game, and relax. Huge half-pound burgers require a two-fisted respect. If burgers aren't your thing, you can try the Garbage Salad, filled with every manner of leafy green and vegetable you can think of. *164 E. Grand Ave., near St. Clair St., Streeterville, 312/938–8700. AE, D, DC, V. $$*

5 b-8

BREAKFAST CLUB

The well-out-of-the-way Breakfast Club serves AM standards worth cruising around the area's warehouses to locate. The cottage turned commercial kitchen turns out omelets, French toast, and frittatas to the universal acclaim of local blue collars and emigrating hipsters who file in on the much-crowded weekends. *1381 W. Hubbard St., at Noble St., West Loop, 312/666–3166. AE. $*

5 b-3

CHARLIE'S ALE HOUSE

The handsome dark-wood bar elevates the tavern from just-another-corner-boîte status. Though the food fails to equal the setting, features are filling and various, with fish specials and Caesar salads alongside meat loaf, chicken pot-pie, and hamburgers. Limited seating expands greatly in summer when the tavern's lovely ivy-walled patio opens. *1224 W. Webster Ave., at Magnolia Ave., Lincoln Park, 773/871–1440. AE, D, DC, MC, V. $*

5 h-8

600 E. Grand Ave., Navy Pier, 312/595–1440.

7 e-6

CHICAGO FLAT SAMMIES

Shoppers and tourists crowd this place at lunch for flat-bread sandwiches, pizza, soup, and cookies generously portioned and uniformly fresh, served cafeteria-style. Lettuce Entertain You reliable, Sammies has the added attraction of inhabiting the Pumping Station, a sister of the Water Tower across the avenue; both buildings survived Chicago's Great Fire. Muffins and coffee make up the breakfast fare. *811 N. Michigan Ave., between Chicago Ave. and Pearson St., Magnificent Mile, 312/664–2733. AE, D, DC, MC, V. $*

4 b-1

DELLWOOD PICKLE

This Andersonville staple serves ably when local cupboards run dry. Pasta is the central focus of the eclectic menu which also includes seafood and more adventurous New Orleans shepherd's pie. The small, funky space, which encourages patrons to draw on the tabletop butcher paper by hanging the best on the walls, still maintains its outsider appeal despite area gentrification.

1475 W. Balmoral Ave., at Clark St., Andersonville, 773/271–7728. AE, D, DC, MC, V. Closed Mon. $

7 g-8

DICK'S LAST RESORT

Dinner at Dick's is like a late-night adolescent romp. You can eat with your hands, see bras hanging over the bar, and throw food on the floor, all the while listening to the tunes of Dixieland jazz or a gospel choir. Long picnic tables in the 500-seat dining room are usually crammed with a good-mood bunch, eating everything from ribs to shrimp out of metal pails. In nice weather you can eat outside along the river, or just stay in and watch two huge televisions, usually showing the big game of the day. *435 E. Illinois St., near McClurg Ct., Streeterville, 312/836–7870. AE, D, DC, V. $$*

7 c-7

ED DEBEVIC'S

Tourists and teenagers pack this retro '50s diner, where sass is a staple side dish. Gum-snapping servers in period

---

SPLENDID BRUNCHES

For a super start to Sunday, stop in at one of these spots:

Erwin (American)
  Perhaps the city's best brunch (try the daily coffeecake) in a pleasant, wood-floored room.

Brett's (American)
  Top baked goods and Southwest-inflected eggs generate lines.

Signature Room at the 95th (Contemporary)
  Best meal to savor atop the Hancock with all of Chicago at your feet.

Atwood Café (American)
  This whimsical café is best appreciated in daylight, serving delicious coffee-toast-egg fare.

House of Blues (Cajun/Creole)
  Gospel Brunch features a live choir jamming with your meal.

Ann Sather (Scandinavian)
  Queue up with the crowds for fab cinnamon rolls and Swedish starters.

Wishbone (Southern)
  Savory eats in an art-filled setting glean a far-and-wide following.

costume give you a hard time when they're not jitterbugging on the bar. Hamburgers, hot dogs, sandwiches, and shakes are the customary big sellers, but there's also Americana of a heartier variety—i.e., meat loaf, pot roast, and chicken potpie. Only the most jaded won't be amused. Unlike a real 1950s diner, Ed's serves liquor. *640 N. Wells St., at Ontario St., River North, 312/664–1707. Reservations not accepted. AE, DC, MC, V. $*

7 *g-7*
ELAINE'S
Breakfast is the big draw at Elaine's, a bright, clean Streeterville café. Fluffy three-egg omelets and rich, vanilla-scented French toast are popular in the morning. Lunch offers fresh renditions of modern midday classics like Caesar salad, cheese ravioli, curried chicken salad, pasta frittata, and fish specials. A bakery case vends muffins, cookies, and other assorted goodies to go. There are plenty of outdoor tables in summer. *448 E. Ontario St., near Lake Shore Dr., Streeterville, 312/337–6700. AE, D, DC, MC, V. $*

8 *c-2*
ENCORE
Coming here after a show is like seeing a show in itself. Right next door to the Cadillac Palace Theater, it has a pre- and post-theater crowd that nibbles on updated bar food like deviled crabcakes. Those in the know jostle for drinks at the sumptuous bar, ordering such specialty martinis as the Midnight in Chicago (Kettle One citrus vodka, Cointreau, and Chambord liqueur). There's also a full lunch menu during the day for those who find cubicle life theater enough. *171 W. Randolph St., near Wells St., Loop, 312/338–3788. AE, D, DC, MC, V. Closed Sun. $$*

7 *b-6*
GREEN DOOR TAVERN
Office lunch breakers, tourists, and recent college grads keep the Green Door revolving. Built just one year after the famous 1871 fire, the historic wood frame building leans perceptibly, adding to its ramshackle allure. Loads of memorabilia keep diners occupied while noshing on standard pub grub including burgers and chili. Given the atmosphere, it's a great place to have a beer and a nosh. *678 N. Orleans St., at Huron*

St., River North, 312/664–5496. AE, D, MC, V. Closed Sun. $

4 *b-8*
HARMONY GRILL
Run by the neighboring rock-folk club Schuba's, this spot gets its share of musicians along with Lakeview locals for quite-good sandwiches, burgers, and mac and cheese. Service is laid-back and lines can form on weekends. But Harmony keeps its considerable cool even when baby strollers crowd the aisles. *3159 N. Southport Ave., at Belmont Ave., Lakeview, 773/525–2528. AE, D, DC, MC, V. $*

6 *d-2*
JAK'S TAP
In the midst of an ethnic food enclave, this completely American bar and grill offers down-home grub like burgers and sandwiches and a wide selection of specialty beers and microbrews. The pool tables and televisions (often tuned to sports) at Jak's provide entertainment, as does a modest schedule of live blues and jazz. Weekends start early here: late hours begin Thursday night. *901 W. Jackson Blvd., near Peoria St., Greektown, 312/666–1700. No credit cards. $$*

5 *c-3*
JOHN'S PLACE
A superpopular Lincoln Parker, John's cooks up comfort food with an organic bent better than most. The whole-foods philosophy plays big in this neighborhood of young families that pile into John's, along with DePaul denizens, for creative sandwiches at lunch and more ambitious tuna steaks for dinner. *1202 W. Webster Ave., at Racine Ave., Lincoln Park, 773/525–6670. AE, D, DC, MC, V. Closed Mon. $*

3 *h-7*
KITSCH'N ON ROSCOE
Vintage Formica tables topped with '60s toasters turned napkin holders crowd this itty-bitty witty diner. A '70s sound track and memorabilia in the form of Mr. Potato Heads and Partridge Family lunch boxes provide amusement. Novelty menu items—Pop Tart Sundae, anyone?—accompany short-order hits like spinach pesto scrambled eggs (making them "green eggs"), *chilaquiles* (corn tortillas in tomato and chili sauce), and homemade sweet-potato chips. *2005 W. Roscoe Ave., at Damen Ave., Roscoe Vil-*

lage, 773/248–7372. AE, MC, V. Closed
Mon. No lunch Fri.–Sat. $

8 a-4
LOU MITCHELL'S
Since 1923 Lou Mitchell's has been serving high-fat breakfasts to legions of
fans. Don't ask for Egg Beaters here;
instead, there's whipped butter, real
cream for the coffee, and double yolk
eggs to up the calorie and cholesterol
ingestion. Don't miss the homemade
hash browns, served in a skillet. The
staff doles out doughnut holes and Milk
Duds to keep waiting patrons happy.
Although waits are common, tables turn
quickly. 565 W. Jackson Blvd., near Jefferson St., West Loop, 312/939–3111. No
credit cards. No dinner. $

5 c-1
THE LUCKY STRIKE
Though the barflies who crowd this
place consider its food an alcohol-sop
only, the kitchen does an admirable job
with sandwiches and burgers showing
flare. Not perhaps what you'd expect
from a neo-vintage bowling alley, but the
Strike has style to spare. There's a
decent selection of wines and microbrews. 2747 N. Lincoln Ave., at Diversey
Ave., Lakeview, 773/549–2695. AE, D, DC,
MC, V. No lunch weekdays. $

2 f-4
MARGIE'S CANDIES
A true Chicago gem, Margie's Candies
is a throwback to old-fashioned soda
fountains serving tuna on white bread
but distinguishing themselves with
dessert. White aproned-waitresses dish
out enormous sundaes served in giant-
clam-shape bowls to patrons happily
stuffed into its aging black vinyl booths.
A dusty collection of dolls for sale and
candy boxes occupies the rest of the
available space. Unless it's February,
expect to wait. 1960 N. Western Ave., at
Armitage Ave., Bucktown, 773/384–1035.
AE, MC, V. $

2 f-2
MOODY'S PUB
For burgers with atmosphere, it has no
match. Allow your eyes to adjust to the
candle glow inside the pitch-dark tavern
before navigating its warren of wood
tables. Burgers are king on the limited
menu. In season the brick-walled, two-
tiered, tree-shaded patio provides some
of the city's best outdoor seats. Despite

its convincing pub character, the beer
selection is slim, a matter of little
import to Moody's legions of lovers.
5910 N. Broadway, near Hollywood Ave.,
Uptown, 773/275–2696. No credit cards. $

5 f-4
NOOKIE'S
A staple diner with the breakfast and
post-bar-hours munchie crowds,
Nookie's does an able job with eggs as
you like them. Regulars return for the
wallet-friendly prices and the no-rush-
when-there's-no-wait attitude of servers.
1746 N. Wells St., north of North Ave.,
Lincoln Park, 312/337–2454. No credit
cards. $

5 d-3
Nookie's Too, 2112 N. Halsted St., at
Armitage Ave., 773/327–1400.

4 d-7
Nookie's Three, 3334 N. Halsted St., at
Buckingham Pl., 773/248–9888.

2 f-4
NORTHSIDE CAFÉ
There's a lot to be said for location—
near the Damen-North-Milwaukee intersection—ensuring the café's success.
It's certainly not the ordinary food: bar
staples with some upscale spins like
grilled tuna steak on pita. But the hip
groove provided by pierced servers,
alternative sound tracks, and a generous
outdoor patio (glassed-in in winter)
makes the Northside feel a little less like
Lincoln Park. 1635 N. Damen Ave., at
North Ave., Bucktown, 773/384–3555. AE,
D, DC, MC, V. $

5 g-6
ORIGINAL PANCAKE HOUSE
This starch-and-syrup specialist has fans
lined up and down the block regularly
on weekends. Devotees tout the apple
flapjacks and waffles as the day's best
starters. Bring the Sunday paper to bide
the inevitable wait. 22 E. Bellevue St., at
Rush and State Sts., Gold Coast, 312/642–
7917. No credit cards. $

4 a-1
PAULINE'S
A classic corner diner tucked away on
the fringe of Andersonville, Pauline's is
as casual as they come with specials on
the blackboard and board games on the
tables. Despite the red-vinyl retro trap-
pings the place stays unaffected, a

favorite of local loyalists for eggs (served all day), burgers, and sandwiches. *1754 W. Balmoral Ave., at Ravenswood Ave., Andersonville, 773/561–8573. No credit cards. No dinner. $*

7 *d-3*
PJ CLARKE'S
A Lettuce Entertain You restaurant that doesn't scream theme, PJ's serves very good pub grub that ranges from traditional burgers and fries to contemporary chicken Caesar salads. Its mini-hamburgers are a big hit for a light bite. The tavern draws its share of Division Street bar-hoppers, but the dinner hour is quite safe from that set. *1204 N. State Pkwy., at Division St., Gold Coast, 312/664–1650. AE, D, DC, MC, V. $$*

5 *d-3*
POTBELLY SUBS
Long Chicago's best hero fixer, this eatery is quickly replicating around town. The original Lincoln Park locale, popular with area university and hospital folk, moves the considerable lines along swiftly, preparing subs to order with top-flight ingredients (read: real turkey). If you can't cop one of the scarred wood tables, get it to go to Oz Park. *2264 N. Lincoln Ave., between Webster and Belden Aves., Lincoln Park, 773/528–1405. No credit cards. $*

6 *e-2*
303 W. Madison St., at Franklin St., Loop, 312/346–1234. Closed Sun.

6 *f-1*
190 N. State St., at Lake St., Loop, 312/683–1234. Closed Sun.

5 *b-3*
1422 W. Webster Ave., at Clybourn Ave., Lincoln Park, 773/755–1234.

5 *e-3*
R. J. GRUNTS
The original Lettuce Entertain You restaurant, R. J. Grunts was founded in 1971 and faithfully adheres to its counter-culture-for-the-masses spirit with dark wooden booths, period R&B, and unpretentious food. More than 30 ingredients crowd the signature salad bar, Chicago's first ever compile-it-yourself station. Oversize burgers and chili earn raves. Tourists and townies alike love the casual parkside location, a great place to stop after visiting the Lincoln Park Zoo. *2056 Lincoln Park W, at Dick-*

ens Ave., Lincoln Park, 773/929–5363. AE, D, DC, MC, V. $–$$

5 *c-2*
SALT & PEPPER DINER
A classic diner with booths lining the windows and swivel stools along the counter, the black-and-white linoleumed Salt & Pepper even has swift short order cooks from central casting. Food is what you'd expect: patty melts, coffee refills, and a light tab. Other than being overcrowded Saturday and Sunday mornings, this is a decent hangout. *2575 N. Lincoln Ave., at Sheffield Ave., Lincoln Park, 773/525–8788. No credit cards. $*

4 *c-7*
3537 N. Clark St., near Addison St., Wrigleyville, 773/883–9800.

5 *d-3*
TOAST
Vintage toasters that ring the room speak to its emphasis on style along with sustenance. Look for flared classics (like mascarpone-stuffed French toast) at breakfast and contemporary bites (like Thai chicken wraps) at lunch. Fans range from hipster patrons of owner Dion Antic's other trendy spots (Iggy's, Fahrenheit) to stroller-pushing mamas. *746 W. Webster Ave., at Halsted St., Lincoln Park, 773/935–5600. AE, D, DC, MC, V. No dinner. $*

2 *f-4*
2046 N. Damen Ave., near Armitage Ave., Bucktown, 773/772–5600.

7 *c-6*
228 W. Chicago Ave., near Franklin St., River North, 312/944–7023.

5 *b-8*
THE TWISTED SPOKE
Once a biker bar outpost, it found fame with its juicy burgers, killer Bloody Marys, and jocular attitude. Expansion followed. Nonetheless the joint manages to hold on to its outlaw ways with programs like the porno at breakfast Smut-N-Eggs. Not for everyone, the Spoke tests your tolerance for testosterone. *501 N. Ogden Ave., at Grand Ave., West Loop, 312/666–1500. AE, MC, V. $*

3 *h-7*
THE VILLAGE TAP
A Roscoe Village tavern, the Tap draws fans from beyond the neighborhood

with more than 30 tap microbrews and food that exceeds typical bar fare. It leans toward healthy Tex-Mex in generous burritos and quesadillas, with a smattering of Middle Eastern dishes like falafel and hummus, as well as burgers, chicken sandwiches, and salads. A retractable awning, outdoor fireplace, and space heaters make garden seating seasonless. *2055 W. Roscoe Ave., at Hoyne Ave., Roscoe Village, 773/883–0817. AE, D, DC, MC, V. No lunch weekdays. $*

ARGENTINE

2 *f-3*
EL NANDU
Empanadas (small meat- and/or vegetable-filled pies) are the specialty at this spiffed-up storefront. Exciting stuffings include ground beef with olives and raisins, chopped steak, corn and peppers, and egg-lace spinach. Order two or three plus a green salad for a meal. On weekends a live guitarist plays tango and pop tunes under a slide screen devoted to rotating images of Argentina. Exposed brick walls, open wine racks, original art, and papered tables add charm to this cheap-eats emporium. *2731 W. Fullerton Ave., near Western Ave., Logan Square, 773/278–0900. AE, D, MC, V. No lunch Sun. $*

4 *b-6*
TANGO SUR
At Tango Sur, South America meets Italy in a fusion of cuisines that owner Sergio DiSapio says defines Argentina. Pastas and *noqui* (the Argentine version of Italian gnocchi) mingle with char-grilled meats on the menu. Diners bring their own beer and wine to the cozy storefront pumped up with tango tunes and painted with a mural of a couple entwined in the sensual dance. DiSapio and his family provide a genuine welcome. *3763 N. Southport Ave., at Grace St., Lakeview, 773/477–5466. BYOB. No lunch Mon.–Sat. MC, V. $$*

AUSTRIAN

4 *b-8*
METRO
This place stands out as the lone Austrian in Chicago's ethnic eats stew. Mounted game and hanging cowbells establish the theme in the otherwise uninspiring rec-roomish interior. The great selection of European beers accompanies a menu of meat classics topped by the enormous Wiener schnitzel. A regular pool of old-timers occupies the bar. *3032 N. Lincoln Ave., near Belmont and Southport Aves., Lincoln Park, 773/929–0622. AE, MC, V. Closed Tues. $$*

BARBECUE

4 *c-8*
BROTHER JIMMY'S BBQ
Ribs and blues team to entertain the college and postcollege crowds that consider Brother Jimmy family. The look is Southern rib shack, though the 'cue rarely gets the raves earned by other slow smokers in town. Instead the club-restaurant endears fans with live music and no cover charge. *2909 N. Sheffield Ave., north of Diversey Ave., Lincoln Park, 773/528–0888. AE, DC, MC, V. $–$$*

7 *c-7*
CARSON'S
A Chicago classic for richly slathered ribs, Carson's barbecue leans to the sweet side with a smoky finish. Rib platters come with coleslaw, rolls, and choice of potatoes—indulge in the au gratin option—a filling meal priced for value. Juicy barbecue chicken and sirloin strip steak make fine non-rib options. Take-out is as popular as dine-in, where waits can be considerable given convention and/or weekend traffic. All meals come with a protective plastic bib. Word to the wise: tie one on. *612 N. Wells St., near Ontario St., River North, 312/280–9200. AE, DC, MC, V. $$*

2 *f-2*
5970 N. Ridge Rd., at Ashland Ave., Edgewater, 773/271–4000.

7 *d-6*
FAMOUS DAVE'S
Hot-sauce specialist Dave burst out of Minnesota with a chain of rib shacks including this outpost. This spot's glory is its variety, with Texas, Carolina, and other barbecue methods on its menu. Its blues stage manages to draw a decent lineup of live artists playing primarily for tourists. *739 N. Clark St., at Superior St., River North, 312/266–2400. AE, D, DC, MC, V. $$*

7 c-1

FIREPLACE INN

For ribs without the rib-shack-shtick try the Fireplace, an Old Town old-timer. The dim and cozy surroundings hinge on a fireplace behind the bar. Regulars rave about the ribs but not much more. In summer the outdoor patio with an outdoor bar is one of the neighborhood's nicest. *1448 N. Wells St., at Burton Place, south of North Ave., Old Town, 312/664–5264. AE, D, DC, MC, V. No lunch weekdays. $$*

7 h-8

JOE'S BE-BOP CAFÉ

Ribs and jazz share top billing here. Aimed at tourists with its Navy Pier location, Joe's deserves the attention of locals, too. Co-owner Wayne Segal, who runs the Jazz Showcase founded by father Joe Segal, books the swing, blues, Latin jazz, ragtime, and boogie-woogie acts that play nightly. The long, narrow room backstopped by an elevated bandstand even looks like a jazz listening club. Jambalaya, sandwiches, and salads join ribs on the menu. Sunday brunch provides an all-you-can-eat buffet, a Bloody Mary bar, and a big band to boot. *700 E. Grand Ave., at Navy Pier, 312/595–5299. AE, D, DC, MC, V. $–$$*

2 h-8

LEON'S BAR-B-Q

Here, and at the three carry-out-only locations, people line up early to dive into the secret sauce and rib tips of a 60-year-old Chicago institution. While full slabs and tips are the specialty, don't miss the chicken or hot links. There's a solution if your out-of-town friends have Leon envy: it ships its food to cities across the country. *1640 E. 79th St., near East End Ave., South Shore, 773/731–1454. No credit cards. $*

2 f-7

1158 W. 59th St., near Racine Ave., Sherman Park, 773/778–7838.

1 f-6

8251 S. Cottage Grove, near 83rd St., Chatham, 773/488–4556.

2 e-7

4550 S. Archer Ave., near 46th St., Brighton Park, 773/247–4171.

4 b-5

N. N. SMOKEHOUSE

A friendly neighborhood barbecue joint patronized by area families, students, and outlying barbecue fans, N. N. Smokehouse does top smoked pork ribs as well as Memphis pulled pork sandwiches. Rib alternatives include good barbecued chicken, broccoli salad, and great pecan and sweet-potato pies. *Pancit* noodles, a Filipino dish, pays homage to the owner's homeland. This is an extremely casual spot with an active take-out counter. *455 W. Irving Park Rd., near Ashland Ave., Lakeview, 773/868–4700. MC, V. No lunch Sun.–Thurs. $–$$*

5 d-3

ROBINSON'S NO. 1 RIBS

It ain't about atmosphere at regular-joe Robinson's. The storefront carry-out counter obscures the dining room and backdoor patio. But who needs looks when you've got great pulled pork? The fall-off-the-bone barbecue regularly earns the unassuming restaurant raves in local dining polls. *655 W. Armitage Ave., near Halsted St., Lincoln Park, 312/337–1399. AE, D, DC, MC, V. Closed Mon. $*

2 f-2

SMOKE DADDY

"Rhythm & barbecue" is the slogan at Smoke Daddy, a rib-and-blues emporium in a funky corner bar setting. Pass under the neon WOW! over the door, grab a booth or a bar stool, and dig into spareribs, baby backs, or rib tips. Pulled pork, beef, chicken, and turkey come in 5-ounce sandwiches and 10-ounce platters. Swab stray sauce with generously supplied paper towels. Most orders include fries and coleslaw, so come hungry. Dessert pies entice from the counter. Stick around for live blues nightly after 9:30. *1804 W. Division St., at Damen Ave., Wicker Park, 773/772–6656. AE, D, DC, MC, V. $–$$*

5 e-5

TWIN ANCHORS

An Old Town institution as popular for its dark tavern setting as its sauce-rich ribs, this place is perpetually jammed by Lincoln Parkers. Those who choose not to gnaw on a rack will find plenty of other rib-sticking choices in steaks, burgers, and seafood. Plan on dining early if you don't want to wait. Better yet, savor the nautical atmosphere and Sinatra on the jukebox over a beer; then take your ribs to go. *1655 N. Sedgewick St., near North Ave., Old Town, 312/266–1616. AE, DC, MC, V. No lunch weekdays. $$*

CAFÉS

4 *c-8*

BITTERSWEET

One of the city's best bakeries, it also serves light meals at tidy marble-top tables. Soups such as potato–red pepper and sandwiches like chicken liver pâté appear as daily specials. If you're just looking for a nosh, try a café au lait with a superb fresh-fruit scone. Service is extremely laid-back, so don't go if rushed. Bring reading material to bide the wait. *1114 W. Belmont Ave., near Racine Ave., Lakeview, 773/929–1100. No credit cards. Closed Mon. $*

2 *f-4*

CAFFE DE LUCA

Coffeehouse, bar, pizzeria, hangout: Caffe de Luca is a café in the use-it-as-you-will Italian style. Crumbling walls evoking European ruins and a menu of *panini* (rolls) and *crostini* (toasted bread cubes) abet the Continental character. But the slacker service is, alas, thoroughly American. *1721 N. Damen Ave., at Wabansia Ave., Bucktown, 773/342–6000. AE, D, DC, MC, V. $*

3 *g-3*

CAFÉ SELMARIE

Anchoring Lincoln Square's old-world retail district, the café holds a dear place in the hearts of locals for its elegant baked goods and flavorful light meals. The menu changes frequently but always includes soups, salads, and sandwiches served in a bright, restful setting. Save room for desserts like cherry streusel and Florentine cookies. Sunday brunch bustles. *4729 N. Lincoln Ave., at Lawrence Ave., Lincoln Square, 773/989–5595. Closed Mon. BYOB. MC, V. $*

8 *e-2*

CORNER BAKERY

For bread lovers, Corner Bakery is a slice of heaven. This Lettuce Entertain You venture, with a string of urban locations, turns out up to 25 varieties daily, including crusty baguettes, rustic country loaves, dense raisin-pecan goodies, and aromatic olive rolls. From smoked turkey to chicken with pesto, sandwiches excel on the bread foundation. Salads, soups, cookies, and muffins make the bakery a good lunch choice. The Cultural Center location is one of the best, with marble-top tables and a rotating roster of poets, musicians, and other entertainers at peak hours. *Chicago Cultural Center, 78 E. Washington St., at Michigan Ave., Loop, 312/201–0805. AE, D, DC, MC, V. $*

5 *f-6*

1121 N. State St., at Cedar St., Gold Coast, 312/787–1969.

7 *d-7*

516 N. Clark St., at Grand Ave., River North, 312/644–8100.

8 *e-4*

224 S. Michigan Ave., at Jackson Blvd., Loop, 312/431–7600.

7 *f-7*

676 N. St. Clair St., at Erie St., Streeterville, 312/266–2570.

8 *b-4*

Sears Tower, 233 S. Wacker Dr., at Adams St., the Loop, 312/466–0200. Closed weekends.

7 *e-5*

CRU CAFÉ & WINE BAR

By the glass or half- or full-bottle, Cru pours 400 wines from around the world on a chic, shady corner, one block from the madness of Michigan Avenue Its all-day menu features deluxe café fare such as charcuterie, mussels, Cobb salads, and lobster club sandwiches. Spend a chic afternoon with a sampler of blue cheeses and French wines in this sophisticated spot. *888 N. Wabash Ave., at Rush and Delaware Sts., Gold Coast, 312/337–4001. AE, DC, MC, V. $$*

CAJUN/CREOLE

7 *c-8*

CLUB CREOLE

In a town short on Creole joints, it does a welcome job with spiced-up sandwiches and entrées, providing tasty and reasonable lunches in the oft-expensive River North area. Decor earns no raves, but that doesn't stop the mobs from the neighboring Merchandise Mart from crowding in at midday. *226 W. Kinzie St., between Franklin and Wells Sts., River*

North, 312/222–0300. AE, D, DC, MC, V.
Closed Sun. $

7 *e-7*

**HEAVEN ON SEVEN
ON RUSH**

Original Heaven on Seven owner Jimmy
Bannos created this buoyant ode to
New Orleans. Under the expansive
"Wall of Fire," a collection of hot sauces
from around the world, shoppers,
tourists, and office workers crowd in for
lunches of red beans and rice, gumbo,
and an array of po'boy sandwiches. Din-
ners are more ambitious, à la grilled
salmon on andouille sausage with
potato hash and vidalia onion crisp. To
get a feel for the girth of the menu, go
hungry and order the "Jimmy Feed Me!"
special—seven demi-courses for a bargain $35. Don't miss the rich coconut
cream cake for dessert. 600 N. Michigan
Ave., at Ontario St., Magnificent Mile,
312/280–7774. AE, D, DC, MC, V. $$

4 *c-7*

Heaven on Seven on Clark, 3478 N. Clark
St., one block south of Addison St.,
Wrigleyville, 773/477–7818.

7 *d-8*

HOUSE OF BLUES

Spicy Cajun and Creole fare, in an out-
sider art–filled room on the first level of
this boisterous music club, draws River
North professionals to lunch and club-
goers to dinner. The fun atmosphere fills
in where the cuisine fails to impress.
Sunday brunch with a gospel choir is
among the city's best. 329 N. Dearborn
St., at Chicago River, River North, 312/
923–2000. AE, D, DC, V. $

2 *h-8*

JACKSON HARBOR GRILL

The only restaurant in Chicago that is
literally lapped by the lake, Jackson
Harbor Grill occupies the former har-
bormaster's house on its namesake
marina. Everyone from Lycra-clad
cyclists to families in their Sunday best
vie for one of the Grill's nine porch-
front tables to catch a cool lake breeze.
Zesty fare ranges from banana-rum-
roasted chicken to blackened scallop
and spinach salad to multilayer muf-
falettas and rock-salted fries. Heaven
dwells here on a summer's afternoon.
6401 S. Coast Guard Dr., at 63rd St.,
Jackson Park, 773/288–4442. AE, DC,
MC, V. $$

8 *e-3*

**ORIGINAL HEAVEN
ON SEVEN**

Jimmy Bannos opened this Creole-Cajun
diner in 1980 on the seventh floor of the
Loop's Garland Building. The lunch
crowd still lines up daily to squeeze into
the tiny room decorated with Mardi
Gras beads and an extensive collection
of hot sauces. The food is not as elaborate as at Heaven's sister's Mag Mile
location due to its closet-size kitchen.
But you won't regret ordering po'boys,
jambalaya, fried oyster salad, collard
greens, or fried chicken salad. 111 N.
Wabash Ave., 7th floor, at Washington St.,
Loop, 312/263–6443. No credit cards. No
lunch on 1st and 3rd Fri. of month. $

CARIBBEAN

2 *h-7*

CALYPSO KITCHEN

Calypso takes its island persona seriously. The tiki-bar-like interior is decorated with whimsical folk art and has
booming island tunes. There are jerk
chicken and beef standards, plus extra-
spicy Cuban black bean soup, made
with Scotch, bonnet peppers, and
cilantro. If you're in the mood for something more unusual, try the tropical linguine flavored with coconut and lime.
5211-C S. Harper Ave., near 53rd St., Hyde
Park, 773/955–0229. Reservations not
accepted. AE, D, DC, MC, V. $$

5 *a-5*

EZULI

From late night into the early morning,
this 50-seat dining room is packed with
revelers sipping mango-infused marti-
nis, eating Gorgonzola and mango
bruschetta, and just enjoying the party
atmosphere. The tables are well spaced,
so even with the crowds, you don't feel
sardined. And unlike at most other after-
hours eateries, dinner is available until
1:30 AM. 1415 N. Milwaukee Ave., near
Wolcott St., Wicker Park, 773/227–8200.
AE, D, MC, V. Closed Mon. No lunch. $$

2 *f-4*

WATUSI

The suave, neutral-toned Watusi draws a
hipster crowd to chef Suzy Crofton's
bold Latin-Caribbean dishes. In tribute
to the Caribbean's melting pot of
French, African, Indian, and Spanish cultures, Crofton centers dishes on indige-

nous fish, root vegetables, pig, and spices. Top efforts include jerked shark with black bean relish and sea bass with corn, curry, and red pepper. But Watusi doesn't take itself too seriously: witness the playful menu of cocktails named after vintage dances. *1540 W. North Ave., at Ashland Ave., Bucktown, 773/862–1540. AE, D, DC, MC, V. $$*

CHINESE

7 *d-8*
BEN PAO
Chic Chinese is hard to find, but this place suits up in style with a red-and-black interior, dramatic pinpoint lighting, and granite pillars streaming with water. The food doesn't outshine the setting, but with a long list of small starters, diners are encouraged to graze until sated. Standouts include shrimp dumplings, eggplant pot stickers, and duck spring rolls. Among entrées, black-pepper scallops are the house specialty. Ideal for a quick bite, a satay bar vends skewered, grilled meats in a variety of sauces. *52 W. Illinois St., at Dearborn St., River North, 312/222–1888. AE, D, DC, MC, V. $$*

5 *c-3*
DEE'S
Lincoln Parkers swear by Dee's for both takeout and eat-in. The menu is a cut above that at most other Chinese restaurants, with such treats as drunken chicken, eggplant in garlic sauce, and a good variety of noodle dishes. However, even the Szechuan dishes are tame spice-wise; if you like your food hot, speak up. Servers are excellent and articulate—and very knowledgeable about the ambitious wine list. *1114 W. Armitage Ave., near Racine St., Lincoln Park, 773/477–1500. AE, MC, V. No lunch. $$*

6 *f-7*
EMPEROR'S CHOICE
One of few Chinatown restaurants that puts effort into creating atmosphere, it manages to make a crowded room intimate with soft lighting and framed art. The food also leads the pack of area eateries with expertly prepared fresh seafood dishes like steamed oysters and Peking-style lobster. A separate menu touts "delicacies" of rattlesnake soup and pork bellies. Be prepared to wait on

weekends. There's free parking (with validation) in the Cermak-Wentworth lot. *2238 S. Wentworth Ave., near Cermak Rd., Chinatown, 312/225–8800. AE, D, DC, MC, V. $–$$$*

3 *d-3*
GREAT SEA
Among the Lawrence Avenue multiethnic stew, Great Sea stands out with flavorful cooking in a clean, inviting interior. Chinese clans gather here to share generous platters of fried chicken with hot sauce—spicy glazed wings with the meat pushed down on the bone. Kung-pao chicken, moo shoo, and noodle dishes also shine; the assorted chow mein mingles shrimp, chicken, beef, pork, and vegetables. Servings are generous. Unless you want a doggie bag, two dishes feed three hungry people. *3254 W. Lawrence Ave., near Kedzie Ave., Albany Park, 773/478–9129. MC, V. $*

6 *f-7*
HONG MIN
Though the Chinatown pick of budget-minded diners, Hong Min actually does its best with the higher-priced dishes, especially stir-fried lobster (the most expensive item on the menu) and oysters. The storefront hole-in-the-wall is split into two nondescript dining rooms that make you feel you've discovered a diamond in the rough when the crustacean arrives, shell intact. Large Formica tables are extended-family-friendly. *221 W. Cermak Rd., near Wentworth Ave., Chinatown, 312/842–5026. Reservations accepted for parties of 6 or more. MC, V. BYOB. $–$$*

2 *f-2*
MEI SHUNG
Of the two menus, it's the Taiwanese list rather than the Chinese that deserves most attention. For well-seasoned recipes prepared with vegetables unwilted by the wok, try sliced chicken with basil, pork in satay sauce, or sautéed shrimp with leeks or dry-cooked string beans. There's a refreshing lack of MSG-bogged sauces in this simple storefront. If you can't decide from the lengthy list of choices, ask the helpful waitstaff for their picks. But pace your order; service is speedy. *5511 N. Broadway, near Bryn Mawr Ave., Edgewater, 773/728–5778. AE, DC, MC, V. BYOB. $*

7 *e-7*

PF CHANG'S CHINA BISTRO

A link in a national chain, this restaurant cooks up Chinese favorites from throughout the country, including spicy Szechuan and Hunan and familiar Canton. Chang's winningly combines solid, flavorful cooking with budget-friendly prices, much appreciated by lunchtime regulars from area offices. *530 N. Wabash Ave., at Grand Ave., River North, 312/828–9977. AE, DC, MC, V. $*

6 *f-6*

PHOENIX

A room with a view is hard to come by in Chinatown; Phoenix, one flight up from street level, has it with a wall of north-facing windows that take in the sweep of the Loop skyline. Some of the best dim sum in town is served here on weekdays and to huge weekend crowds (arrive by 9 AM or wait). Return for dinner; there are lots of good seafood choices on the wide-ranging menu. *2131 S. Archer Ave., near Cermak Rd., Chinatown, 312/328–0848. AE, D, MC, V. $–$$$*

COLOMBIAN

2 *f-4*

LA CUMBAMBA

Mismatched seats surround just a few tables, and odd artwork adorns the walls. But the backyard patio says it all—what other restaurant has a hammock? Relax while eating *sanchocho,* a hearty dish of vegetables, plantains, and yucca that doesn't skimp on garlic. *2311 W. North Ave., near Western Ave., Wicker Park, 773/384–9546. No credit cards. No lunch. $$*

4 *b-8*

LAS TABLAS

This casual neighborhood South American does a superior job with meat as well as seafood. In the Colombian tradition, steak is a big seller. The hunger-handling house special, Matrimonio, unites steak and chicken as well as plantains and fried yucca. Paella is good, generously portioned, and worth the wait. The room can feel crowded, but everything tastes homemade and the welcome is genuine. *2965 N. Lincoln Ave., near Southport Ave., Lakeview, 773/871–2414. AE, DC, MC, V. BYOB. $*

CONTEMPORARY

7 *d-8*

BIN 36

This industrial-chic wine bar–restaurant–wine shop uncorks 50 wines by the glass before a romantic panorama of the district, drawing a significant after-work following. Tasting flights flirt with reds from Spanish rioja to California zinfandel. Mix and match sips with savory bites of hand-rolled gnocchi and crispy striped bass with kalamata-olive mashed potatoes. Appetizers that encourage grazing though entrées are worth the commitment. *339 N. Dearborn St., at Kinzie St., inside the House of Blues, River North, 312/755–9463. AE, D, DC, MC, V. $$*

6 *d-1*

BLACKBIRD

Without a reservation only the early bird-diner may catch Blackbird, where close-set tables in the chic storefront spot make for entertaining eavesdropping. With a plate-glass facade, white walls, mohair banquettes, and aluminum chairs, the minimalist setting sets the stage for exuberant dishes like wild bass with roasted fennel and baby clams. Chef Paul Kahan made the cover of *Food & Wine* as one of the nation's top new talents, which explains why everyone from foodies to celebrities (Cindy Crawford, Michael Jordan) piles in. *619 W. Randolph St., near Des Plaines St., West Loop, 312/715–0708. AE, D, DC, MC, V. Closed Sun. No lunch weekends. $$–$$$*

7 *e-6*

BLACKHAWK LODGE

Posing as a vacation lodge of the Ralph Lauren ilk, this comfortable, regional American serves fittingly haute, hearty food. Start with the warm hazelnut-dusted goat cheese salad, smoky corn chowder, or, for heavier tastes, the cheddar cheese grits. Move on to the chili-rubbed turkey fillet or test the baby back ribs, ranked among the best in the city. The regional repertoire spans the nation from New England to the Southwest, the clientele from conventioneer to suburbanite. *41 E. Superior St., at Wabash Ave., Magnificent Mile, 312/280–4080. AE, D, DC, MC, V. $$–$$$*

3 *h-5*

BLUE STEM

A North Center neighborhood storefront with more culinary ambition than expected, this spot serves upscale American bistro fare such as grilled fish and roast chicken in a folksy atmosphere. Husband-and-wife owners provide a friendly welcome to the intimate spot. *1935 W. Irving Park Rd., east of Lincoln and Damen Aves., North Center, 773/665–1340. AE, DC, MC, V. No lunch. Closed Sun. $–$$*

3 *h-7*

BRETT'S

While most of Roscoe Village is populated by bars and cafés that cater to locals, Brett's draws affluent fans from well beyond it. Namesake of chef-owner Brett Knobel, the restaurant champions New American cooking with Caribbean, Asian, and Southwestern accents. The menu, which changes monthly, is full of creative surprises: potato tacos with poblano chili sauce, Thai-style salmon, jerk pork chops, or garlic chicken with pomegranate relish. The homemade bread is worth the trip alone. Like Knobel herself, who often circulates in the front of the house, the atmosphere is unpretentious and inviting: a clean, smoke-free storefront with a wood bar and warm lighting. The pre–6 PM prix-fixe meal includes three budget-friendly courses. *2011 W. Roscoe St., near Damen Ave., Roscoe Village, 773/248–0999. AE, DC, MC, V. No smoking. Closed Mon. and Tues. No lunch weekdays. $$–$$$*

2 *f-4*

CAFÉ ABSINTHE

The address is on North Avenue but the entrance is from the alley behind. Thus begins a journey into the très hip Café Absinthe. Beyond the swagged entry curtains, exposed brick walls frame the front of the store where an open kitchen produces inventive dishes like scallops in fennel bouillon and octopus with watercress-jícama salad on a frequently changing menu. The unwritten dress code is à la mode funk or, all else failing, black. *1954 W. North Ave., near Damen Ave., Bucktown, 773/278–4488. AE, D, DC, MC, V. No lunch. $$–$$$*

7 *f-7*

CALITERRA

This place manages to make the marriage of Italian and Californian cuisine work with such offspring as bruschetta made from polenta with rosemary and mascarpone cheese. The restaurant is still relatively undiscovered, on the second floor of the Wyndham Hotel, without any outside signs. There's live jazz Friday and Saturday evenings. *Wyndham Hotel, 633 N. St. Clair St., near Erie St., Streeterville, 312/274–4444. AE, D, DC, MC, V. $$$*

5 *d-3*

CHARLIE TROTTER'S

One of the nation's best restaurants, Charlie Trotter's makes theater of dining, with each course a new astonishing act. Reserve a table weeks in advance and save your appetite for a multi-course, $100 degustation menu. Chef Trotter's perfectionism shows in complex preparations using the finest raw materials. A sample dish might be seared sea bass with a puree of caramelized fennel and mustard seed vinaigrette. In a renovated town house, the restaurant has a decor that keeps attention riveted on the food. For a special experience, order the wine pairing menu, with a different glass matched to each course. *816 W. Armitage Ave., near Halsted St., Lincoln Park, 773/248–6228. Reservations essential. Jacket required. AE,*

BEST PATIOS

After a Windy City winter, no one enjoys outdoor dining more than Chicagoans, especially at these perfect patios:

Lutz Continental Cafe & Pastry (Continental)
  Green AstroTurf and a gurgling fountain mark the cheerful spot in which to eat cake.

Moody's Pub (American Casual)
  Sun-dappled or candlelit, Moody's marries romance and burgers.

The Palm (Steak)
  See Lake Michigan and Navy Pier from a calming distance.

Resi's Bierstube (German)
  Maple-canopied picnic tables in a hidden, intimate, bloom-bordered patio.

North Pond Cafe (Contemporary)
  Sylvan Lincoln Park setting beside a pond.

Thyme (Contemporary)
  Chic, private, and leafy setting shuts out surrounding grunge.

DC, MC, V. Closed Sun. and Mon. No lunch. $$$$

4 d-7

CORNELIA'S ROOSTERANT

The roosters in question do exist in ceramic form, separating the smoking and no-smoking sections. A Lakeview institution for more than a decade, the casual dining room, decorated in a barnyard motif, and outdoor patio offer perfect people-watching. The pork chops are a specialty, marinated in Dijon mustard, grilled, and served with sour cream, corn, and mashed potatoes. But before diving right in, start with the shiitake mushroom pancakes in balsamic syrup and sun-dried tomato butter. 748 W. Cornelia Ave., near Halsted St., Wrigleyville, 773/248–8333. AE, DC, V. No lunch. $$$

7 c-7

CROFTON ON WELLS

A small, simple but sophisticated room showcases chef-owner Suzy Crofton's American menu prepared with a Gallic accent. For starters, knock back an oyster shooter or dig into a plate of greens with Maytag blue cheese and avocado. The seasonally changing menu features creative combinations like rare ahi tuna with Asian pear-and-mango slaw or barbecue-glazed smoked pork loin with apple chutney. Dessert is a must. 535 N. Wells St., at Grand Ave., River North, 312/755–1790. AE, DC, MC, V. No lunch weekends. $$–$$$

4 b-5

DELEECE

In a neighborhood short on modern cooking, Deleece stands out. The simple exposed-brick room is a comfortable place to try food that borrows from a world of cultures in dishes like coconut chicken with mint couscous, salmon with fennel and roast pepper, and sun-dried tomato pasta. Salads and soups are fresh starters. It's popular with neighbors and the dating circuit. A brunch is offered on alternate Sundays. 4004 N. Southport Ave., near Irving Park Rd., Lakeview, 773/325–1710. AE, DC, V. $$

2 f-4

ECHO

Grazing diners adore this place specializing in small servings—more mini-entrées than tapas. Thus it's possible to do the tuna trio (maki, tartare, and sashimi) as well as the scallops and foie gras or perhaps the quail. Its inventive food is matched by a cool-verging-on-cold hipster setting, though the service is friendly. 1856 W. North Ave., at Wolcott Ave., Bucktown, 773/395–3474. DC, MC, V. No lunch. $$–$$$

5 d-1

ERWIN

A casual neighborhood restaurant with updated American eats, Erwin is carefully attended to by husband-and-wife owners Erwin and Cathy Drechsler. Everything is house-made using heartland produce, down to the multigrain bread and pickles that top the excellent hand-ground burgers. The menu, which changes monthly, might include trout wraps, onion tart, frisée-and-pear salad, and wood-grilled sturgeon. A popular spot for Sunday brunch, Erwin employs top waiters and assembles an inventive wine list. 2925 N. Halsted St., near Wellington Ave., Lakeview, 773/528–7200. AE, D, DC, MC, V. Closed Mon. No lunch. $$–$$$

5 d-8

FAHRENHEIT

Soaring ceilings and curvaceous walls in icy blue hues set the stage for the young and beautiful who throng the Loop-fringe eatery. If any food can stare down this scene it's chef Patrick Concannon's peppered lamb carpaccio, his duck breast with figs, and other inventive dishes. Service, and occasionally the food, gets lax on those packed weekend evenings. 695 N. Milwaukee Ave., north of Grand Ave., River West, 312/733–7400. AE, D, MC, V. No lunch. $$$

5 e-5

FLAT TOP GRILL

Asian wok cooking meets American cafeteria in this do-it-yourself stir-fry storefront. Diners fill their bowls from the 70-ingredient bar including vegetables, meat, fish, rice, and noodles; ladle on the sauce of their choice; and hand it all over to a grill chef, who stir-fries it. A giant chalkboard announces fat, calorie, and sodium content for each item. Prices are so low, you can afford to be experimental. Kitchen-shy twentysomethings flock here. Valets will park bikes and in-line skates. 319 W. North Ave., near Sedgewick St., Old Town, 312/787–7676. Reservations not accepted. DC, MC, V. No lunch Mon.–Thurs. $

6 *c-1*

This sequel near Harpo Studios accepts reservations and serves lunch daily. *1000 W. Washington St., at Carpenter St., West Loop, 312/829–4800.*

4 *b-8*

3200 N. Southport Ave., at Belmont Ave., Lakeview, 773/665–8100.

5 *a-3*

GREEN DOLPHIN STREET

Though most come for the jazz and discover the food, the latter is no afterthought. Despite its urban industrial facade, the club is split between a swanky listening lounge and a white-linen dining room, with a darkly romantic bar in between. The menu changes weekly, relying on luxuries like foie gras and tuna tartare as well as game and fish. The club room serves casual fare during shows. A small patio has a view of a towering train bridge over the river. *2200 N. Ashland Ave., at Webster Ave., Lakeview, 773/395–0066. AE, D, DC, MC, V. Closed Mon. No lunch. $$$*

7 *c-6*

HARVEST ON HURON

Suave and inventive, Harvest lives up to its hype with game dishes that could make fans of vegans. Chef Alan Sternweiler uses global accents on his American menu, while co-owner Oz Schoenstadt oversees the impressive spirits collection (half-pours make experimentation possible without busting the bank). The rich-toned interior includes cozy burgundy horseshoe booths and comfy divans in the lounge. *217 W. Huron St., near Franklin St., River North, 312/587–9600. AE, D, DC, MC, V. No lunch weekends. $$–$$$*

7 *d-8*

HOUSE OF BLUES FOUNDATION ROOM

Tucked away in the rollicking, folk-art-festooned music club House of Blues, it may be the city's best-kept culinary secret. Chef Cheryl Clark boldly combines flavors from Asia and the American Southwest in dishes like asparagus and goat cheese "sushi" and Alaskan halibut with hoisin (sweet and spicy) glaze. Best of all, the 70-seat dining room is rock-club-cool, from its outsider art to its jeans-friendly dress code. *329 N. Dearborn St., north of Wacker Dr., River North, 312/923–7050. AE, D, MC, V. $$$*

7 *b-8*

HUBBARD STREET GRILL

A River North loft restaurant with an open kitchen sounds ho-hum, but chef-owner David Schy has staying power in the genre: his menu is strong in grilled meat and fish sauced with zippy salsas, chutneys, and relishes. Supplemental pastas and salads provide something for every craving. High praise goes to the ahi tuna burger and fries with house-made jalapeño ketchup. It's popular with River North creatives and post-exercise East Bank Club goers. *351 W. Hubbard St., at Orleans St., River North, 312/222–0770. AE, D, DC, MC, V. No lunch weekends. $$–$$$*

5 *g-7*

IRON MIKE'S GRILLE

Former Bears coach Mike Ditka still has considerable draw here if judged by his namesake restaurant. This cozy, wood-paneled old boys' club looks like a meat-and-potatoes joint, and while it does the standards (steak, hamburger, pork chops), Iron Mike's also surprises with phyllo-wrapped duck and seared tuna. To be expected: loads of football memorabilia, sports-broadcasting TVs, logoed T-shirts and caps for sale, and the de rigueur cigar bar. *Tremont Hotel, 100 E. Chestnut St., near Michigan Ave., Magnificent Mile, 312/587–8989. D, DC, MC, V. $$–$$$*

4 *d-8*

JACK'S AMERICAN BLEND

Jack's serves American food in a modern culinary sense: dishes are influenced by Asian, Italian, and Mediterranean cuisines. The grilled pork tenderloin, for example, is served with a vegetable lasagna made with goat cheese and eggplant. The ahi tuna comes with mashed potatoes. Get here early, as Jack's doesn't take reservations after 6:30 PM. *3201 N. Halsted St., near Belmont Ave., Lakeview, 773/244–9191. AE, D, DC, V. No lunch. $$$*

5 *d-3*

JAPONISANTE

You want sushi, but your date wants foie gras. You both want Japonisante, the city's only French-Japanese fusion restaurant. With gelled magenta lights and a single bloom on each table, it makes a low-key modernist statement. Service occasionally stumbles but patience pays off. *2044 N. Halsted Ave.,*

between Armitage and Dickens Aves.,
Lincoln Park, 773/348–8228. AE, DC,
MC, V. $$

2 f-4

MERITAGE

Like the American blended wine for
which it's named, this Bucktown dandy
draws on the Pacific Northwest, itself a
blend of American produce and Asian
techniques. On the menu are lots of fish
and game: seared ahi tuna, striped bass,
and duck breast. Expect architectural
presentations, subdued lighting, smart
servers, and a wine list heavy on the
West Coast namesake blends. In sum-
mer, the outdoor patio defies the ele-
ments with a large awning. 2118 N.
Damen Ave., near Webster Ave., Buck-
town, 773/235–6434. AE, DC, MC, V. No
lunch. $$–$$$

7 b-5

MK

At mk, chef Michael Kornick's signa-
ture restaurant, a three-story ware-
house with exposed wood trusses gets
gussied up in linen-covered tables,
Christofle flatware, and Royal Doulton
china. The kitchen eschews its working-
class frame for upper-crust bites, turn-
ing out exquisite contemporary
American fare from seared foie gras
with Armagnac-soaked prunes to
coriander-crusted ahi tuna. Capacity
crowds energize the room. Tables are
coveted by out-of-towners and urban-
ites alike. 868 N. Franklin St., at Chest-
nut St., River North, 312/482–9179.
Reservations essential. AE, DC, MC, V.
No lunch weekends. $$$

7 f-5

MRS. PARK'S TAVERN

A casual sister of the Park Avenue Café,
Mrs. Park's Tavern is a flavorful find
among mostly upscale neighbors. Savor
the trademarked pastrami salmon or a
chicken Caesar salad upgraded with
bacon, walnuts, and blue cheese in the
bright, Americana-accented room.
Hearty daily specials range from suck-
ling pig to roast duck. There's a pleasant
sidewalk café in summer. From breakfast into the late night, Mrs. Park's feeds
you well at almost any hour. Doubletree
Guest Suites, 198 E. Delaware Pl., at Mies
van der Rohe Way, Gold Coast, 312/280–
8882. AE, D, DC, MC, V. $$

5 e-2

NORTH POND CAFÉ

Over a hill and out of sight beside a Lin-
coln Park pond, this café is a hidden
treasure. A former skater's warming hut
refinished in woody Arts and Crafts
style, North Pond focuses on seasonal
Midwestern cooking inspired by local
farm produce. Lunches of sandwiches,
pastas, and soups are simpler but still
stellar. It's idyllic at any hour. 2610 N.
Cannon Dr., near Diversey Pkwy., Lincoln
Park, 773/477–5845. AE, D, DC, MC, V.
Closed Mon. $$–$$$

6 b-1

ONE SIXTYBLUE

Co-owned by Michael Jordan, designed
by Adam Tihany, and manned by chef
Patrick Robertson, One Sixtyblue has an
excellent pedigree that earns it high
praise all around. Don't miss the
salmon "leaf" with walnut-cucumber-fig
compote. Spacious table arrangements
provide privacy in a room that otherwise
serves people-watching well. The suave
lounge with woven leather chairs and
zinc-topped bar is a seductive spot for
drinks dates. 160 N. Loomis St., at Ran-
dolph St., West Loop, 312/850–0303. AE,
DC, MC, V. Closed Sun. $$$

4 c-7

THE OUTPOST

Inspired by the China clipper airplane,
which ported the privileged around the
Pacific Rim in the 1930s, this place
attempts to re-create the romance of the
era in a handsome wood-and-brick
room decked with period maps. The
American fare is thick with Asian
accents. More than 35 wines by the glass
make Outpost a sampler's delight. 3438
N. Clark St., at Newport St., Wrigleyville,
773/244–1166. AE, DC, MC, V. No lunch.
$$–$$$

7 e-4

PALETTE'S

A restaurant with a rich, slightly decadent lounge look, Palette's pairs a jewel-
toned, arty palette with an eclectic
American palate. Order everything from
pizzas to chops at seats encompassing
both divans and café tables. Candlelight
cultivates romance. A sizable following
shows up just to hear long-time pianist
Dave Green entertain. 1030 N. State St.,
between Maple and Oak Sts., Gold Coast,
312/440–5200. AE, DC, MC, V. $$

7 *f-5*

PARK AVENUE CAFÉ

If you need an excuse to splurge, this café's creative cuisine obliges. A branch of the New York original, Chicago's version does many of the same imaginative American dishes including the trademarked swordfish chop and salmon cured pastrami-style. Down to the desserts, everything is artfully presented by friendly servers in a comfortable second-story room. The inventive Sunday brunch includes American appetizers served tableside à la Chinese dim sum. *Doubletree Guest Suites, 199 E. Walton Pl., at Mies van der Rohe Way, Gold Coast, 312/944–4414. AE, D, DC, MC, V. No lunch; no dinner Sun. $$$–$$$$*

7 *d-7*

PASHA

There's more flash than flavor here, but nightlife lovers have gotta eat, too. And they prefer to do it at hedonist Pasha, festooned in overstuffed velvet and wrought-iron flourishes. Groove to the DJ-spun tunes as you down with-it food (shrimp-strawberry pasta) and check out the scene. Gals, if your date's a drag, head for the loo, which harbors its own bar. *642 N. Clark St., half-block north of Ontario St., Old Town, 312/397–0100. AE, D, DC, MC, V. $$*

8 *d-5*

PRAIRIE

An ode to the best of the Midwest, Prairie conjures the heartland with a Frank Lloyd Wright–inspired interior and a menu that draws on regional recipes. Seasonality determines the menu, but look for homey corn chowder, roasted buffalo with shallot sauce, and fish specialties such as coho salmon and the acclaimed Lake Superior whitefish. Diners range from Bears fans to business folk. *500 S. Dearborn St., at Congress Pkwy., Printer's Row, 312/663–1143. AE, D, DC, MC, V. $$–$$$*

8 *d-5*

PRINTER'S ROW

A South Loop pioneer, chef Michael Foley's regional American restaurant remains a beacon for area businesspeople and foodies from near and far. The clubby wood-panel and ceramic-tile interior is a comfortable room in which to sample game or seafood dishes like seared scallops with truffle oil or grilled peppered duck breast with almond-raisin couscous. The lauded wine list is devoted to mostly American vineyards. *550 S. Dearborn St., at Harrison St., Printer's Row, 312/461–0780. AE, D, DC, MC, V. Closed Sun. No lunch Sat. $$–$$$$*

7 *f-6*

PUCK'S AT THE MCA

This creation by Wolfgang Puck (of Spago fame) replaces the Museum of Contemporary Art's M Café. Like the artwork in the museum, the look is sleek and spare, with aluminum tables and framed prints on the walls. In summer, a three-tier patio overlooks an expansive city park. You don't need to be a museum patron to eat Puck's light fare of chilled gazpacho or buffalo-mozzarella pizza. *220 E. Chicago Ave., near Mies van der Rohe Way, Magnificent Mile, 312/397–4034. AE, MC, V. Closed Mon. No dinner. $*

7 *d-2*

PUMP ROOM

An institution since 1938 made famous by its celebrity clientele and radio broadcasts, the Pump Room no longer rests on its laurels. A new French chef updated the kitchen with inventive dishes like asparagus-crusted salmon with morels. The cobalt-and-gold room has probably seen more engagements, anniversaries, and birthdays than any other in the city. Management is accustomed to the persnickety ways of local Gold Coasters, though even they have to be famous to be seated in the celebrated Booth One. *Ambassador East hotel, 1301 N. State Pkwy., at Goethe St., Gold Coast, 312/266–0360. Jacket required after 4:30 PM. AE, D, DC, MC, V. $$$$*

8 *e-4*

RHAPSODY

Concert-goers and business crowds alike fill the audience for Rhapsody, inside Symphony Center. The restaurant's contemporary French-informed cuisine leans to the light side—lemon sole with tomato caper veal jus, for example—only to dash it all with the Chocolate Symphony dessert, a sinful trio of cake, pot de crème (creamy, rich custard), and cream. Despite its Loop location, Rhapsody manages to feel green, encased in glass windows facing a small park, and has outdoor tables in summer. *65 E. Adams St., near Michigan Ave., Loop, 312/786–9911. AE, D, DC, MC, V. $$–$$$*

RESTAURANTS

7 e-5
SEASONS
Gold Coasters and visiting foodies
flock here for executive chef Mark
Baker's creative cuisine—haute American with some Asian touches. One of
the city's top chefs, Baker constantly
changes his menu, but expect the sub-
lime from a dish like beef tenderloin
with foie gras and vidalia onion–potato
gratin. Save room for the sinful chocolate soufflé. The formal dining room is
refreshingly unstuffy. Sunday brunch
here is one of Chicago's best (and
most expensive). The adjacent Seasons
Café serves more casual fare throughout the day. *Four Seasons hotel, 120 E.
Delaware Pl., at Michigan Ave., Magnificent Mile, 312/280–8800. Brunch
reservations essential. AE, D, DC,
MC, V. $$$–$$$$*

3 g-4
SHE SHE
Chef Nicole Parthemore made Tomboy
trendy only to leave it and eventually
open the funky She She to instant
applause. Her signature porcupine
shrimp leads a menu of sauced fish and
meats with some Asian and Southwest-
ern accents. Crowds surge on the week-
ends, and close-set tables merge rather
uncomfortably. This place is not for
claustrophobes, though it's Lincoln
Square's only option for sophisticated
cuisine. *4539 N. Lincoln Ave., between
Wilson and Montrose Aves., Lincoln
Square, 773/293–3690. AE, DC, MC, V.
Closed Mon. $$*

7 f-5
SIGNATURE ROOM
AT THE 95TH
A tourist's delight, on the 95th floor of
the John Hancock Building, it relies on a
stunning view of the city and shoreline
to sell its food. Dinner is a formal affair
favored by romantics. Brunch, too, is
expensive though popular. The $9.50
lunch buffet served weekdays is the
restaurant's best deal, including roasts,
vegetables, soup, and a salad bar. The
cocktail lounge one floor up offers the
same skyline views for the price of a
drink. *John Hancock Center, 875 N. Michigan Ave., between Delaware Pl. and
Chestnut St., Magnificent Mile, 312/787–
9596. Brunch reservations essential. AE,
D, DC, V. $$$–$$$$*

2 f-4
SOUL KITCHEN
Dine on animal-print tablecloths with
R&B favorites on the airwaves in the
very heart of Wicker Park. The formula
sounds food-lite, but Soul Kitchen's sur-
prise is the strength of its American-
Southern-Caribbean cuisine. Hits
include sautéed Soul Oysters, jambal-
aya, and pecan-crusted catfish. Crowded
is the norm, even at the bar. A few
stools at the raw bar are a good option
for single or double diners. *1576 N.
Damen Ave., at Milwaukee Ave., Wicker
Park, 773/342–9742. Reservations not
accepted. AE, DC, MC, V. No lunch. $$*

7 d-7
SPAGO
Celebrity chef Wolfgang Puck charms
Chicagoans, who appreciate his clean,
creative cuisine dished up from an open
kitchen in a spirited room. Signature
dishes like duck sausage pizza and Chi-
nois chicken salad join more refined
East-meets-West fish, meats, and pastas. Lots of yummy extras, like goat
cheese with the bread basket, help make
eating well at Spago a no-brainer. For a
more casual setting, graze at the bar.
*520 N. Dearborn St., at Grand Ave., River
North, 312/527–3700. Weekend dinner
reservations essential. AE, D, DC, MC, V.
No lunch weekends. $$–$$$*

7 f-7
SPRUCE
This subterranean Streeterville American gained a reputation for elegant,
sophisticated food on the strength of
combinations like sea bass fillets draped
over vivid red-beet risotto and duck with
tomatillo-lavender honey. The American
theme extends to the setting, which
despite its basement location looks like
a stripped-to-the-bones loft, with huge
wood beams, pillars, and exposed brick.
Spacious table arrangements ensure
intimacy. *238 E. Ontario St., at Fairbanks
Ct., Streeterville, 312/642–3757. AE, MC,
V. No lunch Sat. $$$*

8 c-2
312 CHICAGO
Though adjacent to the style-conscious
Hotel Allegro, 312 Chicago stands on
the corner, targeting the downtown
community as well as the transient
trade. The menu is a zesty Italian-
inspired American affair with dishes like
olive oil poached bass, spit-roasted

lamb, and polenta soufflé. Delicious focaccia arrives first to the table with sun-dried tomato and olive tapenade. Spacious booths, low lighting, wood furnishings, and rich colors create a warm welcome. *136 N. LaSalle St., at Randolph St., Loop, 312/696–2420. AE, D, DC, MC, V. $$–$$$*

5 *d-8*
THYME
A chic crowd throngs here for bold fusion food in a see-and-be-seen setting. A pungent olive-anchovy tapenade partners bread and prepares the palate for the zest to come. Menu selections are seasonally inspired, but seafood lovers most appreciate chef John Bubala's deftness with fish. Asian sculptures and chandeliers made from blue Ty Nant water bottles give an international accent to the interior. The large ivy-walled patio is one of the city's best. *464 N. Halsted St., at Grand Ave., River West, 312/226–4300. AE, DC, MC, V. No lunch. $$–$$$*

4 *b-1*
TOMBOY
Funky music, a warm welcome, and an interesting cross-section of Andersonville residents dining here makes Tomboy playful. The food gets fun, too, from a fanciful "porcupine" shrimp appetizer with spikes of phyllo dough to a dessert of a crème brûlée—filled cookie cone served in a martini glass. Matching the exposed-brick storefront set, service is informal and unrushed. This is a great place to relax over a glass of wine, but remember to bring your own bottle. *5402 N. Clark St., at Balmoral Ave., Andersonville, 773/907–0636. AE, DC, MC, V. BYOB. Closed Mon. No lunch. $$*

6 *d-1*
TOQUE
Another affable option on Randolph's burgeoning restaurant row, Toque, despite its French name, does American dishes with French flare à la wood-grilled venison with pumpkin-sage spaetzle and corn-crusted vegetable potpie. The loft-like space is bright and simple, focusing attention on the open kitchen. Toque is popular prior to United Center events. *816 W. Randolph St., near Halsted St., West Loop, 312/666–1100. AE, D, DC, MC, V. No lunch. $$–$$$*

7 *f-6*
TRU
Next time an expense account comes your way, take it to Tru. A selection of prix-fixe meals can start with a staircase of caviars, followed by a chestnut-crusted venison with butternut squash puree in a sour cherry sauce. The decor is just as enticing as the meal—from the private dining areas decorated with Andy Warhols to a striking cobalt-blue female torso in the bar. The dynamic duo behind this dining room are the creators of Evanston's Trio. *676 N. St. Clair St., near Huron St., Magnificent Mile, 312/202–0001. Reservations essential. Jacket required. AE, D, DC, MC, V. Closed Sun. $$$$*

7 *d-8*
VONG
After opening in New York, London, and Hong Kong, marquee chef Jean-Georges Vongerichten chose Chicago for yet another version of his award-winning Vong, fusing French and Thai tastes. Vong's signature "black plate" appetizer and "white plate" dessert reduce decision-making by providing samples of five starters and finishers, respectively, to share. Of-the-moment designer David Rockwell did the harmonious interior. Despite the hype, Vong's intimidation factor is low and servers are friendly. *6 W. Hubbard St., at State St., River North, 312/644–8664. AE, D, DC, MC, V. No lunch weekends. $$$–$$$$*

7 *e-4*
WHISKEY BAR & GRILL
Until it moved into the Sutton Place hotel, hipsters found little reason to consider the conventioneer-crawling Gold Coast. One in a national string of Whiskeys owned by Rande Gerber, husband to superstrutter Cindy Crawford, the minimal-chic barroom and streamlined dining room serve the chic set. Fare ranges from caviar to rack of lamb. *1015 Rush St., between Oak St. and Bellevue Pl., Gold Coast, 312/475–0300. AE, D, DC, MC, V. $$*

7 *c-7*
WILDFIRE
Named for the open, flaming grill spanning the back wall, Wildfire warms to hearth cookery in a cozy, private club setting. Snag a comfy booth, watch the rotisserie-spun chickens, and settle in

for wood-fired or spit-roasted eats strong on meat like prime rib and barbe-cued ribs. The wood-fired oven does well by planked salmon, wood-roasted mussels, and pizzas, too. This is another hit from the Lettuce Entertain You repertoire. *159 W. Erie St., near LaSalle St., River North, 312/787–9000. AE, D, DC, MC, V. No lunch. $$–$$$*

4 *d-7*
YOSHI'S CAFE
This is a neighborhood favorite for French-Asian fare in a jeans-friendly atmosphere where kids are welcome with their own menu. Yoshi Katsumura's exceptional cooking includes inventive dishes such as grilled mahimahi with carrot juice and lobster essence or crab wontons with a ginger-apricot sweet-and-sour sauce. The dining room is a slightly crowded sea of white-linened tables and bentwood chairs. *3257 N. Halsted St., near Belmont Ave., Lakeview, 773/248–6160. AE, D, MC, V. No lunch. Closed Mon. $–$$$*

7 *b-6*
ZEALOUS
In a restaurant named Zealous, you might expect a circus on your plate. Instead rising-star chef Michael Taus serves playful food with refinement. À la carte standouts include foie gras on lob-ster toast and apricot-and-prune-stuffed guinea fowl. But he saves his best for five- and seven-course degustation menus, starting at $75, with each round a surprise to diners. Clustered bamboo plants, ceiling skylights, and a glass-enclosed wine safe provide eye appeal. *419 W. Superior St., near Orleans St., River North, 312/475–9112. AE, DC, MC, V. Closed Sun. $$$$*

7 *d-7*
ZINFANDEL
Regional American cooking updated with contemporary touches distin-guishes it from the River North pack. Chef Susan Goss explores the nation in dishes like burgoos, thick meat-and-veg-etable stews popular in the South; Mid-western pot roast; New England clambakes; and Pacific mahimahi encrusted in pecans. American folk art and a Southwestern color scheme create a homey atmosphere that underlines the culinary theme. *59 W. Grand Ave., near Dearborn St., River North, 312/527–1818. AE, D, MC, V. Closed Sun. $$–$$$*

CONTINENTAL

7 *d-3*
BIGG'S
This Gold Coast classic serves tradi-tional club fare in an arrestingly reno-vated mansion. The rich, wood-paneled rooms model marble fireplaces, chan-deliers, and dining tables that are for-mally appointed with linen, glassware, and cutlery. On the menu, look for American cuisine from another era such as beef Wellington and Dover sole; also try some caviar served at the handsome caviar bar. For an after-din-ner cigar head for the lower lounge. *1150 N. Dearborn St., at Elm St., Gold Coast, 312/787–0900. AE, D, DC, MC, V. No lunch. $$$*

3 *g-4*
LUTZ CONTINENTAL CAFE & PASTRY SHOP
This lost-in-time gem is reassuringly tra-ditional, serving whipped cream confec-tions as well as quiches, salads, and open-face sandwiches in an intimate tearoom with brocade banquettes. Wait-resses in white lace aprons deliver cof-fee and pastries on tiny silver tea trays. Pass through the front-of-the-house bak-ery to reach the *konditorei* pastry salon and, beyond that, the garden, a bloom-bordered patio with AstroTurf underfoot and a central gurgling fountain. Respectful attire among the mostly older clientele does not include jeans or shorts. *2458 W. Montrose Ave., at West-ern Ave., Lincoln Square, 773/478–7785. MC, V. Closed Mon. $–$$*

COSTA RICAN

2 *f-4*
IRAZU
Family-run Irazu, popular with thrifty Wicker Parkers, serves short-order Costa Rican fare with considerable care. Spe-cialties include *bistek tica* (steak with onions and peppers) and *chicharron* (fried pork with yucca and cabbage salad). Mexican-style torta sandwiches and meat-packed burritos are superior and great value for money. Cool your salsa-fired mouth with one of Irazu's exciting shake flavors such as guana-bana or tamarind. Don't be put off by the tiny front room packed by the to-go crowd. Take your meal to the muraled dining room behind the kitchen. *1865 N.*

Milwaukee Ave., near Western Ave., Wicker Park, 773/252–5687. No credit cards. BYOB. Closed Sun. $

CUBAN

2 *f-4*

CAFE BOLERO

The bossa nova piped over the speakers provides the swing in this unpretentious, hybrid neighborhood joint. Island-cuisine standouts include *bifstek palomilla* (steak with onions), shrimp Creole, and tangy chicken kebabs, all served with generous starchy sides. But half of the husband-and-wife team that owns Bolero is Serbian, which accounts for *cevapcici* (small spicy sausage) on the tapas menu and Niksico Pivo on the beer list. The pleasant sidewalk café is shaded by an awning in summer. *2252 N. Western Ave., at Belden Ave., West Bucktown, 773/227–9000. AE, D, DC, MC, V. $*

3 *d-1*

RANCHO LUNA

Named for a Havana eatery, pretty Rancho Luna is a storefront restaurant with far more character than the norm. Surrounded by Cuban paintings, diners dig into plates of grilled onion-topped steaks and chicken marinated in lime and garlic. *Congri* (white rice and black beans cooked together) makes a great side as does yucca *frita* for an ethnic version of french fries. Lunch options include generous Cuban meat sandwiches on crusty, grilled French bread. No booze is served, but there are lots of shakes in exotic fruit flavors. There is live music on weekends. *3357 W. Peterson Ave., near Kimball Ave., West Ridge, 773/509–9332. AE, D, MC, V. BYOB. $*

DELI

4 *d-8*

THE BAGEL RESTAURANT & DELI

In a town short on delis, the Bagel earns most votes as the best. The matzo ball soup contains a giant dumpling surrounded by cure-your-cold broth. Sandwiches are hearty, and fixings—bagels, cold cuts, cheeses, and so on—are available for eat-in and take-out. It's a good place to pick up picnic supplies on your way to nearby Lincoln Park. *3107 N.*

Broadway, at Barry Ave., Lakeview, 773/ 477–0300. AE, MC, V. $

5 *c-7*

FINKL'S

In an area short on lunch stops, everyone from area art-gallery owners to warehouse workers and high school students flocks to Finkl's. Satisfying deli sandwiches and salads center the menu. The decor is heavy on Chicago memorabilia; best looks are out the huge plate-glass windows to the busy Ogden-Milwaukee-Chicago intersection. *752 N. Ogden Ave., at Milwaukee and Chicago Aves., River West, 312/829–1699. AE, D, MC, V. Closed Sun. $*

6 *d-4*

MANNY'S COFFEE SHOP & DELI

A South Side institution, this place takes a no-nonsense approach that sends diners through the cafeteria line while jesting counter cooks provide commentary. Select from gargantuan corned beef sandwiches, potted Swiss steak, braised ox-tail stew, goulash, calves' tongue, brisket—a you-name-it selection from the Jewish larder. Search for a table in two teeming fluorescent-lit rooms crowded cheek-by-jowl with politicians, salesmen, firefighters, and kibitzing old-timers. You pay on your way out. *1141 S. Jefferson St., near Roosevelt Rd., South Loop, 312/939–2855. No credit cards. Closed Sun. No dinner. $*

EASTERN EUROPEAN

2 *f-2*

CAFÉ CROATIA

Cozy Northwest Sider Café Croatia is a slice of old country in the new. Dim lighting, polished wood, and servers in ethnic costumes set the scene for meat-rich dishes like spicy cevapcici, veal cutlet, and stuffed cabbage. On weekends, a tamburitza band adds to the exotic atmosphere that draws fans from the considerable Croatian community. *5726 N. Western Ave., between Bryn Mawr and Peterson Aves., West Ridge, 773/276–2842. AE, MC, V. Closed Sun.–Wed. $–$$*

2 f-6

HEALTHY FOOD LITHUANIAN RESTAURANT

Not every word in this eatery's name can be taken for face value. Although it's more of a diner than a full-blown restaurant, and the hearty meat-and-potatoes menu is not the contemporary definition of "healthy," Lithuanian fare is the staple here. Try the *blyani* (pancakes) for breakfast; for dinner, the *kolduan* (boiled meat dumplings) are quite filling. The place has been around for more than half a century, maintaining its original size of 14 tables and counter service. *3226 S. Halsted St., near 33rd St., Bridgeport, 312/326–2724. No credit cards. $*

3 g-4

SIMPLON ORIENT EXPRESS

Dishing up the cuisines found along the famed Istanbul-to-Paris *Orient Express* train route, this offbeat eatery throws in a selection of Serbian favorites such as *cevapcici* and *raznjici*, making this a polyglot Eastern European. Homey decor and a sincere welcome provide a comfortable journey. *4520 N. Lincoln Ave., between Montrose and Wilson Aves., Lincoln Square, 773/275–5522. AE, DC, MC, V. $$*

CHICAGO LANDMARKS

For a bite of quintessential Chicago sample these unique locales:

The Berghoff (German)
> *Since Prohibition, Berghoff has been pouring beer in its historic, stand-up bar.*

Billy Goat Tavern (American/Casual)
> *Immortalized on Saturday Night Live, Billy Goat serves "No Coke! Pepsi!"*

Charlie Trotter's (Contemporary)
> *Perhaps Chicago's—and the nation's—top chef draws devotees from far and wide to his Lincoln Park namesake.*

Lou Mitchell's (American/Casual)
> *Famous, high-fat breakfasts at this gregarious diner established in 1923.*

Pizzeria Uno (Pizza)
> *The home of deep-dish pizza. 'Nuf said.*

Wiener's Circle (Hot Dogs)
> *Char dogs served with attitude at 2 AM is an original Chicago experience.*

ECLECTIC

7 b-5

THE CHIC CAFÉ

Students at the Cooking and Hospitality Institute of Chicago staff the stoves at this school café, turning out ambitious gourmet fare at budget-friendly prices. The best deal is the three-course prix-fixe for about $12. The menu changes daily but might include such heady fare as poached lobster medallions with corn relish or goat cheese–stuffed chicken. Sandwiches, too, are available. Chefs are a little stingy with the salt, but other than that, the food is first rate. First-term pupils compose the well-intentioned waitstaff. *361 W. Chestnut St., at Orleans St., River North, 312/944–0882. MC, V. BYOB. No dinner Sun.–Thurs. $*

6 a-6

DEKEGAR

Dekegar is unique in many ways. Not only is it a good old American soul food–West African hybrid, but it's smack dab in the middle of a heavily Hispanic neighborhood. Each patron chooses a main course of meat, chicken, or fish and three sides ranging from creamy macaroni and cheese to cassava leaves and candied yams. Specials change daily or faster, keeping the 30-seat diner buzzing. *1530 W. 18th St., near Ashland Ave., Pilsen, 312/243–3863. No credit cards. BYOB. Closed Sun. $*

4 b-6

DISH

The tiny quarters are a funky setting for tasty food that ranges from Southwest to Northeast. Fish dishes and salads are particularly pert. And the presence of the young chef-owner milling about the vintage-radio-ringed room ensures consistency and service. It's a good stop before or after a movie at the Music Box. Tables are one atop the other, so don't expect privacy. *3651 N. Southport Ave., between Addison St. and Waveland Ave., Lakeview, 773/549–8614. AE, MC, V. Closed Mon. $–$$*

2 f-4

FEAST

Restaurateur Debbie Sharpe lets her hair down in the casual, colorful Feast, a neighborhood joint with global fare. American, Asian, and Mediterranean notes are blended in dishes like coconut-curry chicken quesadillas and grilled duck with tart cherry sauce. Other times they stand alone, as in Southern fried chicken with collard greens. Sharpe also tends the appetizingly lush garden that makes her patio so popular. A seasonless atrium area defies the elements. *1835 W. North Ave., near Damen Ave., Bucktown, 773/235–6361. AE, DC, MC, V. No dinner Sun. $$*

7 *f-5*

FOODLIFE

Lettuce Entertain You takes the mall-food-court concept and ups the interest by creating food stations of astounding variety. Among the warren of aisles and tables are stands hawking Asian noodles, made-to-order wrap sandwiches, homemade pasta, soups, salads, hamburgers, fresh-squeezed juice, and assorted desserts including pies, cakes, and frozen yogurt. This self-service spot has lots of great to-go options popular with Gold Coasters and office lunchers. *Water Tower Pl., Mezzanine level, 835 N. Michigan Ave., at Pearson St., Magnificent Mile, 312/335–3663. AE, D, DC, MC, V. $*

2 *f-4*

JANE'S

The motto here is "clean cuisine." Vegetarian options include a garden burger, mesclun greens, and a veggie burrito. Those less limited in their diets will find pastas and fish dishes in ethnic-inspired arrangements. There are also a few red meat choices. A cozy, converted Bucktown cottage with an exposed peaked ceiling, the building alone draws a considerable crowd. When the beautiful people want low key, they go to Jane's. Expect to wait behind them. *1655 W. Cortland St., near Ashland Ave., Bucktown, 773/862–5263. MC, V. $$*

2 *f-4*

LEO'S LUNCHROOM

This funky storefront diner keeps the artists in the neighborhood from starving. Breakfast and lunch both include updated versions of standards like buckwheat pancakes and grilled sandwiches. Frequently changing dinner options—more ambitious though less successful—roam the culinary range and might include roast duck, blackened catfish, or wild mushroom risotto. The groove is very laid-back, even when there's a line to get in. *1809 W. Division St., near Damen Ave., Wicker Park, 773/276–6509. No credit cards. BYOB. Closed Mon. $*

5 *b-1*

LUCCA'S

Lucca's offbeat delights encompass its decor—candlelight, gilt frames, unusual oil paintings—as well as its food from the Mediterranean and beyond. Presentation clearly matters to the kitchen. Best of all, Lucca's has the sort of service-style-satisfaction quotient not normally found on a neighborhood corner. Locals love it. Expect frequent waits. *2834 N. Southport Ave., at Wolfram St., Lincoln Park, 773/477–2565. AE, DC, MC, V. Closed Mon. No lunch. $$*

7 *f-5*

MITY NICE GRILL

Shoppers and office workers who disdain food-court dining pass through the thronged Foodlife at Water Tower Place to get to Mity Nice Grill, a casual, '40s-flared grill from Lettuce Entertain You. The food aims for comfort—meat loaf, mac and cheese, prime rib—but reaches out globally with offerings such as seafood linguine, grilled flat bread, and Chinese chicken salad. Comfortable booths are conversation-friendly, but beware efficiency-minded servers and too-speedy cooks. *Water Tower Pl., Mezzanine level, 835 N. Michigan Ave., at Pearson St., Magnificent Mile, 312/335–3663. AE, D, DC, MC, V. $–$$*

5 *a-8*

MUNCH

This bright, tiny West Loop storefront took over when Wishbone moved out and is working hard to fill big-following shoes. Solid breakfasts stick to classics, with some trendy touches in scrambled egg wraps. Lunch on sandwiches and salads or hold out for more substantial fare at dinner, including ground lamb pasta or mustard-crusted pork. It has a comfortable, casual-arty vibe. *1800 W. Grand Ave., at Wood St., West Loop, 312/226–4914. AE, MC, V. $–$$*

4 *d-4*

PASTICHE

Just a block from the lake on the third floor of a high-rise, Pastiche plays hard-to-find in this eatery-poor part of town. The global menu, printed with international icons like the Eiffel Tower and the Leaning Tower of Pisa, includes Caribbean conch fritters, Mexican quesadillas, Asian pot stickers, Jamaican jerk chicken, and Italian fettuccine Alfredo. Sandwiches and the all-American burger are available, too. The nice outdoor deck in summer is patronized by actors and area residents. *4343 N. Clarendon St., at Montrose Ave., Uptown, 773/296–4999. AE, MC, V. Closed Mon.–Tues. $$*

5 *a-5*
SAVOY TRUFFLE
This quirky, charming café, infused by outgoing owner Wendy Gilbert's personality, turns out gorgeous meals—pastas, fish, salads—borrowing from Indian, Italian, Asian, and other cultures. Only eight tables populate the sunny yellow room, where Gilbert both cooks for and chats with guests. Hours, like seats, are limited, so Savoy virtually demands you plan for it. *1466 N. Ashland Ave., between Division St. and North Ave., Wicker Park, 312/772–7530. No credit cards. Closed Sun.–Tues. $$*

5 *f-5*
TANZY
Glass chandeliers and vibrant color-block walls tip Tanzy's lighthearted hand. The globe-trotting menu should satisfy most palates. Try the trilogy of tartares—tuna, salmon, and scallop—for a light, zesty bite, or three-cheese macaroni for more heft. Across the street from Piper's Alley movie theater and Second City, it makes a great before- or after-show stop. The patio with a wall of individually potted flowers greens the urban scene. *215 W. North Ave., near Wells St., Old Town, 312/ 202–0302. AE, MC, V. $$*

5 *d-3*
TILLI'S
Friendly neighborhood globalist Tilli's does decent versions of everything from rigatoni with fennel sausage to Caesar salad with chicken to Thai barbecue salmon. A cozy fireplace divides the two brick-exposed rooms and abets the warmth of the staff. Windows open onto Halsted street, extending an invitation to stop by while you're in the Armitage-Halsted district. The sizable bar stocks some interesting brews. *1952 N. Halsted St., at Armitage Ave., Lincoln Park, 773/ 325–0044. AE, D, DC, MC, V. $–$$*

ENGLISH

5 *d-2*
RED LION PUB
Beloved of regulars, Red Lion serves as a popular pub with pretty good grub for

Anglophiles. Service is erratic and the place is rather dog-eared, but the piping-hot fish-and-chips are worth the occasional inconvenience. The balance of the authentic fare includes Welsh rarebit, bangers and mash, and shepherd's pie. There are great English ales on tap and in bottles. Conversation can be challenged by videotaped movies playing—sound track intact—on some evenings. *2446 N. Lincoln Ave., near Halsted Ave., Lincoln Park, 773/348–2695. AE, MC, V. $*

2 *g-3*
ROSE & CROWN
This woody British barroom does right by its fish-and-chips though the balance of the menu cleaves to the American model. Beers are straight from the Isles, and the Anglophile decor underlines the theme. Eat, drink and throw darts. *420 W. Belmont Ave., at Lake Shore Dr., Lakeview, 773/248–6654. D, DC, MC, V. $*

ETHIOPIAN

4 *c-7*
ADDIS ABEBA
Perhaps Chicago's best Ethiopian, and certainly its most attractive, this restaurant sets the scene with native art and decor to introduce its flavorful eat-with-your-hands stews, breads, and vegetarian specialties from North Africa. Dishes are served family style, ideal for groups to sample widely from the exotic menu. Use *injera* (flat bread) to pick up roasted lentils, cardamom-spiced steak tartare, and garlicky chicken stir-fry. *3521 N. Clark St., near Addison St., Wrigleyville, 773/929–9383. AE, D, MC, V. No lunch. $*

4 *c-7*
ETHIOPIAN VILLAGE/ ETHIO CAFÉ
It's mostly vegetarian here, but even hard-core carnivores can find something to their liking. Alhough you can order individually, meals with more than one person tend to become intimate family-style occasions. A relaxing diversion is the Ethiopian coffee ceremony, an hour-long meditation involving roasted coffee on Thursday afternoons. Saturday night, come for the live jazz and try the homemade honey wine. *3462 N. Clark St., near Newport St., Wrigleyville, 773/929–8300. AE, D, DC, V. $$*

4 *d-8*

MAMA DESTA'S RED SEA

Chicago's matriarch among Ethopian restaurants, Mama Desta's sanctions eating with your hands. Tear a hunk from the large, spongy and slightly sour flat-bread injera, served beneath main courses, and use it to scoop up toppings such as the spicy chicken called *doro wat,* or lamb stew with pureed lentils. Spices are insistent and the eating is hearty—come ravenous. *3216 N. Clark St., near Belmont Ave., Wrigleyville, 773/935-7561. AE, DC, MC, V. No lunch Sun.–Thurs. $*

FONDUE

2 *e-2*

FONDUE STUBE

Remember when fondue was at its most popular? Fondue Stube does, especially with its Regal Beagle decor; circa 1970s wood paneling and stained glass provide a dim illumination over a small dining room crowded with tables. Couples and groups don't have to lean far to dip meats, breads, and fruits into oil, cheese, and chocolate fondue pots. *2717 W. Peterson Ave., near Fairfield St., West Ridge, 773/784-2200. AE, D, DC, MC, V. No lunch. $$*

5 *e-3*

GEJA'S CAFE

Courting couples duck below street level into romantic Geja's dimly lit alcoves, where Sterno flames keep the fondue oozing while a flamenco guitarist softly strums. Interactive foods that emerge from the fondue pot include the Swiss cheese classic as well as beef, vegetable, and the irresistible liquid chocolate dessert accompanied by dip-ready pound cake and strawberries. A much-lauded wine list adds more incentive to the pot. Don't expect to get near Geja's on Valentine's Day without weeks of advance planning. *340 W. Armitage Ave., between Clark St. and Lincoln Ave., Lincoln Park, 773/281-9101. AE, D, DC, MC, V. No lunch. $$*

FRENCH

5 *e-2*

AMBRIA

A top special occasion and expense-account splurge, Ambria inhabits a refined art nouveau room rich in dark woods. The sophisticated setting houses chef Gabino Sotelino's contemporary French cuisine. The modestly understated menu dazzles with items like blackberry-sauced venison, lobster gazpacho, and rosemary-infused lamb loin. Do end with the sensational dessert soufflé. Highly regarded sommelier Bob Bansberg oversees the wine list. The service is polished, the clientele well dressed. *2300 N. Lincoln Park W, near Fullerton Ave., Lincoln Park, 773/472-5959. Reservations essential. AE, D, DC, MC, V. No smoking. Closed Sun. No lunch. $$$–$$$$*

5 *d-3*

AUBRIOT

With a blue ribbon résumé—apprentice to Alain Ducasse, chef at Carlos—twentysomething chef Eric Aubriot showcases his precociously seasoned palate in this intimate 56-seater. Contemporary French star turns include smoked-salmon-draped crab salad, signature potato-wrapped goat cheese salad, and seared sea bass in seafood emulsion. Don't miss the daily dessert soufflé. To snare a seat in the tiny Halsted-facing sunflower room, phone ahead. *1962 N. Halsted St., at Armitage Ave., Lincoln Park, 773/281-4211. AE, D, DC, MC, V. Closed Mon. $$–$$$*

7 *e-5*

BISTRO 110

Bistro 110 remains a lively neighborhood favorite by courting the locals, seating regulars even when there's a wait. The wood-burning oven dishes are tops on the classic French menu, from the whole roasted garlic accompanied by crusty bread to the roast chicken entrée. Other highlights include the Brie-stuffed artichoke, cassoulet *toulousain* (white beans, duck confit, sausage, and lamb) and bouillabaisse. The chalkboard in the dining room announces happenings from today's headlines to movie showtimes. The Sunday jazz brunch is a standout. *110 E. Pearson St., at Michigan Ave., Magnificent Mile, 312/266-3110. AE, D, DC, MC, V. $$*

5 *f-5*

BISTROT MARGOT

This French toast of the town serves fine bistro fare in a gorgeous art nouveau interior for few francs—a combination of traits that sends neighborhood natives storming for escargots, moules, and steak frites. No item exceeds $20. They only taste like they do. Expect close quarters. *1437 N. Wells St., north of Schiller St., Old Town, 312/587–3660. AE, DC, MC, V. No lunch. $$*

4 *b-7*

BISTROT ZINC/CAFÉ ZINC

These popular French twins cater to a neighborhood crowd. In the more casual Café, a zinc-topped bar, round marble tables, and wicker chairs surrounded by potted palms aptly emulate a Parisian boîte with beer *au pression* (on tap), a good selection of wines by the glass, and light bites like crepes, *salade niçoise* (salad with green beans, onions, tuna, hard-cooked eggs, and herbs), quiches, and croque sandwiches. The bistro with its tomato-red walls and dim lighting is more formal and features French classics such as steak *frites* (with crispy ribbon fries), *poulet grandmère* (chicken roasted with onions and mushrooms), and duck confit. *3443 N. Southport Ave., at Roscoe Ave., Lakeview, 773/281–3443. AE, D, MC, V. Closed Mon. $–$$$*

7 *d-4*

Unlike the original bifurcated North Side location, the downtown Bistrot Zinc blends bistro and café in one room. *1131 N. State St., between Cedar St. and Elm St., Gold Coast, 312/337–1131. $$–$$$*

7 *d-8*

BRASSERIE JO

Chef Jean Joho, who also owns the gourmet Everest, revisited his Alsatian roots in Brasserie Jo. La crème de la crème consists of *choucroute* (Alsatian sauerkraut), onion tart, and the classic coq au vin. Don't skip the grease-less frites, which come in a paper-lined cup. Authentic brasserie trimmings—brass rails, mirrors, ferns—garnish this stylish spot, which also draws a considerable crowd of drinkers and nibblers to its marble-top bar. There, hard-boiled eggs in a wire egg rack are, in the French café tradition, free. *59 W. Hubbard St., at Dearborn St., River North, 312/595–0800. AE, D, DC, MC, V. No lunch weekends. $$–$$$*

5 *d-3*

CAFÉ BERNARD

This aging Lincoln Parker does surprisingly solid French fare despite its rather dark appearance. If you want nouveau cuisine, head down the street to

Aubriot. But if you crave duck à l'orange and similar French pantry staples, stop in and see the laid-back Bernard. There's usually room for you. *2100 N. Halsted St., between Armitage and Webster Aves., Lincoln Park, 773/871–2100. AE, D, DC, MC, V. $$*

2 *f-4*

CAFÉ MATOU

For simple, earthy, uncomplicated French fare, Café Matou satisfies. Though situated on the still-ragged fringes of Bucktown, it is quietly upscale. Classics like pâté, snail-stuffed tomatoes, trout amandine, and grilled chicken in lemon and olive oil are lick-your-plate good. A list of daily specials accompanies the menu (hope for the duck confit salad). Presentation eschews the fussy. Service can occasionally be slow. *1846 N. Milwaukee Ave., near Ashland Ave., Bucktown, 773/384–8911. AE, D, DC, MC, V. Closed Mon. $$*

7 *c-7*

CYRANO'S BISTROT & WINE BAR

This is one of the prettiest French bistros in the city and features the food of chef-owner Didier Durand's native French southwest. Rotisserie meats—chicken, duck, and lamb served with your choice of sauce (wine and herb, jus, or mustard) and sides (such as *pommes frites* or spinach)—are the focus of the flexible menu. At midday, the Grand Lunch Express combines four courses on a large platter—ideal for the time-constrained. Under a sky-blue ceiling, yellow walls showcase ornately framed mirrors. *546 N. Wells St., between Ohio St. and Grand Ave., River North, 312/467–0546. AE, D, DC, MC, V. Closed Sun. No lunch weekends. $$*

7 *f-5*

THE DINING ROOM

James Beard Society award-winning chef Sarah Stegner whips up outstanding nouvelle French cuisine at the Ritz-Carlton's Dining Room. Using infused oils and vegetable reductions, Stegner's signature is full flavor without the normally attendant fat content. From caviar-and-lobster salad, move on to the perfected seared rack of lamb or the sea bass with a tomato-saffron remoulade. Save room for the cheese course, a heaving cart of 20-plus cheeses. Service is gracious and the elegant room is outfitted in classic French style: walnut paneling, tapestry carpets, and crystal chandeliers. *Ritz-Carlton, 160 E. Pearson St., near Michigan Ave., Magnificent Mile, 312/266–1000. Reservations essential. Jacket and tie. AE, D, DC, MC, V. No lunch. $$$–$$$$*

8 *c-4*
EVEREST
Alsatian-born chef Jean Joho makes Everest a food lover's mecca for fine French cuisine, using top American ingredients like Pennsylvania lamb, Wisconsin veal, and Maine halibut. Joho is renowned for mixing the lowly (i.e., cauliflower) with the luxurious (caviar) in dishes such as pheasant wrapped in savoy cabbage. Like scaling its namesake mountain, Everest requires effort to get to (three elevators), but diners are compensated by a stellar West Side view of streaming traffic and twinkling city lights from the 40th floor of the Chicago Stock Exchange. Prices are also steep, making this a strong special-occasion choice. *440 S. LaSalle St., at Van Buren St., Loop, 312/663–8920. Reservations essential. AE, D, DC, MC, V. Closed Sun.– Mon. $$$$*

2 *h-7*
LA PETITE FOLIE
With so few good upscale restaurants in the area, the tiny "Little Madness" has become a mecca for university types and other locals hungry for haute cuisine. The menu is as perfectly appointed as the high-back chairs and crisp white linen. The foie gras appetizer comes with gossamer slices of pears, and the lime-cured salmon is simple and tangy. The wine list is moderately priced— almost half the bottles are less than $30. *1504 E. 55th St., near Lake Park Ave., Hyde Park, 773/493–1394. AE, D, DC, MC, V. Closed Mon. $$$*

6 *c-1*
LA SARDINE
The younger, urban sister to Le Bouchon, La Sardine is chef Jean-Claude Poilevey's step in the trendy direction. Befitting the warehouse-lined West Loop, the restaurant is less intimate than its elder sibling, packing in a smart crowd that makes for lively people-watching. Fear not the scene; food is foremost here. Start with the savory leek tart or the warm goat cheese salad, but be sure to leave room for the stuffed

pheasant and seafood-rich bouillabaisse. *111 N. Carpenter St., between Randolph St. and Washington Blvd., West Loop, 312/421–2800. AE, D, DC, MC, V. Closed Sun. No lunch Sat. $$–$$$*

2 *f-4*
LE BOUCHON
When Chicago's famed "hawk" wind blows there's no better bistro to duck into than this cozy Bucktowner serving authentic food at budget-friendly prices. Thanks to its high value quotient, Le Bouchon has hordes of fans among urban neighbors and suburban sojourners. They come for classics like snails in garlic butter, duck confit salad, steak frites, and herb-roasted chicken. This is a great place to linger over a bottle of *vin rouge*; there's a nice list of regional wines. *1958 N. Damen Ave., at Armitage Ave., Bucktown, 773/862–6600. AE, D, DC, MC, V. Closed Sun. No lunch. $$*

7 *f-7*
LES NOMADES
Owned by the acclaimed Mary Beth and Roland Liccioni, formerly of Le Français, Les Nomades prepares classic French

---

BIG DEAL DINNER SPOTS

When it's time to celebrate, bust the budget at one of these worth-the-splurge spots:

Ambria (Contemporary)
Seductive art nouveau interior showcases fine food and top wines.

Arun's (Thai)
Exquisite Thai prix-fixe meals redefine the ethnic category in a clean, contemporary setting.

Charlie Trotter's (Contemporary)
Everyone must dine at Trotter's once for the gorgeous food and refined service.

The Dining Room (French)
Nouveau French from a top chef in a classic chandeliered and tapestried room.

Spiaggia (Italian)
Romantic, multitiered room with a view of the lake and imaginative contemporary Italian.

TRU (Contemporary)
Whimsical presentations of serious food in multiple courses with art all around.

food in a formal setting. Lodged in a handsome Streeterville graystone, the dining room has a starched atmosphere that's softened by nautical accents. Plan on two to three hours for a meal, but you're likely to agree that the almond-crusted foie gras, pâté trio, lamb shank, and roasted monkfish are worth the wait—and the significant expense. *222 E. Ontario St., near St. Clair Ct., Streeterville, 312/649–9010. Reservations essential. Jacket and tie. AE, MC, V. Closed Sun.–Mon. No lunch. $$$*

6 *d-1*
MARCHÉ
A bustling open kitchen, a spacious loft trimmed in collage and paint, curvaceous metal chairs, a waiter dressed like a *Braveheart* warrior: Marché is restaurant as theater. The chic scene is amplified by a trendy and celebrity clientele. Not to be overshadowed, the brasserie fare gets high marks for generous portions of French onion soup, seasonal salads, spit-roasted rabbit, and braised lamb shank. Choose from 12 items—one of the largest selections in town—on the dessert tray. *833 W. Randolph St., near Halsted St., West Loop, 312/226–8399. AE, DC, MC, V. No lunch weekends. $$–$$$$*

5 *e-2*
MON AMI GABI
Casual cousin to formal Ambria across the lobby, Mon Ami Gabi allows chef Gabino Sotelino to play with bistro classics. Service details have *esprit*: wine is poured from bottles on an elegant wood trolley and baguettes arrive in bakery bags. The cozy oak-paneled room is trimmed with copper cooking pots, mirrors, and black-and-white photos. Window tables have a view of the Lincoln Park Conservatory. In summer, take advantage of Gabi's proximity to the park at one of its smart outdoor café tables. *2300 N. Lincoln Park W, at Fullerton Ave., Lincoln Park, 773/348–8886. AE, D, DC, MC, V. No lunch. $$–$$$*

8 *e-1*
MOSSANT BISTRO
This Parisian-style bistro has all the standards like foie gras and duck. Breakfast, lunch, and dinner sittings are separated by several hours, so getting a table at the popular theater district spot is harder than usual. It's worth the trouble for the signature beef tenderloin. *Hotel*

Monaco, 225 N. Wabash Ave., near Lake St., Loop, 312/236–9300. Reservations essential. AE, DC, MC, V. $$$

4 *d-7*
OO-LA-LA!
The name is fun to say, especially after a few sips from the extensive wine list. Most of the menu is French-focused, but you don't have to look too hard to find Italian dishes like *fusilli con pollo* (pasta with chicken) or veal piccata. The outdoor patio is a great way to spend a summer's evening before going dancing along the strip. Two events not to miss: Wednesday's jazz trio and Sunday's border brunch. *3335 N. Halsted St., near Roscoe St., Wrigleyville, 773/935–7708. AE, V. No dinner Sun. $$$*

5 *a-2*
RUDI'S WINE BAR & CAFÉ
For well-priced classic bistro bites—think snails and pâté—in this restaurant-poor part of town, Rudi's earns raves. Friendly servers are adept at orienting the less knowledgeable to the wine list. With close-set tables populating a tiny room, Rudi's gets convivial quickly though second-hand smoke sometimes intrudes. *2424 N. Ashland Ave., between Fullerton and Diversey Aves., Lakeview, 773/404–7834. AE, DC, MC, V. No lunch. $$*

7 *c-6*
SAVARIN
Named for 19th-century gourmet Jean Anthelme Brillat-Savarin, Savarin pays homage to classic French foods. The crisp downstairs dining room specializes in savory Gallic staples like sausage and pâté, onion soup, and roast duck under the expert direction of chef John Hogan. Ideal for cocktailing, the sophisticated club room upstairs is ringed by a dozen or so specially commissioned portraits of chefs—all Hogan's mentors and contemporaries. Despite the insider trappings, you need know nothing about epicureans to enjoy the spectacle. *713 N. Wells St., between Huron and Superior Sts., River North, 312/255–9520. AE, D, DC, MC, V. No lunch. $$$*

5 *f-6*
YVETTE'S
Classic French fare romanced by a live piano player draws legions of Gold Coast regulars to this restaurant. The reliable versions of escargots and steak

au poivre can also make great late-night meals while listening to a jazz trio. Apart from its boisterous neighbors, Yvette's aims for an older crowd than normally spotted at the State-Division intersection. *1206 N. State St. at Division St., Gold Coast, 312/280–1700. AE, DC, MC, V. $$*

GERMAN

8 *d-4*
THE BERGHOFF
A Chicago institution for more than 100 years, the Berghoff is beloved by townies and tourists alike. The former pack the wood-paneled, standing-room-only bar, propped up belly-to-belly over sandwiches and beer (Berghoff, holder of city liquor license number 1, has been tapping kegs since the end of Prohibition). Out-of-towners frequently line up for the old-world chow—Wiener schnitzel, sauerbraten, etc.—as well as some modernized lighter fare in the atmospheric dining room. Service, once you are seated, is swift. *17 W. Adams St., near State St., Loop, 312/427–3170. AE, MC, V. Closed Sun. $–$$*

3 *g-3*
CHICAGO BRAUHAUS
This lively Lincoln Square landmark serves up swelling Wiener schnitzel and other plentiful German standards as well as live entertainment—think concertina and accordion—nightly. Family friendly, the Brauhaus bends over backward to please patrons. The effort is infectious, and the dim Bavarian interior grows on you, too. *4732 N. Lincoln Ave., near Lawrence Ave., Lincoln Square, 773/784–4444. AE, D, DC, MC, V. Closed Tues. $–$$*

3 *h-5*
RESI'S BIERSTUBE
For authenticity and warmth it's tough to beat family-run Resi's. The tiny wood-paneled bar-restaurant draws young urbanites as well as old immigrants with its sausage-heavy menu and 13 German beers on tap (plus 100 more varieties in the bottle). In summer, the well-hidden beer garden, with two large maple trees towering over a flower box–trimmed patio, is an urban idyll, where, in the company of a lemon-garnished *weissbier*, you can work up an appetite for less seasonal schnitzel from the kitchen.

2034 W. Irving Park Rd., near Damen Ave., North Center, 773/472–1749. AE, D, DC, MC, V. $

GREEK

5 *d-3*
ATHENIAN ROOM
The serviceable Greek fare here suits the neighborhood regulars who pop in for solid standards at low prices—rare in pricey Lincoln Park. The gyros are good, as is the Greek chick with fries. The patio is pleasant in season. *807 W. Webster Ave., at Halsted Ave., Lincoln Park, 773/348–5155. MC, V. $*

6 *d-2*
COSTA'S
Though the menu resembles other Greektown establishments, Costa's outshines its neighbors in atmosphere and attitude. Whitewashed walls, arches, and terra-cotta tile floors evoke the Aegean islands. Choose from a long list of hot and cold meze to share. For entrées, the grilled meat kebabs and baked moussaka are excellent. Nightly live piano adds to the energy and the noise level. This is a great spot to take the clan. *340 S. Halsted St., at Van Buren St., Greektown, 312/263–9700. AE, D, DC, MC, V. $$–$$$*

6 *d-2*
GREEK ISLANDS
One of the largest restaurants in Greektown, it has 400 seats, several dining rooms, and an outdoor patio. Peek into the kitchen to see what's good today—the cooking is done in plain view. If you're both hungry and brave, try the "Spartan Warrior Feast," a huge pork tenderloin with vegetables, rice, and potatoes. Or, just stick with the daily selections of fresh seafood, lamb, or chicken. *200 S. Halsted St., near Adams St., Greektown, 312/782–9855. AE, D, DC, V. $$*

1 *b-4*
300 E. 22nd St., near Stewart Ave., Lombard 630/932–4545.

7 *d-7*
PAPAGUS
Lettuce Entertain You's excellent Greek number, Papagus, re-creates a rustic family taverna. The menu starts off with *mezethes*, or "little bites," of classic fare

like *saganaki* (flaming cheese), *skordalia* (potato-garlic spread), and eggplant spread. For dessert order the unusual cherry baklava. The all-Greek wine list has some wonderful inexpensive bottles; trust your waiter's recommendation. *Embassy Suites, 620 N. State St., at Ontario St., River North, 312/642–8450. AE, D, DC, MC, V. $$–$$$*

6 *d-2*

THE PARTHENON
Not only does the Parthenon claim to have invented saganaki—the Greek flaming cheese that prompts cries of "Opaa!" around the world—but the venerable Greektown spot also takes credit for serving the first gyro in America. Spirits run high here and checks low as buoyant customers seated in two muraled rooms dig into simple preparations of fish and lamb as well as Greek favorites like spinach pie and stuffed grape leaves. *314 S. Halsted St., at Van Buren St., Greektown, 312/726–2407. AE, D, DC, MC, V. $–$$$*

6 *d-2*

PEGASUS RESTAURANT AND TAVERNA
Bright is definitely the word for this place with a huge skylight over the dining room and a front wall of windows that opens onto the street during summer. In warm weather, the rooftop café offers a great view and light eats. On weeknights, a live trio plays easy-listening music. The medium-size restaurant seats 220 and specializes in mezethes and Greek antipasti. A sign of Greek hospitality—it will bus you to Bulls and Blackhawks home games and to and from area hotels. *130 S. Halsted St., near Monroe St., Greektown, 312/226–3377. AE, D, DC, V. $$*

7 *f-5*

QP
Far away from Greektown, this establishment in the Seneca Hotel offers an upscale Greek dining experience. Navy sconces and light Mediterranean music give the dining room an authenticity, as does the big burly maître d' who greets you at the door with a heavy Chicago accent. Prices are higher than at Halsted Street restaurants, but an extensive wine list and top-notch chef can make you forget. The specialty of the house is *yuvetsi*, beef or lamb baked in a pastry, brought steaming hot to the table.

Seneca Hotel, 200 E. Chestnut St., near Mies van der Rohe Way, Magnificent Mile, 312/751–2100. AE, D, DC, MC, V. $$

6 *d-2*

RODITYS
Traditional favorites abound here, from saganaki (flaming cheese) to *spanakotiropita* (phyllo-wrapped cheese and spinach pies), but lamb dishes, such as village-style cutlets, shish kebabs, and lamb with artichokes, have been drawing crowds since 1972. Locals come for the daily and weekly lunch special, and by the weekend, it's standing room only at the bar. The ocean-inspired murals and traditional music create a festive mood. *222 S. Halsted St., near Quincy St., Greektown, 312/454–0800. AE, V. Reservations not accepted Fri. and Sat. nights. $$*

6 *d-2*

SANTORINI
The seafood here is the biggest draw—there's an extensive array of delicious and not-too-expensive ocean, freshwater, and shell fish. The red snapper and sea bass are broiled simply and seasoned with oregano, and the grilled octopus is tender and tasty. Other traditional dishes are prepared only a few days a week. A favorite, *exohiko* lamb (phyllo-wrapped braised lamb and Greek cheese) is only available Monday, Wednesday, and Friday. *800 W. Adams St., near Halsted St., Greektown, 312/829–8820. AE, V. $$*

GUATEMALAN

3 *h-7*

EL TINAJON
Owner Olga Pezzarossi, a native of Guatemala, travels home several times each year to bring back spices for her tidy storefront restaurant. With less grease and spice-heat than Mexican food, Guatemalan cooking stresses soups and meat stews. El Tinajon also does a brisk business in more familiar enchiladas and burritos. With the rise of Roscoe Village gentrification, El Tinajon has caught on and can be crowded on weekend nights when live musicians entertain. *2054 W. Roscoe Ave., near Damen Ave., Roscoe Village, 773/525–8455. AE, DC, MC, V. $*

HAWAIIAN

8 *d-3*

TRADER VIC'S

Two sides of island invasion are represented here: one side of the restaurant is a sandy tiki bar, and the other looks like Mr. Howell decorated it. It's enough to make you reach for the signature mai tai made with two kinds of rum. When you don't have time for a complete roast pig, the Asian-inspired lunch buffet is a quick, inexpensive treat. *17 E. Monroe St., near State St., Loop, 312/917–7317. AE, D, DC, V. $$$*

HOT DOGS

7 *d-8*

GOLD COAST DOGS

Popular pups purveyor, Gold Coast crowds the bun with tomatoes, pickles, onions, hot peppers, celery salt—you name it—along with the frank. Fries are a must: the cheddar versions are worth the cholesterol overdose. Most of the crowd go for the dogs, but Gold Coast also serves sandwiches, chili, and breakfast items. *418 N. State St., at Hubbard St., River North, 312/527–1222. No credit cards. $*

2 *e-1*

SUPERDAWG DRIVE-IN

For the sake of nostalgia, pile the troops in the car and park it at Superdawg, where carhops deliver your meal on a window tray. A pair of larger-than-life hot dogs perch atop the low-slung drive-in, a 1948 Windy City landmark now surrounded by competing fast-food drive-thru lanes. But spirited Superdawg wraps, burgers, dogs, and shakes in '50s-era graphics salute diners with "Hiya!!" Don't forget to tip the carhops. *6363 N. Milwaukee Ave., at Devon Ave., Jefferson Park, 773/763–0660. No credit cards. $*

5 *e-1*

WIENER'S CIRCLE

Char dogs—hot dogs split lengthwise and grilled—are a Chicago institution and Wiener's Circle is the place to score 'em late night. "Hey buddy, whadd'll ya have?" cry Wiener's wags, who work seven to a window hawking dogs and razzing the post-barroom clientele. Verbal abuse comes with "the works"—mustard, relish, onion, celery salt, hot peppers, and so on, but it's all in good fun. *2622 N. Clark St., near Wrightwood Ave., Lincoln Park, 773/477–7444. No credit cards. $*

HUNGARIAN

2 *d-3*

PAPRIKASH

This place serves regional dishes that taste like they might in a Budapest home: hearty, meaty, and with more than just a touch paprika. Wash down your meal with one of almost 30 kinds of Hungarian wines. The dining room is open through the wee hours, serving food until 1 AM every day—so you know where to go if you get a craving for *lecso* (tomato stew with peppers and onions) in the middle of the night. There's gypsy music on the weekends. *5210 W. Diversey Ave., near Lockwood Ave., Belmont Cragin, 773/736–4949. V. $$*

INDIAN

7 *d-6*

GAYLORD

For a sultan-worthy feast in a more-gracious-than-most atmosphere seek out Gaylord. This River North spot does a superior job with dishes from the northern region of Punjab. Lamb is a big seller here (try lamb *biryani*, a rice dish) or chicken in *masala* sauce. Clay oven-cooked breads are addictive, including the basic nan as well as *kulcha*, a heavier version of nan made with onion and potato. Service is attentive. *678 N. Clark St., at Huron St., River North, 312/664–1700. AE, DC, MC, V. $$*

7 *f-7*

INDIAN GARDEN

Creativity and a healthful orientation help distinguish Indian Garden from the ethnic pack. Gravy-based dishes derive their flavor from spices rather than fats, producing a lighter version of northern Indian specialties. Unusual dishes from the clay tandoor oven include the signature *reshmi* kebab, a yogurt- and spice-marinated chicken dish cooked in a copper pan. There are plenty of meatless choices. Combination plates are a good way to sample from the extensive menu. *247 E. Ontario St., 2nd floor, near Fairbanks St., Streeterville, 312/280–4910. AE, D, DC, MC, V. $–$$*

7 *d-8*

JAIPUR PALACE

Take off for India in this seductive restaurant with a spice-hued palette. Linen-covered tables set the stage for fine food from the tender tandoori chicken to the fresh-and-hot nan (bread) and good vegetarian options. As at most other Indian spots, the lunch buffet is a bargain, which draws loads of value-seeking office escapees. *22 E. Hubbard St., at State St., River North, 312/595–0911. AE, D, DC, MC, V. $$*

2 *f-1*

2548 W. Devon Ave., near Western Ave., West Ridge, 773/338–2929.

5 *e-8*

KLAY OVEN

For Indian cuisine in an upscale atmosphere, cop a seat in this airy dining room decorated with Indian artifacts. The bargain lunch buffet satisfies area workers while dinner draws a haven-seeking clientele. And the food outshines many others with a keen emphasis on freshness. *414 N. Orleans St., at Hubbard St., River North, 312/527–3999. AE, DC, MC, V. $$*

5 *d-1*

RAJ DARBAR

Raj occupies an important niche in Chicago's Indian dining scene: It is, perhaps, the ideal spot for novices. The menu covers the basics, and the knowledgeable, mostly American waitstaff serves above-average food. Begin with a traditional sampling of Indian appetizers, and then move on to the fine curried entrées; also try the soft, delicious Indian breads. Though dishes are spicy, none is particularly hot. Wine and a wide selection of beers, including three from India, are reasonably priced. *2660 N. Halsted Ave., near Wrightwood Ave., Lincoln Park, 773/348–1010. AE, D, DC, MC, V. $–$$*

4 *c-8*

STANDARD INDIA RESTAURANT

As far as supercasual, cheap eats go, Standard India sets the, well, standard. An expansive homemade buffet of tandoori favorites, lamb, kebabs, and paneer runs less than $10 for dinner (even less for lunch). Huge tables are perfect for groups. *917 W. Belmont Ave., near Wilton St., Wrigleyville, 773/929–1123. AE, V. BYOB. Closed Tues. $*

2 *f-1*

TIFFIN: THE INDIAN KITCHEN

Heavy wooden doors lead to a huge dining room paneled in dark wood with a mahogany bar on one side. Try the tandoori specialties, including the shrimp marinated in freshly ground spices and roasted in the clay oven. Vegetarians looking for a kick will be pleased with the vegetable *jalfazie* (stir-fried veggies, lightly spiced with coriander, red and green chilies, and cumin), to be washed down with a citrusy lime soda. Weekend nights are crowded. *2536 W. Devon Ave., near Maplewood Ave., West Ridge, 773/338–2143. AE, D, DC, V. $$*

2 *f-1*

UDUPI PALACE

In the Devon Avenue soup of competing Indian restaurants, Udupi Palace ranks tops for vegetarian dishes from southern India. The rice-based cuisine is lighter than the sauce- and meat-based northern cooking. Top choices include tamarind rice, coconut curry, *idli* (steamed rice patties), and *masala dosa* (potato- and onion-filled crepes eaten with soup and coconut chutney). Despite the name, the setting is less than palatial. *2543 W. Devon Ave., near Western Ave., West Ridge, 773/338–2152. AE, D, DC, MC, V. $*

2 *f-1*

VICEROY OF INDIA

Viceroy is a popular destination for parties of vegetarians and carnivores who don't want to be confined to one meal choice or the other. The *matter paneer* (homemade cottage cheese and peas cooked in onion, tomato, yogurt, and spices) is simultaneously cool and spicy; lamb dishes are the specialty. There's a take-out and bakery next door. *2516 W. Devon Ave., near Maplewood Ave., West Ridge, 773/743–4100, AE, DC, V. $*

INDONESIAN

6 *f-8*

AUGUST MOON

Although half the menu at this modest Chinatown restaurant is indeed Chinese, the Indonesian dishes are what set the place apart. Make a reservation and place your order a day in advance for *rijsttafel*, a feast devised by Indonesian cooks to impress the Dutch colonists, featuring small dishes (18 here) made with fish, meat, or vegetables and served with rice. The banquet is best experienced with a large, hungry group. Speak up if you like things spicy. *225 W. 26th St., near Wentworth Ave., Chinatown, 312/842–2951. Reservations essential. MC, V. BYOB. Closed Mon. $–$$$*

IRISH

7 *c-7*

FADO

From the sea of Guinness-swilling patrons you'd guess Fado ain't about food. But the popular Irish bar also aims for sustenance. There's no fear of famine with hearty mains like corned beef served in a potato pancake, Irish lamb stew, and shepherd's pie. For closers savor the brown bread ice cream. The Oz-like version of an Irish interior should stoke conversation. For the best service arrive well before 9 PM, when drinkers begin to boisterously outnumber diners. *100 W. Grand Ave., at Clark St., River North, 312/836–0066. AE, D, DC, MC, V. $–$$*

ISRAELI

5 *f-5*

OLD JERUSALEM

This cheap, quick-service spot serves up tasty falafel sandwiches and luscious veggie dips like hummus and baba ghanouj. Decor is bare-bones basic, but Old Jerusalem stalwarts swear by it as Old Town's only good-food budget option. *1411 N. Wells St., near North Ave., Old Town, 312/944–0459. AE, D, DC, MC, V. BYOB. $*

ITALIAN

4 *d-6*

ANGELINA RISTORANTE

This stylish yet cozy storefront Italian eatery earns accolades from neighboring Lakeview noodle lovers. Exposed brick and faux-finished walls encompass intimate rooms that are popular among courting couples. The menu breaks no barriers but turns in solid renditions of salad, pasta, and tiramisu. Waits can stretch to hours on weekends, but the hostess will fetch diners-to-be from Joe's on Broadway bar next door where they can wait over a drink. *3561 N. Broadway, at Addison St., Lakeview, 773/935–5933. AE, MC, V. $$*

2 *f-2*

A TAVOLA

This tiny Italian West Sider focuses on doing dishes right by limiting the menu to fit the confines of the space. The tempting grilled antipasti spread practically sits on top of the coat rack. The *primi piatti* feature a gnocchi to rave about. *Secondi* usually include a grilled fish, meat, and chicken option. Mixed greens are offered pre-dessert in Continental style. Save room for great *panna cotta* (cold custard) and flourless chocolate torte. Servers are knowledgeable and gracious. Come early: there are only 56 seats. *2152 W. Chicago Ave., near Damen Ave., Ukrainian Village, 312/276–7567. Closed Sun. $$*

2 *f-4*

BABALUCI

A neighborhood Italian restaurant that seems to please Bucktownies, Babaluci does decent traffic in pastas and veal preparations. The muraled, exposed brick walls keep the funky area beat. It's not a bad choice for take-out pizza when the pantry pales. There's live music on weekends. *2152 N. Damen Ave., at Webster Ave., Bucktown, 773/486–5300. AE, D, DC, MC, V. No lunch weekends. $–$$*

7 *f-7*

BICE

A gilded link in a chic, international chain, Bice serves a stylish clientele elegant northern Italian dishes. Though the menu changes monthly, regulars rave about the veal Milanese. For openers, try beef, tuna, or salmon carpaccio; panna cotta and gelato are simple but superior finishes. In summer the sidewalk café is inviting. Limited budgets will appreciate Bice Café, a less costly, more casual sibling next door. *158 E. Ontario St., near Michigan Ave., Streeterville, 312/664–1474. AE, D, DC, MC, V. No lunch Sun. $$$*

2 *f-6*

BRUNA'S RISTORANTE

In business since the 1930s when Oakley Avenue was the heart of a thriving Italian community on the Southwest Side, Bruna's is a comforting throwback to the old ways. The menu specializes in plentiful veal options as well as tasty, familiar pastas including linguine in clam sauce, lasagna, and tortellini Bolognese. The cozy room is ringed in murals and presided over by a portrait of Bruna herself, the original chef. *2424 S. Oakley Ave., at 24th Pl., Heart of Italy, 773/254–5550. AE, D, DC, MC, V. $$*

5 *g-7*
CAFÉ LUCIANO
A cheerful café that evokes the Mediterranean, Luciano specializes in rustic Italian epitomized by its signature rigatoni with sausage and pancetta. Thincrust pizzas and salads please lighter appetites. Portions are generous and prices reasonable, offering value that keeps customers coming back. Come expecting tight seating; Luciano packs 'em in. *871 N. Rush St., at Chestnut St., Gold Coast, 312/266–1414. AE, D, DC, MC, V. $$*

5 *g-6*
CARMINE'S
Prodigious portions of familiar Italian-American dishes distinguish Carmine's from the Rush Street lot. The same people who brought you oodles of noodles at Rosebud and Centro do so at Carmine's too, along with garlic-loving clams and several fish options, which you can digest to live piano in the bar. Crowds are the rule, not the exception. *1043 N. Rush St., between Cedar and Oak Sts., Gold Coast, 312/988–7676. AE, D, DC, MC, V. $$–$$$*

7 *c-6*
CENTRO
This place is as much about style as sustenance. A suave room with dark wood paneling, white tile floor, and black-and-white photos of stars like Frank Sinatra beckons a beautiful set who make securing a seat difficult (even with a reservation expect to be kept waiting). The food isn't daring but it is sizable. Expect to find delicious bread salad, linguine in an ocean of seafood, and popular standards like chicken Vesuvio. Prices are reasonable, considering you'll be taking home tomorrow's lunch. *710 N. Wells St., between Superior and Huron Sts., River North, 312/988–7775. AE, D, DC, MC, V. No lunch Sun. $$–$$$*

7 *b-6*
CLUB LAGO
It's still 1952 inside this colorful corner of Old Chicago anchoring trendy River North. Snare a bar-adjoining red vinyl booth or a checker-clothed back table to savor both traditional ambience and Italian fare. In clubby style, Lago serves many dishes omitted from the menu, so be sure to ask. Atmosphere beats food, but the Pasta Francois (with tomato, broccoli, and romano cheese) sings. *331 W. Superior St., at Orleans St., River North, 312/951–2849. AE, DC, MC, V. Closed Sun. No dinner Sat. $–$$*

2 *f-4*
CLUB LUCKY
A Bucktown social club remodeled into a '40s-style supper club with spacious booths and checked floors, Club Lucky plays the retro card. Cooking up a similar swagger, dishes are generous and include hearty classics like *pasta e fagioli* (pasta and bean soup), rigatoni and meatballs, and pork chops with peppers. There are tasty, substantial sandwiches at lunchtime. The popular bar in the front room specializes in mammoth martinis. *1824 W. Wabansia Ave., near Damen Ave., Bucktown, 773/227–2300. AE, D, DC, MC, V. $$*

7 *b-8*
COCO PAZZO
The who's who in Chicago embrace this River North branch of the New York Italian hot spot founded by celebrity restaurateur Pino Luongo. Coco Pazzo tends to draw Hollywood actors passing through town, the accolades of local food critics, and the regular patronage of opera and symphony performers. Its vast loft space, ideal for viewing the open kitchen, is softened by blue velvet swagging. Specialties on the Tuscan bill include pasta, risotto, and wood-roasted meats and pizzas; bread is made on the premises. Service is polished. *300 W. Hubbard St., at Franklin St., River North, 312/836–0900. AE, DC, MC, V. No lunch weekends. $$$*

7 *f-7*
COCO PAZZO CAFÉ
Where sister restaurant Coco Pazzo is an occasion eatery, Coco Pazzo Café aims for the everyday trade. The intimate, 95-seat room is warmed by glazed terracotta tile underfoot and enlivened by Modigliani-esque murals. The Tuscan

menu touts rustic, simple fare like gnocchi in tomato sauce and mushroom risotto. Don't pass up the salads, especially the seven vegetable version. For sides, try the inventive Tuscan fries: french fries tossed with caramelized onions, rosemary, and rock salt. It is one of the city's best summer sidewalk cafés, shaded by a generous awning. *636 N. St. Clair St., at Ontario St., Streeterville, 312/664–2777. AE, DC, MC, V. $$*

5 *d-8*
COMO INN

This Chicago staple since 1924 doesn't dare update its standard American fare—steaks, pastas, seafood. A metropolis of regulars might object. They come for the Marchetti family hospitality, which infuses this enormous, isolated West Loop eatery. The warren of distinctively decorated rooms includes some dedicated to a Florentine courtyard and a carnival. Popular on the event circuit, Como Inn also shuttles diners to and from the United Center. *546 N. Milwaukee Ave., at Ohio St., River West, 312/421–5222. AE, D, DC, MC, V. No lunch weekends. $$–$$$*

5 *b-3*
FILIPPO'S

Solid Italian cooking with some inventive touches keep Lincoln Parkers crowding—and overcrowding—this Clybourn storefront. The loft-style decor is softened by assorted dishware and floral linens. The risotto and veal scallopini are popular with regulars. Helpful staffers ensure a good experience at the family-run trattoria. *2211 N. Clybourn Ave., at Webster Ave., Lincoln Park, 773/528–2211. AE, DC, MC, V. $$*

6 *b-4*
FRANCESCA'S ON TAYLOR

Another popular restaurant run by some of the same partners behind Wrigleyville's Mia Francesca, Francesca's on Taylor brings the street up to date with a contemporary Italian kitchen. Pastas and entrées change regularly, but typical dishes include spinach-stuffed ravioli and roast halibut. With the exception of an occasional veal dish, few meat choices make the menu. Prices, as a result, are low. This is a good pre-event choice for the United Center–bound. *1400 W. Taylor St., at Loomis St., Little Italy, 312/829–2828. AE, MC, V. No lunch weekends. $–$$$*

7 *d-8*
HARRY CARAY'S

It's fun to play tourist at Harry Caray's, namesake of the legendary Cubs announcer who died in 1998. Inside the redbrick building emblazoned with Caray's famous "Holy Cow!" cry, you'll find yourself among passionate baseball fans as well as out-of-towners sharing in Harry's favorite food: Italian. The menu sets no records, but it's a solid hitter with pastas and ample steaks and chops. The memorabilia-laden room is casual and unpretentious. For barroom eats, elbow your way into the boisterous saloon and catch a Cubs game. *33 W. Kinzie St., at Dearborn St., River North, 312/828–0966. AE, D, DC, MC, V. $$–$$$*

8 *d-3*
THE ITALIAN VILLAGE RESTAURANTS

There are really three restaurants here: La Cantina, an intimate seafood dining room, great for a pre-theater meal without the crowd; Vivere, a trendy, modern eatery with a classy feel; and the namesake Village, a Loop institution since 1927. The theme here is outdoor trattoria, with a ceiling mural painted to look like the night sky. Intimate booths allow for privacy. The trio offers nightly specials and Italian classics into the wee hours. *71 W. Monroe St., near Dearborn St., Loop, 312/332–7005. AE, D, DC, MC, V. $$$*

3 *g-4*
LA BOCCA DELLA VERITA

For good Italian eats, the kind you normally have to go downtown for, North Siders luck out with La Bocca. This modest restaurant does classic foods well, including an outstanding duck breast ravioli, generous seafood risotto, and a time-honored sea bass baked in salt. La Bocca's three modest rooms aren't much to look at, but friendly servers provide some spark. Among La Bocca's collection of celebrity photos, Sylvester Stallone signed his "Your pasta's a knock-out." *4618 N. Lincoln Ave., near Montrose Ave., Lincoln Square, 773/784–6222. AE, D, MC, V. Closed Mon. $$*

4 *b-2*
LA DONNA

Paper-covered tables clustered together in this warmly accented storefront make customers feel like part of a very large party. The top choice in Andersonville for

Italian, La Donna serves great pastas like pumpkin ravioli in creamy balsamic sauce and spicy penne arrabiata. Pizzas are also excellent. The wine list is well chosen and fairly priced, and there's a bargain-price Sunday brunch. *5146 N. Clark St., near Foster Ave., Andersonville, 773/561–9400. AE, D, DC, MC, V. $$–$$$*

8 *d-3*

LA ROSETTA

With butter-toned walls, wood paneling, white tablecloths, and soft lighting, La Rosetta manages to defy its office-building atrium setting. A link in the Rosebud Restaurants chain (which also includes sister properties Rosebud and Centro), it speedily serves clock-watchers—working lunchers and theater-going diners. The menu includes enormous pasta portions, excellent chicken Vesuvio, and a handful of veal dishes. Arrive after 7:30 for a more leisurely meal. *70 W. Madison St., at Dearborn St., Loop, 312/332–9500. AE, D, DC, MC, V. Closed Sun. $$–$$$*

5 *d-8*

LA SCAROLA

Devotees of satisfying, fill-'em-up hearty Italian meals line up to get into the unassuming La Scarola. There's nothing trendy on the menu. But pleasers include pasta Vesuvio, eggplant parmigiana, and the house specialty, veal dishes in portions that mandate a doggy bag. The '80s time-warp decor is big on photos of buxom blonds and has-been celebs, though Sinatra on the sound track improves the mood. *721 W. Grand Ave., near Halsted St., River West, 312/ 243–1740. AE, D, DC, MC, V. No lunch weekends. $–$$*

8 *e-2*

LA STRADA RISTORANTE

Underground but not unknown, La Strada manages to be bright and sophisticated even below street level. The piano lounge has a pretty glass ceiling and the dining room embodies a dark-wood and white-tablecloth elegance. The signature dish here is veal, whether in scallopini, chops, or stuffed form. In summer the restaurant offers entertainment packages that include dinner and an open-air concert at Grant Park, followed by dessert and drinks. *155 N. Michigan Ave., near Randolph St., Loop, 312/565–2200. AE, D, DC, V. Closed Sun. $$$*

7 *c-7*

MAGGIANO'S LITTLE ITALY

Huge portions of familiar Italian-American favorites served in a boisterous room make you feel you're part of the old neighborhood. The Palermo–in–New York-style food is heavy on hearty, including brick-size lasagna, escarole with white beans and sausage, and country-style rigatoni. Two entrées easily feed three. Great bread, the foundation of excellent lunchtime sandwiches, comes from the Corner Bakery next door. There's no intimacy here, but it's a good choice for entertaining the entire clan. *516 N. Clark St., at Grand Ave., River North, 312/644–7700. AE, D, DC, MC, V. $$–$$$*

4 *d-7*

MIA FRANCESCA

Insanely popular, Mia Francesca taps a winning formula that combines chef-owner Scott Harris's good authentic Italian cooking, moderate prices, and a minimal-chic storefront setting. Butcher-papered tables are crowded together urban-style, all the better to people-watch over plates of pizza and pasta. Arrive before 6 or expect to wait. Many complain about the din, though it adds to the energy. For sometimes quicker and always quieter service in summer, get on the separate waiting list for a table in the intimate garden. *3311 N. Clark St., near Belmont Ave., Wrigleyville, 773/281–3310. Reservations not accepted. MC, V. No lunch. $$–$$$*

5 *c-8*

MISTO

Misto, Italian for "mixed," combines Asian, French, and American elements in its recipes prepared by chummy chef Danny Greco. This is Italian with a trendy twist—think tuna tartare and saffron crab cakes—though pastas deliver a straight-ahead punch. Lunch puts a spin on sandwiches and salads. Warm lighting and generous booths encourage indulgence. *1118 W. Grand Ave., at May St., River West, 312/226–5989. AE, D, DC, MC, V. No lunch weekends. $$*

7 *b-6*

MR. BEEF

For classic Italian beef sandwiches, no one makes 'em meatier than Mr. Beef, a Chicago institution. This fast-food purveyor wads up thin slices of beast on a bun and piles on the extras—don't miss the peppers—along with the jus. Each mammoth hero is a two-fister. Mr. Beef gets down to serious business at the lunch hour, when the dining room's solo picnic table is packed. *666 N. Orleans St., near Erie St., River North, 312/337–8500. No credit cards. Closed Sun. No dinner. $*

5 *f-8*

NANA'S CAFÉ

Italian like Grandma might have made it were she a generous soul, this café delivers homey, well-priced pastas, salads, and eggplant sandwiches. Nana's loyalists, many of them neighboring *Sun-Times* workers, relish the unpretentious spot tucked into an out-of-the-way corner of River North. It is busiest at lunch and there is street seating in season. *7 W. Kinzie St., at State St., River North, 312/527–0300. AE, D, DC, MC, V. Closed Sun. $*

7 *e-4*

PAPA MILANO

If you're a Papa Milano fan, chances are you're a regular. The old-fashioned, '50s-era Italian does chicken parmigiana and spaghetti marinara that won't startle your taste buds. But the dark room with pictures of local celebs and coveted booths somehow creates a cozy welcome that keeps customers returning. It's the anti-chic chic on the Prada-and-Barneys-lined shopping street. *951 N. State St., at Oak St., Gold Coast, 312/787–3710. AE, DC, MC, V. $$*

8 *f-1*

PRIMAVERA

Don't be surprised if the waiter serving your scallops sporadically bursts into song. All of the waiters here are professional singers, belting out arias and old standards. The menu is standard as well, with dishes like veal scallopini and bruschetta. There are some surprises, too: the cannoli alla primavera is made with white and dark chocolate mousse. *Fairmont Hotel, 200 N. Columbus Dr., near Lake St., Loop, 312/565–6655. AE, D, DC, V. $$$*

4 *b-7*

RED TOMATO

Despite the neighborhood location, Red Tomato aspires to sophistication with a menu that doesn't rest on its pastas and a brick storefront outfitted with trendy trims. Look for house specialties like veal scallopini, grilled eggplant, and pizzas (the restaurant got its start with the sister pizza joint LoGalbo's next door). It's generally crowded on weekends but there's a nice bar in which to wait. *3417 N. Southport Ave., at Roscoe St., Lakeview, 773/472–5300. AE, D, DC, MC, V. $$*

7 *e-6*

RL

Luxurious yet comfortable, Ralph Lauren's signature and initial restaurant—pun intended, this is his first foray into food—serves up some of the best Italian in the city. Low lights play off the crisp white tablecloths, and leather couches are the perfect place to show off your purchases from the adjoining store. Ladies-who-lunch will appreciate the East Coast aesthetic, but the portions are generously Midwestern. Modeled after Lauren's favorite New York eatery, Vico, the menu's standouts include signature dish *Milanese alla Vico* (breaded veal chop). *115 E. Chicago Ave., near Michigan Ave., Magnificent Mile, 312/475–1100. AE, MC, V. $$$*

5 *b-2*

ROSE ANGELIS

Cheap and abundant fare keeps the yuppies filing through this restaurant inside a renovated house. Though occasionally bland, generous homemade pastas are particular hits here, and waits of several hours are not uncommon on weekends. The series of connected rooms provides an intriguing atmosphere. *1314 W. Wrightwood Ave., between Southport and Racine Aves., Lincoln Park, 773/296–0081. D, MC, V. Closed Mon. $$*

6 *b-4*

THE ROSEBUD CAFE

Taylor Street's marquee attraction, Rosebud serves traditional Italian food highlighted by one of the city's best red sauces. You can also get good roasted peppers, homemade sausage, and hearty pastas. Patrons are zealously attached to this sentimental favorite. Expect to wait practically any time, reservation or no reservation. While waits stretch to an hour-plus, tables in the bustling bar are often available. *1500 W. Taylor St., near Ashland Ave., Little Italy, 312/942–1117. AE, DC, MC, V. No lunch weekends. $$*

7 b-6
SCOOZI!

A perennially popular part of the Lettuce Entertain You chain, Scoozi! shines with good country-style Italian food in a cavernous loft with leather banquettes and exposed truss beams. The lively restaurant entertains both tourists and locals, starting with selections from the 12-ft antipasti bar. The thin, wood-fire pizzas and roast chicken are favorites, and satisfying pastas come in small or large sizes. Look for the giant tomato outside and expect to wait for a table inside. *410 W. Huron St., near Orleans St., River North, 312/943–5900. AE, D, DC, MC, V. No lunch weekends. $$–$$$*

7 e-4
SPIAGGIA

Matching the stellar location—a romantic, trilevel room overlooking Oak Street Beach—with a contemporary kitchen, Spiaggia raises the bar on Italian cooking in the city. The menu changes frequently; choices are always innovative and fresh. Look for wood-roasted squab, grilled scallops with porcini mushrooms, and rich veal-filled pasta. Save room for equally inventive desserts. Service is professional and informed and the wine list scholarly. While Spiaggia is a special-occasion destination, its informal sister, Cafe Spiaggia (312/280–2755) next door, is a good place to sample superior pizzas, pastas, and antipasti at everyday rates. *980 N. Michigan Ave., at Oak St., Magnificent Mile, 312/280–2750. Reservations essential. Jacket required. AE, D, DC, MC, V. No lunch Sun. $$$–$$$$*

5 c-3
TARANTINO'S

A neighborhood Italian with hipster appeal, Tarantino's anchors its panache in an exposed-brick-walled room popular with young area cocktailers. Food takes a light, contemporary turn that thankfully eschews the breaded and the creamed. There is a cozy, convivial bar, as well as sidewalk seating in season. *1112 W. Armitage Ave., at Seminary Ave., Lincoln Park, 773/871–2929. AE, DC; MC, V. Closed Mon. $$*

5 f-5
TOPO GIGIO RISTORANTE

This popular restaurant tends to be packed to its not-so-pleasant gills. But polished service and reliable dishes— veal saltimbocca, pastas a-plenty, and, yes, tiramisu—make up for the clamor. The large, leafy outdoor patio plays up Old Town's charm. *1516 N. Wells St., at North Ave., Old Town, 312/266–9355. AE, DC, MC, V. No lunch Sun. $$*

5 d-5
TRATTORIA GIANNI

Favored by Steppenwolf and Royal George theater-goers, Gianni cooks flavorful pre-curtain grilled calamari and rigatoni with sun-dried tomatoes that won't have you nodding off by Act II. Try for a streetside seat in the tiny wood-floor front room. Chef-owner Gianni Delisi makes the trattoria one of the few personal spots in a neighborhood without much character. *1711 N. Halsted St., at North Ave., Lincoln Park, 312/266–1976. AE, D, DC, MC, V. Closed Mon. $$*

8 d-3
TRATTORIA NO. 10

For romance in the Loop, descend the winding staircase at Trattoria No. 10 to a dramatically lit subterranean dining room with niches created by arches and awash in warm colors. Pastels of the Italian countryside decorate the walls. Homemade pasta and risotto are special here—ravioli is a particular passion and the menu may include a half-dozen choices. Farfalle with duck confit also earns raves, and bread with sun-dried tomatoes is a zesty freebie. More upscale than a true trattoria, No. 10 does a big lunch business and is a good pretheater pick. *10 N. Dearborn St., near Madison St., Loop, 312/984–1718. AE, D, DC, MC, V. Closed Sun. No lunch Sat. $$–$$$*

5 f-5
TRATTORIA PIZZERIA ROMA

This tiny Old Town Italian's popularity exceeds its capacity. Selections of salads, pizzas, pastas, and daily specials are refreshingly light and tasty. A wine bar alleviates the crush on weekends. *1535 N. Wells St., near North Ave., Old Town, 312/664–7907. AE, D, DC, MC, V. No lunch. $$*

7 e-5
TUCCI BENUCCH

At this "outdoor" patio on the fifth floor of the Bloomingdale's building overlooking the escalators, you can enjoy trattoria-style staples like stuffed grilled eggplant, goat cheese antipasti, and five-cheese lasagna. It's perfect for an after-shopping or pre-movie bite. *900 N. Michigan Ave., near Walton St., Magnificent Mile, 312/266–2500. AE, D, DC, V. $$*

6 *c-3*
TUFANO'S
Also known as the Vernon Park Tap, Tufano's is a neighborhood Italian old-timer in a newly gentrifying area. Cheap prices draw students from the University of Illinois at Chicago campus across the street. But the bustling, casual, family-run joint appeals to diners citywide with reliable red-sauce pastas, lasagna, antipasto salad, and, on Friday, fish dishes. *1073 W. Vernon Park Pl., near Morgan St., Little Italy, 312/733–3393. No credit cards. Closed Mon. $–$$*

6 *c-4*
TUSCANY
A bright spot at the east end of Taylor, Tuscany cultivates true trattoria-style informality. As the name suggests, this restaurant focuses on the hearty, rustic flavors of the Tuscan countryside. The rotisserie-grilled chicken is especially good, as are the thin-crust pizzas, the rack of lamb Vesuvio, and, in season, soft-shell crab Vesuvio. Unlike many other Italian menus this one offers traditional *salsiccia* (homemade sausage) entrées. *1014 W. Taylor St., at Morgan St., Little Italy, 312/829–1990. AE, D, DC, MC, V. No lunch weekends. $$–$$$*

4 *c-6*
3700 N. Clark St., at Waveland Ave., Wrigleyville, 773/404–7700.

5 *e-3*
VIA EMILIA
For a taste of contemporary Italy, seat yourself at one of only 50 places at lively Via Emilia. The handsome waiters call back and forth to each other in Italian. The music switches to high-energy dance tunes when the joint gets jumping. And the chef takes pride in his food, a list heavy on homemade pastas, with second plates featured as specials. The Bolognese meat ragout on paper-thin tagliatelle is a house specialty, and the kitchen does wonders with veal. If you're feeling gregarious, *mangia qui*. *2119 N. Clark St., near Fullerton Ave., Lincoln Park, 773/248–6283. AE, DC, MC, V. No lunch. $$–$$$*

3 *d-1*
VIA VENETO
This spot serves up regional Italian home cooking far from the Little Italy neighborhood. It's consistently crowded, and dishes like *vitello carrozzella alla salvia* (puffs of mozzarella and veal sautéed in white wine and sage) are part of the reason. The dinner menu has more items, but luckily both lunch and dinner feature a pumpkin ravioli that you shouldn't just save for Thanksgiving. *3449 W. Peterson Ave., near Bernard Ave., West Ridge, 773/267–0888. AE, D, V. $$*

5 *d-4*
VINCI
Chef-owner Paul LoDuca turns out robust regional Italian dishes in this casual dining room, a comfortable setting with rustic flare. Carpaccio, grilled polenta, and savory pizza *dell'Ortolano* make appetizing starters. Among pastas, twirl your fork around homey

---

ROOMS WITH A VIEW

From modernist architecture to sprawling shoreline, Chicago's best assets are framed from these seats:

Everest (French)
From the 40th floor city lights and traffic streams head westward-ho to the horizon.

Jackson Harbor Grill (Creole)
Three steps from the marina and Lake Michigan's lapping waters.

North Pond Café (Contemporary)
Leafy Lincoln Park and a tranquil pond cultivate serenity.

Phoenix (Chinese)
A clear shot to the Loop from south-side Chinatown takes in all the landmarks.

Riva (Seafood)
Stepped back on Navy Pier, Riva takes in the lake and Loop panorama.

Signature Room at the 95th (Contemporary)
Skyline view from skyscraper height in this John Hancock topper.

Spiaggia (Italian)
Trilevel room gives every diner a blissful view of Oak Street Beach and Lake Shore Drive.

Grandma's linguine, tossed with bread crumbs, zucchini, and tomato. Just down the street from the Steppenwolf, the restaurant is a pretheater hit. *1732 N. Halsted St., at Willow St., Lincoln Park, 312/266–1199. Reservations essential. AE, DC, MC, V. Closed Mon. No lunch. $$–$$$*

8 *d-3*
VIVERE
The fine dining room at Italian Village, Vivere is a visual and victual feast. The theatrical interior demands attention with doodlelike gilded scrolls and glowing ceiling light cones. Despite distracting decor, the food stands its ground, with dishes like prosciutto rosettes accompanied by fig slivers and bass-stuffed squid-ink tortellini. For lunch try the excellent homemade sausage with grilled polenta. The restaurant, now run by the third generation of the Capitanini family, has one of the country's best Italian wine lists. *71 W. Monroe St., at Dearborn St., Loop, 312/332–7005. AE, D, DC, MC, V. Closed Sun. No lunch Sat. $$–$$$*

6 *d-1*
VIVO
Despite competition from newer restaurants on Randolph, Vivo, a pioneer in upscale eats on the street, remains a see-and-be-seen spot. The industrial aesthetic embraces dramatic spot lighting, open wine racks against exposed-brick walls, a granite bar, and one high-demand booth in a former elevator shaft. Food is reliable Italian with modern touches. Go for the good antipasto assortment, hearty pastas like rigatoni and ravioli, and veal chops. Stay for the scene. *838 W. Randolph St., near Halsted St., West Loop, 312/733–3379. AE, D, DC, MC, V. No lunch weekends. $$–$$$*

2 *c-1*
ZIA'S TRATTORIA
Charcoal sketches of the owner's aunts—his *zias*—line the wall of this tidy house-proud family Italian. But the food—excellent Bolognese sauce, inventive bread salad, and juicy roast Portobello mushrooms—exceeds neighborhood expectations. Seats in the small storefront are appreciably harder to get on weekends. *6699 N. Northwest Hwy., between Touhy Ave. and Park Ridge, 1 mi north of Harlem, Edison Park, 773/775–0808. AE, DC, MC, V. $$*

JAMAICAN

4 *b-3*
BLUE MOUNTAIN RESTAURANT
In a revitalized neighborhood (note the Starbucks on the corner), Blue Mountain retains the aim-to-please attitude with a menu constantly updated according to customers' requests and daily specials such as shrimp Jamaica (sautéed in coconut milk) on Wednesday or curried goat on Saturday. The dining area is bright and spacious with a good mixture of island and contemporary decor. A spicy Sunday brunch offers a respite from the usual fruit-and-Danish offerings. *1319 W. Wilson Ave., near Beacon St., Uptown, 773/334–6488. No credit cards. Closed Mon. $*

2 *f-2*
LINNETTE'S JAMAICAN KITCHEN
With soul food becoming increasingly trendy, ethnic eateries like Linnette's are shaping up to fill the gap. Large portions of hearty island favorites are warm and welcoming and the dining room relaxation-inducing, as it is dimly lit even on a summer day. There aren't too many options on the menu—and almost all items are the same price—but this place is a firm believer in doing a few things well. The jerk pork and chicken are standouts, as is the *gungo* soup (a thick pea soup with steak and ham). Take care at night. *7366 N. Clark St., near Jarvis St., Roger's Park, 773/761–4823. MC, V. Closed Sun. $*

JAPANESE

7 *c-7*
COCORO
Unique among its competitors, Cocoro specializes in *shabu-shabu*, the Japanese fondue. Diners cook their own shaved beef and vegetables in salted seaweed water warmed at the table. Sushi lovers, fear not: the restaurant also serves excellent sushi. Its main problem, in fact, is its low-key exterior, very hard to spot in this much-hyped eating district. *668 N. Wells St., at Erie St., River North, 312/943–2220. AE, DC, MC, V. Closed Sun. $$*

7 *f-7*
HATSUHANA
For some of Chicago's best sushi in a serene spot, save your pennies for the

pricey raw fish served at Hatsuhana. A seat at the long bar gives you a good view of the chefs at their delicate work. Choosing lunch or dinner specials—which include soup and tea as well as maki rolls and sushi pieces—help keep the check reasonable. Japanese lanterns, white stucco walls, and blond-wood trim make Hatsuhana a peaceful retreat from the commercial buzz outside. *160 E. Ontario St., near Michigan Ave., Streeterville, 312/280–8808. AE, D, DC, MC, V. Closed Sun. No lunch Sat. $$–$$$*

5 *f-5*
KAMEHACHI
Fine fresh fish and a trendy setting deliver the hip hordes to Kamehachi. The blond-wood, brightly lit lower level showcases the culinary arts of its sushi chefs, while the magenta-hued night-clubby second story serves poser patrons. Interesting non-sushi items like green tea noodles round out the menu. A peaceful garden patio operates in season. *1400 N. Wells St., between North Ave. and Division St., Old Town, 312/664–3663. AE, D, DC, MC, V. No lunch. $$*

4 *c-7*
MATSUYA
Japanese twentysomethings crowd Matsuya's two appealingly minimal, blond-wood rooms along Clark. Large cones of hand-rolled maki are the hallmark of the sushi menu. But the appetizer list is extensive, making this a good place to dig your chopsticks into sesame spinach, deep-fried spicy chicken wings, or gyoza dumplings. Waits are common, but tables have a quick turnaround under the attentions of fleet servers. *3469 N. Clark St., near Newport Ave., Wrigleyville, 773/248–2677. MC, V. No lunch weekdays. $$*

2 *f-4*
MIRAI SUSHI
This place combines freshly prepared sushi with a cutting-edge atmosphere that keeps the relatively small dining room and patio packed on weekends. The menu changes daily, and it's best to ask the knowledgeable staff what they suggest. If they say *aji* (horse mackerel), go for it. You get the entire fish as sashimi, with the body used as a garnish. An upstairs lounge serves a full menu and has curvy, plush couches that are nice places to relax and listen to the nightly DJ. Floor-to-ceiling windows let

in the soft glow of streetlights. *2020 W. Division St., near Damen Ave., Wicker Park, 773/862–8500. AE, D, DC, MC, V. No lunch. $$$*

7 *c-7*
NANIWA
This sushi seller is low on atmosphere but distinguishes itself with superior fresh raw fish and inventive maki (rolls). Finish off your meal with the everything-in-it house-special dragon roll. Service is friendly and a side patio enables you to eat outside. *607 N. Wells St., between Ohio and Ontario Sts., River North, 312/255–8555. AE, DC, MC, V. No lunch weekends. $$*

5 *c-3*
SAI CAFÉ
Neighborhood sushi does not get better than Sai Café, a longstanding Lincoln Park favorite with top-quality fish. Exposed-brick-walled rooms eschew the cheesy ethnic artifacts to create a contemporary, comfortable space. To enjoy the entertaining sushi chefs, however, you have to tolerate the smoking section. Remarkably friendly staffers apparently follow the example of the affable owner. Expect big waits at peak hours. *2010 N. Sheffield Ave., at Armitage Ave., Lincoln Park, 773/472–8080. AE, MC, V. $$*

4 *b-1*
SUNSHINE CAFÉ
A spartan, unassuming Japanese noodle house, Sunshine presents excellent noodle soups, donburi, and tempura made by veteran restaurateurs now in their '80s. The restaurant has many Japanese customers as well as gentrified locals. You're in good hands with the friendly staffers, who bring you a huge mug of steaming green tea at the start of your meal. *5449 N. Clark St., north of Foster Ave., Andersonville, 773/334–6214. D, MC, V. Closed Mon. $*

6 *d-1*
SUSHI WABI
With only 50-some seats, a disc jockey, and industrial decor, Wabi pushes the hip quotient, which means a reservation is quite useful, even off peak. Most of the black-clad crowd come for the quite inventive sushi and maki, though a small kitchen in the back both sears and cooks a tender selection of alternatives. For all the intimidation potential,

the servers are really quite helpful. *842 W. Randolph St., at Halsted St., West Loop, 312/563–1224. AE, D, DC, MC, V. $$–$$$*

7 *d-3*
TSUNAMI
Befitting its location just off party-hearty Division Street, Tsunami swings with low lighting, faux-finished walls, and a club-inspired soundtrack. Couch-side coffee tables upstairs allow you to eat and lounge at once. But the best seats in the house are at the sushi bar (a must-reserve on weekends) where the entertaining chefs turn out gorgeous maki and sushi on wood trays. The menu has all the usual choices, but the cooks are happy to whip up a special roll on request. *1160 N. Dearborn St., at Division St., Gold Coast, 312/642–9911. AE, D, DC, MC, V. No lunch weekdays. $$–$$$$*

KOREAN

5 *a-5*
SOJU
Soju is Korean vodka and a popular ingredient in many of the dishes in this upscale restaurant. In the exposed-brick dining room, a hipster crowd of locals dines on Soju Chicken, the restaurant's signature dish of deep-fried boneless chicken in hot bean paste. Complimentary *pajun* (side dishes) change daily but include various *kimchis* (fermented cabbage), marinated soybeans, and pickled cucumbers. *1745 W. North Ave., near Hermitage St., Wicker Park, 773/782–9000. AE, MC, V. BYOB. Closed Mon.–Tues. No lunch. $$*

3 *h-3*
WOO CHON
The bucket of red-hot coals dumped in the center pit of your table should convince you Woo Chon is an authentic joint for Korean barbecue. Grill marinated beef, short ribs, and pork strips on a grate over the coals. Wrap your meat in lettuce leaves stuffed with crisp bean sprouts, pickled daikon radish, and a host of other options from the sidekick veggie dishes. Appetizers, including delicious green-onion pancakes, are the size of entrées. Though pleasant, servers are often harried, rushing between large tables in the intimate shop. It's the most fun with a crowd.

5744 N. California Ave., at Lincoln Ave., Albany Park, 773/728–8001. AE, MC, V. Closed Wed. $–$$

KOSHER

2 *f-1*
GOOD MORGAN KOSHER FISH MARKET
Good Morgan combines a busy fish market with an even busier seafood restaurant. The food here is "parve," a term used to describe kosher food that is neither meat nor dairy. Inside it's small, clean, and simple, with blue- and white-tile walls and a handful of tables, each with a little prayer card in Hebrew and English. The place is inherently healthy: tuna and salmon salads are made fresh, and soups and salads are organic. *2948 W. Devon Ave., near Richmond Ave., West Ridge, 773/764–8115. No credit cards. BYOB. Closed Sat. $*

5 *e-2*
SHALLOTS
Kosher-conscious diners gush over Shallots. But they aren't alone. The stylish Mediterranean fare pleases palates with you-won't-miss-the-dairy eats like Moroccan-style snapper, pomegranate-glazed lamb, and warm pistachio cake. White linens add elegance and a fireplace brings warmth to the Clark Street storefront. *2324 N. Clark St., at Fullerton Ave., Lincoln Park, 773/755–5205. Closed Fri. AE, DC, MC, V. $$$*

LATIN

4 *a-5*
CAFÉ 28
A pleasant double storefront with exposed-brick walls and marble-top café tables, Café 28 serves a mix of Cuban and Mexican dishes. From the island nation, top picks include tomato-beef *ropa vieja* casserole, chicken-stuffed fried potatoes, and Cuban roast pork sandwiches. From south of the border, try the chicken quesadillas and torta sandwiches. Owner Berta Navarro eagerly makes friends of customers, and if she's got something she's proud of on the stove she'll coax you back to see it. *1800 W. Irving Park Rd., at Ravenswood Ave., North Center, 773/528–2883. AE, V. BYOB. No lunch. $*

2 *f-2*

FLOWER'S POT

No frills and down home, this 50-seat eatery tucked into a strip mall serves a straightforward menu of traditional Central American fare, varying daily. You can usually find some combination of stewed chicken, beer, pork, or oxtails, served with beans, rice, or *ducunu* (a boiled sweet corn bread with the husks inside). But only on Saturday do the real specials appear. Try the Boil Up, consisting of yams, cocoa, cassava, sweet potato, and plantain cooked in tomato sauce and served with steamed fish and pig tails. *7328 N. Clark St., near Jarvis St., Roger's Park, 773/761–4388. MC, V. No smoking. $*

7 *d-8*

MAMBO GRILL

Inventive dishes from Central and South America as well as the Caribbean islands keep the pan-Latin beat at Mambo. And the mambo beat—along with the margaritas—moves a friendly crowd. Back booths provide intimacy at this little River North spot. The lunch menu sandwiches Latin flavors between a bun for appreciative River North office workers. *412 N. Clark St., between Kinzie and Hubbard Sts., River North, 312/467–9797. AE, D, DC, V. Closed Sun. No lunch Sat. $$*

5 *a-6*

MAS

It's loud and crowded, and it doesn't take reservations—not surprising, considering it's one of the most popular places among the see-and-be-seen scene in Wicker Park. Small tapas-style dishes and full-flung new Latin meals vie for your attention, almost all served as hot as the Brazilian beaches that inspired them. The black bean soup comes thick with a shot glass of *cachaca*, a fire-hot liquid made from sugarcane that you add to the soup to taste. The portions are big enough to share, including the ceviche of the day served in a martini glass. *1670 W. Division St., near Ashland, Wicker Park, 773/276–8700. Reservations not accepted. AE, DC, MC, V. No lunch. $$$*

7 *b-6*

NACIONAL 27

Flirt with Beautiful People over a Havana sidecar or a *pisco* (Peruvian grape brandy) sour in the sexy, palm-fringed, white-curtained cocktail lounge at Nacional 27, named for the 27 Central and South American countries represented on its menu. Or you can dine late on Cuban grouper or Brazilian snapper in the swanky supper club. Stick around after 11 PM, when tables get pushed back and Latin dancers crowd the floor. *325 W. Huron St., at Orleans St., River North, 312/664–2727. AE, D, DC, MC, V. No lunch. $$*

MEDITERRANEAN

5 *e-1*

CLARK STREET BISTRO

A big hit with Lincoln Parkers and dating couples, this bistro scores with its comfortable atmosphere and good fish dishes at reasonable prices. Preparations exceed storefront expectations, from the complex bouillabaisse to the simple saffron couscous with cilantro and cumin. *2600 N. Clark St., at Wrightwood Ave., Lincoln Park, 773/525–9992. AE, D, DC, MC, V. $$–$$$*

MEXICAN

2 *e-3*

ABRIL

A sunny Logan Square staple, Abril draws fans from near and far for hearty portions of Mexican standards. Big burritos, lavish nachos, and teeming tostadas join rich mole enchiladas and special fish dishes among the favorites of regulars. Booths along the window walls are the best seats for neighborhood gazing over a margarita. Arrive early or off-peak, as this colorful place packs quickly. *2607 N. Milwaukee Ave., at Logan Blvd., Logan Square, 773/227–7252. AE, D, DC, MC, V. $*

7 *c-1*

ADOBO GRILL

Swirl, sip, swallow: tequila gets the connoisseur treatment at Adobo Grill, where a tequila sommelier guides venturesome palates through a list of 70-some varieties. Absorb the alcohol with fine regional Mexican fare including pumpkinseed mole duck, guacamole prepared tableside, and exquisite desserts. Both the room and the servers maintain sunny dispositions. *1610 N. Wells St., near North Ave., Old Town, 312/266–7999. AE, DC, MC, V. $$–$$$*

5 *b-3*

CHIPOTLE GRILL

Where most fast foodies grease the taste buds, Chipotle nuances them with lime-and-cilantro-tossed rice, black beans spiced with cumin, and adobo-marinated chicken. Most importantly, Chipotle heeds the quick-service mantra, charging less than $5 for each enormous 22-ounce burrito, which is prepared to order in minutes. Chipotle takes another step most chains don't, using industrial materials to outfit the hip, minimalist dining rooms. *2000 N. Clybourn Ave., near Armitage Ave., Lincoln Park, 773/935–5710. MC, V. $*

4 *d-8*

3181 N. Broadway, at Belmont Ave., Lakeview, 773/525–5250.

5 *d-2*

2256 N. Orchard Ave., at Lincoln Ave., Lincoln Park, 773/935–6744.

2 *c-1*

DON JUAN'S

This friendly family-run Edison Park restaurant has an enormous following and woos a range of diners with a split menu. Mexican standards like enchiladas and fajitas compose the bulk of orders. But chef Patrick Concannon also cooks his own menu-within-the-menu of fusion foods, which changes frequently. *6730 N. Northwest Hwy., near Touhy Ave., Edison Park, 773/755–6438. AE, D, DC, MC, V. $*

7 *d-8*

FRONTERA GRILL

Credited with bringing authentic regional Mexican food north of the border, chef Rick Bayless started a culinary revolution at Frontera Grill. Thus, you can't go wrong here. Though the menu changes frequently, expect salsas and moles of rich, chili-roasted character found among grilled fish, tacos, and roasted meats. Singles and couples may find a few spots at the kitchen bar, but should prepare for the inevitable two-margarita wait. Since Bayless takes his staff with him to Mexico for annual research outings (the restaurant closes during these trips, which usually occur around July 4), servers are informed foodies. The colorful room is decorated with Mexican folk art. *445 N. Clark St., at Illinois St., River North, 312/661–1434. AE, D, DC, MC, V. Closed Sun.–Mon. $–$$$*

5 *a-7*

HACIENDA TECALITLAN

An expansive indoor courtyard hosting tables set around a trickling fountain makes Hacienda Tecalitlan the prettiest Mexican restaurant around. Standard burritos and tacos accompany more ambitious fare such as aromatic tomatillo-and-roasted-pepper *molcajete*-sauced game hen. Heat lovers can ask for the sweat-producing salsa *diablo* to go with their chips. The servers are highly informed but can become over-whelmed by weekend crowds. *820 N. Ashland Ave., near Chicago Ave., Near West Side, 312/243–6667. AE, MC, V. $–$$*

2 *e-3*

IXCAPUZALCO

Critics went wild when Rick Bayless protégé Geno Bahena opened this authentic storefront restaurant. Success—and some evident stress on the kitchen—followed. Go off-peak for the best experience. Bahena's unique appeal is a daily Oaxacan mole special, and regulars argue about whether Thursday's trumps Saturday's. An out-of-place piano player entertains with schmaltzy tunes. *2919 N. Milwaukee Ave., north of Diversey Ave., Logan Square, 773/486–7340. AE, D, DC, MC, V. $$*

5 *b-2*

MI CASA SU CASA

At Mi Casa Su Casa you feel welcomed into owner Felix Gomez's casa. Food ranges from standards—burritos, tostadas, etc.—to regional meat preparations. But the welcome is genuine and the cozy atmosphere thankfully spares diners the Mexican fiesta look. There is sidewalk dining in season. *2524 N. Southport Ave., at Lill Ave., Lincoln Park, 773/525–6323. AE, DC, MC, V. No lunch. $$*

6 *b-6*

NUEVO LEON

Cascading faux flowers on the brightly painted facade herald Nuevo Leon, a popular Mexican outpost run by the Guitiérrez family since 1962. Inside, two clean and simply furnished rooms are attended by waitresses in traditional flounced skirts. The extensive menu includes enchiladas, tacos, and tamales as well as *menudo* (tripe soup), steak dishes, and the house special, sizzling fajitas. Served with chips, the house salsa is fiery. Not all servers are fluent in English, but cheerful goodwill prevails. *1515 W. 18th St., near Ashland Ave., Pilsen, 312/421–1517. Reservations not accepted. No credit cards. BYOB. $–$$*

7 *c-3*
¡SALPICÓN!
Mexico City native Priscila Satkoff, chef-owner at ¡Salpicón!, serves up sophisticated Mexican food to rival Frontera Grill. The meats in rich sauces, such as ancho chili quail, and deftly grilled fish are outstanding. Drinks receive equivalent attention from the 50-strong tequila list to the award-winning wine list. The colorful room, managed by husband Vincent Satkoff, reflects the chef's liveliness in the kitchen. The service is knowledgeable and accommodating. This is not a chips-and-salsa joint; if you want them you have to ask. *1252 N. Wells St., near Division St., Old Town, 312/988–7811. AE, D, DC, MC, V. No lunch. $$*

7 *d-8*
TOPOLOBAMPO
The more polished half of the twin-set storefront that includes Frontera Grill, Topolobampo is chef Rick Bayless's upscale take on Mexican regional cuisine. The richly colored room is a more sober setting in which to appreciate dishes that emphasize game, seasonal fruits and vegetables, and exotic preparations such as homemade tortillas with pumpkinseed sauce and pheasant roasted in banana leaves. Good service and interesting wine selections add to the appeal. Since Topolobampo takes reservations, it is often easier to get into than the ever-crowded Frontera. *445 N. Clark St., at Illinois St., River North, 312/661–1434. Reservations essential. AE, D, DC, MC, V. Closed Sun.–Mon. No lunch Sat. $$–$$$*

MIDDLE EASTERN

4 *b-1*
COUSIN'S
The rather sprawling menu draws on cuisines from Morocco to Turkey. Locals favor Cousins for its lamb chops, salads, hummus, and baklava at budget-beating prices. Lots of vegetarian selections are served in the Mid-East–theme rooms, and there is efficient delivery service. *5203 N. Clark St., at Foster Ave., Andersonville, 773/334–4553. AE, MC, V. $*

5 *d-1*
2833 N. Broadway, at Diversey Ave., Lincoln Park, 773/880–0063.

2 *f-1*
HASHOLOM
The kitschy vinyl-covered seats and small, clean tables in this place would be retro anywhere else, but here they're charming. Big portions of Middle Eastern favorites like hummus and baba ghanouj are made fresh, and the soups are overflowing with chunks of veggies. On Friday night only you can get the Moroccan couscous with chicken, vegetables, almonds, and raisins. You'll have plenty to take home to eat on Saturday and Sunday as well. *2905 W. Devon Ave., near Francisco Ave., West Ridge, 773/465–5675. No credit cards. BYOB. Closed weekends. $*

4 *b-1*
REZA'S
Substantial dishes, served quickly, keep the registers ringing at Reza's. Skewered kebabs, grilled meats, and saucy stews dominate the Persian menu in chicken, meat, and vegetable combinations preceded by pita bread, feta cheese, and soup. There's also plenty here for vegetarians. If you still have room for dessert after the multiple courses, try the rich, homemade baklava. Both locations are spacious, though the original North Side location is more laid-back. *5255 N. Clark St., near Foster Ave., Andersonville, 773/561–1898. AE, D, DC, MC, V. $–$$*

7 *b-7*
432 W. Ontario St., near Orleans St., River North, 312/664–4500.

2 *f-4*
SOUK
This ultrahip Wicker Park restaurant takes its name from the Arabic word for market and creatively draws on a melting pot of Middle Eastern cultures. Familiar starters include hummus and baba ghanouj. But the bulk of the menu is devoted to adventurous dishes such as pistachio-crusted veal brains and tahini- and onion-crusted red snapper. *Saj*, a rustic Lebanese flat bread, comes to the table with olive oil and a sesame-sumac spice blend. The hide-covered banquettes are ideal for lounging with a *shisha*, a postprandial waterpipe packed with fruit-blended tobacco. *1552 N. Milwaukee Ave., at North Ave., Wicker Park, 773/227–9110. AE, D, DC, MC, V. $$*

4 *b-8*

ZOUZOU

Tasty Middle Eastern bites issuing from this tiny shop's grill keep the Lakeview neighbors happy. You can't go wrong with anything on the tightly focused menu, but best bets include the moist pita-wrapped shawirma sandwiches, spicy falafel, and lemony tabbouleh salad. Take-out is speedy. *1406 W. Belmont Ave., at Southport Ave., Lakeview, 773/755–4020. MC, V. BYOB. Closed Sun.*

MOROCCAN

5 *d-5*

L'OLIVE

Chef-owner Mohamed Ben Mchabcheb takes pride in his food, visiting each table to inquire after it. You could easily make a meal of appetizers like roast eggplant, *marguez* sausages, and goat cheese hummus. But save room for the *bastilla*, an exotic phyllo pie loaded with spices, lemon, olives and chicken. Given the generous entrées, most patrons leave the exotically tiled dining room with doggy bags. *1629 N. Halsted St., near North Ave., Lincoln Park, 312/573–1515. D, DC, MC, V. Closed Mon. No lunch. $$*

7 *c-7*

TIZI MELLOUL

Moroccan with a modern streak, Tizi Melloul teases the senses, from the spice-scented foyer to the cumin-color palette. Designer Suhail accents fez finds with white glass light globes inspired by nomadic tents. For Tizi Melloul's most exotic experience, cop a floor cushion in the lantern-lit, circular communal dining room and dig, with your hands, into couscous or chicken saffron pie. *531 N. Wells St., at Grand Ave., River North, 312/670–4338. AE, D, DC, MC, V. No lunch weekends. $$*

PAN-ASIAN

7 *e-4*

BIG BOWL

In typical Lettuce Entertain You fashion, Big Bowl takes the Asian-noodle-shop concept to the nines. The result is a wide-ranging menu of flavorful dishes in a zippy setting ideal for area shoppers and neighborhood regulars. The large selection of noodle dishes swings from

Shanghai wheat noodles to Chinese lo mein. Stir-fry fans can choose their own ingredients from a do-it-yourself bar and then have cooks prepare it. There are many interesting Asian beers and teas, and service is superior. *6 E. Cedar St., near State St., Gold Coast, 312/640–8888. AE, D, DC, MC, V. $–$$*

7 *c-7*

159½ W. Erie St., near LaSalle St., River North, 312/787–8297.

7 *e-7*

60 E. Ohio St., near State St., Magnificent Mile, 312/951–1888.

4 *b-6*

HI RICKY ASIAN NOODLE SHOP AND SATAY BAR

Brightly lit, with exposed brick and an open kitchen, Hi Ricky has inexpensive and filling dishes from Vietnam, Thailand, China, and Indonesia. Start with a satay before moving on to more adventurous fare like the Spicy Drunken Noodles. Meat-and-potatoes types will go for the Crispy Chinese Chow Fun— broad noodles and broccoli served in a mild sauce. This is one of three locations in the city. Right across from the Music Box Theater, it has pre- and post-movie crowds that keep the place filled, especially on weekends. *3730 N. Southport Ave., near Waveland Ave., Wrigleyville, 773/388–0000. AE, V. $$*

6 *d-1*

941 W. Randolph St., near Halsted St., West Loop, 312/491–9100.

5 *a-5*

1852 W. North Ave., near Honore Ave., Wicker Park, 773/276–8300. AE, D, DC, V.

6 *e-7*

JOY YEE'S NOODLE SHOP

If you blink you might miss this small storefront restaurant right in the heart of a bustling neighborhood. But don't let size fool you. The menu is chock-full of Chinese, Korean, Vietnamese, and Thai noodle dishes, including a thinly cut pad thai. *2159 Archer Ave., near Cermak Ave., Chinatown, 312/328–0001. AE, D, DC, MC, V. BYOB. $*

5 *e-2*

OODLES OF NOODLES

The name almost says it all—big portions, big Asian pastas—but omits a key allure: its low prices. Not surprisingly, it's popular with the post-college crowd who populates Lincoln Park apartments. *2540 N. Clark St., at Fullerton Ave., Lincoln Park, 773/975–1090. AE, D, DC, MC, V. BYOB. $*

4 *c-7*

PENNY'S NOODLE SHOP

Penny's introduced Chicago to the noodle shop in this wedge-shape storefront, and Chicagoans took to its fresh preparations at very low prices overnight. Expect to wait for a counter or table seat at almost any hour. But then you'll only spend about $10 for an order of excellent pot stickers followed by a bowl brimming with pad thai or noodles, bean sprouts, and beef, all washed down by sweet, strong Thai iced coffee. Clean, contemporary decor and efficient service enhance both locations. *3400 N. Sheffield Ave., at Roscoe St., Lakeview, 773/281–8222. No credit cards. BYOB. Closed Mon. $*

5 *d-1*

950 W. Diversey Pkwy., near Halsted St., Lakeview, 773/281–8448.

6 *d-1*

RED LIGHT

Like sister restaurants Marché and Vivo, Red Light is something to see as well as sample. The undulating art nouveau–inspired interior sets the stage stylishly for an exotic array of Asian dishes from China, Thailand, Vietnam, and Indonesia. An assortment of condiments at each table lets diners adjust the heat level. Desserts, which come from Marché, are very Western—and very good. Expect a trendy crowd and a noisy buzz. *820 W. Randolph St., near Halsted St., West Loop, 312/733–8880. AE, DC, MC, V. No lunch weekends. $$–$$$*

PERUVIAN

2 *f-2*

RINCONCITO SUDAMERICANO

This inexpensive and unpretentious storefront trades in unusual Peruvian fare that's popular with South Americans and Bucktowners alike. There are many interesting sauces such as nut cream. Seafood—from ceviche to paella to fish specials—is plentiful. Though Peru is the native land of potatoes, don't pass up the plantain side dish. Friendly servers are good guides to the menu.

1954 W. Armitage Ave., at Damen Ave., Bucktown, 773/489–3126. AE, MC, V. $

PHILIPPINE

5 *a-6*

RAMBUTAN

In its new and improved Wicker Park home, Rambutan promises to draw an even bigger crowd than did its previous, tiny incarnation. *Humba* (chunks of meat with yellow mung beans) is a nice way to start your meal, while the delicious desserts, such as the warm egg rolls with fruit and chocolate, make a perfect ending. The portions are medium-size but inexpensive and meant to be eaten family-style, like tapas. *2049 W. Division St., near Damen Ave., Wicker Park, 773/773–2727. AE, D, DC, MC, V. BYOB. $$*

PIZZA

5 *d-3*

BACINO'S

A star in the stuffed-pizza category, Bacino's combines fresh ingredients with a measured amount of mozzarella and tops the pie with a zesty tomato sauce. Gourmet-about-town Charlie Trotter calls it "the best pizza I know of," according to the menu. The cheese-laced stuffed spinach even earns a recommendation from the American Heart Association. Fortunately for tables where tastes are divided, Bacino's offers "bambino" sizes, individual portions of thin or stuffed pizzas. Be prepared with conversation or the Sunday paper for a 30-minute cook-time wait. *2204 N. Lincoln Ave., at Webster Ave., Lincoln Park, 773/472–7400. AE, D, DC, MC, V. $*

8 *a-3*

118 S. Clinton St., between Monroe and Adams Sts., West Loop, 312/876–1188.

4 *c-8*

3146 N. Sheffield Ave., at Belmont Ave., Lakeview, 773/404–8111.

8 *e-1*

75 E. Wacker Dr., between Michigan and Wabash Aves., Loop, 312/263–0070.

5 *e-4*

BRICKS

What do you need in a pizza joint beside the pies and some salads? Good beer.

And Bricks offers all three with invention. The semi-subterranean pizzeria tops its thin crusts with the usual suspects and some unusual ones like Gouda cheese and pureed artichoke. Salads are fresh and creative and beers number two dozen. Intimate brick-walled rooms are a stylish step above the norm. *1909 N. Lincoln Ave., at Wisconsin St., Lincoln Park, 312/255–0851. AE, D, DC, V. No lunch. $*

5 *e-3*

CHICAGO PIZZA & OVEN GRINDER CO.

When your waitress turns over your pot-pie pizza at this Lincoln Park original, you'll understand why you waited in line for the rather dim parlor and barroom. The unusual upside-down pie joins a list of Italian sausage subs on the hearty menu. *2121 N. Clark St., between Webster and Dickens Aves., Lincoln Park, 773/248–2570. No credit cards. No lunch weekdays. $*

5 *f-6*

EDWARDO'S NATURAL PIZZA

Herbs growing in the windows at this chain indicate the freshness of its pizza ingredients. Other healthful elements include the lauded wheat crust and stuffed spinach number. The decor is no great shakes. In fact, take-out makes an excellent option. *1212 N. Dearborn St., at Division St., Gold Coast, 312/337–4490. AE, D, DC, MC, V. $*

8 *d-5*

521 S. Dearborn St., at Congress Pkwy., Printer's Row, 312/939–3366.

5 *d-1*

2662 N. Halsted Ave., near Diversey Ave., Lincoln Park, 773/871–3400.

2 *g-7*

1321 E. 57th St., near Woodlawn Ave., Hyde Park, 773/241–7960.

7 *f-6*

GINO'S EAST

Join the tourists and queue up along the sidewalk for a table in the cavernous headquarters of this deep-dish mecca. Gino's serves substantial 'za in sizes as small as individual. The thin crust isn't bad, but if you're not at all in the mood, try a sausage or Italian beef sandwich. Bide the 30-minute cook time by adding to the graffiti. The Lakeview shop is considerably smaller but does brisk delivery

business. *633 N. Wells St., at Ontario St., River North, 312/943–1124. AE, D, DC, MC, V. $*

5 *c-1*

2801 N. Lincoln Ave., at Racine Ave., Lakeview, 773/327–3737.

2 *e-6*

HOME RUN INN

For really excellent pizza beyond tourist range, slide into Home Run Inn. Join beat cops, softball teams, families, and packs of teens digging into traditional pizzas loaded with fresh toppings and based on thin, more-bread-than-brittle crusts. There are lots of entertainment options, including video games and TVs broadcasting Sox/Bulls/Bears efforts, in this lively neighborhood joint. *Chicago Magazine* critics picked this for the best thin-crust pizza in the city. *4254 W. 31st St., between Cicero Ave. and Pulaski Rd., South Lawndale, 773/247–9696. AE, MC, V. $*

5 *c-2*

LOU MALNATI'S

Malnati's fans champion the family-run chain over the more famous Uno's in the perpetual pizza debate. And indeed the deep dish satisfies. But so do the antipasto salads and thin-crust-pizza versions. The restaurant is chock-full of memorabilia and trumpets the Chicago of sporting fame with jerseys from the likes of Michael Jordan and Ryne Sandberg on the wall. It's a family favorite. *958 W. Wrightwood Ave., at Sheffield and Lincoln Aves., Lincoln Park, 773/832–4030. AE, DC, MC, V. $*

7 *c-8*

439 N. Wells St., at Hubbard St., River North, 312/828–9800.

7 *e-7*

PIZZERIA UNO/ PIZZERIA DUE

Heavily trafficked by out-of-towners, this is the original deep-dish pizza purveyor, established in 1943 (and later franchised). A meal in a slice, the rich cheese-filled pies issued from these ovens have spawned a world of imitators, as well as sister restaurant Pizzeria Due down the street. Due handles the overflow, which accumulates quickly in the dark and narrow Uno. A $5 lunch special, including individual pizza and choice of soup or salad, is a weekday bargain. *29 E. Ohio St., at Wabash Ave.,*

River North, 312/321–1000. Reservations not accepted. AE, D, DC, MC, V. $–$$

7 *e-7*

Due, 619 N. Wabash Ave., at Ontario St., River North, 312/943–2400. Reservations not accepted. AE, D, DC, MC, V. $–$$

4 *c-8*

POMPEII LITTLE ITALY

Fantastic pizza by the slice and loads of other flavorful Italian options served cafeteria-quick win Pompeii considerable patronage. Pies are lightly sauced, loaded with generous toppings, and have a bready crust. Alternatives include homemade pasta (a cook labors over noodles in the front window), fresh salads, and burrito-like pizza strudels. Diners order at the counter and helpful servers bring food to your table. The North Side location really bustles. *2955 N. Sheffield Ave., at Wellington Ave., Lakeview, 773/325–1900. AE, D, DC, MC, V. $*

6 *b-4*

1455 W. Taylor St., between Ashland Ave. and Loomis St., Little Italy, 312/421–5179.

5 *e-3*

RANALLI'S

Ranalli's never quite challenges Chicago's best pizza purveyors on food, but aficionados love it for its social sports-bar setting. Drinking one of the dozens of beers on Ranalli's impressive international list inevitably brings on a yen for decent calamari or passable pizza. The chain's Lincoln Avenue location is especially prized for its large, leafy outdoor café. *1925 N. Lincoln Ave., at Armitage Ave., Lincoln Park, 312/642–4700. AE, D, DC, MC, V. $*

7 *d-3*

24 W. Elm St., at Dearborn St., Gold Coast, 312/440–7000. AE, D, DC, MC, V.

4 *b-4*

1522 W. Montrose Ave., east of Ashland Ave., Ravenswood, 773/506–8800. AE, D, DC, MC, V.

6 *e-2*

138 S. Clinton St., at Adams St., West Loop, 312/258–8555. AE, D, DC, MC, V. Closed Sun.

3 *h-7*

VILLAGE CAFÉ & PIZZA

One of few New York–style pizzerias around, the Village Café puts together exceptional pies on airy, yeasty crusts.

One giant slice—served separately—nearly satisfies a hungry guy at lunch. Sandwiches, fries, and salads round out the menu in this unsung local corner, which deserves a citywide reputation. *2132 W. Roscoe Ave., at Hamilton Ave., Roscoe Village, 773/404–4555. No credit cards. Closed Mon. $*

POLISH

3 *c-8*

HOME BAKERY

Poles pile in for filling, four-square meals at the no-frills Home. Monday is Swiss steak day, Tuesday is chopped steak day, and so on. But the regular menu has loads of hits, including buttery pierogi, thick breaded pork chops, and the overloaded Polish plate encompassing blintz, kielbasa, sauerkraut, stuffed cabbage, pierogi, and potato—all this, plus dessert for around $10. Wash it all down with an imported beer from Home's impressive collection, which includes both Polish Zywiec and Jamaican Red Stripe. Lunch packs a crowd. Sausages and baked goods are sold at the adjoining deli. *2931 N. Milwaukee Ave., at Central Park Ave., Polish Village, 773/252–3708. AE, MC, V. $*

2 *d-3*

LUTNIA

Formally outfitted in red carpet, white tablecloths, and candelabra, Lutnia provides a polished setting for Polish and Continental cuisine. Waiters flame dishes tableside and a live pianist entertains—accents that cheer the convivial and embarrass the bashful. Stick with the Polish food, including starters of pierogi or the hunter's stew called *bigos*, moving on to stuffed quail with cranberry sauce. *5532 W. Belmont Ave., near Central Ave., Portage Park, 773/282–5335. AE, D, MC, V. Closed Mon. No lunch weekends. $$–$$$*

3 *b-8*

THE RED APPLE/ CZERWONE JABLUSZKO

Rock-bottom prices sticker an all-you-can-eat buffet, earning the Red Apple a following among Chicago's extensive Polish community as well as its artists, students, and cheap eaters. Chafing dishes brim with ethnic specialties like pierogi, stuffed cabbage, goulash, blintzes, kielbasa, and roast meats.

Dessert and coffee is included in the under-$10 meal. Generous booths, pleasant servers, and a clean interior make the Apple a good pig-out place. *3121 N. Milwaukee Ave., near Belmont Ave., Avondale, 773/588–5781. D, MC, V. $*

2 *d-1*
6474 N. Milwaukee Ave., near Devon Ave., Forest Glen, 773/763–3407. D, MC, V. $

ROMANIAN

4 *a-8*
LITTLE BUCHAREST
Old-world ambience and a genuine welcome distinguish Little Bucharest, Chicago's Romanian king. Generous portions of chicken paprikash, beef goulash, veal schnitzel, and stuffed pork accompanied by spaetzle make for hearty eating. Management works hard for your business, even dispatching a limousine to pick diners up and hiring a Latin band on weekends. Every September the restaurant sponsors a lively outdoor festival—one of the best of the city's summer street gigs—with spit-roasted pig, lamb, and beef. *3001 N. Ashland Ave., at Wellington Ave., Lakeview, 773/929–8640. AE, D, DC, MC, V. No lunch Mon. $–$$*

RUSSIAN

8 *e-4*
RUSSIAN TEA TIME
Don't let the name fool you; this is no chintz-and-china tearoom. Think Continental glitz (burgundy leather booths, brass chandeliers, mahogany trim, and tuxedoed waiters) and old-world Russian food—borscht, blinis with caviar and salmon, lamb kebabs, and stuffed cabbage. Among 22 desserts are homemade strudel and farmer's-cheese blintzes. Portions are generous, though prices high. Just steps from the Art Institute, this is an indulgent lunch choice. *77 E. Adams St., near Michigan Ave., Loop, 312/360–0000. AE, D, DC, MC, V. $$–$$$$*

SCANDINAVIAN

4 *d-8*
ANN SATHER
Chicago's Swedish diner, Ann Sather is renowned for its huge, gooey cinnamon rolls, which bring on breakfast cravings

at any hour. Scandinavian specialties start with *limpa* (Swedish rye) toast and eggs at breakfast and move onto afternoon-evening specialties like lingonberry-glazed duck and Swedish meatballs, all at value prices. Belmont is particularly jammed on weekends, when other locations are better bets. *929 W. Belmont Ave., near Clark St., Lakeview, 773/348–2378. Reservations not accepted. AE, MC, V. $*

4 *b-1*
5207 N. Clark St., near Foster Ave., Andersonville, 773/271–6677. No dinner.

4 *b-7*
3415 Southport Ave., near Roscoe St., Lakeview, 773/404–4475. No dinner.

4 *b-1*
SVEA
This cozy, sweet-smelling little diner is tops in the morning. Choose a seat at the counter or snare a table and indulge in a breakfast with old-world touches like Swedish pancakes or eggs over easy with a side of limpa toast. Try an open-face sandwich, salt pork, or fruit soup for lunch. Friendly servers, flavorful meals, and regular coffee refills ensure a brisk business. *5236 N. Clark St., near Foster Ave., Andersonville, 773/275–7738. No credit cards. $*

3 *d-1*
TRE KRONOR
Open the door of this cute family-run corner shop and you'd swear Grandma had just pulled coffeecake from the oven. The highly appetizing aromas issue from a kitchen that does a steady trade in all three meals. Among Scandinavian options, try crunchy muesli, mild Norwegian sausage, Danish blue-cheese omelet, open-face or Swedish meatball sandwiches, or roast pork with figs and prunes. Salads and quiches are also available on the ever-changing menu. Service is cheerful as are frolicking troll murals, Carl Larsson prints, and tidy café curtains. *3258 W. Foster Ave., near Kedzie Ave., North Park, 773/267–9888. No credit cards. BYOB. Closed Mon. $–$$*

SCOTTISH

4 *d-8*
DUKE OF PERTH
Part bar, part restaurant, the Duke draws votes on both sides of the food

divide. Its 100 or so single-malt Scotch whiskeys bolster its bar status. The restaurant wins customers with its menu of unique-to-Chicago highland fare including leek pie and Scottish eggs as well as fish-and-chips and Sean Connery burgers. The combination of drinks and eats ensures a cheerful crowd. *2913 N. Clark St., at Oakdale Ave., Lincoln Park, 773/477–1741. AE, DC, MC, V. $*

SEAFOOD

4 *b-2*

ATLANTIQUE
At Atlantique, locals don't have to leave the 'hood for the kind of creative fare you would normally expect downtown. Chef Jack Jones draws foodies on a reverse commute to Andersonville for his exquisite seafood, highlighted by lobster salad, shrimp and sweetbreads, and whatever's on special. The seafood theme extends to the mounted-marlin decor in this cozy, classy find. *5101 N. Clark St., near Foster Ave., Andersonville, 773/275–9191. DC, MC, V. No lunch. $$*

6 *d-1*

BLUE POINT OYSTER BAR
Named for the famous Long Island mollusk, Blue Point is a handsome seafarer. Wooden portholes separate bar and dining room, both staffed by waiters in captains' jackets. The menu, printed daily, often contains more than 12 oyster varieties. Warm up your gullet with a Spicy Oyster Shot, a short Bloody Mary with an oyster. In addition to bivalves, Blue Point serves a variety of fish dishes with American accents, like grouper in key lime butter and blackened amberjack with spicy remoulade. *741 W. Randolph St., at Halsted St., West Loop, 312/207–1222. AE, D, DC, MC, V. No lunch weekends. $$–$$$$*

7 *f-4*

CAPE COD ROOM
This Chicago classic mimics the dark-galleon look and gingham-tablecloth style of New England chowder houses. The house Bookbinder soup (red snapper in a tomato base) is famed, and fish preparations like buttered Dover sole and lobster thermidor are quaintly old-fashioned. Traditional oysters Rockefeller are right at home under the hanging brass pots. A small marble-top bar is an intimate nook in which to nosh

on raw shellfish. It's very cozy but also very Gold Coast, so look sharp. *Drake Hotel, 140 E. Walton St., at Michigan Ave., Magnificent Mile, 312/787–2200. AE, D, DC, MC, V. $$–$$$*

8 *d-1*

CATCH 35
In the lobby of the Leo Burnett Building, Catch 35 nets advertising types, particularly after office hours, for cocktails over a platter of raw oysters in the lively piano bar. Entrées tout Pacific fish such as ahi tuna and mahimahi, often prepared with an Asian flair; Thai curries and ginger make frequent appearances. The marble-and-wood dining room is arrayed on several levels, affording some privacy. *35 W. Wacker Dr., at Dearborn St., Loop, 312/346–3500. AE, D, DC, MC, V. No lunch weekends. $$$–$$$$*

7 *c-6*

JOE'S CRAB SHACK
Ersatz backwater decor draws Midwest Key Westerners and plenty of tourists for shell-busting, bib-wearing seafood shucking. With loads of butter to dip 'em in, it's hard to go wrong with the crab legs here. Picnic-table seating and raucous good-time music encourage interaction with neighbors. *745 N. Wells St., between Chicago Ave. and Superior St., Old Town, 312/664–2722. AE, D, DC, MC, V. Closed Sun. $$*

7 *e-5*

MCCORMICK & SCHMICK'S
The menu changes not just daily but twice daily, effectively showcasing the dozens of fresh seafood varieties received that day. In addition to several oysters available, the fish ranges from Wisconsin trout to Atlantic char and is prepared every which way from plank roasted to horseradish crusted. The handsome, high-ceiling dining room boasts enough wood to feign oldness. Cheap appetizers and a live pianist combine to pack the bar. Private alcove tables make a great romantic choice. *41 E. Chestnut St., at Rush St., Gold Coast, 312/397–9500. AE, D, DC, MC, V. $$–$$$*

8 *d-3*

NICK'S FISHMARKET
Popular with expense-account business folk as well as splurging couples, Nick's is a bilevel Loop institution occupying romantic digs. Fish, of course, high-

lights the menu, but the restaurant also touts plenty of red meat, pasta, and shellfish options. The tuxedo-clad wait-staff is smooth and attentive. Patrons are treated like royalty; expect to pay handsomely during your reign. *1 BankOne Plaza, 51 S. Clark St., between Madison and Monroe Sts., Loop, 312/621–0200. AE, D, DC, MC, V. Closed Sun. No lunch Sat. $$$–$$$$*

7 h-7

RIVA

A wall of floor-to-ceiling windows along Navy Pier's second story overlooking the lake and city skyline gives Riva a stunning setting in which to serve seafood. The expansive menu includes raw-bar options, mesquite-grilled fish, and, among specialties, filet mignon of tuna. Unlike the rest of Navy Pier, Riva requires proper attire, thus maintaining its dignity among mostly french fries–and–burgers purveyors. For a less pricey nosh, order appetizers at the elegant wood bar, which has the same view as the dining room. Café Riva, one floor below, serves casual sandwiches. *700 E.*

Grand Ave., at Navy Pier, 312/644–7482. AE, D, DC, MC, V. $$$–$$$$

7 e-8

SHAW'S CRAB HOUSE AND BLUE CRAB LOUNGE

Chicago's liveliest seafood emporium, Shaw's is two restaurants in one: the more formal Crab House and the casual Blue Crab Lounge. The wood-paneled dining room serves excellent, simple, and classic fish dishes like fried perch and grilled grouper. Fun seekers prefer the bustling Lounge, often swinging to live music; it's set around a convivial 25-seat oyster bar that stocks up to a dozen varieties. Most items like crab, lobster, and hearty clam chowder are available in either setting. Knowledgeable servers keep meals apace on both sides. *21 E. Hubbard St., between State St. and Wabash Ave., River North, 312/527–2722. AE, D, DC, MC, V. $$–$$$$*

SOUTHERN

2 g-8

ARMY & LOU'S

A Chicago institution, Army & Lou's is tops for Southern comfort food. The fried chicken is arguably the city's best; barbecued ribs, roast turkey, collard and mustard greens, and crunchy fried catfish are other standouts. The food may be down-home, but the room is uptown with white linens on the tables and African and Haitian art on the walls. It's especially crowded after church on Sunday. *422 E. 75th St., at Martin Luther King Dr., South Shore, 773/483–3100. AE, DC, MC, V. Closed Tues. $–$$$*

2 h-7

DIXIE KITCHEN & BAIT SHOP

A kitschy bayou-esque shack setting tacked with fishing poles, old Coca-Cola ads, and oodles of yard-sale kitchenware, the thematic Dixie thrives on masterful versions of jambalaya, gumbo, red beans and rice, and catfish po'boys. Subbing for bread, warm johnnycakes start the meal in step. Keep from overdosing, as main courses are generous. Brisk business means waits are not uncommon. Friendly servers help make Dixie fun for the whole family. *5225 S. Harper Ct., near Lake Park Ave. and 53rd St., Hyde Park, 773/363–4943. AE, D, DC, MC, V. $*

COOL FOR KIDS

Bring the family and don't fret—the kids will love these locales:

Ed Debevic's (American/Casual)
  A '50s setting with jitterbugging, gum-popping servers and fab burgers, fries, and shakes.

Foodlife (Eclectic)
  Something for the whole family in this imaginative food court.

Home Run Inn (Pizza)
  Great pies in teeming pizzeria with pastimes including video games.

R. J. Grunts (American/Casual)
  Ideal stop after visiting the Lincoln Park Zoo, Grunts is used to kid-heavy traffic.

Sesi's Seaside Café (Turkish)
  Some basic American choices among the exotic Turkish fare plus a playground out back.

Superdawg Drive-In (Hot Dogs)
  Pile the kids in the minivan for a taste of yesteryear.

Wishbone (Southern)
  Extremely family-friendly policy doesn't diminish adult appeal of food and drink here.

2 g-7

GLADYS' LUNCHEONETTE

This place serves cheap and delicious soul standards in a no-nonsense setting. Rock-bottom prices ensure a hungry following among South Siders, who keep the tables turning. Though the neighborhood is rough, the diner provides a measure of security, with a guarded parking lot adjacent to it. *4527 S. Indiana Ave., at 45th St., Kenwood, 773/548–4566. No credit cards. Closed Mon. $*

7 e-6

PAIGE'S PLACE

Homey Southern eats make a unique addition to the chichi River North scene. Look for classics like fried catfish, fried green tomatoes, and chicken wings served in an African American art–filled family room. Kool-Aid comes in mason jars. *16 E. Huron St., between State St. and Wabash Ave., River North, 312/397–9390. AE, MC, V. Closed Mon. $$*

6 c-1

WISHBONE

Casual, cheap, and tasty, Wishbone packs 'em in for sweet-corn pancakes, zesty blackened catfish, huge Hoppin' John, and rib-sticking mac and cheese. Breakfast is spicy; eggs are accompanied by irresistible corn muffins. Hung with "outsider" art, Wishbone unites everyone in the neighborhood from *Oprah* attendees to area loft dwellers to plumber's-union stewards. Families thankful for the kids-love-it-too menu crowd the newer Roscoe Village location. *1001 W. Washington Blvd., at Morgan St., West Loop, 312/850–2663. AE, D, DC, MC, V. No dinner Sun.–Mon. $*

3 h-7

3300 N. Lincoln Ave., at School St., Roscoe Village, 773/549–2663.

SOUTHWESTERN

5 d-4

BLUE MESA

The perennially popular, adobe-wall Blue Mesa looks and tastes New Mexican. Margaritas are a must here, shared over blue tortilla chips with guacamole. Mains make zesty use of hot peppers (dried varieties hang from the ceiling) in dishes like green-chili chicken enchilada and grilled shrimp with jalapeño-and-pineapple salsa. Tacos, fajitas, and bur-

ritos are also available. The brunch menu is full of eye-opening, spicy selections. The private patio is pleasant in summer. *1729 N. Halsted St., at Willow St., Lincoln Park, 312/944–5990. AE, D, DC, MC, V. Closed Mon. No lunch Fri.–Sat. $$*

SPANISH

4 d-7

ARCO DE CUCHILLEROS

Not a chain, and not as crowded as other tapas places, Arco offers nibblers and imbibers—you can't forget the sangria—plenty to satiate their appetites. The family-style atmosphere makes for a lively crowd, especially after a couple of drinks. If you don't like to share, get your own plate of the paella with chicken, fish, and chorizo. If you can handle squid, try the calamari *a la plancha* (with lemon juice and white wine). In good weather, the glass front opens and the Sunday brunch crowd spills onto the street. *3445 N. Halsted St., near Roscoe Ave., Wrigleyville, 773/296–6046. AE, V. $$*

5 d-3

CAFÉ BA-BA-REEBA!

For crowd-pleasing Spanish food, visit this branch of the Lettuce Entertain You empire. Ambria chef Gabino Sotelino, a native of Spain, oversees the kitchen here, which means most dishes are successful. Consider the entertaining, colorful murals over a pitcher of sangria and a few tapas (try goat cheese marinara or tuna cannelloni) while you wait for the paella to cook. Though Ba-Ba-Reeba sprawls over a series of rooms, on weekends you will most surely wait for a table. *2024 N. Halsted St., near Armitage Ave., Lincoln Park, 773/935–5000. AE, D, DC, MC, V. $$*

7 c-6

CAFÉ IBERICO

For the most authentic, least expensive Spanish experience in town, head to Iberico. Tapas are the star here. Order a bunch—grilled octopus, tuna cannelloni, tortilla (a Spanish omelet), and *patatas bravas* (potatoes) are good starters—and share with friends over a basket of bread and glasses of Rioja. Notable Spaniards passing through town, including Placido Domingo, soccer players, flamenco stars, and figures of state, have been known to call at Iberico. A store-deli sells Spanish foods to go. *739 N. LaSalle St., near Chicago Ave., River North, 312/573–1510. D, DC, MC, V. $*

5 *e-2*

EMILIO'S TAPAS

Superior cooking keeps the small plates spinning. Entrées are available but a meal of shared tapas allows you to taste more. Among the stars: beef brochette, chicken-stuffed red peppers, and grilled calamari. Munch on the small bowl of olives while contemplating the good selection of Spanish wines, sangria, and brandy. The L-shape restaurant is deceptively large, with sunny details like window flower boxes. Helpful servers are good guides to the extensive menu. *444 W. Fullerton Ave., at Clark St., Lincoln Park, 773/327–5100. AE, MC, V. No lunch Mon.–Thurs. $$*

STEAK

7 *f-7*

THE CAPITAL GRILLE

In the Capital Grille the City of Big Shoulders bulks up on dry-aged steaks dished up by the Rhode Island–based chain. Humidity-controlled lockers sequester meat for 21 to 28 days, thus intensifying the flavor. Thick slabs of steak suit the masculine interior. Buffalo and deer heads, oil portraits, art-deco light fixtures, and mahogany paneling lend an exclusive men's-club feel to the dining room. A handsome bar is cigar-friendly, of course. *633 N. St. Clair Ct., at Ontario St., Streeterville, 312/337–9400. AE, D, DC, MC, V. No lunch weekends. $$–$$$$*

6 *c-2*

CARMICHAEL'S

A steak house that chases the United Center–bound beef eaters, Carmichael's takes care of prime business, serving juicy steaks and chops. The vintage-inspired room and woody bar generate a casual warmth that devotees praise. Enormous martinis pair well with the sizable stogies available in the bar. *1052 W. Monroe St., at Aberdeen St., West Loop, 312/433–0025. AE, D, DC, MC, V. No lunch weekends.*

7 *d-7*

CHICAGO CHOP HOUSE

Chicago's best steaker? Many say so. And flocks of tourists follow. The vintage

photos of famous Chicago figures—from mobsters to mayors—underscores a sense of place in this clubby steak house occupying a 100-year-old brownstone. Generous cuts are priced to please—including salad and side, a tremendous value. *60 W. Ontario St., between Clark and Dearborn Sts., River North, 312/787–7100. AE, D, DC, MC, V. $$$*

7 *f-6*

ELI'S THE PLACE FOR STEAK

Clubby and inviting in leather and warm wood, Eli's developed its outstanding reputation through an unflagging commitment to top-quality ingredients prepared precisely to customers' tastes. Prime aged steaks are the specialty here, among the best in Chicago. Save room for dessert; Eli's is almost as famous for its rich cheesecakes (in endless flavors like chocolate chip and almond) as it is for its steaks. *215 E. Chicago Ave., near Michigan Ave., Streeterville, 312/642–1393. AE, D, DC, MC, V. No lunch weekends. $$–$$$$*

7 *a-7*

ERIE CAFÉ

The great atmosphere at this Italian meatery makes it deserving of a look by even the most ardent vegan. The meat packer gets dressed up in white linens and warm wood paneling that says clubby without saying upper crust only. Large servings appeal to hearty appetites, though additional Italian pastas please lighter ones. *536 W. Erie St., near Kingsbury St., River North, 312/266–2300. AE, DC, MC, V. $$$*

7 *b-6*

GENE & GEORGETTI

This guy's joint of the old-neighborhood variety is worth visiting for its so anti-trendy-it's-hip atmosphere and the collection of power diners. The core menu is based on massive prime, aged steaks with cottage fries, good chops, and the famed Garbage Salad—a kitchen-sink creation of greens with vegetables and meats. If they don't know you here, you won't get a good table. No matter: the people-watching, as well as the eating, is as good in the boonies as it is elsewhere. Expect generally crusty waiters. *500 N. Franklin St., at Illinois St., River North, 312/527–3718. AE, DC, MC, V. Closed Sun. $$–$$$$*

7 *d-4*

GIBSONS STEAKHOUSE

Size is everything at Gibsons, from the huge signature martinis to the fat stogies puffed by the patrons. An energizing mix of politicians, celebs, sports figures, and conventioneers packs the place nightly. Matching the outsized personalities, steaks are substantial and flavorful. Soup and salad are included, and titanic desserts easily serve two, if not a crew. Lobster tail is a popular meatless option. The smoky piano bar is usually thronged with drinkers and those awaiting tables. *1028 N. Rush St., near Oak St., Gold Coast, 312/266–8999. Reservations essential. AE, D, DC, MC, V. No lunch. $$$–$$$$*

7 *c-8*

KINZIE CHOPHOUSE

A handsome steak house behind the Merchandise Mart, it creates a comfortable setting for settling into meat and potatoes. Kinzie doesn't have the food-meets-quantity reputation of competitors around town, but it does have a warm, welcoming style aided in part by cushy banquettes and caricatures of regulars on the walls. *400 N. Wells St., at Kinzie St., Old Town, 312/822–0191. AE, D, DC, MC, V. Closed Sun. $$–$$$$*

7 *e-7*

LAWRY'S THE PRIME RIB

Unique-to-Chicago Lawry's wheels its signature prime rib to the table, atop a silver cart for carving. Out-of-towners and special-occasion celebrants love the Italian Renaissance–style setting created by carved wood and chiseled stone throughout the various rooms. The much-lauded chef, Jackie Shen, turns out tasty fish dishes for non-meat eaters. Do save room for her signature sinful finish, the Chocolate Bag. The entire experience is elegantly old-fashioned. *100 E. Ontario St., near Michigan Ave., Magnificent Mile, 312/787–5000. AE, D, DC, MC, V. $$$*

7 *b-7*

MAGNUM'S STEAK & LOBSTER

Very big aged steaks and lobster tails star, the perfect companions to mammoth martinis. Bring your substantial appetite as well as your tolerance here. The steak house adjoins Faces dance club next door and resounds with the disco beat. But most afficionados like the combination of loud music and large meals. *225 W. Ontario St., at Franklin St., River North, 312/337–8080. AE, D, DC, MC, V. $$$*

6 *d-1*

MILLENNIUM STEAKS & CHOPS

Those bound for the United Center—with a steak hankering—check into this West Loop meat purveyor. The satisfying dry-aged slabs come with more modern options in the form of side dishes. The soothing wood-and-glass interior merits a sit, particularly the upstairs room, which offers a dramatic downtown skyline panorama. *832 W. Randolph St., near Halsted St., West Loop, 312/455–1400. AE, D, DC, MC, V. Closed Sun. $$$–$$$$*

7 *d-4*

MORTON'S OF CHICAGO

Steak lovers consider this Chicago's best. Ensconced in the lower level of an apartment building, Morton's cozy room is the place to carve into a 24-ounce porterhouse or a 20-ounce New York sirloin. Servers show off raw steaks, softball-size potatoes, and even giant tomatoes at the table before they are grilled, baked, and sliced. Non-meat eaters should try the large lobster or grilled swordfish. Sides are big enough to feed two. Service is enthusiastic and the wine list is a good match to the menu. *1050 N. State St., at Rush St., Gold Coast, 312/266–4820. AE, D, DC, MC, V. No lunch. $$$–$$$$*

6 *e-1*

NINE

The name is simply Nine, as in decked to the nines. The chic newcomer blends nightclub-trendy design—a circular champagne-and-caviar bar, plasma TVs in the lounge, a domed ceiling that changes color—with edible indulgences from caviar to tartare to porterhouse. The ultrahip vibe bears no resemblance to other steak houses in the city. Don't miss the upstairs Ghost Bar, where signature Midori martinis glow in the dark. *440 W. Randolph St., at Canal St., West Loop, 312/575–9900. AE, D, DC, MC, V. Closed Sun. No lunch Sat. $$$–$$$$*

8 *f-1*

THE PALM

This clubby wood-trim room with high-back booths is a bit of old Chicago in the modern Swissôtel. Big portions of steak (36 ounces, anyone?) and even bigger lobsters are the draws, but the Palm does a good job with veal and the occasional fish, too. Save room for the strongly recommended desserts. Caricatures of city celebrities and regular customers make this link in the steakhouse chain feel local. The patio has a lovely view of Lake Michigan and Navy Pier. *Swissôtel, 323 E. Wacker Dr., near Columbus Dr., the Loop, 312/616–1000. Reservations essential. AE, DC, MC, V. $$–$$$$*

7 *d-8*

RUTH'S CHRIS STEAK HOUSE

An outpost of the New Orleans–based chain, Ruth's Chris manages to score in the crowded steak house category with excellent, juicy steak preparations nicely accompanied by garlic-mashed potatoes, outstanding service, and Louisiana-style options like turtle soup, Cajun shrimp, and gumbo. The lobster is good although expensive—largely because the smallest lobster in the tank is about 3 pounds. The setting is masculine. *431 N. Dearborn St., at Hubbard St., River North, 312/321–2725. AE, D, DC, MC, V. Closed Sun. No lunch Sat. $$–$$$$*

7 *f-5*

THE SALOON

In addition to the requisite meat, this place updates the image of a steak house by offering loads of seafood and other steak-less options in a refreshingly bright and cheery interior. Not that the steaks don't rule; the Kansas City strip (a New York strip with the bone left in), the massive porterhouse, and the double pork chop are top picks here. Convention goers, Streeterville residents, and Michigan Avenue shoppers patronize the Saloon. *200 E. Chestnut St., near Michigan Ave., Gold Coast, 312/280–5454. AE, D, DC, MC, V. $$–$$$*

8 *d-1*

SMITH & WOLLENSKY

A satellite of the New York original, Smith & Wollensky landed one of the best locations in town. The glass-wall, bilevel restaurant overlooks the Chicago River, giving it a clubby and sunny feel simultaneously. S&W does big box office in grilled sirloin and rib-eye steaks accompanied by chili-laced whipped potatoes and signature creamed spinach. There are lots of lighter and/

or nonmeat alternatives, too. The high-energy upper level is noisier than the cozy lower level, which is shared by Wollensky's Grill, a good lunch or late-night option that serves steaks as well as sandwiches, burgers, salads, and pizzas. *318 N. State St., at the Chicago River, River North, 312/670–9900. AE, D, DC, MC, V. $$–$$$$*

5 *f-8*

SULLIVAN'S STEAKHOUSE

The supper club–theme restaurant delivers its colossal steaks (signatures include a 24-ounce porterhouse and 20-ounce Kansas City strip) in a winsome, wood-paneled dining room that, thankfully, doesn't repeat the clichéd men's-club look. There are great sides and plenty of seafood options for nonmeat eaters. The classy bar with louvered windows and a live jazz trio serves the full menu more informally. *415 N. Dearborn St., at Hubbard St., Old Town, 312/527–3510. AE, D, DC, MC, V. Closed Sun. $$$*

5 *g-6*

TAVERN ON RUSH

This clubby Gold Coast steak house owned by Phil Stefani (Riva, Tuscany) appeals to fans of big portions. Because of its location, the Tavern draws its share of conventioneers and Division Street swillers. But the bilevel joint is attractive, and Stefani reliably serves good food, including 16-ounce porterhouses and New York strips. Starters make great meals for lighter appetites. For drinks with dash try the convivial bar. *1031 N. Rush St., at Bellevue Pl., Gold Coast, 312/664–9600. AE, DC, MC, V. $$–$$$$*

TEA

7 *e-6*

JOY OF IRELAND TEA ROOM

A quainter version of the bookstore-café phenomenon, the tearoom is in a tiny, tucked-away corner of the store, providing a view of the city. A selection of tea sandwiches includes the popular cucumber and cream as well as the more contemporary crab finger with avocado. For the purist, the Traditional Tea Service will bring to your table a nibbler's delight of sandwiches, scones, petits fours, and fresh fruit—

and tea, of course. *700 N. Michigan Ave., near Huron St., Magnificent Mile, 312/664–7290. AE, D, DC, MC, V. Closed Sun. No dinner.* $

7 *f-4*
PALM COURT
Take tea in another era at the Drake Hotel's Palm Court. The high ceiling, palm-draped room, outfitted with cushy divans and inviting armchairs, is the perfect throw-back setting in which to linger thoughtfully over a cup of Orange Pekoe while nibbling on cucumber finger sandwiches, raisin scones, and French pastries. A harpist provides a soothing accompaniment. Plan your genteel escape carefully; the line for seats forms early on weekends and throughout the holiday season. *Drake Hotel, 140 E. Walton St., at Michigan Ave., Gold Coast, 312/787–2200. Reservations for groups of 8 or more only. AE, D, DC, MC, V.* $

7 *f-5*
THE GREENHOUSE AT THE RITZ-CARLTON CHICAGO
The fabulously genteel Ritz-Carlton pours nearly two dozen different tea blends during afternoon tea. The sunlit and flower-festooned lobby retreat will soothe the most harried of break-takers. The scones with cream, homemade lemon curd, and elegant tea sandwiches are finger-licking good. For peace of mind, reserve your own overstuffed couch in advance. *Ritz-Carlton Chicago, 160 E. Pearson St., near Michigan Ave., Gold Coast, 312/266–1000. AE, D, DC, MC, V.* $–$$

3 *g-4*
VILLA KULA
An American arts-and-crafts room is lit with Asian rice-paper lamps at this tranquil teahouse. The tableside tea directory lists black, green, white, and oolong teas as well as herbal-infused tisanes. Sandwiches, salads, and quiches join the traditional afternoon tea bites on the light menu. A great place to read by day, Villa Kula is filled with Old Town School musicians in the evening. The outdoor patio gets the same loving attention of the owner as the teahouse itself. There is live jazz Friday through Sunday. Beware slow service. *4518 N. Lincoln Ave., between Wilson and Sunnyside Aves., Lincoln Square, 773/728–3114. AE, DC, MC, V. Closed Tues.* $

TEX-MEX

5 *f-6*
BLUE AGAVE
Every neighborhood needs its reliable, no surprises Tex-Mex. Blue Agave is the Gold Coast's. Americanized Mexican classics twinned with tequila-laced drinks compose the menu at this cactus-studded corner joint. *1 W. Maple St., at State St., Gold Coast, 312/335–8900. AE, MC, V.* $–$$

4 *c-7*
EL JARDÍN RESTAURANT
This is not the dance club that bears the same name just down the street, nor is it the place to go before or after a Cubs game—unless you want to wait a couple hours. El Jardín has been a Wrigleyville institution for more than 30 years, so eating fajitas in one of the two main dining rooms, the sidewalk

LATE NIGHT NOSHES
Where can you eat late without resorting to fast food? Check out one of these night owls:

Nine (Steakhouse)
Steak house meets nightclub in this swanky West Looper, where image is everything.

Pasha (Contemporary)
A DJ, dancing, and ambitious fare draw late-night supper seekers.

Nacional 27 (Latin)
Sensuous Latin cuisine really swings when the dancing starts after 11 PM.

Echo (Contemporary)
Graze through mini-entrée-size portions at this hip Bucktownie.

Black Duck Tavern & Grille (American/Casual)
Upscale barroom serves late theater and pub-crawling crowds.

Red Light (Pan-Asian)
Very groovy Asian Randolph Street resident draws hungry nightclubbers.

Sushi Wabi (Japanese)
A DJ and industrial decor only improve as the night progresses.

The Twisted Spoke (American/Casual)
Top burger and beer joint popular with some of the city's top chefs when their shifts end.

café, or garden is a historic experience. Game or no game, there's nothing more relaxing than having a drink on the ensconced patio. The Fiesta Buffet on Sundays is like a meet-and-greet for a 5-mi radius. *3335 N. Clark St., near Buckingham Pl., Wrigleyville, 773/528–6775. AE, D, DC, V. $$*

5 *d-2*

LAS FUENTES

Serve standby Mexican in the heart of Lincoln Park and the college kids will come. The party-train spirit buoys Las Fuentes, where the food earns few raves. Nevertheless the large patio packs 'em in for margaritas in the open air. *2558 N. Halsted Ave., at Wrightwood Ave., Lincoln Park, 773/935–2004. AE, D, DC, MC, V. $–$$*

5 *c-1*

LINDO MEXICO

A Lincoln Park fixture on the Tex-Mex scene, Lindo Mexico's has as its best feature color-bright decor and festive atmosphere. Food hovers around average, but the vast menu thankfully provides choices rivals don't, including heart-smart low-fat foods along with the caloric chimichangas. Savor strong margaritas in season in the pleasant garden patio. *2642 N. Lincoln Ave., between Sheffield and Seminary Aves., Lincoln Park, 773/871–4832. AE, D, DC, MC, V. $–$$*

5 *c-4*

TWISTED LIZARD

Excellent house margaritas draw hordes of postcollege Lincoln Park drinkers, but don't underestimate the Lizard's food. Salsas come at various heat levels, and tortillas are fresh and fajitas juicy. The basement setting provides some intrigue. Eat early to avoid the tequila-slamming tipplers. *1964 N. Sheffield Ave., at Armitage Ave., Lincoln Park, 773/929–1414. AE, DC, MC, V. $–$$*

TIBETAN

4 *c-5*

TIBET CAFÉ

A star in the ethnic-storefront melting pot, Tibet Café serves foods strong on vegetarian preparations in a spiffy plywood-paneled interior. Unusual specialties include cold potato salad with peas

and tofu, potato and vegetable fried dumplings, mild chicken curry with cabbage and potatoes, and *deysee*, a Tibetan rice pudding. Food takes 10 to 15 minutes "for total readiness"—plenty of time to relax into a state of mellowness under the gaze of the Dalai Lama and a series of relief sculpture panels made of dyed butter. *3913 N. Sheridan Rd., near Irving Park Rd., Lakeview, 773/261–6666. AE, DC, MC, V. BYOB. No lunch weekdays. $*

THAI

4 *a-5*

ALWAYS THAI

This clean and simple Asian distinguishes itself with solidly prepared Thai standards that have an emphasis on fresh ingredients—worth going out of your way for among ethnic storefronts. Inexpensive fare and a BYOB policy ensure low checks, another satisfying feature of this find. *1825 W. Irving Park Rd., between Wolcott and Ravenswood Aves., North Center, 773/929–0100. AE, D, DC, MC, V. BYOB. Closed Sun. $*

3 *d-5*

ARUN'S

Perhaps the best Thai restaurant nationally—per the James Beard Society—Arun's is worth every dear penny for freshness, innovation, and presentation. Chef Arun Sampanthavivat sets the courses at the $75 per person prix-fixe-only restaurant. Choice courses may include intricate shrimp-filled golden pastry baskets or tamarind red snapper. Familiar dishes like pad thai and curries will spoil you for versions elsewhere. Desserts such as custard cubes and sticky rice are slightly sweet, starchy delights. The pleasant, warmly lit dining room is quiet and conversation-friendly. *4156 N. Kedzie Ave., between Irving Park Rd. and Montrose Ave., Irving Park, 773/539–1909. AE, D, DC, MC, V. Closed Mon. No lunch. $$–$$$*

7 *f-7*

DAO THAI

You can sit in traditional Thai style here, with your legs in the little foxhole under the table. There are conventional tables as well—125 in all, some on a small patio—making this one of the most spacious Asian restaurants in the neighborhood. Huge helpings will make your dog happy. *230 E. Ohio St., near St. Clair St., Streeterville, 312/337–0000. AE, D, DC, V. $$*

3 *g-3*

OPART THAI HOUSE

A find among neighborhood storefront restaurants, Opart Thai House does tasty and zesty noodle, hot pot, and stir-fry dishes cheaply. Once you get past the dingy facade, the wood-panel joint gives you more to ogle than average, including portraits of Thai royalty alongside Abe Lincoln's mug. Match your favorite meat to various sauces with spice levels adjusted to spec. Opart caters to a faithful neighborhood following and fills lots of take-out orders. *4658 N. Western Ave., near Lincoln Ave., Lincoln Square, 773/989–8517. AE, D, MC, V. $*

4 *c-7*

P. S. BANGKOK

Both the menu and restaurant itself are filled to the brim—the former with traditional and exotic dishes, the latter with traditional and exotic decorations. Despite its appearance from the outside, the dining room is spacious and never gets too crowded. In spring and summer, you can get a 20% discount with your theater or sporting-event ticket stub, making the restaurant an appealing alternative for the post-Cubs-game meal. If you're in an adventuresome mood, try the Banana Blossom Salad, or stick with the pad thai or a satay option. A Sunday brunch has more than 100 items. *3345 N. Clark St., near Buckingham Pl., Wrigleyville, 773/871–7777. AE, D, V. Closed Mon. $$*

4 *c-3*

SIAM CAFÉ

The deceptively small Uptown exterior fronts an expansive Thai restaurant within. Cozy booths, gingham-topped tables, and Thai architectural accents make this cheap eatery more comfortable than most. Hot food lovers will find the list of spicy dishes compelling. Generous noodle dishes, such as crispy *mee krob* and satay, rank above average. When your lunch budget dips below $10, make for the all-you-can-eat lunch buffet. *4712 N. Sheridan Rd., near Lawrence Dr., Uptown, 773/769–6602. AE, MC, V. Closed Tues. $*

7 *e-8*

STAR OF SIAM

Among the first to suit Thai food to downtown tastes, Star of Siam earns the loyalty of the professional lunch crowd with well-priced noodle, meat, and stir-fry dishes. Nights are less hectic, offering a chance to appreciate the Thai-import decor. Request a floor seat for the most fun. *11 E. Illinois St., at State St., River North, 312/670–0100. AE, D, DC, MC, V. $*

4 *c-7*

THAI CLASSIC

Thai food lovers generally single out this simple Wrigleyville storefront for fresh dishes in a clean, attractive setting that includes seating on floor pillows (those with bad backs will appreciate the availability of standard tables and chairs). The expansive menu includes noodle dishes as well as meats and veggies prepared in curry, basil, peanut, and other sauces. Beware weekend crowds. *3332 N. Clark St., near Roscoe St., Wrigleyville, 773/404–2000. AE, MC, V. BYOB. $–$$*

7 *e-7*

THAI STAR CAFÉ

The marquee attraction here sure isn't the atmosphere-free dining room. The very good food draws local business folk and residents. Low prices match reasonable portions. *660 N. State St., at Erie St., River North, 312/951–1196. BYOB. DC, MC, V. $*

TURKISH

2 *f-1*

SESI'S SEASIDE CAFÉ

Tucked between a playground and the lake, Sesi's has location, location, location. An elm-shaded patio just steps from the rocky shoreline is the city's most restful in summer. But Sesi's also has good Turkish eats from *kofte* (spiced meat patties) to *doner kebab* (the Turkish gyro). Try the Mediterranean Sampler for a plate of pita and fresh salads. American lunch and breakfast standards service domestic palates. *6219 N. Sheridan Rd., at Granville Ave., Edgewater, 773/764–0544. No credit cards. $*

4 *b-8*

A LA TURKA

Turkish delights served on engraved copper tables mimic an Istanbul eatery. You could make a meal from the 23 starters on the menu: sample several in the *karisik meze*, a plate of addictive bread spreads. Likewise the house-specialty grilled meats are well represented in the mixed-grill dish. Linger afterward over a muddy Turkish coffee. The more dexterous can grab a pillow and lounge on the floor, though the best seats—all upright—are at the back of the house after 10:30 on weekends when a band and belly dancer entertain. *3134 N. Lincoln Ave., near Belmont Ave., Lakeview, 773/935–6101. DC, MC, V. $–$$*

UKRAINIAN

2 *f-4*

SAK'S UKRAINIAN VILLAGE RESTAURANT AND LOUNGE

This is your neighborhood bar—if your neighborhood is Kiev. The family-run joint with cozy booths and superfriendly staff is a bit out of place among the urban hipsters, but that only makes the borscht and pierogi better. Meat, potatoes, and beer, the staples here, are great in combination. *2301 W. Chicago Ave., near Claremont Ave., Ukrainian Village, 773/278–4445. AE, MC, V. $*

VEGETARIAN

4 *b-7*

AMITABUL

Nary a spice-bland dish emerges from the kitchen at Amitabul, home of Korean Buddhist vegetarian cuisine. The vegan menu is 60 items strong and the portions are considerable. In addition to seaweed-wrapped maki rolls, noodle soups, and vegan pancakes, the restaurant specializes in stir-fried or steamed vegetables over rice. A daily special gets you a bargain plate, often $6, including tea and soup. Decor is stripped down to monkish, but value seekers from students to families crowd in regardless. *3418 N. Southport Ave., near Roscoe St., Lakeview, 773/472–4060. AE, DC, MC, V. $*

4 *d-7*

THE CHICAGO DINER

If the word "vegetarian" makes your mouth yawn rather than water, check out the Chicago Diner. This funkster takes the grease out of diner cooking, offering meat-free versions of normally animal fatted foods like burgers, fajitas, burritos, and chili. Going against the multigrain, the veggie diner also serves alcohol and has a style-conscious staff. *3411 N. Halsted St., near Roscoe St., Lakeview, 773/935–6696. AE, DC, MC, V. $*

2 *f-1*

HEARTLAND CAFÉ

Birkenstock-wearing granola crunchers have a home in this tie-dye friendly Rogers Parker, popular as a community gathering spot as well as a food destination. A Berkeley-in-the-'60s spirit thrives among earthy staffers, who truck out vegetarian staples as well as burgers and fish dishes from the meat-tolerant-but-healthful menu. The Heartland also programs live musical acts, sells alternative literature, and stocks a health food store. There's a great sidewalk patio in summer. *7000 N. Glenwood Ave., at Lunt Ave., Rogers Park, 773/465–8005. AE, MC, V. $*

4 *b-5*

JIM'S GRILL

Jim's treats a strong band of loyalists to heart-healthy fare in a greasy-spoon setting. The diner dishes up zesty Korean noodles, soups (don't miss the *mandoo* wheat noodle version), and rice-based dishes, many of them vegetarian. You can still get eggs in the AM, but Bi-Bim-Bop bests them. Expect to wait for a counter stool on weekends. *1429 W. Irving Park Rd., near Southport Ave., North Center, 773/525–4050. No credit cards. Closed Sun. No dinner. $*

VIETNAMESE

7 *e-4*

LE COLONIAL

This romantic Gold Coast outfit re-creates a Saigon club during the French occupation circa 1920. Low lighting, slowly revolving ceiling fans, potted palms, and louvered windows engender nostalgia of the sophisticated sort. The French-Vietnamese menu earns raves for fresh *chao tom*, elegant beef tenderloin salad, and juicy gingered duck. Patronized by a smart set, Le Colonial warrants dressing up. Solo diners will appreciate the out-of-the-way tables reserved for them. Weather-dependent, balcony seats require same-day reservations. The dimly lit, slightly decadent bar upstairs is a great spot for a nightcap. *937 N. Rush St., at Oak St., Gold Coast, 312/255–0088. AE, D, DC, MC, V. No lunch Sun. $$–$$$*

4 b-2

JULIE MAI'S LE BISTRO

Presided over by the namesake owner, this offbeat North Sider works hard to please. In addition to Vietnamese standards, the menu also touts French classics such as beef in wine sauce. For intimacy request a table in one of the semiprivate alcoves with dimmable lamps. *5025 N. Clark St., near Foster Ave., Andersonville, 773/784–6000. AE, D, DC, M, V. No lunch. $$*

4 c-2

NHU HOA CAFÉ

Nua Hoa may be your best bet among the competing Vietnamese restaurants lining Argyle. Two golden lions outside mark the clean, ornately trimmed eatery. With more than 200 Vietnamese and Laotian dishes on the menu, ordering can create a quandary. Try the stir-fried Laos noodles, similar to pad thai but with seafood and richer spices. If you feel like crooning in Vietnamese, check out the karaoke set-up in the back of the house. Lunch is popular with area business folk. *1020 W. Argyle St., near Sheridan Rd., Edgewater, 773/878–0618. MC, V. $–$$*

4 c-1

PASTEUR

A pretty, romantic setting for satisfying Vietnamese, Pasteur is arguably Edgewater's most popular restaurant. For starters, wrap yourself a rice-paper spring roll or slurp some *pho,* a Hanoi rice noodle soup. Clay-pot chicken and stuffed beef rolls are good entrée selections. Dessert sorbets are frozen in cute coconut halves. Service is amiable. Even when the kitchen slows, a pitfall here, it's hard not to be seduced by the glow of candlelight, arching ferns, and cheongsam-clad waitresses. *5525 N. Broadway, near Bryn Mawr Ave., Edgewater, 773/878–1061. AE, D, DC, MC, V. No lunch Mon.–Tues. $$–$$$*

4 c-2

PHO 777

As you might guess from the name, this place specializes in pho; one of the 20 different kinds is bound to please anybody. Dac Biet 777 has it all—steak, flank, brisket, tendon, tripe, and meatballs—and, like all the other pho, it comes steaming to the table along with a plate of mesculin-like greens you add to the broth yourself. A complete array of traditional noodle and rice dishes is also available. *1065 W. Argyle St., near Kenmore Ave., Uptown, 773/561–9909. MC, V. Closed Wed. $*

chapter 2

SHOPPING

The Magnificent Mile, Chicago's affectionate moniker for the northernmost stretch of Michigan Avenue, has the crème de la crème of stores, including Neiman Marcus, Marshall Field's, and Saks Fifth Avenue.

A few blocks south is State Street, which has improved remarkably in the last few years thanks to a massive overhaul of the streets and sidewalks. Bargain stores, including Old Navy, Toys 'R' Us, Filene's Basement, and T. J. Maxx, have the upper hand on the Great Street.

You won't find many bargains on Oak Street, between Michigan Avenue and Rush Street, but that doesn't stop the legions of well-dressed Europeans who come out of stores loaded down with carrier bags marked Hermès, Giorgio Armani, and Gianni Versace.

Andersonville, Lincoln Park, Hyde Park, and Bucktown and Wicker Park are neighborhoods that attract shoppers with festive, offbeat stores and restaurants.

shopping areas

DEPARTMENT STORES

7 e-4
BARNEYS NEW YORK
A scaled-down version of the Manhattan flagship with a reputation for austere men's and women's designer fashions, this store is heavy on private-label merchandise. Brides-to-be will want to visit the Vera Wang salon, if only for inspiration. 25 E. Oak St., Magnificent Mile, 312/587–1700.

7 e-5
BLOOMINGDALE'S
Looking quite unlike the New York flagship, this store has a light, airy feel brought about by its Prairie School and postmodern design. Architecture aside, it gives you plenty of room to sift

through an assortment of designer labels and check out its stylish housewares. 900 N. Michigan Ave., Magnificent Mile, 312/440–4460.

8 d-3
CARSON PIRIE SCOTT
Check out famed architect Louis Sullivan's superb iron scrollwork at the corner of State and Madison streets, and then venture inside to peruse the array of clothing, housewares, accessories, and cosmetics, all with an emphasis on moderately priced merchandise. 1 S. State St., Loop, 312/641–7000.

2 d-3
JCPENNEY
This department store is similar in feel to others in this popular, reasonably priced chain. Who couldn't love the store's good bargains, especially in the areas of shoes and underwear? Brickyard Mall, 6445 W. Diversey Ave., Belmont-Craigin, 773/745–1550.

7 e-5
LORD & TAYLOR
Chicago mainstay, this downtown store carries moderate to upscale clothing for men and women, plus shoes and accessories, often at sale prices. Water Tower Place, 835 N. Michigan Ave., Magnificent Mile, 312/787–7400.

8 d-2
MARSHALL FIELD'S
It was the place your mothers and grandmothers went to for an afternoon of Loop shopping, dressed in gloves and hats. Smart man that Marshall Field was, his motto became "Give the lady what she wants!" So for many years both ladies and gentlemen have been able to find everything from furs to personalized stationery on one of the store's nine levels. The basement level, called Down Under, contains a series of small boutiques that sell kitchenware, luggage, books, gourmet food, wine, and Field's famous Frango mints, which many consider to be among the store's finest merchandise. After a Frango mints break, you'll want to see the Tiffany Dome designed in 1907 by Louis Comfort Tiffany and visible from the fifth floor near women's lingerie. The glossy Water Tower branch also stocks an array of superb goods but lacks the charm of the flagship store. 111 N. State St., Loop, 312/781–1000.

7 *e-5*
Water Tower Place, 835 N. Michigan Ave., Magnificent Mile, 312/335–7700.

7 *e-6*
NEIMAN MARCUS
Prices are on the high side at this first-class branch of the Dallas-headquartered chain. There's a phenomenal selection of merchandise, especially of designer clothing and accessories for men and women; visit even if only to check what's fashionable this year. The gourmet food area on the top floor carries hard-to-find delicacies, delicious chocolates, and exquisite hostess gifts. *737 N. Michigan Ave., Magnificent Mile, 312/642–5900.*

7 *e-7*
NORDSTROM
The flagship of the new North Branch shopping complex, this huge outpost of the Seattle-based chain consists of close to 300,000 square ft spread over four floors. It has a reputation for extraordinary service, not to mention a killer shoe department. *55 E. Grand Ave., Magnificent Mile, 312/464–1515.*

7 *e-6*
SAKS FIFTH AVENUE
A tinier version of the original New York store, it still has an excellent selection of designer clothes for men and women. *Chicago Place, 700 N. Michigan Ave., Magnificent Mile, 312/944–6500.*

2 *c-4*
SEARS
Though not necessarily one of the hippest, Sears is one of the oldest department stores in the country and remains quite popular. Shoppers often sing the praises of the store's excellent tool supply and reasonably priced merchandise. *1601 N. Harlem Ave., Austin, 773/804–5000.*

MALLS AND SHOPPING CENTERS

2 *d-3*
BRICKYARD MALL
If you're in the mood for a can of paint and some brushes, you'll find your heart's desire here. Store giants JCPenney and Kmart sell wares to suit every family member's need. *6465 W. Diversey Ave., Avondale, 773/745–8838.*

5 *d-1*
CENTURY MALL
In a former movie palace, this mall targets the young-and-hip crowd. Here you'll find Victoria's Secret, Lady's Foot Locker, Structure, and other trendy stores. *2828 N. Clark St., Lakeview, 773/929–8100.*

7 *e-6*
CHICAGO PLACE
Just a stone's throw from Water Tower Place and 900 North Michigan Avenue, this art deco–inspired building is home to Saks Fifth Avenue, Talbots, Ann Taylor, the Teddie Kossof Salon & Spa, and several boutiques carrying distinctive art for the table and home, including Chiaroscuro, Tutti Italia, Design Toscano, and companion furniture stores Room & Board and Retrospect. After shopping, you can replenish your stamina at the mall's lovely food court on the top floor, which has a wonderful view. *700 N. Michigan Ave., Magnificent Mile, 312/266–7710.*

8 *c-1*
MERCHANDISE MART
Just north of the Chicago River, this huge building is noted most for its art deco design, not for its shopping. While most of the building is reserved for the design trade, the first two floors have been turned into retail. Stores are predominantly standard mall fare (such as the Limited and Athlete's Foot). *Merchandise Mart Plaza, 320 N. Wells St., River North, 312/527–4141. Closed Sun.*

7 *e-5*
900 NORTH MICHIGAN SHOPS
Slightly more upscale than other malls, here you'll find Bloomingdale's, along with dozens of smaller boutiques and specialty stores, such as Gucci, J. Crew, Club Monaco, Mark Shale, and Oilily. There's a Four Seasons hotel on top and a movie theater. *900 N. Michigan Ave., Magnificent Mile, 312/915–3916.*

2 *e-3*
RIVERFRONT PLAZA
This suburbanlike outdoor mall is quite popular, since it's in easy driving distance from the city and has plentiful parking. Its attractive, nicely laid-out buildings are home to such major draws as Microcenter and Jo-Ann Fabrics. *Elston Ave. and Logan Blvd., Bucktown.*

7 *e-5*
WATER TOWER PLACE
Shoppers spend more than $300 million a year at what is one of the city's most popular vertical malls. This marble-clad structure is home to branches of Marshall Field's and Lord & Taylor, as well as seven floors of specialty stores. Most are standard mall stores, but there are quite a few more exceptional shops, including Alfred Dunhill. The tony Ritz-Carlton hotel sits atop the entire complex. *835 N. Michigan Ave., Magnificent Mile, 312/440–3165.*

SHOPPING NEIGHBORHOODS

BUCKTOWN AND WICKER PARK
Once a hangout for gangs and artists, this northwest neighborhood is now home to trendy coffeehouses, nightclubs, restaurants, an eclectic array of clothing boutiques, art galleries, alternative music stores, and antiques shops. The most seductive shopping can be found along Milwaukee and Damen avenues from Division Avenue to Webster Street; here you'll find a mind-boggling array of merchandise, including home furnishings, decorative accessories, antiques, clothing, and art. Most stores don't open until at least 11 AM; some shops are closed on Monday and Tuesday.

CLYBOURN CORRIDOR
Formerly a derelict industrial area, the Clybourn Corridor bustles with chain superstores, strip shopping centers, outlet stores, and small boutiques. Most shops are on Clybourn Avenue between North Avenue (1600 N.) and Fullerton Avenue (2400 N.). You'll want to drive to explore these stores, since they're spread out over a wide area.

THE MAGNIFICENT MILE
This shopping area looks like magazine maven Martha Stewart laid a hand to it, with its high-gloss, tony-looking stores and lovely, ever-changing plant beds that skirt the sidewalks. Along this northernmost stretch of Michigan Avenue, all within a few blocks, you'll find the Crate & Barrel hometown flagship, NikeTown, Neiman Marcus, Nordstrom, and Water Tower Place, with Lord & Taylor and Marshall Field's anchoring a substantial portion of its square footage. Nearby you'll find Ultimo, Ralph Lauren, Paul Stuart, Giorgio Armani, Jil Sander, and Urban Outfitters.

specialty shops

ANTIQUES

antiques centers & flea markets

7 *c-8*
ANTIQUARIANS BUILDING
Right outside the mammoth Merchandise Mart is the heaviest concentration of antiques stores in River North, and this is the largest antique mall in the area. About 20 dealers ply their wares in this rambling space, where you can find mostly fine 18th- and 19th-century furnishings from Asia and Europe, with a smattering of 20th-century pieces. The true strength of the place is its robust selection of pieces with Oriental and Chinoiserie styling. *159 W. Kinzie St., River North, 312/527–0533.*

7 *c-8*
ANTIQUES CENTRE AT KINZIE SQUARE
With its series of meandering rooms, the center has a homey feeling created

by the domestic nature of the wares. While there is a good mix of furnishings ranging from the 18th to 20th century, the strong suits here are the cutlery, bowls, serving pieces, candlesticks, silverware, and dishes of every ilk—with an especially deep stash of silver. It's no wonder that this mall, home to about 20 dealers, was the first antiques source in the city to offer a wedding registry. *220 W. Kinzie St., River North, 312/464–1946.*

2 *f-4*
THE ANTIQUE MALL AT YELLO GALLERY
Designed to resemble a quaint country shop, this mall is at the back of a contemporary art gallery. Once you enter the cool art deco doors, everything's old or vintage. Here you'll find cocktail shakers, coffee urns, and gaming pieces. *1630 N. Milwaukee Ave., Bucktown, 773/235–9731.*

5 *c-3*
ARMITAGE ANTIQUE GALLERY
This unique mall showcases diverse collectibles and antiques. Toys, costume jewelry, porcelain, lighting, and more are strengths here, but be prepared to sift through booths so packed that you'll need a few moments to register exactly what there is to scoop up. *1529 W. Armitage Ave., Clybourn Corridor, 773/227–7727.*

2 *f-1*
BROADWAY ANTIQUE MARKET
This is Chicago's brightest star on the vintage circuit, and for good reason. This spacious mall features 75 dealers spread out over 20,000 square ft. The emphasis is on 20th-century collectibles and furnishings. Costume jewelry, Heywood Wakefield furniture, '50s dinette sets, Arts and Crafts pottery, Art Deco serving pieces, and kitchenware are wonderfully displayed for full effect. *6130 N. Broadway, Edgewater, 773/868–0285.*

4 *b-8*
CHICAGO ANTIQUE CENTRE
This antiques mall has 35 dealers hawking their various wares and collectibles. Housewares ranging from lamps to dishes are the stars, though several dealers have solid collections of mid-20th-century costume jewelry. *3045 N. Lincoln Ave., Lakeview, 773/929–0200.*

4 *b-8*
LINCOLN ANTIQUE MALL
This neighborhood mall is filled with dozens of dealers carrying fashionable treasures, mostly post-1920. *3141 N. Lincoln Ave., Lakeview, 773/244–1440.*

6 *e-4*
MAXWELL STREET MARKET
The infamous market's not even on Maxwell Street anymore, sigh. Scaled down considerably as it moved and as the neighborhood gentrified, this largely outdoors, year-round, Sundays-only flea market has a few antiques, some collectibles, but mostly junk. Go for the experience, if nothing else. *Clinton St. and Roosevelt Rd., University Village.*

auction houses

7 *c-6*
CHRISTIE'S
Paintings, jewelry, furniture, and art objects can be bid on at this River North auctioneer. *875 N. Michigan Ave., Magnificent Mile, 312/787–2765. No credit cards. Closed weekends.*

7 *c-7*
SOTHEBY'S MIDWEST
Similar to its New York City counterpart, this River North auction house hosts bidding four or five days a month. It's only open during auctions; call for a recording of upcoming events. *215 W. Ohio St., River North, 312/396–9599.*

8 *c-1*
SUSANIN'S AUCTIONEERS & APPRAISERS
You'll find good deals on furniture, paintings, and collectibles and spectacular deals on Oriental rugs, which range from really worn to barely used. This general-line auction house is also pioneering an unusual format by holding its live sales weekly yet offering most of the preview items for sale on the floor immediately. *138 Merchandise Mart, River North, 312/832–9800.*

6 *c-1*
WRIGHT
This gallery and auction house is aiming to become the consummate local resource for mid 20th-century furniture and decorative accessories. Thanks to its stock—which includes a wide range of American and European furnishings,

textiles, pottery, and glass by the masters of modern design—as well as monthly auctions and interior design counsel, it may accomplish this goal. *1140 W. Fulton St., West Loop, 312/563–0020.*

collectibles

7 *c-6*

FLY BY NITE GALLERY

This shop is filled with an exquisite oeuvre of decorative and functional art objects from 1890 to 1930. Every item is chosen with a curatorially discerning eye and is a prime example of its genre, with prime prices to match. But the shop is probably the best source in the city for European art, glass, ceramics, pottery, and metalwork vases from the mid-19th through early 20th century and is renowned for its stellar and rich collection of silver and fine antique jewelry. *714 N. Wells St., River North, 312/664–8136.*

3 *g-3*

GENE DOUGLAS
ART & ANTIQUES

Douglas is known as a dealer's dealer and opened a retail establishment only recently. His shop is a must-see for serious collectors of late-19th- to mid-20th-century pieces. Douglas concentrates on clean-line, classic furniture; decorative home accessories; and fine art; he also has a remarkable stash of glassware, silver serving and tabletop pieces, and pottery. The shop has perhaps the best collection of Modernist and mid-20th-century jewelry in town as well. *4621½ N. Lincoln Ave., Lincoln Square, 773/561–4414. Closed Mon.*

3 *h-8*

THE GOOD OLD DAYS

Hankering for the sound of yesteryear? This Lakeview store carries a wide selection of vintage radios along with bar and sports memorabilia. *2138 W. Belmont Ave., Lakeview, 773/472–8837.*

5 *c-1*

STEVE STARR STUDIOS

This quaint store pays homage to the film stars of the 1930s and 1940s with its huge array of vintage art deco frames filled with stunning black-and-white images of James Stewart, Judy Garland, Shirley Temple, and many more. Stop by and stay a while. *2779 N. Lincoln Ave., Lincoln Park, 773/525–6530.*

furniture

2 *f-4*

ABN

Named for the identical initials of the two sisters who own the shop, this quirky store has a playful, romantic feel. You'll find old fences, telephones, and letters, all presented in an appealing way that makes you want to buy. A smattering of new wares made by artists adds to the well-rounded mix. *1472 N. Milwaukee Ave., Wicker Park, 773/276–2525. Closed Mon.–Tues.*

4 *a-8*

ANTIQUE RESOURCES

This large, well-stocked store begins the stretch of Belmont Avenue known as Antique Sellers Row. It is rife with choice Georgian antiques at fair prices and is an excellent source for stately desks, dignified dining sets, and handsome bureaus in lustrous dark woods. But the true find here is a huge collection, numbering in the hundreds, of antique crystal and gilt chandeliers from France. *1741 W. Belmont Ave., Lakeview, 773/871–4242.*

2 *f-4*

BLEEKER ST.

While most of the antiques shops in Bucktown embrace an edgy aesthetic, at this place provincial styling prevails. The specialties are country furnishings for the home and garden from England, Ireland, and France, and decorative home accessories—once perfectly proper but eccentric and fanciful today—such as cigarette card sets or Brighton bamboo furniture. *1946 N. Leavitt St., Bucktown, 773/862–3185. Closed Mon.–Wed.*

7 *c-8*

CHRISTA'S LTD.
ART AND ANTIQUES

With chests, cabinets, tables, and bureaus piled in attractive stacks three or four high, the 3,500-square-ft shop gives new meaning to the phrase "packed to the gills." Besides furniture of every ilk, it has bronzes, lamps, clocks, porcelains, mirrors, tableware, fine silver, serving pieces, urns, crystal, fireplace equipment, garden ornaments, and more. The jam-packed, narrow aisles make for adventurous exploring. *217 W. Illinois St., River North, 312/222–2520.*

3 *h-8*

DANGER CITY

Near Roscoe Village, it's a good place to scout for fun and unusual remnants of the mid-20th century. There are furniture, lighting fixtures, and jewelry, but the barware and kitchen accoutrements from the 1940s through the '60s are noteworthy. *2129 W. Belmont Ave., Lakeview, 773/871-1420.*

4 *a-6*

DANIELS ANTIQUES

This cavernous shop has a huge stock of Victorian through 20th-century furnishings, especially larger pieces and complete sets. There is also an exceptional collection of chandeliers, lighting fixtures, and rugs. *3711 N. Ashland Ave., Lakeview, 773/868-9355.*

7 *f-7*

DECORO

It has long been known for its substantial collection of Japanese tansu, Chinese country furniture, and Asian textiles, sculptures, ceramics, and accessories, but Decoro has recently gone global and expanded its offerings. It now has antiques from more than two dozen countries, including magnificent contemporary Venetian silks and velvets for sale by the yard. *224 E. Ontario St., Streeterville, 312/943-4847.*

2 *f-5*

2000 W. Carroll St., West Loop, 312/850-9260.

3 *h-3*

GRIFFINS & GARGOYLES LTD.

Find a large stash of provincial pine furniture from all over Europe here at fabulous prices. All items have been stripped to perfection and restored, save for the ornately painted pieces. Sometimes dark-wood furnishings also turn up. *2140 W. Lawrence Ave., Ravenswood, 773/769-1255. Closed Tues.–Wed.*

7 *d-8*

GOLDEN TRIANGLE

This is a must for anyone enamored with the East-meets-West aesthetic. Golden Triangle's two roomy floors are an ordered yet abundant mix of exotic and beguiling antiques, including British colonial furniture from Burma and Chinese furniture. Choose from among the Japanese utilitarian storage tansu and

library cabinets, campaign chests and divans, and decorative accessories, with such items as Chinese wedding baskets and Burmese lunch boxes. *72 W. Hubbard St., River North, 312/755-1266.*

7 *c-8*

JAY ROBERT ANTIQUE WAREHOUSE

Years of buying trips to Europe have yielded the deep stock in the 60,000-square-ft showroom, which specializes in 18th- and 19th-century fine furnishings. There are oversize formal dining tables, sets of dining chairs, armoires, hutches, bureaus, sideboards, breakfronts, benches, trunks, and a great selection of hard-to-find beds. There is also a decent collection of architectural artifacts, such as fireplace mantels and iron gates. *149 W. Kinzie St., River North, 312/222-0167.*

7 *b-6*

MICHAEL FITZSIMMONS DECORATIVE ARTS

If you're looking for vintage merchandise to stock your old-fashioned bungalow or just want to add a touch of hand craftmanship to your modern high-rise apartment, you might want to take a look at this River North store. It stocks an impressive array of furniture and artifacts from the American Arts and Crafts movement. On display are works by Frank Lloyd Wright, Louis Sullivan, and Gustav Stickley, along with some quality reproductions. *311 W. Superior St., River North, 312/787-0496.*

2 *f-4*

MODERN TIMES

The name says it all, as this spacious shop celebrates 20th-century home furnishings, particularly those of the 1940s, '50s, and '60s. There are always storage cabinets, shelving units, desks, and dining tables and chairs on hand, as well as pottery, silver, and glass (especially vintage Higgins pieces). A few cases of jewelry are usually stocked with prime pieces of mid 20th-century silver and copper jewelry. A second-story loft has good pickings for vintage-clothing fans. *1538 N. Milwaukee Ave., Wicker Park, 773/772-8871.*

2 *f-4*

PAGODA RED

Though it looks spare, it is actually packed with a wide range of exceptionally well priced Asian pieces. There are traditional, clean-line pieces from northern China—such as carved-wood wedding chests, immortal tables, cinnabar lacquer coffers, and leather storage trunks—as well as Tibetan storage pieces from monasteries and handwoven carpets from Katmandu. Two highlights are the rare collection of vintage 20th-century Chinese advertising posters and the 19th-century Chinese garden pieces. *1714 N. Damen Ave., Bucktown, 773/235–1188. Closed Mon.*

2 *f-4*

PAVILION

This airy corner store has the kind of curious mix of merchandise that reflects the collecting insight of its owners, who hand-pick their merchandise in Europe and the Midwest. While the stock is ever-changing, many of the quirky pieces reflect opulent decay or have great visual appeal. Fixtures, mirrors, furniture, decorative pieces, industrial items, and art by anonymous makers are available. At times pieces by noted French and American designers show up here. *2055 N. Damen Ave., Bucktown, 773/645–0924. Closed Mon.–Tues.*

7 *c-6*

PRIMITIVE ART WORKS

The focus here is on authentic objects intended for use by their makers rather than export. Items fall into four general categories: sculptural artifacts such as passport masks and pre-Columbian pottery; textiles ranging from shawls to rugs; furniture in a wide range of precious or exotic woods; and ethnic beads and jewelry. There are also collections of rare and remarkable items found nowhere else in the city, such as Ottoman cut-glass lamps, Tantric lingams from India, and painted spirit spouses from the Ivory Coast. *706 N. Wells St., River North, 312/943–3770.*

4 *b-8*

RED EYE ANTIQUES

This large shop begs to be browsed—it's so overloaded with prime furnishings, accessories, artifacts, and textiles that there's plenty to catch any shopper's eye. Items tend to the odd and unusual and span a wide range of ages and prices. Occasionally there is an excellent stash of pottery and garden statuary. Expect to spend some time here to poke around. *3050 N. Lincoln Ave., Lakeview, 773/975–2020. Closed Mon.*

7 *c-8*

RITA BUCHEIT, LTD.

This elegant gallery carries the equally elegant furniture of the Biedermeier era. You'll find an ever-changing array of pieces from Germany and Vienna with the streamlined silhouette and honey-toned burnished woods that exemplify this style, including an exceptional cache of original pieces by Michael Thonet. *449 N. Wells St., River North, 312/527–4080.*

quilts

3 *h-6*

TURTLE CREEK ANTIQUES

After 25 years in Lincoln Park, this source for antique quilts relocated to Lakeview. Besides quilts, it has tabletop pieces, Victorian furniture, and estate jewelry. Perfection is paramount here: just about every piece is in mint condition. The shop also buys and rents the quilts, and appraisal and design consultations are available. *3817 N. Lincoln Ave., Lakeview, 773/327–2630. Closed Mon.*

ART SUPPLIES

4 *c-7*

AIKO'S ART MATERIALS

Creative types love this wonderful Wrigleyville shop with its hundreds of stenciled, marbled, textured, and tie-dyed papers, mostly from Japan. *3347 N. Clark St., Lakeview, 773/404–5600. Closed Sun.–Mon.*

6 *f-3*

BRUDNO ART SUPPLY

This is a primary source of materials and supplies for students who attend the nearby School of the Art Institute of Chicago. But the shop, smack in the midst of architects' offices, caters to the architecture trade as well. The Streeterville store is in the heart of an advertising agency district and has everything an art director could desire. *700 S. Wabash Ave., South Loop, 312/787–0030. Closed Sun.*

7 *e-6*

601 N. State St., Streeterville, 312/751–7980. Closed Sun.

6 *d-4*

CREATIVE REUSE WAREHOUSE

Near the Dan Ryan Expressway, this emporium stocks paint, foam core, paper, and other hard-to-find art essentials. You can get real bargains like a $3 bag full of stuff that could easily set you back $30 elsewhere. *721 W. O'Brien St., West Loop, 312/421–3640. No credit cards.*

6 *g-2*

FLAX ART & FRAME

Besides having a range of art materials, portfolio and presentation binders, and picture framing services and supplies, this is one of the premier spots in the city to buy fine writing implements and accessories. *220 S. Wabash Ave., Loop, 312/431–9588.*

7 *c-6*

PEARL ART & CRAFT SUPPLIES

You must stop by this incredible River North store if you have any artistic instinct. It's easy to believe its claim that it's one of the world's largest arts-and-crafts discount centers. There are drafting, silk-screen, etching, carving, and batik supplies and much more. *225 W. Chicago Ave., River North, 312/915–0200.*

2 *d-3*

RICH'S ART SUPPLY & FRAMING SHOP

It stocks just about everything an artist needs, including silk-screen supplies. Custom-made picture frames are available, as is some handmade paper. *3838 N. Cicero Ave., Portage Park, 773/545–0271. Closed Sun.*

5 *c-5*

THE ART STORE

It's smack in the center of a new shopping district that caters to families, and it has everything families will want for school and more. *1574 N. Kingsbury Ave., West Town, 312/573–0110.*

2 *e-8*

TROST HOBBY SHOP

Brush right up to this Chicago Lawn store, with artists' materials and crafts supplies: brushes, paints, and canvases. *3111 W. 63rd St., Marquette Park, 773/925–1000.*

8 *e-4*

UTRECHT SUPPLY CENTER

The company makes its own stock of paint, art, and drafting supplies, all high quality and reasonably priced. Other manufacturers' supplies are also discounted at this downtown store. *332 S. Michigan Ave., South Loop, 312/922–7565.*

BEADS

8 *e-2*

INTERNATIONAL BEAD CO.

In business since 1918, it sells beads—including those made from bone, wood, clay—and Indian handmade glass. It also stocks exotic African and Asian beads. *111 N. Wabash Ave., 7th floor, Loop, 312/332–0061. Closed Sun.*

5 *d-3*

MAYET BEAD DESIGN

Similar to a candy store, this shop stocks a tempting array of thousands of glass, ethnic, and vintage beads in dishes and containers. You also can sign up for beading classes. *826 W. Armitage Ave., Lincoln Park, 773/868–0580.*

7 *c-6*

PRIMITIVE ART WORKS

It has ethnic beads and jewelry, as well as sculptural artifacts, textiles, and furniture. *706 N. Wells St., River North, 312/943–3770.*

BEAUTY

fragrances & skin products

7 *e-5*

AVEDA

This chain caters to the natural-products crowd with its line of yummy-smelling hair and skin products, makeup, bath preparations, and home fragrance, all made with natural ingredients. *John Hancock Center, 875 N. Michigan Ave., Magnificent Mile, 312/664–0417.*

7 *e-6*

THE BODY SHOP

Environmentally sensitive products that cleanse, polish, and protect skin and hair are available at this successful worldwide chain. The manufacturer uses biodegradable or recyclable packaging and doesn't test products on animals. *Chicago Place, 700 N. Michigan Ave., Magnificent Mile, 312/482–8301.*

8 *d-3*
1 N. State St., Loop, 312/553–4503.

5 *d-1*
623 W. Diversey Ave., Lakeview, 773/935–9645.

7 *e-4*
BRAVCO DISCOUNT STORE
This beauty store has a huge array of expensive shampoos, conditioners, and gels, including the Paul Mitchell and Nexus brands. It's all discounted, so your stressed tresses look their best without the price. *43 E. Oak St., Magnificent Mile, 312/943–4305. No credit cards.*

5 *d-1*
COSMETIC CENTER
Everything from generic cotton swabs to designer makeup, all discounted, is sold by this chain. The main attraction is designer cosmetics, including Clinique, Estée Lauder, Chanel, and Lancôme. *2817 N. Broadway, Lakeview, 773/935–2600.*

7 *e-5*
CRABTREE & EVELYN
This is the place to find England's scrumptious toiletries and beautifully presented and packaged edible items, such as imported jams, teas, oils, cookies, honey, and other edible items. *Water Tower Place, 835 N. Michigan Ave., Magnificent Mile, 312/787–0188.*

7 *c-8*
222 Merchandise Mart Plaza, River North, 312/644–5551. Closed Sun.

7 *e-7*
634 N. Michigan Ave., Magnificent Mile, 312/944–4707.

5 *d-3*
ENDO-EXO APOTHECARY
Get down and funky and shop for lotion at the same time. At this store, where a DJ sometimes spins for shoppers and vintage pharmacy cabinets mingle with mod furnishings, you can sample from a well-chosen array of hard-to-find beauty lines like Peter Thomas Roth and Bliss. *2034 N. Halsted St., Lincoln Park, 773/525–0500.*

7 *e-4*
MAC
Spokespeople like cross-dresser RuPaul and rapper L'il Kim help tout this cosmetics line—a testament to its bold, fun dynamic. The lipstick names make you want to stock up just for the heck of it, from Viva Glam and Diva to Rizzo and Film Noir. *40 E. Oak St., Magnificent Mile, 312/951–7310.*

5 *f-7*
MARLENA'S FACTORY OUTLET STORE
Named for local makeup diva Marilyn Miglin's daughter, it sells overruns of Marilyn Miglin cosmetics and a changing selection of other fine cosmetic and skincare lines, as well as roughly 80 fragrances. *127 W. Huron St., River North, 312/943–2626. Closed Sun.*

5 *d-5*
ULTA 3
A haven for beauty junkies, this chain got its start in the Chicago suburbs. These self-serve superstores carry a vast array of hair products (including salon brands), cosmetics, and fragrances at competitive prices. In-store salons do cuts and color, too. *1000 W. North Ave., Clybourn Corridor, 312/664–0230.*

4 *c-8*
3015 N. Clark St., Lakeview, 773/348–7315.

hair & skin care

7 *e-4*
CHANNING'S
This "secret retreat in the middle of Oak Street" is in a revamped Victorian house on Chicago's ritziest shopping stretch. It's the place to go for customized facial treatments, which include steaming the skin with the help of essential oils, plus manicures, pedicures, massages, and more. *54 E. Oak St., Magnificent Mile, 312/280–1994. Closed Sun.–Mon.*

7 *e-4*
CHARLES IFERGAN SALON
Ifergan and crew are well known among the tony downtown crowd, who flock to this swanky full-service hair salon to tame their tresses. Makeup consultations are also available. *106 E. Oak St., Magnificent Mile, 312/642–4484. Closed Sun.–Mon.*

7 *f-6*

CHARLES OF THE BARCLAY

Tucked away on the lower level of the Summerfield Suites Hotel, this old-fashioned barbershop offers men's haircuts, shoe shines, pedicures, massages, and manicures. *166 E. Superior St., Streeterville, 312/337–3317. Closed Sun.–Mon.*

7 *e-5*

ELIZABETH ARDEN RED DOOR SALON & SPA

One knock on salon's signature red door and you will enter the world of head-to-toe pampering. A recent renovation has gussied up the place; it's doing a good job of moving away from its blue-hair image. Makeup applications and expert facials are among the salon's specialties. *919 N. Michigan Ave., Magnificent Mile, 312/988–9191.*

7 *e-5*

GEORGETTE KLINGER

Men and women alike get wonderfully soothing hour-long facials as well as manicures, pedicures, massage, and waxing at this salon. Skin-care regimens are available. *Water Tower Place, 835 N. Michigan Ave., Magnificent Mile, 312/787–4300.*

7 *e-4*

JACQUES DESSANGE

Come for the highlights, and stay for a French lesson. This international salon is famous for producing sun-kissed blonds with its unique no-cap, no-foil, hand-painted highlights. The result is a more natural look. *45 E. Oak St., Magnificent Mile, 312/951–6270. Closed Sun.–Mon.*

7 *e-5*

JANET SARTIN
SKIN CARE INSTITUTE

New to Chicago, Janet Sartin developed a huge following in New York City for her serious approach to skincare. Choose from a variety of facials, massages, manicures, pedicures, and other skin treatments. Sartin also makes her own line of skincare products. *46 E. Pearson St., Streeterville, 312/397–1550.*

7 *f-5*

KIVA

There are so many things to try at Kiva, it's hard to decide where to start. How do you choose among the Native American cocoon body wraps, ayurvedic massages, the plethora of facials? All have a nurturing-healing bent and borrow from the traditions of cultures around the globe. The space has a Zen-like calm about it—you feel relaxed just being here. A store boutique carries hard-to-find makeup lines. *196 E. Pearson St., Streeterville, 312/840–8120.*

7 *b-5*

MARIANNE
STROKIRK SALON

Oprah's stylist, Andre Walker, cuts at this top salon when he's not tied up with the media maven. Marianne, whose father cut hair for the Swedish royal family, has her own share of big-shot clientele, from local anchor people to Hillary Rodham Clinton. The rest of the staff is held in pretty high regard, too, as an attempt to make an appointment here can convey. *361 W. Chestnut St., River North, 312/944–4428. Closed Sun.–Mon.*

7 *e-4*

41 E. Oak St., Magnificent Mile, 312/640–0101. Closed Sun.–Mon.

7 *e-4*

MARILYN MIGLIN

This salon is completely devoted to making you look your best. It provides lessons in makeup application and sells the eponymous owner's complete line of wonderful (and pricey) makeup and face and body skin-care products and applicators. *112 E. Oak St., Magnificent Mile, 312/943–1120.*

7 *e-4*

SALON BUZZ

There's always a buzz at this salon, where the hub of activity increases late in the day, when the postwork crowd comes in for experts cuts and color, as well as facials, manicures, pedicures, and waxing. *1 E. Delaware Pl., Gold Coast, 312/943–5454.*

7 *e-5*

TRUEFITT & HILL

Precise haircuts, hot lather shaves, herbal steam facials, manicures, pedicures, and shoe shines are among services offered by this shop. The flagship has served the British Royal Family since 1805; the staff here will treat you like royalty, too. *900 N. Michigan Ave., Magnificent Mile, 312/337–2525.*

7 e-5

VIDAL SASSOON SALON
The old motto "If you don't look good, we don't look good" still holds true. Makeup and hair-care products are available, as are discount cuts by students under the supervision of established stylists. *Water Tower Place, 835 N. Michigan Ave., Magnificent Mile, 312/751–2216.*

BICYCLES

5 e-2

CYCLE SMITHY
Ride on over to this Lakeview shop to check out Trek, Cannondale, Zipp, and other well-priced used bikes. It will even repair your bike for you. *2468½ N. Clark St., Lincoln Park, 773/281–0444.*

4 e-8

JOHNNY SPROCKET'S
Find the most cutting-edge equipment for every aspect of bicycling, from the cycles themselves to the shoes, togs, and accessories to outfit your bike. There are unusually good selections of road and hybrid bikes and extras such as panniers. The sales staff is exceptionally helpful, and there is a respected repair department. *3001 N. Broadway, Lakeview, 773/244–1079.*

2 f-2

1052 W. Bryn Mawr Ave., Edgewater, 773/293–1695.

8 c-5

KOZY'S BICYCLE SHOP
Why not get the whole family in the act? There are bikes for everyone here at this well-stocked downtown store. Lifetime-parts guarantees, an excellent service department, and free parking are available. *601 S. LaSalle St., South Loop, 312/360–0020.*

4 d-6

3713 N. Halsted St., Lakeview, 773/281–2263.

BUCKTOWN AND WICKER PARK

Creative types cluster in hip, somewhat grungy Bucktown and Wicker Park, centered on Milwaukee, Damen, and North avenues. These neighborhoods harbor an unusual bazaar of shops—plus the best people-watching in the city:

Around the Coyote Gallery (Fine Art Galleries)
Bucktown gallery exhibiting work of 30 city artists and designers.

Casa Loca (Home Furnishings, Furniture & Accessories)
Filled with rustic furniture from Mexico and south-of-the-border folk art, this Bucktown and Wicker Park shop also stocks gorgeous Guatemalan and Mexican textiles.

Cielo Vivo (Home Furnishings, Furniture & Accessories)
Step into another world at this shop, which is so densely layered with exotic ethnic items you'll be transported to a Middle Eastern market.

Eclectic Junction for Art (Gifts and Souvenirs)
Bucktown shop selling functional yet whimsical art.

**Jean Alan Upholstered Furniture and Furnishings
(Home Furnishings, Furniture & Accessories)**
Former set decorator Alan has a penchant for the dramatic. Look for quirky lamps with feather-covered shades or outrageously opulent Victorian sofas.

Modern Times (Antiques, Furniture)
Wicker Park store with furniture from the '40s, '50s, and '60s.

Occult Bookstore (Bookstores, Specialty)
Consult with the on-premises astrologer, and then peruse the New Age and occult books and paraphernalia at this Wicker Park bookstore.

Robin Richman (Clothing for Women/General, Designer)
Knitwear, antiques, and hand-carved wood furniture in an eclectic Bucktown store.

Una Mae's Freak Boutique (Clothing for Women/General, Vintage)
Wicker Park vintage clothing boutique with the funkiest dressing rooms in the city.

8 *e-8*

RECYCLE BIKE SHOP
This store truly lives up to its name. It sells new and used bikes, all reasonably priced. Used bikes are reconditioned in-house. *1465 S. Michigan Ave., South Loop, 312/937–1080.*

2 *d-2*

SPORTIFF IMPORTER LTD.
This large Jefferson Park shop offers a choice of more than 50 imported brands, including Trek, Schwinn, and Raleigh. *5225 W. Lawrence Ave., Jefferson Park, 773/685–0240.*

7 *c-2*

VILLAGE CYCLE CENTER
This shop has a huge selection of mountain bikes that are perfect for riding along the lakefront or simply getting across town. *1337 N. Wells St., Old Town, 773/751–2448.*

BOOKS

antiquarian

7 *d-4*

**CHICAGO
RARE BOOK CENTER**
About 25 dealers rent shelf space in this addition to Chicago's antiquarian book scene, representing a wide range of interests. Strengths include children's books, literature, and Chicago history. *56 W. Maple St., Near North, 312/988–7246.*

7 *e-5*

HARRY L. STERN, LTD.
Antiquarian books, maps, and prints are among the treasures to be found at this downtown store. *919 N. Michigan Ave., Magnificent Mile, 312/337–1401. By appointment only.*

2 *f-7*

JOHN RYBSKI
You'll want to check out the out-of-print American history books, especially those about Chicago. *2319 W. 47th Pl., Back of the Yards, 773/847–5082. By appointment only.*

2 *h-7*

**O'GARA AND WILSON,
BOOKSELLERS LTD.**
Near the University of Chicago, the city's oldest bookstore has one of the best selections of used books, especially fiction, but you'll also find some science, military, American history, psychology, religion, Midwest, film, and kids' lit. New acquisitions arrive every weekend. *1311 E. 57th St., Hyde Park, 773/363–0993.*

2 *h-7*

POWELL'S BOOKSTORE
Powell's is for the family intellectual: it carries used books and remainders on such topics as Marxism, the occult, and philosophy. *1501 E. 57th St., Hyde Park, 773/955–7780.*

8 *e-6*

828 S. Wabash Ave., South Loop, 312/341–0748.

5 *c-1*

2850 N. Lincoln Ave., Lakeview, 773/248–1444.

8 *e-4*

RAIN DOG BOOKS
A welcome respite from the frenzy of Michigan Avenue, this small shop has a good selection of fine art, architecture, and travel titles to choose from. *404 S. Michigan Ave., Loop, 312/922–1200.*

4 *d-7*

SELECTED WORKS
There are books galore at this huge shop. Used books cover topics in the humanities, including literature, philosophy, and music. The used sheet music will bring the singer within you out of the closet. *3510 N. Broadway, Wrigleyville, 773/975–0002.*

general

8 *b-4*

BARBARA'S BOOKSTORE
A wonderful source for small- and alternative-press books, this chain excels in literature, politics, African and African-American studies, science fiction, women's studies, poetry, and the performing arts. It also has a reputable kids' selection. You'll find stores in the suburbs as well as downtown. *Sears Tower, 233 S. Wacker Dr., Loop, 312/466–0223. Closed weekends.*

7 *c-2*

1350 N. Wells St., Old Town, 312/642–5044.

7 h-7

700 E. Grand Ave., Navy Pier, 312/222–0890.

8 a-3

2 N. Riverside, Loop, 312/258–8007. Closed weekends.

7 g-6

Northwestern Memorial Hospital, 201 E. Huron St., Streeterville, 312/926–2665.

5 d-1

BARNES & NOBLE

The motto, "Books As Far As the Mind Can Reach," about says it all. This chain store stocks more than 150,000 titles and has a huge children's department. Both locations have Starbucks coffee bars inside. 659 W. Diversey Ave., Lakeview, 773/871–9004.

5 b-3

1441 W. Webster Ave., Clybourn Corridor, 773/871–3610.

8 e-2

B. DALTON BOOKSELLERS

This very large, well-known, and well-stocked nationwide chain stocks some 15,000 paperbacks. One floor is for bargains. You'll also find current fiction titles as well authors to sign them. 129 N. Wabash Ave., Loop, 312/236–7615.

7 c-8

222 Merchandise Mart Plaza, River North, 312/329–1881. Closed Sun.

7 e-5

BORDERS BOOKS & MUSIC

Aiming to outdo its competitors, this chain has more than 200,000 titles plus author readings and a café. There are also a good selection of CDs and tapes and a card and stationery section. 830 N. Michigan Ave., Magnificent Mile, 312/573–0564.

5 d-1

2817 N. Clark St., Lakeview, 773/935–3909.

8 b-2

BRENT BOOKS AND CARDS

The specialty of this jam-packed bookstore is business, but you'll find all the bases covered. It's a homey place despite a location in the heart of the Loop. 309 W. Washington Blvd., Loop, 312/364–0126. Closed Sun.

8 e-3

CROWN BOOKS

This chain sells discounted tomes by the thousands. You can also find significant savings on books on tape. 105 S. Wabash Ave., Loop, 312/782-7667.

5 c-4

1714 N. Sheffield Ave., Clybourn Corridor, 312/787–4370.

5 e-2

LINCOLN PARK BOOK SHOP

This wonderful neighborhood bookstore, easy to find on busy Clark Street, is homey and cozy, with chairs in the back where you can plop down and read. Fiction and nonfiction topics like history and travel are strengths, but you'll find a full range of subjects. 2423 N. Clark St., Lincoln Park, 773/477–7087.

8 d-2

MARSHALL FIELD'S

After you sample some Frangos, check out America's premier department-store bookstore. There are good cookbook and children's book sections. 111 N. State St., Loop, 312/781–1000.

7 d-5

NEWBERRY LIBRARY'S A.C. MCCLURG BOOKSTORE

Tucked inside a library nook, this little shop sells a great selection of postcards, stationery, maps, and gift items. There's also a considerable selection of books on calligraphy, music, cartography, Native American studies, and genealogy. 60 W. Walton St., Gold Coast, 312/255–3520. Closed Sun.–Mon.

7 e-5

RIZZOLI INTERNATIONAL BOOKSTORE & GALLERY

Rizzoli is an exquisite downtown backdrop for fine-art books and a graphics gallery. Here you'll discover magazines and newspapers, as well as classical and international CDs and tapes. Water Tower Place, 835 N. Michigan Ave., Magnificent Mile, 312/642–3500.

6 f-3

SANDMEYER'S BOOKSTORE INCORPORATED

Family-owned and operated since 1982, Sandmeyer's is a nice change of pace from the bookselling giants. There's an intriguing mix of books here, and the travel and children's departments are

stars. *714 S. Dearborn St., Printer's Row,
312/922–2104.*

2 *h-7*

**SEMINARY COOPERATIVE
BOOKSTORE, INC.**
Established by students, this store has
18,000 co-op owners. It's easy to get
lost in the maze of shelves crammed
with some 50,000 often-arcane titles in
theology, political science, social sciences, humanities, philosophy, and, in
fact, just about any academic area. The
South University store's emphasis is on
academics and often original editions in
foreign languages. The East 57th location, a general bookstore, has a large
selection of literature, children's books,
and cookbooks. *5757 S. University Ave.,
Hyde Park, 773/752–4381.*

2 *g-7*

*1301 E. 57th St., Hyde Park, 773/684–
1300.*

4 *c-7*

THE BOOKWORKS
It has more than 40,000 titles, with an
emphasis on sports (for Cubs fans
strolling by) and contemporary fiction.
There's a neat vintage-vinyl-record area,
too. *3444 N. Clark St., Wrigleyville, 773/
871–5318.*

2 *g-7*

**UNIVERSITY OF CHICAGO
BOOKSTORE**
It has a majestic selection: general
books on the first floor, and texts on the
second, including sociology, medicine,
philosophy, poetry, and reference. *970 E.
58th St., Hyde Park, 773/702–8729. Closed
Sun.*

8 *d-3*

WALDENBOOKS
This large national chain focuses on
practical how-tos and consumer-ori-
ented titles. *127 W. Madison St., Loop,
312/236–8446. Closed weekends.*

specialty

7 *b-6*

**ABRAHAM LINCOLN
BOOK SHOP**
This used-books store attracts Civil War
buffs nationwide. The store emphasizes
Lincolniana, historical documents, and
Civil War books. *357 W. Chicago Ave.,
River North, 312/944–3085. Closed Sun.*

8 *d-4*

AFROCENTRIC BOOKSTORE
This bookshop carries an array of books,
ranging from novels to religious titles,
all with an African-American slant. The
store regularly hosts prominent authors
for signings. *Chicago Music Mart at
DePaul Centre, 333 S. State St., Loop, 312/
939–1956. Closed Sun.*

2 *e-1*

**CHICAGO HEBREW
BOOKSTORE**
You'll want to dig through this treasure
trove of Jewish books, hardcover and
paperback, and gifts. *2942 W. Devon
Ave., West Rogers Park, 773/973–6636.
Closed Sat.*

7 *d-5*

EUROPA BOOKS
The place to come for foreign language
books, newspapers, and magazines, this
downtown bookstore stocks French,
Spanish, German, and Italian titles and
is famous for its selection of Latin
American literature. *832 N. State St.,
Gold Coast, 312/335–9677.*

4 *b-6*

**HIT THE ROAD
TRAVEL STORE**
It carries a good selection of travel
books, both of the practical, theoretical,
and coffee-table varieties (covering
North America only), with a heavy
emphasis on driving and road-trip information. *3758 N. Southport Ave., West
Lakeview, 773/388–8338. Closed Mon.*

2 *f-4*

OCCULT BOOKSTORE
In addition to New Age books, you'll
find all sorts of weird paraphernalia. An
astrologer is available by appointment.
*1561 N. Milwaukee Ave., Wicker Park, 773/
292–0995.*

8 *e-5*

**PRAIRIE AVENUE
BOOKSHOP**
It draws architecture buffs worldwide for
its nearly 7,000 new, rare, and out-of-
print titles on architecture, interior
design, and urban planning. Spread
your books on massive conference
tables to browse. *418 S. Wabash Ave.,
Loop, 312/922–8311. Closed Sun.*

5 *f-7*
PRINTWORKS, LIMITED
The artistic process of printmaking and drawing are the focus here, but there's a decent selection of other art books as well. A good representation of local artists like Frances Whitehead and Hollis Sigler is also on hand. *311 W. Superior St., River North, 312/664–9407. Closed Sun.–Mon.*

2 *f-4*
QUIMBY'S BOOKSTORE
Looking for something to read that's bizarre, surreal, or just downright weird? Head to this cool store, where the quirkier the book it is, the more likely they'll carry it. There's also a good selection of comics and magazines, including a particularly thorough range of tattoo titles. Readings and events match the inventory. *1854 W. North Ave., Wicker Park, 773/342–0910.*

7 *e-8*
RAND MCNALLY—THE MAP AND TRAVEL STORE
World-renowned for its travel aids, Rand McNally supplies guidebooks galore as well as thousands of maps, loads of travel literature, and luggage, gifts, and accessories in two locations in the heart of downtown and at four suburban stores (Oakbrook, Northbrook, the Woodfield Mall in Schaumburg, and the Old Orchard Mall in Skokie). *444 N. Michigan Ave., Magnificent Mile, 312/321–1751.*

8 *b-4*
150 S. Wacker Dr., Loop, 312/332–2009. Closed weekends.

8 *e-4*
SAVVY TRAVELLER
This bookshop stocks a majestic selection of travel books, maps, luggage, and videos, along with gadgets that can improve your life while you're on the road. *310 S. Michigan Ave., Loop, 312/913–9800.*

5 *d-5*
TRANSITIONS BOOKPLACE
One of the country's top New Age/self-improvement bookstores, it stocks books on subjects like alternative healing, religion, mythology and folklore, and recovery and addiction. There's a lively program of author appearances and self-improvement workshops, and a wonderful café; and the store is right

next door to Whole Foods, so you can stock up on organic and natural foods while your motivation is still high. *1000 W. North Ave., Clybourn Corridor, 312/951–7323.*

2 *f-4*
UKRAINIAN BOOKSTORE
Ukrainian books, magazines, newspapers, and music are available along with transfer embroideries and materials. *2315 W. Chicago Ave., Ukrainian Village, 773/276–6373. No credit cards. Closed Sun.*

4 *d-7*
UNABRIDGED BOOKSTORE
Chicago's top gay bookstore is small, but you'll find a full range of general titles, including some good kids' books. A plus: the knowledgeable staff is good at helping you find what you want. *3251 N. Broadway, Lakeview, 773/883–9119.*

4 *b-1*
WOMEN & CHILDREN FIRST
This feminist shop stocks fiction and nonfiction, periodicals, journals, small press publications, and children's books. *5233 N. Clark St., Andersonville, 773/769–9299.*

BUTTONS

7 *e-4*
TENDER BUTTONS
An institution in New York, where it was founded, the Chicago branch of this button haven carries thousands of new, vintage, and antique button designs ranging from classic to whimsical. Prices run the gamut. *946 Rush St., Gold Coast, 312/337–7033. Closed Sun.*

CAMERAS

8 *e-4*
CENTRAL CAMERA
This century-old store is stocked to the rafters with cameras and darkroom equipment at competitive prices. *230 S. Wabash Ave., Loop, 312/427–5580. Closed Sun.*

6 *c-2*
HELIX CAMERA & VIDEO
Professional and amateurs alike will delight in the array of camera and dark-

room paraphernalia at these camera shops. The stores, which specialize in underwater photography, also offer an excellent selection of used equipment. *310 S. Racine Ave., West Loop, 312/421–6000.*

8 *d-3*

70 W. Madison St., Loop, 312/444–9373.

8 *e-1*

233 N. Michigan Ave., Loop, 312/565–5901. Closed Sun.

4 *c-1*

JOHN'S ELECTRONICS

Although this shop specializes in stereo and electronics, it also sells cameras. The used cameras are good buys. *5322 N. Broadway, Uptown, 773/878–3716. Closed Sun.*

4 *d-7*

TRIANGLE CAMERA

It sells an excellent assortment of new camera equipment and related accessories, all competitively priced. The used-camera department is equally excellent. *3445 N. Broadway, Lakeview, 773/472–1015.*

7 *e-6*

WOLF CAMERA & VIDEO

It has a variety of popular film and cameras and does high-quality one-hour film processing. *750 N. Rush St., Gold Coast, 312/943–5531.*

CAKE DECORATING EQUIPMENT & SUPPLIES

2 *c-3*

KITCHEN KAPERS

Thirty-five years in business, this shop sells cake and candy decorating supplies and wedding and shower favors. *3821 N. Harlem Ave., Elmwood Park, 773/283–3767. Closed Sun.–Mon.*

CANDLES

6 *d-2*

ATHENIAN CANDLE CO.

After you grab a gyro for dinner, saunter on over to this very kitschy Greek candle and icon shop. It has an interesting array of statues, herbs, incense, books, and, oh yes, candles. *300 S. Halsted St., Greektown, 773/721–3442.*

7 *e-5*

ILLUMINATIONS

This chain store carries a wealth of candles and accessories. Unique items include chandeliers and sconces for candles, and a large assortment of aromatherapy scents. *Water Tower Place, 835 N. Michigan Ave., Magnificent Mile, 312/867–0445.*

4 *b-8*

WAXMAN CANDLES

There's a hippie feel to this shop, where all the candles are made on the premises and come in countless shapes, colors, and scents. There's an incredible selection of holders for votives and pillars, and incense, too. *3044 N. Lincoln Ave., Lakeview, 773/929–3000.*

2 *f-4*

WAXY BUILDUP

Handmade candles and a serious sense of cool set it apart from the ordinary candle store. Candles come in funky flavors like "downpour," "beach encounter," and "shocking pink grapefruit." For Valentine's Day, you can buy a package of 270 votives and holders to create a truly smoldering experience. *1942 N. Hoyne Ave., Wicker Park, 773/292–9299.*

CLOTHING FOR CHILDREN

5 *d-3*

ACTIVE KIDS

Just a stone's throw from the adult-size Active Endeavors, this shop's strength is its sizable supply of Patagonia outerwear for children. *1967 N. Fremont St., Lincoln Park, 773/281–2002.*

5 *d-3*

ALL OUR CHILDREN

You'll find clothes, infant to size 10, including a large selection of Flapdoodles, West & Willy, Petite Bateau, and Sweet Potatoes, at this adorable boutique. *2217 N. Halsted St., Lincoln Park, 773/327–1868.*

7 *e-5*

BABYGAP

Here you'll find tot-wear, Gap-style: trendy, cute, and comfy. Prices are reasonable, but the best bargains are on the sale racks, which are well worth sifting through. *Water Tower Place, 835 N. Michigan Ave., Magnificent Mile, 312/486–5530.*

7 *e-6*
679 N. Michigan Ave., Magnificent Mile, 312/335–1892.

5 *d-3*
2108 N. Halsted St., Lincoln Park, 773/549–2065.

4 *b-8*
3155 N. Lincoln Ave., Lakeview, 773/883–9050.

5 *b-3*
CRADLES OF DISTINCTION
It has added more high-end clothing to its mix of furniture and toys for babies and children. Baby Dior, Cakewalk, and Petit Bateau are a few of the lines carried. *1445 W. Webster Ave., Clybourn Corridor, 773/472–1001.*

7 *e-5*
GAP KIDS
It has clothing for the rough-and-tumble junior set. It's all essentially miniature versions of the adult line, again reasonably priced. *Water Tower Place, 835 N. Michigan Ave., Magnificent Mile, 312/944–3053.*

7 *e-6*
679 N. Michigan Ave., Magnificent Mile, 312/335–1892.

5 *d-3*
2123 N. Halsted St., Lincoln Park, 773/528–6884.

4 *b-8*
3155 N. Lincoln Ave., Lakeview, 773/883–9050.

7 *e-5*
GYMBOREE
Plop your little one down in the play area while you shop for comfortable, well-coordinating kids' clothes in sizes newborn through seven. This chain has locations throughout the suburbs as well. *Water Tower Place, 835 N. Michigan Ave., Magnificent Mile, 312/649–9074.*

8 *d-3*
KIDS 'R' US
This Toys 'R' Us relative is for the diaper and preschool crowd. Parents love the discounted garb in more than 250 brands. *10 S. State St., Loop, 312/857–0727.*

7 *e-4*
MADISON & FRIENDS
David and Wendi Shelist opened this shop filled with great kids' clothes when they couldn't find hip duds for their newborn, Madison. The orginal Oak Street location is now dedicated solely to baby clothes. The store just across the road on Rush Street carries sizes 2T to 16. *11 E. Oak St., Gold Coast, 312/642–6403.*

7 *e-4*
1003 N. Rush St., Gold Coast, 312/642–8811.

7 *e-5*
OILILY
If the cute magazine ads don't get you one day, the undeniably sweet but pricey children's clothing will. *900 N. Michigan Ave., Magnificent Mile, 312/642–1166.*

7 *e-5*
PENNIES FROM HEAVEN
The precious clothes that grandparents love to ogle their grandchildren in can be found here. Prices reflect the very upscale neighborhood. *838 N. Rush St., Gold Coast, 312/266–2700.*

5 *c-2*
RUBENS & MARBLE
This is a DePaul University–area factory outlet for no-frills diapers, undies, and waterproof pants for kids from birth to 3 years. *2340 N. Racine Ave., Lakeview, 773/348–6200. No credit cards. Closed weekends.*

5 *c-3*
SECOND CHILD
This boutique bills itself as "an upscale children's resale boutique," but that's understating it. It sells a wondrous array of children's fashions, some of it barely worn, at a fraction of original prices. Maternity fashions are also available. *954 W. Armitage Ave., Lincoln Park, 773/883–0880.*

7 *e-6*
TALBOTS KIDS
Next to the mother shop, Talbots, it stocks tiny, preppy clothes with adult-size prices. *Chicago Place, 700 N. Michigan Ave., Magnificent Mile, 312/943–0255.*

7 *e-5*

TARTINE ET CHOCOLAT

Part of a chain of high-end children's boutiques, this place has all the fabulous stuff: cashmere bodysuits, hand-knit coats, plush accessories, in sizes for newborns to 12-year-olds. It also carries blankets, sheets, and cribs. *900 N. Michigan Ave., Magnificent Mile, 312/649–9401.*

7 *e-5*

WARNER BROS. STUDIO STORE

Who can resist the cartoon appeal of this downtown store? As gimmicky as it looks, it actually surprises with cute, reasonably priced, and durable children's clothes. Of course, it stocks a great assortment of stuffed animals à la the cartoons and funky kitchen items. Adult collectors will like the animation gallery. *Water Tower Place, 845 N. Michigan Ave., Magnificent Mile, 312/664–9440.*

5 *b-1*

WEAR ME OUT

Mom shop-workers and their kids hang out at this friendly, small boutique with particularly charming clothes for babies and children. The inventory includes pieces by Baby LuLu, Cozy Toes, and Geo Rags in sizes infant through 7. *2944 N. Lincoln Ave., Lakeview, 773/868–6781. Closed Sun.*

children's shoes

4 *b-1*

ALAMO SHOES

This family shoe store's strength is children's shoes. Salespeople take time to measure children's feet properly and even treat buyers to balloons. Many Chicago children get their first shoes here. *5321 N. Clark St., Andersonville, 773/784–8936.*

5 *d-3*

PIGGY TOES

Mother and daughter Mary Fink and Jennifer Thomas opened this cute shop after the birth of Jennifer's daughter, Olivia. Shoes, sandals, and booties from designers like Buckle My Shoe, Magnolia, Moschino, and Shoe Be Do come in European sizes infant 17 to children's 5. The store also carries hand-crafted dolls, hair accessories, socks, and tights. *2205 N. Halsted St., Lincoln Park, 773/281–5583.*

CLOTHING FOR MEN/GENERAL

classic & casual

7 *e-5*

AGNÈS B.

This downtown boutique is as much a great source of French basics for men who create their own distinct style as it is for their style-conscious female counterparts. *46 E. Walton St., Gold Coast, 312/642–7483.*

7 *e-5*

BANANA REPUBLIC

Easy pieces that work well together make for simple men's shopping at this popular national chain. *744 N. Michigan Ave., Magnificent Mile, 312/642–0020.*

8 *c-4*

BROOKS BROTHERS

A veritable institution of good taste since 1818, this store offers men who adore the classic look a line of navy blazers, chinos, and well-made shirts. *209 S. LaSalle St., Loop, 312/263–0100.*

7 *e-6*

713 N. Michigan Ave., Magnificent Mile, 312/915–0060.

7 *e-6*

GAP

The comfy, basic styles for women and children are available for men, too. *679 N. Michigan Ave., Magnificent Mile, 312/335–1896.*

7 *e-5*

Water Tower Place, 835 N. Michigan Ave., Magnificent Mile, 312/787–7992.

5 *b-3*

1740 N. Sheffield Ave., Clybourn Corridor, 312/944–6774.

7 *e-5*

J. CREW

It's a great store for men who hate to shop. You can quickly scan the selection of reasonably priced, comfortable, and just-fashionable-enough clothes, leave with a few bags full, and be set for the season. *900 N. Michigan Ave., Magnificent Mile, 312/751–2739.*

7 e-5
MARK SHALE
Looking for classy clothes for work? This store has conservative yet stylish attire geared to the corporate world. *900 N. Michigan Ave., Magnificent Mile, 312/440–0720.*

8 d-2
OLD NAVY
Basics at value prices are the draw for men at this popular chain, where you can get everything from underwear to winter coats, and all the stuff in between. *35 N. State St., Loop, 312/551–0522.*

5 c-5
1569 N. Kingsbury St., Clybourn Corridor, 312/397–0485.

5 a-2
1730 W. Fullerton Pkwy., Bucktown, 773/871–0601.

7 e-5
PAUL STUART
It sells top-quality traditional men's clothing for the boardroom and the golf course and some women's clothing. *John Hancock Center, 875 N. Michigan Ave., Magnificent Mile, 312/640–2650.*

7 e-6
POLO/RALPH LAUREN
This place pays tribute to the genteel world of Ralph Lauren for men, women, children, and the home. At 30,000 square ft, it's the designer's largest U.S. store, and it even contains a respected restaurant, RL (named for guess who). *750 N. Michigan Ave., Magnificent Mile, 312/280–1655.*

7 e-5
ST. CROIX SHOP
The finest knitwear and outerwear for men can be found at this downtown shop. *900 N. Michigan Ave., Magnificent Mile, 312/787–2888.*

7 e-5
STRUCTURE
Another offshoot of the popular Limited chain, this store offers men a basic, casual look with a hip, young bent. Expect more fashion than quality. *Water Tower Place, 835 N. Michigan Ave., Magnificent Mile, 312/654–0447.*

8 c-3
SYD JEROME
This menswear shop caters to Board of Trade types who fancy a more straightforward, European style. *2 N. LaSalle St., Loop, 312/346–0333. Closed Sun.*

7 e-4
URBAN OUTFITTERS
When you're young and stylin', this is the place to shop for clothes, housewares, and gifts. *935 N. Rush St., Gold Coast, 312/640–1919.*

5 e-2
2352 N. Clark St., Lincoln Park, 773/549–1711.

contemporary

7 e-5
CACHE
It stocks expensive designer fashions, accessories, sportswear, and hats. *900 N. Michigan Ave., Magnificent Mile, 312/787–3054.*

7 e-4
DIESEL
There's a heavy emphasis on up-to-the-minute men's fashions at this hip chain, most famous for its well-fitting denims. *923 N. Rush St., Gold Coast, 312/255–0157.*

7 e-4
GIANNI VERSACE
You'll find definitive Italian style from the design house now run by the late Gianni's sister, Donatella. *101 E. Oak St., Magnificent Mile, 312/337–1111. Closed Sun.*

7 e-5
GIORGIO ARMANI
It has all the signature, refined Armani men's clothing and furnishings. *800 N. Michigan Ave., Magnificent Mile, 312/427–6264.*

7 f-5
GIOVANNI
High-end sportswear and designer collections for men are available in this Drake-hotel boutique. *140 E. Walton St., Gold Coast, 312/787–6500. Closed Sun.*

7 *e-5*

NORTH BEACH LEATHER

This unique downtown store carries very special leather fashions—from the totally outrageous to the subdued—for women and men. *Water Tower Place, 835 N. Michigan Ave., Magnificent Mile, 312/ 280–9292.*

custom

7 *e-5*

ALFRED DUNHILL OF LONDON, INC.

As famous for its custom men's clothing as it is for its tobacco products and accessories, this store is indeed for a man's man. *Water Tower Place, 835 N. Michigan Ave., Magnificent Mile, 312/ 467–4455.*

8 *e-3*

CUSTOM SHOP

Tailors here fashion made-to-measure shirts at no extra charge (prices based on the cutting of four). A wide choice of fabrics (including imported) and styles is available. The store also caters to women. Expect a 5- to 10-week delivery. *38 S. Michigan Ave., Loop, 312/263–3816. Closed Sun.*

7 *e-5*

900 N. Michigan Ave., Magnificent Mile, 312/337–7979.

8 *c-4*

D DEBARTOLO & COMPANY

This downtown shop specializes in custom-made suits, ties, and shirts using imported materials. *330 S. Wells St., South Loop, 312/939–3169. Closed weekends.*

discount & off-price

6 *e-4*

MORRIS & SONS

This downtown shop has discounts on this season's couture, for both men and women. Discounts begin at 30%. Knowledgeable staff will help you find good buys. *555 W. Roosevelt Rd., South Loop, 312/243–5635.*

resale, vintage, surplus

5 *c-3*

MCSHANE'S EXCHANGE

Store owners Denise McShane and Chuck Caffrey oversee these well-

stocked shops carrying gently worn quality—including designer—sportswear, dresses, and suits, as well as shoes, belts, and jewelry. *1141 W. Webster Ave., Lincoln Park, 773/525–0211.*

5 *d-3*

815 W. Armitage Ave., Lincoln Park, 773/ 525–0282.

8 *e-2*

SUITSMART

A resale shop for men's suits in the heart of the city's tony downtown? Yes! *115 N. Wabash Ave., 2nd floor, Loop, 312/ 236–7848.*

4 *e-8*

ULTIMATELY YOURS

This shop stocks clothes with a practical, snob appeal for fashionable yet budget-savvy women and men. American and European designers include Missoni, Albert Nippon, Calvin Klein, Ralph Lauren, and Giorgio Armani. It has Gucci bags and Maude Frizon shoes previously—though in most cases gently—worn. *2931 N. Broadway, Lakeview, 773/975–1581. Closed Tues.–Wed.*

unusual for men/ specialties

4 *c-3*

WALLIS Z SURPLUS DEPARTMENT STORE

Psst! Don't tell your friends but this is a great, if a little bit out-of-the-way, army surplus store. It carries military clothing, duffel bags, metal trunks, military insignias, camping equipment (including backpacks and tents), and work boots. *4647 N. Broadway, Uptown, 773/ 784–9140.*

formalwear

6 *d-4*

BUY-A-TUX

Why rent when you can buy a brand-new tuxedo that fits you perfectly? Remember, there are no rentals at this store. *615 W. Roosevelt Rd., South Loop, 312/243– 5465.*

8 *e-2*

DESMONDS FORMALWEAR

This store is perfect for the marrying man or a band member. You'll find sale and rental formalwear with such names

as Pierre Cardin, Perry Ellis, and Chaps
Ralph Lauren. Grooms-to-be, take note:
you're free with five paid rentals! *6 E.
Randolph St., Loop, 312/782–1115.
Closed Sun.*

8 *e-3*

GINGISS
FORMALWEAR CENTER

There are tuxedos for rent or sale at this
chain. It has traditional and designer
names such as After Six, Pierre Cardin,
Adolfo, YSL, Lord West, and Bill Blass.
*151 S. Wabash Ave., Loop, 312/263–7071.
Closed Sun.*

5 *c-4*

MODERN TUXEDO

Whether it's for a wedding or a black-tie
event, this chain will help you dress up
in style. Stores carry formalwear by
Christian Dior, Perry Ellis, and Oscar de
la Renta as well as accessories by
Michael Newell. *1953 N. Clybourn Ave.,
Clybourn Corridor, 773/388–0800. Closed
Sun.*

hats

2 *e-3*

HATS PLUS

Russian cossacks, earflap hats, fedoras,
homburgs, top hats—you name it and
this store with more than 10,000 hats in
stock is likely to have it. Both Michael
Jordan and Scottie Pippen have worn
chapeaux bought here. *4706 W. Irving
Park Rd., Portage Park, 773/286–5577.*

2 *e-5*

NEW WORLD HATTERS

More than 50 years old, this store stocks
quite an array of hats, including fedoras,
derbies, and homburgs for the stylish
man. It also renovates hats. *4146 W.
Madison St., East Garfield Park, 773/638–
4900. Closed Sun.*

shirts

8 *e-3*

CUSTOM SHOP

Tailors here fashion made-to-measure
shirts at no extra charge (prices based
on the cutting of four). There's a wide
choice of fabrics and styles. Expect a 5-
to 10-week delivery window. *38 S. Michigan Ave., Loop, 312/263–3816.
Closed Sun.*

7 *e-5*

*900 N. Michigan Ave., Magnificent Mile,
312/337–7979.*

8 *b-1*

RIDDLE MCINTYRE

A fitting is required for custom shirts,
and there is a four-shirt minimum order.
The delivery period is four weeks. This
store also carries pajamas and shorts.
*175 N. Franklin St., Loop, 312/782–3317.
Closed weekends.*

shoes & boots

5 *a-7*

ALCALA'S WESTERN WEAR

An out-of-the-way, eclectic store—with
more than 10,000 pairs of cowboy boots
for men, women, and children—it's a
must-see for the cowboy (or -girl) within
you. *1733 W. Chicago Ave., West Town,
312/226–0152.*

7 *e-7*

ALLEN-EDMONDS

In business for more than 75 years, this
downtown shop manufactures high-
quality wing-tip, cap-toe, and slip shoes
for men. Sizes 5–18, AAAA–EEE are
available. *541 N. Michigan Ave., Magnificent Mile, 312/755–9306.*

8 *c-3*

ALTMAN'S MEN'S
SHOES AND BOOTS

It's usually jammed with men testing
everything from Alden oxfords and Tony
Lama boots to Allen-Edmonds and Timberland, all discounted. Don't be hood-
winked by the store's tiny size—the
stockrooms contain more than 10,000
pairs of men's shoes in sizes from 5 to
19 and in widths from AAAA to EEE. *120
W. Monroe St., Loop, 312/332–0667.
Closed Sun.*

7 *e-5*

AVVENTURA

This is a favorite stop for professional
basketball players who need European-
style footwear. The shop stocks men's
sizes up to 16. *Water Tower Place, 835 N.
Michigan Ave., Magnificent Mile, 312/
337–3700.*

7 *e-5*

FLORSHEIM SHOE SHOP

It's a fashionable shop with moderately
priced shoes for men and women,

including Timberland and Rockport. *845 N. Michigan Ave., Magnificent Mile, 312/ 944–7891.*

unusual sizes

3 g-3

MARTIN'S BIG AND TALL STORE FOR MEN

If your tall guy perennially has trouble finding clothes that fit, you might want to give this store a try. It claims to have the largest selection in the Midwest with sizes up to 10X and 80-inch waist, all of it moderately priced. *4745 N. Lincoln Ave., Ravenswood, 773/784–5853.*

2 c-2

NAPOLEON'S TAILOR

It stocks clothes for men 5'8" and shorter. *7254 W. Foster Ave., Jefferson Park, 773/594–9800.*

ties

7 e-5

KNOT SHOP

If you don't find a tie you like here, you're not looking hard enough. There are about 5,000 ties from designers including Jerry Garcia and Nicole Miller, as well as some ladies' scarves. *845 N. Michigan Ave., Magnificent Mile, 312/ 944–7121.*

7 e-4

TESSUTI

This downtown store has an exceptional selection of ties, sweaters, and sport shirts. There are also Paul Ziler suits, sports jackets, pants, and dress shirts. *50 E. Oak St., Magnificent Mile, 312/ 266–4949.*

CLOTHING FOR WOMEN/GENERAL

classic & casual

7 e-5

AGNÈS B.

Timeless and beautifully crafted pieces are this French designer's signature. Her snap-front tops, crisp jackets, and skinny pants are coveted but often in short supply. *46 E. Walton St., Gold Coast, 312/642–7483.*

7 e-7

ANN TAYLOR

This popular chain caters to the career woman, selling a great selection of contemporary clothes, footwear, and accessories. Stock is well organized and attractively displayed. The chain took over the giant Viacom store on the Mag Mile to create a giant corner flagship. *600 N. Michigan Ave., Magnificent Mile, 312/587–8301.*

7 e-6

Chicago Place, 700 N. Michigan Ave., Magnificent Mile, 312/335–0117.

8 c-4

231 S. LaSalle St., Loop, 312/332–5572. Closed weekends.

7 e-4

103 E. Oak St., Magnificent Mile, 312/ 943–5411.

5 d-3

2010 N. Halsted St., Lincoln Park, 773/ 296–6090.

7 e-6

BANANA REPUBLIC

Banana Republic stores are stocked to the rafters with moderately to high-price natural fiber, earth-tone active and casual wear. There are also leather and canvas belts, bags, shoes, and men's and women's boots. *744 N. Michigan Ave., Magnificent Mile, 312/642–0020.*

7 e-5

Water Tower Place, 835 N. Michigan Ave., Magnificent Mile, 312/642–7667.

5 d-3

2104 N. Halsted St., Lincoln Park, 773/ 832–1172.

8 e-2

EDDIE BAUER

Casual clothes with a nod toward the outdoors are sold at this chain. There's an Eddie Bauer Home section, filled with home furnishings and accessories, at the Michigan Avenue store. *123 N. Wabash Ave., Loop, 312/263–6005.*

7 e-7

600 N. Michigan Ave., Magnificent Mile, 312/951–5888.

7 e-6

EXPRESS

An offshoot of the Limited, this chain provides younger, hipper clothing with a decidedly faux-French accent. The good buys are, however, real; clothes tend to be more fashionable than durable. 676 N. Michigan Ave., Magnificent Mile, 312/944–5770.

7 e-5

Water Tower Place, 835 N. Michigan Ave., Magnificent Mile, 312/943–0344.

5 d-1

Century Mall, 2828 N. Clark St., Lakeview, 773/871–5883.

7 c-8

222 Merchandise Mart Plaza, River North, 312/836–0051. Closed Sun.

7 e-6

GAP

Young and old, who doesn't love this store? Jeans, T-shirts, sport separates, athletic wear—this popular chain has it all, and at reasonable prices to boot. It also has a great selection of rugged but stylish shoes. 679 N. Michigan Ave., Magnificent Mile, 312/335–1896.

7 e-5

Water Tower Place, 835 N. Michigan Ave., Magnificent Mile, 312/787–7992.

5 c-4

1740 N. Sheffield Ave., Clybourn Corridor, 312/944–6774.

7 e-4

GIOVANNI

In the city's famous Drake hotel, this store stocks luxurious designer collections, au courant sportswear, and unique accessories for socialites, partygoers, and ladies who lunch. 140 E. Walton St., Gold Coast, 312/787–6500. Closed Sun.

7 e-5

J. CREW

J. Crew is about classic American style with a modern edge. Originally famous for its roll-neck sweaters and barn jackets, the retailer-cataloger has expanded to include a good selection of more dressy clothes, shoes, and lingerie. 900 N. Michigan Ave., Magnificent Mile, 312/751–2739.

7 e-5

THE LIMITED

This familiar retailer sells moderately priced fashions, including many of its own designs. You'll also find a good choice of stylish accessories. Water

Tower Place, 835 N. Michigan Ave., Magnificent Mile, 312/527–2725.

5 d-1

Century Mall, 2828 N. Clark St., Lakeview, 773/549–2075.

8 d-2

OLD NAVY

A value concept from the people behind Gap, Old Navy has developed a solid following for its very reasonable, of-the-moment fashions for the whole family. Fun, seasonal accessories, like beach towels and flip-flops in summer and school clothes in fall, are a steal. 35 N. State St., Loop, 312/551–0522.

5 c-5

1569 N. Kingsbury St., Clybourn Corridor, 312/397–0485.

5 a-2

1730 W. Fullerton Pkwy., Bucktown, 773/871–0601.

7 e-6

POLO/RALPH LAUREN

There's quite the selection for Ralph fans at this giant, four-story flagship store, carrying Ralph, Polo, the Women's Collection, Collection Classics, Polo Sport, the handmade Purple Label, Purple Label Sportswear, and Polo Golf. 750 N. Michigan Ave., Magnificent Mile, 312/280–1655.

7 e-5

ST. CROIX SHOP

Knitwear and outerwear can be found at this upscale shop, which carries an extensive men's line. 900 N. Michigan Ave., Magnificent Mile, 312/787–2888.

conservative

8 c-3

BROOKS BROTHERS

More well known for its men's classics, this fashion institution is nonetheless equally popular for its classic, conservative womenswear. 209 S. LaSalle St., Loop, 312/263–0100.

7 e-6

713 N Michigan Ave., Magnificent Mile, 312/915–0060.

7 e-6

BURBERRY

This store has revamped its image with the help of hot young Italian designer

Roberto Menechetti. Besides his more cutting-edge designs, there's also a wide selection of business attire and casual wear. *633 N. Michigan Ave., Magnificent Mile, 312/787–2500.*

7 *e-5*
TALBOTS
This well-known chain pulls few punches, and that's what customers prefer. You'll find primarily classic suits and dresses. *Chicago Place, 700 N. Michigan Ave., Magnificent Mile, 312/ 944–6059.*

7 *e-5*
Water Tower Place, 835 N. Michigan Ave., Magnificent Mile, 312/664–3852.

8 *e-3*
139 S. Wabash Ave., Loop, 312/944–6059.

contemporary

5 *d-3*
ART EFFECT
If you seek a clothing store for garb that doesn't pinch or squeeze, you might want to check out this chic little boutique. Here you can count on comfortable yet creative clothes. Several local designers are represented with an impressive contemporary jewelry collection. *651 W. Armitage Ave., Lincoln Park, 312/664–0997.*

5 *d-2*
BLAKE
It specializes in really hip clothes, including Dries Van Noten, Ann Demeulemeest, Martin Margiela, and Helmut Lang, all displayed in a stark setting. *2448 N. Lincoln Ave., Lincoln Park, 773/477–3364.*

7 *e-5*
CLUB MONACO
This Canadian-based chain stocks superstylish separates that capture the key items of the season at very appealing prices and is, consequently, very popular with fashion-savvy shoppers. An in-house line of cosmetics has a strong following. *900 N. Michigan Ave., Magnificent Mile, 312/787–8757.*

7 *e-5*
DIESEL
This place is for those who don't blink at paying $100 for jeans. Loud music and an upbeat atmosphere attract a young

crowd with plenty of money to spend. *923 N. Rush St., Gold Coast, 312/255–0157.*

7 *e-7*
GUESS?
The company that made a splash in the '80s with its sexy jeans is still going strong, now with a complete line of clothes for men, women, and kids, as well as home furnishings. *605 N. Michigan Ave., Magnificent Mile, 312/440–9665.*

7 *e-4*
HINO & MALEE
Known for its top-quality clothing with distinctive asymmetrical cuts, this downtown boutique is owned by a locally based husband-and-wife design team with a great sense of style. *50 E. Oak St., Magnificent Mile, 312/664–7475. Closed Sun.*

5 *c-3*
KRIVOY
At the atelier of Chicago designer Cynthia Hadesman, you'll find bridal wear, linen, silk and alpaca knits, chunky shoes, and exceptional hats. *1145 W. Webster, Lincoln Park, 773/248–1466. Closed Sun.–Mon.*

7 *d-5*
ONLY SHE
This downtown shop carries unique apparel and accessories, focusing on hand-painted scarves, one-of-a-kind jewels, and custom hats and handbags. You will also find items by Olsen European Fashions, Louben, and Harari. *8 E. Delaware Pl., Gold Coast, 312/335–1353.*

5 *c-3*
OUT OF THE WEST
But not out of your hemisphere. This store stocks Western-influence fashions that don't look out of place up here in the North. *1000 W. Armitage Ave., Lincoln Park, 773/404–9378.*

7 *e-5*
PLAZA ESCADA
This downtown boutique showcases the Escada line, in all its variations, including the Escada Magaretha Ley Collection, Escada Couture, and more. You will also find a shoe salon and leather goods here. *840 N. Michigan Ave., Magnificent Mile, 312/915–0500.*

7 *e-4*

SUGAR MAGNOLIA

Named for the Grateful Dead song, it has women's clothing and accessories that tap into trends with a romantic, Bohemian spin. T-shirts come in all kinds of colors, sizes, and styles. *34 E Oak St., Magnificent Mile, 312/944–0885.*

2 *f-4*

TANGERINE

This store, on a hot shopping block in a cool neighborhood, is filled with fun, trendy clothes. It's the type of place you happen to wander into, then return to again and again. *1659 N. Damen Ave., Bucktown, 773/772–0505.*

5 *d-2*

TRIBECA

Named for the trendy New York City neighborhood, this boutique brings New York know-how to Chicago, with pieces from designers like BCBG, Max Studio, Cousin Johnny, and Easel. Juliet custom jewelry designs and Hobo handbags are also for sale. *2480½ W. Lincoln Ave., Lincoln Park, 773/528–5958.*

4 *c-8*

TRAGICALLY HIP

A young, good-looking crowd that shops for cutting-edge clothes and accessories can be found at this hip shop. *931 W. Belmont Ave., Lakeview, 773/549–1500.*

7 *e-4*

URBAN OUTFITTERS

If you're looking for something that'll set you apart from the crowd, look no further. This funky chain carries clothes and accessories for young hipsters, along with a slew of unique home accessories. *935 N. Rush St., Gold Coast, 312/640–1919.*

5 *e-2*

2352 N. Clark St., Lincoln Park, 773/549–1711.

designer

5 *d-3*

CELESTE TURNER

Owner Celeste has impeccable taste, and it shows in her selection of frocks, sweaters, and slender black pants. The store's very popular with shoppers along this busy shopping strip. *859 W. Armitage Ave., Lincoln Park, 773/549–3390.*

7 *e-4*

CHANEL BOUTIQUE

Inside the Drake hotel, this classic boutique carries the complete line of Chanel products, including fragrances, ready-to-wear, cosmetics, and accessories. *935 N. Michigan Ave., Magnificent Mile, 312/787–5500.*

5 *d-3*

CYNTHIA ROWLEY

Rowley, a Chicago-area native, lines her store with her ever-popular, spirited, well-priced dresses and separates. The store also carries her shoes and other Rowley products, such as books and tablewear. *808 W. Armitage Ave., Lincoln Park, 773/528–6160.*

7 *e-4*

GIANNI VERSACE

Namesake of the late Italian designer, this tony store stocks high-style day and evening fashions. *101 E. Oak St., Magnificent Mile, 312/337–1111. Closed Sun.*

7 *e-5*

GIORGIO ARMANI

This understated, airy two-story space is devoted to Armani's discreetly luxurious clothes and accessories. It features his top-price Black Label collection, considered a cut above the department-store line. *800 N. Michigan Ave., Magnificent Mile, 312/427–6264.*

5 *d-3*

INNUENDO

A neighborhood favorite, this shop specializes in uniquely trimmed suits; they're not cheap, though. *844 W. Armitage Ave., Lincoln Park, 773/929–9944.*

5 *d-3*

ISIS ON ARMITAGE

Especially eye-catching in this Lincoln Park boutique are white linen and lacy ensembles. *823 W. Armitage Ave., Lincoln Park, 773/665–7290.*

5 *c-3*

JANE HAMILL

This Chicago designer sells her own interpretations of the season's latest fashions at fair prices. If you seek sophisticated bridesmaid's dresses, Hamill's designs might fit the bill. *1115 W. Armitage Ave., Lincoln Park, 773/665–1102.*

2 *f-4*

I'M LU

The clothes at this store exude a fresh simplicity, thanks to the clean lines and linens used by designer Luisa Gasiewski. Women's separates are relaxed, no nonsense, and generously cut. *2042 N. Damen Ave., Bucktown, 773/862–9808.*

7 *e-4*

JIL SANDER

A striking, two-story building showcases the German designer's entire collection for men and women. You will also find shoes, handbags, belts, and the designer's exclusive fragrance. *48 E. Oak St., Magnificent Mile, 312/335–0006. Closed Sun.*

7 *e-4*

NICOLE MILLER

Miller's fun, urban fashions have been a hit for some now, but her reasonably priced bridalwear—bridesmaid's dresses and outfits for less-formal brides-to-be—has really taken off in the past few years. *63 E. Oak St., Magnificent Mile, 312/664–3532.*

7 *b-7*

PATRICIA RHODES CUSTOM COUTURE

Rhodes takes sumptuous fabrics like silks, laces, organzas, and velvets and transforms them into custom gowns at her new workshop-salon. *434 W. Ontario St., River North, 312/664–4200. By appointment only Sat., closed Sun.*

7 *e-4*

PRADA

The glowing pistachio walls are a sign to fashion worshipers that they've come to the right temple. Three floors of women's and men's clothing, footwear, bags, and luggage are stocked for ogling by this trendsetting Italian company. *30 E. Oak St., Magnificent Mile, 312/951–1113.*

2 *f-4*

P. 45

This boutique stocks new styles by a cadre of up-and-coming designers. Clothes range from adventurous to elegant, and prices don't get out of hand. Still, the size range is limited and popular pieces fly out of the store quickly. *1643 N. Damen Ave., Bucktown, 773/862–4523.*

2 *f-4*

ROBIN RICHMAN

In this art gallery–retail store, nationally known knitwear designer Robin Richman stocks her knits and antique goods as well as wood furniture made by sculptor Floyd Gompf. *2108 N. Damen Ave., Bucktown, 773/278–6150. Closed Mon.*

7 *e-4*

SONIA RYKIEL

Known as the "Queen of the Knits," Parisian designer Sonia Rykiel creates a warm array of knit coordinates, crepes, and cottons for women and children. You'll also find the designer's unique signature hats, jewels, scarves, and shoes. *106 E. Oak St., Magnificent Mile, 312/951–0800. Closed Sun.*

5 *c-3*

STUDIO 910

This neighborhood boutique has loads of cool, fashionable finds and a friendly sales staff. *910 W. Armitage Ave., Lincoln Park, 773/929–2400.*

7 *e-4*

ULTIMO

It has changed hands twice in the last few years and is branding itself to appeal to a less rarified customer. But this boutique still carries Marc Jacobs, John Galliano, and Zoran, the chic-of-the-chic. *114 E. Oak St., Magnificent Mile, 312/787–0906. Closed Sun.*

5 *c-3*

ZONE

It features unique designs by local Pamela Vanderelinde, who likes simple silhouettes that utilize unusual fabrics, contrast linings, and one-of-a-kind buttons. *1154 W. Armitage Ave., Lincoln Park, 773/472–4007. Closed Mon.–Tues.*

discount & off-price

8 *d-3*

FILENE'S BASEMENT

You'll find great buys here if you're patient. The State Street branch probably has the best merchandise outside the Boston original. Women can get great bargains at either the State Street or Michigan Avenue store. Men will find a superior selection of designer names at State Street. Watch newspaper ads midweek for special shipments and such events as the bridal-gown sale. *1 N. State St., Loop, 312/553–1055.*

7 *e-5*

830 N. Michigan Ave., Magnificent Mile, 312/482–8918.

5 *e-2*

FITIGUES OUTLET

This outlet is within the headquarters of Fitigues, which made its name in upscale thermal loungewear popular with the likes of Oprah Winfrey, an avowed fan. Discounts range from 60% to 70%, depending on how recent the stock is. Tip: Get on the mailing list to learn about the periodic warehouse sales at the outlet, when prices are *really* slashed. *1535 N. Dayton St., Near North, 312/255–0095.*

5 *d-3*

FOX'S

This local outlet chain sells designer clothes, including suits, dresses, sportswear, and outwear at great discounts. Most of the labels have been ripped out, but those with an eye for fashion will likely know who made what. *2336 N. Clark St., Lincoln Park, 773/281–0700.*

2 *e-3*

GAP FACTORY OUTLET

This store is worth a stop to clear significant savings on overruns and seconds on men's, women's, and children's clothing from the Gap, Banana Republic, and Old Navy. *2778 N. Milwaukee Ave., Logan Square, 773/252–0594.*

5 *a-6*

KMART

The popular chain sells housewares, apparel, and hardware. It distinguishes itself from the competition with exclusive designs by popular celebrities such as Kathy Ireland and Jaclyn Smith. Kmart's coup is decorating maven Martha Stewart. Her line of towels, bedding, and whatnot is well coordinated, but fabric quality is on the low end. *1360 N. Ashland Ave., Wicker Park, 773/292–9400.*

2 *f-3*

MARK SHALE OUTLET

In a strip shopping center near the Kennedy Expressway, this store stocks corporate and weekend clothing from the likes of Polo and Joseph Abboud. It decreases the prices on unsold men's and women's clothing from Mark Shale stores by 30% to 70%. *2593 N. Elston Ave., West Lakeview, 773/772–9600.*

4 *d-8*

MARSHALL'S

This popular chain has become better organized in recent years, so you don't have to sift through just about everything in the store to find your favorite brand. There's an array of popular name-brand apparel, shoes, and accessories for men, women, and children, all of it discounted. *3131 N. Clark St., Lakeview, 773/327–2711.*

8 *d-3*

T. J. MAXX

Plates, vases, and other gift items are some of the bargains that shoppers swear by at this perennially loved discount store, but the big draw is apparel, shoes, accessories, underwear, and a great jewelry selection. *11 N. State St., Loop, 312/553–0515.*

2 *f-3*

TARGET

Knockoffs of the latest styles at low prices are the draw at this branch of the Minneapolis-based megachain, where it's good to shop for fast-fading trends that you've got to have but don't plan on investing in. Moms and students alike adore the store's back-to-school supplies. Other good buys are high-quality but inexpensive towels, socks, and housewares by designer Michael Graves. *2656 N. Elston Ave., West Lakeview, 773/252–1994.*

resale

5 *d-1*

BUY POPULAR DEMAND

This store sells on consignment better designers' suits, shoes, and jackets for men and women. *2631 N. Halsted St., Lincoln Park, 773/868–0404.*

5 *d-3*

CACTUS TRADE

Not the least bit prickly, it sells new and used designer clothes for women. It also has a charming selection of new, hand-crafted jewelry. *2040 N. Halsted St., Lincoln Park, 773/472–7222.*

5 b-3

CYNTHIA'S CONSIGNMENTS
This store has an excellent selection of used designer and upper-end brand label clothes, all in nearly mint condition, priced at the low end. *2218 N. Clybourn Ave., Clybourn Corridor, 773/248–7714.*

7 e-4

DAISY SHOP
You'll have to search to find this gem, but it'll be worth it. It stocks gently worn current and vintage couture clothing, accessories, and signed costume jewelry. *67 E. Oak St., 6th floor, Magnificent Mile, 312/943–8880.*

7 d-7

DESIGNER RESALE OF CHICAGO
It sells a glitzy array of used designer clothes for women at wonderful prices. *658 N. Dearborn St., River North, 312/587–3312.*

unusual sizes

8 c-3

AUGUST MAX WOMAN
This chain carries moderately priced contemporary looks for the contemporary woman, size 14–24. *39 S. LaSalle St., Loop, 312/759–9306. Closed weekends.*

7 e-5

Water Tower Place, 835 N. Michigan Ave., Magnificent Mile, 312/266–6416.

7 e-7

THE FORGOTTEN WOMAN
This store has fashionable clothes for women sizes 14–26. It has day and evening dress, sportswear, sweaters, and swimsuits. *535 N. Michigan Ave., Magnificent Mile, 312/329–0885.*

8 e-2

LANE BRYANT
Here you'll find designer sportswear and lingerie in sizes 14–28. Accessories are also available. *29 N. Wabash Ave., Loop, 312/332–7063.*

7 e-6

TALL GIRL
This downtown shop caters to tall, long-waisted, and long-legged women. Leggy fashions include sportswear, dresses, suits, outerwear, lingerie, and hosiery in tall sizes 8–20. *Chicago Place, 700 N. Michigan Ave., Magnificent Mile, 312/649–1303.*

vintage

4 d-7

FLASHY TRASH
This boutique is filled with men's and women's vintage clothing and accessories in superb condition. The reasonable prices attract prom-goers as well as more mature buyers. You'll also find new, supertrendy clothes here. *3524 N. Halsted St., Lakeview, 773/327–6900.*

4 c-7

HUBBA HUBBA
Looking for something different to wear to that next party? This shop splits its merchandise between select vintage clothing and new clothing. Clothes, jewelry, and accessories all have a retro feel. *3309 N. Clark St., Lakeview, 773/477–1414.*

3 h-7

SHANGRILA
If you're searching for clothes for a night of swing dancing, you've come to the right place. Shangrila sells lots of vintage duds from the 1930s through the 1970s. You also can sometimes find older period pieces such as 1920s lingerie. Rayon dresses that date to the 1940s will set you back between $10 and $40. Hard-to-find vintage shoes cost $10 to $25, depending on condition. *1952 W. Roscoe St., Roscoe Village, 773/348–5090.*

4 d-7

SILVER MOON
Known for its impressive selection of vintage wedding dresses, this store is also a favorite with the swing crowd because it specializes in 1930s and 1940s fashion. It sells period hats, gloves, jewelry, and dresses. *3337 N. Halsted St., Lakeview, 773/883–0222.*

4 d-7

STRANGE CARGO
Named after a popular Clark Gable and Joan Crawford movie, it sells vintage clothes from the 1940s through the 1980s. Ladies will especially like the 1940s day dresses, which are reasonably priced. *3448 N. Clark St., Wrigleyville, 773/327–8090.*

5 *a-5*

UNA MAE'S FREAK BOUTIQUE

This boutique with vintage clothes and accessories has the funkiest dressing rooms in the city. *1422 N. Milwaukee Ave., Wicker Park, 773/276–7002.*

4 *b-8*

WACKY CATS

Favored by those who lindy hop, Wacky Cats carries garb from the 1940s through 1960s, with heavy emphasis on women's 1940s clothes. Vintage hats and gloves to match are available, too. *3109 N. Lincoln Ave., Lakeview, 773/929–6701.*

4 *d-8*

WILD THING

This store's 1940s through 1970s vintage fashions include antique wedding gowns. *2933 N. Clark St., Lakeview, 773/549–7787.*

4 *b-6*

WISTERIA

It sells an array of 1940s-era togs, gloves, and dresses. The average price is $36. *3715 N. Southport Ave., Lakeview, 773/880–5868.*

CLOTHING FOR WOMEN/ SPECIALTIES

furs

7 *f-6*

CHICAGO FUR MART

In business for more than 60 years, this downtown shop is one of the largest importers and wholesale fur distributors in the Midwest. It sells designs by Christian Dior, Mary McFadden, Saga Mink, and many more. *166 E. Superior St., Streeterville, 312/951–5000. Closed Sun.*

5 *d-1*

CHICAGO FUR OUTLET

Discounts on new and used furs just might warm you up. *777 W. Diversey Ave., Lincoln Park, 312/348–3877. Closed Sun.*

7 *e-6*

ELAN

From barguszin sable to long-hair beaver, it's all available at this swanky fur store, which sells designs by Pisani, Louis Feraud, Zuki, Zandra Rhodes, Bob Mackie, and many other well-known designers. *675 N. Michigan Ave., Magnificent Mile, 312/640–0707.*

handbags & gloves

7 *e-5*

GLOVE ME TENDER

This shop exclusively stocks gloves in a wide price range. It has a huge supply of the practical, the elegant, and the lavish for women, men, and children. *900 N. Michigan Ave., Magnificent Mile, 312/664–4022.*

7 *e-4*

KATE SPADE

The designer who makes the purses everyone's just got to have has, at last, opened a shop on Oak Street. The 2,100-square-ft, two-level store carries Kate luggage, stationary, and shoes, plus the new Jack Spade line of men's accessories. *101 E. Oak St., Magnificent Mile, 312/604–0808.*

7 *f-5*

LOUIS VUITTON

You'll find the LV moniker on everything from key cases to steamer trunks. There's also a line without the statusy initials. *Water Tower Place, 835 N. Michigan Ave., Magnificent Mile, 312/944–2010.*

8 *e-1*

THAT'S OUR BAG

Bag great bargains here on discounted luggage, briefcases, wallets, and more. Don't miss the end-of-season (after Christmas and July 4) clearances. *200 N. Michigan Ave., Loop, 312/984–3510.*

hats

5 *e-2*

RAYMOND HUDD

A Chicago institution that has a reputation for wildly whimsical hats (such as a dreidl hat for Hannukah), Hudd is also quite adept with the everyday as well. Many collectors snap up his creations. *2545 N. Clark St., Lincoln Park, 773/477–1159. Closed Sun.–Mon.*

leather

7 e-5

NORTH BEACH LEATHER

This unique downtown store carries very special leather fashions—from the totally outrageous to the subdued—for women and men. *Water Tower Place, 835 N. Michigan Ave., Magnificent Mile, 312/280–9292.*

lingerie

6 d-4

CHICAGO HOSIERY & UNDERWEAR CO.

You'll find those impossible-to-find large bras, designer undies, sweatshirts, and much more at this indispensable emporium. *601 W. Roosevelt Rd., South Loop, 312/226–0055.*

7 e-5

ENCHANTE

It has frilly, feminine, mainly French underthings. *900 N. Michigan Ave., Magnificent Mile, 312/951–7290.*

5 d-3

UNDERTHINGS

This lovely boutique stocks pretty, feminine lingerie and loungewear. *804 W. Webster Ave., Lincoln Park, 773/472–9291.*

7 e-5

VICTORIA'S SECRET

Here you'll find lush lingerie and sleepwear in an inviting boudoir setting, just like you find in the catalog that your husband likes to "read." *Water Tower Pl., 835 N. Michigan Ave., Magnificent Mile, 312/440–1169.*

maternity

7 e-5

MIMI MATERNITY

This chain stocks fashionable clothing throughout your pregnancy. *900 N. Michigan Ave., Magnificent Mile, 312/951–0359.*

5 c-2

MOTHERS WORK MATERNITY OUTLET

You can find bargains on casual items like denim overalls or jumpers and T-shirts direct from the factory. *1730 W. Fullerton Pkwy., Lakeview, 773/529–0564.*

7 e-4

A PEA IN THE POD— MATERNITY REDEFINED

The name might be lighthearted, but the clothes are seriously comfortable. It stocks well-made casual and career clothes. Bathing suits are also available. *46 E. Oak St., Magnificent Mile, 312/944–3080.*

shoes & boots

3 c-5

ADAMS FACTORY SHOE OUTLET

This store discounts all kinds of shoes for men, women, and children. It also sells accessories like hosiery and handbags. *3655 W. Irving Park Rd., North Center, 773/539–4120.*

7 e-5

BROWNS

It supplies such pricey brands as Charles Jourdan, DKNY, and Doc Martens, as well as private labels. *Water Tower Place, 835 N. Michigan Ave., Magnificent Mile, 312/642–4762.*

5 d-3

ENTRATA

The place to go for bridal and formal footwear, it carries very high-end lines like Emma Pope. *826 W. Armitage Ave., Lincoln Park, 773/244–1807.*

8 d-3

FAMOUS FOOTWEAR

This chain is well known for discounting all shoes. *7 W. Madison St., Loop, 312/236–3218.*

5 d-3

HANIG'S BIRKENSTOCK SHOP

Stock up on Birkenstock shoes and sandals for men and women in an array of styles and colors. *847 W. Armitage Ave., Lincoln Park, 773/929–5568.*

5 d-1

HANIG'S SLIPPER BOX

This store stocks moderately priced boots and shoes of such brands as Rockport and Zodiac. *2754 N. Clark St., Lincoln Park, 773/248–2235.*

5 *d-3*

LORI'S DESIGNER SHOES

Many fine-footed women consider this the best show shop in the city. Shoes by great designers like Franco Sarto, Joan & David, Gastone Luciole, janet & janet, and Steve Madden are here at competitive prices, stacked among a flurry of terrific handbags, jewelry, and other accessories. It has great bridal shoes, too. *824 W. Armitage Ave., Lincoln Park, 773/281–5655.*

4 *d-8*

SOLE JUNKIES

Catering to a young and very mobile clientele, this store specializes in platform and skateboard shoes. *3176 N. Clark St., Lakeview, 773/348–8935.*

7 *e-4*

TOD'S

Tod's began with the nubby-soled driving shoes designer Diego Della Valle invented for Gianni Agnelli but now has more, including styles sought after by fashionistas and celebrities. The handbags are great, too. *121 E. Oak St., Magnificent Mile, 312/943–0070.*

swimsuits

2 *f-4*

BODY BODY

This bikini superstore also sells resort wear. *508 N. Hoyne St., West Loop, 312/733–0700.*

7 *d-4*

LONDO MONDO

It sells swimsuits you'll want to be seen in. Mossimo, Robin Piccone, and Body Glove are among the brands stocked. In-line skates are also sold and rented here. *1100 N. Dearborn St., Gold Coast, 312/751–2794.*

5 *d-3*

2148 N. Halsted, Lincoln Park, 773/327–2218.

COINS

2 *d-1*

ARCHIE'S COINS

It buys and sells U.S. gold and silver coins and some paper money. *5516 W. Devon Ave., Saugaunash, 773/774–1433. Closed Sun.*

8 *d-2*

HARLAN J. BERK

Besides classical Greek, Roman, and Byzantine coinage from 700 BC to the fall of Byzantium, this shop also sells historical autographs and antiquities such as Greek and Roman pottery, statues, and bronzes. It also has U.S. and foreign coins, gold bullion, and currency. *31 N. Clark St., Loop, 312/609–0016. Closed weekends.*

8 *d-2*

MARSHALL FIELD'S STAMP & COIN DEPARTMENT

U.S. coins, gold, and limited medals are available here. *111 N. State St., lower level, Loop, 312/781–4237. Closed Sun.*

COMPUTERS & SOFTWARE

5 *c-4*

BEST BUY

It's easy to get lost in this megastore, but if you can find your way around, you'll discover a phenomenal selection of computers and related gadgets (but not much help). There are also audio equipment and CDs. *1000 W. North Ave., Lincoln Park, 312/988–4067.*

7 *b-7*

COMPUTER CITY

It's conveniently located next to the highway, so PC shoppers don't have far to go. *352 W. Grand Ave., River North, 312/840–5900.*

2 *f-3*

MICROCENTER

This Riverfront Plaza store is an excellent place to buy game software and computers. It also has a mammoth computer books and programming manuals section. *2645 N. Elston Ave., Bucktown, 773/292–1700.*

6 *e-2*

SECOND CITY COMPUTERS, INC.

Whether you want something new, used, or to rent, this full-service store is likely to have it. It also takes trade-ins and has an excellent repair and maintenance department. *600 W. Van Buren St., 3rd floor, South Loop, 312/382–9282.*

COSTUME RENTAL

1 e-6

BEVERLY COSTUME SHOP

Whether you feel like Cleopatra or Carmen Miranda, chances are this store's got something for you to play dress-up in. There's a huge selection of costumes for children and adults; most are rentals, but "everything's negotiable" according to the store manager. *11628 S. Western Ave., Beverly, 773/779–0068. Closed Sun.*

6 c-7

BROADWAY COSTUMES, INC.

A move to a new location in 1999 meant room for more stock at the city's oldest costumer, which has been in business since 1886. The rental business stocks some 150,000 costumes, and often outfits community and high school theater productions. *1100 W. Cermak Rd., Pilsen, 312/829–6400. Closed Sun.*

5 d-2

CHICAGO COSTUME COMPANY

If you don't find what you're looking for at this popular shop, which stocks thousands of costumes and makeup for all age groups, you can arrange to have a custom order made especially for you. But be prepared to thin your wallet if you do: prices start at about $800. *1120 W. Fullerton Pkwy., Lincoln Park, 773/528–1264.*

2 d-3

FANTASY HEADQUARTERS

You're sure to find a get-up that's perfect at this block-long costume emporium, which stocks more than 1 million costumes. *4065 N. Milwaukee Ave., Portage Park, 773/777–0222.*

CUTLERY & GADGETRY

7 e-5

BROOKSTONE

Here you can find products for the home, garden, and auto care and repair, all practical and attractive. *Water Tower Place, 835 N. Michigan Ave., 4th level, Magnificent Mile, 312/943–6356.*

8 d-2

CORRADO CUTLERY

What began in the Loop as a grinding shop in 1908 has become a great source for the world's best knives, from Swiss Army to stag-handled pocket cheese knives and boning knives. *26 N. Clark St., Loop, 312/368–8450. Closed weekends.*

6 d-1

NORTHWESTERN CUTLERY & SUPPLY

In the heart of the Fulton Market District, this is where chefs shop. You can find the sharpest knives at a variety of prices. Knife-sharpening is also done. *810 W. Lake St., River West, 312/421–3666. Closed Sun.*

DISCOUNT

2 f-3

EDWARD DON & CO. OUTLET

This restaurant-supply store is open to the public. In the front, you'll find regular-priced kitchen accessories and party goods. In back, discontinued and closeout kitchen supplies and appliances beckon. *2525 N. Elston Ave., Bucktown, 773/489–7739.*

5 d-3

LORI'S DISCOUNT DESIGNER SHOES

This self-service store undercuts department-store prices with its women's designer shoes from Joan & David and others. The selection of bridal footwear is particularly good. *824 W. Armitage Ave., Lincoln Park, 773/281–5655.*

ELECTRONICS & AUDIO

7 d-4

BANG & OLUFSEN CHICAGO

It sells unique and high-quality entertainment centers made in Denmark. Its specialties are home theater, custom installation, and pre-wiring. *15 E. Oak St., Gold Coast, 312/787–6006.*

8 e-1

RADIO SHACK

This chain offers mostly its own brand of consumer electronics, including telephones, pagers, and stereos. It also sells a handy cache of electronic converts for use overseas. Service and follow-up are excellent. *310 N. Michigan Ave., Loop, 312/236–1485.*

4 *d-8*

SATURDAY AUDIO EXCHANGE

Vintage-vinyl junkies, don't despair. Here is the place to find those indispensable record turntables so you can play your Frank Sinatra LPs. This store also sells other new and used audio equipment. But beware: it's only open a few days a week. *2919 N. Clark St., Lincoln Park, 773/935–8733. Closed Mon.– Wed. and Fri.*

7 *e-6*

SONY GALLERY OF CONSUMER ELECTRONICS

This downtown shop doesn't offer any deals on electronic gadgets, but it does provide a lot of high-tech fun. *663 N. Michigan Ave., Magnificent Mile, 312/ 943–3334.*

7 *e-5*

UNITED AUDIO

Audiophiles are in heaven at this nirvana, containing home and car stereos and portable audio equipment. *900 N. Michigan Ave., Magnificent Mile, 312/ 664–3100.*

2 *e-1*

6181 N. Lincoln Ave., Rogers Park, 773/ 478–7505.

5 *d-1*

2825 N. Clark St., Lincoln Park, 773/525– 7005.

EROTICA

4 *d-7*

CUPID'S TREASURES

It has novelty gifts and clothing, plus a wide selection of videos and magazines organized by taste and sexual orientation. The helpful salespeople don't flinch when asked to explain how some of the more unusual devices operate. *3519 N. Halsted St., Lakeview, 312/943–3393.*

4 *d-8*

TABOO-TABOU

This place has a combination of silver jewelry, cigars, and erotic accou-

trements—no kidding. There's an extensive choice of for-your-eyes-only outfits (from firefighters to French maids) and lingerie (from see-through to studded leather) as well as condoms and playthings. *858 W. Belmont Ave., Lakeview, 773/723–3739.*

4 *d-7*

THE PLEASURE CHEST

This is an adults-only emporium that has done its best to do away with the seedy atmosphere usually prevailing at such stores. The decor says "bedroom" not "bordello." Clever edibles, videos, adult games, and bath and massage potions are available. *3155 N. Broadway, Lakeview, 773/525–7151.*

ETHNIC ITEMS

7 *e-4*

THE ALASKA SHOP

Just stepping inside this store on a hot summer day makes the temperature drop. It has Eskimo art, including sculpture and jewelry made of soapstone, scrimshaw, whalebone, ivory, antlers, and jade. Very warm clothing is also offered. *104 E. Oak St., Magnificent Mile, 312/943–3393. Closed Sun.*

4 *c-7*

CASA COMPOS

Instead of going south of the border to buy, you can find an outstanding selection of artisan-made Mexican furniture and accessories here. Styles range from rustic to contemporary, and there is also an exceptional selection of Talavera pottery. *3326 N. Clark St., Lakeview, 773/281– 2272. Closed Mon.*

4 *b-7*

FOURTH WORLD ARTISANS

Handcrafted treasures, including textiles, artifacts, and jewelry from India, Africa, and the Americas, can be found in this exotic store. Be sure to check out the Turkish tearoom in the back. *3440 N. Southport Ave., Lakeview, 773/404–5200.*

2 *e-2*

JAPAN BOOKS & RECORDS

For a touch of Asia, mosey down to this Lincoln Square shop, which sells Japanese records and books. *3450 W. Peterson Ave., West Rogers Park, 773/463–7755.*

4 d-8

J. TOGURI MERCANTILE COMPANY

Warehouse-size dimensions make this the largest and most comprehensive spot for all things Asian outside of Chinatown. Find everything from chinaware, tea sets, and rice cookers to lanterns, origami papers, floral arrangements, and bonsai pots. There are also kimonos and martial arts uniforms. *851 W. Belmont Ave., Lakeview, 773/929–3500.*

7 e-6

JOY OF IRELAND

You'll find the luck of the Irish at this cute downtown shop with cladagh rings in gold, "Parking for Irish Only" signs, Guinness glasses, books, and other Emerald Isle mementos. *Chicago Place, 700 N. Michigan Ave., Magnificent Mile, 312/664–7290.*

7 e-5

LA MAISON DE NICOLE

The Parisian touch is evident at this lovely Gold Coast store, owned and managed by France natives. There are table tops from Limoges, Quimper, Gien, and Provence; designers including Laure Jany and Patrick Frey are represented. *66 E. Walton St., Magnificent Mile, 312/943–3988.*

2 d-2

THE POLONIA BOOKSTORE

At this store you'll find Polish-language books, magazines, newspapers, and records. *4738 N. Milwaukee Ave., Jefferson Park, 773/481–6968. Closed Sun.*

7 e-6

RUSSIAN CREATIONS

Authentic, unique art items from Russia make fabulous gifts. You'll find crystal pieces, custom-designed Palekh boxes, hand-painted nesting dolls, Fabergé eggs, and Baltic amber. *Chicago Place, 700 N. Michigan Ave., Magnificent Mile, 312/573–0792.*

3 d-1

THE SWEDEN SHOP

Near North Park College, this shop stocks Scandinavian imports, including cookware, china, dinnerware, and accessories. You'll find items made by Dansk, Orrefors, and Royal Copenhagen. It also sells clogs for the whole family. *3304 W. Foster Ave., North Park, 773/478–0327. Closed Sun.*

2 f-1

UMA SAREES

It has traditional silk saris and sari fabric. *2535 W. Devon Ave., Rogers Park, 773/338–6302. Closed Tues.*

EYEWEAR

5 a-8

AARDVARK EYEWEAR

With its exclusive focus on eyewear for children and teens, this is the place to take style-conscious kids for glasses. No appointments are necessary. *1917 W. Fullerton Pkwy., Lakeview, 773/880–5400. Closed Sun.*

4 d-8

CONTACTS & SPECS UNLIMITED

This store carries lots of attractive frames and accessories, and it specializes in modern, sleek specs such as those by Calvin Klein, Modo, and Red Rose. But beware: all this style comes at a price. *3144 N. Broadway, Lakeview, 773/880–5400. Closed Sun.*

3 h-6

EYE SPY OPTICAL

It's the hippest optical shop in Chicago. Eye Spy's got it all going on—frames by funky designers like Maui Jim, Anne et Valentine, and Eyephorics 2.5; digital pics of you in your prospective purchases; a resident dog; and even singles parties for unattached clientele. *3350 N. Lincoln Ave., Roscoe Village, 773/477–2670.*

5 e-2

FOR EYES

You can't beat the bargains at this popular optical chain. Top brand-name and designer eyewear is 30%–50% off. *2555 N. Clark St., Lincoln Park, 773/929–5553.*

5 d-3

SUN KING OPTICAL SHOP

It's an emporium of bargains: Ray-Bans, Vuarnets, and other brands, including designer eyeglass frames, are discounted here. *826 W. Armitage Ave., Lincoln Park, 773/975–7867.*

4 *c-1*

UHLEMANN OPTICAL
This outlet store focuses on prescription lenses but provides good bargains on sunglasses. *1135 W. Berwyn Ave., Rogers Park, 773/878–5197. Closed Sun.*

5 *c-4*

VISUAL EFFECTS OPTICAL
Supertrendy frames and sunglasses from designers like Oliver Peoples, Matsuda, and BADA bring in a fashionable (and deep-pocketed) clientele. Helpful and patient sales staff make browsing fun. *1953 N. Clybourn Ave., Clybourn Corridor, 773/281–0200. Closed Sun.*

FABRICS

2 *g-8*

A PART OF THE SOLUTION, INC.
On the city's South Side, this store supplies African fabrics, fashions, and artifacts. *321 E. 79th St., Grand Crossing, 773/723–9519.*

7 *c-1*

CALICO CORNERS
If you're seeking a fresh look for your home decor, head for this shop, which stocks all sorts of fabrics suitable for slipcovers and pillows. The staff is knowledgeable and helpful. *1525 N. Wells St., Old Town, 773/280–9707.*

8 *b-4*

FRAERMAN'S FABRICS
Across the street from the Sears Tower, this decades-old (established 1927) store offers a complete array of fabrics and provides custom drapes, slipcovers, and upholstery. *314 W. Adams St., Loop, 312/236–6886.*

6 *d-4*

FISHMAN'S FABRICS
This warehouse-size store may be the largest fabric store in the city. In addition to a huge selection of fabrics for every type of garment ranging from fine silks to imported suitings, and textiles for decorating the home, there is an exceptional department for bridal and evening wear. You will also find imported beaded and embroidered laces, ornate headpieces, exotic trims, and more. *1101 S. DesPlaines St., University Village, 312/922–7250.*

4 *a-8*

HANCOCK FABRICS
This full-service chain supplies all your sewing needs, down to patterns and tools, and even offers sewing classes. *3016 N. Ashland Ave., Lakeview, 773/549–6300.*

2 *e-3*

3326 W. Belmont Ave., Logan Square, 773/463–0180.

2 *f-1*

6101 N. Broadway, Edgewater, 773/743–6446.

2 *3-d*

4848 W. Irving Park Rd., Portage Park, 773/286–8550.

2 *f-6*

3000 S. Halsted St., Bridgeport, 312/808–0491.

1 *e-6*

JEROME FABRICS
This well-stocked store offers high-fashion fabrics as well as an outstanding selection of buttons. Bridal and formal fabrics are also available. *1750 W. 95th St., Beverly, 773/238–5560.*

2 *f-3*

JO-ANNE FABRICS & CRAFTS
Find everything you need for your sewing and art projects at the chain's Riverfront Plaza store. *2647 N. Elston Ave., Bucktown, 773/645–9075.*

7 *c-7*

LOOMCRAFT
This downtown shop pegs itself as "the home decorator fabric store," with an array of drapery, bedding, and upholstery fabrics, all at affordable prices. *640 N. LaSalle St., River North, 312/587–0055.*

2 *e-7*

SUPREME NOVELTY FABRICS
About a mile from Midway Airport, this shop has a large supply of bridal fabrics, laces, and accessories. *5954 S. Pulaski Rd., Brighton Park, 773/735–9595.*

6 *d-4*

TENNER FABRICS
This store, just off the Dan Ryan Expressway, has a great array of crepes and bridal fabrics. *605 W. Roosevelt Rd., University Village, 312/666–7980.*

7 *e-5*

VOGUE FABRICS

With two city locations, this store boasts one of the Midwest's best selection of fabrics. Designer collections, fine silks, and buttons are major attractions. *Water Tower Place, 835 N. Michigan Ave., Magnificent Mile, 312/787–2521.*

6 *d-4*

621 W. Roosevelt Rd., University Village, 312/829–2505.

8 *e-4*

WHITES FABRIC SHOP AND EMPORIUM

This downtown mart has a laundry list of fabrics: drapery, upholstery, leather, vinyls, silks, woolens, linens, ribbons, and much, much more. *226 S. Wabash Ave., Loop, 312/939–4930.*

FINE ART GALLERIES

2 *f-4*

AROUND THE COYOTE GALLERY

An offshoot of the annual Around the Coyote Walk, this gallery is open year-round and exhibits work by 30 city artists and designers. *1579 N. Milwaukee Ave., Wicker Park, 733/342–6777. Closed Mon.–Wed.*

7 *c-6*

CARL HAMMER GALLERY

It emphasizes outsider and self-taught artists, such as Lee Godie and Mr. Imagination. *740 N. Wells St., River North, 312/266–8512. Closed Sun.–Mon.*

7 *b-6*

CATHERINE EDELMAN GALLERY

It specializes in contemporary photography. *300 W. Superior St., River North, 312/266–2350. Closed Sun.–Mon.*

7 *c-6*

DOUGLAS DAWSON

This gallery brings the spirit of ancient peoples to life with art, textiles, furniture, and urns from Africa, China, and Tibet. *222 W. Huron St., River North, 312/751–1961. Closed Sun.*

7 *c-6*

G. R. N'NAMDI GALLERY

Check out the works by contemporary painters and sculptors, with an emphasis on black and Latin-American artists. *230 W. Huron St., River North, 312/587–8262. Closed Sun.–Mon.*

5 *c-2*

LILL STREET GALLERY

Contemporary, functional art and sculptures are the highlights here. It represents more than 100 emerging and established artists nationwide. *1021 W. Lill St., Lincoln Park, 773/477–6185.*

7 *e-7*

R. S. JOHNSON FINE ART

This downtown gallery carries both old masters and 20th-century works worthy of many museums. *645 N. Michigan Ave., Magnificent Mile, 312/943–1661.*

7 *e-5*

RICHARD GRAY GALLERY

An out-of-the-way gallery, on the 25th floor of the John Hancock Center, it displays modern masters. *John Hancock Center, 875 N. Michigan Ave., Magnificent Mile, 312/642–8877.*

FLOWERS & PLANTS

florists

5 *f-6*

BELLA BELLO

The flowers are good here, but the Portuguese and French imported soaps are outstanding. *12 W. Maple St., Gold Coast, 773/252–9538.*

4 *c-8*

FLOWER BUCKET

Prices are a drop in the old bucket at this chain. Can you beat $8.99 for a dozen roses, cash and carry? Similar bargains can be had on other posies. *1201 W. Belmont Ave., Lakeview, 773/281–9773.*

4 *d-6*

THE FLOWER CART

Unique fresh floral arrangements with unusual choices of flowers are the forte of this Lakeview shop. Accessories and giftware in a range of prices are also on offer. *3819 N. Broadway, Lakeview, 773/477–7755. Closed Sun.*

5 *f-4*
A NEW LEAF
Put this one on your "A" list. This shop stocks an astonishing and enticing choice of flowers, pottery, and copperware, all reasonably priced. The expansive second location is two blocks north and devoted to rustic American antique furnishings and objects as well as unusual decorative accessories from all over the world. *1645 N. Wells St., Old Town, 312/642–1576.*

5 *f-4*
1818 N. Wells St., Old Town, 312/642–8553.

4 *b-1*
POTPOURRI FLOWER SHOP
This is a wonderful spot for cut flowers, European silk flowers, imported dried flowers, and plants. *5243 N. Clark St., Andersonville, 773/561–2253.*

6 *d-1*
VILLARI FLORIST
You'll find an antidote to the Loop's concrete in the form of freshly cut flowers and plants, particularly bonsai and orchids. *601 W. Randolph St., West Loop, 312/382–1600. Closed Sun.*

7 *d-7*
ZUVERINK
Look once, they look real; look twice, they still look pretty real, but the flowers at this downtown store never wilt. These deceivingly "fresh" silk and dried flowers are beautifully arranged—and expensive. *1 E. Erie St., Magnificent Mile, 312/751–2290. Closed Sun.*

nurseries

5 *c-1*
FERTILE DELTA
City gardeners swear by this plant and garden center, which stocks an outstanding selection of unique and hard-to-find plants. Most notably, it sells straight-from-the-farm Christmas trees. *2760 N. Lincoln Ave., Lincoln Park, 773/929–5350.*

2 *f-2*
GETHSEMANE GARDEN CENTER
Hard-core gardeners can find everything they need at this complex, which includes outdoor areas filled with plants and an extensive indoor shop filled with garden items, decorative home accessories, and gifts. There is an outstanding selection of annuals, perennials, trees, garden ornaments, fountains, tools, and structural components such as bricks and arbors. Landscape, design, and installation services are also available. *5739 N. Clark St., Edgewater, 773/878–5915.*

5 *c-3*
JAYSON HOME & GARDEN
This spacious Lincoln Park store sells various topiaries, plants, flowers, and gardening tools. Here you can buy your pumpkin for Halloween and a tree at Christmastime. Huge stocks of home furnishings and accessories are also sold. *1915 N. Clybourn Ave., Clybourn Corridor, 773/525–3100.*

5 *c-4*
SMITH & HAWKEN
The swank catalog springs to life in this gargantuan store near Lincoln Park. Pretty gardening supplies, accessories, and books are all a bit expensive. *1780 N. Marcey St., Clybourn Corridor, 312/266–1988.*

5 *c-3*
URBAN GARDENER
In a quaint, turn-of-the-20th-century building, with boxes of flowers dripping from the eaves during the summer, this Lincoln Park store sells plants, interesting garden architectural salvage, a wide range of classy garden furniture, pots, and gardening-related books. *1006 W. Armitage Ave., Lincoln Park, 773/477–2070.*

FOOD & DRINK

2 *e-7*
BOBAK SAUSAGE
Though there is a renowned meat counter laden with sausages of every ilk, don't be deceived by the name of this place. It is actually a gleaming, full-service, traditional European grocery that has every food imaginable, including a good produce section, hard-to-find imported groceries, and a cafeteria for eating on-premises. *5275 S. Archer Ave., Brighton Park, 773/735–5334.*

2 *e-7*

GILMART
This South Side market is a few blocks south of Bobak Sausage and the stock is very similar, right down to the comprehensive meat department and excellent, on-premises cafeteria. It's just a bit more old world and less glitzy. *5050 S. Archer Ave., Brighton Park, 773/585–5514.*

4 *c-2*

OLD WORLD MARKET
Cosmopolitan comestibles, including foods from the Caribbean, Africa, and Latin America, are for sale at this Uptown mart. *5129 N. Broadway, Uptown, 773/989–4440.*

breads & pastries

4 *a-1*

A TASTE OF HEAVEN
Despite its quaint, low-key appearance, this is one of several bakeries that supply high-profile stores such as Neiman Marcus with sumptuous cakes, which are the specialty here. There is also a café on the premises. *1701 W. Foster Ave., Andersonville, 773/989–0151.*

7 *d-3*

ALBERT'S CAFÉ
The traditional European pastry counter is stocked with an irresistible and ever-changing array of pastries, pies, tarts, and cakes; the wedding cakes are a strong suit. The café has an excellent bistro-style menu as well. *52 W. Elm St., Gold Coast, 312/751–0666.*

2 *f-4*

ANN'S BAKERY
Follow your nose to this wonderful old-world bakery for yummy rye and black bread, rolls, and cakes. *2158 W. Chicago Ave., Ukrainian Village, 773/384–5562.*

4 *c-8*

BITTERSWEET
There's an airy European-style café in the front half of this bakery just in case you can't wait to get home to sample the wares. And for good reason, since it is considered one of the city's best sources for pastries and cakes and it supplies posh restaurants and department stores with its desserts. Though taste comes first, the fare here is also exquisitely crafted. *1114 W. Belmont Ave., Lakeview, 773/929–1100.*

8 *e-2*

BOUDIN SOUR DOUGH BAKERY
The standout here is San Francisco sourdough bread, baked fresh daily. *20 N. Michigan Ave., Loop, 312/332–1849.*

8 *a-3*
500 W. Madison St., West Loop, 312/715–1255.

8 *e-1*
225 N. Michigan Ave., Loop, 312/565–2323.

7 *e-5*
900 N. Michigan Ave., Magnificent Mile, 312/649–3570.

3 *g-3*

CAFÉ SELMARIE
Although the address suggests otherwise, this charming old-fashioned café and bakery is on Giddings Avenue, around the corner from Lincoln and facing a little park. Besides picking up great baked treats, or even ordering a wedding cake, it's a great place for sandwiches and salads along with dessert. *4729 N. Lincoln Ave., Lincoln Square, 773/989–5595. Closed Mon.*

7 *d-7*

CORNER BAKERY
You won't be able to resist the enticing and wonderfully aromatic array of breads, including raisin pecan, fig anise, potato dill, rosemary olive oil, onion, and whole wheat sourdough. There's also a café selling scones, muffins, toast, and coffee in the morning; weekend brunch is in an adjacent restaurant. *516 N. Clark St., River North, 312/644–8100.*

8 *d-3*
140 S. Dearborn St., Loop, 312/920–9100.

7 *f-6*
676 N. St. Clair St., Streeterville, 312/266–2570.

7 *e-5*
900 N. Michigan Ave., Magnificent Mile, 312/573–9900.

7 *d-4*
1121 N. State St., Gold Coast, 312/787–1969.

8 *e-2*
78 E. Washington St., Loop, 312/201–0805.

4 *a-7*
DINKEL'S BAKERY
With more than 50 years of sweet-temptation experience, this huge, third-generation Lakeview bakeshop knows how to please with its stollen, coffee cakes, decorated cakes for all occasions, chocolate-chip cookies, and almond, apple, poppy-seed, and walnut strudel. *3329 N. Lincoln Ave., West Lakeview, 773/281–7300.*

2 *d-2*
GLADSTONE PARK BAKERY
Named for the neighborhood it serves, this wonderful bakery sells luscious whipped- or butter-cream cakes with interesting fillings like white fudge, apricot, and banana cream. The staff will decorate your cake while you wait. *5744 N. Milwaukee Ave., Gladstone Park, 773/774–4210.*

7 *d-6*
LET THEM EAT CAKE
The best ingredients can be put together in the form of your favorite pet, car, or person. Wedding cakes are a specialty. *60 E. Chicago Ave., Magnificent Mile, 708/863–4200.*

8 *e-2*
66 E. Washington St., Loop, 708/863–4200.

8 *d-4*
17 W. Jackson Blvd., Loop, 708/863–4200.

8 *c-2*
179 W. Washington St., Loop, 312/863–4200.

3 *g-4*
LUTZ CONTINENTAL CAFÉ AND PASTRY SHOP
This fabulous bakery, which also houses one of the city's most charming European cafés, gets raves for producing the best and richest baked goods in Chicago. Try the glorious Viennese pastries and incredible Black Forest cake, or order a portrait cake for a special occasion. *2458 W. Montrose Ave., Ravenswood, 773/478–7785. Closed Mon.*

4 *d-8*
RHAMIG'S HOUSE OF FINE CHOCOLATES
This classic old-world bakery makes fine chocolates on the premises. Selections include truffles, butter creams, and chocolate-covered fruits and nuts. *3109*

N. Broadway, Lakeview, 773/525–8338. Closed Mon.

2 *f-4*
RED HEN BREAD
The fresh, authentic French provincial decor of this bakery is fitting for the kind of food served here. Breads range from hale and hearty whole grain and country loaves to offerings made with spices or chocolate, and all are elegantly wrapped in wax paper and string to go. This is another bakery that supplies the local restaurants of note with its goods. *1623 N. Milwaukee Ave., Bucktown, 773/342–6825. Closed Mon.*

2 *e-4*
ROESER'S
This German bakery stocks good breads, rolls, pastries, and coffee cakes. You'll also find homemade ice cream. *3216 W. North Ave., Humboldt Park, 773/489–6900. Closed Sun.*

4 *b-1*
SWEDISH BAKERY
One of the anchors of a once-Swedish, but now diverse, neighborhood, this bakery serves pastries, cookies, and traditional butter-cream cakes. The coffee cakes are a standout. *5348 N. Clark St., Andersonville, 773/561–8919.*

4 *b-7*
SWEET MYSTERIES
"Killer cakes" is the motto here, and it may very well kill you to cut these masterpieces, since they are uncommonly beautiful, crafted by the artist turned baker who owns this shop. They also taste as good as they look and are supplied to chic restaurants and department stores such as Neiman Marcus. The place is renowned for its carrot, fudge, and mousse cakes, and ruggeleh, as well as a whopping yet reasonably priced 6-pound pound cake in four flavors. *3335 N. Southport Ave., Lakeview, 773/404–2900. Closed Mon.*

coffee & tea

6 *d-1*
CAFÉ APOLLO
Illycafe, an excellent Italian coffee, is the brand used here. But there's more than just top-notch coffee at this cute café, especially for the sweet-toothed, who can choose between homemade cook-

ies, cakes, and gelato. *800 W. Washington Blvd., West Loop, 312/850–4124.*

4 *d-7*

COFFEE & TEA EXCHANGE
Get a cuppa Joe from people who know their beans. This store stocks coffee in bulk or ground to order. It also has a good assortment of teas. *3311 N. Broadway, Lakeview, 773/528–2241.*

5 *d-3*

833 W. Armitage Ave., Lincoln Park, 773/ 929–6730.

4 *d-8*

**INTELLIGENTSIA
COFFEE ROASTERS
AND TEA BLENDERS**
This roaster and blender wins lots of local "Best of" awards, and with good reason. The widely varied teas are bold and flavorful, and the coffee has such a popular following that many area restaurants use the beans. If you buy a pound of coffee you get a free cup—a perfect excuse to linger in the comfortable shop and sip slowly. *3123 N. Broadway, Lakeview, 773/348–8058.*

5 *c-5*

PEET'S COFFEE AND TEA
The California company famous for its very strong beans has come to Chicago, and the locals couldn't be happier or more alert. The coffee shop, which has some seating, also serves pastries and teas. Although situated in the busy Whole Foods Shopping Center, it is blissfully devoid of chaos. *1000 W. North Ave., Clybourn Corridor, 312/475–9782.*

5 *f-4*

SAVORIES
A recent move across the street didn't slow business down for one minute at this homespun shop, where comfy couches, unsophisticated service, and less-than-perfect presentation are part of the charm. In addition to standard coffee drinks, there's a creative array of smoothies and a small menu of tasty sandwiches, muffins, and the like. *1700 N. Wells St., Old Town, 312/951–7638.*

5 *c-1*

SOMETHING'S BREWING
This area shop will wake you up with its fresh roasted and ground coffee. You can sit or stand at the coffee-and-tea bar while contemplating purchasing

espresso machines, teapots, mugs, coffeepots, and grinders. *2677 N. Lincoln Ave., Ravenswood, 773/871–7475.*

B *c-3*

STARBUCKS
In case you hadn't noticed, they're everywhere. Why fight it? Treat yourself to a latte and relax. Besides the basic menu of coffee-based drinks and baked goods, there are also a small lunch menu and several ground coffees by the pound. *105 W. Adams St., Loop, 312/855–0099.*

6 *e-7*

**TEN REN TEA
& GINSENG COMPANY**
It's always teatime at this Chinese tea company, where sample cups of green, black, oolong, and more exotic varieties like our favorite, hibiscus spice, are yours for the sipping. Feeling decadent? Splurge on one of the specialty teas, kept in gold urns behind the counter, that can cost upwards of $100 a pound. *2247 S. Wentworth Ave., Chinatown, 312/ 842–1171.*

cheese

**GOLD STANDARD &
CHALET WINE SHOPS**
This award-winning wine store carries a wide variety of cheese. *3000 N. Clark St., Lakeview, 773/935–9400.*

SAM'S LIQUORS
Try some of the 250 different cheeses sold at this store, in addition to the wide selection of fine wines. The erudite staff can assist you in your selection. *1720 N. Marcey St., Lincoln Park, 312/664–4394.*

chocolate & other candy

2 *f-1*

AFFY TAPPLE, INC.
Itching for a taffy apple or frozen banana? Indulge here—seconds are 50% off. *7110 N. Clark St., Rogers Park, 773/338–1100. Closed Sun.*

7 *e-5*

**AUNT DIANA'S
OLD-FASHIONED FUDGE**
Forget your waistline at this downtown sweet shop. You'll find homemade fudge in nine mouthwatering flavors. *Water Tower Place, 835 N. Michigan Ave., 5th level, Magnificent Mile, 321/664–1535.*

7 a-8

BLOMMER'S CHOCOLATE FACTORY

This River North store is the place to come to buy the absolutely scrumptious chocolate chefs use to make their goodies. *600 W. Kinzie St., River West, 312/226–7700. Closed weekends.*

2 f-2

DELICATESSEN MEYER

This European delicatessen stocks a wide variety of imported sweets. There are candies from Austria and Germany and chocolate eggs at Easter filled with marzipan, kirsch, nougat, and truffle. *4750 N. Lincoln Ave., Lincoln Square, 773/561–3377.*

7 e-5

FANNIE MAY

Chicago's own for more than 70 years has more than 100 types of scrumptious chocolates in addition to fudge and peanut brittle. *638 N. Michigan Ave., Magnificent Mile, 312/337–7363.*

7 c-1

THE FUDGE POT

You don't want to go to this shop on an empty stomach . . . or maybe you do. Ever since 1963, this heavenly spot has sold personalized lollipops, handmade chocolates, homemade fudge, caramel apples, truffles, toffee, chocolate-dipped strawberries, and chocolate-dipped bananas. *1532 N. Wells St., Old Town, 312/943–1777.*

7 e-5

GHIRARDELLI CHOCOLATE

In addition to buying the myriad products made by this famous San Francisco chocolatier, you can have a sinfully dreamy treat in the old-fashioned ice cream parlor. *118 E. Pearson St., Magnificent Mile, 312/337–9330.*

7 e-5

GODIVA

At 80 years and ticking, this Belgian retailer offers the ultimate in sweet indulgence—painstakingly wrapped chocolates for instantaneous consumption or gifts. *Water Tower Place, 845 N. Michigan Ave., 3rd level, Magnificent Mile, 312/280–1133.*

2 f-4

MARGIE'S CANDIES

This Bucktown family business, open for more than 70 years, concocts sensational fountain creations as well as hand-dipped (in view in the window) chocolates. Here you'll find the "world's largest sundae" with a half gallon of fresh homemade ice cream topped with homemade fudge. *1960 N. Western Ave., Bucktown, 773/384–1035.*

8 d-2

MARSHALL FIELD'S

Frangos, a Field's and Chicago staple treat, have been made on the premises since 1921. The original mint has been joined by almond, coffee, lemon, orange, raspberry, rum, and one of the newest, peanut butter. Related specialties and imports are also available. *111 N. State St., at Randolph St., 1st floor, Loop, 312/781–1000.*

4 d-8

RHAMIG'S HOUSE OF FINE CHOCOLATES

Though this is a classic European-style bakery that specializes in "old world" treats, such as dobosh tortes and Linzer tortes, it is most famous for its made-on-premises fine chocolates. *3109 N. Broadway, Lakeview, 773/525–8338. Closed Mon.*

5 c-3

VIVANTE CHOCOLATIER

This Lincoln Park store crafts mouthwatering, luscious chocolates and wondrous gift baskets. It makes 90% of its chocolates on the premises. Try the chocolate-dipped potato chips. *1056 W. Webster Ave., Lincoln Park, 773/549–0123.*

2 f-4

VOSGES HAUT CHOCOLAT

You'll find exotic and creative handmade truffles with names like "Woolloomooloo," "Black Pearl," and "Viola" at this fine chocolate shop. They look almost too good to eat and, in fact, are divine. *2105 W. Armitage Ave., Bucktown, 773/772–5349. Closed Sun.*

ethnic foods

6 b-4

CONTE-DI-SAVOIA EUROPEAN SPECIALTIES

This Little Italy shop is a veritable international foods bazaar with Russian, Polish, English, French, Italian, and German goods. You'll find imported oils, vinegars, dried fruits, coffees, teas, homemade pastas and cheese, and barrels of spices, grains, and olives. *1438 W. Taylor St., University Village, 312/666–3471.*

4 b-1
ERIKSON'S DELICATESSEN
It has a smorgasbord of delights, including herring, Scandinavian cheeses such as Norway's clove-studded nokkelost limpa, and flat breads. *5250 N. Clark St., Andersonville, 773/561–5634.*

3 f-3
HELLAS PASTRY
This North Side Greek bakery sells mouthwatering phyllo rolls filled with cheese or spinach, and baklava and custard pastries. *2627 W. Lawrence Ave., Ravenswood, 773/271–7500.*

7 e-5
L'APPETITO
If it's a taste of Italy you crave, the Italian specialties such as pastries, gelato, and delicious panini here just might cure you. *John Hancock Center, 875 N. Michigan Ave., lower level, Magnificent Mile, 312/337–0691.*

7 e-6
30 E. Huron St., Gold Coast, 312/787–9881.

2 f-2
DELICATESSEN MEYER
The mouthwatering smell of garlic-infused meats hits you as you step in the door of this European delicatessen, where products from Austria and Germany dominate the stock. It also sells sausages and brats made by different local butchers; whole grain pumpernickels and ryes from small bakeries around the city; prepared meats and salads; and imported candies and chocolates. *4750 N. Lincoln Ave., Lincoln Square, 773/561–3377.*

5 a-8
MIKOLAJCZYK SAUSAGE CO.
You'll find the Polish foods, including good sausages, that your grandma loves in this shop near the Loop. *1737 W. Division St., Ukrainian Village, 773/486–8870. Closed Sun.*

6 f-6
ORIENTAL FOOD MARKET
In the heart of Chinatown is this emporium filled with all the ingredients—including great egg rolls, bok choy, and tofu—for your next Chinese or Japanese meal. *2002 S. Wentworth Ave., Chinatown, 312/949–1060.*

4 a-7
PAULINA MARKET
Stroll here for delicious Swedish-style smoked meats and fish, including ham, salmon, lake trout, and goose breast. *3501 N. Lincoln Ave., Lakeview, 773/248–6272. Closed Sun.*

2 c-3
RIVIERA ITALIAN IMPORTED FOODS
Looking for authentic Italian foods? Try this North Side shop, which stocks a wide selection of Italian sausage and beef, cheeses, salads, and breads. *3220 N. Harlem Ave., Elmwood Park, 773/637–4252.*

7 d-3
TREASURE ISLAND
Chef Julia Child calls this "the best grocery in the nation." *75 W. Elm St., Gold Coast, 312/440–1144.*

fish & seafood

5 d-5
BURHOP'S
This store has been specializing in the finest fresh fish and seafood since 1926. It sells cooked shrimp, crab cakes, seafood salad, poached salmon, and smoked fish, along with fresh bread and wine. *Father & Son Plaza, 609 W. North Ave., Old Town, 312/642–8600.*

health foods

2 e-1
ALL THE BEST NATURAL FOODS
Sandwiches, groceries, and herbal teas can be found at this West Rogers Park store. Kosher products including Freeda Natural Vitamins are also available. *3008 W. Devon Ave., Rogers Park, 773/274–9478.*

2 *e-3*

CHICAGO NUTRITION CENTER

This store sells whole grains and flours, dairy products, vegetables, books, and vitamins at a 10% discount. *1924 W. Chicago Ave., Wicker Park, 773/227–8022. No credit cards. Closed Sun.*

2 *f-1*

HEARTLAND

This general store and café was one of the first health food spots in the city and will take you back to the '60s, with its stock of teas, grains, baked goods, and natural cosmetics. *7000 N. Glenwood Ave., Rogers Park, 773/465–8005.*

4 *d-8*

LIFE SPRING

Near Lincoln Park, this shop has a juice bar and sells health foods, sandwiches, and ice cream. *3178 N. Clark St., Lakeview, 773/327–1023.*

5 *d-1*

SHERWYN'S HEALTH FOOD STORES

Dairy products, whole grains, flours, nuts, herbs, organic produce, and decaffeinated coffee are sold here. You will also find one of the best selections of vitamins around, along with a staff that really knows its business to help you make appropriate choices. *645 W. Diversey Ave., Lakeview, 773/477–1934.*

2 *h-7*

SUNFLOWER SEED HEALTH FOODS

This shop stocks dairy products, herb teas, freshly ground peanut butter, vitamins, and minerals. *5210 S. Harper Ave., Hyde Park, 773/363–1600.*

4 *a-7*

WHOLE FOODS MARKET

If you've never tasted a fresh orange that hasn't been injected with dye, you will absolutely love the organic produce at this store, ever popular with strict vegetarians. But be forewarned: you will pay a hefty price for the superb produce. There's a great selection of spices, which you buy by the gram. *3300 N. Ashland Ave., Lakeview, 773/244–4200.*

5 *c-4*

1000 W. North Ave., Clybourn Corridor, 312/587–0648.

5 *f-7*

50 W. Huron Ave., Gold Coast, 312/932–9600.

herbs & spices

2 *f-2*

DR. MICHAEL'S HERB CENTER

Long before herbs became a fad, the aromatic plants were a specialty here. The 70-year-old shop stocks more than 400 varieties of herbs. *5109 N. Western Ave., Ravenswood, 773/271–7738. Closed Sun.*

2 *f-2*

MERZ APOTHECARY

This shop imparts an old-world air with its homeopathic and herbal remedies. The store also sells hard-to-find European toiletries. *4716 N. Lincoln Ave., Lincoln Square, 773/989–0900. Closed Sun.*

2 *d-2*

MONK'S HERB CENTER

You can choose from the many, many prepackaged herbs here. *4732 N. Milwaukee Ave., Jefferson Park, 773/205–0639.*

meats & poultry

6 *d-1*

COLUMBUS MEAT MARKET

Buy where the restaurants buy at this mart, which mostly sells wholesale. *906 W. Randolph St., West Loop, 312/829–2480.*

2 *f-2*

MUELLER MEATS

This West Ridge butcher shop sells a variety of meats, including pork, beef, and lamb, at reasonable prices. The staff are on hand to aid in your selection. *2439 W. Peterson Ave., West Rogers Park, 773/561–7580. Closed Tues.*

7 *c-1*

OLD TOWNE BUTCHER SHOP

Despite its Old English spelling, this shop is decidedly hip, even if it looks old-fashioned with the ceiling fans lazily spinning overhead. You'll not only find prime cuts, a delicatessen, and specialty produce, but proprietor Dan Noonan also stocks turkey veggie patties. *1547 N. Wells St., Old Town, 312/640–0256.*

6 *d-1*

PEPE'S MEAT PACKING
Save big bucks on a wide array of meats, competitively priced. *853 W. Randolph St., West Loop, 312/421–2488.*

nuts & seeds

4 *c-6*

NUTS ON CLARK
Go nuts for pistachios, almonds, even chocolate at this downtown shop. Yummy samples are available. Call to find other locations around the city. *3830 N. Clark St., Lakeview, 773/549–6622.*

7 *c-6*

RICCI & COMPANY
In business since 1919, this River North shop sells salters and roasting nuts on premises. It also has a discount retail outlet. *162 W. Superior St., River West, 312/787–7660. Closed Sun.*

2 *d-3*

SUPERIOR NUTS
Nut lovers come from all over to buy the delicious cashews and pistachios at this shop, which also proffers candies. *4038 N. Nashville Ave., Dunning, 773/282–3930. Closed Sun.*

produce

5 *b-5*

STANLEY'S FRUITS & VEGETABLES
Seemingly in the middle of nowhere, this tiny shop in between Lincoln Park, Bucktown, and Wicker Park stocks an incredible fresh selection of vegetables and fruits that brings shoppers from all over the city, including the Gold Coast. *1558 N. Elston Ave., West Town, 773/276–8050. No credit cards.*

WHOLE FOODS MARKET
The organic produce comes at a price here, but the quality is superb. There is also a wide selection of spices sold by the gram. *3300 N. Ashland Ave., Lakeview, 773/244–4200.*

wines & spirits

5 *b-7*

CASEY'S
Stock up on beer before the next big game or important barbecue at this liquor store. with more than 700 brews in stock. *1444 W. Chicago Ave., River West, 800/213–2337.*

4 *d-8*

GOLD STANDARD & CHALET WINE SHOPS
This award-winning store carries an impressive array of wine, spirits, cheese, and cigars. *3000 N. Clark St., Lakeview, 773/935–9400.*

5 *e-3*

405 W. Armitage Ave., Lincoln Park, 312/266–7155.

7 *e-5*

40 E. Delaware Pl., Streeterville, 312/787–8555.

2 *h-7*

1531 E. 53rd St., Hyde Park, 773/324–5000.

7 *c-3*

HOUSE OF GLUNZ
This atmospheric store is the city's oldest wine shop. *1206 N. Wells St., Old Town, 312/642–3000.*

7 *b-7*

JOHN HART FINE WINE LTD.
There's no showroom for this wine store, just a temperature-controlled warehouse. But you can get just about any fine or rare wine, all competitively priced. Sales are by phone, fax, or e-mail only. *363 W. Erie St., lower level, River West, 312/482–9996.*

5 *d-5*

LEONARD SOLOMON WINES & SPIRITS
This boutique sells Italian, French, Australian, Californian, Spanish, and other wines. *1456 N. Dayton St., Old Town, 312/915–5911.*

5 *c-4*

SAM'S LIQUORS
This store is the place to buy sensational fine wine. There's a dizzying selection of more than 300,000 reasonably priced bottles as well as an impressive collection of 250 different types of cheese. Ask the knowledgeable staff for help. *1720 N. Marcey St., Lincoln Park, 312/664–4394.*

7 *d-7*

SANDBURG WINE CELLAR

It sells reasonably priced wines. *1525 N. Clark St., Gold Coast, 312/337–7537.*

5 *b-4*

WINE DISCOUNT CENTER

The name says it all for this Bucktown store selling thousands of different wines. You can sample varieties at Saturday wine tastings. *1826½ N. Elston Ave., West Town, 773/489–3454.*

7 *c-7*

ZIMMERMAN'S CUT RATE LIQUOR STORE

This River North shop stocks a superb selection of French, Italian, and German wines. *213 W. Grand Ave., 312/332–0012.*

FRAMING

5 *c-4*

ARTISTS' FRAME SERVICE

This gargantuan operation enjoys a citywide reputation for the excellent job it consistently performs on both routine and intricate framing projects. It is also known for its trained design staff that aids in making framing decisions, the huge range of frames available, and its exceptionally broad selection of archive-quality materials. *1915 N. Clybourn Ave., Clybourn Corridor, 773/248–7713. Closed Sun.*

5 *c-4*

ARTISTS' FRAME SERVICE OUTLET

There are no framing services here, but you can save 50%–80% on framing materials at this outlet for Artists' Frame Service (see above). *1855 N. Clybourn Ave., Clybourn Corridor, 773/880–1165. Closed Mon.–Wed.*

4 *d-8*

BILLY HORK FRAMING

At this excellent Lakeview frame source, you'll find metal moldings, wood frames, and museum-quality mats. *3033 N. Clark St., 773/935–9700.*

4 *a-8*

FRAME FACTORY

The price is often right at this large, warehouse-style framing source, where every imaginable option is available. Choose from ready-made frames or con-

trive your own creations. Wholesale and conservation-quality framing services are also available. *3030 N. Ashland Ave., Lakeview, 773/929–1010.*

2 *e-3*

3400 N. Pulaski Ave., Old Irving, 773/427–1010.

7 *b-5*

FRAMEWAY STUDIOS, INC.

This shop does complete custom framing, including photo and specialty mounting and, for your significant art works, conservation framing. *875 N. Orleans St., River North, 312/751–1660. Closed weekends.*

2 *f-2*

GRANVILLE GALLERY

The staff at this Edgewater gallery doesn't put on airs but does do museum-quality work, so don't expect a quick turn-around on your frames. *6200 Broadway, Edgewater, 773/764–1919. Closed Sun.*

5 *b-7*

THE GREAT FRAME UP

This frame-it-yourself store offers step-by-step instruction as well as a great selection of frames, moldings, mats, and dry mounting. *2905 N. Broadway, Lakeview, 773/549–3927.*

7 *d-3*

21 W. Elm St., Gold Coast, 312/939–0914.

2 *h-7*

1418 E. 53rd St., Hyde Park, 773/752–2020.

2 *b-1*

7055 Higgins Ave., Norridge, 773/763–0310.

5 *c-3*

HELLMAN FRAME SHOP

This friendly little custom frame shop specializes in conservation framing and is more intimate than the big warehouse-style shops that dominate the market. *953 W. Webster Ave., Lincoln Park, 773/525–7757. Closed Fri. and Sun.*

GIFTS & SOUVENIRS

8 *b-4*

ACCENT CHICAGO

These area stores are stocked with the mandatory souvenirs and Chicago memorabilia. *Sears Tower, 233 S. Wacker Dr., Loop, 312/993–0499.*

8 *e-6*

Chicago Hilton & Towers, 720 S. Michigan Ave., South Loop, 312/360–0115.

8 *d-4*

333 S. State St., Loop, 312/922–0242. Closed Sun.

7 *d-4*

ANTHROPOLOGIE

This outpost of the national chain offers an interesting mix of new and antique home furnishings, including upholstered pieces, small decorative items, clothing, and accessories. Well-edited home and fashion selections are reasonably priced. *1120 N. State St., Gold Coast, 312/255–1848.*

8 *e-3*

ART INSTITUTE OF CHICAGO'S MUSEUM SHOP

These gift shops feature museum reproductions in the form of jewelry, posters, and books, along with impressive tabletop accents, decorative accessories, and toys. *111 S. Michigan Ave., Loop, 312/443–3535.*

7 *e-3*

900 N. Michigan Ave., Magnificent Mile, 312/482–8275.

5 *f-6*

BELLA BELLO

The imported French and Portuguese soaps and the wide selection of fresh flowers here make great gifts. *12 W. Maple St., Gold Coast, 773/252–9538.*

7 *e-5*

CHIASSO

This Magnificent Mile boutique emphasizes high-style contemporary home and office accessories; there's plenty that appeals to men. *Water Tower Place, 835 N. Michigan Ave., Magnificent Mile, 312/280–1249.*

7 *e-6*

CHIAROSCURO

This eclectic downtown shop represents artists who create whimsical jewelry, home accessories, and furniture. *Chicago Place, 700 N. Michigan Ave., Magnificent Mile, 312/988–9253.*

8 *e-4*

CHICAGO ARCHITECTURE FOUNDATION

Architecture buffs will love the stylish Windy City mementos such as books, posters, T-shirts, toys, and ties, as well as decorative home accessories related to architecture. Find Frank Lloyd Wright–designed china and glasses, plaster casts of Louis Sullivan terracotta panels, and stained-glass lamps with Prairie or Arts and Crafts motifs. *224 S. Michigan Ave., Loop, 312/922–3432.*

7 *e-5*

John Hancock Center, 875 N. Michigan Ave., Magnificent Mile, 312/751–1380.

7 *e-5*

CITY OF CHICAGO STORE

This store sells unusual city souvenirs, ranging from a street sign to a brick from the old Comiskey Park. It's also an excellent source for guidebooks, posters, and T-shirts. *Chicago Waterworks, 811 N. Michigan Ave., Magnificent Mile, 312/744–9197.*

2 *f-4*

ECLECTIC JUNCTION FOR ART

This wacky Bucktown store features an array of functional yet whimsical art, from drawer pulls to toilet seats. *1630 N. Damen Ave., Bucktown, 773/342–7865. Closed Mon.*

5 *d-3*

EXPRESSLY WOOD

Gifts and home accessories crafted in domestic and exotic wood are plentiful at this downtown find. You'll love the various clocks, picture frames, toys and games, and executive accessories. *825 W. Armitage Ave., Lincoln Park, 773/477–7050.*

4 *b-7*

FLY PAPER

This Lakeview shop sells zany greeting cards and gifts. *3402 N. Southport Ave., Lakeview, 773/296–4359. Closed Thurs.–Fri.*

8 *e-2*

GALLERY 37 STORE

Talk about talent! This store carries the work of student artists in the nonprofit Gallery 37 programs; proceeds are then pumped back into the group. The selection varies but may include everything from hand-painted birdbaths to small ceramics, all at affordable prices. At press time, the store was slated to move, but call ahead to be certain. *66 E. Randolph St., Loop, 312/744–7274. Closed Sun.*

7 *e-8*

HAMMACHER SCHLEMMER

Near the Chicago River, this cool shop entices with upscale gadgets and unusual gifts. Kids of all ages gravitate to the space where visitors can play with some of the toys. *Tribune Tower, 445 N. Michigan Ave., Magnificent Mile, 312/527–9100.*

4 *d-7*

HE WHO EATS MUD

This shop stocks whimsical gifts, including interesting cards, gifts, candles, soaps, and costume jewelry. *3247 N. Broadway, Lakeview, 773/525–0616.*

5 *c-2*

HEALING EARTH RESOURCES

Sooth and nurture your spirit and senses with the wide range of practical and ethereal offerings at this shop, which may be the largest of its kind in the city. There's everything from Tibetan bowls, sculptures and artworks with a spiritual component, and artisan-made jewelry studded with mood-enhancing or protective stones to incense, candles, natural toiletries and cosmetics, books, and toys. *3111 N. Ashland Ave., Lakeview, 773/327–8459.*

8 *c-2*

ILLINOIS ARTISANS SHOP

It chooses the best work of craftspeople statewide, including jewelry, ceramics, glass, and African-American dolls, selling them at affordable prices. *James R. Thompson Center, 100 W. Randolph St., Loop, 312/814–5321. Closed weekends.*

7 *h-7*

ILLINOIS MARKET PLACE

A joint venture between the city and state, this shop features Illinois products and artists and has museum merchandise, including gift items related to Abraham Lincoln, Frank Lloyd Wright, and Route 66. *Navy Pier, 700 E. Grand Ave., Navy Pier, 312/595–5400.*

7 *f-5*

THE MUSUEM OF CONTEMPORARY ART STORE

Forget the traditional art-museum offerings and visit this large shop for the hippest gift-shop items in town. Besides cutting-edge dishes, serving pieces, jewelry, wearable accessories, and home accessories, there are artist-made T-shirts and an excellent book section on contemporary art. *220 E. Chicago Ave., Magnificent Mile, 312/397–4000. Closed Mon.*

7 *f-5*

THE SHARPER IMAGE

The gadgets catalog springs to life here in downtown Chicago, where you can find all those fascinating items you can't bear to be without such as a talking scale and a safari hat with a built-in fan. *845 N. Michigan Ave., Magnificent Mile, 312/335–1600.*

8 *d-3*

55 W. Monroe St., Loop, 312/263–4535.

HOME FURNISHINGS

5 *e-1*

AFFORDABLE PORTABLES

If you seek an inexpensive way to furnish your abode, this lively Lincoln Park shop just might be what you need. It specializes in bargain-price futons, sofas, and contemporary furniture. *2608 N. Clark St., Lincoln Park, 773/935–6160.*

7 *d-4*

ANTHROPOLOGIE

This chain features both new and antique home furnishings, including upholstered pieces and decorative objects, at reasonable prices. *1120 N. State St., Gold Coast, 312/255–1848.*

4 *a-6*

CB2

CB2, a stylish and sprawling home furnishings store in an up-and-coming area, is so named for its parent company, Crate & Barrel. Unlike Crate, it is aimed at first-time apartment dwellers who own nothing save their computers. There are lots of clean-lined, colorful basics for every room in the home, but the special emphasis is on unique yet utilitarian multifunctional storage pieces and decorative accessories that can be used in any room—all sans a big price tag. *3745 N. Lincoln Ave., Lakeview, 773/ 755–3900.*

7 *c-8*

CAMBIUM

This full-service showroom is loaded with tempting furniture and decorative accessories for every room in the home, but kitchens are the foundation here. You will find unfitted kitchen components, cooking accoutrements, and tabletop lines, ranging from winsome handmade ceramics and linens to sleek serving pieces and china by well-known designers. *113 W. Hubbard St., River North, 312/832–9920.*

5 *g-7*

CRATE & BARREL

This is the place to buy glassware, housewares, and decorative items. The new, ultramodern store on North Avenue also sells fresh flowers and has a café. Specialty items are dinnerware and glassware, including Marimekko, Kosta, and Pilgrim. *676 N. Michigan Ave., Magnificent Mile, 312/787–5900.*

5 *e-6*

850 W. North Ave., Clybourn Corridor, 312/573–9800.

1 *a-1*

CRATE & BARREL OUTLET STORE

Every day is sale day at this outlet. Seconds, closeouts, and special-purchase items are available; some of it is first-quality, too. *800 W. North Ave., Clybourn Corridor, 312/787–4775.*

5 *d-4*

ETHAN ALLEN

For a classic style, look no further than this store. It provides an interactive computer program that enables you to see how your choice of fabric and frame will look before you buy. *1700 N. Halsted St., Lincoln Park, 312/573–2500.*

7 *e-5*

LIGNE ROSET

This French furniture giant is known for its pared-down but sumptuous pieces by world-renowned European designers such as Pascal Mourgue, who is known for his use of sleek tubular steel, golden pearwood, and ripely shaped forms. Spaniard Dider Gomez, whose pieces

display a Modernist bent, is also a best-seller here. *56 E. Walton St., Magnificent Mile, 312/867–1207.*

7 *b-6*

LUMINAIRE

The city's largest and most comprehensive showroom for edgy contemporary furnishings and accessories sprawls over 20,000 square ft and three floors and features a star-studded lineup of international names and more than 80 lines. Find the work of designers Philippe Stark and Antonio Citterio and furniture by B&B Italia, Cassina, Kartell, Cappellini, Driade, Montis, Porro, and Vitra. The store has a lighting and large home accessories section, both with cutting-edge items and free design services. All staff members are trained interior designers. *301 W. Superior St., River North, 312/664–9582.*

7 *c-6*

MANIFESTO

You'll find a sizable stable of international contemporary design lines that employ warm woods, mellow metals, or richly textured fabrics. There is everything from large-scale cabinets and clean-lined upholstered pieces to sculptural decorative accessories, all with styling that is grounded in modern design but revitalized with a softer aesthetic. *755 N. Wells St., River North, 312/ 664–0733.*

7 *b-7*

MODERNICA

It makes high-quality reproductions of mid-20th-century designs as well as a line of furniture that takes its cues from the aesthetic of the modernist period. There are replicas of hard-to-find period icons by Ray and Charles Eames, George Nelson, Isamu Noguchi, Eero Saarinen, and Alvar Aalto, and the price-to-quality ratio is surprisingly reasonable. *555 N. Franklin St., River North, 312/ 222–1808.*

5 *a-1*

PIER 1 IMPORTS

Widely known for its affordable and attractive furnishings, this national chain is a prime source for contemporary wicker furnishings and goods. Many products, however, don't hold up over time. *2868 N. Ashland Ave., Lakeview, 773/975–1033.*

7 *e-6*

POTTERY BARN

This glitzy store sells lots of candles, picture frames, and other knickknacks, all with a hip, retro feel, and has almost all the furniture from the catalog as well. *734 N. Michigan Ave., Magnificent Mile, 312/587–9602.*

7 *e-6*

RETROSPECT

The period options are endless as this 14,000-square-ft sister store to Room & Board, and the name refers to the furniture that pays homage to historic influences. Collections are based on themes ranging from the Ming Dynasty to the Art Deco and Arts and Crafts movements. *Chicago Place, 700 N. Michigan Ave., Magnificent Mile, 312/266–0656.*

7 *e-6*

ROOM & BOARD

It sprawls over 40,000 square ft and has an impressive selection of furniture, all of it sturdy and attractive. There's a resemblance to Crate & Barrel. *Chicago Place, 700 N. Michigan Ave., Magnificent Mile, 312/266–0656.*

7 *c-7*

SAWBRIDGE STUDIOS

This huge studio displays custom-hand-crafted furniture, decorative accessories, and tablewares by the premier artisans and furniture makers in the U.S. There are sterling Frank Lloyd Wright, Macintosh, and Shaker reproductions as well as contemporary furniture with a crafted attitude. The tabletop, copper, and pottery lines are extensive, often exclusive to the shop, and jibe with the craft-oriented aesthetic of the furniture. *153 W. Ohio St., River North, 312/828–0055. Closed Sun.*

7 *d-6*

SHABBY CHIC

The cushy, slipcovered look reigns supreme here, but besides the upholstered pieces there is a good range of housewares, including an extraordinary cache of mostly vintage lighting, a sweet retro-inspired private line of bedding for babies and adults, and lots of vintage decorative accessories. *46 E. Superior St., Streeterville, 312/649–0080.*

7 *c-7*

WORKBENCH

The handsome American and European contemporary furniture is reasonably priced. Watch for the great sales. *640 N. LaSalle St., River North, 312/266–0089.*

2 *h-8*

7048 S. Stoney Island Ave., South Shore, 773/363–1957.

7 *d-7*

10 E. Ontario St., Streeterville, 312/944–7928.

architectural artifacts

4 *a-4*

ARCHITECTURAL ARTIFACTS

While this salvage warehouse stocks the usual array of architectural castoffs, its selection of mantelpieces, garden appointments, grills, and tiles is particularly strong. If you seek something really unusual, such as a Victorian gazebo made out of metal, an old church altar, or marble Corinthian columns, you've come to the right place. Owner Stuart Grannen travels worldwide to find the best pieces. *4325 N. Ravenswood Ave., Ravenswood, 773/348–0622.*

6 *c-5*

SALVAGE ONE

Situated in a huge building, this 100,000-square-ft Pilsen salvage warehouse draws home remodelers and restaurant designers from across the nation. It fairly brims with stained lead glass, garden ornaments, fireplace mantles, hutches, bars, hardware, tiles, and other architectural artifacts. *1524 S. Sangamon St., University Village, 312/733–0098. Closed Sun.*

carpets & rugs

7 *c-6*

CASPIAN ORIENTAL RUGS

This showroom has more than 5,000 new, antique, and used rugs. *700 N. LaSalle St., River North, 312/664–7576.*

5 *c-3*

FORTUNATE DISCOVERIES

It has a wide selection of kilims and other ethnic rugs, as well as tribal and ethnic furniture, accessories, and artifacts. *1022 W. Armitage Ave., Lincoln Park, 773/404–0212.*

7 *c-8*

OSCAR ISBERIAN RUGS

Fine antique carpets and kilims mix with new hand-knotted and woven rugs here. But the Isberian brothers scour workshops in India, Pakistan, Armenia, and Turkey for rich, densely patterned Persian and Caucasian carpets that have all the character and depth of the antiques thanks to the use of hand-spun wools, organic dyes, and traditional weaving techniques. *122 S. Kinzie St., River North, 312/467–1212.*

4 *b-8*

PEERLESS RUG COMPANY

You'll find an amazing array of Oriental and Navajo rugs as well as ceramic and vinyl tiles. *3033 N. Lincoln Ave., Lakeview, 312/525–4876.*

7 *c-7*

SOTHEBY'S MIDWEST

This counterpart of the New York Sotheby's is only open during auctions; call for a recording of upcoming events. *215 W. Ohio St., River North, 312/396–9599.*

8 *c-1*

SUSANIN'S AUCTIONEERS & APPRAISERS

There are spectacular deals to be had here on Oriental rugs, from well-worn antiques to exquisitely preserved ones. The auction house holds weekly sales but also offers most of the preview items for sale on the floor immediately. *138 Merchandise Mart, River North, 312/832–9800.*

ceramic tiles

7 *c-8*

ANN SACKS

This tony shop stocks marble and ceramic tiles that are on the pricey side. *501 N. Wells St., River North, 312/923–0919. Closed Sun.*

2 *d-2*

HISPANIC DESIGN

Portuguese, Mexican, Dutch, and Italian tiles are sold here in a variety of designs and prices. *6125 N. Cicero Ave., Sauganash, 773/725–3100. No credit cards. Closed weekends.*

4 *b-8*

PEERLESS

At this shop, you'll find mostly ceramic tiles, imported from Spain, Italy, Mexico, and Portugal. *3030 N. Lincoln Ave., Lakeview, 773/525–4876. Closed Sun.*

china, glassware, porcelain, pottery, silver

7 *c-8*

CAMBIUM

Cambium is chock-full of decorative accessories for every part of your home. Kitchens are the specialty, though, for which you will find handmade ceramics, elegant serving pieces, and china by well-known designers. *113 W. Hubbard St., River North, 312/832–9920.*

7 *e-4*

ELEMENTS

The name hints at components rather than foundations, and this shop delivers perhaps the best, and most carefully edited, inventory of cutting-edge elements for both home and fashion in the city. But the strong, varied, and engaging cache of dishes, glassware, serving pieces, and table linens is the true highlight of the shop; there is also a substantial selection of jewelry and a small but prime selection of vintage European Deco furnishings. *102 E. Oak St., Gold Coast, 312/642–6574.*

7 *e-5*

MATERIAL POSSESSIONS

The name suits the merchandising style of this shop, which overflows with batteries of goods in various categories. Although there are decorative accessories, jewelry, and fashion accessories, the most astonishing collections are the tabletop lines. Find perhaps the most comprehensive selection of serving pieces, glassware, cutlery, place mats, and table linens for casual and formal entertaining outside of the major department stores, and a bridal registry. *54 E. Chestnut St., Gold Coast, 312/280–4885.*

7 *b-7*

NO PLACE LIKE

The modernist sensibility of this store is reflected clearly in its selections of ceramic and china, fused and blown glassware, and the boldly glazed pottery that comes in streamlined shapes. *300 W. Grand St., River North, 312/822–0550.*

4 *b-6*

P.O.S.H.

This tiny store charmingly displays never-used, vintage hotel and restaurant china. There's also a grand selection of silver gravy boats, creamers, and flatware from ocean liners and private clubs long gone. *3729 N. Southport Ave., Lakeview, 773/529–7674.*

7 *c-7*

SAWBRIDGE STUDIOS

There is a strong emphasis on artisanal crafts at this store; the extensive collections of pottery and copper are often exclusively sold here. *153 W. Ohio St., River North, 312/828–0055. Closed Sun.*

5 *c-3*

TABULA TUA

This tabletop shop stays away from the format of standard place settings. Instead, the emphasis is on colorful, contemporary, mix-and-match dishes and tabletop accessories, including a range of pottery from Provence. But there are also singular mosaic tables handmade by artisans, rustic shelves and cabinets crafted from old barn wood, and large-scale armoires from France with a vintage demeanor. *1015 W. Armitage Ave., Lincoln Park, 773/525–3500.*

6 *f-7*

THAT PORCELAIN PLACE

This shop sells traditional Eastern crockery, including rice bowls, soup spoons, saucers, figurines, and vases. *2239 S. Wentworth Ave., Chinatown, 312/225–3888.*

furniture & accessories

5 *f-4*

A NEW LEAF

For reasonably priced pieces of pottery and copperware, have a look at the large selection available here. For antique rustic furnishings from around America, as well as decorative objects from around the world, visit the second location two blocks north. *1645 N. Wells St., Old Town, 312/642–1576.*

5 *b-6*

CASA LOCA

Filled with rustic, reasonably priced furniture from Mexico and south-of-the-border folk art, this shop also stocks gorgeous Guatemalan and Mexican pottery and textiles. Anyone with something to display will also appreciate the large selection of vintage repisa shelves. *1130 N. Milwaukee Ave., Wicker Park, 773/278–2972.*

2 *f-4*

CIELO VIVO

Step into another world at this intimate shop, so densely layered with exotic and enticing items you'll think you're in a foreign bazaar rather than an inner-city shop. But there's no bartering for the ethnic art, textiles, rugs, furniture, and decorative accessories from Asia, North and South America, the Middle East, and Africa. *1528 N. Milwaukee Ave., Wicker Park, 773/276–8012. Closed Mon.–Tues.*

5 *c-4*

COST PLUS
WORLD MARKET

Near Lincoln Park, this mart has the feel of an international general store, with furniture and goods from all over the world, ranging from unusual jams to exotic oils and funky things like piñatas for your next party. What's more, it's all fairly priced. *1623 N. Sheffield Ave., Clybourn Corridor, 312/587–0364.*

4 *b-7*

ELIZABETH MARIE

This lovely boutique sells an array of vintage children's furniture. It's also one of the few places in town where you can buy Amy Coe bedding and Maine cottage furniture. *3453 N. Southport Ave., Lakeview, 773/525–4100.*

2 *f-4*

EMBELEZAR

It takes its name from the Portuguese word for "embellish," and its stock lives up to the name. Wares include elegant garden and home items, sumptuous sofas, beautiful teak dining-room sets, and a great choice of silk-covered items made in Venice. *1639 N. Damen Ave., Bucktown, 773/645–9705.*

7 *b-7*

ESTHETICS

All things Eastern, and slightly exotic, reign supreme here, from the wide range of Raj-inspired lustrous teak and wrought-iron furniture from Indonesia and the Philippines to the opulent, richly hued silks from India that are used in table linens, wall hangings, duvet covers, pillows, and upholstery. All the furniture and textiles are specially made for the store and reasonably priced. There are also bronze and sandalwood sculptures of Hindu gods peppered all over the shop for those with a spiritual bent. *300 W. Grand Ave., River North, 312/923–9811.*

5 *c-3*

FORTUNATE DISCOVERIES

A treasure trove of rugs, kilims, furniture, and decorative accessories, all with an ethnic or tribal provenance, makes this shop feel worlds away from the rest of the street. Artifacts are also reworked into functional objects, such as ornate window frames transformed into mirrors. *1022 W. Armitage Ave., Lincoln Park, 773/404–0212.*

7 *b-6*

GALLERIA M

Contemporary furnishings with singular yet complementary points of view are the standard at this shop, which holds local exclusives for two noted furniture lines: Dialogica from New York, with dreamy pieces for every room in the home, and Mike Furniture from San Francisco, serving up tailored sofas, tables, chairs, and wooden storage pieces. *313 W. Superior St., River North, 312/988–7790.*

5 *a-5*

HOLLIS FUNK

The high-tech look meets the new millennium in this shop, which has an amazing stash of steel furniture in every conceivable form and finish. There are immaculately stripped and refinished vintage pieces; new steel pieces that have the character of the old imbued with new stylistic twists; and a comprehensive line of bold, colorful painted steel from Germany, sporting gleaming paint jobs done with auto-body lacquers that come in more than 200 shades. *1463 N. Milwaukee Ave., Wicker Park, 773/862–2530.*

5 *c-3*

JAYSON HOME & GARDEN

This large Lincoln Park store sells a wide selection of home furnishings and accessories. *1915 N. Clybourn Ave., Clybourn Corridor, 773/525–3100.*

2 *f-4*

JEAN ALAN UPHOLSTERED FURNITURE AND FURNISHINGS

The staff at this eponymous atelier works marvels with textiles, especially upholstered furnishings and window treatments. You will also find a great selection of handmade pillows at this shop, which is owned and operated by a former film-set decorator. *2062 N. Damen Ave., Bucktown, 773/278–2345. Closed Mon.*

7 *c-7*

MIG AND TIG

For something different and dramatic, check out this shop, a favorite with interior designers. It sells wrought-iron beds, velvet accessories, and things made with grapevines. Equally dramatic are the prices. *549 N. Wells St., River North, 312/644–8277.*

7 *c-7*

MONTAUK

The second U.S. store in the popular Canadian chain, this shop offers custom upholstery for sofas, loveseats, and chairs. It will even upholster your new furnishings in such fabrics as camel hair. *223 W. Erie St., Near North, 312/951–5688.*

7 *e-5*

MORSON COLLECTION

European contemporary design is celebrated at this showroom just off Michigan Avenue. It has exclusive sales agreements with a lineup of well-known Continental names and discounts furnishings. Find Moroso, Molteni & C., and Giorgetti from Italy and Perobell from Spain, to name a few. The new H2O bath line designed by Antonio Citterio is also sold here. *100 E. Walton St., Magnificent Mile, 312/587–7400.*

7 *b-7*

NO PLACE LIKE

There is currently no other place like this breezy home furnishings shop, which sells contemporary merchandise that pays homage to modernism. It has several exclusive furniture lines that marry metal and wood in uniquely designed and fabricated pieces, and a healthy selection of ceramic and china dishes, fused and blown glassware, and pottery in bold hues and streamlined shapes. *300 W. Grand St., River North, 312/822–0550.*

5 *a-3*

PACIFIC INTERIORS

With an emphasis on furniture from the Pacific Rim, this store sells Chinese armoires, bookcases, cabinets, and chairs in an array of exotic woods, all at reasonable prices. *2076 N. Elston Ave., Bucktown, 773/645–1122. Closed Mon.–Wed.*

2 *f-4*

PAGODA RED

Superior-quality Asian furniture is sold here for an exceptionally reasonable sum. You will find such unusual pieces as carved-wood wedding chests, immortal tables, cinnabar-lacquer coffers, and concubine beds. There are also storage pieces from Tibetan monasteries, hand-woven carpets from Nepal, and antique Chinese garden pieces. *1714 N. Damen Ave., Bucktown, 773/235–1188. Closed Mon.*

5 *e-5*

PINE AND DESIGN IMPORTS

It has a huge selection of European pine antiques and reproductions. On-site artisans help personalize your choice. *511 W. North Ave., Lincoln Park, 312/640–0100.*

7 *d-6*

SHABBY CHIC

Cottage-style furnishings and accessories can be found in abundance at this store. *46 E. Superior St., Streeterville, 312/649–0080.*

5 *c-3*

TABULA TUA

Instead of the standard wedding-registry fare, this store sells crockery that's colorful and contemporary. The range of pottery from Provence would brighten just about any table. The furniture here has a vintage feel, with mosaic tables, shelves, and cabinets handcrafted by artisans. *1015 W. Armitage Ave., Lincoln Park, 773/525–3500.*

5 *c-3*

URBAN GARDENER

Besides plants, pots, and books on gardening, you'll find interesting accessories for your garden as well as a wide range of up-market garden furniture. *1006 W. Armitage Ave., Lincoln Park, 773/477–2070.*

2 *f-4*

WHIZBANG

This furniture store's not for the faint of heart. Bright velvets, leopard prints, and dizzying paisley prints are all material for the dramatic sculptural furniture you'll find at this unique atelier. *1959 W. Cortland St., Bucktown, 773/292–9602. Closed Mon.–Tues.*

lamps & lighting

4 *c-7*

CREST LIGHTING STUDIOS

If the lighting you want isn't on display in this large, jam-packed lighting showroom, hit the dozens of catalogs found here from American and European lighting suppliers and order what you want. There is a huge selection of everything from high-tech tracks to opulent and outrageous blown-glass or crystal chandeliers to exterior lighting, ceiling fans, and electrical supplies. *3300 N. Sheffield Ave., Lakeview, 773/525–8000.*

2 *f-6*

HARRIS LAMPS FACTORY OUTLET

Lighten up your home with excellent buys from this shop, which displays and sells a huge inventory of lighting in contemporary and classic styles. *1200 W. 35th St., Bridgeport, 773/650–7835. Closed Mon.–Thurs. and Sun.*

7 *c-5*

NEW METAL CRAFTS

This shop sells antique and custom-designed lighting. *812 N. Wells St., River North, 312/787–6991. Closed Sun.*

5 *e-3*

STANLEY GALLERIES

Antique lighting, chandeliers, and desk, table, and floor lighting are all available, as are architectural hardware, stained glass, fretwork, and terra-cotta. *2118 N. Clark St., Lincoln Park, 773/281–1614. Closed Sun.*

7 *b-6*

TECH LIGHTING

This is perhaps the best source in the city for lighting with a contemporary bent, be it sleek, elegant, or funky. Find cutting-edge lighting lines from the U.S. and Europe, as well as innovative fixtures and lamps designed in-house and only available here. The staff is well trained and very helpful at this showroom. *300 W. Superior St., River North, 312/944–1000.*

paint & wallpaper

1 *e-6*

PAPER & MORE

This wallpaper store goes by the book and has traditional wall hangings. *1844 W. 95th St., Beverly, 773/233–1421.*

4 *b-1*

THYBONY

Choose from more than 500 wallpaper patterns, including fabric wall coverings, window treatments, paint, and related items. *5440 N. Clark St., Andersonville, 773/561–2275.*

HOUSEWARES & HARDWARE

5 *a-2*

BED, BATH AND BEYOND

You really can find just about any bedding, towels, or anything else related to the bathroom or bedroom at this megastore, but don't count on personal service. *1800 N. Clybourn Ave., Clybourn Corridor, 312/642–6596.*

5 *d-5*

THE CONTAINER STORE

This store near Lincoln Park has billions of different containers for hiding away all the stuff you never want to get rid of. *908 W. North Ave., Clybourn Corridor, 312/654–8450.*

7 *e-8*

HAMMACHER SCHLEMMER

Can't resist playing with the stuff here, can you? It stocks gadgets galore, conveniences, and indulgences for every room in the abode, the car, the sauna, the boat, the plane, and universe. *445 N. Michigan Ave., Magnificent Mile, 312/527–9100.*

5 *b-5*

HOME DEPOT

Everything and anything you could possibly need for your house, patio, or garage can be found in this huge store near Lincoln Park. Snare a store employee to help you find what you need. *1232 W. North Ave., Clybourn Corridor, 773/486–9200.*

2 *g-8*

200 W. 87th St., Chatham, 773/602–1301.

2 *d-3*

2555 N. Normandy Ave., Belmont Central, 773/745–9900.

7 *e-6*

WILLIAMS-SONOMA

With its total understanding of the yuppie aesthetic, the famed San Francisco kitchen-supply company is happily at home on the Magnificent Mile, where it sells its attractive, durable wares. The occasional cooking demonstration beckons the uninitiated. *Chicago Place, 700 N. Michigan Ave., Magnificent Mile, 312/787–8991.*

JEWELRY

8 *e-2*

CARTEAUX INC.

This longtime Loop retailer sells engagement rings and other jewels, but has a significant selection of watches: Rolex, Omega, Oris, Tag Heuer, Cyma, Ventura, and more. *31 N. Wabash Ave., Loop, 312/782–5375.*

8 *e-3*

HAROLD BURLAND & SON

This Loop diamond specialist makes education about stones part of the sales process. *5 S. Wabash Ave., Loop, 312/332–5176. Closed Sun.*

7 *e-5*

HENRY KAY

Diamonds and precious gems are some of the high-profile items at this downtown shop. But it also carries gold and platinum jewelry, which can be customdesigned. It's one of the few authorized Rolex jewelers in the city. *Water Tower Place, 835 N. Michigan Ave., Magnificent Mile, 312/266–7600.*

8 *e-3*

IRVING COHN JEWELERS

Also known as wholesaler M.Y. Finkel-
man Co., this store carries various gems
in classic settings, along with Italian
gold, Breitling watches, and Mont Blanc
pens. *5 S. Wabash Ave., Loop, 312/236–
3021. Closed Sun.*

8 *e-3*

MARSHALL PIERCE & CO.

It significantly discounts well-known
watches, such as Audemars Piguet,
Ebel, Movado, and Rado. *29 E. Madison
St., Loop, 312/372–2415. Closed weekends.*

WINDY CITY STYLE

*There may be no 7th Avenue fashion
shows in Chicago, but there is a vital
group of designers who live in the Windy
City and produce work that ranges from
classic and refined to cutting edge and
funky. Many are nationally known stars
whose lines are sold in designer boutiques, salons, and department stores all
over the U.S., while others have their
own ateliers. Here's a rundown of some
of the highlights:*

**Giovanni (Clothing for Men/
General, Contemporary)**
  *Acclaimed couturier Maria Pinto
  plies sumptuous yet sleek evening
  separates and accessories.*

**Hino & Malee (Clothing for Women/
General, Contemporary)**
  *Find the spare, often asymmetrical
  couture designs of this nationally
  known duo.*

**Krivoy (Clothing for Women/
General, Contemporary)**
  *This is home base for milliner and
  designer Cynthia Hadesman, who
  specializes in hats for cancer
  patients and clothes with classic
  lines emphasized by intricate, elegant detailing.*

**Patricia Rhodes Custom Couture
(Clothing for Women/General,
Designer)**
  *This salon has Rhodes' streamlined,
  body-conscious collection of apparel
  for occasion dressing.*

**Robin Richman (Clothing for Women/
General, Designer)**
  *You'll find whimsical hand-knits for
  women, men, and children.*

---

antique & collectible items

8 *e-2*

COSTUME JEWELRY
REPAIR HOUSE

The name's a bit misleading because it
does more than fix jewels; it also sells
collectible baubles made by the likes
of Miriam Haskell, Ciner, Trifari, Butler
& Wilson, Chanel, Ciro, and Elsa
Schiaparelli, all discounted. *55 E.
Washington Ave., Loop, 312/782–7810.
Closed weekends.*

4 *c-7*

HUBBA HUBBA

This vintage clothing store stocks jewelry and accessories with a retro feel.
3309 N. Clark St., Lakeview, 773/477–1414.

contemporary pieces

5 *d-3*

ART EFFECT

This chic Lincoln Park boutique stocks
an impressive contemporary jewelry
collection representing such designers
as Jeanine Payer and Beth Orduna.
Prices range from $8 to hundreds. *651
W. Armitage Ave., Lincoln Park, 312/
664–0997.*

7 *e-5*

GIA, DESIGNER JEWELRY

Tucked away right off Michigan Avenue,
this small shop packs a big punch with
its outstanding, high-quality selection of
interesting contemporary and avant
garde platinum and gold jewelry crafted
by Gia and other designers from around
the world. *64 E. Walton St., Gold Coast,
312/944–5263.*

7 *e-4*

GREAT LAKES JEWELRY

This tiny gem of a shop stocks a large
selection of sterling silver jewelry,
including designer buckles. Men's and
women's watches are also sold. *104 E.
Oak St., Gold Coast, 312/266–2211.*

5 *e-4*

NONPAREIL

Hip, fun, and funky silver and gold
baubles at cheap to moderate price
points are this store's strength. There's
also a good selection of wearable and
decorative accessories. *2300 N. Clark
St., Lincoln Park, 773/477–2933.*

`7` *e-4*

RIPKA'S BOUTIQUE

Former Chicago area resident Hillary Rodham Clinton owns one of Ripka's bold baubles, a pin she wore to her husband's inauguration. Rings and other jewels are also available at this ever-so-hip boutique. *129 E. Oak St., Gold Coast, 312/642–1056.*

`7` *e-6*

TIFFANY

This world-renowned jeweler has a large array of fine jewels in its downtown showcase, including those designed by Paloma Picasso, Jean Schlumberger, and Elsa Peretti. Also available are china, crystal, and timepieces. *730 N. Michigan Ave., Magnificent Mile, 312/944–7500.*

KITES

`7` *h-8*

A KITE HARBOR

This store stocks a top-flight choice of hundreds of kites, radio-control planes and boats, yo-yos, and boomerangs. *435 E. Illinois St., Streeterville, 312/321–5483.*

LEATHER GOODS & LUGGAGE

`7` *e-5*

BOTTEGA VENETA

Recently relocated to new digs in the Park Hyatt Hotel, this store retains its cache, selling top-quality Italian leathers—most notably shoes and bags—in its signature woven design. *840 N. Michigan Ave., Magnificent Mile, 312/664–3220. Closed Sun.*

`7` *e-5*

COLLECTIONS BY LINDA

A collection of unique handbags (day and evening), accessories, and gift items can be found at this downtown shop. *900 N. Michigan Ave., Magnificent Mile, 312/943–0698.*

`8` *d-4*

DEUTSCH LUGGAGE SHOP

This chain carries most national brands of luggage and small leather goods. Employees will do repairs. *39 W. Van Buren St., Loop, 312/939–2935.*

`8` *d-1*

40 W. Lake St., Loop, 312/236–2935.

`7` *e-5*

GUCCI

For snob appeal, you can't go wrong with the pricey leather goods, luggage, handbags, and travel accessories with or without signature initials at this boutique. The store also stocks luxurious apparel for status-conscious men and women. *900 N. Michigan Ave., Magnificent Mile, 312/664–5504.*

`5` *b-3*

KAEHLER TRAVELWORKS

A major destination for everything from briefcases and laptop carriers to oversized wheelies. The Clybourn location has airline seats so you can make sure the luggage you buy will fit under the seat in front of you. *2070 N. Clybourn Ave., Clybourn Corridor, 773/404–1930.*

`7` *f-5*

835 N. Michigan Ave., Water Tower Place, Magnificent Mile, 312/951–8106.

`7` *e-6*

900 N. Michigan Ave., Magnificent Mile, 312/951–7989.

`7` *f-5*

LOUIS VUITTON

Luggage from here is a bona fide status symbol, and comes at the price that goes along with such. *Water Tower Place, 835 N. Michigan Ave., Magnificent Mile, 312/944–2010.*

`7` *f-5*

NORTH BEACH LEATHER

This shop carries a nice selection of leather apparel in various colors and designs, including furs, shearlings, jackets, winter coats, suits, dresses, and evening wear. *Water Tower Place, 835 N. Michigan Ave., Magnificent Mile, 312/280–9292.*

`8` *d-3*

THE LEATHER SHOP

Visit this store for a fine array of travelware, luggage, handbags, attaché cases, smaller leather goods, wallets, belts, and pens. *190 W. Madison St., Loop, 312/782–5448. Closed Sun.*

2 f-4
STITCH
This stylish shop's emphasis is on fine leather goods from the standard (belts, brief cases, wallets) to the eclectic (picture frames and pillows). There are furniture, jewelry, and sunglasses, too. *1723 N. Damen Ave., Wicker Park, 773/782–1570. Closed Mon.*

LINENS

7 c-8
ARRELLE FINE LINENS
It sells the ultimate in imported textiles for the bed, bath, and table. There are lovely Egyptian cotton duvet covers and sheeting, cashmere blankets, lingerie, table linens, and silk and damask items. *445 N. Wells St., River North, 312/321–3696.*

7 e-7
LINEN'S N THINGS
This is a megastore with all sorts of reasonably priced bed sheets, towels, and more. *600 N. Michigan Ave., Magnificent Mile, 312/787–0462.*

4 d-8
3131 N. Clark St., Lakeview, 773/388–5409.

4 d-7
PASS THE SALT & PEPPER
This North Side specialty tabletop boutique stocks salt and pepper shakers, place mats, napkins, candleholders, and mugs. *3337 N. Broadway, Lakeview, 773/975–9789.*

MAPS

7 e-8
RAND MCNALLY—THE MAP AND TRAVEL STORE
A good source for travel aids, Rand McNally has guidebooks, maps, travel literature, luggage, gifts, and accessories in the heart of downtown. *444 N. Michigan Ave., Loop, 312/321–1751.*

8 e-4
SAVVY TRAVELER
This downtown bookshop stocks an extensive selection of travel books, maps, luggage, and videos, along with gadgets that can improve your life while you're on the road. *310 S. Michigan Ave., Loop, 312/913–9800.*

MEMORABILIA

2 d-3
METRO GOLDWYN MEMORIES
From the '20s to the '60s, this fascinating Belmont-Cragin store stocks original movie stills, posters, books, and magazines. Return to a simpler era with tapes of old favorite radio shows, television shows, and movies. *5425 W. Addison St., Portage Park, 773/736–4133.*

4 c-6
YESTERDAY
This Wrigleyville treasure trove sells hundreds of old baseball cards, scorecards, and other baseball mementos. You can buy cool movie posters, old newspapers, magazines, political buttons, games, and toys, too. *1143 W. Addison St., Lakeview, 773/248–8087. No credit cards.*

MINIATURES

4 d-8
THINK SMALL BY ROSEBUD
Thrill to the tiny but extraordinary detailed dollhouse furniture; you're encouraged to build your own miniature abode on the premises. *3209 N. Clark St., Lakeview, 773/477–1920. Closed Mon.*

MISCELLANY

2 d-2
AMERICAN SCIENCE & SURPLUS
For future Albert Einsteins and Marie Curies, this store is a delight. Science supplies, including telescopes, microscopes, and chemistry kits are available. *5316 N. Milwaukee Ave., Jefferson Park, 773/763–0313.*

2 f-2
MAGIC, INC.
Now you see it, now you don't! This store is a magical source (pun intended) of supplies for magicians and puppeteers. *5082 N. Lincoln Ave., Lincoln Square, 773/334–2855. Closed Sun.*

MUSIC

cds, tapes & vinyl

7 *d-3*
DR. WAX
This shop isn't just about music, although it stocks an admirable selection of new and used CDs, LPs, and cassettes. It also has cool music memorabilia, like Elvis's driver's license and a Sheryl Crow autographed guitar. *1203 N. State St., Gold Coast, 312/255–0123.*

5 *e-2*
HEAR MUSIC
Grab a coffee at the adjoining Starbucks and bop on over to the Chicago branch of this chain, where you can listen to any album in the entire store. Run by die-hard music fans with a wide array of tastes, it carries a thorough cross-section of styles. You'll find lots of world music, folk, and classic torch singers like Billie Holiday and Etta James. *932 North Rush St., Gold Coast, 312/951–0242.*

5 *e-2*
HI-FI RECORDS
There's an emphasis on vinyl here—from albums to truly vintage 45s and 78s—but the store also deals in CDs. You can preview the LPs on a customers' stereo. *2570 N. Clark St., Lincoln Park, 773/880–1002.*

7 *e-8*
JAZZ RECORD MART
This giant sells new and used, domestic and imported jazz and blues CDs, LPs, cassettes, 78s, and 45s dating from the Roaring '20s to the present. *444 N. Wabash Ave., Near North, 312/222–1467.*

4 *d-8*
RECKLESS RECORDS
This is one of the city's major alternative and secondhand record stores. *3157 N. Broadway, Lakeview, 773/404–5080.*

4 *b-3*
SHAKE, RATTLE AND READ
This spunky store sells used books, old magazines, CDs, and records. Vintage vinyls are especially fun to sift through. *4812 N. Uptown, 773/334–5311.*

5 *e-2*
TOWER RECORDS/ VIDEOS/BOOKS
It has more than 150,000 music titles, covering all musical tastes, plus good selections of books—mainly bestsellers, pop culture, music, and art titles. The selection of Latin and world music is particularly good. The Clark Street store is nicer than the one downtown and stays open until midnight. *2301 N. Clark St., Lincoln Park, 773/477–5994.*

8 *e-4*
214 S. Wabash Ave., Loop, 312/663–0660.

7 *e-7*
VIRGIN MEGASTORE
Richard Branson's Virgin Group has brought its own brand of sizzle to Chicago with this huge musical extravaganza. The two-story emporium boasts a broad selection of classical music and imports, sells coffee and muffins in its second-floor café, and offers videos, DVDs, and books. *540 N. Michigan Ave., Magnificent Mile, 312/645–9300.*

musical instruments

2 *d-3*
CHICAGO MUSIC EXCHANGE
Budding and experienced guitarists come to this buyer and seller of guitars, basses, and amps for their expertise and huge selection. They do repairs, too. *3270 N. Clark St., Lakeview, 773/477–0830.*

7 *b-6*
KURT SAPHIR PIANOS
This generations-old shop restores old pianos and sells new ones. *310 W. Chicago Ave., River North, 312/440–1164.*

7 *b-6*
ZZOUNDS
Looking for an Australian Didgeridoo or Brazilian Berimbau to complete your sound? You'll likely need to search no further than Zzounds, as comprehensive a music store as you'll find just about anywhere. They stock thousands of instruments, including a huge selection of hard-to-find world instruments, software, and synthesizers. The staff is fun, friendly, and knowledgeable. *230 W. North Ave., Old Town, 312/280–1164.*

sheet music

8 *d-4*

CHICAGO MUSIC MART

This multi-mart is home to nearly a dozen stores devoted to all things musical—instruments, CDs, sheet music, and music-theme gifts and souvenirs. Listen to a free concert during your lunchtime break. *333 S. State St., Loop, 312/362–6700. Closed Sun.*

NEEDLEWORK & KNITTING

2 *d-3*

MIDWEST DISCOUNT YARNS

This is the place for good buys in wool or acrylic yarn by the skein or cone. You can also purchase cones for hand- or machine-knitting and weaving. *5723 W. Irving Park Rd., Portage Park, 773/481–7944. No credit cards. Closed Sun.*

5 *d-3*

WEAVING WORKSHOP

A fabulous selection of imported and domestic yarns and related paraphernalia can be found. *2218 N. Lincoln Ave., Lincoln Park, 773/929–5776. Closed Mon.*

7 *e-4*

WE'LL KEEP YOU IN STITCHES

This lovely knitting and needlepoint emporium stocks an inviting array of yarns, canvas, needles, patterns, and books. It also offers instruction and personalized service. *67 E. Oak St., Gold Coast, 4th level, 312/642–2540. Closed Sun.*

NEWSPAPERS & MAGAZINES

2 *d-3*

CITY NEWS STAND

It has out-of-town newspapers and 6,000 magazines. *4018 N. Cicero Ave., Portage Park, 773/545–7377.*

2 *d-3*

SUPERSTAND

With titles as varied as Alternative Family and Christian Parenting among its inventory, chances are you'll find what you're looking for at this Texas-based chain. Its stores carry more than 3,500 magazine titles, plus a wide selection of periodicals, journals, and newspapers from around the globe. *1620 N. Wells St., Old Town, 312/397–8880.*

PETS & PET SUPPLIES

4 *d-7*

BARKER & MEOWSKY

How can you not be charmed by this "paw firm" selling great gifts for dogs, cats, and humans? There are beautiful bowls, plush beds, picture frames, treats, and more, and the friendly service would make any tail wag. *3319 N. Broadway, Lakeview, 773/ 880–0200.*

5 *f-5*

PAWS-A-TIVELY

It's easy to tell the owners of this great little shop are pet lovers through and through by the fabulous array of pampering products for sale, their gentle grooming techniques, and their commitment to animal welfare charities. Every pet that paws through the door gets treated like royalty. Owners don't get treated too shabbily, either. *109 W North Ave., Old Town, 312/951–6547. Closed Sun.*

5 *d-3*

THREE DOG BAKERY

This nationwide chain was launched by Dan Dye and Mark Beckloff in 1989 and named for their dogs Sarah, Gracie, and Dottie. They make all-natural dog biscuits, plus food, cakes, and cookies that look like the real thing. The bakery sells coffee and treats for people, too, plus a collection of great pooch-inspired accessories. *2142 N. Halsted St., Lincoln Park, 773/388–2599.*

POSTERS

In most of these stores, you'll find modern works as well as quaint posters—portraying a bygone era when men and women wore hats—that have become hot collectibles, with prices for rare ones doubling, even quadrupling, within a year.

5 *b-2*

CHICAGO CENTER FOR THE PRINT/POSTER

It has vintage posters from Switzerland and France as well as a slew of American movie posters and contemporary printmakers. *1509 W. Fullerton Ave., Lincoln Park, 773/477–1585. Closed Mon.*

7 *e-4*

THE COLLETTI COLLECTION

This garden level gallery transports you to the late 19th century. It's best known form its fine antique posters, but it also features a serious selection of European ceramics and glass in important styles of this era, plus 17th and 18th century drawings and painting. *67 E. Oak St., Gold Coast, 312/664–6767.*

8 *e-4*

POSTER PLUS

A stone's throw away from the Chicago Art Institute, it stocks vintage and reproduction posters. *200 S. Michigan Ave., Loop, 312/461–9277.*

7 *c-7*

SPENCER WEISZ GALLERIES

This eponymous shop sells mostly European advertising from the late 19th century through present day. No reproductions are sold here. *214 W. Ohio St., River North, 312/527–9420.*

7 *c-1*

VINTAGE POSTERS

Find a huge array of posters, including artwork portraying aviation, transportation, food, wines and spirits, opera, and the circus. *1551 N. Wells St., Old Town, 312/951–6681.*

SPORTING GOODS & CLOTHING

5 *c-3*

ACTIVE ENDEAVORS

A favorite spot for the outdoors enthusiast, this store is well known for its hiking, biking, and sports garb, and has expanded its offerings to include more hip, urban clothing, including Chaiken for women. It also sells a very large collection of Patagonia. At press time, another store was slated for the North Bridge shopping center, at 43 E. Grand Ave. *935 W. Armitage Ave., Lincoln Park 773/281–8100.*

8 *e-2*

EDDIE BAUER

This popular chain is a great source for high-quality down-insulated garments. Men's and women's wool outdoor clothing and equi also sold. Backpacking an fits can be bought through the catalog. *123 N. Wabash Ave., Loop, 312/263–6005.*

7 *e-7*

600 N. Michigan Ave., Magnificent Mile, 312/951–5888.

7 *e-6*

NIKETOWN

At this tourist destination/retail shop, you can rub shoulders with professional athletes, check out sports memorabilia, road test sneakers on the mini basketball court, join a Thursday night running club, or stare at the fish behind the aquatic footwear display. Oh yeah—you can buy the company's athletic gear here, too. *669 N. Michigan Ave., Magnificent Mile, 312/642–6363.*

7 *e-6*

PLAY IT AGAIN SPORTS

Not sure you want to invest in pricey in-line skates, hockey equipment or golf clubs before you're sure you're sold on the sport? Check out this chain, which sells new and used equipment for all kinds of sports at a fraction of normal retail prices. *2101 W Irving Park Rd. North Center, 773/463–9900*

7 *c-7*

SPORTMART

Sports fans will want to visit this major chain, with more than 60,000 fairly priced items, including an abundance of team merchandise for athletes and spectators. Check out the handprints of famous athletes (all with a local connection) on the exterior and first floor of the LaSalle Street flagship. *620 N. LaSalle St., River North, 312/337–6151.*

4 *d-8*

3134 N. Clark St., Lakeview, 773/871–8500.

2 *d-3*

6420 W. Fullerton Pkwy., Belmont/Craigin, 773/804–0044.

5 *c-3*

TONY'S SPORTS

Young, urban logo fanatics love Tony's; it draws a hip-hop crowd from all over the city for its always-current footwear and sporty fashions. *3941 N. Sheridan Ave., Lakeview, 773/477–4944.*

boating

5 *a-3*

BOATERS WORLD C Y N

Mostly sails and clothing are sold at this store, but there's also a selection of boating supplies and marine equipment. *1661 N. Elston Ave., West Lakeview, 773/227–7900.*

camping/outdoors

5 *a-2*

EASTERN MOUNTAIN SPORTS

Outdoorsy types love this chain for its depth of product; its laid back, in-the-know sales staff; and its policy that it will repair, replace, or refund any purchase you're not happy with. This store has two floors and lots to blow your paycheck on. *1000 W. North Ave., Clybourn Corridor, 312/337–7750.*

5 *a-2*

EREHWON MOUNTAIN OUTFITTER

Rock climbing equipment is a specialty, and they carry anything you need for camping, hiking, biking and skiing, too. *1800 N. Clybourn Ave., Clybourn Corridor, 312/337–6400.*

7 *e-5*

THE NORTH FACE

This downtown store can spur even the most avid couch potato with its classy outdoor sports equipment, clothing, and accessories. *John Hancock Center, 875 N. Michigan Ave., Magnificent Mile, 312/337–7200.*

5 *d-2*

UNCLE DAN'S GREAT OUTDOOR STORE

This family-run shop h s been outfitting campers since 1972. I stocks eco-friendly products wherever possible and is keen on offering advice to customers. *2440 N. Lincoln Ave., Lincoln Park, 773/477–1918.*

fishing tackle & supplies

2 *f-4*

DAN'S TACKLE SERVICE

It has fly fishing gear; fly tying and rod building are also available. Opening hours are shorter on Sundays, so call before you go. *2237 W. McLean Ave., Bucktown, 773/276–5562.*

2 *g-6*

HENRY'S SPORTS & BAIT SHOP

This South Side store pegs itself as the "how to, where to" fishing store, with tackle and live bait experts available for advice. Fishing licenses for Midwest states are available and the fishing report hotline number is 312/225–3474. It keeps very early and very late hours; call to confirm. *3130 S. Canal St., Bridgeport, 312/225–8541.*

2 *g-6*

ORVIS

A household name among the fly-fishing set, Orvis is also the place to go for cool outdoor-oriented gifts, books, clothing and boots. Think *River Runs Through It*, and you get its take on style. *142 E. Ontario St., River North, 312/440–0662.*

golf

5 *a-2*

CHICAGO TENNIS & GOLF CO.

Near the Kennedy Expressway, this claims to be the city's largest tennis and golf store. It stocks all major brands of rackets, footwear, and apparel and has an indoor demonstration lane. *1880 W. Fullerton Pkwy., Bucktown, 773/489–2999.*

8 *e-1*

NEVADA BOB'S

Part of a chain, this huge golf and tennis store has all the major brands of clubs, footwear, and accessories. *60 E. Lake St., Loop, 312/726–4653.*

running

8 *c-1*

ATHLETE'S FOOT

This national chain offers a great choice of reasonably priced athletic footwear such as Reebok, Nike, Adidas, New Balance, Avia, and Converse, and also sells related accessories and clothes. *222 Merchandise Mart Plaza, River North, 312/329–0998. Closed Sun.*

8 *c-1*

FLEET FEET SPORTS

A move from across the street in 2000 to the newly remodeled Piper's Alley meant more space for running and fitness apparel. The expert salespeople analyze your gait and stride, and have you test run sneakers on a quick jaunt outside to ensure comfort. *Piper's Alley, 210 W. North Ave., Old Town, 312/329–0998.*

5 *b-3*

UNIVERSAL SOLE
An excellent source for runners and walkers, this store carries brands like Adidas, Nike, Mizuno and Brooks, as well as watches, sunglasses, and other sports accessories. They sponsor races throughout the running season, too. *3352 N. Paulina St., North Center, 773/ 868–0893.*

5 *b-3*

VERTEL'S
Runners from all over the city have come to Vertel's since it opened in 1976 for its comprehensive assortment of running and other sports gear. The sports-minded staff knows their stuff. *2001 N. Clybourn Ave., Clybourn Corridor, 773/248–7400.*

2 *d-3*
24 S. Michigan Ave., South Loop, 312/ 683–9600.

skating

5 *e-2*

CITY SWEATS
No wonder in-line skaters love this shop: it's close to their favorite haunts, the zoo and the lake. You can buy or rent high-quality skates. *2467 N. Clark St., Lincoln Park, 773/348–2489.*

7 *d-4*

LONDO MONDO
Serious in-line skaters come to this store for its huge selection of skates and all that goes with them. A staff technician is available for repairs, and lessons and rentals are available. It carries lots of look-at-me swimwear, too. *1100 N. Dearborn St., Gold Coast, 312/751–2794.*

5 *d-3*
2148 N. Halsted St., Lincoln Park, 773/ 327–2218.

4 *c-7*

WINDWARD SPORTS
This store specializes in equipment and clothing for skateboarding, in-line skating, snowboarding, and windsurfing. It has a good selection of swimsuits, too. Check out the skateboarding ramp in

the basement. *3317 N. Clark St., Lakeview, 773/472–6868.*

skiing

2 *e-3*

VIKING SKI SHOP
Chic ski duds and accessories by Tecnica, K2, Marmont, Volkl, and many other manufacturers are sold at this one-stop shop. It does custom boot fittings, ski tunings, and ski and snowboard rentals. *3422 W. Fullerton Pkwy., Logan Square, 773/276–1222.*

tennis

5 *a-2*

CHICAGO TENNIS & GOLF CO.
This large store is located near the Kennedy Expressway and stocks all major brands of rackets, footwear, and apparel. It also has an indoor demonstration lane. *1880 W. Fullerton Pkwy., Bucktown, 773/489–2999.*

2 *f-3*

MID-TOWN TENNIS CLUB
In addition to 18 indoor courts and group and private lessons, the pro shop here sells tennis rackets and gear, and it re-strings rackets, too. *2020 W. Fullerton Pkwy., Bucktown, 773/235–2300.*

STATIONERY & OFFICE SUPPLIES

office supplies

7 *c-7*

ARVEY PAPER & OFFICE PRODUCTS
This brightly lit, cheery chain sells competitively priced basic office materials. *661 N. LaSalle St., River North, 312/951–5051.*

3 *d-8*
3335 N Kimball Ave., Avondale, 773/463– 0822.

4 *a-8*

NATIONAL RUBBER STAMP COMPANY
This store sells stamps, pads, accessories, and custom-made rubber stamps. One-hour service is available on some custom orders. *1704 W. Belmont*

Ave., Lakeview, 773/281–6522. No credit cards. Closed Sun.

5 f-5

OFFICE DEPOT

The stores in this chain have a staggering selection of office supplies, furniture, and equipment, and are a great source for back-to-school supplies. The prices are competitive and the staff is usually helpful. Most stores have fax and copy services. 230 W. North Ave., Old Town, 312/587–0863.

7 b-7

352 W. Grand Ave., River North, 312/670–8200.

5 1-a

2928 N. Ashland Ave., Lakeview, 773/868–6161.

2 e-2

6165 N. Lincoln Ave., Lincoln Square, 773/583–5301.

5 a-2

OFFICE MAX

More than 7,000 office products, furniture, computers, and business electronics are discounted at this store. 1829 W. Fullerton Pkwy., Lakeview, 773/665–2053.

5 d-1

2832 N. Broadway, Lakeview, 773/755–4106.

6 g-2

ORDER FROM HORDER

Chicago companies have come to depend on this local chain, in business since 1901, for a bevy of ever-changing office supply needs. 111 E. Wacker Dr., Loop, 312/648–7272. Closed weekends.

7 c-8

Merchandise Mart Plaza, River North, 312/527–5237. Closed weekends.

8 d-3

135 S. Clark St., Loop, 312/648–7208. Closed weekends.

8 e-2

184 N. Wabash, Loop, 312/648–7212. Closed Sun.

pens & pencils

8 d-4

B. COLLINS PENS

This shop sells a large collection of pens from around the word. It also stocks

exquisite leather desk accessories and stationery. 318 S. Dearborn St., Loop, 312/431–1888. Closed Sun.

7 e-5

MONT BLANC

The complete line of signature white-starred writing instruments is here, as are watches, stationery, and leather goods. 900 N. Michigan Ave., Magnificent Mile, 312/943–1200.

8 c-3

STEVENS MALONEY & CO.

Catering to the true devotees of fine pens, this stationer carries a selective collection of writing instruments from prestigious manufacturers like Pelikan, Tombow, Bexley, and Namiki. 2 N. LaSalle St., Loop, 312/372–4311.

8 c-3

GILBERTSON CLYBOURN INC.

The friendly and knowledgeable sales staff will help you select from among their fine collection, which includes all the big brand names. 55 E. Chicago Ave., Near North, 312/573–8075.

stationery

7 e-4

D B FIRENZE

Some say that if you can afford engraved correspondence cards from this renowned stationer, you've made it. If not, stop in just to ogle the incredibly lush color combinations and paper. Custom leatherwork, bookbinding, and restoration services are available here, and the shop also sells photo albums and leather desk accessories. 1003 N. Rush Street, Gold Coast, 312/867–7474.

5 b-3

I'VE BEEN TO A MARVELOUS PARTY

Get that fab party feeling going from the start with invitations from this store, which has all the major books for ordering social stationery, as well as fill-in invites. Party supplies, thank-you notes, and balloons are available here, too. There's a good selection of kids' stuff. 2121 N. Clybourn Ave., Clybourn Corridor, 773/404–9400.

7 *e-5*

JANE WEBER, INK!

It sells personal and corporate stationery, custom wedding invitations, and all other types of social invitations. Unique frames, desk accessories, and photo albums are also available. Jane Weber and her staff offer personal consultations. *Water Tower Place, 835 N. Michigan Ave., Magnificent Mile, 312/642–0747.*

4 *c-8*

PAPER BOY

Paper Boy is a great source for cards, gift wrap, and invitations with a hip sensibility. It carries many of the popular books for ordering stationery, (William Arthur and Crane's), plus some funkier lines. They've also got some nifty paper-related wedding accessories, including beautiful photo albums, and a small collection of inexpensive vintage cake toppers. *1351 W. Belmont Ave., Lakeview, 773/388–8811. Closed Mon.*

7 *b-6*

PAPER SOURCE

This shop sells reams and reams of different types of paper, a lot of it expensive but worth the price for its uniqueness. There's a good selection of rubber stamps, bookbinding supplies, and a custom invitation department. The store also runs lots of nifty do-it-yourself-with-paper classes. *232 W. Chicago Ave., River North, 312/337–0798.*

7 *e-4*

THE WATERMARK

You'll find custom-designed stationery, invitations, announcements, and personal and business writing paper at this high-end store, plus greeting cards, distinctive desk accessories, and photo albums. *109 E. Oak St., Magnificent Mile, 312/337–5353. Closed Sun.*

7 *c-6*

WRITE IMPRESSIONS, LTD.

This shop proffers custom personal and corporate stationery, printed party supplies, business cards, desk accessories, and gift items. *211 W. Huron St., River North, 312/943–3306. Closed Sun.*

THEATRICAL ITEMS

8 *f-3*

THE GOODMAN THEATRE STORE

It sells autographed scripts and plays, T-shirts from past and present productions, posters, coloring books, and mugs. It is generally open one hour before, during, and half an hour after performances. *Goodman Theatre, 170 N. Dearborn Ave., Loop, 312/443–3800.*

TOBACCONISTS

7 *f-5*

ALFRED DUNHILL NORTH AMERICA

This shop is famous for its custom-blended tobacco, but the renowned tobacconist also stocks carved briar pipes, humidors, cigars, and gifts, including its celebrated expensive lighters. It has men's clothes and leather accessories as well. *Water Tower Place, 835 N. Michigan Ave., Magnificent Mile, 312/467–4455.*

4 *c-8*

AROUND THE WORLD TOBACCO

Name your brand—this tobacconist near Wrigley Field will most likely have it. It stocks a good selection of pipes, too. *1044 W. Belmont Ave., Lakeview, 773/327–7975.*

8 *e-3*

IWAN RIES & CO.

Cigars aren't the latest fad for this family store that's been around since 1857. Cigar smokers can light their stogies in the smoking area, where antique pipes are displayed. Nearly 100 brands of cigars are in stock, as are 10,000 pipes, deluxe Elie Bleu humidors, and all manner of smoking accessories. *19 S. Wabash Ave., 2nd floor, Loop, 312/372–1306. Closed Sun.*

8 *e-3*

OLD CHICAGO SMOKE SHOP

Most of the cigars at this large retailer's shop are handmade in the Dominican Republic, Honduras, Jamaica, or Mexico. The buy-five-cigars-get-one-free deal is popular with patrons. *10 S. LaSalle St., Loop, 312/236–9771. Closed Sun.*

2 *e-3*

LOGAN SQUARE CIGAR STORE

It stocks a huge array of imports as well as domestic cigars and 25 blends of tobacco. It carries Nat Sherman cigarettes and cigars to celebrate newborns' births. *2541 N. Kedzie Ave., Logan Square, 773/278–4554. No credit cards.*

7 *c-1*

THE UP DOWN TOBACCO SHOP

This shop will sell you loose cigarette tobacco and more than 250 brands of cigars, including many imports. It has one of the world's largest (over 40 ft long) humidors for cigar storage and is home of the Chicago Pipe Smoking Contest every April, as well as a three-day free cigar party in November. It has late hours (until 11 PM Sun.–Thurs., midnight Fri.–Sat.) for those looking for after-dinner smokes. *1550 N. Wells St., Old Town, 312/337–8505.*

2 *e-4*

WORLD WIDE TOBACCO INC.

The faintly sweet smell of tobacco and a helpful staff enhance the browsing experience at this store, which has an impressive selection of tobacco products and accessories. It stays open until 11 PM from Sunday to Thursday and 1 AM on Friday and Saturday. *1587 N. Milwaukee Ave., Wicker Park, 773/862–2226.*

TOYS & GAMES

collectibles

3 *g-4*

QUAKE COLLECTIBLES

Owner David Gutterman named his shop after a now-defunct cereal. Anybody who grew up in the '70s will love the range of toys, and die-hard collectors flock to the store for its always-changing stock of *Star Wars* paraphernalia. *4628 N. Lincoln Ave., Lincoln Square, 773/878–4288.*

new

5 *g-7*

AMERICAN GIRL PLACE

The only American Girl retail store in the country (products are also sold through catalog and Internet business) attracts little girls from just about everywhere with the company's signature dolls in tow. There's easily a day's worth of activities for visitors here, who can shop at the boutique, take in a live musical revue, and have lunch, afternoon tea, or dinner at the café, where "sassy seats" are available especially so dolls can partake in the meal. Be prepared for lines to get in during busy shopping seasons. *111 E. Chicago Ave., Magnificent Mile, 312/943–9400.*

5 *h-8*

CHICAGO CHILDREN'S MUSEUM STORE

Educational and purely fun goodies intermingle at this store attached to the museum. *700 E. Grand Ave., Navy Pier, 312/595–0600.*

5 *g-7*

F.A.O. SCHWARZ

The Chicago outpost of this giant fantasy toy-store chain has an impressive array of playthings, including an extensive selections of Barbie and *Star Wars* items. Play on the floor keyboard like Tom Hanks did in *Big* and you're guaranteed to leave smiling. *840 N. Michigan Ave., Magnificent Mile, 312/587–5000.*

5 *a-2*

FUNCOLAND

This national chain sells all sorts of used computer games, including the Nintendo and Gameboy brands. *1730 W. Fullerton Pkwy., West Lakeview, 773/549–0885.*

2 *d-3*

6560 W. Fullerton Pkwy., Norridge, 773/637–2727.

5 *g-7*

GALT TOYS

This small shop with a large variety of fun, fabulous, and pricey goodies appeals most strongly to indulgent grandparents. *900 N. Michigan Ave., Magnificent Mile, 312/440–9550.*

2 *d-8*

K. B TOYS

This chain stocks preschool playthings, electronic toys, sports equipment, and traditional toystore fare. *222 Merchandise Mart Plaza, River North, 312/645–1949. Closed Sun.*

2 g-7

1730 W. Fullerton Pkwy., West Lakeview, 773/281–4852.

2 g-7

4620 W. Irving Park Rd., Avondale, 773/ 283–4852.

5 f-3

LINCOLN PARK ZOO GIFT SHOP

After touring the zoo, stop in here for puppets, coloring books, hats, and stuffed creatures that match the live ones on exhibit but don't require feeding and clean-up. Proceeds support the zoo. *2200 N. Cannon Dr., Lincoln Park, 773/294–4660.*

5 b-3

NOODLE KIDOODLE

The "please touch" policy at the branch of this national chain is a guaranteed kid pleaser, but adults often get caught tinkering, too. Toys here emphasize learning, and there are thousands of them to please everyone from junior scientists to budding artists. Designated play and video-watching areas are nice touches. *2163 N. Clybourn Ave., Clybourn Corridor, 773/281–2371.*

5 d-3

SATURDAY'S CHILD

This shop feels like a quaint, old-fashioned toy store with an emphasis on educational and creative toys. The doll selection is unusually good. *2146 N. Halsted St., Lincoln Park, 773/525–8697.*

4 b-7

SWEET PEA

It contains toys made with natural materials like wood, wool, and cotton (no plastic trucks or dolls here). There's a refreshing absence of big-name licensed brands. *3447 N. Southport Ave., Lakeview, 773/281–4426.*

5 b-3

THE RIGHT START

Developmental toys and baby equipment are the strengths of this store, part of a chain that also sells via the Web and catalogs. The staff really knows its stuff and can be especially helpful in pinpointing appropriate gifts for children based on age. *2121 N. Clybourn Ave., Clybourn Corridor, 773/296–4420.*

4 f-2

TOYS 'R' US

This is the store parents love to hate. Yes, it's got great prices on toys, games, videos and video games, and you can find most any toy and baby product here. But service is frequently lacking, and checkout lines can try the patience of adults as well as children. *10 S. State St., Loop, 312/857–0667.*

2 g-7

3350 N. Western Ave., Roscoe Village, 773/ 525–1690.

5 d-1

TOYSCAPE

It emphasizes handcrafted toys, including wood trains and puppets, and lots of musical toys. *2911 N. Broadway, Lakeview, 773/665–7400.*

4 b-8

UNCLE FUN

This store is jammed with every novelty toy you can imagine. Some merchandise, like the 1950s wind-up cars, is old enough to be classified as collectible. *1338 W. Belmont Ave., Lakeview, 773/477– 8223. Closed Mon.–Tues.*

5 h-8

WINSTON'S GAME COMPANY

Winston's stocks a wide variety of games for kids and adults, including board games, puzzles, casino, and some electronic games. It makes a pleasant change from the usual touristy shops on the pier. *700 E. Grand Ave., Navy Pier, 312/464–0554.*

UMBRELLAS & RAINWEAR

7 e-5

BURBERRY

Leave it to the fashionistas. The label's signature plaid—de rigueur among the conservative, moneyed set—has become a must-have for young trendoids. Luckily for them, the store brightens up such nasty-weather gear as umbrellas, scarves, and trench-coat linings, all things you can't do without here in the Windy City. *633 N. Michigan Ave., Magnificent Mile, 312/787–2500.*

VIDEOS

BLOCKBUSTER VIDEO

In virtually every neighborhood, this national-chain megastore handles rentals and sales of both VHS tapes and DVDs and stocks the requisite popcorn and candy to complete your cocooning experience. Most stores are open until midnight. Check the business listings in the White Pages for the nearest location.

5 *b-2*

FACETS VIDEOTHEQUE

Film buffs all over the country know Facets as the ultimate video resource. It stocks 40,000 titles, plus a nice selection of film magazines and books. Rare titles like *The Decalogue Series*—for which the store has exclusive rights—draw mail orders from big-name directors like John Sayles, but Chicagoans have the advantage of being able to stop in to browse. An annual membership costs $35 and gets you six free rentals and theater discounts. *1517 W. Fullerton Pkwy., DePaul, 773/281–9075.*

4 *d-8*

SPECIALTY VIDEO

The specialties here include foreign, cult, and gay and lesbian titles, and the store has one of the largest collections of DVD rentals in the city. The Broadway location's bigger, but both stores draw throngs of serious North Side film fans. *3221 N. Broadway, Lakeview, 773/248–3434.*

4 *b-1*

5307 N. Clark St., Andersonville, 773/878–3434.

5 *f-1*

SPORTLITE FILM-VIDEO

Visits to this store are by appointment only. It sells one of the most extensive collections of sports videos around, including baseball, golf, tennis, boxing, auto racing, football, and soccer games

from the 1950s to the present. *2970 N. Lake Shore Dr., Lakeview, 773/477–1517.*

5 *e-1*

VIDEO BEAT

This shop stocks mostly music videos and movies along the lines of *Purple Rain*, but you will also find used records, CDs, and tapes. *2616 N. Clark St., Lincoln Park, 773/871–6667.*

WATCHES & CLOCKS

antique

2 *f-3*

FATHER TIME ANTIQUES

In the heart of Antiques Row, this shop sells fully restored vintage timepieces. *2108 W. Belmont Ave., Lakeview, 773/880–5599. Closed Mon.–Tues.*

contemporary

7 *e-6*

LESTER LAMPERT

This shop has an excellent selection of watches. Hold out for the international watch festival and sale in November. *57 E. Oak St., Gold Coast, 312/944–6888. Closed Sun.*

7 *e-6*

TIME US

It has Guess, Swiss Army, and other stylish watches, although pickings can be slim. *Chicago Place, 700 N. Michigan Ave., Magnificent Mile, 312/266–0330.*

7 *e-5*

WATCHWORKS

This store stocks new, often unusual watches, both for the wrist and the pocket. Employees repair watches. *Water Tower Place, 835 N. Michigan Ave., mezzanine level, Magnificent Mile, 312/266–9377.*

chapter 3

PARKS, GARDENS & SPORTS

Chicagoans always tell lost travelers to remember the lake is east. The lake is integral to the Windy City, determining property values and transportation routes and, to the delight of visitors and natives, creating a place for recreation. Because the Cubs and Bears play baseball and football at different points near the lake, their stadiums have far more personality than the more centralized homes of the Bulls and White Sox. In summer, no matter how hot and humid the weather, Chicagoans strap on in-line skates, jump on bicycles, unsheath tennis racquets, walk, run, and use any means possible to fully experience the lakefront parks and beaches. Even in colder weather, locals put on furry hats and earmuffs and give their all while they ice-skate, cross-country ski, and even play football along the eerily silent lakeshore. Once you endure the challenging weather between early December and late February, you'll understand why there are so many functional indoor park facilities as well.

parks

For such an urban center, Chicago has a remarkable abundance of green. From the city's tree-lined streets to the numerous parks and playgrounds, Chicagoans can always find a great place for activities ranging from barbecue to boccie ball. And regardless of what political shenanigans have occurred over the years, the city fathers have always worked to preserve the parks. There's a certain sanctity about Chicago's green spaces, evidenced by the lack of big business along the city's expansive lakefront.

More than 900,000 residents use a park at least once a week; the long stretches of green are antidotes to concrete.

park information

The Chicago Park District is in charge of more than 550 parks, from the fenced-in little neighborhood spots where residents walk dogs and play with kids to the massive Grant Park and Lincoln Park. In addition to maintaining facilities for ice-skating, softball, bicycling, volleyball, and many other outdoor activities, the district sponsors programs such as Theatre on the Lake and swimming lessons. Most parks have individual phone numbers, but for general information the **Chicago Park District Hotline** is 312/742–7529. The district also has five regional offices: **North**, 312/742–7879; **Central**, 312/746–5962; **Southeast**, 312/747–7661; **Southwest**, 312/747–6136; and **Lakefront**, 312/747–2474.

permits

Use of city parks and facilities is almost always free, but permits are required for events with more than 50 people. (The city recommends reserving space 60 days in advance for big events.) Lakefront permits can be ordered at 312/747–0974.

chicago

2 g-5, g-6, g-7
BURNHAM PARK
Many Near South Side residents moved north, to ritzier areas like the Gold Coast, when early 20th-century city planners built practical but unsightly train stations and warehouses in the area. In 1909, architect Daniel Burnham's city plan led to this huge lakefront area, which helped keep people in the neighborhood. The thin 598-acre park, extending south of Grant Park to Hyde Park, surrounds Soldier Field and includes facilities for baseball, softball, football, basketball, volleyball, tennis, horseback riding, and bicycling. With three beaches and a boat harbor, it's a central spot for sun-worshiping Loop residents and people from the South Shore neighborhood. *East McFetridge Dr. to East 56th St. at Lake Michigan, 312/747–6620 (Promontory Point).*

2 e-5
DOUGLAS PARK
This 174-acre park, where the city's first outdoor gymnasium and public swimming pool were built in 1896, is filled with soccer fields, tennis courts, softball diamonds, sandboxes, basketball hoops, a beach, a fitness center, and a bicycle path. *Roosevelt Rd. to 19th St. between Albany and California Aves., Lawndale, 312/747–7670.*

2 *e-5*

GARFIELD PARK

Originally named Central Park, this 184-acre area was dedicated in 1869 and, in addition to a big lagoon in the center and the many indoor and outdoor facilities for all kinds of team and individual sports, it contains the world's largest enclosed conservatory (*see Botanical Gardens, below*). *Hamlin Ave. to Central Park Ave. between Kinzie St. and Eisenhower Expressway and from Lake St. to Madison St., along Trumbull Ave., Near West Side, 312/746–5100.*

2 *g-5*

GRANT PARK

As famous for its sports celebrations as for its reputation as one of the best outdoor music venues, Grant Park is a beautiful buffer zone between the city's elegant skyscrapers and soothing lakeshore. Fun-seekers of every stripe have discovered audible bliss by the wide array of entertainment that finds its way into the park every summer. From the Taste of Chicago to the city's gospel, blues, and jazz fests, Grant Park serves as a kind of town square where business executives and bus drivers alike mix as easily as the different types of entertainment that grace the stage.

This 304-acre grass-and-concrete world-class park surrounds both the massive Buckingham Fountain and the Art Institute of Chicago. In September 1996, during the Democratic National Convention, thousands of Bill Clinton supporters streamed to the park to remember a different kind of rally 28 years earlier—in which "the Boss," Mayor Richard J. Daley, instructed his police officers to shoot to kill peaceful Vietnam War protesters. But unlike in August 1968, there were no bashed heads, tear-gassed lungs, or police riots; Daley's son, current mayor Richard M. Daley, decorated the city streets with flowers.

Originally part of Lake Michigan, until the Great Chicago Fire of 1871 filled it with rubble, Grant Park briefly played host to the Cubs and it was the site of a 1979 mass by Pope John Paul II. Bulls rallies and important structures such as the Art Institute of Chicago and the Goodman Theater have typically drawn people to the park, as have the softball games.

Grant Park's centerpiece, Buckingham Fountain, regularly pumps a million-and-a-half gallons of water, and the four bronze sea horses are usually surrounded by 8,000 rose bushes. Dedicated in 1927, the fountain has elaborate lights—shining from May 1 to October 1—that complement the sparkling lights running endlessly up Michigan Avenue. The Petrillo Band Shell is a nice outdoor stage to see the Grant Park Society Concerts, Tom Jones, Ray Charles, Aretha Franklin, Lonnie Brooks, Koko Taylor or any of the other artists who perform here in warm weather. Show up early to claim the best view. *Bounded by lakefront, Randolph St., Roosevelt Rd., and Michigan Ave., Loop, 312/742–7648.*

2 *d-4*

HANSON PARK

Maintained by the Board of Education near Archbishop Weber and Prosser Vocational high schools, this park is a central spot in Belmont Cragin, a northwest neighborhood of historically Polish, German, and Italian residents. *From Fullerton St. to W. Armitage Ave. and from Central Ave. to Long Ave., northwest of West Town.*

2 *e-4*

HUMBOLDT PARK

Near the exact center of the city, Humboldt Park was originally established as North Park in 1857. Named for German naturalist Alexander von Humboldt, the 207-acre park shares its name with the neighborhood to its immediate west. With a big lagoon in the center, it's a prominent West Side spot for swimming, and it has facilities for baseball, soccer, basketball, cross-country skiing, ice-skating, and bicycling—plus a field house with boxing and health-club facilities. *Between Kedzie Pkwy. and California Ave., south of W. North Ave., Humboldt Park, 312/742–7549.*

2 *h-7*

JACKSON PARK

This South Side park near the University of Chicago and the Museum of Science and Industry was designed by Frederick Law Olmsted specifically for the World's Columbian Exposition of 1893. There are lagoons for swimming and fishing, the Wooded Island (*see Bird-Watching, below*), and a Japanese garden (*see Botanical Gardens, below*). *Bounded by*

E. 56th and 67th Sts., S. Stony Island Ave., and the lakefront, Jackson Park, 312/747–6187.

2 e-2
LEGION PARK
A vertical strip of land on the North Side, this park surrounds the Chicago River, although it's fenced in so there's no swimming. But the vast open space includes a jogging path, four playgrounds, outdoor basketball courts, and tennis courts. *From Foster Ave. to Peterson Ave. on east and west sides of the Chicago River, Albany Park, 312/742–7516.*

2 f-2, g-3, g-4
LINCOLN PARK
The first day of genuinely warm spring sun is always a cause for celebration in Chicago, as if long months of meteorological punishment have finally let up. All at once, it seems, thousands of people drop everything, shed their winter layers and—using bicycles, in-line skates, buses, and cars, although it's usually impossible to find a parking space—head to the city's largest park. The onslaught continues all spring and summer; on weekends, especially, if there's a patch of open grass anywhere, somebody has staked it out with a blanket or a Frisbee game. Even in winter, when the lake is quiet, the sky is gray, and the windchill is inhumane, cross-country skiers and football players fight cabin fever in the park's wide-open spaces.

In addition to being a cozy place to read or play sports, and a scenic, tree-filled spot to tour its bisecting bicycle path, Lincoln Park houses attractions beloved by residents but not quite as well known among visitors. Walkers can pass through the 110-year-old Lincoln Park Zoo (*see* Zoos, Aquariums, & Animal Preserves, *below*) to visit with animals such as penguins, giraffes, elephants, and monkeys. The most famous of the many statues in the park is of Abraham Lincoln, completed in 1887 by American sculptor Augustus Saint-Gaudens and located just east of the Chicago Historical Society off North Avenue; less familiar but equally stately is Alexander Hamilton, enshrined in a circular bed of flowers near Diversey Avenue. The Chess Pavilion, at the south end of the park, is evident by the statues of a king and queen on either side; avoid getting

too close to the intense, quiet types hunched over their boards.

In 1842, Chicago acquired the 1,200 acres encompassing the 250-acre park for $8,000 from the state of Illinois, which had received the land through a federal grant. Originally, officials used the land as a cemetery, which came in handy in the wake of the Civil War and during the 1852 cholera epidemic. In 1864, city fathers converted the land to a park, which meant the bodies had to be dug up and transferred to other cemeteries. In addition to its statues, zoo, and conservatory, the park has four beaches and well-maintained facilities for miniature golf, tennis, yachting, and ice-skating. *Bordered by W. Armitage Ave., N. Clark St., N. Lake Shore Dr., and W. North Ave. to W. Hollywood Ave., Lincoln Park, 312/742–7726.*

2 f-6
MCKINLEY PARK
A small park in the center of a historically tough southwest Chicago neighborhood of the same name, this 69-acre plot contains the country's first field house, designed by architect Daniel Burnham and erected in 1905. This typical city park has a swimming pool, baseball and softball fields, basketball, volleyball, tennis and racquetball courts, and a playground. *From Western Blvd. to Damen Ave. and from 37th St. to Pershing Rd., McKinley Park, 312/747–6527.*

2 g-7, h-7
MIDWAY PLAISANCE PARK
The horizontal strip that connects Washington Park and Jackson Park in the center of the University of Chicago campus, Midway Plaisance Park was once the formal entrance to the World's Columbian Exposition of 1893. It has a bicycle path and a winter ice-skating rink and is a popular spot for students to sunbathe. *From E. 59th St. to E. 60th St. and S. Stony Island Ave. to S. Cottage Grove Ave., Hyde Park, 312/747–7661.*

2 g-4
MILLENNIUM PARK
Largely built on top of a former railyard, this new 24½-acre park at the northwest corner of Grant Park has turned an eyesore into another of the city's jewels; it was scheduled for completion in summer 2001. Renowned architect Frank Gehry's stunning new music pavilion is

KEY

Beaches

Bike paths

Fishing

Golf Courses

Marinas

Tennis Courts

W Hollywood Ave.

W Bryn Mawr Ave. 5600N

Bike Way
(18.5 miles from
Hollywood Ave. to 71st St.)

Foster Avenue Beach

N Broadway

N Sheridan Ave.

5200N

W Foster Ave.

Lincoln Park

W Argyle St.

N Marine Dr.

W Ainslie St.

4800N

W Lawrence Ave.

W Lawrence Dr.

N Racine Ave.

N Broadway

W Leland Ave.

N Clarendon St.

W Simonds Dr.

W Wilson Ave.

W Wilson Dr.

Montrose Beach

Chicago Corinthian
Yacht Club

CLARENDON
PARK

4400N

W Montrose Ave.

N Sheridan Ave.

W Montrose Dr.

Montrose Harbor

Montrose Harbor Dr.

GRACELAND
CEMETERY

W Buena Ave.

800 W

SYDNEY R. MAROVITZ
(WAVELAND)
GOLF COURSE

*Lake
Michigan*

4000N

W Irving Park Rd.

N Fremont St.

W Sheridan
Rd.

N Halsted St.

Sheridan Rd.

Waveland Field House

W Grace St.

N Sheffield Ave.

Bird Sanctuary

W Waveland Ave.

Wrigley Field

W Addison St.

N Broadway

Belmont Harbor Dr.

*Lincoln
Park*

N Clark St.

W Cornelia Ave.

Chicago
Yacht Club

W Roscoe St.

Belmont Harbor

W Aldine Ave.

W Melrose St.

3200N

W Belmont Ave.

N Sheridan Rd.

N Lake Shore Dr.

U.S. Military
Reservation

N Sheffield Ave.

N Broadway

600 W

W Wellington Ave.

Lake Shore Drive

W Diversey Ave.

2800N

N Lakeview Ave.

Diversey
Driving Range

Diversey Pkwy.

N Lincoln Ave.

Diversey
Harbor

W Wrightwood

Ave.

N Halsted St.

N Clark St.

Diversey
Yacht Club

W Altgeld St.

North Pond

Theatre on the Lake

Peggy Notebaert Nature Museum

2400N

W Fullerton Ave.

N Geneva Ter.

W Fullerton Pkwy.

N Lincoln Ave.

Conservatory

N Stockton Dr.

*Lincoln
Park*

W Belden Ave.

N Lincoln Park
West

W Webster Ave.

Lincoln
Park
Zoo

W Dickens

Ave.

N Larrabee St.

N Cleveland Ave.

N Sedgwick St.

N Clark St.

N LaSalle Dr.

South
Pond

North Avenue
Beach

W Armitage Ave.

2000N

N Kingsbury St.

N Clybourn Ave.

*LINCOLN
PARK*

Chicago
Historical
Society

N Stone Pkwy.

North Avenue
Beach House

64

W North Ave. 1600N

64

North Blvd.

N Park St.

N Wells St.

N LaSalle
St.

N Clark St.

N State Pkwy.

41

N
Orleans
St.

N

0   1500 feet

0   500 meters

the show-stopper here. Gehry designed the music pavilion with dramatic ribbons of stainless steel that look like flower petals wrapping the stage. The sound system is suspended by a trellis that spans the great lawn, promising to give concert-hall sound in the great outdoors.

The pavilion, which replaces Grant Park's Petrillo bandshell, is to be the home of the Grant Park Music Festival—a free classical music series—as well as the city's popular free summer concerts, including the jam-packed blues fest and jazz fest. The high-tech, sand-based lawn is designed to handle the hordes and shed rain quickly. Another good addition is the indoor Music and Dance Theater of Chicago, a long-needed space for midsize performing-arts companies. Gracing the park between Washington and Madison streets is Anish Kapoor's 60-ft-long, 30-ft-high elliptical sculpture of gleaming seamless polished steel, which was likened to a giant jelly bean before it ever was unveiled. An outdoor ice-skating rink on Michigan Avenue is to become an activity plaza the rest of the year. *Bounded by Michigan Ave., Columbus Dr., Randolph Dr., and Monroe St., Loop.*

2 *g-4*
OLIVE PARK
Though it was built for an unromantic reason—to disguise a water filtration plant—the tiny park has become one of the Loop's best outdoor spots for handholding and skyscraper-gazing. At the center of a beach, the lake, and Navy Pier, it's filled with paved walkways, benches, and—even though the Near North Side's concrete and traffic are less than a block away—greenery. It's also the site of several summer festivals. *Just north of Navy Pier and Lake Point Tower (505 N. Lake Shore Dr.), on Grand Ave. at the lakefront, Loop.*

5 *d-3*
OZ PARK
Though the metallic statue of the Tin Man from *The Wizard of Oz* initially seems out of place, it's there because the book's author, L. Frank Baum, once lived nearby. This tiny park fills quickly with sunbathers in summer, and it has well-kept volleyball courts and great

kids' wooden play equipment. *2021 N. Burling St., Lincoln Park, 312/742–7898.*

2 *e-2*
PETERSON PARK
The city acquired this 23-acre park, previously owned by the Municipal Tuberculosis Sanitarium, in 1977. Though it's near two large cemeteries and the still-existing sanitarium, the North Side park is nonetheless vibrant with outdoor activity, including baseball, football, volleyball, basketball, tennis, and cross-country skiing. *From Central Park Ave. to the east end of North Park Village and from Peterson Ave. to Bryn Mawr Ave., North Park, 312/742–7584.*

2 *d-3*
RIIS PARK
Due east of the Brickyard, a huge shopping center built in 1977, Riis has an outdoor pool, indoor basketball camp (and an outdoor one in summer), and softball diamonds. *From Wrightwood Ave. to Fullerton Ave. and from Narragansett Ave. to Meade Ave., Belmont Cragin, 312/746–5363.*

2 *f-5*
UNION PARK
At this large park at the border of the growing Near West Side area, the main attraction is a large basketball court with lights for night games. (Furthering interest in the sport are Michael Jordan's second restaurant, One Sixtyblue, and the indoor Hoops the Gym, just across the Ogden-Randolph intersection.) There are also lots of great new restaurants nearby. The park contains a field house with an indoor gymnasium, outdoor softball fields, a playground, and places to ice-skate and cross-country ski. Take note that it gets very isolated at night; though the nearby roads are well lit, walking alone isn't recommended. The park was established in 1854, when the city bought its 13 acres for $18,000. *From Ashland Ave. to Ogden Ave. between Washington Blvd. and Lake St., Near West Side, 312/746–5494.*

2 *g-7*
WASHINGTON PARK
The centerpiece of a long-depressed area, just west of the University of Chicago, this 367-acre park was the site of the World's Columbian Exposition of

1893. The *Fountain of Time* sculpture (by artist Lorado Taft) has been admired almost since Frederick Law Olmsted originally laid out the park. After years of declining population, the area, which surrounds a landscaped rose garden and borders the Du Sable Museum of African-American History (*see* Museums & Galleries *in* Places to Explore, *below*), has recently been undergoing development. There's the usual mix of baseball fields, shuffleboard courts, bowling greens, playgrounds, field house, pool, bicycle path, archery range, and lagoon for fishing. *From Hyde Park Blvd. to 60th St. between Cottage Grove Ave. and Russell Dr., Hyde Park, 312/747–6823.*

2 *f-4*
WICKER PARK
In the early '90s, young Chicago artists and musicians made this neighborhood of mostly warehouses famous as a growing alternative-culture mecca. The area has lost some of its hipster luster, but the park at its center is still a pretty place for parents to take their kids. One of the city's smallest parks (at 4 total acres), it was donated by the Wicker brothers in 1870. There's a softball field, volleyball court, basketball hoops, field house, a nicely kept playground, and plenty of posing by locals to entertain even the most finicky people watchers. *East of 1425 N. Damen Ave., bordered by Wicker Park Ave. and Schiller St., Wicker Park, 312/742–7553.*

wheaton

1 *b-4*
CANTIGNY
Because of Colonel Robert McCormick, who edited and published the *Chicago Tribune* from 1925 to 1955, Cantigny is perhaps the most elegant and stately park in Chicagoland. The park used to be McCormick's 500-acre estate, but he willed it all—the restored 1870s mansion; a park of tanks from World War II, the Korean War, and the Vietnam War; and the First Division Museum of war history—to Wheaton for recreational and educational purposes. You can view the mansion's antiques, artwork, art deco-style theater, formal rooms, and dumbwaiters. *1 S. 151 Winfield Rd., 630/668–5161.*

other green spaces

BEACHES
One of the great advantages to living in Chicago—in the summer, anyway—is the ability to cross Lake Shore Drive and immediately go from cement and honking horns to sand and sun block. For decades, city planners have taken great pains to make sure no big buildings or businesses encroach on the lakefront beaches and parks. Of course, this means it's usually impossible to find a secluded spot, but there's always the Bahamas for that. Swimming is allowed in many places, but brave the cold and pollution at your peril. The city's 33 beaches are open, officially, from 9 AM to 9:30 PM from Memorial Day to Labor Day. Following are some of the best.

2 *h-7*
57TH AVENUE BEACH
Near the Museum of Science and Industry, this South Side beach is perhaps the best diving spot in the city, thanks to a ledge known as Promontory Point. Since drivers have to endure parking problems caused by the museum, bike or take public transportation. *57th Ave. and the lakefront, Hyde Park. Changing rooms, drinking water, grills, picnic tables, phones, rest rooms, showers, snack bar.*

2 *f-2*
FOSTER BEACH
It's unclear why, but this family-oriented beach with shallow lake depths has been a high-school-student gathering point for decades. *Foster Ave. and the lakefront, Lincoln Park. Changing rooms, drinking water, grills, picnic tables, phones, rest rooms, showers, snack bar.*

2 *f-1*
KATHY OSTERMAN BEACH
With the pastel and cream-colored low-rise buildings separating this idyllic little-known beach from the up-and-coming Edgewater neighborhood, you might think you're in a remote stretch of Miami Beach. This beach is popular with the city's gay population, many of whom live in the surrounding area. *Ardmore Ave., south of Hollwood Ave., and the lakefront, Edgewater. Changing rooms, drinking water, phones, rest rooms, showers.*

2 g-2

MONTROSE AVENUE BEACH

A long beach on the North Side that stretches nearly to Wilson Avenue, Montrose is a spacious alternative to the closer-to-downtown North Avenue and Oak Street areas. It's good for team athletes, who use the big fields to practice, then plunge in the water. *Montrose Ave. and the lakefront, Uptown. Changing rooms, drinking water, phones, rest rooms, showers, snack bar.*

5 g-5

NORTH AVENUE BEACH

The annual Pro-Am Beach Volleyball Series and sporadic events like the traveling X-Treme Games show up regularly in the pavilions at this hugely popular, frequently crowded North Side beach. The good news, at least for bicyclists and in-line skaters, is once you roll north of North along the lakefront path, the traffic begins to thin out. *North Ave. and the lakefront, Gold Coast. Changing rooms, drinking water, grills, picnic tables, phones, rest rooms, showers, snack bar.*

5 g-6, h-6

OAK STREET BEACH

Chicago's most popular beach is always packed, so don't even think about head-

---

---

ing in this direction if seclusion is on your mind. It's yuppie-dominated, which means lots of seeing and being seen. Sunbathers park top-of-the-line bicycles and in-line skates next to their blankets, but the primary sport is spying on the opposite sex. (The beach lures its fair share of families, but not nearly as many as North Avenue Beach to the north or Ohio Street Beach, near Navy Pier, to the south.) There are bathrooms, but the nearest changing facilities are at North Avenue Beach. *Oak St. and the lakefront, Gold Coast. Drinking water, phones, rest rooms, showers, snack bar.*

7 h-7

OHIO STREET BEACH

In a V-shape nook just north of Navy Pier, this small but central beach has a great view of the skyline. Because it's adjacent to the wonderful Olive Park, it has more personality and intimacy than most of the North Side's other crowded beaches. But that doesn't mean fewer crowds. *Ohio St. and the lakefront, Near North Side. Drinking water, phones, rest rooms, showers, snack bar.*

2 h-8

RAINBOW BEACH

The sandy floor beneath the lake at this South Side beach slopes dramatically, which means good deep areas for swimming. There is also a big park and lots of parking. *76th St. and the lakefront, South Shore.*

2 h-8

SOUTH SHORE COUNTRY CLUB BEACH

This beautiful beach looks like a snapshot of the past, anchored by the intriguing South Shore Cultural Center and Spanish-style architecture. Police occasionally train their horses in the entry area. *71st St. and South Shore Dr., South Shore. Changing rooms, drinking water, grills, picnic tables, phones, rest rooms, showers, snack bar.*

BOTANICAL GARDENS

chicago

1 d-2

CHICAGO BOTANIC GARDEN

This 300-acre garden, which contains a desert, a rain forest, and a topiary garden in three biodomes, is a haven for Chicagoans who desperately need their occasional nature fix. In addition to 10 flower-filled greenhouses and year-round weekend shows and events, such as the Japan Festival in May and the daffodil show in spring, the sprawling landscape has many different kinds of gardens. There is a three-island Japanese garden, an aquatic garden, a learning garden, and a 3½-acre fruit-and-vegetable garden. The Education Center includes the Museum of Floral Arts, the Food for Thought Café, the Plant Information Service, and a gift shop. Anybody with even the remotest interest in the outdoors will find something worthwhile: the lagoons are central spots for bird-watching; a nature trail winds through 15 wooded acres; and a 45-minute tram tour runs the whole year, for an additional fee. *Lake Cook Rd., east of the Edens Expressway, Glencoe, 847/835–5440. Parking $7, tram $4. Open daily 8 AM–dusk.*

7 *h-7*

CRYSTAL GARDENS

One of the many tourist attractions at Navy Pier, this six-story glass atrium includes 69 desert fan palms, plus tropical and flowering plants and long, arching fountains. All are on display during the Flower & Garden Show every March. *600 E. Grand Ave., Near North Side, 312/595–7437.*

2 *e-5*

DOUGLAS PARK
FORMAL GARDEN

This 160- by 60-ft garden on the West Side includes a natural lagoon, open pergola, and water-lily pool—plus 60 lilies that bloom at different times of day. *South of Ogden Ave., east of Sacramento Blvd., Lawndale.*

6 *h-3*

DANIEL L. FLAHERTY
MEMORIAL ROSE GARDEN

With more than 8,000 plants, including Floribunda roses, the rose garden is a colorful supplement to the nearby Buckingham Fountain in Grant Park. *Grant Park, near Congress Pkwy., in the vicinity of Buckingham Fountain, Loop.*

2 *e-5*

GARFIELD PARK
CONSERVATORY

Despite its size, this 4½-acre plot at the tip of the West Side's Garfield Park doesn't get as much attention as, say, the Chicago Botanic Garden, because the surrounding neighborhood has been in decline since the 1968 riots. With eight halls enclosing 5,000 types of plants, trees, and flowers—plus the annual Azalea Flower Show in February, the Spring & Easter Flower Show in spring, and the Chrysanthemum Show in fall—it's one of the most impressive green spots within city limits. The Garfield Park Garden for the Blind, with planting areas marked in braille and more than 1,500 plants, is surrounded by a 360-ft-long brick wall due south of the conservatory. *300 N. Central Park Ave., Garfield Park, 312/746–5100. Open daily 9–5.*

2 *e-4*

HUMBOLDT PARK
FLOWER GARDEN

Some 114,000 flowers fill this circular formal garden on the West Side. It's flanked by two life-size bison. *North of Division St., west of Sacramento Blvd., Humboldt Park.*

2 *h-7, h-8*

JACKSON PARK
JAPANESE GARDEN

At the north end of the Wooded Island, a nature retreat with 300 bird species, this quiet park with a waterfall, water lilies, and Japanese lanterns has been here since the World's Columbian Exposition in 1893. The Japanese government built it, but anti-Japanese sentiment during World War II led to its vandalism in 1945. Thirty-six years later, it was finally restored and rededicated so University of Chicago romantic types could pause from their studies here forever after. (It's also called the Osaka Memorial Garden.) *Bordered by Hayes Dr., S. Stony Island Ave., 67th Pl., and the lakefront, Jackson Park, 312/747–6187.*

5 *f-5*

LINCOLN PARK
CONSERVATORY

A beautiful, quiet jungle in the middle of otherwise-bustling Lincoln Park, this 3-acre conservatory houses four glassed buildings and many outdoor gardens, which contain about 20,000 flowers every spring. The main building, erected in 1892, surrounds a palm house, a show house (with mounted displays), a fernery, and a cactus house. Three annual shows, which coincide with the ones at Garfield Park Conservatory (*see above*), include

February's Azalea Flower Show, the Spring & Easter Flower Show, and the late-fall Chrysanthemum Show. Outside the conservatory, the Lincoln Park Grandmother's Garden covers about 130,000 square ft, and the park's main garden, due south, includes 25,000 blooming plants in formal beds. *2400 N. Stockton Dr., at Fullerton Ave., Lincoln Park, 312/ 742–7736. Open daily 9–5.*

2 *e-8*

MARQUETTE PARK ROSE & TRIAL GARDEN
One of the Midwest's largest municipal rose gardens, with about 4,000 roses in 80 varieties, this southwestern Chicago spot also has a pool, fountains, swans, trees, shrubs, and 17,000 non-rose plants. *3540 W. 71st St. (enter at 67th St. and Kedzie Ave. and follow the signs), Marquette Park.*

oak park

1 *d-4*

OAK PARK CONSERVATORY
With about 10,000 display plants, plus 22,000 herb plants and 18,000 bedding plants for village parks, this Oak Park–run conservatory began in 1914. It was originally a homey garden for residents to display the plants they brought from abroad but expanded into several

PLAYGROUNDS

Many Chicago parks, like those listed here, have elaborate playground equipment where city kids can climb, hang, slide, swing, and generally frolic.

Andersonville Playlot Park, *3748 S. Prairie Ave.*

Cricket Hill Playlot Park, *Lake Shore Drive north of Montrose Ave.*

Dean Playground Park, *1344–1368 N. Dean Ave. in Wicker Park*

Donovan Playground Park, *3620 S. Lituanica Ave.*

Garibaldi Playground Park, *1520 W. Polk St.*

Kiwanis Playground Park, *7631 N. Ashland Ave.*

Morrie Mages Playground Park, *3800 N. Irving Park Rd. in Lincoln Park*

houses 15 years later. There are three showrooms, plus group tours and a plant clinic. *615 Garfield St., Oak Park, 708/386–4700.*

zoos, aquariums & animal preserves

chicago

2 *f-1*

INDIAN BOUNDARY PARK ZOO
After some of the animals were shipped out in 1995, some nearby residents feared this North Side neighborhood zoo would have to close. But it has persevered, thanks to a $50,000 boost from the park district and constant supervision by the larger Lincoln Park Zoo. *2555 W. Estes Ave., Rogers Park, 312/ 742–7862. Free. Open daily 8:30–4:30.*

5 *f-2, f-3*

LINCOLN PARK ZOO
The 24 gorillas in the Ape House are probably the most popular attraction of this free 35-acre urban zoo; but all the 1,600 alert, lively animals, reptiles, and birds are fascinating to watch. An elephant will occasionally show off by lifting a huge tractor tire with its trunk and hurling it into the distance. The tigers consistently win stare-down contests with even the most determined of gawking visitors. The penguins perform like stand-up comics, wobbling and squawking and working the crowds for cheap laughs.

The zoo officially began in 1868, when New York's Central Park donated two swans; thanks to animal and financial donations from local residents, and a purchase of a Barnum and Bailey Circus collection, it has become one of the most popular outdoor zoos in the country. Even the zoo's facilities are thoughtful and designed for comfort, of both visitors and animals—the outdoor habitats approximate the animals' wild homelands, and the structures, including the big Lion House, are strong and steady in brick and metal. Though many of the animals aren't available for public viewing during the colder months, it's almost always possible to see giraffes, black rhinos, an elaborate birdhouse

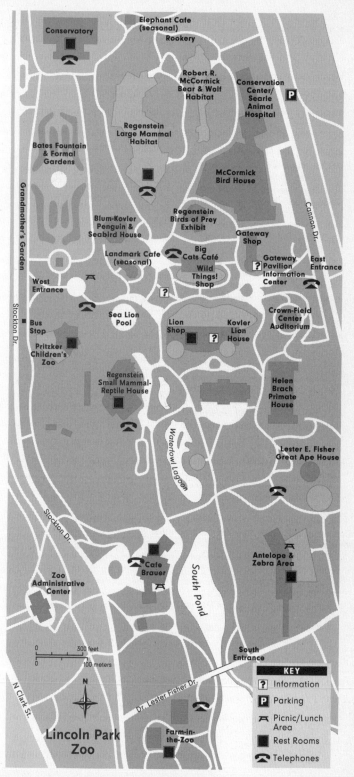

Conservatory

Elephant Cafe
(seasonal)

Rookery

Robert R.
McCormick
Bear & Wolf
Habitat

Conservation
Center/
Searle
Animal
Hospital

Regenstein
Large Mammal
Habitat

Bates Fountain
& Formal
Gardens

McCormick
Bird House

Grandmother's Garden

Blum-Kovler
Penguin &
Seabird House

Regenstein
Birds of Prey
Exhibit

Gateway
Shop

Stockton Dr.

Landmark Cafe
(seasonal)

Big
Cats Café

Gateway
Pavilion
Information
Center

East
Entrance

Wild
Things!
Shop

Cannon Dr.

West
Entrance

Sea Lion
Pool

Lion
Shop

Kovler
Lion House

Crown-Field
Center
Auditorium

Bus
Stop

Pritzker
Children's
Zoo

Regenstein
Small Mammal-
Reptile House

Helen
Brach
Primate
House

Waterfowl Lagoon

Lester E. Fisher
Great Ape House

Stockton Dr.

Cafe
Brauer

Antelope &
Zebra Area

Zoo
Administrative
Center

South Pond

N Clark St.

0   300 feet

0   100 meters

South
Entrance

N

Dr. Lester Fisher Dr.

Farm-in-
the-Zoo

Lincoln Park
Zoo

KEY	
?	Information
P	Parking
⚷	Picnic/Lunch Area
■	Rest Rooms
☎	Telephones

143

with plenty of air space for flying, the rare spectacle bear, a children's zoo, the educational Farm in the Zoo, and lots and lots of monkeys. There are several entrances, but watch for the inviting bronze statue of Hans Christian Andersen, erected in 1896, and his swan from *The Ugly Duckling. 2200 N. Cannon Dr., Lincoln Park, 312/742–2000. Free. Open daily 9–5.*

6 *h-4*
JOHN G. SHEDD AQUARIUM

Pacific black whales, beluga whales, sea otters, and especially dolphins make like vaudeville performers behind a long glass wall in the Oceanarium, which opened in 1990. Attached to the aquarium on the Lake Michigan side, the world's largest indoor facility for marine mammals is a terrific viewing spot. Dolphins sail speedily from side to side, and whales frequently swim right up to the glass, behind which are rows of spectator benches. The regular aquarium facility includes the 90,000-gallon Coral Reef exhibit, filled with sea anemones, sharks, and river otters and regular exhibits of divers feeding the fish.

Shedd, donated to the city by its namesake, former Marshall Field & Co. president, is the largest indoor aquarium in the world. Even if you can't afford the Oceanarium, which costs extra, the regular building is filled with 4,500 sea creatures of all colors, types, and temperaments—electric eels, piranhas, sea turtles, even goldfish—in lovingly recreated habitats of streams, rocks, and reefs. Plus, there's a gift shop, a slide show, a massive penguin habitat, and live jazz Thursday evenings from mid-June to late August on the Oceanarium's north terrace. *1200 S. Lake Shore Dr., South Loop, 312/939–2438. Oceanarium package $13 adults, $9 senior citizens and children; aquarium only, $5 adults. Tickets available in advance at Ticketmaster, 312/559–0200, or at box office. Open Memorial Day–Labor Day, Fri.–Wed. 9–6, Thurs. 9–9; Labor Day–Memorial Day, weekdays 9–5, weekends 9–6.*

brookfield

1 *d-5*
BROOKFIELD ZOO

The 2,000 animals abide in lovingly created replicas of their natural habitats. This huge suburban zoo, spread out on 204 acres, covers all things animal:

Tropic World reproduces rain forests of Asia, Africa, and South America and makes a rock-and-waterfall-filled home for monkeys, otters, and birds; the Seven Seas Panorama is the most impressive dolphin exhibit this side of the John G. Shedd Aquarium; the Aquatic Bird House contains interactive machines where visitors can test their simulated wing-flapping strength; Fragile Kingdom, an indoor safari, tours lion and tiger habitats in a faux-African desert and Asian rain forest; Indian Lake Nature Trail is a great vantage point for bird-watchers; and other exhibits, such as Australia House and Predator Ecology, are nicely crafted cross-sections of other animal cultures.

To add spice to this massive main animal-watching course, the zoo offers a lecture series, annual events such as Boo! At the Zoo on Halloween; a bookstore with more than 4,000 relevant titles; a Children's Zoo with goats, lambs, and horses; and in-depth Backstage at the Zoo tours. To make tours easier, the Motor Safari Tram operates from April to October for a small charge and the heated winter Snowball Express runs for free. *8400 West 31st St., at 1st Ave., Brookfield, 14 mi west of downtown Chicago, 708/485–0263. $7 adults, $3.50 senior citizens and children; free Oct.–Mar., Tues.–Thurs. Open daily 10–4:30.*

stadiums

2 *g-6*
COMISKEY PARK

This 44,000-capacity stadium was rebuilt in 1991 to house the Chicago White Sox and replace the oldest baseball park in the major leagues. There are some neighborhoods nearby, although you have to walk several blocks in questionable safety to get to them, but mostly the surrounding area is the massive Dan Ryan Expressway and a housing project. *333 W. 35th St., off the Dan Ryan Expressway, Douglas, 312/674–1000.*

2 *g-5*
SOLDIER FIELD

Though the Chicago Bears haven't been much fun to watch in recent years, they've resided in this cavernous, old-fashioned stadium since 1971. The field itself opened in 1924 for many events,

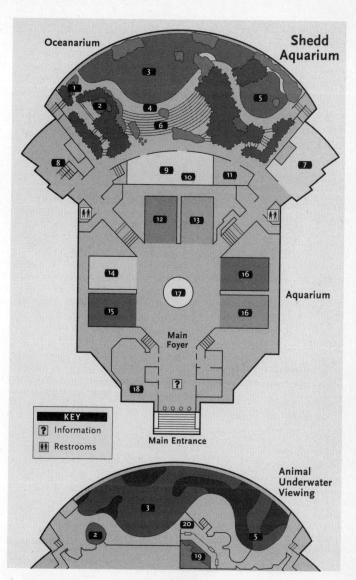

Oceanarium

Shedd Aquarium

3
1
2
4
5
6
8
7
9
10
11
12
13

Aquarium

14
16
17
15
16

Main Foyer

18
?

KEY
? Information
👫 Restrooms

Main Entrance

Animal Underwater Viewing

3
20
2
5
19

1   Tide Pool
2   Sea Otter Cove
3   Dolphins
4   Nature Trail
5   Beluga Whales
6   Marine Mammal Presentation Seating
7   Phelps Auditorium
8   Restaurant and Food Counter
9   Seahorse Symphony
10   Special Exhibit
11   Big Blue Gift Shop
12   Illinois Lakes and Rivers

13   Ocean Coasts
14   Tropical Waters
15   Asia, Africa and Australia
16   Amazon Rising
17   Caribbean Dive
18   Go Overboard Gift Shop and Café
19   Penguins
20   A Resource for the Curious

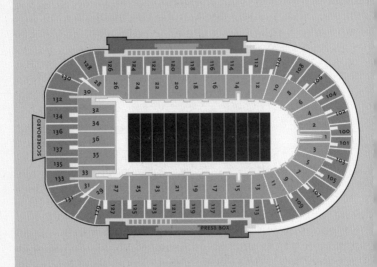

Soldier Field

Wrigley Field

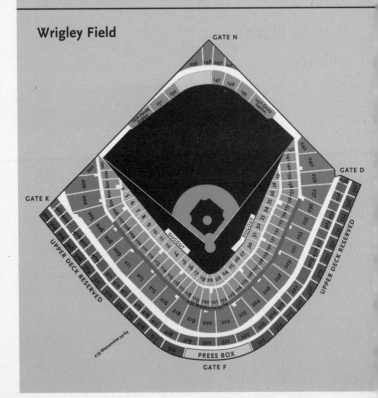

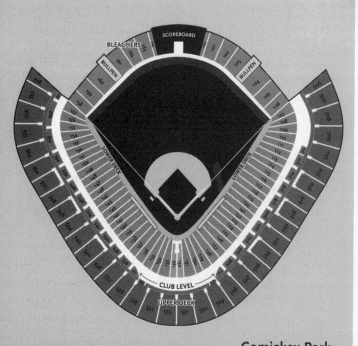

Comiskey Park

United Center

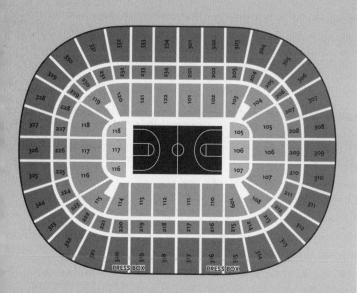

Jack Dempsey–Gene
ɪgular rock concerts
ɪs (who opened their
, the Grateful Dead,
Pearl Jam, Madonna, and Bruce Springsteen. Traffic on game days, especially
on the Lake Shore Drive areas surrounding the southwest Chicago stadium, is
murder. *425 E. McFetridge Dr., just south
of the Field Museum of Natural History,
South Loop, 847/295–6600.*

2 *f-5*
UNITED CENTER
Tickets used to be hard to come by, but
now that Michael Jordan has retired,
this venue has become more famously
known as the home of the city's hockey
team, the Blackhawks. Though the area
around the stadium used to be barren
and worth avoiding while not attending
a Bulls game, it's beginning to attract
many new condo and loft developments
and may be the city's hip new growth
area. *1901 W. Madison St., Near West
Side, 312/455–4000.*

4 *d-6*
WRIGLEY FIELD
Even without Harry Caray to lead them,
the Bleacher Bums will always holler
goofy, drunken invectives and crowds
will always gather on bordering Wave-

WRIGLEY FIELD SINGERS

*Since the great Chicago Cubs broad-
caster Harry Caray died before the 1998
baseball season, the following notables
have sung "Take Me Out to the Ballgame" at Wrigley Field:*

Ernie Banks, *Mr. Cub*

Lonnie Brooks, *blues singer*

Billy Corgan, *Smashing Pumpkins
singer*

Mike Ditka, *former Bears coach,
current New Orleans Saints coach*

Jeff Foxworthy, *comedian*

Steve Kerr, *Bulls three-point specialist*

Jay Leno, *talk show host*

Ryne Sandberg, *retired Cubs second
baseman*

Tom Skilling, *WGN weatherman*

Eddie Vedder, *Pearl Jam singer*

---

land Avenue when a slugger like Sammy
Sosa slams balls out of the classic
39,000-seat stadium during batting
practice. And with luck, despite the
installment of lights for night games in
1988, the grass will always be real and
ivy will always cover the outfield walls of
the friendly confines. *1060 W. Addison
St., Wrigleyville, 773/404–2827.*

sports & outdoor activities

BASEBALL & SOFTBALL

teams to watch

4 *d-6*
CHICAGO CUBS
Nothing says baseball like a sunny afternoon at Wrigley Field (*see Stadiums,
above*). The team has its ups and
downs, but no matter what the action
on the field, Cubs fans know how to
have fun. Even though the ambience
took a big hit in 1998, when "Take Me
Out to the Ballgame" singer Harry
Caray, the team's beloved announcer,
died before the baseball season, the
team has continued to find ways to
entertain the masses. For example, later
that year the famously hapless team
received a boost when Sammy Sosa (following the Cardinals' Mark McGwire)
broke Roger Maris's vaunted seasonal
home run record. Kerry Wood, a 20-year-
old phenom, tied a major-league record
for most strikeouts in one game, and
the Cubs, for the first time since 1989,
made it (barely) to postseason play.
*Wrigley Field, 1060 W. Addison St.,
Wrigleyville, 773/404–2827.*

2 *g-6*
CHICAGO WHITE SOX
While the Cubs nestle in Wrigleyville,
with packed bars and crowded burger
joints in every direction, the concrete-
and-metal Comiskey Park (*see Stadiums,
above*) is in the middle of nowhere. The
stadium and its bordering parking lots
and streets are aggressively patrolled
and very safe, and the White Sox often
play better baseball than their crosstown
rivals. So once you're inside, a Sox game
is an enjoyable experience. It's just an

unfair reminder that the North Side, with its friendly bars, packed streets, and ivy-covered stadium, always gets the marketing edge over the South Side. *Comiskey Park, 333 W. 35th St., off the Dan Ryan Fwy., Douglas, 312/674–1000.*

where to play

The Chicago Park District sponsors many baseball leagues on its 150-plus senior diamonds and 320-plus junior diamonds. There are teams for all ages, from T-ball to advanced fast-pitch, and summer leagues run from May until August. The park district, at 312/742–7529, will have specifics about leagues in particular neighborhoods.

Chicago parks contain more than 300 softball diamonds. It's best to join a league, through your company or a sports organization like the Chicago Social Club, because established teams don't take kindly to individual players who show up unannounced with glove and bat. Take note: Chicagoans play with a 16-inch ball and no glove. Summer softball season starts in April. Contact the park district (*see* Park Information, *above*) for more information.

BASKETBALL

teams to watch

 f-5

CHICAGO BULLS

Nowhere in Chicago is it more evident that the '90s are over than at the United Center (*see* Stadiums, *above*), where the formerly unstoppable Chicago Bulls are in a period of, er, rebuilding in the post–Michael Jordan years. His impressive form is permanently anchored in front of the building in the form of a statue of the crown prince emeritus mid-jump-shot. His departure from the team prompted a mass exodus of the former Dream Team, leaving Chicagoans no choice but to transfer their zeal to another sport for the time being. Good things take time, so it shouldn't take forever till the new-school Bulls gain some respect throughout the NBA and, more importantly, win some games. Meanwhile, tickets are definitely easier to get! *United Center, 1901 W. Madison St., Near West Side, 312/455–4000.*

where to play

The Chicago Park D[istrict] 1,254 outdoor backboar[ds] often packed with players or su[me] rusty rims and torn nets. The park district, at 312/742–7529, has information about available courts. For more reliable games, consult your neighborhood health club or YMCA. Hoops the Gym, at 1380 West Randolph Street (*see* Health Clubs, *below*), has pay-to-play facilities at two near-downtown locations; if you can get enough players to commit regularly, it's a great deal.

events

SHOOT-THE-BULL 3-ON-3 BASKETBALL TOURNAMENT

Hoops aficionados are still talking about Marcus Sheffield's buzzer-beating lay-up that gave his team the title in 1995. With more than 9,000 playgrounders in shorts, tennis shoes, tube socks, and jerseys, it's an annual (if hot) chance to Be Like Mike. *Grant Park, Loop, 312/455–4000. 1st wk in Aug.*

BICYCLING

As in any big city, it takes an experienced and aware biker to navigate through the sometimes gnarling traffic Chicago provides. Since Chicago drivers have become very lax in their attention to traffic laws overall, the chance for collision with cell-phone-calling or otherwise distracted drivers is elevated. This said, it behooves bikers to wear their helmets and do their part in observing bike laws, which include staying off sidewalks and using hand signals when making turns, as well as following general laws of traffic.

Bike theft is high in the city, so equip your ride with one of those bulky black U-Locks and try to stitch the lock through the front wheel at racks. It also helps to register the bike by filling out a small card at any Chicago police department. And don't forget—most renters' and homeowners' insurance policies cover bikes, too. For tips and strategies on avoiding theft, contact any bike shop or police station; suffice it to say, many of the locked bike rooms in apartment buildings aren't as safe as they seem.

Including the lakefront path (*below*), the park district maintains more than 20 paths snaking through parks all over the city. (The Lincoln Park path, which

.tours through the Lincoln Park Zoo, is among the most scenic and satisfying.) Call 312/742–7529 for more information. The Cook County Forest Preserve also maintains 50 mi of trails in Chicago and the suburbs, which are usually far less crowded and easier in which to find secluded spots; call 800/870–3666.

clubs and federations

The following groups help bicyclists acclimate themselves to city riding.

6 *f-2*

CHICAGOLAND BICYCLE FEDERATION

Has a truck ever tried to run you off the road? If so, contact the CBF, a nonprofit advocacy group whose volunteers fight to improve bicycle parking and lanes and smoothly work bikes into the city's car-dominated transportation mix. The quarterly "ACBF News" lists upcoming events, and the federation sponsors the Boulevard Lakefront Tour (*see below*) and publishes a giant bicycling map. *417 S. Dearborn St., Loop, 312/427–3325.*

CHICAGO CYCLING CLUB

This informal group organizes rides to Chicagoland locations, from the nuclear power plant in Zion to the Ba'hai Temple in Wilmette. The club, one of about 15 in Chicago and the suburbs, also holds weekly meetings with guest speakers who have cycled through India, Cuba, and other exotic locales. *773/509–8093.*

1 *e-3*

EVANSTON BICYCLE CLUB

As much a social group as a cycling advocacy club, the EBC holds monthly meetings and sponsors the annual North Shore Century Ride in July. *1700 Maple St., 847/866–7743.*

2 *d-4*

OAK PARK CYCLE CLUB

Like most of the roughly 14 other cycling clubs in the Chicago area, the OPCC organizes rides, including intense 100-mi trips on Sundays and shorter ones during the week. It also holds monthly meetings with guest speakers. *Some meetings held at 1 Fox Center, Oak Park Ave. and Jackson Blvd., 708/802–2453.*

where to cycle

2 *f-1, f-2, g-2, g-3, g-4, g-5, g-6, h-7, h-8*

LAKEFRONT BICYCLE PATH

There are many advantages to biking on this smoothly paved, clearly marked, 20-mi bike road between Lake Shore Drive and the Lake Michigan beaches. The scenery is incredible, especially when you're heading south, past the North, Oak, and Olive Park beaches, staring at the Drake hotel and John Hancock Building with the lake breeze in your face. It's also a fast way to get around, with no lights or stop signs and few built-in traffic obstacles. The disadvantage is the crowds: no matter how careful you are, it's possible to bump against an oblivious in-line skater, careless runner, meandering walker, or belligerent fellow cyclist. Needless to say, with pedestrians of all ages wandering in and out of the path, use caution and don't pretend you're in a triathlon. And wear a helmet.

Some businesses rent bikes for the day: Bike Stop (1034 W. Belmont Ave., 773/868–6800) is near the entrance of Lincoln Park at Fullerton Avenue; On the Route (3167 N. Lincoln Ave., 773/477–5066) is in the Lincoln Park neighborhood, far from the path, but it also rents by the hour; Bike Chicago (312/755–0488 or 800/915–2453) has several different locations (Oak Street Beach, Lincoln Park Zoo, Buckingham Fountain, and Navy Pier) and delivers bicycles to visitors' hotels.

events

BOULEVARD LAKEFRONT BIKE TOUR

The point of this annual 35-mi ride, in which 6,000 amateur bicyclists snake through many different Chicago neighborhoods, isn't competition. It's a chance to learn about local history at a much faster pace than museums provide. *Begins at Midway Plaisance Park, 59th St. and Woodlawn Ave., Near West Side, 312/427–3325. 3rd wk in June.*

BILLIARDS

Shooting pool is one of those perennial sports that just seem to attract everyone from barroom regulars to people who travel great distances to compete in tournaments. It's tough to find a bar without a table, but serious billiards players should try one of the following.

chicago

2 d-2

CHRIS'S BILLIARDS

This North Side hall has lessons, regular tournaments, and food to go with its 48 tables. *4637 N. Milwaukee Ave., Bucktown, 773/286–4714.*

2 e-2

MARIE'S GOLDEN CUE

To go with 20 tables (1 for billiards, 19 for pool), this West Side hall repairs cues, hosts the occasional tournament, and gives weekly lessons. *3241 W. Montrose Ave., Ravenswood, 773/478–2555.*

oak park

1 d-4

OAK PARK BILLIARDS

No lessons, leagues, or other frills here—just 32 tables and lots of players. *1019 South Blvd., Oak Park, 708/848–9085.*

willow springs

1 d-6

ILLINOIS BILLIARD CLUB

You have to be a member to play at this private club, but the fee includes leagues, occasional tournaments, and, if the owner's schedule permits, private lessons. *8442–46 Archer Ave., 708/839–1331.*

BIRD-WATCHING

More than 200 species of birds fly through the Chicago area every year, but they vary widely depending on the migration season. To determine what birds are where, contact the Chicago Audubon Society (773/539–6793), which organizes bird walks, field trips, and workshops. The society's Bird Report (847/265–2118) describes bird-sighting conditions. Some of the many bird-watching areas (interesting birds congregate all over the city and suburbs) are listed below.

barrington

1 b-2

CRABTREE NATURE CENTER

Every May, on International Migratory Bird Day, this suburban center encourages experienced bird-watchers and novices to see the magnolia warblers, black-throated blue warblers, yellow-breasted chats, sandpipers, plovers, terns, and gulls. But it's not the only time of year for good birding: egrets and herons pass through in March. *Palatine Rd., 1 mi west of Barrington Rd., 847/381–6592. Free. Open weekdays 8–5, weekends 8–5:30.*

chicago

2 g-2

MONTROSE HARBOR

In the '60s, the U.S. government permitted trees to grow near a missile site fence on the lakefront. The spot no longer shrouds missiles, but the Magic Hedge has become one of the best bird-watching areas in the city. *Montrose Ave. and the lakefront, Lincoln Park.*

2 h-7

PAUL H. DOUGLAS NATURE SANCTUARY

This 1-mi stretch of land was landscaped as a bird sanctuary for the 1893 Columbian Exposition. In what used to be called Wooded Island, in the Jackson Park lagoon near the University of Chicago, the area attracts phoebes, yellow warblers, meadowlarks, Cooper's hawks, and about 240 other species. *South of the Museum of Science and Industry, 57th St. and Lake Shore Dr., Jackson Park.*

2 g-3

THE SANCTUARY

This dense area of trees and bushes that attracts all kinds of birds year-round is on park district land but doesn't seem to be formally maintained by any group. It's fenced off so birders can't actually walk inside, but there's plenty to see on the fringes. *East of Wrigley Field, off Addison Ave. near the totem pole, Wrigleyville.*

lisle

1 b-5

MORTON ARBORETUM

This 1,500-acre arboretum is famous for its hiking paths, woodlands, wetlands, and prairie grasslands—but that makes it the ultimate bird-watching spot as well. Established in 1922 by Morton Salt Co. founder Joy Morton, it's right off Arbor Lake, a beautiful winter spot to catch migrating waterfowl. You can take bus tours, and cars are allowed in some areas, but walking is recommended. The arboretum's showpieces are the Hedge Gardens and the Fragrance Garden. There's also Gingko, a good restaurant. *4100 Rte. 53, at east–west tollway, 630/ 968–0074. $7 per car Thurs.–Tues., $3 per car Wed. Grounds open daily 7–7, buildings daily 9–5.*

evanston

1 *e-3*

LADD ARBORETUM

Not as large or impressive as the better-known Morton Arboretum, this 22-acre ecology center includes a nice bird sanctuary. It also has hiking trails and gardens, all run by the Evanston Environmental Association. *2024 McCormick Blvd., 847/864–5181. Free. Weekdays 9–4:30.*

zion

1 *d-1*

ILLINOIS BEACH STATE PARK

Hawks and eagles are among the variety of birds you'll see at this lakeside park. *300 Lakefront, Zion, 847/662–4811. Free.*

BOATING

Hundreds of motorized boats sit idly in Chicago harbors, just waiting for the first sunny day of spring. When that day comes, lakefront boat traffic can resemble the Dan Ryan Expressway. To dock your own boat in one of the park district's many harbors, call the harbor division at 312/747–0737; you'll need to fill out an application and pay a deposit of $15 per foot of the boat. Launching the boat each time you take it out is less cost-effective than keeping it in the harbor year-round, but the fee is $15 a day or $100 for the entire boating season, which lasts from May 15 to October 15.

There are six major harbors on the Chicago lakefront: Belmont (Belmont Ave. and the lakefront, 312/742–7673); Burnham (1559 S. Lake Shore Dr., 312/ 747–7009); Diversey (150 W. S. James Pl., 312/742–7762); Jackson (6500 S. Coast Guard Dr., 312/747–6189); Monroe (Monroe St. and the lakefront, 312/ 742–7643); and Montrose (Montrose Ave. and the lakefront, 312/742–7527).

BOCCIE

Chicago still has a few outdoor courts for boccie, a traditional Italian game involving heavy balls knocking against each other, including the following.

2 *c-3*

HIAWATHA PARK

Two courts are at this park on the northwest edge of Chicago, south of Norridge near Addison and Forest Preserve avenues. *8029 W. Forest Preserve Ave., Norridge, 312/746–5559.*

2 *f-6*

MCGUANE PARK

There are three courts on this tiny park just south of Interstate 55. *2901 S. Poplar Ave., Bridgeport, 312/747–6497.*

BOWLING

Those heavy rolling balls are part of everything from your aunt's Friday night bowling league to an offbeat nightlife activity for hipster yuppies to a supplemental activity for punk-rock concerts. Many bowlers take their leagues and scores seriously, so call first to make sure a lane is available. Of course, some bars showcase bowling purely as a drinking activity, so don't worry if you never learned the right form and technique.

chicago

2 *f-3*

DIVERSEY RIVER BOWL

With 36 lanes, this is one of the most popular North Side bowling spots. It's also an offbeat party place, with a cocktail lounge and facilities for private soirees and candlelight bowling. *2211 W. Diversey Pkwy., Roscoe Village, 773/227–5800.*

2 *f-3*

FIRESIDE BOWLING ALLEYS

The main draw at this beat-up alley is not necessarily the bowling—it's the loud punk-rock bands that play in the corner while fans clank balls against pins. *2646 W. Fullerton Ave., Logan Square, 773/486–2700.*

4 *c-5*

MARIGOLD ARCADE

This serious bowlers' haven has 32 lanes, plus private instruction through the pro shop. *828 W. Grace St., Lakeview, 773/935–8183.*

4 *b-7*

SOUTHPORT LANES
The four alleys are great fun, with pin boys doing the work that machines normally do, but the adjoining bar in this heavily yuppie area practically screams "non-serious bowlers only." *3325 N. Southport Ave., Lakeview, 773/472–6600.*

2 *f-3*

WAVELAND BOWL
You'll find just the basics—computer scoring, snack machines, shoes—at these 40 lanes. *3700 N. Western Ave., Roscoe Village, 773/472–5900.*

1 *d-4*

oak forest

OAK FOREST BOWL
With 32 alleys, this southern-suburb spot caters mostly to score-conscious bowlers—and offers free instruction on changing days. Call for open bowling times. *15240 S. Cicero Blvd., 708/ 687–2000.*

BOXING
Big-name boxers haven't fought for years in Chicago, but some local promoters, most prominently 8 Count Productions, have brought some relatively big names (such as Mike "The Fly" Garcia and Rocky "The Mexican Kid" Martinez) to the city. The gyms below have all the basics for instruction and practice.

2 *f-2*

DEGERBERG MARTIAL ARTS & FITNESS ACADEMY
This relatively new facility has a regulation-size ring, speed bags, heavy bags, mirrored walls, and instruction for men and women. *4717 N. Lincoln Ave., Lincoln Park, 773/728–5300.*

2 *e-5*

WINDY CITY BOXING CLUB
For members, this northwest club has a regulation-size ring, weights, and classes. *4401 W. Ogden Ave., West Town, 773/277–4091.*

CRICKET
Though most Chicagoans are more enamored of baseball, it's still possible to find pitches (which is to say fields) for this venerable British sport. The Suburban Cricket Club had been keeping the sport of flat bats and occasional four-day contests alive in Hyde Park since 1993. The club doesn't really have a phone number or address, however, so peruse its Web page (www.suburbancc.org) or show up on a sunny weekend at Washington Park, from Hyde Park Boulevard to 60th Street, between Cottage Grove Avenue and Russell Drive. Also, call the park district (*see Park Information, above*) for nearby facilities, or at least spaces where you can set up your own facilities.

CROQUET
Bring your own mallets, balls, and hoops to any spacious park and presto, you've got a croquet match. To determine the nearby park with the most available space, call the park district (*see Park Information, above*).

CROSS-COUNTRY SKIING
Midwesterners are forever defending the legitimacy of their skiing hills from Colorado, Utah, and Vermont skeptics. With cross-country, they actually have a case. Especially in parks near the lakefront, cross-country skiing is a great way both to explore the city and stay in touch with its outdoor beauty. The park district has about 50 free cross-country ski areas, open in decent weather while it's light outside in the winter. Some parks provide equipment rental and skiing lessons, both for a fee. Call the district (*see Park Information, above*) for nearby locations.

3 *f-4, f-5, f-6*

HORNER PARK
One advantage to skiing this long, thin North Side park off the Chicago River is its field house (for bathroom breaks). *2741 W. Montrose Ave., North Center, 312/ 742–7572.*

2 *e-2*

LEGION PARK
Though there's no field house and little parking, this fenced-in vertical North Side park surrounds the Chicago River

and has a surprisingly high level of nature for a big city. *From Foster Ave. to Peterson Ave., on east and west sides of the Chicago River, Albany Park, 312/742–7516.*

2 *f-2, g-3, g-4*
LINCOLN PARK
Though there are no official cross-country skiing facilities such as rentals or maps, many frustrated downhillers brave the lakeshore winds to follow these woodsy paths. Park officials recommend skiing north of Diversey Avenue, to avoid running out of grassland and running into boat areas and bridges. *Bordered by W. Armitage Ave., N. Clark St., N. Lake Shore Dr., and W. North Ave. to W. Hollywood Ave., Lincoln Park, 312/742–7726.*

FENCING

You don't have to be a swashbuckler like Errol Flynn to appreciate the finer points of foiling an opponent. At the location below, you can find instruction for recreational and competitive fencing.

6 *e-2*
FENCING 2000 ACADEMY
This group teaches students grace, motor skills, timing, and what the academy calls personal-combat psychology. Founded in 1993, the academy is one of the few places for lessons and information in Chicago and a congregating point for fencers all over the Midwest. *328 S. Jefferson St., Near West Side, 312/879–0430.*

FISHING

It's pretty easy to score a fishing license in Illinois; you have to be older than 16 (those over 65 qualify for a special rate) and willing to stop in at any bait shop, major sporting-goods tore, currency exchange, or city clerl s office (the last, given bureaucracy, is not recommended). For a brief primer on where to fish in Illinois, the state's Department of Natural Resources, at 312/814–2070, will send thorough guidebooks and answer questions over the phone. You can fish pretty much anywhere off Lake Michigan; some of the best harbors are listed below, along with parks and non-Chicago locations.

CHICAGO PARK DISTRICT
Many of Chicago's parks contain lagoons, filled with smelt (for about six weeks beginning in early April), salmon, and other hauls for children and nonex-

perts. The Chicago Park District sponsors free fishing clinics, focusing on catching coho salmon, among other things, at various parks. Parks with prime fishing include Lincoln (2400 N. Fullerton Ave. on the park, and 2200 North Cannon Dr. behind the zoo); Jackson (6401 S. Stony Island Ave.); Marquette (6700 S. Kedzie Blvd.); McKinley (2210 W. Pershing Rd.); Washington (5531 S. Martin Luther King Jr. Dr.); Columbus (500 S. Central Ave.); Douglas (14th St. and S. Albany Ave.); and Garfield (1400 N. Sacramento Blvd.).

COOK COUNTY FOREST PRESERVE
With more than 28 lakes, ponds, and sloughs for hook-and-line fishing, the forest preserve is for slightly more experienced fisherfolk, or at least those bored with the sailboat-infested Lake Michigan harbors. Save for largemouth and smallmouth bass, northern pike, rainbow trout, and a few others, there are no seasons or limits on fishing season. (Ice fishing is available on certain lakes if the ice is more than four inches thick, but you need a license.) Call the forest preserve at 800/870–3666 for more information. Some of the best lakes are Belleau, on 12 acres west of the Tri-State Tollway off Busse Highway, with largemouth bass, bluegill, yellow perch, bullhead, and trout; Busse, south of Higgins Road, between I-90 and Arlington Heights Road, with three huge, separate pools full of largemouth bass, bluegill, bullhead, northern pike, carp, sunfish, crappie, and channel catfish; Des Plaines, between the towns of Wheeling and Lemont, featuring a natural stream containing northern pike, largemouth bass, bluegill, sunfish, bullhead, crappie, goldfish, and many others; McGinnes Slough, off Mannheim Road, about ½ mi north of Orland Park, with bullhead and goldfish; Powderhorn, near a wildlife refuge, 2 mi north of Calumet City, ½ mi east of Burnham Avenue on the north side of Brainard Avenue, with northern pike, largemouth bass, channel catfish, sunfish, carp, and others; and Skokie Lagoons, between Willow and Dundee Roads, east of the Edens Expressway, with some bass, sunfish, carp, bluegill, and crappie.

LAKE MICHIGAN HARBORS
Perch, carp, bass, and northerns (in summer) and chinook salmon and rainbow trout (in fall) are the pickings along Lake Michigan's Chicago shore. The most popular harbors include Belmont

(Belmont Ave. and the lakefront, 312/742–7673); Diversey (Diversey Pkwy. and the lakefront, 312/742–7762); Montrose (Montrose Ave. and the lakefront, 312/742–7527); Burnham (1559 S. Lake Shore Dr. at the lakefront, 312/747–7009); 59th St. (59th St. and the lakefront, 312/747–7012); and Monroe (Monroe St. and the lakefront, 312/742–7643).

Many fishing-friendly shops charter boats near the lake (and some parks)—the Chicago Sportfishing Association (Burnham Harbor, 312/922–1100), Henry's Sport and Bait (3130 S. Canal St., 312/922–1100), and Park Bait (Montrose Harbor, 312/271–2838) are among them.

FLYING

A pilot's license is required to fly planes in Chicagoland; some of the following places can help you earn one.

2 *g-5*

A FLIGHT CENTER OF CHICAGO

Catering to beginners, the flight center has aircraft rentals, aerial tours, and flying lessons out of Chicago's small Meigs Field airport. *800/494–5535.*

2 *d-7*

AVIATION PROFESSIONALS INC.

This flight school offers graded instruction, including single- and multi-engine planes, for fliers seeking a private license. API also rents planes and sells pilot supplies. *5300 W. 63rd St., north of Bedford Park, 773/284–1220.*

2 *d-7*

CHICAGO AVIATION INC.

Based at Midway Airport, Chicago Aviation rents planes and gives flying lessons. *4943 W. 63rd St., north of Bedford Park, 773/767–9800.*

FOOTBALL

teams to watch

2 *g-5*

CHICAGO BEARS

It's possible that Da Bears—to quote the name coined by *Saturday Night Live*—are finally starting to hit their stride. After many years of disappointing scores and highlights, this legendary team is starting to win some games, and some fans back to Solider Field (*see* Stadiums, *above*). The untimely passing in 1999 of former Bears hero Walter Payton may have galvanized the team's spirit and inspiration. Most tickets are sold through subscriptions, but ticket brokers throughout the city can score tickets to any individual game—for a fee, of course. *Soldier Field, 425 E. McFetridge Dr., just south of the Field Museum of Natural History, South Loop, 847/295–6600.*

evanston

1 *e-3*

NORTHWESTERN UNIVERSITY WILDCATS

Though their 1996 and 1997 successes were mostly due to graduated running back Darnell Autry, the Wildcats have permanently made the leap from Big Ten doormat to legitimate Midwestern powerhouse. They beat out Michigan, Ohio State, Illinois, Michigan State, and the other more conventional Big Ten champs for entry into the 1996 Rose Bowl and continued the success with a 1997 trip to the Citrus Bowl. Like most other college football teams, Northwestern plays Saturday afternoons in the fall. *Ryan Field, 1501 Central St., 847/491–2287.*

where to play

Any ambitious group with a pigskin can set up a game at one of the city's many wide-open park spaces. It's usually first-come, first-served, and part of the fun is casually asking football-throwing strangers to meet for a game on an upcoming fall weekend. For information on fields near you, call the park district (*see* Park Information, *above*).

GOLF

You can always join a private club in the suburbs, but that would be expensive and remove the pleasure of driving in the shadow of Loop skyscrapers. Though just one of the city's six public golf courses—Jackson Park—has the full 18 holes, they're all in decent shape. The park district's automated registration service, at 312/245–0909, accepts reservations seven days in advance with a credit card. Fees vary, but they're usually about $10, more on weekends, with cheaper deals for junior golfers and senior citizens. Courses are open from mid-April to November.

2 *d-5*

COLUMBUS

This 2,867-yard course is far from downtown, on the western edge of the city at the suburban Oak Park border. But it's off the Eisenhower Expressway and easy to reach when there's no traffic. *Bordered by Adams Blvd., Central Ave., the Eisenhower Expressway, and Austin Blvd., West Garfield Park.*

2 *h-7*

JACKSON PARK

The city's sole 18-hole course is 5,538 yards, including a 298-yard 11th hole full of trees and water hazards and a 560-yard 14th hole. It's convenient for Hyde Park residents and University of Chicago students. *Bordered by Hayes Dr., S. Stony Island Ave., 67th Pl., and the lakefront, Jackson Park.*

2 *e-8*

MARQUETTE PARK

There's a new irrigation system at this 3,300-yard course in southwestern Chicago. *At Marquette Rd. and Kedzie Blvd., near Midway Airport, Marquette Park.*

1 *e-3*

ROBERT A. BLACK

Near the Evanston-Chicago border, this 2,600-yard course is the newest of the park-district golf courses. *Between Western Ave. and Ridge Blvd., and Pratt Blvd. and Arthur Ave., Edgewater.*

2 *h-8*

SOUTH SHORE

A former private club, this 2,903-yard city course affords great views of the Loop. *South Shore Dr. at 71st St. on the lakefront, South Shore.*

4 *e-5*

SYDNEY MAROVITZ/WAVELAND

The most difficult of city golf courses, this 3,290-yard lakeside area is filled with small trees and water hazards. *Lake Shore Dr. and Irving Park Rd. on the lakefront, Lakeview.*

6 *g-1*

CHICAGO FAMILY GOLF CENTERS

Supplementing the city golf greens is a 9-hole, par-3 course open all year. It's $12 for 9 holes Monday–Thursday and $15

Friday–Sunday; for 18 holes, $18 Monday–Thursday and $22 Friday–Sunday. *221 N. Columbus Dr., Loop, 312/616–1234.*

suburban chicago

There are more than 125 public golf courses in the Chicago suburbs, and greens fees go from $10 to $100. They include Cantigny (27 W. 270 Mack Rd., Wheaton, 630/668–8463); Cog Hill Golf and Country Club (12294 Archer Ave., Lemont, 630/257–5872), host of the PGA tour's Western Open in early July; Kemper Lakes (Old McHenry Rd., Long Grove, 847/320–3450), a superexpensive course costing $120 with mandatory cart rental included; and Village Links of Glen Ellyn (485 Winchell Way, Glen Ellyn, 630/469–8180). The Cook County Forest Preserve maintains 10 courses throughout the city and suburbs, open from mid-April through November for varying fees; to make a reservation by phone or get more information about specific courses and tee times, call 708/366–9466.

HANDBALL

Though racquetball facilities have cut into this old-fashioned sport's popularity, there are still thousands of courts in the city and suburbs. Call the park district (*see Parks Information, above*), a health club, or a YMCA near you for more details.

HIKING

The city's park trails are good for extremely short hikes, but hardcore hikers who can't afford to fly to Colorado or Alaska must content themselves with the Cook County Forest Preserve's almost 200 mi of hiking trails. For maps and more information, call 800/870–3666. Also contact Friends of the Chicago River (312/939–0490), which offers two-hour guided walks along the Chicago River on summer weekends.

HOCKEY

teams to watch

2 *f-5*

CHICAGO BLACKHAWKS

Though the balance of power in the National Hockey League has shifted to the Midwest, the Hawks have yet to become a beneficiary. Chris Chelios and company have given the team more talent than luck, which is always depressing when playoff time rolls around. The Blackhawks play at the United Center from October to April, unless they make the playoffs, which would extend their season into June. Games usually start at 7:30 PM. *United Center, 1901 W. Madison St., Near West Side, 312/455–7000.*

1 *c-4*

CHICAGO WOLVES

Though the International Hockey League continues to earn far less respect and has far less sales power than its older sibling, the National Hockey League, the Wolves are more fun to watch these days than the Blackhawks. Thousands of fans, who had paid comparatively little money for tickets, waved Howlin' Hankies as their team won the Turner Cup in May 1998 and again in 2000. Buy tickets by calling Ticketmaster at 312/559–1212 or 800/843–9658. *Allstate Arena, 10550 Lunt Ave., 847/390–0404.*

where to play

There's only one city-run place to play ice hockey year-round: the McFetridge Sports Center (3845 N. California Ave., Irving Park, 312/742–7585). Otherwise, nine of the city's outdoor ice rinks (including Riis, Rowan, McKinley, and Midway Plaisance parks) have hockey leagues and time slots for rat hockey or first-come, first-served pickup games. Call 312/747–5283.

HORSEBACK RIDING

Save for the rare police officer on horseback and a few equestrian enthusiasts, Chicago tends to worship its cars, buses, and subways much more reverently than its horses. It's impossible to find any facilities to keep horses in the city, although visitors can use the four bridle paths in the parks. Outside Chicago, you can ride on Cook County Forest Preserve trails with a valid rider's license, available for a small fee wherever you rent a horse.

tinley park

1 *d-7*

FOREST VIEW FARMS

The suburban farm gives English riding lessons in its indoor and outdoor rings, plus trail rides. *16717 S. Lockwood Ave., 708/560–0306.*

palos hills

1 *d-6*

PALOS HILLS RIDING STABLES

Though the stables have no trails, they offer both group and private riding lessons. *10100 S. Kean Ave., 708/598–7718.*

HORSE RACING

Until the Arlington International Racecourse gave up horse racing in 1997, the northwest suburban track was the premier place to bet and watch in the country. It's still possible to watch jockeys win by a nose, just not in fancy, flower-covered Arlington, whose managers have since tried to reinvent the place as a concert venue.

cicero

2 *d-6*

HAWTHORNE RACE COURSE

Thoroughbred racing is from early July through late December at this track just beyond Chicago's city limits. *3501 S. Laramie Ave., 708/780–3700.*

2 *d-6*

SPORTSMAN'S PARK

This park with live Thoroughbred racing from early March through late June is just down the street from Hawthorne. Without Arlington Heights in the game, Cicero has become the ultimate horse-racing city in the Chicago area. *3301 S. Laramie, 773/242–1121.*

crete

1 *e-8*

BALMORAL PARK

This course has no live Thoroughbred racing (simulcasts only) but does provide year-round live harness racing. *26435 S. Dixie Hwy., 708/672–7544.*

maywood

2 b-4

MAYWOOD PARK

Harness racing is from late February
through early May and late September
through late December. *8600 W. North
Ave., 708/343–4800.*

HORSESHOES

2 f-2, g-3, g-4

LINCOLN PARK

There are a few pitches at the south end
of the Lincoln Park Zoo. *Bordered by W.
Armitage St., N. Clark St., N. Lake Shore
Dr., and W. North Ave. to W. Hollywood
Ave., Lincoln Park, 312/742–7726.*

3 g-4

WELLES PARK

This park on the Northwest Side has
some pitches. *2333 W. Sunnyside Ave.,
Ravenswood, 312/742–7511.*

ICE-SKATING

One thing you may know about Chicago:
It's cold in the winter. Most people hibernate from roughly November through
February. Others, to stave off cabin fever,
do outside exercise. Even when the wind-
chills are ridiculous, it's possible to work
up a sweat while skating, near the lake
and otherwise. The park district runs 11
rinks in the winter, all of which are outdoors save the McFetridge Sports Center.
For information about rinks near you, call
312/747–5283. All the following rinks rent
skates. Of course, to avoid improper fits
and even less proper smells, it pays to
bring your own.

6 h-1

**DALEY
BICENTENNIAL PLAZA**

When it's freezing, the in-the-know skating obsessives hail a cab or walk a few
blocks to the intimate and charming
downtown rink near the lake. Despite
frequently thick crowds, skate rental is
indoors and the whole experience is
quick and easy. *337 E. Randolph St.,
Grant Park, Loop, 312/742–7648.*

2 e-2

**MCFETRIDGE
SPORTS CENTER**

Though most skating enthusiasts brave
the cold and pack Navy Pier on chilly

weekends, more practical Chicagoans
head to this popular indoor rink. The
center provides lessons and time slots
for hockey games. *3843 N. California
Ave., Irving Park, 312/742–7585.*

2 g-7

MIDWAY PLAISANCE PARK

Like all city ice rinks, this South Side
facility is Olympic-size. *Woodlawn Ave.
and 59th St., Hyde Park, 312/747–7661.*

2 g-4

NAVY PIER

This 80- by 108-ft rink is appealing for
its proximity to the Navy Pier's touristy
indoor restaurants, shops, and the
Chicago Children's Museum. The
views are terrific from this lakeside
vantage point adjacent to a Ferris
wheel. *600 E. Grand Ave., Near North
Side, 312/595–7437.*

schiller park

2 b-2

SCHILLER WOODS

In the middle of a suburban forest near
Chicago's North Side, this pond is one of
the many ice-skating facilities maintained
by the Cook County Forest Preserve. (Call
first at 773/261–8400 to make sure the
pond has the four inches of ice required
for skating.) *Irving Park and River Rds.,
800/870–3666 (forest preserve).*

IN-LINE SKATING
& ROLLER-
SKATING

Though some outdoor parks, notably
Daley Bicentennial Plaza in the Loop,
have skating facilities, in-line skating is
mostly unorganized. Some skaters ride
in the streets and some on sidewalks,
but there's just one place in Chicago
that directly accommodates the bladers.
That's the Lakefront Bicycle Path (*see
below*), and even there, we recommend
wearing pads wherever you can wear
them and staying to the right out of
respect to bicyclists.

In-line skating has mostly taken over
from the consummate '70s sport, roller-
skating, although retro movies such as
Boogie Nights have given the latter a
pop-culture boost. You might get some
funny looks zipping past the bladers in
one of the Chicago Park District's 300-

plus paved areas (most notably the lake-front path), but nobody will arrest you or anything. By the way, some ice-skating rinks, such as those in McKinley (2210 W. Pershing Rd.), Mt. Greenwood (3721 W. 111th St.), and West Lawn (4233 W. 65th St.) parks, transform into in-line-skating arenas in summer.

2 *f-1, f-2, g-2, g-3, g-4, g-5, g-6, h-7, h-8*
LAKEFRONT BICYCLE PATH
Nowhere is the boom in in-line skat-ing—from nonexistent a decade ago to a multimillion-dollar business today—more evident than near Lake Michigan on Chicago's Near North Side. It's impossible to walk or bicycle more than a foot, especially on sunny summer weekends, without narrowly avoiding a side-to-side skater. The sport looks easy, but it's hard to pick up, in case you hadn't noticed from the multitudes of weak-kneed rookies who dive hands-first into the grass. It's fun to watch the best ones zoom around carefully placed traf-fic cones next to the lake between North Avenue Beach and Olive Park Beach. Skates are available for rent at Londo Mondo (1100 N. Dearborn St., 312/751–2794); Windward Sports, (3317 N. Clark St., 773/472–6868); Bike Chicago (*see* Bicycling, *above*); and at a stand, with unpredictable hours during the summer, near the North Avenue beach house.

4 *b-2*
RAINBOW SKATING CENTER
With pizza and birthday parties, the city's largest roller-skating rink will bring any '70s-era teen back to childhood. During slow songs, ask strangers to skate with you and hold hands. *4836 N. Clark St., Uptown, 773/271–5668.*

JUGGLING

bensenville

1 *b-4*
ILLINOIS JUGGLING INSTITUTE
If you're looking for a great party trick, or you just want to distract the kids, you can learn to juggle at this facility. *143 Pershing St., 630/766–1437.*

LAWN BOWLING

Lawn bowling, a sport in which competi-tors wear white, shake hands, and wish

each other "good bowling" before going at it, has struggled to stay alive amid Chicago's unpredictable weather condi-tions. The park district continues to maintain a few greens (*see* Park Infor-mation, *above*).

2 *h-7*
LAKESIDE LAWN BOWLING CLUB
To play, you need 120 square ft of well-kept lawn—and even this South Side club's two greens have been endangered recently by heat waves and grass-eating fungi. But the club members, who prac-tice near the University of Chicago in Hyde Park, know lawn bowlers have faced adversity in the past. According to legend, Sir Francis Drake had to finish his game in 1588 before staving off the Spanish armada. *5800 S. Lake Shore Dr., South Shore, 773/684–9799.*

MARTIAL ARTS

Dozens of Chicago-area businesses pro-vide training in Eastern self-defense techniques—most offer karate, jujitsu, tae kwon do, kung fu, and judo. Some add more Western styles such as kick-boxing, wrestling, and standard boxing to the mix. Either way, you'll be able to take care of yourself after a few lessons. Consult the Yellow Pages for a listing.

2 *f-2*
DEGERBERG MARTIAL ARTS & FITNESS ACADEMY
In addition to its general fitness facili-ties (*see* Boxing, *above*), the exhaustive Degerberg offers hundreds of karate, jujitsu, tae kwon do, kung fu, and tai chi courses. Like many martial-arts acade-mies, it supplements the instruction with classes on "skills for highly effec-tive living" and "grappling and weapon arts." *4717 N. Lincoln Ave., Lincoln Park, 773/728–5300.*

2 *f-3*
IRON FIST KUNG FU
Focusing more on the basics than the frill-filled Degerberg, Iron Fist offers self-defense lessons for men, women, and children. *3845 N. Broadway, Uptown, 773/248–3478.*

6 *e-1*
656 W. Lake St., Loop, 630/582–4140.

2 *f-3*

K. S. HYUN'S HAPKIDO

Specializing in a Korean street fighter's technique known as hapkido, this fitness center teaches kicking, joint locks, hand strikes, punching, and weapons. It also advertises "special police guard training." *2743 N. Western Ave., North Center, 773/252–8300.*

2 *e-8*

3722 W. 79th St., Marquette Park, 773/284–1300.

MINIATURE GOLF

chicago

2 *g-4*

NAVY PIER

Everything touristy, from cotton candy to a Ferris wheel, can be found at Navy Pier, the lakeside amusement park near the Magnificent Mile. The miniature golf is fun and goofy, with trick shots like lofting the ball into a drinking cup. *600 E. Grand Ave., Near North Side, 312/595–7437.*

hickory hills

1 *d-6*

JUMP N' FUN

Despite the odd cage and waterfall, these two 18-hole courses are pretty standard. There's also a lighted double-deck driving range for the real golfers. *8125 W. 95th St., 708/599–6100.*

joliet

1 *b-2*

HAUNTED TRAILS FAMILY AMUSEMENT CENTER

Conveniently down the road from two riverboat gambling ca′ nos, this center allows you to drop off the kids and put a few tokens down on blackjack. The center is thorough, with go-carts, batting cages, amusement-park rides, and a restaurant to supplement the miniature golf. *1425 N. Broadway (Rte. 53), 815/722–7800.*

morton grove

1 *d-3*

PAR-KING SKILL GOLF

In a shopping center (which is to say popular with high school students), this challenging and elaborate course makes you hit balls into elevators, pipes, and other obstacles. There's a 48-inch height requirement, so don't bring the really young kids. *6711 Dempster Ave., 847/965–3333.*

MULTI-SPORT EVENTS

MRS. T'S TRIATHLON

Multidimensional athletes of all ages pack the city's lone annual triathlon, which, by definition, includes running, bicycling, and swimming. *Begins at Monroe Street Harbor, South Loop, 773/404–2372. August.*

SPORTFEST CHICAGO

This inexpensive tribute to team ground games includes a rugby tournament and softball, basketball, and hockey competitions and entertainment. *2200 W. Winnemac Ave. May.*

PADDLEBALL

This sport of one wall and one ball is easy to learn but difficult to master. Contact the park district (*see Park Information, above*), a YMCA, or health clubs to find facilities near you.

PADDLING

There are several places to rent paddleboats and canoes.

COOK COUNTY FOREST PRESERVE

Though it's hard to escape the city's urban clutches, even in a boat, call the forest preserve at 800/870–3666 for a woodsier sailboat, rowboat, or canoe experience. You can rent crafts at most of the lakeside concession stands. Some of the available suburban areas include Beck Lake, at Central Avenue and East River Road; Big Bend Lake, at Golf and East River Road; Maple Lake, at 95th Street west of Willow Springs Road; Powderhorn Lake, at Brainard and Burnham avenues in Calumet City; Saganashkee Slough, at 107th Street, west of Willow Springs Road (private rowboats only); Skokie Lagoons, east of the Edens Expressway, west of Winnetka between Willow and Dundee Roads; and Tampier Lake, at Wolf Road and 131st Street.

5 *f-3*
LINCOLN PARK PADDLEBOATS

It's not quite the same as buying a huge boat and cruising around Lake Michigan, but renting a paddleboat here, just footsteps away from the zoo, is a quiet way to spend a lazy, sunny Saturday. *2021 N. Stockton Dr., Lincoln Park, 312/742–2038.*

RACQUETBALL

A racquetball court is one of the only places where the act of bouncing off the walls doesn't mean you're certifiably insane. Because the walls always seem to be closing in, the sport is more intense than tennis, but it's easier to learn than, say, squash or hockey. Almost 20 city-run parks have racquetball courts, and they're a staple of health clubs, including the following.

2 *d-2*
EDENS ATHLETIC CLUB

The club sponsors leagues, but individual members can play without much hassle on five courts. *5130 N. Cicero Ave., North Park, 773/286–6700.*

2 *c-2*
PRESIDENT'S FITNESS CENTER

Members book time in advance on one of the center's three courts. *8600 W. Bryn Mawr Ave., Harwood Heights, 773/693–6500.*

6 *g-1*
RIVIERA HEALTH CLUB

The downtown club's one court is desirable, so members should sign up in advance. *400 E. Randolph Ave., Loop, 312/527–2525.*

RUGBY

Scrums aren't quite as common in Chicago parks as touchdowns and rushes, but there's nothing stopping you from organizing a game in any park.

2 *f-3*
CHICAGO LIONS RUGBY FOOTBALL CLUB

To join a more formal team, start by calling the Lions, who organize various leagues throughout the year. *1801 W. School St., Roscoe Village, 773/404–1441.*

5 *f-3*
LINCOLN PARK RUGBY FOOTBALL

Everyone's seen them—devoted rugby fans, kicking their way through another Sunday afternoon. Find out how you can become one of the group. *2019 N. Fremont St., Lincoln Park, 773/528–8844.*

RUNNING & WALKING

The Lakefront Path (*see Bicycling, above*) is the most prominent route for Chicago joggers, and runners of all skill levels regularly create a route of any length at any entry point. Beware: the path gets extremely congested, especially on nice weekends, so for a quiet, thoughtful run, get up early or stay out late. The park district's 25-plus oval tracks and seven or so straightaways are scattered throughout the city: Among the best are Avalon, Bessemer, California, Dunbar, Foster, Lake Shore, Legion, Riis, Union, and Warren parks (*see Park Information, above*). The Parcour path, with stations designed for joggers and walkers to exercise their muscles, begins in Lincoln Park at Fullerton Avenue. Call for a free packet of maps detailing routes (847/968–3335). The Lakewood Forest Preserve (708/526–5290), at Route 176 and Fairfield Road, in Wauconda, is a year-round ¾-mi trail with 20 exercise stations.

associations

6 *g-1*
CHICAGO AREA RUNNERS ASSOCIATION

The largest runners' club in the Midwest organizes several local races and provides training information for marathon and beginning runners. *203 N. Wabash Ave., Loop, 312/666–9836.*

events

AIDS WALK CHICAGO

Over the past decade or so, this annual 6.2-mi walk—which isn't a race by any means—has raised more than $8 million for people with HIV and AIDS. In addition to the cause, its biggest selling point is location, beginning downtown and heading along the lakefront toward the John G. Shedd Aquarium. *Begins at Monroe Street Harbor, South Loop, 312/739–9255. 3rd wk in Sept.*

BALLY'S TOTAL FITNESS RACE-TO-TASTE

This race's starting point and destination—the massive Taste of Chicago festival, which draws millions of hungry people to Grant Park for 10 days every summer—have a much higher profile than the race itself. But the 5K event is growing in popularity, and it makes sense to work off the food before you eat it. *Begins in Grant Park, 312/744–3370. Early July.*

CHICAGO MARATHON

The huge marathon isn't as influential as, say, the Boston Marathon, but it has its moments. In the mid-'80s, it was arguably the premier fall marathon, and in recent years, thanks to participation by Olympians such as Keith Brantly and Kim Jones, it has regained some of the lost popularity. *Begins in Grant Park, Loop, 773/868–3010. 3rd wk in Oct.*

SAILING

Sailing is part of the city's culture, what with regular regattas far into Lake Michigan and the annual Chicago-to-Mackinac Island Yacht Race (*see below*). On any clear day in spring and summer, the hundreds of docked yachts in the city's six harbors, some of which are within walking distance from the Loop, set sail for the open lake. The sport is much harder than it looks, however, so take your first several trips with an experienced sailor or try one of several boating schools, listed below. Also, contact the Chicago Yacht Club (312/861–7777) for more information. The park district (*see* Park Information, *above*) also has sailing programs, at Burnham Harbor, North Avenue Beach, and South Shore Beach.

clubs and schools

4 *e-8, f-8*

CHICAGO SAILING CLUB

Hearty yachtsman Bill Gladstone teaches classes in Belmont Harbor for beginners and wanna-be racers during boating season. With both private and group lessons, Gladstone and staff can remove seasickness from even the most landlubbing urbanite. *Belmont Ave. and the lakefront, Lincoln Park, 773/871–7245.*

2 *h-8*

OFFSHORE SAILING SCHOOL

This national company offers three-day courses but doesn't rent boats—except to members, who pay an initiation fee and regular dues. *6401 S. Coast Guard Dr., 10 minutes south of Soldier Field, 773/643–7289.*

2 *g-5*

RAINBOW FLEET SAILING INSTRUCTION

Run by the Chicago Park District, this school has affordable local classes and boat rental. *1362 S. Lynn White Dr., in Burnham Harbor near Soldier Field, 312/747–7684.*

docks

LAKEFRONT HARBORS

Many local boat owners pay the $15 a day or $100 for the boating season, which lasts from May 15 to October 15, to dock in one of the lakefront's six major harbors. (Call the harbor division, at 312/747–0737, for more information.) The harbors are Belmont (Belmont Ave. and the lakefront, 312/742–7673); Burnham (1559 S. Lake Shore Dr., 312/747–

STATUES IN THE PARKS

Some of the better-known Chicago parks monuments:

The **Bison** guard the east entrance to the rose garden in Humboldt Park.

Buckingham Fountain, in Grant Park, is one of the most impressive and famous city monuments.

Alexander Hamilton watches over sunbathers in Lincoln Park, near the corner of Stockton Drive and Diversey Parkway.

Abraham Lincoln sits at the Grant Park Court of Presidents.

Abraham Lincoln stands in Lincoln Park.

The **Big Beaver**, a wooden totem pole, is next to the Field Museum of Natural History.

The **Fountain of Time**, in Washington Park, portrays the passing of humanity.

The **Haidan Indian Totem Pole**, in a lakefront park near Addison Avenue and Lake Shore Drive, is said to be haunted.

7009); Diversey (150 W. St. James Pl., 312/742–7762); Jackson (6500 S. Coast Guard Dr., 312/747–6189); Monroe (Monroe St. and the lakefront, 312/742–7643); and Montrose (Montrose Ave. and the lakefront, 312/742–7527).

events

CHICAGO-TO-MACKINAC ISLAND YACHT RACE

This fancy competition, sponsored by the Chicago Yacht Club, celebrated its 100th anniversary in 1998 and included its first all-women team. It's expensive to participate, with some of the 300 sailboats costing as much as $1 million, but it's cheap and exciting to watch. Some spectators plan summer trips around the event, which winds up in Michigan's Upper Peninsula. *Begins near the lighthouse at Monroe Street Harbor, South Loop, 773/404–2372. 3rd wk in July.*

SCUBA DIVING

Lake Michigan might not be the great blue sea, but in the event that you travel out of the Windy City, Chicago offers some ways to get your sea legs by learning scuba diving.

5 *a-2*

ADVENTURES IN SCUBA

This place offers a variety of courses, from beginning to advanced. It has an in-store training pool and flexible training times. *1730 W. Fullerton Ave., DePaul, 773/935–3483.*

6 *f-4*

MAGNUM SCUBA

This scuba school has instruction as well as diving trips. *14 E. 11th St., South Loop, 312/341–3483.*

SOCCER

teams to watch

2 *g-5*

CHICAGO FIRE

One of the stronger U.S. teams, Major League Soccer's Chicago Fire put together an impressive 11-game winning streak in 1998 and sent several team members to the 2000 Olympics in Sydney. *Soldier Field, 425 E. McFetridge Dr., South Loop, 888/657–3473.*

where to play

You can't throw a soccer ball in Chicago parks without hitting one of the 200-plus fields. The park district (*see Park Information, above*) runs leagues for players of all ages, and two excellent private resources are the Illinois Soccer Association (5306 W. Lawrence Ave., 773/283–2800) and the National Soccer League of Chicago (4534 N. Lincoln Ave., 773/275–2850).

events

MAYOR'S CUP SOCCER FEST

Some 600 teams compete in Chicago's two-day answer to the World Cup every year, and the sidelights include dancers, tumblers, and singers. *Montrose Ave. and Lake Shore Dr., Lakeview, 312/744–3315. 2nd wk in July.*

SQUASH

Some private clubs have facilities for squash.

2 *g-4*

LAKESHORE ATHLETIC CLUB

For members, the downtown clubs have three courts for free, or $15 during prime time. The Lincoln Park outlet's two courts are available for $11, or $15 in prime time (they're never free). *441 N. Wabash Ave., Loop, 312/644–4880.*

2 *g-4*

211 N. Stetson Ave., Loop, 312/616–9000.

2 *f-3*

1320 W. Fullerton Ave., Lincoln Park, 773/477–9888.

SWIMMING

Even in winter, when the idea of stepping into any body of water is enough to make a Chicagoan's toes freeze instantly, pools are open in the city. Summer is prime swimming time, though, and the park lagoons, outdoor pools, and Lake Michigan fill with splashers and kickers of all ages. Most of the city's 65 outdoor pools are open daily from noon to 9 PM from the end of June to Labor Day; the park district also runs day-camp programs for preteens and sponsors swimming lessons at all locations. The 35 indoor pools are open year-round, with extended hours from October through May. The city also contracts pools at several high schools, and if all else fails, there's always the YMCA and health clubs.

2 d-4

AUSTIN TOWN HALL PARK

There's an average-size indoor pool at this West Side park. 5610 W. Lake St., West Garfield Park, 312/746–5006.

2 d-4

BLACKHAWK PARK

Kids dominate this large indoor pool; it's quieter during designated hours for adults. 2318 N. Lavergne St., West Garfield Park, 312/746–5014.

1 e-6

CARVER PARK

The indoor pool at this far South Side park is much bigger than average. 939 E. 132nd St., South Side, 312/747–6047.

2 f-4

ROBERTO CLEMENTE

This is an adult-oriented pool, larger than usual, and as deep as 12 ft. 2334 W. Division St., Ukrainian Village, 312/742–7538.

2 e-5

DOUGLAS PARK

This 500-meter outdoor pool attracts a lot of kids, especially teens, in the evenings. 1401 S. Sacramento Blvd., Lawndale, 312/747–7670.

2 g-7

DYETT SCHOOL

This large pool is on the South Side, near Lake Michigan. 513 E. 51st St., Hyde Park, 312/747–6118.

2 e-3

INDEPENDENCE PARK

At 20 meters long, this pool is the smallest in the city, but that gives it a certain calmness. 3945 N. Springfield Ave., Irving Park, 312/742–7590.

LAKE MICHIGAN

One of the great things about living in Chicago is you don't have to travel far to hit a sandy beach (even if it flows into concrete and cement on the opposite edge of the lake). Though it's frigid most of the year, and some residents are still wary of pollution, it's warm at the end of summer and cleaner than people think. On the most popular beaches, such as Oak Street and North Avenue, it's difficult to find space to air out the old breast stroke. But out-of-the-way spots, especially as you head farther north or farther south of the Loop, exist for explorers (see Beaches, above). The lake is open for swimming, with lifeguards, from Memorial Day through Labor Day.

2 e-4

ORR SCHOOL PARK

This North Side pool is Olympic-size. 730 N. Pulaski Rd., Humboldt Park, 312/746–5354.

1 e-6

RIDGE PARK

This pool is Olympic-size. 96th St. and S. Longwood Dr., South Side, 312/747–6639.

2 d-1

WHEALAN AQUATIC CENTER

The only Cook County Forest Preserve–run pool in Chicago, Whealan is open seven days a week. 6200 W. Devon Ave., at Milwaukee Ave., North Park, 773/775–1666.

5 d-5

YMCA

Most of the Chicago-area YMCAs have pools, swimming lessons, and varying water activities such as aerobics and meets. The two largest YMCA pools are at the Austin (501 N. Central Ave., 773/287–9120) and South Side (6330 S. Stony Island Ave., 773/947–0700) branches. Bring your own towels and locks.

The central location is the New City "Y," which divides two starkly different neighborhoods, the affluent Lincoln Park to the north and the Cabrini-Green housing project to the south; bright lighting and tall fences make the facilities safe. 1515 N. Halsted St., Clybourn Corridor, 312/266–1242. $10 with guest pass.

calumet city

1 f-7

GREEN LAKE

One of three Chicago-area pools run by the Cook County Forest Preserve, this outdoor facility has actual sand at the bottom and Lake Michigan water piped through a filter. Torrence and 159th St., 708/862–4730.

lyons

1 *d-5*

CERMAK POOL

Maintained by the Cook County Forest Preserve, Cermak is Olympic-size. *7600 W. Ogden Ave., at the Des Plaines River, 708/447–3226.*

TENNIS

where to play

Most of the city's 600-plus courts are free, and players sign up using the racking system: hang a tennis racket (preferably an old one) on a pegboard near the court to sign up for specific time slots. Then show up and claim the court. There are courts all over the place, but the most popular ones are along the lakefront. Tennis season usually begins in mid-April, weather permitting, and the park district offers lessons; call 773/248–2063.

The following Chicago tennis listings are city-owned, except where noted.

7 *e-5*

CHICAGOLAND INDOOR TENNIS ASSOCIATION

It's hard to play on the city's many courts without help from an expert group. Call weekdays 9–5. *919 N. Michigan Ave., Loop, 312/337–0145.*

6 *h-1*

DALEY BICENTENNIAL PLAZA

This outdoor spot is hugely popular because it's downtown, and you can play beneath the skyscrapers. Each of the 12 courts, unlike most free city-run tennis facilities, costs $5 per hour. It also sponsors its own lesson program. *337 E. Randolph St., Loop, 312/742–7648.*

5 *e-1*

DIVERSEY

Because of city maintenance complications, these are the only four clay courts left in the city. They cost $10 an hour, tennis shoes are required, and be forewarned that it's impossible to play after a rainstorm. *138 W. Diversey Pkwy, Lincoln Park.*

8 *f-2*

GRANT PARK

The city levies fees to play at the two sets of courts in this beautiful downtown park. *Off Randolph St. at the northern tip of Grant Park, Loop.*

2 *e-2*

MCFETRIDGE SPORTS COMPLEX

The price of playing indoors is high but, as most Chicago residents know, invaluable given unpredictable weather. Each of the six indoor courts costs $10.50 an hour and $16 an hour after 6 PM; weekends, $10.50 an hour until 5 PM. Winter rates are roughly the same. Before playing, you must sign up for a membership card. *3845 N. California Ave., Logan Square, 312/742–7585.*

2 *f-6*

MCKINLEY PARK

With 10 courts, this West Side park is becoming a major tennis headquarters. *2210 W. Pershing Rd., McKinley Park.*

2 *f-3*

MID-TOWN TENNIS CLUB

With 18 metropolitan club locations, the Tennis Club is an excellent central point for private lessons (in foreign languages, too) and group instruction. *2428 N. Elston Ave., Bucktown, 773/235–2300.*

5 *d-3*

OZ PARK

In the shadow of the Tin Man, these 10 recently resurfaced courts are the next best thing to being in Lincoln Park. *2021 N. Burling St., Lincoln Park.*

2 *d-3*

RIIS PARK

These 10 courts make up one of the West Side's most popular tennis spots. *6100 W. Fullerton Ave., Logan Square.*

2 *h-8*

SOUTH SHORE CULTURAL CENTER

There are four good outdoor courts, but individual players should call first to make sure Midwest Tennis isn't holding a camp. Otherwise, courts are available on a first-come, first-served (excuse the pun) basis. *7059 South Shore Dr., South Shore, 312/747–2536.*

4 *e-5*

WAVELAND

A hotbed for tennis, with passes costing $3 for a day, this area has 20 courts and

is in Lincoln Park near the golf course.
37 N. Recreation Dr., Lakeview.

2 *h-7*
HAROLD WASHINGTON
Several courts are near the University of
Chicago, just on the edge of Jackson
Park. *5200 S. Hyde Park.*

niles

1 *e-3*
TAM TENNIS & FITNESS COMPLEX
A pro-rated health club that offers racquetball and complete fitness facilities
to members, this suburban complex
also rents its eight indoor tennis courts
by the hour. *7686 N. Caldwell Ave., 847/
967–1400.*

oak lawn

1 *e-6*
OAK LAWN RACQUET CLUB
This members-only club supplements
its racquetball, weight-training, sauna,
whirlpool, and bar facilities with six
indoor tennis courts. *10444 S. Central
Ave., 708/857–2215.*

oak park

2 *d-4*
TENNIS & FITNESS CENTER
With eight indoor courts, tennis is the
bottom line of this club in the near western suburbs, but it also includes six racquetball courts, a workout room, and
standard health-club facilities. *301 Lake
St., 708/386–2175.*

VOLLEYBALL

Maybe because of the constantly filled
pickup games at North Avenue Beach,
spiking and setting are huge in the Windy
City. There's the Pro-Am Beach Volleyball
Series, which always draws summer
crowds to the beach, and the park district
keeps more than 400 indoor and outdoor courts. There are leagues and training activities aplenty; call the district at
312/871–8008 (for equipment rental) or
312/742–7841 (for league and court information). Most health clubs and YMCAs
have volleyball facilities, too.

where to play

4 *d-1*
FOSTER BEACH
Beach volleyball is big at this relatively
uncrowded beach on the North Side. If
you can't find an available court, try
Montrose Beach due south or Hollywood to the north. *Foster Ave. and the
lakefront, Andersonville.*

5 *g-5*
NORTH AVENUE BEACH
Pickup volleyball games are less mean-
spirited than, say, pickup hoops or rat
hockey—how can anybody snarl effectively in bare feet and bikinis?—but just
as competitive. Show up early to get a
court at this beach volleyball paradise,
or prepare to wait all day. *North Ave. and
the lakefront, Gold Coast.*

events

CHICAGO PRO-AM BEACH VOLLEYBALL SERIES
Because amateurs belong to the 16
competing divisions in this occasional
weekend series, it doesn't have the pres-
tige of the professional volleyball tournaments. But the open registration
makes the event more democratic, and
it's a fun way to spend a lazy summer
weekend. *North Avenue Beach, Gold
Coast, 312/266–8580. Several weekends in
summer, beginning in May.*

WINDSURFING

Chicagoans rarely pretend they're Cali-
fornians, especially with the lack of killer
waves in Lake Michigan, but occasionally they get the urge to surf anyway.

4 *e-4*
MONTROSE BEACH
This northern harbor is near a treeless
hill and kite-flyers by the dozen. It's not
too crowded, and the beach area
attracts practicing windsurfers. *Montrose
Ave. and the lakefront, Uptown.*

WRESTLING

We're talking about real wrestling,
here—the difficult sport where athletes
engage each other in pure, fair hand-to-
hand-to-leg combat, not the "sport" of
the World Wrestling Foundation. For
non-fake wrestling classes and tourna-

ments, contact the park district (*see* Park Information, *above*).

YOGA

Call one of the Chicago Park District's regional offices (*see* Park Information, *above*) to find a park with morning, afternoon, and evening yoga classes, for a fee.

2 *f-4*

GLOBAL YOGA AND WELLNESS CENTER

It has classes in hatha yoga, meditation, and stress reduction. *1608 N. Milwaukee St., Bucktown, 773/489–1510.*

2 *f-3*

PEACE SCHOOL

For more than 25 years, the Peace School has been giving workshops on yoga, women's self-defense, martial arts, acupressure, and massage. *3121 N. Lincoln Ave., Lincoln Park, 773/248–7959.*

2 *f-2*

SIVANANDA YOGA CENTER

The center combines yoga with meditation, breathing, and dietary techniques. *1246 W. Bryn Mawr Ave., Uptown, 773/878–7771.*

fitness centers, health clubs & spa services

CLUBS

Parks and recreation centers, not to mention the YMCA, have some of the best workout deals in the city. But for a membership fee, the following health clubs will sweat all the small stuff— everything's air-conditioned in the summer and well heated in the winter; the shower facilities are usually immaculate, with lotions and shampoos available on the counters; and weight-training equipment is state-of-the-art. Plus, scheduling is simply more convenient at health clubs; if you want to shoot hoops immediately after getting off work, odds are a court will be available. Aside from the price, the payoff for all this comfort is the fashion distraction. Whether you're there to work out or not, somebody is there to check you out or be checked out. At some clubs, it's hard to concentrate with all the Lycra, makeup, and posing flashing before your StairMaster-addled eyes. Membership fees are all pretty expensive, but some have deals at certain times of the year.

7 *b-5*

BALLY TOTAL FITNESS

This huge national health-club chain, which has everything from aerobics classes to indoor pools, has 23 outlets in Chicagoland. One-day entry will cost you $15. *820 N. Orleans St., River North, 312/664–6537.*

4 *b-8*

CHICAGO FITNESS CENTER

Other than karate, boxing, and kickboxing classes and facilities, this North Side club is refreshingly devoid of frills. The workout equipment, from Nautilus to Cybex, is in good shape and the fees are reasonable. You can use the gym for one day for just $7 and a picture ID. *3131 N. Lincoln Ave., Lakeview, 773/549–8181.*

2 *f-5*

HOOPS THE GYM

Finding a decent place to play basketball in Chicago is more difficult than it sounds. Cheaper places like park gyms and YMCAs often have regular hours and chuckers who refuse to pass the ball. Even the health clubs are crapshoots. So for serious Michael Jordan emulators, Hoops the Gym has been a godsend. The fees are large ($110 per hour for a group of up to 20), but the inexpensive idea is to gather a bunch of like-minded players for regular timeslots. The facilities are well maintained. *1380 Randolph St., West Loop, 312/850–4667.*

2 *f-5*

1001 W. Washington St., West Loop, 312/850–9496.

2 *g-4*

LAKESHORE ATHLETIC CLUB

At three Chicago locations, this 25-year-old club has pretty much everything a conscientious exerciser needs, including StairMasters, NordicTrack stationary bicycles, a big indoor swimming pool, kids' activities, and a health bar. Plus, there are facilities for racquetball, tennis, handball, and track. Try it for one day for $15. *441 N. Wabash Ave., Loop, 312/644–4880.*

2 *f-3*

1320 W. Fullerton Ave., Lincoln Park, 773/477–9888.

2 *g-4*

211 N. Stetson Ave., Loop, 312/616–9000.

5 *e-1*

LEHMANN SPORTS CLUB

In the heart of trendy Lincoln Park, Lehmann is almost as appearance-oriented as the Lake Bicycle Path. It's also one of the most thorough health clubs in the city, with equipment and courts available for hoops, dancing, aerobics, indoor swimming, racquetball, boxing, and tae kwon do. We're not sure what sun-tanning has to do with fitness, but that's here, too. A one-day guest pass is $15. 2700 N. Lehmann Ct., Lincoln Park, 773/871–8300.

7 *g-7*

MCCLURG COURT SPORTS CENTER

What separates McClurg from its Loop competitors is massage—two therapists are on hand to help with the cooldown after working out in the free-weight room, lap pool, basketball court, racquetball courts, tennis courts, or free aerobics classes. 333 E. Ontario St., Streeterville, 312/944–4546.

8 *b-3*

WORLD GYM AND FITNESS CENTER

A sauna and steam room are available after hard workouts with the cardiovascular equipment, aerobics classes, or weight-training machines. 100 S. Wacker Dr., South Loop, 312/357–9753.

DAY SPAS

Even the "city that works" has to pamper itself every once in a while. Try a soak at these, or any of the other dozen or so spa facilities in Chicago. They're usually expensive.

4 *d-8*

A THOUSAND WAVES SPA

This women-only spa is in the heart of a fun, populated area on the North Side (just down the street from B.L.U.E.S. Etc. and the Ann Sather restaurant). It has sauna, hot tub, massage, steam bath, and beauty facilities. A half-hour massage will run you $45. 1212 N. Belmont Ave., Lakeview, 773/549–0700.

7 *c-7*

EMBASSY STUDIO

"Total indulgence," says the ad for this salon just north of the Loop, which emphasizes beauty (hair styling, body waxing, pedicures) but also includes massage and sauna. 770 N. LaSalle St., River North, 312/642–9800.

2 *g-4*

WAVES SPA

Inside the Athletic Club Illinois Center, this downtown spa offers massage and skin care facilities—and a pass to the health club for the day. A 20-minute massage session costs $45 for non-members. 211 N. Stetson Ave., Loop, 312/616–1087.

8 *g-1*

SPA DI LA FRONZA SALON

This full-service spa is on the east side of the Loop, near several fancy hotels. A one-hour massage costs $75. 233 E. Wacker Dr., Loop, 312/565–0505.

MASSAGES

A spa is not the only place in town to get a massage. Try one of the following, which have professional, fully trained massage therapists.

4 *b-8*

CHICAGO SCHOOL OF MASSAGE THERAPY

Students charge reasonably for half-hour or full-hour sessions (a half-hour massage costs $25). The agency also refers clients to professional therapists. 2918 N. Lincoln Ave., Lincoln Park, 773/477–9444.

4 *a-7*

KNOW NO LIMITS FITNESS AND WELLNESS CENTER

Staff members specialize in treating sports-related aches and pains. Non-members of the adjacent fitness center can make massage appointments, too. 3530 N. Lincoln Ave., Lakeview, 773/404–1950.

6 *f-1*

ULTIMATE BACK STORE

This downtown store offers seated-chair massage on a walk-in basis. Full-body table massage is also available by appointment. 27 W. Lake St., Loop, 312/263–4782.

7 *d-4*

URBAN OASIS

This soothing, upscale downtown hide-away specializes in all types of massage, from Swedish to shiatsu. *12 W. Maple Ave., Magnificent Mile, 312/587–3500.*

5 *e-3*

**ZENERGY
MASSAGE THERAPY**

In a charming old building close to Lincoln Park, this center has an aura of soothing and calm. *346 W. Armitage St., Lincoln Park, 773/975–9300.*

chapter 4

PLACES TO EXPLORE

galleries, gargoyles, museums & more

To watch Lake Michigan lie glittering in the sun, as turquoise as the Caribbean, from where you sit trapped in your office is a Windy City brand of torture. Especially in the warm summer months, the pristine beaches, wide-open green parks, and sheltered harbors constantly whisper in your ear: "Why are you sitting behind a desk? Everybody's having fun outside except you. Take the day off!"

On the dreariest days of winter, when white-capped waves crash up against Lake Shore Drive, the spectacular buildings dotting the city's skyline are enough to lure even the most snow-bound to come out and explore.

When you live in Chicago, it's easy to be content with the simple routines of life: watching Bulls games with friends at a favorite watering hole, even if Michael Jordan and Scottie Pippen have long since been replaced by Elton Brand and Ron Artest; stopping by the Art Institute when yet another world-class exhibit comes to town; taking the kids to see Lincoln Park Zoo's giraffes, elephants, monkeys and hyenas; hanging out in the bleachers at Wrigley Field; shopping on the Magnificent Mile when the holidays arrive.

But those are the basics. In Chicago, you can always pick the more offbeat option.

Start by looking out the window as you ride the El. Attend an art gallery opening in the River North district. Wander through Graceland Cemetery, where prominent Chicagoans rest. Take a day for book-shopping in Hyde Park. Climb to the top of the John Hancock Center and try to figure out where you live. Grimace at the tiny patches of human hair hanging at the Museum of Contemporary Art. Visit Sue the dinosaur at the Field Museum of Natural History. And slowly begin to understand that with suburbs like Oak Park, with its Frank Lloyd Wright–designed homes, a venture outside the city doesn't have to start at O'Hare Airport.

Of course, your opinion of Chicago already is sky-high. Where else can you find some of the world's tallest skyscrapers and an abundance of people who are nice to you on the street? Even though the Bulls will never be the same without Michael Jordan, and the Cubs will never finish higher than second place, there's no place like home.

where to go

ARCHITECTURE

Each site is introduced with the name of its architect and the year the project was completed. A telephone number is given if the building is open to the general public beyond its lobby and other public areas.

8 f-2
AMOCO BUILDING
(Edward D. Stone, 1974; addition, Perkins & Will Partnership, 1985.) This tall, white rectangle on the city's skyline claimed the title "world's highest marble-clad sculpture" when erected in 1974. Unfortunately, after a few harsh Chicago winters, the delicate slabs—taken from the same quarry Michelangelo used—began to warp and fall off. Speckled granite now covers the building, best viewed from a distance, which rises 80 stories and offers spectacular city views. It contains Harry Bertoia's chime sculpture *Sounding*, which uses copper rods to make interesting sounds when the wind blows. *200 E. Randolph St., Loop.*

7 c-7
ANTI-CRUELTY SOCIETY
(Leon E. Stanhope, 1935; addition, Stanley Tigerman, 1982.) Don't forget to have your pet spayed or neutered, and don't forget to admire the building that houses the Anti-Cruelty Society. The Depression-era building was spruced up by architect Stanley Tigerman's whimsical wood-and-glass addition, which bears strange resemblance to a can of dog food. Architecture aside, it's a great place to find a new pet. Through the curved green windows, cats and dogs in cages attempt to use their endearing

cuteness to hypnotize passersby into taking them home. *157 W. Grand Ave., Streeterville, 312/644–8338.*

7 *d-1*

ARCHBISHOP'S RESIDENCE

(Alfred F. Pashley, 1880.) Since 1880, this stunning Victorian mansion has been home to Chicago's Roman Catholic archbishops, including the much-loved Joseph Cardinal Bernadine who died in 1996. Children love to count all the chimneys on this three-story landmark—19 in all. *1555 N. State Pkwy., Gold Coast.*

8 *e-3*

ART INSTITUTE OF CHICAGO

(Shepley, Rutan & Coolidge, 1892; McKinlock Court: Coolidge & Hodgdon, 1924; North Wing: Holabird & Root, 1956; Morton Wing: Shaw, Metz & Associates, 1962; East Wing: Skidmore, Owings & Merrill, 1976.) As if its world-renowned collections weren't enough, the two massive lions flanking the Art Institute's entrance certainly give the museum an aura of importance. The building, however, was not meant to intimidate people: designers deliberately chose a Classical Renaissance style to make art seem accessible and familiar to the people of the city. Judging from the crowds who casually hang out on the museum's steps, especially on sunny days, that goal has been achieved. *S. Michigan Ave. and Adams St., Loop, 312/443–3600.*

8 *e-5*

AUDITORIUM THEATRE

(Adler & Sullivan, 1889; restoration, Harry Weese, 1967.) A reputation for unimpeded views and near-perfect acoustics are icing on the cake for the building's architectural splendor. The 1889 building is a monument to the engineering skill of Dankmar Adler and the design genius of Louis Sullivan; even Frank Lloyd Wright was impressed with the theater, calling it "fifty years ahead of its time." The lobby facing Michigan Avenue has marble wainscot-

ing and a truly grand staircase. The interior ornamentation, including arched rows of lights along the ceiling, is breathtaking. Another beautiful (though less well-known) space is the library on the 10th floor of the building. Although the theater is normally closed to the public unless there's a show or concert, a 45-minute tour, usually given once a day on weekdays, is worthwhile even for seen-it-all Chicago architecture devotees. *50 E. Congress Pkwy., South Loop, 312/922–2110.*

8 *e-1*

CARBIDE AND CARBON BUILDING

(Burnham Brothers, 1929.) This striking Art Deco building has a deep green terra-cotta tower and a sleek gold-and-black exterior. Designed by the sons of famed Chicago architect Daniel H. Burnham, the 40-story building has a spectacular lobby with brass, marble, and glass ornamentation. *230 N. Michigan Ave., Near North.*

8 *d-3*

CARSON PIRIE SCOTT & COMPANY STORE

(Louis H. Sullivan, 1899, 1903–4; additions, Daniel H. Burnham & Co., 1906, and Holabird & Root, 1960.) Striking flower-and-leaf designs on the main entrance, and movable windows around a large fixed central pane developed by the so-called Chicago School of architects give this building architectural significance. But the department store might be best known for its key location at the intersection of State and Madison, the "0,0" coordinates of Chicago's map grid. *1 S. State St., at Madison St., Loop, 312/641–7000.*

7 *e-2*

CHARNLEY HOUSE

(Adler & Sullivan, Frank Lloyd Wright, 1891.) This three-story, 11-room private residence built for lumberman James Charnley shows off the talent of renowned architects Louis Sullivan and Frank Lloyd Wright, who was a 25-year-old draftsman in Sullivan's office at the

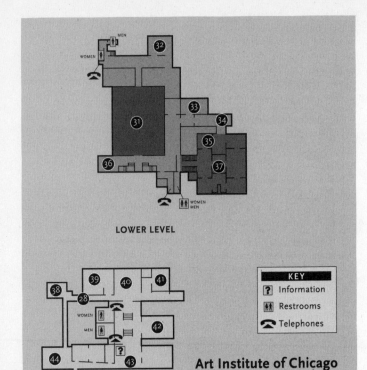

LOWER LEVEL

KEY

? Information

🚻 Restrooms

☎ Telephones

Art Institute of Chicago

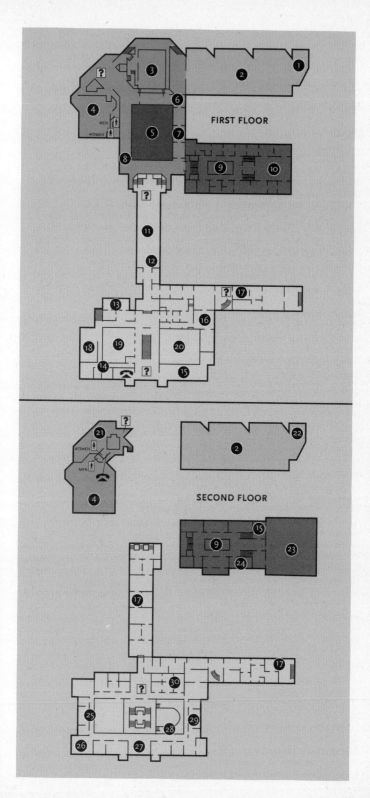

FIRST FLOOR

SECOND FLOOR

time. Wright later claimed to have been the building's sole designer, although many architects say the protruding covered balcony, with its stark horizontal roof and thin vertical columns, is clearly a mark of Sullivan. *1365 N. Astor St., Gold Coast, 312/915–0105.*

8 *c-4*

CHICAGO BOARD OF TRADE BUILDING

(Holabird & Root, 1930.) Inside, traders scramble madly in the pits, making deals for corn, wheat, soybeans, and other commodities. But outside, a gilded statue of Ceres, the Roman goddess of grain and harvest, sits serenely atop this 45-story skyscraper. Along with the Civic Opera House and the Carbide and Carbon Building, it's a stunning example of Art Deco architecture, with breathtaking light and dark marbles and rectilinear designs. It stands 526 ft tall, casting shadows over LaSalle Street's southern end and anchoring Chicago's financial district. A 24-story glass-and-steel addition, facing south, was completed in 1980. *141 W. Jackson Blvd., Loop, 312/435–3590.*

8 *e-2*

CHICAGO CULTURAL CENTER

(Shepley, Rutan & Coolidge, 1897; restoration, Holabird & Root, 1977.) This elegant building began its existence in 1872 as the Chicago Public Library, handling books sent from England to replace those destroyed by the Great Fire of 1871. Now a cultural center, the building has an elegant Romanesque-style entrance with marble and mosaic decoration, a stunning back-lighted Tiffany dome, and a white Carrara marble grand staircase. Scene of lunchtime concerts and other civic events, it also houses the Museum of Broadcast Communications, dedicated to exhibits about television and radio. *78 E. Washington St., at Michigan Ave., Loop, 312/744–6630.*

6 *g-3*

CHICAGO HILTON AND TOWERS

(Holabird & Roche, 1927.) Once billed as the largest hotel in the world, the former Stevens Hotel has transformed several times, most recently with a $150 million renovation in the mid-'80s. With its endless chandelier-filled ceilings, sweeping stairway, and spec-tacular Grand Ballroom, the hotel is a great place to wander through during a walk around the Loop. Maintaining the old-fashioned ambience is a brass quartet, which plays at the top of the big stairway on opening Lyric Opera nights. *720 S. Michigan Ave., South Loop, 312/922–4400.*

5 *f-4*

CHICAGO HISTORICAL SOCIETY

(Graham, Anderson, Probst, & White, 1932.) A stately Georgian-style building houses Chicago's oldest cultural institution (founded in 1856). A terra-cotta arch designed by Daniel Burnham graces the building's south end; it originally framed National Livestock Bank's doorway near the old Chicago stockyards. The striking, rather modern addition facing Clark Street was completed in 1971. *1601 N. Clark St., Lincoln Park, 312/642–4600.*

8 *b-3*

CHICAGO MERCANTILE EXCHANGE

(Fujikawa Johnson and Associates, 1983.) From the visitors' galleries, you might be too distracted by the frenetic activity, as traders wheel and deal over commodities, to notice the Merc's architecture. But it's worth a peek: the top 38 floors of this 40-story building are cleverly cantilevered over the trading floors. *30 S. Wacker Dr., Loop, 312/930–8249.*

7 *e-6*

CHICAGO PLACE

(Base: Skidmore, Owings & Merrill; tower: Solomon Cordwell Buenz & Associates; 1990.) This 58-story tower, smack in the middle of the Mag Mile, houses Chicago Place Mall, which has 50 shops on eight floors and is anchored by Saks Fifth Avenue. Its eighth-floor Garden Food Court, an airy space filled with fountains and ficus trees, is quite possibly the best food court on Michigan Avenue. From the food court, a stunning 65-ft barrel vault glass window overlooks the city. *700 N. Michigan Ave., Near North, 312/642–4811.*

7 *e-8*

CHICAGO SUN-TIMES BUILDING

(Naess & Murphy, 1957.) While undeniably less attractive than the Gothic-inspired Tribune Tower, where rival *Chicago Tribune* is published just across the street, this modern no-frills building seems an appropriate home for the newspaper that covers "The City That Works." Cut through the lobby to view the *Sun-Times*'s printing plant through windows. *401 N. Wabash Ave., Loop.*

8 d-1

CHICAGO THEATER
(C. W. and George Rapp, 1921.) Restored in 1986 after years of neglect, this Beaux Arts–style building (and its siren-red CHICAGO marquee) anchors Chicago's revitalized theater district. The 3,800-seat theater, called the "world's wonder theater" when it opened in 1921, was the first major movie palace to be built in a downtown area. *175 N. State St., at Lake St., Loop.*

8 a-3

CITICORP CENTER
(C. F. Murphy/Jahn Associates 1911; renovation 1987.) This is a commuter train station and an office building, rolled into one convenient—and striking— structure. Broad bands of mirrored and smoked glass alternate up the building's exterior for a ribbon effect, and on the inside, the marble floors and exposed grayish-blue girders are reminiscent of grand old railroad stations. The railroad station was built in 1911 and torn down in 1984 to make way for the Northwestern Atrium Center, which was renamed the Citicorp Center in 1993. You can reach the gates to the tracks, elevated above street level to allow traffic to proceed east and west via underpasses, by going up one level and heading to the north end of the building. Go up another flight for a view northward looking out over the tracks; at this level you'll also find the entrance to the building's office spaces. *500 W. Madison St., West Loop.*

8 c-2

CITY HALL–COOK COUNTY BUILDING
(Holabird & Roche, 1907, 1911.) The place where Chicago politicians toil, this 1911 building has Corinthian columns and huge twin Classical Revival edifices. It's easy to get lost in the spacious halls of this stately building, claimed by the city at one end and the county at the other. *121 N. LaSalle St., Loop.*

8 b-3

CIVIC OPERA HOUSE
(Graham, Anderson, Probst & White, 1929.) Once known as the Kemper Insurance Building, this 45-story skyscraper houses offices and, most notably, the Lyric Opera's 3,500-seat auditorium. The Art Deco building, with its marble pillars, crystal chandeliers, and elegant grand staircase, was put up in 1929 at a cost of $20 million by utilities magnate Samuel Insull, shortly before his financial ruin. *20 N. Wacker Dr., at Madison St., Loop.*

8 d-6

DEARBORN STREET STATION
(Cyrus L. W. Eidlitz, 1885; restoration, Hasbrouck and Hunderman, 1986.) Designed in Romanesque Revival style, Chicago's oldest standing passenger train station now serves as a mixed-use mall. The interior has white, red, and green marble floors; a wraparound walkway with brass railings; handsome grillwork; and arching doorways. On the outside, this South Loop landmark has a tall clock tower and a red-sandstone-and-brick facade with terra-cotta. *47 W. Polk St., South Loop.*

8 d-6

DONOHUE BUILDING
(Julius Speyer, 1883; renovation, Hasbrouck & Peterson, 1999.) With its beautiful ironwork and woodwork, this building claims to be the very first factory in the country to be converted into condominium lofts. Marble columns flank the main entrance, and intricate tilework enlivens its granite arch. *711 S. Dearborn St., South Loop.*

7 f-5

DRAKE HOTEL
(Marshall and Fox, 1920.) At the crook of Lake Shore Drive is the Drake Hotel, the beloved Chicago landmark and meeting spot that opened on New Year's Eve in 1920. This elegant hotel, placed on the National Register of Historic Places in 1981, has exquisite decor and superb lake views. Cecil B. DeMille, Hillary Clinton, heavy-metal singer Ozzy Osbourne, and countless others have laid their weary heads to rest here; Princess Diana stayed at the Drake on her only visit to the Windy City. Built on a landfill, the Drake serves as the north

anchor of the Mag Mile. *140 E. Walton Pl., Near North.*

5 *e-1*

ELKS NATIONAL MEMORIAL BUILDING

(Egerton Swartout, 1926; Magazine Building: Holabird & Root, 1967.) A standout among Lincoln Park's brownstones and high-rise condos is this massive, building. Its central rotunda is 75 ft in diameter and 100 ft high. Two bronze elks (by Laura Gardin Fraser) stand guard at the memorial, dedicated to Elks members who died in World War I. *2750 N. Lake View Ave., Lincoln Park.*

5 *g-8*

EQUITABLE BUILDING

(Skidmore, Owings & Merrill and Alfred Shaw & Associates, 1965.) An attractive steel-and-glass building on the bank of the Chicago River, the Equitable stands 40 stories above Pioneer Court plaza, scene of summer entertainment and lunchtime crowds. The plaza also is the site of Chicago's first house—that of pioneer Jean Baptiste-Pointe Du Sable (1750–1818). *401 N. Michigan Ave., Near North.*

8 *c-5*

EXCHANGE CENTER

(Skidmore, Owings & Merrill, 1984.) Traffic on Congress Parkway flows right underneath this red polished-granite complex. At this financial powerhouse are the seven-story Chicago Board of Options Exchange, the six-story Midwest Stock Exchange, and One Financial Plaza, a 40-story office tower that includes the very posh Everest restaurant among its tenants. *440 S. LaSalle St., Loop, 312/663–2980.*

8 *d-4*

FEDERAL CENTER & PLAZA

(Mies van der Rohe; Schmidt, Garden & Erikson; C. F. Murphy & Associates; A. Epstein & Sons, Inc.; 1964, 1975.) The 40-story John C. Kluczynski and 27-story Everett Dirksen federal buildings are classic examples of Mies van der Rohe's trademark glass-and-steel boxes. Alexander Calder's *Flamingo,* an arching red mobile-like sculpture dedicated in 1974, is the plaza's dominant image. *219 S. Dearborn St. (Dirksen), 230 S. Dearborn St. (Kluczynski), Loop.*

8 *e-5*

FINE ARTS BUILDING

(Solon S. Beman, 1885.) Built to house the Studebaker Co.'s carriage and wagon showroom (that's the reason for the large windows on the lower floors), this creaky old building ended up enjoying a long life dedicated to the arts. In 1898, it was converted into a performing-arts center with artists' studios, crafts shops, concert halls, and a theater. The building is still home to professional musicians, those who cater to musicians' needs, and a four-screen cinema that shows art films and independent movies. The motto engraved in the marble as you enter says, appropriately, "All passes—art alone endures." *410 S. Michigan Ave., Loop.*

8 *d-3*

FIRST NATIONAL BANK BUILDING & PLAZA

(C. F. Murphy & Associates and Perkins & Will Partnership, 1969.) Get a sense of First National Bank's height by standing at its base and gazing up 60 stories at its imposing granite "A" shape. You

---

HONORARY CHICAGO AVENUES

The Chicago Department of Transportation has named more than 800 "honorary streets" after celebrities and bigwigs, always marked with the brown signs. Here are some of the honorees:

Hugh Hefner, *Playboy magazine publisher and Viagra supporter*

Frank Sinatra, *singer of "Chicago" ("My kind of town")*

Bob Fosse, *theater director and choreographer*

Harold Washington, *former Chicago mayor*

Siskel and Ebert, *movie critics*

Harry Caray, *former Chicago Cubs announcer*

Ruth Page, *dance impresario*

Swami Vivekenanda, *19th-century writer of Raja Yoga*

Albertina Walker, *Chicago-based gospel singer*

Diana, *Princess of Wales*

King Sargon, *ancient royalty of Assyria*

won't be surprised to learn that this is the world's tallest bank. Of course, the bank's real treasure—other than its assets—is its 70-ft-long Chagall mosaic, "The Four Seasons," in its airy, bilevel plaza. *Bounded by Dearborn, Clark, Monroe, and Madison Sts., Loop.*

8 *d-4*

FISHER BUILDING

(Daniel H. Burnham & Co., 1896; addition, Peter J. Weber, 1907.) The 20-story, Gothic-inspired Fisher Building made from steel-frame construction is now an architectural landmark. Carved cherubs float over the glass-enclosed Van Buren Street entrance. *343 S. Dearborn St., Loop.*

5 *e-1*

FRANCIS J. DEWES HOUSE

(Adolph Cudell and Arthur Herez, 1896.) A popular place for wedding receptions, the Dewes House was designed in a lavish baroque style that captured the over-the-top, old world tastes of wealthy brewery owner Dewes and his European architects. Inside, you'll find a beautiful winding staircase, intricate woodwork, and lovely stained-glass windows. *503 W. Wrightwood Ave., Lincoln Park, 773/477-3075.*

2 *c-4*

FRANK LLOYD WRIGHT HOME & STUDIO

(Frank Lloyd Wright, 1889-1909.) Wright designed this home for his bride when he was just 22 years old. Throughout the years, he remodeled it constantly as he worked to perfect his Prairie style of design. In 1898 he built a new studio to keep up with the demands of his successful practice. Over the next 20 years, he designed and built 120 buildings, including the fantastic Robie House. Stroll through the neighborhood to find more beautiful homes designed by Wright or his students. *951 Chicago Ave., Oak Park, 708/848-1976.*

8 *d-6*

FRANKLIN BUILDING

(George C. Nimmons, 1888.) This beautifully ornamented structure, now a condominium building, was built in 1888 to house the Franklin Company's printing business. Over the front door a medieval scene called "The First Impression" illustrates the history of the printer's craft. The motto inscribed above the entryway reads, "The excel-

lence of every art must consist in l complete accomplishment of its purpose." *720 S. Dearborn St., South Loop.*

6 *g-6*

GLESSNER HOUSE

(Henry H. Richardson, 1886.) Simple and graceful, the Romanesque Revival house is the sole remaining building in Chicago by famed Boston architect H. H. Richardson. Chicago's first designated landmark, it was built for John J. Glessner, founder of the International Harvester Company. Tiny windows face the street, but the L-shape construction allows larger windows to face a private courtyard on the interior—some might call it the quintessential city dwelling. *1800 S. Prairie Ave., Near South Side, 312/326-1480.*

2 *g-7*

HELLER HOUSE

(Frank Lloyd Wright, 1897.) Note the smoothly sculpted nymphs frolicking at the top. Built for Isidore H. Heller, this private residence is an early Wright with just hints of the Prairie style achieved in the Robie House. *5132 S. Woodlawn Ave., Hyde Park.*

8 *d-1*

IBM REGIONAL OFFICE BUILDING

(Mies van der Rohe Office and C. F. Murphy & Associates, 1971.) A truly sleek structure built on the north bank of the Chicago River, the IBM Building has 52 stories of bronze-colored aluminum and tinted glass. Its sunny, rather hidden plaza is a popular hangout for the lunchtime business crowd. In the building's lobby is a bust of the master of modernity, Mies van der Rohe. *Wabash Ave. and State St., Loop.*

8 *c-2*

ILLINOIS CENTER

(One Illinois Center [111 E. Wacker Dr.], Two Illinois Center [233 N. Michigan Ave.]: Mies van der Rohe, 1970, 1973; Hyatt Regency Chicago [151 E. Wacker Dr.]: A. Epstein & Sons, Inc., 1974, 1980; Three Illinois Center [303 E. Wacker Dr.]: Fujikawa Johnson and Associates, 1980; Fairmont Hotel [200 Columbus Dr.]: Hulmuth, Obata, & Kassabaum, 1987.) Built over the Illinois Central Railroad tracks, this enormous mixed-use urban development includes the soaring bronze-aluminum-and-glass Illinois

well as the Hyatt
landscaped
strian walkways
ings. *Loop.*

INLAND STEEL BUILDING
(Skidmore, Owings & Merrill, 1957.)
This 19-story classic skyscraper was one
of the first stainless-steel-and-glass
buildings entirely supported by external
steel columns, which allow office spaces
to be completely open. The elevator and
stairs are actually in the taller structure
behind the main building. *30 W. Monroe
St., Loop.*

2 *g-7*
INTERNATIONAL HOUSE
(Holabird & Root, 1932.) At the University of Chicago, many international students and staff have passed through
this limestone Gothic structure. It looks
like a square castle, with small red roofs
offsetting the earthy color. *1414 E. 59th
St., Hyde Park.*

8 *c-2*
**JAMES R. THOMPSON
CENTER**
(C. F. Murphy/Jahn Associates and
Lester B. Knight & Associates; completed
1983.) Former governor James Thompson selected the Helmut Jahn design for
this state government building, and people either love it or hate it. One thing
most can agree on: its features are
almost overwhelming. The atrium is one
of the largest enclosed spaces in the
world; its 13 floors of open, balconied
state offices rise above a 160-ft rotunda,
and two glass elevators shoot up toward
a skylight 75 ft above the roofline. On the
concourse level, a 900-seat food court
surrounding a marble rosette is one of
the busiest places in the city at
lunchtime. A waterfall streams down
glass panels from the first floor, and the
escalators are open on the sides to reveal
their mechanics. The idea behind the
unusual design is to break down barriers
between government and people, which
explains the retail shopping mall on the
concourse and first two floors—an
unusual feature for a government building. *100 W. Randolph St., Loop.*

7 *f-5*
JOHN HANCOCK CENTER
(Skidmore, Owings & Merrill, 1969.)
The unique X's running up and down

this 1,107-ft skyscraper are actually
cross-bracings to deal with that unre-
lenting Chicago wind. The observation
deck on the 94th floor provides spectacular vantage points as does the Signature Room lounge on the 95th floor,
which almost makes up for the exorbi-
tant prices of drinks. Women should be
forgiven for spending so much time in
the lounge's ladies' room; the view,
believe it or not, is the best from there.
The lower floors house offices and posh
residences. *875 N. Michigan Ave., Near
North, 312/751–3681.*

7 *h-8*
LAKE POINT TOWER
(Schipporeit-Heinrich Associates and
Graham, Anderson, Probst & White,
1968.) The fascinating cloverleaf design
of this beautiful 70-story bronze-tinted-
glass structure makes it an architectural
showstopper. The tallest residential
building in the world, it is also the only
apartment building east of Lake Shore
Drive. *505 N. Lake Shore Dr., Streeterville.*

7 *g-5*
**LAKE SHORE DRIVE
APARTMENTS**
(Mies van der Rohe, with PACE and
Holsman, Holsman, Klekamp & Taylor,
1952; 900–910 completed in 1956.)
Mies van der Rohe's "glass houses" are
widely thought to be some of his best
works—and certainly the most imitated.
*860–880 and 900–910 N. Lake Shore
Dr., Near North.*

5 *b-6*
LASALLE TOWERS
(Renovation, Weese, Seegers, Hickey
and Weese, 1979–80.) This 1920s-era
building is familiarly known as the
Trompe L'Oeil Building—that's French
for "fool the eye," a style of art that uses
optical illusion to create an entirely different appearance. On LaSalle Towers'
windowless south side, an elaborate
painting by Richard Haas cleverly makes
the building look like it has a rose window, ornate arched doorway, stone
steps, columns, and sculptures. *1207 W.
Division St., West Town.*

2 *g-7*
**LUTHERAN SCHOOL
OF THEOLOGY**
(Perkins & Will Partnership, 1968.) Built
in three sections, this stunning struc-
ture is lightened by the transparency of

its smoked-glass exteriors. *1100 E. 55th St., Hyde Park.*

5 *f-5*

MADLENER HOUSE

(Richard E. Schmidt, 1902; interior remodeling, Brenner, Danforth & Rockwell, 1963.) Austere but elegant, the Madlener House is a Prairie-style landmark. The decorative elements around the entrance reflect the influence of architect Louis Sullivan, who designed nearby Charnley House. *4 W. Burton Pl., Gold Coast.*

2 *g-7*

MANDEL HALL

(Shepley, Rutan & Coolidge, 1903.) In the Reynolds Club Building at the University of Chicago, this beautifully restored 900-seat concert hall hosts performances by professional music organizations, including the Chicago Symphony Orchestra. Funded by Chicago merchant Leon Mandel, the exterior is patterned after the English Gothic manor house of Sir John Crosby. Inside the theater, gold leaf and soft greens contrast pleasantly with the dark woodwork. *1131 E. 57th St., Hyde Park.*

8 *d-1*

MARINA CITY

(Bertrand Goldberg Associates, 1964, 1967.) These peculiar, twin corncob towers never fail to draw comments from out-of-towners. A Chicago landmark often featured in photographs and prints, Marina City is home to wedge-shape apartments, four restaurants, the House of Blues nightclub, a huge bowling alley, and, at ground level, a marina. *300 N. State St., Near North.*

8 *d-3*

MARQUETTE BUILDING

(Holabird & Roche, 1894.) This 17-story building, named for Jesuit missionary and explorer Jacques Marquette, is built around a central court for natural light, with a steel skeleton and wide windows typical of the Chicago School of Architecture. The lobby has Tiffany-glass mosaics and brass reliefs depicting Marquette's adventures. *40 S. Dearborn St., Loop.*

8 *d-2*

MARSHALL FIELD'S

(Daniel H. Burnham & Co., 1893, 1902, 1906–7.) During the holiday season,

gazing at the world-famous department store's festive window displays is a beloved tradition. The rest of the building is worth admiring, too. Occupying an entire city block, the store has a stunning Tiffany-glass mosaic dome in the southwest corner and two ornate clocks weighing nearly 8 tons each on the exterior. The interior of the building, renovated in 1992, still imbues a turn-of-the-20th-century charm. Tea at the landmark Walnut Room on the seventh floor is a treat. *111 N. State St., Loop, 312/781–1050.*

6 *h-7*

MCCORMICK PLACE COMPLEX

(Gene Summers for C. F. Murphy & Associates, 1971.) The largest convention center in North America, McCormick Place has 2.2 million square ft of exhibit space. Named for *Chicago Tribune* newspaperman Colonel Robert R. McCormick, the colossal center has Mies-inspired bare-boned steel architecture. It suffered extensive fire damage only seven years after it was built but reopened in 1971. In 1993, a $987-million renovation project disrupted Lake Shore Drive traffic when the 23rd Street bridge was replaced with a glass-enclosed pedestrian concourse, and a section of Martin Luther King Drive was relocated to allow an expansion to the center's South Building. Today, conventions take place on alternating weekends. Some of the shows are open to the public. The Arie Crown Theatre is a nice place to see a play or concert. *2301 S. Lake Shore Dr., Near South.*

5 *g-8*

MEDINAH SHRINERS TEMPLE

(Huehl & Schmid, 1912.) Odd among its urban surroundings is this large Moorish-style building, home to the annual Medinah Shrine circus each February. The building, which has a large auditorium, also hosts high school and college graduation ceremonies, fashion shows, and other events. *600 N. Wabash Ave., Near North.*

5 *f-8*

MERCHANDISE MART

(Graham, Anderson, Probst & White, 1931.) This building is amazing from any angle simply because of its colossal size. With 4.2 million square ft, the Mer-

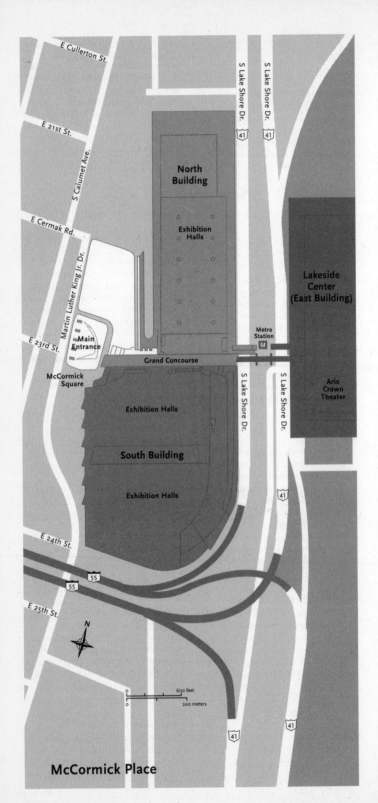

E Cullerton St.

E 21st St.

S Calumet Ave.

E Cermak Rd.

Martin Luther King Jr. Dr.

S Lake Shore Dr.

S Lake Shore Dr.

41

41

North Building

Exhibition Halls

Lakeside Center (East Building)

Metra Station

M

E 23rd St.

Main Entrance

Grand Concourse

McCormick Square

Arie Crown Theater

Exhibition Halls

South Building

Exhibition Halls

S Lake Shore Dr.

S Lake Shore Dr.

41

E 24th St.

55

55

E 25th St.

N

600 feet

200 meters

41

41

McCormick Place

chandise Mart is bigger than any other building in the country except the Pentagon. Inside the mammoth Mart are more than 600 permanent trade showrooms for all sorts of home furnishings; the 13th-floor showrooms with their kitchen and bath merchandise are open to the public during the week. In 1992 the first two floors were turned into a retail mall, with limited success; prepare to spend a lot of time walking down marble floors with lofty ceilings for quick stops at the Limited and at Crabtree & Evelyn. The Kennedys sold their interest in the Mart in 1998. You can access the Brown Line El stop on the second floor. *300 N. Wells St., Near North.*

8 d-4

METROPOLITAN CORRECTIONAL CENTER

(Harry Weese, 1975.) Perhaps it's fitting that the city Al Capone once called home could build such a fine-looking prison. The infamous mobster never stayed here, but it has certainly been the home of other dangerous criminals. With its slit windows (no bars required) and triangular shape, the 27-story building is impressive even before you realize it's a prison. If you pay close attention from the ground, or from nearby Loop buildings, you can sometimes see prisoners walking around outside at the very top. As one writer notes, "Even a jail can be an architectural show-stopper in Chicago." *71 W. Van Buren St., Loop.*

8 d-4

MONADNOCK BUILDING

(Burnham & Root, 1891; south-side addition, Holabird & Roche, 1893.) This is a magnificent example of an all-masonry building. With this type of construction, the base walls must be thick enough to support the building's height; for Monadnock's 16 stories, the base walls are 6 ft thick! You can see why modern steel-frame construction became such a bit hit. The Monadnock's designers deliberately kept its ornamentation simple—the idea was to prevent pesky pigeons from roosting there. The building has been tastefully renovated inside by Katahdin and Associates (the original wrought-iron banisters, for example, have been retained) and cleaned outside. *54 W. Van Buren St., Loop.*

2 h-7

MUSEUM OF SCIENCE AND INDUSTRY

(D. H. Burnham & Company; Charles B. Atwood, designer, 1891; restoration, Graham, Anderson, Probst & White, 1929–40.) This Classical Revival building houses one of Chicago's best-loved museums. Built during the World's Columbian Exposition of 1893 as a temporary structure for the Palace of Fine Arts, it is the fair's only surviving building. Details of the edifice are copied from the Parthenon. *5700 S. Lake Shore Dr., Jackson Park, 773/684–1414.*

7 h-7

NAVY PIER

(Charles Sumner Frost, 1916; restoration, Jerome R. Butler Jr., 1976; VOA, 1995.) What was once a mess of dilapidated buildings and trash-ridden walkways now is one of Chicago's most appealing lakefront destinations. An awe-inspiring renovation completed in 1995 turned this once-deserted pier into a unique setting for indoor shopping promenades and outdoor landscaped areas with a fountain, carousel, and pretty gardens, not to mention an enormous 15-story Ferris wheel. There are also the Chicago Children's museum; a spectacular grand ballroom for premier events; restaurants; an IMAX theater; the Crystal Gardens; the lakefront Skyline Stage; the round, relaxing Chicago Shakespeare Theatre; and an outdoor beer garden. On a historical note, the 3,000-ft-long peninsula, part of Daniel H. Burnham's Chicago Plan of 1909, was built as a commercial-shipping pier but subsequently was used by the navy during World War II. *600 E. Grand Ave., at lakefront, Near North, 312/595–7437.*

5 g-8

NBC TOWER

(Skidmore, Owings & Merrill, 1989.) An elegant limestone-and-granite skyscraper topped by the corporation's peacock emblem, the tower is suspiciously reminiscent of another NBC home, the GE Building at the Rockefeller Center complex in New York. *455 N. Cityfront Plaza Dr., Near North.*

7 f-5

900 NORTH MICHIGAN AVENUE

(Perkins & Will Partnership; Kohn, Pedersen & Fox Associates, 1989.) Within this glitzy $450 million building are 60 glitzy shops and several restaurants surrounding a six-story atrium. Above that are offices, the Four Seasons Hotel, and residential condos. The 2.7-million-square-ft building occupies an entire city block. *900 N. Michigan Ave., Near North.*

7 *e-4*
ONE MAGNIFICENT MILE
(Skidmore, Owings & Merrill, 1980–83.) With an address like that, you'd expect the building's architecture to be, well, magnificent. Luckily, the same architects who came up with the Hancock Center and the Sears Tower didn't fail us, although One Magnificent Mile's three hexagonal pinkish granite towers, set on a shiny metallic base, are a departure from their usual work. Inside you'll find clothing, leather, and fur shops; the award-winning restaurant Spiaggia; offices; and pricey condos. *N. Michigan Ave. at Oak St., Near North.*

8 *e-4*
ORCHESTRA HALL BUILDING
(D. H. Burnham & Co., 1905; restoration, Harry Weese, 1969.) This distinguished hall has been home to the world-renowned Chicago Symphony Orchestra since 1898. Look for the names of composing greats Bach, Mozart, Beethoven, Schumann, and Wagner carved into the entrance design. *220 S. Michigan Ave., Loop, 312/294–3333.*

8 *d-2*
PAGE BROTHERS BUILDING
(John Mills van Osdel, 1871.) The Page Brothers Building, listed on the National Register of Historic Places, is one of only two buildings in the entire city with cast-iron facades, used to imitate stone in the late 19th century. (The other is the Berghoff Restaurant, which dishes up German food at 17 W. Adams Street.) It was saved from the wrecker's ball during the North Loop development project and is the home of WLS-TV, Chicago's ABC affiliate. *177 N. State St., Loop.*

8 *d-3*
PALMER HOUSE
(Holabird & Roche, 1927.) This gorgeous hotel is a Chicago landmark. The ballrooms are a must-see, most notably the Empire Room, a former supper club decorated in dramatic shades of green and 24-karat gold leaf; and the Red Lacquer Room, a gem of a room with red-stained walls and chandeliers dripping dangerous-looking red crystal prisms. The hotel's lavishly decorated lobby has a restored Beaux Arts ceiling: this magnificent room is one of the few remaining examples of opulent elegance once expected in Chicago's fine hotels. *17 E. Monroe St., Loop.*

8 *d-5*
PONTIAC BUILDING
(Holabird & Roche, 1891.) This early Chicago School skyscraper, with the classic rectangular shape, flat roof, red brick, and 14 stories, is the city's oldest surviving building. Booth/Hansen and Associates renovated the 14-story building for office use in 1985. *542 S. Dearborn St., South Loop.*

2 *h-7*
PROMONTORY APARTMENTS
(Mies van der Rohe with PACE; Holsman, Holsman & Klekamp; 1949.) This unfinished-concrete residential building is named for Promontory Point, which juts out into the lake. The first Chicago high-rise designed by Mies van der Rohe, the building demonstrates the postwar trend toward a cleaner, simpler style. Even from the street level, the wide Lake Michigan views here are breathtaking. *5530 South Shore Dr., Hyde Park.*

8 *e-2*
PRUDENTIAL BUILDING
(Naess & Murphy, 1955.) Until the late '60s, this 41-story gray limestone monolith was the city's tallest skyscraper. Rising like a rocketship behind it is the 64-story Two Prudential Plaza at 180 North Stetson (Loebl, Schlossman and Hackl, 1988), which is the city's fourth-tallest building (after the Sears Tower, the Amoco Building, and the Hancock Center, in that order). The adjacent 1-acre plaza, with its waterfalls and terracing, is pleasant. *130 E. Randolph St., Loop.*

8 *d-1*
QUAKER OATS BUILDING
(Skidmore, Owings & Merrill, 1987.) This tall glass building on the Chicago River's north bank is the headquarters of the famous maker of breakfast cereals. In case you didn't know that, the two enormous replicas of oatmeal boxes, featuring the smiling Quaker emblem, plunked down in the lobby

would likely tip you off. *321 N. Clark St., Near North.*

8 *d-2/3*

RELIANCE BUILDING

(Charles Atwood, Daniel H. Burnham & Co., 1894–95.) An important predecessor to the modern skyscraper, this State Street landmark is 15 floors of white terra-cotta and glass. When it was built, the upper stories of the former structure on the site had not been vacated. Not letting that stop them, builders went ahead and built a new ground level; then three years later the rest of the old building was demolished and replaced. In September 1999, the Reliance reopened as the fancy, 122-room Hotel Burnham. *32 N. State St., Loop.*

8 *d-2*

RICHARD J. DALEY CIVIC CENTER & PLAZA

(C. F. Murphy & Associates and Skidmore, Owings & Merrill, 1964.) Named after the late great Richard J. Daley, father of the current mayor, this is the headquarters of the Cook County court system. The architecture is most notable: the building is made from Cor-Ten steel, a low-maintenance metal that weathers naturally and attractively. To boot, a landmark Picasso sculpture rises from the plaza. But what's really noteworthy about the Daley Center is that the police chase in the legendary Chicago movie *Blues Brothers* was filmed here. *Bounded by Washington, Randolph, Dearborn, and Clark Sts., Loop.*

8 *c-6*

RIVER CITY

(Bertrand Goldberg Associates, 1985–88.) Built alongside the Chicago River, this 17-story curving complex offers great views of beautiful boats docked year-round at its marina (the water is aerated to keep it from freezing). The complex, with its 446 apartments, was built by Marina City architect Bertrand Goldberg as a self-contained "city within a city." Interior spaces are used for shops, walkways, and a health club; residents also can enjoy a 1-acre rooftop park off the building's fifth floor. *800 S. Wells St., Near South.*

7 *g-8*

RIVER EAST PLAZA

(Original pier built 1905; renovation, MCL Cos., 1998.) Formerly known as North Pier, this onetime shipping terminal and pier was converted to a glitzy shopping mall and office space in the late '80s. A 1998 renovation spruced up the interior of the mall, home to specialty shops and outdoor-dining restaurants. *435 E. Illinois St., Streeterville.*

8 *b-3*

RIVERSIDE PLAZA BUILDING

(Holabird & Root, 1928.) This early skyscraper, originally the Chicago Daily News Building, maintains its vintage charm. *2 N. Riverside Plaza, Loop.*

2 *g-7*

ROBIE HOUSE

(Frank Lloyd Wright, 1909.) Frank Lloyd Wright's Prairie-style masterpiece has been called "one of the most significant buildings in the history of architecture." Wright credited the prairies of the Midwest with influencing the exterior's horizontal lines, from the brickwork and the limestone sills to the sweeping roofs. Wright himself pronounced it his best residence, which he built for bicycle manufacturer Frederick C. Robie. Interestingly, considering that the Midwest is tornado country, Wright built the house without a basement (he thought they were unhealthy). Instead, the house sits on a pedestal. A cantilevered roof allows light to filter in while also providing privacy. Notice the leaded-glass windows, the built-in cupboards, and the spacious kitchen of the house, which is open to the public. Like most of Wright's buildings, it seems compact from the outside, but inside it's a complex, fully thought-out maze of glass windows and 174 doors. What was recently a three-car garage is now a bookstore. Restored in the 1960s, the house is part of the University of Chicago. *5757 S. Woodlawn Ave., Hyde Park, 773/834–1847.*

2 *g-7*

ROCKEFELLER MEMORIAL CHAPEL

(Bertram G. Goodhue, 1928.) An important example of the Gothic Revival style, this imposing structure has a spectacular vaulted ceiling, a hand-carved organ, and intensely colored stained glass in the north window above the altar. The chapel, named for the University of Chicago's founder, is decorated inside and out with ornate carvings, sculpture, and inscriptions. Seventy-two bells peal regularly from inside the 207-ft carillon. Across the street to the east, Buky Schwartz' boxy aluminum sculpture "Untitled," built in 1976, gives the block a metallic, orderly feeling. *5850 S. Wood-lawn Ave., Hyde Park, 773/702–2100.*

8 *c-3*

THE ROOKERY

(Burnham & Root, 1886.) This distin-guished structure was built partly using masonry and partly using the modern steel-frame construction. It stands on the exact site of a post-Great Fire tem-porary city hall much loved by pigeons—hence the name Rookery. Frank Lloyd Wright remodeled its lobby, with a large skillet central court, in 1905. A 1992 renovation maintained his vision of airy marble and gold leaf. *209 S. LaSalle St., Loop.*

8 *e-4*

SANTA FE BUILDING

(Daniel H. Burnham & Co., 1904.) Also known as the Railway Exchange Build-ing, it has a rooftop Santa Fe sign that is a familiar sight on the city skyline. It was put there early in the 20th century by the Sante Fe railroad, which had offices in the building when Chicago was the country's rail center. Chicago architect Daniel Burnham later had his office here; now, appropriately, the Chicago Architecture Foundation Shop makes its home on the ground floor. The building underwent a renovation in 1985, and the atrium lobby with its marble floor is spectacular. *224 S. Michigan Ave., Loop.*

8 *b-4*

SEARS TOWER

(Skidmore, Owings & Merrill, 1974.) Forget those Petronas Towers in Kuala Lumpur, Malaysia, whose measly spires allegedly give them a ttle extra height over this building. To most Chicagoans, the Sears Tower remains the world's tallest building. On some days, the top is obscured in cloud cover; other days, its two antennae are visible from the farthest outreaches of the Kennedy Expressway. A feat of modern architec-ture, the Sears Tower stands 1,454 ft tall; its 110 stories occupy 129,000 square ft of a city block. Its steel frame is covered in sleek black aluminum and bronze-tinted glass. A 1985 refurbishing added the 56-ft-tall glass atrium at the main entrance. When the weather is clear, the views from the 103rd-floor observation deck are stunning. *233 S. Wacker Dr., Loop, 312/875–9696.*

8 *e-2*

STONE CONTAINER BUILDING

(A. Epstein & Sons Inc., 1983.) One of the more striking additions to the Chicago skyline is the Stone Container Building, with its diamond-shape sliced-off top, which looks like a giant pencil sharpener. The building houses the paper company's corporate offices. *150 N. Michigan Ave., Loop.*

8 *b-4*

311 SOUTH WACKER DRIVE

(Kohn, Pedersen & Fox Associates, 1991.) This pale pink building's most distinctive feature is its White Castle–type crown, illuminated to an ultrabright white at night. In fact, so many birds crashed into the tower during migration season that the building management had to tone down the light to slightly-less-than-blinding levels. Inside the building, an airy atrium has palm trees and a splashy fountain. *311 S. Wacker Dr., Loop.*

8 *b-1*

333 WEST WACKER DRIVE

(Kohn, Pederson & Fox Associates, 1983.) Keep in mind that this beautiful modern building was designed with the Chicago River in mind. The exterior curves gracefully along the river's bend; the glass windows reflect the water's blues and greens, as well as other build-ings that appear smaller than they actu-ally are. *333 W. Wacker Dr., Loop.*

7 *f-7*

TIME-LIFE BUILDING

(Harry M. Weese & Associates, 1971.) This 30-story concrete structure, with curtain walls of weathering steel and gold-toned mirrored-glass windows, is home to *Time* magazine's Chicago bureau. *303 E. Ohio St., Near North.*

7 *e-8*

TRIBUNE TOWER

(Hood & Howells, 1925.) One of Chicago's classiest buildings, the Tri-bune Tower has a Gothic edifice impres-sive from any vantage point. In 1922 *Trib* owner Colonel Robert McCormick held an international contest to select an architectural design for his building; Chicago's skyline was most definitely the winner. Embedded on the outside of the building, at street level, are chunks of famous structures from around the world: the Taj Mahal, Westminster Abbey, the Berlin Wall, the Moon, and the Alamo, among others. Inside the glorious main lobby, phrases carved into marble panels sing the praises of First Amendment rights to freedom of the press. *435 N. Michigan Ave., Near North, 312/222–3232.*

8 *a-4*

UNION STATION

(Graham, Anderson, Probst & White, 1925.) A grand old station, with a 10-story skylighted waiting room, Corinthian columns, and gilded statues, Union Station has welcomed thousands to the Windy City. The steps from Canal Street into the waiting area were in the famous scene from Brian de Palma's 1987 film *The Untouchables*, where Kevin Costner's character kills all the bad guys while a baby carriage rolls down in slow motion. *210 S. Canal St., West Loop.*

2 *g-7*

UNIVERSITY APARTMENTS

(I. M. Pei; Harry M. Weese & Associates; Loewenberg & Loewenberg; 1959–62.) Twin 10-story university apartment buildings sit on an island in the middle of the street. They were designed by famed architect I. M. Pei, well known for his controversial glass pyramids in front of the Louvre. *1400–1450 E. 55th St., Hyde Park.*

7 *e-5*

WATER TOWER

(W. W. Boyington, 1867.) Most people, especially tourists, are charmed by this sand castle–like structure, built to hide a 138-ft standpipe that equalizes the pressure of water from the pumping station across the street. Others, however, have remarked on the unsophisticated design of the Water Tower, which manages to look like something out of a fairy tale. Oscar Wilde uncharitably called it a "monstrosity." Regardless, the Water Tower has a spot in history as the only public building to survive the Great Fire, making it a worthy symbol of Chicago's motto, "I will." *835 N. Michigan Ave., Near North.*

2 *g-7*

WINDERMERE HOUSE

(Rapp and Rapp, 1924.) Once one of the area's grandest hotels, with guests including John D. Rockefeller, Babe Ruth, and Edna Ferber, the Windemere House is now an apartment building. It was designed by the architectural team known for their movie palaces. A grand gatehouse stands in front of the sweeping, semicircular carriage path at the entrance. *1642 E. 56th St., Hyde Park.*

7 *e-8*

WRIGLEY BUILDING

(Graham, Anderson, Probst & White, 1921.) This Chicago landmark, headquarters of the chewing gum company, is sheathed in white terra-cotta. When illuminated at night, the building gracefully marks the south end of the Mag Mile. The tower was based on the Giralda Tower in Seville, Spain. *400 N. Michigan Ave., Near North.*

ART EVENTS

may

7 *h-7*

ART CHICAGO

This mid-May exhibition at Navy Pier showcases modern and contemporary art with 200 international exhibitors. Featured artists in past years have included Andy Warhol, Willem de Kooning, Louise Bourgeois, and Joseph Beuys. Prices for individual works range from $200 to—this isn't a typo—$3 or $4 million. *Near North, 312/587–3300.*

june

2 *h-7*

57TH STREET ART FAIR

The 57th Street Art Fair is the oldest juried art fair in the Midwest. Enjoy paintings, sculpture, jewelry, ceramics, clothing, and textiles in Ray School yard, at 57th Street and Kimbark Avenue. *Hyde Park, 773/493–3247.*

5 *e-4*

OLD TOWN ART FAIR

Stroll through the quaint streets of this historic neighborhood while admiring the work of local and national artists. This much-loved summer event offers fine art and fine food, at an outdoor food court hosted by local eateries. *Old Town, 312/337–1938.*

september

2 *f-5*

DÍA DE LOS MUERTOS

The Día de los Muertos (Day of the Dead) celebration at the Mexican Fine Arts Center Museum includes a display of the work of Mexican and Mexican-American artists. *1852 W. 19th St., Pilsen, 312/738–1503.*

2 *f-4*

AROUND THE COYOTE

In early September, this festival in Chicago's most bohemian neighborhoods includes theater performances, poetry and fiction readings, dance, film, and a gallery walk that begins at the intersection of Milwaukee, North, and Damen avenues. *Wicker Park and Bucktown, 773/342–6777.*

ART GALLERIES

fine art

7 *g-5*

ALICE ADAM, LTD.

Specializing in German Expressionists and Bauhaus works on paper, Alice Adam also stocks 19th- and 20th-century master prints and drawings. Call for the address. *Near North, 312/787–7295. By appointment only.*

7 *h-7*

ANNE & JACQUES BARUCH COLLECTION

For those with an eye for contemporary Slavic art, the Baruch Collection stocks tapestries from Poland and fine art from the Czech Republic, Slovakia, Hungary, and former Yugoslavia. *680 N. Lake Shore Dr., Near North, 312/944–3377. By appointment only.*

5 *c-7*

ARC GALLERY (ARTISTS, RESIDENTS OF CHICAGO)

Established in 1973, the oldest cooperative gallery of Chicago women artists features contemporary art and sponsors seven shows each month. You might also be lured by the gallery's RAW space, which is dedicated to installation art, and a video program on computer art. *1040 W. Huron St., River West, 312/733–2787. Closed Sun.–Mon.*

5 *c-7*

ARTEMISIA GALLERY

This cooperative gallery of women artists shows the work of members and guests, in all mediums. The gallery also has performance-art series. *700 N. Carpenter St., River West, 312/226–7323. Closed Sun.–Mon.*

7 *f-7*

ARTS CLUB OF CHICAGO

A private club whose gallery is open to the public, the Arts Club sponsors exhibits of contemporary art and sculpture that change every two months. *201 E. Ontario St., Streeterville, 312/787–3997. Closed Sat. July; Aug.*

7 *e-7*

ATLAS GALLERIES

With a range of original oils, sculptures, and limited-edition graphics, this gallery also stocks master prints by Renoir, Rembrandt, and Whistler. *535 N. Michigan Ave., Near North, 312/329–9330.*

7 *e-5*

900 N. Michigan Ave., Near North, 312/649–0999.

7 *d-7*

AUSTRALIAN EXHIBITION CENTER

Director Tom Spender, an Aussie who lives part-time in Chicago, displays the boxy, repeating designs of aboriginal painters in this loft several months every year. Artists such as Ronnie Tjampitjinpa paint with both emotional complexity and primitive geometrical shapes. *114 W. Kinzie St., 2nd fl., Near North, 312/645–1948.*

4 *d-8*

BILLY HORK GALLERIES, LTD.

Here you'll find a variety of wall-hangers: contemporary European and American lithographs, serigraphs, etchings, and fine art, not to mention vintage French posters. *109 E. Oak St., Gold Coast, 312/337–1199.*

4 *d-8*

3033 N. Clark St., Lincoln Park, 773/528–9090.

7 *c-6*

CARL HAMMER

Forget famous water lilies. This unusual gallery spotlights the work of self-taught and "outsider" artists, both historic and contemporary. Carl Hammer also stocks contemporary furniture and quilts. *740 N. Wells St., Near North, 312/266–8512. Closed Sun.*

7 *d-8*

CHICAGO ARTISTS' COALITION

Those who wish to take the catalog approach to art purchases can mull over the gallery's extensive slide registry, featuring the works of 1,200 contemporary artists. *11 E. Hubbard St., 7th fl., Near North, 312/670–2060. Closed weekends.*

5 *e-3*

CONTEMPORARY ART WORKSHOP

Founded by sculptor John Kearney, this non-profit workshop provides exhibition space for fresh talent. *542 W. Grant Pl., Lincoln Park, 773/472–4004. Closed Sun.*

6 *c-1*

GALLERY 312

A nonprofit gallery focusing mostly on Chicago-area artists, Gallery 312 gives its proceeds to the PEACH Club charity. There's never an admission charge, exhibits rotate frequently, and it sponsors a yearly display of high-level children's artwork. *312 N. May St., Fulton Market, 312/942–2500.*

7 *c-6*

GILMAN/GRUEN GALLERIES

You'll find an extensive collection of African, Haitian, and Oceanic art, as well as contemporary paintings and sculpture. *226 W. Superior St., 1st fl., Loop, 312/337–6262. Closed Sun.*

6 *d-1*

JAN CICERO GALLERY

Contemporary paintings, drawings, prints, and the occasional sculpture are on sale here. *835 W. Washington St., Near West Side, 312/733–9551. Closed Sun.–Mon.*

5 *d-8*

KLEIN ART WORKS

If the old masters aren't your thing, check out Klein's contemporary abstract paintings and sculpture. *400 N. Morgan St., West Town, 312/243–0400. Closed Sun.–Mon. except by appointment.*

5 *e-7*

MARY BELL

You'll find contemporary American art, from abstract to traditional. *740 N. Franklin St., Near North, 312/642–0202. Closed Sun.–Mon.*

7 *e-5*

MERRILL CHASE

Drop by if you want to add Picasso, Miró, Chagall, or Dalí to your collection. Merrill Chase's established galleries have paintings, prints, and sculpture of contemporary and historic artists. *Water Tower Place, 835 N. Michigan Ave., Near North, 312/337–6600.*

1 *b-3*

Woodfield Mall, between Golf Rd. and W. Frontage Rd., Schaumburg, 847/330–0300.

1 *c-5*

Oak Brook Center, 294 Oak Brook Mall, Oak Brook, 630/572–0225.

7 *e-5*

Gallery Lara, 900 N. Michigan Ave., Near North, 312/943–0500.

7 *c-6*

MONGERSON WUNDERLICH

Collectors beckoned by the call of the desert will enjoy this gallery's 19th- and 20th-century American Western art and sculpture. *704 N. Wells St., Near North, 312/943–2354. Closed Sun.–Mon.*

5 *d-8*

THE VAN STRAATEN GALLERY

Featuring some noted names, this gallery offers original prints and works on paper. *470 N. Milwaukee Ave., Near North, 312/455–2900. By appointment only.*

7 *e-6*

PETER BARTLOW GALLERY

With graphics by modern masters, including Miró, Picasso, and Chagall, this gallery is a feast for the eyes. Peter Bartlow specializes in abstract and realist paintings by modern and contemporary artists. *44 E. Superior St., Near North, 312/337–1782. Closed Sun. and, except by appointment, Mon.*

7 b-6

PETER MILLER GALLERY

This place has contemporary art and sculpture. *740 N. Franklin St., Near North, 312/951–1700. Closed Sun.–Mon.*

7 e-7

R. H. LOVE GALLERIES

Take time to peruse R. H. Love's 19th- and 20th-century American paintings. *40 E. Erie St., Near North, 312/640–1300. Closed Sun.*

7 e-7

R. S. JOHNSON FINE ART

A gallery with historical flair, R. S. Johnson offers master graphics from the 15th through 20th centuries. There are also 19th- and 20th-century paintings, drawings, watercolors, and sculpture. *645 N. Michigan Ave., Near North, 312/943–1661. Closed Sun.*

6 c-1

RHONA HOFFMAN GALLERY

For art aficionados, this gallery has major international contemporary works in all mediums. *312 N. May St., Fulton Market, 312/455–1990. Closed Sun.–Mon.*

7 e-5

RICHARD GRAY GALLERY

This gallery concentrates on contemporary and modern European and American masters. *Hancock Center, 875 N. Michigan Ave., Suite 2503, Near North, 312/642–8877. Closed Sun.–Mon.*

7 c-6

ROY BOYD GALLERY

This gallery has a regional spotlight, often shining on contemporary American art and sculpture from Chicago-area artists. *739 N. Wells St., Near North, 312/642–1606. Closed Sun. By appointment Mon.*

1 e-6

VANDERPOEL GALLERY

It has a permanent collection of late-19th- and early 20th-century realist works and monthly changing exhibits. *2153 W. 111 St., 773/445–9616, or 773/779–0007 for appointments. Closed Mon., Wed., Fri., and Sun.*

5 g-6/7

WALLY FINDLAY GALLERIES

At Chicago's oldest gallery, established in 1870, you'll find pretty pictures far more expensive than a Bulls play-off ticket. Depending on the size of your bank account, you might leave with an original Monet, Renoir, or Matisse priced at more than $1 million. Walter Findlay stocks other fine works, too, but not much for under $1,500. *188 E. Walton Pl., Near North, 312/649–1500.*

2 g-8

WOODSHOP ART GALLERY

Focusing on African-American paintings, sculpture, and furniture, this 25-year-old gallery has showcased the works of Margaret Burroughs and Jacob Lawrence, among other huge figures. *441 E. 75th St., Park Manor, 773/994–6666.*

7 e-7

WORTHINGTON

Specializing in German Expressionism, Worthington also stocks contemporary American and European prints, drawings, sculpture, and paintings. *645 N. Michigan Ave., Near North, 312/266–2424. Closed Sun.–Mon.*

7 b-6

ZAKS GALLERY

This is a good place to browse through contemporary paintings, drawings, and sculpture. *311 W. Superior St., Suite 207, Near North, 312/943–8440. Closed Sun.–Mon.*

7 b-6

ZOLLA/LIEBERMAN

Factor in some extra time when you visit Zolla/Lieberman, one of Chicago's largest galleries. With its extensive collection of contemporary sculpture, paintings, and drawings, you'll be glad there's no rush. *325 W. Huron St., Near North, 312/944–1990. Closed Sun.–Mon.*

crafts

7 c-6

ANN NATHAN

This gallery specializes in artist-made furniture, sculpture, and contemporary paintings and also carries some American and African folk art. *218 W. Superior St., Near North, 312/664–6622. Closed Sun.–Mon.*

1 *e-3*

THE ARTISAN SHOP & GALLERY

There's an array of contemporary American handicrafts here. *Plaza del Lago, 1515 Sheridan Rd., Wilmette, 847/251–3775.*

4 *e-8*

JOY HORWICH GALLERIES

This gallery features contemporary Chicago-area and national artists working in a variety of media: painting, sculpture, ceramics, woodcarvings, jewelry. Owner Joy Horwich also leads personalized art tours, with stops at Chicago art collectors' homes and other cultural places. *3180 N. Lake Shore Dr., Suite 16H, Lakeview, 773/327–3366. By appointment only.*

5 *c-2*

LILL STREET GALLERY

Bowing to the notion that inspiration may strike those who view Lill Street's ceramics and large-scale ceramic artworks, the studio has children's and adult art classes. *1021 W. Lill St., DePaul, 773/477–6185. Closed Mon.*

1 *e-3*

MINDSCAPE

A perfect place to shop for the person who has everything, Mindscape offers a whimsical collection of jewelry, wearable art, and contemporary American crafts in all media: fiber, metal, wood, ceramics, leather, and glass. *2114 Central St., Evanston, 847/864–2660.*

eastern and african art

7 *c-6*

DOUGLAS DAWSON

Ancient and historic ethnographic art from Asia, Africa, and the Americas, including textiles, ceramics, furniture, and sculpture, may be found here. *222 W. Huron St., Near North, 312/751–1961. Closed Sun.*

7 *b-6*

MICHAEL WYMAN

It has traditional primitive art of Africa and Oceania. *217 W. Huron St., Near North, 312/787–3961. By appointment only.*

7 *c-6*

PRIMITIVE ART WORKS

This is Chicago's largest collection of tribal and ethnic artwork from around the world, featuring extensive collections of furniture, jewelry, artifacts, textiles, and rugs. *706 N. Wells St., River North, 312/943–3770. Closed Sun.*

photography, prints, posters

5 *b-2*

CHICAGO CENTER FOR THE PRINT, LTD.

Contemporary fine-art prints and vintage European posters are sold here; custom framing is done. *1509 W. Fullerton Ave., DePaul, 773/477–1585. Closed Mon.*

7 *e-8*

KENYON OPPENHEIMER INC.

It shows John James Audubon and natural history artists. There's a paper-conservation laboratory; services include paper restoration and archival framing. *Wrigley Building, 410 N. Michigan Ave., Near North, 312/642–5300.*

8 *e-4*

POSTER PLUS

Sure, the masterpieces in the Art Institute would look great hanging in your apartment, but cross the street to this gallery, where you can study some pieces you can actually take home with you. Poster Plus is well known as one of the city's largest poster sources. Periods represented include art nouveau, Art Deco, and WWI. Reproductions and vintage posters are also available. *200 S. Michigan Ave., Loop, 312/461–9277.*

7 *b-6*

PRINTWORKS

Contemporary prints, drawings, photography, and artists' books are sold here. *311 W. Superior St., Near North, 312/664–9407. Closed Sun.–Mon.*

7 *c-1*

VINTAGE POSTERS INTERNATIONAL LTD.

Mainly antique European lithographic advertising posters are among the art nouveau, Art Deco, and European decorative art works. *1551 N. Wells St., Old Town, 312/951–6681.*

ART MUSEUMS

8 *e-3/4*

ART INSTITUTE OF CHICAGO

A world-class museum like the Art Institute forces even the haughtiest East and West coasters to stand up and look at Chicago. Among the familiar and favorite paintings on exhibit are Grant Wood's *American Gothic*, Edward Hopper's *Nighthawks*, Pablo Picasso's *The Old Guitarist*, and George Seurat's *A Sunday on La Grande Jatte–1884*. The Art Institute is particularly celebrated for its stunning collection of Impressionist and post-Impressionist paintings; in recent years, the museum has hosted spectacular, sold-out exhibits of works by Monet, Renoir, van Gogh, and Degas. The museum also has impressive collections of medieval, Renaissance, and modern art. Less well known are its fine holdings in Asian art and photography.

A fantastic find for those who have visited only the main exhibit halls are the Thorne Miniature Rooms, on the lower level. These delicious little dollhouse-size rooms, set behind glass, show interior decoration in every historical style down to the most exacting detail. There's also the shimmering Rubloff paperweight collection, donated by a Chicago real-estate magnate. Those who have attended the museum's After-Hours social event should be familiar with the Stock Exchange Room, a splendid reconstruction of the trading floor of the old Chicago Stock Exchange, which was demolished in 1972. The Daniel F. and Ada L. Rice Building has three floors of exhibition galleries, a large space for temporary exhibitions, and a skylighted central court dotted with sculptures and plantings. The Galleries of Contemporary Art showcases post–World War II–era paintings, sculptures, and videos. The museum store carries fantastic gift items, such as art books, calendars, stationery, and jewelry; you can even buy small replicas of the mighty lions that stand guard outside the museum's entrance.

Especially helpful for those who want to become intimately familiar with the museum is the 45-minute "Introduction to the Collections" tour, daily at 2. If you have a youngster with you, make an early stop at the Kraft Education Center downstairs. Kids can choose from an assortment of 25 or so Gallery Games, some of which come with picture post-cards. The delightful and informative games help keep children from becoming hopelessly bored as you tramp through the galleries. *S. Michigan Ave. and Adams St., Loop, 312/443–3600. $8, free Tues. Open Mon. and Wed.–Fri. 10:30–4:30, Tues. 10:30–8, weekends 10–5.*

2 *g-7*

DAVID AND ALFRED SMART MUSEUM OF ART

Small but beautiful, the museum features an eclectic 8,000-piece permanent collection ranging from classical Greek vases to contemporary paintings by Chicago imagist Roger Brown. The museum was founded in 1974 with a gift from the Smart Family Foundation (David and Alfred Smart founded *Esquire* magazine). Now it houses the fine-arts collection of the University of Chicago, which includes works by old masters; sculptures by Degas, Matisse, Rodin, and Henry Moore; ancient Chinese bronzes; and modern Japanese ceramics. There are also photographs by Walker Evans and furniture by Frank Lloyd Wright. Outside the museum is a noteworthy sculpture garden. *5550 S. Greenwood Ave., Hyde Park, 773/702–0200. Free. Open Tues.–Wed. and Fri. 10–4, Thurs. 10–9, weekends noon–6.*

2 *f-5*

THE MEXICAN FINE ARTS CENTER

This gallery, the first Mexican cultural center and museum in the Midwest, has changing exhibits of the work of contemporary Mexican artists. *1852 W. 19th St., Pilsen, 312/738–1503. Free. Open Tues.–Sun. 10–5.*

7 *f-6*

MUSEUM OF CONTEMPORARY ART

Depending on your level of appreciation for contemporary art, prepare to be blown away or underimpressed by the changing exhibits in this museum. Founded in 1967 by art patrons who felt the mighty Art Institute was unresponsive to modern work, the MCA remains an alternative to the Institute's more conventionally pleasing paintings. Though some of the all-black works typically evoke the "my 5-year-old could do that!" reaction, others are more complex and twisted. Joseph Beuys's hanging gray *Filzanzug* (Felt Suit), for example, brings to mind the ghost of a bored

Loop-office employee. Ann Hamilton's close-up videos of a person squishing water around her marble-filled mouth are striking juxtapositions of the everyday and the bizarre.

The museum reopened in June 1996 in a breathtaking location with unobstructed views of the lake. Among its features are four barrel-vaulted galleries on the fourth floor and a terraced sculpture garden with outdoor café tables. MCA's growing 7,000-piece collection concentrates on 20th-century art, principally works created after 1945. Artists represented include René Magritte, Alexander Calder, Bruce Nauman, Sol LeWitt, Franz Kline, and June Leaf. The museum also has regular exhibits of performance art, some conducted on its front lawn. *220 E. Chicago Ave., Near North, 312/280–2660. $7, free Tues. Open Tues. 10–8, Wed.-Sun. 10–5, 1st Fri. of month 10–5 and 6–10.*

6 *c-1*

MUSEUM OF HOLOGRAPHY

For those unfamiliar with this art form, holograms are three-dimensional images produced by lasers. If you've never seen a holograph before, check out this museum, just west of the Loop; the images seem to leap out at you from their frames. Exhibits of holographic art from around the world include computer-generated holograms, moving holograms, pulsed portraits of people, and color holograms. *1134 W. Washington Blvd., Near West, 312/226–1007. $3. Open Wed.–Sun. 12:30–5.*

6 *g-6*

NATIONAL VIETNAM VETERANS' ART MUSEUM

You know the creepy, gray-and-green van Goghs hanging in the Art Institute that remind you of death even though they're beautiful? This lesser-known museum is exclusively filled with stuff like that, notably *Dressed to Kill*, in which shell casings make up a guy's mohawk hairdo. From straightforward paintings and sculptures to more elaborate displays of poetry and diaries, the Veterans' Art Museum captures the emotional intensity of last century's least victorious American war. *1801 S. Indiana Ave., Near South, 312/326–0270. $5, free for veterans. Open Tues.–Fri. 11–6, Sat. 10–5, Sun. noon–5.*

7 *e-7*

TERRA MUSEUM OF AMERICAN ART

Famed art patron Daniel Terra, ambassador-at-large for cultural affairs under Ronald Reagan, made his collection of American art available to Chicago in 1980; in 1987 it was moved to this Mag Mile location from Evanston. The museum's superb collections highlight American Impressionists and folk art. In particular, look for works by Whistler, Sargent, Winslow Homer, Cassatt, and three generations of Wyeths. *664 N. Michigan Ave., Near North, 312/664–3939. $7, free Tues. Open Tues. 10–8, Wed.–Sat. 10–6, Sun. noon–5.*

2 *f-4*

UKRAINIAN INSTITUTE OF MODERN ART

This unusual gallery on the West Side focuses on contemporary paintings and sculpture by artists of Ukrainian descent. *2320 W. Chicago Ave., Ukrainian Village, 773/227–5522. Free. Open Wed.–Thurs. and weekends noon–4.*

BRIDGES

7 *e-8*

MICHIGAN AVENUE BRIDGE

This gateway to the Magnificent Mile has impressive sculptures on its four pylons representing significant Chicago events: its exploration by Frenchmen Marquette and Joliet, its settlement by Haitian trader Jean Baptiste Point du Sable, the Fort Dearborn Massacre of 1812, and the rebuilding of the city after the fire of l871. The bridge can be opened to allow tall-masted boats to pass, which, while charming, can be excruciatingly irritating if you're in a hurry to get someplace and suddenly you're cooling your heels while waiting for a spindly little sailboat to pass underneath. In any event, the Michigan Avenue bridge is always bedecked with a host of colorful flags, making it a picturesque spot often featured in movies filmed in Chicago. *Chicago River at E. Wacker Dr., Loop.*

CHILDREN'S MUSEUMS

1 *e-6*

BRONZEVILLE CHILDREN'S MUSEUM

The only African-American children's museum in the country, Bronzeville is filled with magnetic maps, toys, and, of course, video games. It's not nearly as elaborate as the Loop's Chicago Children's Museum, but its recent exhibits on George Washington Carver and aviation, for example, explore fascinating territory. *9500 S. Western Ave., Evergreen Park, 708/636–9504. $3, $2 children. Open Tues.–Sat. 10–5.*

7 *h-7*

CHICAGO CHILDREN'S MUSEUM

This big museum, conveniently located at Navy Pier, offers loads of fun, hands-on exhibits for kids to enjoy. Within the museum's 57,000 square ft are appealing educational exhibits. Some favorites

are an early-childhood exhibit with a kid-size neighborhood complete with a bakery, service station, and construction site; a hands-on art studio; science exhibits on such subjects as recycling and inventing; and an activity-filled exhibit that provides children and adults with tools for addressing prejudice and discrimination. *Navy Pier, 700 E. Grand Ave., Near North, 312/527–1000. $6.50. Open Tues.–Sun. 10–5.*

CHURCHES & SYNAGOGUES

1 *e-3*

BAHA'I HOUSE OF WORSHIP

This intriguing nine-sided building, with its delicate lacelike details and massive dome, lends an exotic flavor to this very proper North Shore neighborhood. The 191-ft-tall building surrounded by formal gardens contains a visitor center with exhibits explaining the Baha'i faith, which celebrates the unity of all religions. Fittingly, the temple, which serves as the U.S. center for the Baha'i faith, incorporates architectural styles and symbols from many of the world's religions. *100 Linden Ave., Wilmette, 847/853–2300.*

2 *g-7*

BOND CHAPEL

Inside this Gothic-style chapel, a simple interior of dark wood, stained glass, and delicate ornamentation imbues intimacy and warmth. On the outside of the building, fanciful gargoyles ward evil spirits away. For services, given regularly, contact Chicago University's Divinity School at 773/702–8200. *1025 E. 58th St., Hyde Park.*

5 *f-7*

CHICAGO SINAI CONGREGATION

In addition to its liberal rabbis and Classical Reform principals, this congregation is known for its Outreach Program, which counsels interfaith (Jewish and non-Jewish) couples. It recently reopened in a large building designed by Chicago's Lohan & Associates. *15 W. Delaware Pl., Near North, 312/867–7000.*

8 *d-2*

CHICAGO TEMPLE

The eight-story spire of this Gothic-inspired temple, the headquarters of the

---

ESCAPES FROM A RAINY DAY

Rain in itself isn't so bad in Chicago—what really makes you want to hibernate is the umbrella-crunching wind and the December through February blizzard season. But here are a few fun reasons to leave the house:

Chicago Children's Museum (Children's Museums)
Don't forget the extensive web of rope ladders snaking through every floor.

Harold Washington Library Center (Libraries)
In addition to having loads of books and the city's most extensive magazine collection at your fingertips, you can rent pianos and visit the eight-floor Blues Archives.

Ravenswood El (Viewpoints)
The most scenic, and usually least crowded, elevated train rolls into the Loop from the north, overlooking some of the best city views. Call 312/733–7000 for a schedule.

Robie House (Architecture)
This is Frank Lloyd Wright's South Side masterpiece. If you're in the mood, drive to Oak Park and tour the rest of his creations.

First United Methodist Church of Chicago, is best viewed from the bridge across the Chicago River at Dearborn Street. Get closer, though, to observe the stained-glass windows along the building's east wall, which relate the history of the church in Chicago. Inside the building is a first-floor sanctuary and office space. Joan Miró's sculpture *Chicago* (1981) is in the small plaza just east of the church. *77 W. Washington St., Loop, 312/236–5050.*

2 *g-7*

CHICAGO THEOLOGICAL SEMINARY

More for book lovers than spiritualists, this nondenominational seminary is known for its basement Seminary Cooperative Bookstore. But it's a fun building in which to get lost, with the Reneker organ, a handcrafted replica of an 18th-century organ, in the Graham Taylor Chapel on the second floor; the small first-floor Thorndike Hilton Memorial Chapel; and, outside, elaborate redbrick designs, pinlike green spires, stained-glass windows, and, most excitingly, gargoyles. *1164 E. 58th St., Hyde Park, 773/752–5757.*

2 *g-7*

FIRST UNITARIAN CHURCH

Built in 1931, this Gothic church contains the Hull Memorial Chapel and, from a distance, appears quiet and unassuming. Up close it's a different story—the adjacent Pennington Center offers worship classes and youth activities, and kids run around the grounds all day long. *5650 S. Woodlawn Ave., Hyde Park, 773/324–4100.*

7 *e-5*

FOURTH PRESBYTERIAN CHURCH

This beautiful church would be better located on a peaceful village road rather than on one of the most heavily trafficked streets in the Midwest. Its grassy courtyard has doubtlessly provided respite for many a weary shopper. The granite structure is a prime example of the Gothic Revival style popular at the turn of the 20th century. Noontime organ concerts are given occasionally in the sanctuary. *Michigan Ave. and Delaware Pl., Near North, 312/787–4570.*

7 *d-6*

HOLY NAME CATHEDRAL

Built from yellow stone between 1874 and 1875, this Victorian cathedral serves as the principal church of the Diocese of Chicago—the largest Catholic diocese in the country. The glorious interior often echoes with heavenly music from the huge, beautiful organ in back. *735 N. State St., Near North, 312/787–8040.*

7 *e-3*

LAKE SHORE DRIVE SYNAGOGUE

Arguably the city's most magnificent synagogue, this late-1800s structure is decorated with ornate stained glass. *70 E. Elm St., Near North, 312/337-6811.*

5 *e-4*

MIDWEST BUDDHIST TEMPLE

Built in 1971, the temple has plain walls, landscaped gardens, and a pagodalike roof that are striking amid the brick in this neighborhood. The temple draws its congregation, about 80% Japanese-American, from all over the city and the suburbs. *435 W. Menomonee St., Lincoln Park, 312/943–7801.*

7 *d-1*

MOODY MEMORIAL CHURCH

One of the largest Protestant churches in the nation, this enormous redbrick church was named after 19th-century evangelist Dwight L. Moody and is affiliated with the nearby Moody Bible Institute. The nondenominational Protestant church, built in 1925, seats 4,000. *1630 N. Clark St., Lincoln Park, 312/943–0466.*

4 *d-8*

OUR LADY OF MT. CARMEL CHURCH

The mother church for the North Side Catholic parishes, a serene oasis in the midst of urban cacophony, Our Lady Of Mt. Carmel was built in 1913 for what was then a predominantly Irish and German neighborhood. *690 W. Belmont Ave., Lakeview, 773/525–0453.*

4 *b-8*

ST. ALPHONSUS REDEMPTORIST CHURCH

With its vaulted ceiling and stained-glass windows, this Gothic church took eight years to build. The beautiful structure originally served a German neighborhood when it was completed in 1897. *1429 W. Wellington Ave., Lakeview, 773/ 525–0709.*

5 *f-5*
ST. CHRYSOSTOM'S EPISCOPAL CHURCH
This English Gothic church has beckoned Gold Coast dwellers since it opened in 1895. Known for its 43-bell carillon imported from England, the church received a gold medal for outstanding design from the American Institute of Architects in 1926. *1424 N. Dearborn St., Gold Coast, 312/944–1083.*

5 *d-2*
ST. CLEMENT'S CHURCH
Inside this French Romanesque–style church, beautiful mosaics and lavish stained glass come together in almost dizzying detail. The intricate design traces the rich history of Christianity, which is why those with eyes heavenward might notice an unusual touch inside the painted dome—the signs of the zodiac. *642 W. Deming Pl., Lincoln Park, 773/281–0371.*

2 *g-7*
ST. GABRIEL CHURCH
Designed more than 100 years ago by Daniel Burnham and John Root, this church has an exterior that has been considerably altered, although the interior retains its original feeling of breadth and spaciousness. It is just south of the Bridgeport neighborhood, Chicago's longtime Irish community. *4522 S. Wallace St., Bridgeport, 773/268–9595.*

7 *e-6*
ST. JAMES CATHEDRAL
This glorious cathedral, Chicago's oldest Episcopal church, was built in 1875 after the Chicago Fire destroyed its original 1856 building. Look for its magnificent stenciled nave in the Arts and Crafts style. If the church doors are locked, ask at the church office (in the building next door, east of the cathedral) for admission. *65 E. Huron St., Near North, 312/787–7360.*

5 *e-4/5*
ST. MICHAEL'S CHURCH
There's a story behind this massive brick Romanesque church, which was partially destroyed during the Chicago Fire. German residents who lived in the

neighborhood came together to restore the church's interior, and their work is a legacy of exquisite craftsmanship. Inside are beautiful stained-glass windows and a stunning altar of carved wood. Outside are classical columns of different heights, elaborate capitals, many roofs with stonework at the top, and an elegant spire. Interestingly, Michael Diversey (the early beer baron after whom Diversey Parkway is named) donated the land in the 1850s so that the German community could build a place to worship. *1633 N. Cleveland Ave., Lincoln Park, 312/642–2498.*

2 *f-6*
ST. MICHAEL'S ITALIAN ROMAN CATHOLIC CHURCH
Beautifully ornate, St. Michael's is a Pilsen neighborhood institution. *2325 W. 24th Pl., Bridgeport, 773/847–2727.*

2 *f-4*
ST. NICHOLAS UKRAINIAN CATHOLIC CATHEDRAL
This 1914 cathedral has 13 copper-clad domes modeled after the Basilica of St. Sophia in Kiev. *2238 W. Rice St., Ukrainian Village, 773/276–4537.*

2 *g-7*
ST. THOMAS THE APOSTLE CHURCH
Designed by former Frank Lloyd Wright apprentice Barry Byrne, the church has an open, modern look inside and terracotta ornamentation outside. Built in 1922, it also has impressive bronze bas-reliefs of the stations of the cross. *5472 S. Woodlawn Ave., Hyde Park, 773/324–2626.*

6 *g-6*
SECOND PRESBYTERIAN CHURCH
Originally designed by noted New York architect James Renwick, the 1874 church has seven Tiffany stained-glass windows. *1936 S. Michigan Ave., Near South, 312/ 225–4951 or 312/922–4533 for tours.*

2 *c-4*
UNITY TEMPLE
One of Frank Lloyd Wright's early public buildings, the temple was built in 1906 for a Unitarian congregation. The stark concrete building, considered one of the great religious buildings of the century, consists of two spaces, a sanctuary and a parish house, connected by the low-

ceiling main entrance. The cubical sanctuary, stucco with wood trim, is lighted by high windows of stained glass. It conveys a sense of calm and balance that also invokes the spiritual. Wright would no doubt be delighted to find his original furniture still in use here. *875 W. Lake St., Oak Park, 708/383–8873.*

GRAVEYARDS & CEMETERIES

5 f-4
CROUCH TOMB
This tomb serves as a reminder of Lincoln Park's past as public cemetery. Ira Crouch was a pioneer hotel owner whose family successfully prevented movement of his tomb when the cemetery was discontinued. *Stockton Dr., Lincoln Park.*

4 b-5
GETTY TOMB
(Louis Sullivan, 1890.) Built for Carrie Eliza Getty, wife of a prominent Chicago businessman, this stone tomb features ornamentation of unmatched delicacy and beauty. It is listed as an Architectural Landmark for being "a requiem for the dead, an inspiration for the living." *Graceland Cemetery, 4001 N. Clark St., northeast section, Uptown.*

4 b-5
GRACELAND CEMETERY
Many prominent Chicagoans have come to rest on these serene acres, including Marshall Field, George Pullman, and Potter Palmer. Also interred here are some of the masterminds behind Chicago's architecture: Louis Sullivan, John Wellborn Root, Daniel Burnham, and the incomparable Ludwig Mies van der Rohe. A tour map is available at the front gate so you can explore on your own. *4001 N. Clark St., Uptown, 773/525–1105.*

2 g-8
OAK WOODS
This cemetery, founded in 1853 on 183 acres, is the final resting place of Enrico Fermi, father of the atomic bomb. An obelisk marks Federal Mound, the burial place of 6,000 Confederate prisoners from Camp Douglas who died in 1867. *1035 E. 67th St., Hyde Park.*

2 f-2
ROSEHILL CEMETERY
This 1859 graveyard is on Chicago's highest natural point. Buried here are 230 Union soldiers, including casualties of General Grant's Mississippi River campaign. In 1864 a city ordinance prohibited further burial in Chicago City Cemetery and decreed that 3,000 tombs be moved to Rosehill. *5800 N. Ravenswood St., Edgewater.*

2 g-6
STEPHEN A. DOUGLAS TOMB
(Leonard W. Volk, 1881.) The 96-ft-tall bronze sculpture of the "Little Giant" stands on what was part of Douglas's 53-acre estate. A U.S. senator who debated the merits of slavery with political rival Abraham Lincoln, Douglas moved to Chicago in the late 1840s and died in 1861. *636 E. 35th St., Douglas.*

HAUNTED PLACES

6 c-4
HOLY FAMILY CHURCH
Legend has it that in 1890 church founder Rev. Arnold Damen was awakened by two young altar boys who led him to their seriously ill mother. The story gets creepier. As it turns out, the boys had died six years earlier. Today a statue of each boy, carved out of wood, stands on either side of the altar. *1080 W. Roosevelt Rd., University Village.*

2 b-3
INDIAN BOUNDARY DIVISION
According to Indian folklore, the ghost of Potawatomi lays claim to the woods after dark. *8800 W. Belmont Ave., River Grove.*

2 c-8
RESURRECTION CEMETERY
"Resurrection Mary" died in a car crash on her way home from a dance in 1931. Yet she is said to be "seen" hitchhiking along Archer Avenue, on her way to another dance. *7200 S. Archer Ave.*

5 e-3
ST. VALENTINE'S DAY MASSACRE SITE
The S-M-C Cartage garage, where Bugs Moran's gang received Al Capone's

message on February 14, 1929, was demolished long ago, and nowadays there's not even a building on North Clark with the 2122 street number. The city refused to commemorate the massacre—a black spot in its history—with any sort of marker. Several trees grow on the grassy massacre site, although not even neighborhood dogs go near them. *2122 N. Clark St., Lincoln Park.*

4 *e-6*

TOTEM POLE

According to Chicago writer Norman Mark, the second-from-the-top man on the totem pole has changed the position of his hands at least four times. *Lincoln Park at Addison St.*

HISTORIC STRUCTURES & AREAS

4 *c-2*

ARGYLE STREET

Why go to Southeast Asia when you can walk down Argyle Street? Vietnamese, Cambodian, Laotian, Thai, and other immigrants have transformed this stretch of Argyle Street, between Sheridan Road and Broadway on the North Side, into a bustling Asian shopping and dining district. In fact, English is a second language in this ethnic Uptown neighborhood.

5 *d-2*

BIOGRAPH THEATER

Watch a first-run movie in the same theater where Public Enemy No. 1 John Dillinger was shot by the FBI in 1934. The movie house, now a four-screen cinema complex, was rolling *Manhattan Melodrama* when the notorious gangster met his end. *2433 N. Lincoln Ave., Lincoln Park, 773/348–4123.*

2 *g-6*

BRONZEVILLE

This historic community, originally settled by waves of African-Americans fleeing the South after World War I, is enjoying renewed interest as it undergoes renovation. The evocative name comes from the *Chicago Bee*, a black newspaper of the time, which held a contest in 1930 to elect a "Mayor of Bronzeville." The *Chicago Defender* also has roots in Bronzeville; the influential newspaper, which has attracted the likes of talent such as Langston Hughes, originally was based here. Among Bronzeville's more poignant landmarks is the 15-ft statue at 26th and King Drive (the neighborhood's symbolic entrance) that depicts a new arrival from the South bearing a suitcase held together with string. *Bounded roughly by 31st and 39th Sts. and by State St. and King Dr.*

6 *h-1*

BUCKINGHAM FOUNTAIN

(Bennett, Parsons & Frost; bronzes, Marcel Loyau, 1927.) There's nothing like summer in Chicago, and to observe Buckingham Fountain in all its glory— even if you happen to be stuck in traffic on nearby Lake Shore Drive—makes you wish the long hot days would never end. With jets reaching 200 ft in the air, it is purportedly the world's largest fountain. Patterned after a Latona Fountain in Versailles (but about twice as large), the fountain was donated to the city by Kate Sturges Buckingham in memory of her brother, Clarence. Between May 1 and October 1, it's elaborately illuminated at night. *Grant Park between Columbus and Lake Shore Drs. east of Congress Plaza.*

2 *e-3/4 and f-3*

BUCKTOWN AND WICKER PARK

Artsy Greenwich Village wanna-bes hang out in these hip, somewhat grungy enclaves called Bucktown and Wicker Park, centered at Milwaukee, Damen, and North avenues. Both neighborhoods, set miles back from Lake Michigan, are still among Chicago's lesser-known destinations, yet they harbor an intriguing mix of eclectic restaurants, nightclubs, cafés, theaters, coffeehouses, cutting-edge galleries, small businesses, and an unusual bazaar of shops. Musicians, artists, and young professionals call this area home, and an abundance of Latin American–run shops and restaurants indicates the strong ethnic influences. In the early 1990s, hip young rock-and-roll artists such as Liz Phair and Urge Overkill declared bohemian Wicker Park their home base, symbolizing the revitalization of the neighborhood. Bucktown, by the way, is said to have taken its name from the goats kept by the area's original Polish and German immigrants.

7 *g-8*

CENTENNIAL
FOUNTAIN AND ARC
In other cities, bells may ring or a fire horn might blow to mark the passing of the hour. Not in Chicago. A truly unusual sight to behold, the Centennial Fountain shoots an arc of water clear across the river for 10 minutes daily on the hour from 10 to 2 and from 5 to midnight, between May 1 and October 1. The idea is to commemorate the availability of clean water in and around the city. On sunny days you might see the hues of a rainbow in the arc. *300 N. McClurg Ct., Streeterville.*

7 *e-1*

CHESS PAVILION
(Maurice Webster, 1957.) Just south of the North Avenue beach house is this open-air limestone structure beloved by chess enthusiasts, who meet here for matches, rain or shine. The pavilion, which features nearly two dozen chess boards set into stone, was financed by Chicago businessman and chess aficionado Laurens Hammond, who felt sorry for the hundreds of chess players who met in Chicago's parks with no protection from the elements. Look for hand-carved limestone sculptures on either end of the pavilion—the chess king and chess queen. *Between Lake Shore Dr. and Lake Michigan, just south of North Ave. beach house, Lincoln Park.*

8 *d-2*

CHICAGO THEATER SIGN
You can't miss the neon lights of this bright red, upright marquee with white letters that spell C-H-I-C-A-G-O downwards. Affixed to the Chicago Theater building, this landmark sign in the heart of State Street's revitalized theater district recalls Hollywood's golden era. *Chicago Theater, 175 N. State St., Loop, 312/443–1130.*

6 *g-6*

CLARKE HOUSE
This Greek Revival structure, built in 1836, is Chicago's oldest house. Also known as the Widow Clarke House, the restored building is a focal point of the Prairie Avenue Historic District. Moved to another site for safekeeping after the Great Fire, Clarke House is back near its original location and operates as a museum. *1826 S. Indiana St., Near South, 312/326–1480 for tour dept. Tours*

Wed.–Sun. at noon, 1, and 2. $7 ($11 in combination with Glessner House).

2 *g-7*

COBB HALL
The University of Chicago's oldest structure (dating to 1892) houses classrooms, offices, and the Renaissance Society, which was founded in 1915 to identify living artists whose work would be of lasting significance and influence. It was one of the first hosts of works by Matisse, Picasso, Braque, Brancusi, and Miró. *5811 S. Ellis Ave., Hyde Park, 773/702–8670 for gallery. Free. Open Tues.–Fri. 10–5, weekends noon–5.*

7 *d-8*

COURTHOUSE PLACE
Now an office building, this former Cook County Criminal Courts building was the site for many trials-of-the-century long before television was allowed in the courtroom. Sensational judicial events that took place here include the Leopold and Loeb murder trial, in which Clarence Darrow defended two University of Chicago students who killed a 13-year-old boy just for a thrill. The *Front Page* authors Ben Hecht and Charles MacArthur, as well as poet Carl Sandburg, worked as reporters in the building's pressroom. *54 W. Hubbard St., Near North.*

2 *g-7*

COURT THEATRE
(Harry M. Weese & Associates, 1981.) The intimate Court Theatre offers unimpeded views and some of the city's finest professional productions. *5535 S. Ellis Ave., Hyde Park, 773/753–4472.*

7 *c-1, b-1*

CRILLY COURT
Made up of lovely tree-lined streets, Crilly Court was created in 1884 when South Side contractor Daniel Crilly built the row houses on the west side and the four-story apartment buildings on the east side. Look for the names of his children carved above the doors of the eastside buildings: Isabelle, Oliver, Edgar, and Erminnie. The buildings were later renovated by son Edgar Crilly, and their restoration marked the beginning of gentrification of the Old Town Triangle in particular and Lincoln Park in general. *Bounded by Eugenie and Wells Sts. and N. Park and St. Paul Aves., Old Town.*

7 *c-1, c-2, c-3, c-4, d-1, d-2, d-3, d-4, e-1, e-2, e-3, e-4*

GOLD COAST

Chicago's toniest turf, the Gold Coast neighborhood, wears the city's greatest treasure—the Lake Michigan shoreline—like a gilded necklace. Here you'll find fashionable residences with outstanding views. This is where those who can afford the beautiful homes have lived ever since the Great Chicago Fire. Nearby are some of the ritziest Mag Mile shops. *Bounded by the lake, North Ave., Oak St., and LaSalle St.*

2 *h-7*

JACKSON PARK

Created for the World's Columbian Exposition of 1893, this park contains lagoons, the Wooded Island, and a Japanese garden. The park, designed by Frederick Law Olmsted, is just south of the Museum of Science and Industry. *Bounded by E. 56th and 67th Sts., S. Stony Island Ave., and the lakefront.*

2 *f-2, g-2, g-3, g-4*

LINCOLN PARK

An outstanding city neighborhood, Lincoln Park offers the best urban comforts—hot restaurants, stylish boutiques, and a variety of watering holes—while providing easy access to open green spaces and the lakeshore path. Once a run-down immigrant neighborhood, and later gang turf, Lincoln Park now counts young urban professionals, who snap up restored brownstones and condos, as residents. At the heart of this trendy neighborhood, extending from North Avenue to Hollywood Avenue, is the giant park for which it is named. Since the 1960s the gentrification of Lincoln Park has moved steadily westward, spreading as far as Clybourn Avenue, formerly a light industrial strip. *Bounded by North Ave., Diversey Pkwy., the lake, and the Chicago River.*

7 *e-4, e-5, e-6, e-7, e-8*

MAGNIFICENT MILE

Call it a tourist wasteland. Call it heaven-on-earth, if you need to finish your holiday shopping on the quick. Just don't call it the Miracle Mile, which has more to do with great moments in track-and-field history than swanky shops that line Michigan Avenue between the Chicago River and Oak Street. The modest "Mag Mile" moniker was provided by developer Arthur Rubloff way back in 1947,

but for some reason, out-of-towners—especially New Yorkers, due to having their own Miracle Mile on Long Island—never seem to get it right. In any event, the Magnificent Mile still boasts the most elegant shops around (e.g., Tiffany, Chanel, and Saks), but has made room in recent years for popular chain stores like the Gap, Express, and (gasp!) Filene's Basement, which caused quite a stir when it opened in 1995 as the Mag Mile's only discount retailer. *Michigan Ave. from the Chicago River (400 N.) to Oak St. (1000 N.).*

8 *c-1*

THE MERCHANDISE MART HALL OF FAME

The giant bronze busts towering over the Chicago River portray "titans of retail" Marshall Field, F. W. Woolworth, Edward A. Filene, and five other American merchants. Four times life-size, the row of heads make up the Merchandise Mart Hall of Fame, erected in 1953 at Joseph P. Kennedy's behest. *300 N. Wells St., Near North, 312/527–4141.*

4 *e-4*

MONTROSE HARBOR

A treeless hill near this harbor off Lincoln Park draws kite-flying enthusiasts of all ages on sunny weekends; dog walkers, runners, sailboaters, and Rollerbladers abound as well. Windsurfers often practice at nearby Montrose Beach. *W. Montrose Ave. at lakefront, Uptown.*

6 *d-2*

OLD ST. PATRICK'S CHURCH

In a town of many faithful souls, St. Patrick's has achieved recognition as Chicago's oldest church, built between 1852 and 1856. Perhaps through an act of God, the structure withstood the Great Fire of 1871. Its towers, one Romanesque and one Byzantine, are symbolic of West and East. *700 W. Adams St., West Loop, 312/648–1021.*

5 *f-4*

OLD TOWN TRIANGLE

This historic district filled with charming courts and lanes has some of the oldest—and most expensive—residences in the city. It's quite a departure from its meager beginnings in the 1850s as a modest neighborhood for working-class German families. In recent decades, many of its beautiful homes have been preserved. Besides its interesting architecture, Old Town also is notable for being home to the comedy club Second City. *Wisconsin Ave. and Lincoln Park West.*

2 g-4
OLIVE PARK

A green oasis just north of Navy Pier and Lake Point Tower (505 N. Lake Shore Dr.), it has benches, trees, shrubs, and grass and absolutely no big buildings that would impede the views of the posh homes behind it. Jutting out into Lake Michigan, the park provides a marvelous city skyline vista. *Grand Ave. at lakefront, Near North.*

2 f-5/6
PILSEN

This formerly Bohemian neighborhood on the South Side is home to artists and, more recently, Mexican immigrants. Note the murals along 18th Street and elsewhere, which depict scenes from Mexican history, culture, and religion. *Bordered by Halsted St. and Damen Ave., extending from 18th St. to 26th St.*

7 e-2
PLAYBOY MANSION

Once the scene of wild parties attended by women with cleavage and bunny ears, this ornate building now is a quiet private residence. Up into the 1980s, though, *Playboy* magazine's Hugh Hefner lived and worked here—often, legend has it, using his circular bed as a desk. Until his move to Beverly Hills, Hef even used his posh home and its indoor pool (no longer there) as a backdrop for the mag's photo shoots. In early 2000, in the face of feminist protesters and sarcastic newspaper columnists, city fathers (probably not mothers) named an honorary street downtown for Hef. *1340 N. State Pkwy., Gold Coast.*

6 g-6
PRAIRIE AVENUE
HISTORIC DISTRICT

Several blocks south of Downtown South, two important historic homes, Clarke House and Glessner House, and a beautiful church, Second Presbyterian Church, recall a vanished era. Many prominent merchants and manufacturers from the 1870s to the turn of the

century built their homes in the area around Prairie Avenue. Later, houses of vice and the laying of train tracks led these residents to leave. *1800 S. Prairie Ave., Near South.*

7 e-5
QUIGLEY SEMINARY

Modeled after the famous Sainte-Chapelle in Paris, the St. James Chapel in this 1918 Gothic-style building is a little jewel, with perfect acoustics and a splendid rose window. The Rev. James Edward Quigley, looking stately in statue form, overlooks the intersection at the southeast corner. *103 E. Chestnut St., Near North, 312/787–9343.*

2 g-4
RIVER NORTH

This lively neighborhood, swollen with art galleries, was settled by Irish immigrants in the mid-19th century but fell into disrepair when economic conditions changed and factories moved out. Craftspeople moved into River North in the 1970s, attracted by low rents and spacious, abandoned shop floors. Today, a slew of art galleries, restaurants, and shops thrive here. The area is nearly devoid of contemporary construction; most of the renovated buildings are large, rectangular, solidly built structures made of Chicago redbrick, with high ceilings and hardwood floors. *Bounded on the south and west by branches of the Chicago River and by Oak and Clark Sts.*

5 f-5
SECOND CITY

Some of the world's biggest comedic television and movie stars—Elaine May, Mike Nichols, Alan Arkin, Joan Rivers, the late John Belushi, Shelley Long, and, most recently, *Saturday Night Live* comedienne Rachel Dratch and head writer Tina Fey, to name a few—launched their careers from this once-grassroots improvisational theater in Chicago. In late 1999, the club celebrated its 40th anniversary with a huge reunion, for which actors Arkin, Harold Ramis, Fred Willard, writers for *The Late Show With David Letterman* and *Saturday Night Life*, and dozens of others waxed nostalgic in panels and skits. *1616 N. Wells St., Old Town, 312/337–3992.*

5 *f-8*

SPORTMART BUILDING

Famous Windy City athletes have gathered here at the "Chicago Sports Wall of Fame" to press their hands into cement. Scattered on the outside of the building are the handprints of Blackhawks winger Bobby Hull, Bears quarterback Sid Luckman, and White Sox outfielder Minnie Minoso, among others. And yes, Michael Jordan's handprints are here, too, but are cleverly located in the store to draw gawkers inside. *620 N. LaSalle Dr., Near North.*

8 *d-1, d-2, d-3, d-4, d-5*

STATE STREET

Thanks to an overhaul, State Street is recovering that "great street" status, as Sinatra sung. For a long time, though, Chicago's main drag was a dismal place. A 1979 attempt to turn State Street into a pedestrian mall failed, largely because a bus-traffic-only rule meant shoppers couldn't drive there. In 1996, city officials conceded defeat and "de-malled" the street, allowing traffic to return. Also, nine blocks stretching from Congress Parkway on the south to Wacker Drive on the north were given a $24.5 million face-lift. The street was widened, trees and shrubs were planted, and old-fashioned streetlights installed, giving the revitalized area a 1920s look. The firm Skidmore, Owings & Merrill oversaw the design.

5 *g-7*

STREETERVILLE

This upscale area began life as a disreputable landfill presided over by notorious lowlife Cap Streeter and his wife, Maria. The couple left Milwaukee in the 1880s on a steamboat headed for Honduras but then decided to claim squatter's rights when their boat beached on a sandbar between Chicago Avenue and Oak Street. Cap claimed about 180 acres as his own and built a shantytown there, thus becoming, technically, one of the city's first urban developers. The area known as Streeterville, where building contractors were once invited to dump their debris, today is one of Chicago's most valuable properties. The Hancock Center marks the spot where Cap's own shanty sat. *East of Michigan Ave. and south of Chicago Ave.*

2 *f-4*

UKRAINIAN VILLAGE

This neighborhood still maintains its ethnic roots, with a largely Ukrainian population. At the heart of the village is Holy Trinity Cathedral, a Russian Orthodox church that, legend has it, received a $4,000 donation from Czar Nicholas of Russia during its construction. There's also St. Nicholas Ukrainian Catholic Cathedral, with its resemblance to the Basilica of St. Sophia in Kiev, and the Ukrainian Institute of Modern Art, which focuses on contemporary paintings and sculpture by artists of Ukrainian descent. *Bounded by Damen Ave. on the east and Western Ave. on the west, between Chicago Ave. and Division St.*

HISTORY MUSEUMS

2 *e-8*

BALZEKAS MUSEUM OF LITHUANIAN CULTURE

For a taste of 10 centuries of Lithuanian history and culture, stop by this little-known museum, a half-hour drive southwest of Hyde Park. On its three floors are exhibits on rural Lithuania; concentration camps; rare maps, stamps, and coins; textiles; and amber. The library can be used for research. *6500 S. Pulaski Rd., West Lawn, 773/582–6500. $4, free Mon. Open daily 10–4.*

8 *e-2*

CHICAGO CULTURAL CENTER

Dedicated to all things cultural, this ornate building has concerts and changing exhibits, as well as "Round & About the Loop," an information center that shows a seven-minute video about Chicago's downtown. The Museum of Broadcast Communications, housed within the building, has exhibits about television and radio, a large archive of programs and commercials, and an anchor's desk where you get to play anchor while the cameras roll (for a fee). *78 E. Washington St., Loop, 312/346–3278. Open Mon.–Wed. 10–7, Thurs. 10–9, Fri. 10–6, Sat. 10–5, Sun. noon–5.*

5 *f-4*

CHICAGO HISTORICAL SOCIETY

A great place for history buffs, the society has permanent exhibits that include the much-loved Diorama Room, which portrays scenes from Chicago's history, and the popular Illinois Pioneer Life Gallery, which has daily crafts demonstrations. There are also collections of costumes, Chicago's first locomotive (which visitors may board), and a wonderful gift shop with historical prints and photographs for sale. A beautiful spiral staircase makes the building an elegant setting for weddings. *1601 N. Clark St., Lincoln Park, 312/642–4600. $5, free Mon. Open Mon.–Sat. 9:30–4:30, Sun. noon–5.*

2 g-7
DUSABLE MUSEUM OF AFRICAN-AMERICAN HISTORY

Named for Haitian trader Jean Baptiste Pointe du Sable, a black man who was Chicago's first permanent non–Native American resident, this museum has a collection of art and objects related to the African-American experience. Of note is the poignant slavery exhibit, which displays disturbing artifacts such as rusted shackles used on slave ships. The museum, which opened in 1961, also has a cinema series, jazz and blues concerts, lectures and symposiums, and special programs for children. *740 E. 56th Pl., Hyde Park, 773/947–0600. $3, Sun. free. Open Mon.–Sat. 10–5, Sun. noon–5.*

6 d-3
HULL HOUSE MUSEUM

The redbrick Victorian building where Jane Addams started the American settlement movement in 1889 is now a museum, with moving displays about the experience of German, Irish, Greek, Bohemian, and Jewish immigrants. Now affiliated with the University of Illinois at Chicago's School of Social Work, the museum is in what was once a slum neighborhood for new immigrants. The building is named for Charles J. Hull, who owned the building before it became a settlement home. *800 S. Halsted St., University Village, 312/413–5353. Free. Open by appointment only, weekdays 10–4, Sun. noon–5.*

2 g-7
HYDE PARK HISTORICAL SOCIETY

This group, which focuses on area history and sponsors lectures and tours, has its headquarters in this restored redbrick building. Originally a cable car station, the building dates to the 1893 Columbian Exposition. *5529 S. Lake Park Ave., Hyde Park, 773/493–1893.*

2 g-7
ORIENTAL INSTITUTE

A 40-ton sculpture of a winged bull from an Assyrian palace is just one of the many fascinating items on display at the institute. Also here are art and artifacts from the ancient Near East, including small-scale amulets, mummies, limestone reliefs, gold jewelry, and pottery from the 2nd millennium through the 13th century. *1155 E. 58th St., Hyde Park, 773/702-9520. Free. Call for current schedule.*

2 f-4
POLISH MUSEUM OF AMERICA

In a town like Chicago, home to the largest Polish population outside Warsaw, having "ski" affixed to your last name is like a badge of honor. This museum, dedicated to gathering materials on the history of Polish people in America, has exhibits on the Shakespearean actress Helena Modjeska, the American Revolutionary War hero Tadeusz Kosciuszko, and the pianist and composer Ignacy Paderewski. The stations of the cross from the first Polish church in America (which was in Texas) are on display; there is a library and art gallery, too. *984 N. Milwaukee Ave., West Town, 773/384–3352. $2. Open daily 11–4.*

8 e-5
SPERTUS MUSEUM OF JUDAICA

A tattered concentration-camp uniform and haunting Holocaust photos are some of the poignant items on display in this museum, part of the Spertus Institute of Jewish Studies. A hands-on children's museum called the Artifact Center entertains kids with a simulated archaeological dig. *618 S. Michigan Ave., South Loop, 312/322–1747. $5, Fri. free. Sun.–Wed. 10–5, Thurs. 10–8, Fri. 10–3; children's museum Sun.–Thurs. 1–4:30.*

4 b-1
SWEDISH-AMERICAN MUSEUM CENTER

Proving that good things come in little packages (take Swedish meatballs, for instance), this tiny but welcoming museum has changing exhibits that focus on the art and culture of Sweden.

On permanent display are personal items brought to this country by Swedish immigrants, including trunks, clothes, and tools. *5211 N. Clark St., Uptown, 773/728–8111. $4. Open Tues.–Fri. 10–4, weekends 10–3.*

LIBRARIES

8 *d-4*

HAROLD WASHINGTON LIBRARY CENTER

(Hammond, Beeby & Babka, 1991.) The county's central (and largest) library took 70 years to build, but the result is impressive. The massive granite-and-brick building features some of the most spectacular terra-cotta work seen in Chicago since the 19th century: ears of corn, faces with puffed cheeks (representing the Windy City), and the logo of the Chicago Public Library are among the embellishments. Within its 10 stories are more than a million volumes; its holdings include the Chicago Blues Archives, the Jazz/Blues/Gospel Hall of Fame, and the Balaban and Katz Theater Orchestra Collection. The center, named for the first black mayor of this city, has an impressive Winter Garden on the ninth floor that is used for special events. There's also an excellent children's library, with a charming story-

---

PLACES TO MEET "THE ONE"

"It's hard to meet people in Chicago!" singles complain all the time. And unlikely saviors—museums—have come to the rescue. Here are some surprising daytime exploring spots that mysteriously transform into singles bars in the evenings:

Museum of Contemporary Art (Art Museums)
Attracts mostly high-culture singles on the first Friday of every month, from 6 to 10 PM.

Shedd Aquarium (Science Museums)
"Jazzin' at the Shedd," with fish and background music, runs Thursday nights until 10 PM.

The Art Institute of Chicago (Art Museums)
Offers food, music, and the occasional treasure hunt on the third Tuesday and Saturday of every month, from 5:30 to 8:30 PM.

---

telling alcove and vibrant wall-mounted figures by Chicago imagist Karl Wirsum. *400 S. State St., Loop, 312/747–4300. Open Mon.–Thurs. 9–7, Fri.–Sat. 9–5, Sun. 1–5. Tours Mon.–Sat. at noon and 2, Sun. at 2.*

2 *g-7*

JOHN CRERAR SCIENCE LIBRARY

(Stubbins Associates and Loebl Schlossman & Hackl, 1984.) A large part of the University of Chicago's extensive biological, medical, and physical sciences collections is housed in this library, which is open to the public. A sight to see is Chicago sculptor John David Mooney's work *Crystara*, made of Waterford crystal and aluminum and suspended from the skylight in the library's three-story atrium. *5730 S. Ellis Ave., Hyde Park, 773/702–7715. Open Mon–Sat. 8:30–5.*

5 *C-2*

JOHN T. RICHARDSON LIBRARY

(Lohan Associates of Chicago, 1992.) DePaul University's library has soaring ceilings, oak woodwork, and antique Tiffany stained-glass windows, not to mention an impressive two-story reading room on the third floor. The statue in the courtyard is of St. Vincent de Paul. *2350 N. Kenmore Ave., DePaul. Open Mon.–Thurs. 8 AM–midnight, Fri. 8–9, Sat. 10–9, Sun. noon–midnight.*

2 *g-7*

JOSEPH REGENSTEIN LIBRARY

(Skidmore, Owings & Merrill, 1970.) The University of Chicago's massive graduate research library has a distinctly modern look, with rough limestone instead of concrete, the more prevalent material for campus exteriors. The underground Map Collection, with 390,000 maps, atlases, aerial photos, and other directional documents, is a gold mine for navigation buffs. The Center for Children's Books, on the fourth floor, supplements the usual college-library mix (on separate floors) of film, music, geography, and the rest. And the Chicago Jazz Archive, filled with classic sheet music, reviews, and old handbills, recalls the period early last century when such jazz greats as Louis Armstrong, Joe "King" Oliver, and Benny Goodman held court at South Side clubs. It has seven floors, two of them belowground.

Note: The library is closed to non-students, although visitors can make special research arrangements by calling in advance. *1100 E. 57th St., Hyde Park.*

5 *f-6*
NEWBERRY LIBRARY
(Henry Ives Cobb, 1892; remodeling, Harry M. Weese & Associates, 1968.) This wonderful institution, endowed by early Chicago businessman Walter Loomis Newberry, houses superb book and document collections, including Indian-language grammars, genealogical records, and rare bound and unbound manuscripts in the fields of literature, history, and music. Flocks turn out each summer for the annual book fair; the library also hosts changing exhibits in a small gallery space. *60 W. Walton St., Old Town, 312/943–9090. Free. Open Tues.–Thurs. 10–6, Fri.–Sat. 9–5.*

SCHOOLS

6 *g-3*
COLUMBIA COLLEGE
Not to be confused with the more prestigious Columbias in Missouri and New York City, this downtown campus has a liberal-arts (specifically art, music, and journalism) focus that benefits from the nearby Art Institute. *600 S. Michigan Ave., South Loop, 312/663–1600.*

5 *c-2*
DEPAUL UNIVERSITY
Founded in 1898 by the Vincentian Fathers, DePaul is one of the largest Catholic universities in the country. Its 28-acre Lincoln Park campus serves more than 17,000 students; four other campuses are in the Loop and suburbs. The university has received national recognition for its music and drama programs and, on the odd occasion, its basketball team. DePaul also has a large continuing-education program, which thousands of Chicago adults attend on evenings and weekends. On its Lincoln Park campus, three buildings were designed by Holabird & Root: the Stone Building (1968), McGaw Memorial Library (1963), and James McClure Memorial Chapel (1963). *Lincoln Park Campus: 2320 N. Kenmore Ave., bounded by Fullerton, Racine, and Belden Aves. and Halsted St., 773/325–7000.*

6 *f-2*
Downtown Campus: 1 E. Jackson Blvd., Loop, 312/362–8000.

2 *g-6*
ILLINOIS INSTITUTE OF TECHNOLOGY
(Mies van der Rohe & Ludwig Hilberseimer; Friedman, Alschuler & Sincere; PACE; 1942–58; Skidmore, Owings & Merrill, 1963.) Considering the great Mies van der Rohe spent some time here (he was actually a dean at the School of Architecture) it's not surprising that many IIT structures bear Mies' trademark, the box shape. The master designed much of the 100-acre campus, including the Administration Building, the Commons Building, and the Chapel. S. R. Crown Hall, made of black steel and clear glass, is the jewel of the collection; the other buildings—mostly low-rises—have a certain sameness and sterility. *S. State St. between 31st and 35th Sts., Douglas, 312/567–3000.*

5 *g-7*
LOYOLA UNIVERSITY
(Schmidt, Garden & Erikson, 1925.) Loyola has the distinction of being Chicago's oldest university and largest Jesuit institution in North America. The original building on Loyola's downtown campus was donated by Chicago philanthropist Frank Lewis. *Water Tower Campus: 820 N. Michigan Ave., Near North, 312/915–6000.*

2 *f-1*
Lake Shore Campus: 6525 N. Sheridan Rd., Rogers Park, 773/274–3000.

7 *c-6*
MOODY BIBLE INSTITUTE
Though it isn't as open as sprawling urban colleges like DePaul University or the University of Illinois–Chicago, this conservative Christian college is in a huge contemporary brick structure on the North Side. *820 N. LaSalle St., Near North, 312/329–4000.*

5 *g-7*
NORTHWESTERN UNIVERSITY CHICAGO CAMPUS
(John Gamble Rogers, 1926–32; Holabird & Root, 1929–67; Schmidt, Garden & Erikson, 1966; Bertram Goldberg & Associates, 1974.) This prestigious university has its main campus just across the city

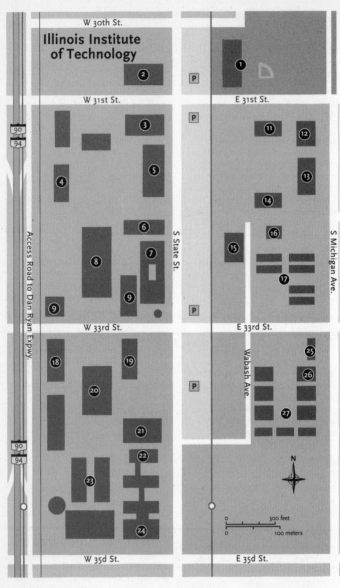

**Illinois Institute
of Technology**

W 30th St.

W 31st St.　　　E 31st St.

90
94

Access Road to Dan Ryan Expwy.

S State St.

S Michigan Ave.

W 33rd St.　　　E 33rd St.

Wabash Ave.

90
94

N

0　　300 feet
0　　100 meters

W 35d St.　　　E 35d St.

1	Keating Sports Ctr	12	Cunningham Hall Apts	22	World Learning Center
2	Stuart	13	Gunsaulus Hall Apts	23	IITRI Complex
3	Life Sciences	14	Carman Hall Apts	24	IITRI Tower
4	VanderCook College of Music	15	Commons Building	25	Farr Hall
5	Eng 1 Building	16	Chapel	26	Res Hall Annex
6	Alumni Memorial Hall	17	Residence Hall Complex	27	Fraternity Complex
7	Hermann Union	18	Main Building		
8	Perlstein Hall	19	Siegel		
9	Machinery Hall	20	Galvin Library		
10	Wishnick	21	Crown Hall		
11	Bailey Hall Apts				

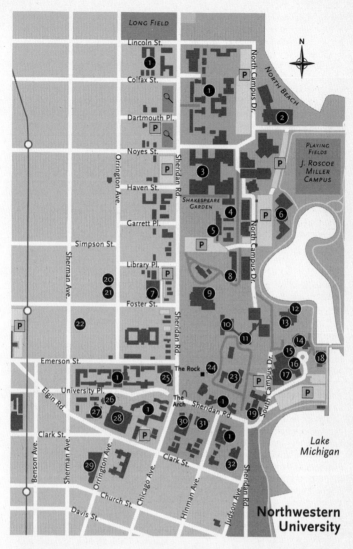

Northwestern University

1 Student Residences
2 Crown Sports Pavilion
3 McCormick Technological Institute
4 Dearborn Observatory
5 Garret Evangelical Theological Seminary
6 Allen Center
7 Blomquist Recreation Center
8 Cresap Laboratory
9 Owen L Coon Forum
10 Deering Library
11 University Library
12 McCormick Auditorium
13 Norris University Ctr
14 Pick-Staiger Concert Hall
15 Block Gallery
16 Theatre and Interpretation Ctr
17 Marjorie Ward Marshall Dance Ctr
18 Regenstein Hall of Music
19 Fisk Hall
20 Chabad House
21 Canterbury House
22 Hillel Foundation
23 Kresge Centennial Hall
24 University Hall
26 Lutkin Hall
27 Music Administration
28 Rebecca Crown Center
29 Omni Orrington Hotel
30 Alice Millar Chapel
31 Levere Temple
32 John Evans Alumni Center

line, in the attractive North Shore suburb of Evanston. But several of N.U.'s graduate schools, including those in dentistry, medicine, business, and law, hold classes in a complex of buildings between the Mag Mile and the lake. Of particular note are the gorgeous law school building and its equally impressive (and extensive) law library. Also included on the downtown campus is the McGaw Medical Center, consisting of Northwestern Memorial Hospital, Prentice Women's Hospital and Maternity Center, the Passavant and Wesley pavilions, the Veterans Administration Research Hospital, and the Rehabilitation Institute of Chicago. If you can make your way up there, the lake views from atop the campus dormitories are magnificent. *710 N. Lake Shore Dr., Near North.*

2 *g-7*
UNIVERSITY OF CHICAGO
(Henry Ives Cobb, 1897; Henry H. Richardson, Shepley, Rutan & Coolidge, 1903.) The University of Chicago was founded in 1892 through the largesse of John D. Rockefeller and has produced, in the ensuing years, 68 Nobel Prize winners—more than any other university in the country. U of C's students attend classes on its 184-acre Hyde Park campus, with its stately Gothic quadrangles made from Indiana limestone. More Midwestern in character than its East Coast Ivy League counterparts, U of C has world-famous economics, law, business, and medical schools. The University of Chicago Hospitals are leading teaching institutions as well. Perhaps the most world-altering event to take place at U of C (or anywhere else, for that matter) was the first self-sustaining nuclear chain reaction, created here in 1942 by Enrico Fermi and his team of physicists under an unused football stadium. Although the stadium is gone, there's a plaque on the spot now, near the Crerar Science Library. *5801 S. Ellis Ave., Hyde Park, 773/702–1234.*

2 *f-5*
UNIVERSITY OF ILLINOIS AT CHICAGO
(Walter A. Netsch of Skidmore, Owings & Merrill, 1965, 1968, 1971; Student Union Building: C. F. Murphy & Associates.) UIC is one of Chicago's major universities, drawing students of all ages from much of the city and surrounding suburbs. Its modern urban campus includes a number of architecturally

exciting buildings; when viewed from a distance, the structures seem to surge and weave toward one another. The state-funded school, which draws more non-traditional students than Chicago's high-brow private universities, was built on a former immigrant-port-of-entry area. The campus incorporates the landmark Hull House, now a museum. *1200 W. Harrison St., Near West, 312/996–7000.*

SCIENCE MUSEUMS

2 *g-5*
ADLER PLANETARIUM
At the far end of a peninsula that juts out into Lake Michigan is the Adler Planetarium, which offers exhibits and a popular program of sky shows. The Adler opened in 1930 as the first public planetarium in the western hemisphere, and it has continued to delight audiences of all ages ever since. In fact, it is one of three museums that make up Chicago's "museum campus" (the others are the Field Museum and the Shedd Aquarium), all located within walking distance of one another. The Adler continues to unveil new and revamped exhibits and gallery space; additions include the high-tech Star-Rider Theater, the Atwood Sphere Planetarium, and exhibits on the solar system, Mars exploration, and the Milky Way galaxy. *1300 S. Lake Shore Dr., Near South, 312/922–7827. $5, free Tues. Open Sat.–Thurs. and Sun. 9–5, Fri. 9–9.*

8 *g-8*
FIELD MUSEUM
Named for its patron, Chicago retailer Marshall Field, the Field Museum was established in 1893 to hold material gathered for the World's Columbian Exposition. Its current home, the imposing building designed in classical style, opened in 1921. This gigantic world-class museum contains more than 6 acres of exhibits that explore cultures and environments around the world. Visitors love to gape at the gigantic posed dinosaur skeletons and 600 other fossils on exhibit. The 65-million-year-old fossilized bones of "Sue," the largest and most complete Tyrannosaurus rex ever found, went on display in early 2000. Originally more than 13 ft tall, 42 ft long, and weighing more than 7 tons—not to mention foot-long teeth and a ferocious disposition—Sue

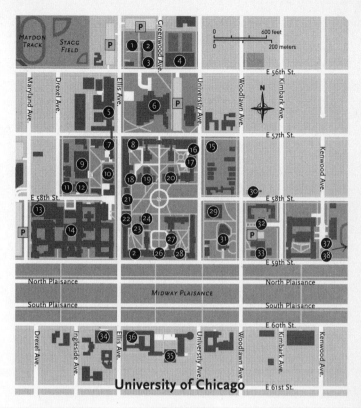

University of Chicago

1 Court Theatre
2 Cochrane-Woods Art Center
3 Smart Museum
4 Henry Crown Field House
5 Research Institutes
6 Regenstein Library
7 Kersten Physics Teaching Center
8 Snell-Hitchcock Halls
9 Crerar Library
10 Hinds Laboratory
11 Kovler Viral Oncology Laboratories
12 Cummings Life Science Center
13 Bernard Mitchell Hospital/Chicago Lying-in Hospital
14 University Hospitals

15 Quadrangle Club
16 Reynolds Club/University Theater
17 Mandel Hall
18 Jones Laboratory
19 Kent Chemical Laboratory
20 Ryerson Physical Laboratory
21 Administration Building
22 Cobb Hall
23 Bond Chapel
24 Swift Hall
25 Classics Building
26 Harper Memorial Library/College Admissions
27 Stuart Hall
28 Social Science Research
29 Oriental Institute

30 Robie House
31 Rockefeller Memorial Chapel
32 Woodward Court
33 Ida Noyes Hall
34 Social Service Administration
35 Laird Bell Law Quadrangle/D'Angelo Law Library
36 Burton-Judson Courts
37 International House
38 Breckinridge House

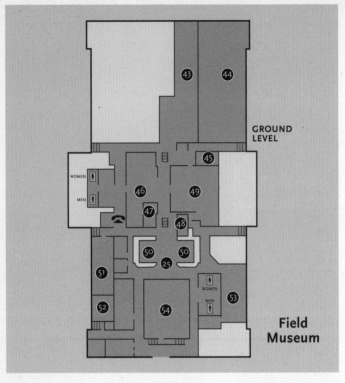

GROUND
LEVEL

Field
Museum

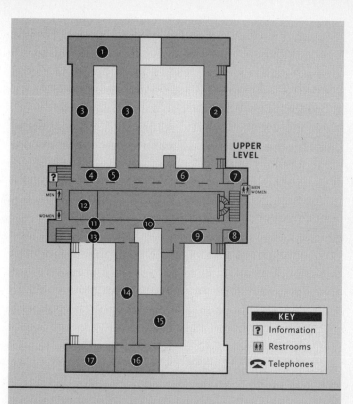

UPPER
LEVEL

KEY
? Information
Restrooms
Telephones

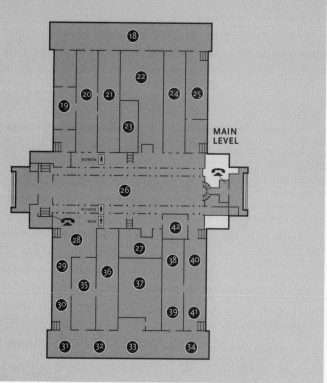

MAIN
LEVEL

is named for South Dakota fossil hunter Sue Hendrickson. Also in the museum is the remarkable Mastaba complex, part of Inside Ancient Egypt, which includes a working canal, a living marsh where papyrus is grown, a shrine to the cat goddess Bastet, burial-ceremony artifacts, and 23 mummies. The reconstructed Pawnee earth lodge was completed with the assistance of the Pawnee tribe of Oklahoma; the museum's glittering gem room contains more than 500 gemstones and jewels.

Kids ages 4–10 should visit the Place for Wonder, where they can pick up and touch everything on display, including a ½-ton stuffed polar bear, shells, animal skins, clothing, toys from China, aromatic scent jars, and gourds. In addition to special exhibits, the museum also schedules music, dance, theater, and film performances. The museum's DinoStore sells a wide assortment of dinosaur-related merchandise. *E. Roosevelt Rd. and Lake Shore Dr., Near South, 312/922–9410. $8, free Thurs. Open Labor Day–Memorial Day, daily 9–5; Memorial Day–Labor Day, daily 8–5.*

2 g-5
INTERNATIONAL MUSEUM OF SURGICAL SCIENCE

Morbid yet fascinating, this unusual museum showcases 4,000-year-old skulls, amputation kits, an iron lung, and other intriguing oddities. The museum occupies four floors of a landmark Lake Shore Drive building patterned after a Louis XVI chateau. *1524 N. Lake Shore Dr., Gold Coast, 312/642–6502. $5 suggested donation. Open Tues.–Sat. 10–4.*

8 h-8
JOHN G. SHEDD AQUARIUM

On the lakefront near Adler Planetarium, the world's largest indoor aquarium has fantastically beautiful fish, electric eels, river otters, piranhas, and hundreds of other aquatic animals. The splashiest attraction is the spectacular Oceanarium, with pools that seem to blend right into Lake Michigan, which is visible through an enormous glass wall. Here, animal trainers show off the skills of the Shedd's Pacific white-sided dolphins by putting on a host of shows throughout the day. In the Oceanarium you also can have a stare-down with one of the knobby-headed beluga whales (they love to people-watch) and explore

the simulated Pacific Northwest nature trail, complete with tall pines, birdsongs, and tide pools. On the lower level, check out the underwater viewing windows for the dolphins and whales and the information-packed, interactive, hands-on activities.

In the original aquarium facility, a highlight is the Coral Reef Exhibit, where visitors can watch divers feed sharks and other creatures of the deep. A special treat on Thursday evenings from mid-June to late August is live jazz on the Oceanarium's north terrace, which has a great view of the lake and skyline. *1200 S. Lake Shore Dr., Near South Side, 312/939–2438 or 312/939–2426. Aquarium and Oceanarium $13, $8 Mon.; Aquarium only, free Mon. Memorial Day–Labor Day, Fri.–Wed. 9–6, Thurs. 9–9; Labor Day–Memorial Day, weekdays 9–5, weekends 9–6.*

2 h-7
MUSEUM OF SCIENCE AND INDUSTRY

It's too bad the stuff here doesn't really work. Although the venerable museum is already Chicago's top tourist attraction, imagine the crowds who would show up to become an actual fairy (in Colleen Moore's Fairy Castle) or sail underwater into Lake Michigan (from the U-505 German Submarine, captured during World War II). Constantly updating itself with new exhibits—*Titanic: The Exhibition* was a huge draw until it closed in late 2000—the museum is a sprawling open space on three floors. Recent additions among the 2,000 exhibits are Lego MindStorms and the Idea Factory; the museum also has the world's first permanent exhibit on HIV and AIDS. Of special interest for families is the Imagination Station on the lower level, with hands-on activities for kids up to age 12. The Omnimax Theater shows science- and space-related films on a giant five-story screen; the latest gigantic attraction is "Michael Jordan at the MAX," which applies fancy special effects to Jordan's non–high-tech hoops heroics. The museum's classical revival building was designed in 1892 by D. H. Burnham & Company as a temporary structure to house the Palace of Fine Arts in the World's Columbian Exposition. It's the fair's only surviving building. On nice days, the giant lawn out front is almost as entertaining—try sunbathing or kite-flying—as the museum itself. Lake Michigan is directly across the street. *5700 S. Lake Shore Dr., Hyde Park, 773/684–1414. Museum $7, free Thurs.; combination museum and Omnimax $10. Memorial Day–Labor Day, daily 9:30–5:30; Labor Day–Memorial Day, weekdays 9:30–4, weekends 9:30–5:30.*

5 *f-2*

NATURE MUSEUM

In this 73,000-square-ft museum, which opened in October 1999, you'll walk among hundreds of Midwest species of butterflies and learn about the impact of rivers and lakes on daily life. Like Chicago's other science museums, it's geared toward children, with educational computer games to play and water tubes in which to get wet. But even jaded adults will have trouble restraining their excitement when bright yellow butterflies land on their shoulders. (You can actually watch them transform from caterpillar to butterfly, too.) Extensive glass and multilevel, open-air terraces enable visitors to connect with nature outside as they view exhibits inside. A Children's Gallery is designed to teach three- to eight-year-olds about the environment. *Fullerton Pkwy. and Cannon Dr., Lincoln Park, 773/755–5100. $6. Open Thurs.–Tues. 10–5, Wed. 10–8.*

STATUES, MURALS & MONUMENTS

As there are more than 100 works of art in Chicago's parks and plazas, these are merely the highlights.

6 *d-2*

BATCOLUMN

(Claes Oldenburg, 1977.) Many feel this 100-ft-high gigantic baseball bat strikes out—especially given its location, across the street from the sprawling Presidential Towers apartments in the middle of the financial district. Still, the sculpture, made of gray-painted-steel latticework, is an amusing sight. *600 W. Madison St., West Loop.*

6 *f-1*

CHICAGO

(Joan Miró, 1981.) Just east of the Chicago Temple is this 37-ft bronze, concrete, and ceramic-inlaid lady with outstretched arms and rather voluptuous proportions. It is said that this lucky girl will become more beautiful with age.

Brunswick Plaza, 69 W. Washington Blvd., Loop.

8 *d-2*

CHICAGO PICASSO

(Pablo Picasso, 1964–67.) It's a horse. It's a woman. It's an Afghan dog. It's the Picasso sculpture in front of the Daley Center. Known simply as "the Picasso" (what else would you call it?), this 50-ft-tall sculpture provoked puzzlement and scoffs when it was unveiled in 1967. Chicago columnist Mike Royko called the sculpture a "big, homely metal thing" that "looks like some giant insect that is about to eat a smaller, weaker insect" with "eyes that are pitiless, cold, mean." Concluded Royko: "Picasso has never been here, they say. You'd think he's been riding the L all his life." Today the sculpture is showered with pride and recognized as an unofficial emblem of Chicago. It does manage to fit in beautifully with its surroundings, largely because it's made of Cor-Ten weathering steel, the same material used to build the Daley Center. *Bounded by Washington, Randolph, Dearborn, and Clark Sts., Loop.*

5 *g-7*

CHICAGO PLACE MALL SCULPTURE

Granted, a mall food court may be an unusual place for a spectacular piece of artwork. But this aluminum sculpture depicting the city skyline arched like a colorful Indian headdress is a sight to see. Underneath the sculpture are the words AND THE ILLINI CALLED IT CHE-CA-GOU. Created by a California artist, Sussman Prejza, the sculpture features large onion balls, as the Indian name *che-ca-gou* means "smell of the onions." Curly pieces of aluminum represent prairie grass. *700 N. Michigan Ave., Near North.*

8 *c-3*

DAWN SHADOWS

(Louise Nevelson, 1983.) No public art collection is ever complete without a Nevelson. The 42-ft, black-painted steel sculpture is reflected in the high-rise behind it. *Madison Plaza, Madison and Wells Sts., Loop.*

5 *f-2*

ELLSWORTH KELLY SCULPTURE

This monolith was erected by the Friends of the Parks with a little help

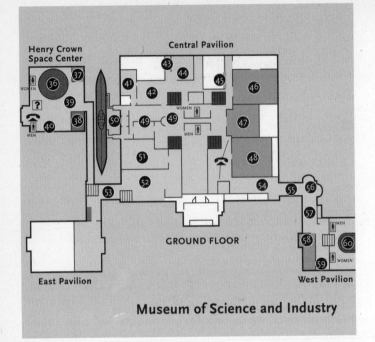

Henry Crown Space Center

Central Pavilion

GROUND FLOOR

East Pavilion

West Pavilion

Museum of Science and Industry

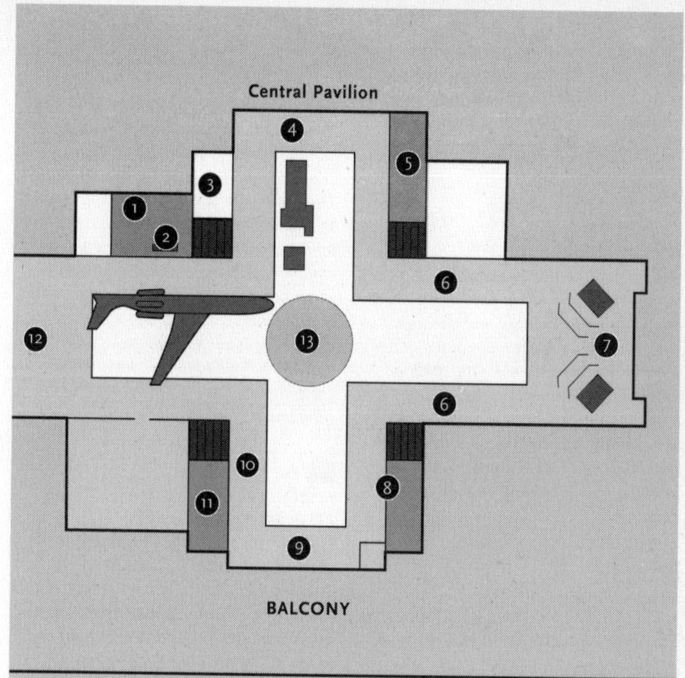
Central Pavilion
1
2
3
4
5
6
7
6
8
9
10
11
12
13
BALCONY

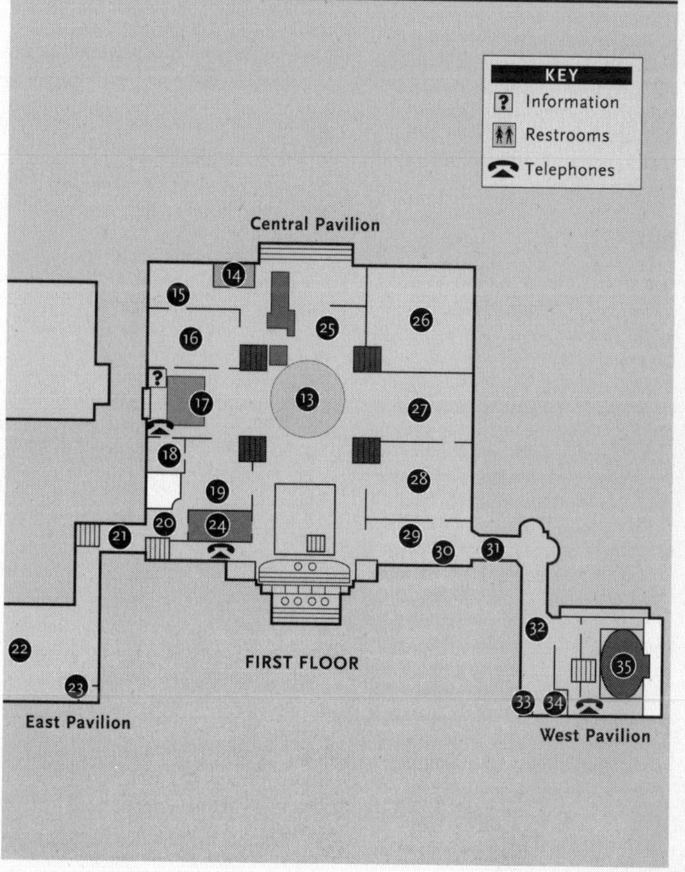
KEY
Information
Restrooms
Telephones
Central Pavilion
14
15
16
17
18
19
20
21
22
23
24
25
26
27
28
29
30
31
32
33
34
35
13
FIRST FLOOR
East Pavilion
West Pavilion

from the National Endowment for the Arts. The 40-ft, sleek stainless-steel sculpture symbolizes Chicago's rise from the ashes of the fire. *Cannon Dr. and Fullerton Pkwy., Lincoln Park.*

8 d-4
FLAMINGO
(Alexander Calder, 1973.) You can't miss this graceful red-painted Calder stabile (a sculpture that looks like a mobile). The 53-ft-high *Flamingo* was dedicated in 1974, on the same day as Calder's *Universe* at the Sears Tower. The artist is said to have had a great time going from one dedication to another, riding in a brightly colored circus bandwagon. *Federal Center Plaza, Dearborn St. between Adams St. and Jackson Blvd., Loop.*

2 g-7
FOUNTAIN OF TIME
(Lorado Taft, 1922.) This haunting sculpture depicts the figure of Time observing humanity passing by. Its designer, Lorado Taft, was one of the most distinguished sculptors and teachers of his time. Taft created numerous pieces for the Columbian Exposition of 1893, and many of his works adorn Chicago's parks and public places. *West end of Midway Plaisance, west of Cottage Grove Ave., Hyde Park.*

6 f-2
THE FOUR SEASONS (LES QUATRE SAISONS)
(Marc Chagall, 1974.) This 70-ft-long mosaic depicts vibrant scenes of a city community: children and musicians playing, men and women dancing. In all, there are more than 3,000 square ft of murals, containing more than 300 shadings of glass, granite, and marble. The French artist created the mural for the city, in an effort to capture what he called America's "continuous motion, the coming and going of machines and people." It's a wonderful piece to contemplate seriously by day or by night, when it is lit. Ironically, considering the theme is the four seasons, Chicago's harsh seasonal weather began causing tiles to pop out, so a glass canopy was erected over the monument in 1996 to provide extra protection. Wondering about vandals? First Chicago NBD's cameras provide 24-hour security. *1 First National Plaza, Monroe and Dearborn Sts., Loop.*

2 f-5
MICHAEL JORDAN STATUE
(Julie and Omri Rotblatt-Amrany, 1994.) The husband-and-wife artist team worked with the Bulls star to design this 11½-ft bronze sculpture, officially named *The Spirit.* The statue, which depicts No. 23 soaring over his opponents, was unveiled outside the United Center in 1994 as a tribute to Michael Jordan upon his initial retirement. Jordan, of course, retired in early 1999, after leading the Bulls to six championships, including 1998's famous winning-shot-pose victory. *United Center, 1901 W. Madison St., West Loop.*

8 d-2
MONUMENT WITH STANDING BEAST
(Jean Dubuffet, 1985.) The crowning glory of the unusual James R. Thompson Center is this fascinating sculpture. The 10-ton, 28-ft-high monument has curved shapes—in white with black traceries, set against the curving red, white, and blue of the center—that add to the visual variety. This fiberglass abstract was a gift from the French artist. *100 W. Randolph St., Loop.*

2 g-7
NUCLEAR ENERGY
(Henry Moore, 1967.) A 12-ft bronze sculpture marks the site where Enrico Fermi and other physicists set off the first controlled nuclear chain reaction on December 2, 1942. The dawn of the atomic age occurred under the bleachers of what was then Stagg Field. The sculpture is said to represent both a human skull and an atomic mushroom cloud. *University of Chicago Campus, east side of Ellis Ave. between 56th and 57th Sts., Hyde Park.*

8 f-2
SOUNDING SCULPTURE
(Harry Bertoia, 1975.) The artist referred to this wind-chime sculpture as "an offering to the wind." Made of copper rods 4 to 16 ft high set in a reflecting pool, it makes interesting sounds when the breeze blows. *Amoco Oil Building Plaza, 200 E. Randolph St., Loop.*

5 f-4
STANDING LINCOLN
(Augustus Saint-Gaudens, 1887.) To create this piece, Saint-Gaudens used a

mask of Lincoln's face and casts of his hands that were made before he became president. The noted American sculptor's portrayals of military heroes and presidents adorn almost every major city east of the Mississippi River. *East of Chicago Historical Society, Lincoln Park.*

8 b-4
UNIVERSE

(Alexander Calder, 1974.) Inside the Sears Tower lobby is this spiraling Calder mobile sculpture, made of brightly painted but slow-moving aluminum abstract. It's actually powered by seven motors placed behind the 55- by 33-ft wall. The simultaneous movements are reminiscent of a three-ring circus, one of Calder's favorite motifs. *233 S. Wacker Dr., Loop.*

VIEWPOINTS

2 g-5
ADLER PLANETARIUM

Because of its location at the far end of a peninsula jutting out onto Lake Michigan, the Adler is a great place to take pictures of the city skyline. Enjoy similar views of the city from the steps of the nearby Field Museum, or the north terrace of the Shedd Aquarium. *1300 S. Lake Shore Dr., Near South.*

8 f-2
AMOCO OIL BUILDING PLAZA

Stand in the shadows of Chicago's second-tallest building to get a wonderful view of the Loop, the lake, and the Art Institute. *200 E. Randolph St., Loop.*

6 h-6
BURNHAM PARK

From this vantage point you have Lake Michigan on both sides of you. Enjoy the sights as you hear the clank of halyards hitting sailboat masts in nearby Burnham Harbor and the whir of planes taking off from Meigs Field. *Achsah Bond Dr. at 1300 Lake Shore Dr., Near South.*

7 f-5
JOHN HANCOCK OBSERVATORY

The 94th floor has an observation deck, which is 1,030 ft high. On a clear day the 60-mi visibility affords fantastic views of Lake Michigan and the states bordering

it. You can also see the ordering a pricey drink Room lounge on the ing a meal at the Signature 95th restaurant. The best time to go is at sunset, when you can see lights blinking across the city as the sky deepens to red and purple. *875 N. Michigan Ave., Near North, 312/751–3681.*

LAKE SHORE DRIVE

Drive along the lakeshore with its parks, marinas, and beaches on one side and the high rises, skyscrapers, and mansions on the other. By day or night, it's an urban delight—except, of course, during rush hour. Slow down on the deadly curve just north of the Loop, and observe the 45 mph speed limits, as the police are always watching. *5700 North to 5900 South.*

2 g-3/4
LINCOLN PARK

It's almost easy to forget your urban setting as you cut through the park with its ponds, parks, and trees. But look to the south for a wonderful view of the Hancock Center and other buildings. *Fullerton Pkwy. at the Lagoon.*

7 e-8
MICHIGAN AVENUE BRIDGE

Look around: in any direction it's a treat for the mind's, or camera's, eye. From here you get a spectacular view of the Wrigley Building and Tribune Tower, which anchor the south end of the Magnificent Mile. To the west, an array of bridges cross the Chicago River; to the east, the river opens up into Lake Michigan. *400 N. Michigan Ave., Near North.*

7 h-7
NAVY PIER

Take a ¾-mi walk along the tree-lined east promenade of the pier to soak up the views. You can do this any time of the year, although summer is the most enjoyable season. Take a ride on the giant Ferris wheel for a truly sensational view of the city and the lake. *East end of Grand Ave., Near North.*

7 f-4
OAK STREET BEACH

A good place to glimpse lots of hard bodies, Oak Street Beach also offers fantastic views of the Drake Hotel and posh Gold Coast residences lining Lake Shore

...ive. Oak St. and N. Lake Shore Dr., Gold Coast.

THE RAVENSWOOD EL (BROWN LINE)

A ride on one of the roller coaster–like elevated Loop trains is very much a part of the Chicago experience. Hop on the Ravenswood El for a heart-stopping ride, as the train makes hideous squeaking noises curving along the tracks and sometimes seems to get a little too close to Loop buildings and back porches.

8 *b-4*

SEARS TOWER SKYDECK

The enclosed Skydeck Observatory on the 103rd floor is 1,353 ft above the streets of Chicago, and the nonstop elevator gets you there in one minute. Once on top, you'll have a 360-degree view and, on a clear day, 60-mi visibility—which means you can see Indiana, Wisconsin, and Michigan. *233 S. Wacker Dr., Loop, 312/875–9696.*

guided tours

AIRPLANE TOURS

8 *h-8*

CHICAGO BY AIR

Enjoy a bird's-eye view of the city, with flights out of Meigs Field scheduled at your convenience. *1521 S. Lynn White Dr., Near South Side, 708/524–1172.*

BICYCLE TOURS

7 *h-7*

BIKE CHICAGO RENTAL & TOURS

This bicycle-rental company offers three guided tours: a two-hour trip from the Loop to Lincoln Park, including the zoo and the conservatory; a five-hour ride along the lakefront to the Baha'i Temple in Wilmette; and a lakefront jaunt to Hyde Park, with the Osaka Japanese Garden and the Fountain of Time statue. The company also provides maps for self-guided tours. *Navy Pier, 600 E. Grand Ave., Near North, 312/755–0488.*

5 *g-4*

North Avenue Beach, at North Ave. and Lake Shore Dr., Lincoln Park, 312/755–0488.

BUS TOURS

6 *g-2*

AMERICAN SIGHTSEEING

The North tour along State Street and North Michigan Avenue covers the Loop, State Street, Wacker Drive, the Magnificent Mile, and the lakefront, with a stop at the Lincoln Park Zoo and Conservatory. The South tour takes in the financial district, Grant Park, the University of Chicago, the Museum of Science and Industry, and Jackson Park. Tours leave from the Palmer House Hilton, at 17 East Monroe Street, or you can be picked up at your hotel (downtown or Near North only). *312/251–3100.*

CHICAGO TROLLEY CHARTERS

Visitors to the city can get a glimpse at all the downtown highlights from the seat of an authentic open-air trolley. Venture from the Sears Tower to the Water Tower, or board at Planet Hollywood for a trip to the Adler Planetarium. These trolleys also stop at the Art Institute, the Lincoln Park Zoo, and Navy Pier, as well as other notable sights. You can get off and reboard at any scheduled stop along the 13-mi route. *312/663–0260.*

BOAT TOURS

Boat-tour schedules vary by season; call for exact times and fares. The season usually runs from May 1 through October 1.

8 *e-1*

CHICAGO ARCHITECTURE FOUNDATION RIVER CRUISE

Step aboard Chicago's First Lady for a cruise that highlights more than 53 sights. The 90-minute tours depart from the southwest corner of Wacker Drive and Michigan Avenue from April to October. Reservations are recommended. *312/922–3432 for information, 312/902–1500 for tickets.*

8 *e-1*

MERCURY CHICAGO SKYLINE CRUISELINE

Enjoy city sights on 90-minute river and lake cruises that leave from Wacker Drive at Michigan Avenue (the south side of the Michigan Avenue Bridge). *312/332–1353 for recorded information.*

SHORELINE MARINE

This outfit runs half-hour boat trips on Lake Michigan: narrated tours leave from the Shedd Aquarium during the day and from Buckingham Fountain in the evening. Tours also depart from Navy Pier every half hour. The company's Shoreline Water Taxi takes you to Chicago's favorite destinations: Sears Tower, Navy Pier, and Shedd Aquarium. The fleet of taxis makes frequent departures daily from Memorial Day to Labor Day. *312/222–9328.*

7 *e-8*

WENDELLA SIGHTSEEING BOATS

From April to October, Wendella has 90-minute guided tours that traverse the Chicago River to south of the Sears Tower and through the locks; on Lake Michigan, they travel between the Adler Planetarium on the south and Oak Street Beach on the north. The company also has evening tours. All tours leave from lower Michigan Avenue at the foot of the Wrigley Building on the north side of the river. *400 N. Michigan Ave., Near North, 312/337–1446.*

7 *h-8*

WINDY OF CHICAGO LTD.

Sail Lake Michigan on *The Windy*, a 148-ft ship modeled on old-time commercial vessels. Ninety-minute cruises offer riders a chance to help the crew or even take a turn at the wheel. Cruises begin at Navy Pier. *312/595–5555.*

SPECIAL-INTEREST TOURS

BRONZEVILLE TOURS

The Black Metropolis Convention and Tourism Council, the Chicago Office of Tourism, Black Coutours, and Willie Dixon's Blues Heaven all offer tours of historic Bronzeville, spotlighting the historic significance of this African-American neighborhood. *Black Metropolis*

Convention and Tourism Council, 773/548–2579; Tour Black Chicago, 312/332–2323; Black Coutours, 773/233–8907; Willie Dixon's Blues Heaven, 312/808–1286.

CARRIAGE RIDES

When the mood strikes, a carriage ride through the Windy City can be very romantic. *Antique Coach and Carriage, 773/735–9400. Chicago Horse & Carriage Ltd., 312/944–9192. Noble Horse, 312/266–7878.*

8 *b-3*

CHICAGO MERCANTILE EXCHANGE

Two visitors' galleries provide views of the often-frenetic trading floors. The eighth-floor gallery overlooks the currency pit; the fourth-floor gallery overlooks agricultural and stock index products trading and has a presentation that explains the activity. Galleries are open weekdays. *30 S. Wacker Dr., Loop, 312/930–8249.*

CHICAGO SUPERNATURAL GHOST TOURS

Visit famous murder sites, local Native American burial grounds, allegedly haunted pubs, and the scenes of various gangster rubouts, such as the St. Valentine's Day Massacre. Two five-hour tours, narrated by veteran "ghost hunter" Richard Crowe, leave from various locations and operate daily during October and November and weekends the rest of the year. A cruise, which leaves from the Mercury boat dock at Michigan Avenue and Wacker Drive, operates in the summer. *708/ 499–0300.*

CHICAGO TOUR GUIDES INSTITUTE, INC.

Non-English-speaking visitors to Chicago will find it easy to follow the tours given by Chicago Tour Guides Institute, Inc. Tour guides fluent in French, Italian, English, German, Spanish, Hebrew, and Portuguese coordinate personal and group tours. Other languages are available. *773/276–6683.*

1 *f-6*

A DAY IN HISTORIC BEVERLY HILLS/ MORGAN PARK

This two-hour tour covers two Southwest Side neighborhoods with fancy Victorians and Frank Lloyd Wright houses. *10924 S. Prospect Ave., 773/881–1831.*

5 *d-7*

FREEDOM CENTER

The *Chicago Tribune* offers free one-hour tours of its Freedom Center production facility. Make reservations in advance. *777 W. Chicago Ave., 312/222–2116.*

6 *g-1*

LOOP TOUR TRAINS

The Chicago Office of Tourism runs Loop Tour Trains on Saturday afternoons from May through September. Tickets are free from the Visitor Information Center on the first floor of the Chicago Cultural Center. *78 E. Washington St., 312/744–6630.*

5 *f-8*

UNTOUCHABLE TOURS

Get a glimpse into the lives of the gangsters who made Chicago famous with a tour of sites where such notables as Al Capone and John Dillinger made history. Untouchable Tours captures the excitement of Jazz Age Chicago at old hoodlum haunts, brothels, gambling dens, and sites of gangland shootouts. Tours last two hours and depart from the corner of Ohio and Clark. Times vary depending on the season; make phone reservations in advance. *773/881–1195.*

WALKING TOURS

6 *g-1*

AUDIO ARCHITECTURE

The Chicago Office of Tourism offers Audio Architecture, a 90-minute taped, self-guided walking tour of historic buildings, skyscrapers, and sculptures in the Loop. The tour, developed by the Landmarks Preservation Council of Illinois, is available at the Shop in the Chicago Cultural Center Welcome Center. *78 E. Washington St., Loop, 312/744–6630.*

6 *g-2, g-7*

CHICAGO ARCHITECTURE FOUNDATION

The CAF offers more than 50 tours. The popular Loop walking tour, which departs from the Santa Fe Building, is given daily throughout the year. The North Michigan Avenue tour departs from the John Hancock Center. The Foundation also leads other tours— Graceland Cemetery, Frank Lloyd Wright's Oak Park buildings, and bicycle tours of Lincoln Park—on an occa-

sional, seasonal, or prescheduled basis. *Tour Centers: Santa Fe Building, 224 S. Michigan Ave., Loop; John Hancock Center, 875 N. Michigan Ave., Near North; 312/922–3432.*

6 *g-1*

CHICAGO NEIGHBORHOOD TOURS

Sponsored by the city's Office of Tourism, these walking tours emphasize Chicago's rich multicultural history and snake through areas removed from the glitzy tourism of Michigan Avenue. The South Side tour, for example, emphasizes Bronzeville, once known as "Black Metropolis," and stops at the Museum of African-American History and the Little Black Pearl Workshop arts center. Other excellent tours: Chinatown/Pilsen, including the Mexican Fine Arts Center; West Side, from the United Center to the Garfield Park Observatory; Near South/Prairie Avenue Historic District, with the onetime "Record Row," where a museum dedicated to the blues label Chess Records still stands; Wicker Park; Uptown; Andersonville; and Devon Avenue. *78 E. Washington St., Loop, 312/742–1190.*

6 *f-3*

FRIENDS OF THE CHICAGO RIVER

This group sponsors Saturday-morning walking tours along the river, as well as boat cruises and canoe days from May to October. Times vary, so call for a schedule. The organization also has maps of the walking routes, available for a small donation. *407 S. Dearborn St., Suite 1580, South Loop, 312/939–0490.*

events

JANUARY

6 *h-7*

CHICAGO BOAT, SPORTS, AND RV SHOW

It's never too early to start thinking about summer vacation. The Chicago Boat, Sports, and RV Show, held each year in early to mid-January, displays more than 900 boats and 300 recreational vehicles at McCormick Place. *312/946–6262.*

FEBRUARY

AFRICAN-AMERICAN HERITAGE MONTH

All month long, African-American Heritage Month celebrations are held at the Museum of Science and Industry (773/684–1414), the DuSable Museum of African-American History (773/947–0600), the South Shore Cultural Center (312/747–2536), the Chicago Cultural Center (312/346–3278), the Field Museum (312/922–9410), the Art Institute of Chicago (312/443–3600), and other Chicago cultural institutions. Events include arts-and-crafts exhibitions and theater, music, and dance performances.

5 *f-3*

AZALEA AND CAMELLIA SHOW

Chase away the winter blues with an early glimpse of spring at the Azalea and Camellia Show, in mid-February at Lincoln Park Conservatory. *312/742–7736.*

6 *h-7*

CHICAGO AUTO SHOW

The Chicago Auto Show, held each year in mid-February, previews the coming year's domestic and imported models at McCormick Place. *312/791–7000 or 312/559–1212 for tickets.*

5 *g-8*

MEDINAH SHRINE CIRCUS

Kids of all ages look forward to the delights of the circus, held each year in mid-February or early March at the Medinah Temple. *312/266–5050.*

WINTERBREAK FESTIVAL

Concerts, skating exhibitions, and other entertainment events are held mid-month at various locations. *312/744–3315.*

MARCH

ST. PATRICK'S DAY PARADE

You know it's St. Patrick's Day when the Chicago River is dyed green (using a secret recipe involving orange food-based powder), shamrocks decorate the street, and the center stripe of Dearborn Street is painted the color of the Irish from Wacker Drive to Van Buren Street. *312/942–9188.*

APRIL

ANNUAL CHICAGO LATINO FILM FESTIVAL

Celebrate Latino culture at the annual Columbia College–sponsored film festival, held at various locations around the city. *312/663–1600.*

MAY

ART CHICAGO

See Art Events, *above.*

6 *h-1*

BUCKINGHAM FOUNTAIN

From May until October 1, Buckingham Fountain in Grant Park flows day and night. Colored lights illuminate the spectacular fountain nightly from 9 until 11.

PRINTER'S ROW BOOK FAIR

A popular springtime event, the two-day fair in the historic Printer's Row district features programs and displays on the printer's and binder's arts. *312/987–9896.*

WRIGHT PLUS HOUSE WALK

Soak in the genius of Frank Lloyd Wright and other Prairie School architects with a look at their masterpieces in suburban Oak Park. *708/848–1976.*

JUNE

BOULEVARD-LAKEFRONT BICYCLE TOUR

In mid-month, 6,000 cyclists hit the city's network of boulevards and parks for a 35-mi ride. *312/427–3325.*

2 *g-5*

CHICAGO BLUES FESTIVAL

Crowds descend on the "Home of the Blues" for this perennial favorite—at which you're guaranteed to hear Robert Johnson's Mississippi Delta standard "Sweet Home Chicago" more than three times a day—held in Grant Park. The four-day, three-stage event stars blues greats from Chicago and around the country. Recent big names have included Ray Charles, Ruth Brown, the late Screamin' Jay Hawkins, Robert Cray, and locals such as Koko Taylor, Honeyboy Edwards, and boogie-woogie master Erwin Helfer. *312/744–3315.*

2 *g-5*

CHICAGO GOSPEL FEST

Though the Gospel Fest doesn't have quite the name recognition as the Blues Fest, organizer Pam Moore has managed to lure headliners such as jazzman Jimmy McGriff and soul hero Al Green, now a Memphis-based minister. It's held in early to mid-June in Grant Park. *312/744–3315.*

57TH STREET ART FAIR
See Art Events, *above.*

2 *g-5*

GRANT PARK SYMPHONY ORCHESTRA AND CHORUS

This popular series of free classical concerts, held at the Petrillo Music Shell, features world-class artists performing with the Grant Park Symphony Orchestra and Chorus. Concerts are scheduled in mid-June through mid-August, Wednesday through Sunday. *312/742–7638.*

OLD TOWN ART FAIR
See Art Events, *above.*

1 *d-2*

RAVINIA FESTIVAL

For some Chicagoans, summer doesn't officially start until the Ravinia Festival kicks off in Highland Park in late June. The festival hosts a variety of jazz, classical, and popular musical artists, with performances through Labor Day. Enjoy a picnic while you sit on the lawn and listen to wonderful music. *847/266–5100.*

2 *g-5*

TASTE OF CHICAGO

This weeklong feast feeds 4 million visitors, who sample culinary delights from scores of Chicago restaurants. (You haven't lived until you've eaten a pickle on a stick.) Taste of Chicago, which begins in late June and takes place in Grant Park, also features entertainment on several stages over the Fourth of July weekend; this includes the Country Music Festival, with rockers and crooners from Travis Tritt to Wayne Hancock. *312/744–3315.*

JULY

4 *e-7, f-7*

CHICAGO TO MACKINAC ISLAND BOAT RACE

Enjoy the picturesque sight of sails filling the horizon, when the Chicago to Mackinac Island Boat Race kicks off in mid-July at Belmont Harbor. *312/861–7777.*

2 *g-5*

INDEPENDENCE DAY

Gather along the lakefront with the rest of the crowd for July 4 fireworks at dusk; bring a blanket and a portable radio to listen to the "1812 Overture" from Grant Park. *312/744–3315.*

5 *f-6*

NEWBERRY LIBRARY BOOK FAIR

The venerable institution sells thousands of good used books at low prices; experienced book-fair goers arrive early and bring their own bags. The park across the street holds the Bughouse Square Debates the same weekend. *312/255–3510.*

TWIN CITIES TO CHICAGO AIDSRIDE

For five days in early to mid-July, bike riders who've raised $2,300 each get to pedal the 500 mi between Minneapolis–St. Paul and Chicago. Registration is $45. *773/880–8812.*

8 *g-3*

VENETIAN NIGHT

As evening falls, boats festooned with lights dot the lakefront at Monroe Street Harbor. The event also features an impressive display of fireworks. *312/744–3315.*

6 *d-2*

WORLD'S LARGEST BLOCK PARTY

Swarms of people gather at Old St. Pat's Church in mid-July for the World's Largest Block Party, which features nationally recognized bands, food, and drinks. *312/648–1021.*

AUGUST

7 *e-1*

AIR AND WATER SHOW

If the weather cooperates, the Air and Water Show in late August makes for a perfect day at the beach. Crowds pack North Avenue Beach, as well as Oak Street and Fullerton beaches, to gape as precision flying teams and antique and high-tech aircraft go through their paces. If you happen to forget about the show, don't worry. Odds are you'll hear the planes roaring overhead from any vantage point in the city. Just find a roof with an unobstructed view of the downtown lakefront area. *312/744–3315.*

2 *g-5*

CHICAGO JAZZ FESTIVAL

The Chicago Jazz Festival, whose recent headliners have included Chick Corea and LaVay Smith and Her Red Hot Skillet Lickers, runs for four days during Labor Day weekend at the Petrillo Music Shell in Grant Park. Many great avant-garde artists perform at night, after festival hours, at small clubs in the area. *312/744–3315.*

7 *h-7*

CHICAGO TRIATHLON

Stalwart Chicago Triathlon participants plunge in at Ohio Street on the lakefront for a 1-mi swim, followed by a 25-mi bike race on Lake Shore Drive, and a 10-km run in the world's largest triathlon, held in late August. *773/404–2372.*

2 *d-2*

TASTE OF POLONIA

The Taste of Polonia, held in late August or early September at Lawrence and Milwaukee avenues, has food, carnival games, polka bands, and Polish handicrafts. *773/777–8898.*

SEPTEMBER

AROUND THE COYOTE

See Art Events, *above.*

DÍA DE LOS MUERTOS

See Art Events, *above.*

8 *d-4*

OKTOBERFEST

You can leave the lederhosen at home, but don't forget to bring your appetite to the Berghoff Restaurant (17 W. Adams St.) for an Oktoberfest celebration with beer and German specialties. A variety of Chicago area pubs also host Oktoberfests. *312/427–3170.*

2 *g-5*

VIVA CHICAGO

The sultry sounds of Latin music delight crowds at this Grant Park festival, held in early to mid-September. *312/744–3315.*

WORLD MUSIC FESTIVAL CHICAGO

Yet another city-sponsored music festival, this late-September event is scattered around various nightclubs, concluding with a big show at the Field Museum of Natural History. Though it's diverse—performers were from 25 different countries one recent year—it has yet to draw Blues Festival–level names. *312/744–3315.*

OCTOBER

CHICAGO INTERNATIONAL FILM FESTIVAL

Film aficionados love this festival, which brings new American and foreign films to various Chicago theaters in mid-October. *312/425–9400.*

COLUMBUS DAY PARADE

Despite controversies pertaining to who actually discovered America, the Columbus Day Parade endures, following a route on Dearborn Street from Wacker Drive to Congress Parkway. *312/828–0010.*

8 *f-6*

LASALLE BANK CHICAGO MARATHON

Cheer on intrepid runners as they weave through 26 mi of the Windy City for the LaSalle Bank–sponsored Chicago Marathon, which starts in Grant Park at Columbus and Balbo streets. *312/904–9800.*

NOVEMBER

2 *h-7*

CHRISTMAS AROUND THE WORLD

Trees decorated in the traditional styles of more than 40 countries are on display at the Museum of Science and Industry from late November through December. *773/684–1414.*

8 *d-2*

CHRISTMAS TREE LIGHTING

The lighting of Chicago's Christmas tree takes place on the Friday of Thanksgiving weekend in the Daley Center Plaza; the Christmas Parade, with balloons, floats, and Santa, travels down Michigan Avenue on Saturday.

5 *f-3*

CHRYSANTHEMUM SHOW
By late November, all the blooms have withered—except for the chrysanthemums that take center stage at the Lincoln Park Conservatory. *312/742–7736.*

7 *e-4*

MAGNIFICENT MILE LIGHTS FESTIVAL
A huge city seems to recall its quaint Midwestern roots with this family event, held on the Saturday before Thanksgiving. The festival kicks off the holiday season with a block-by-block illumination of hundreds of thousands of tiny white lights along Michigan Avenue and Oak Street. *312/642–3570.*

6 *h-7*

THE NUTCRACKER
The Christmas season really begins with annual performances from mid-November through December of *A Christmas Carol,* at the Goodman Theatre (170 N. Dearborn St., 312/443–3800), and *The Nutcracker,* at the Arie Crown Theatre at McCormick Place (2301 S. Lake Shore Dr., 312/791–6190).

5 *f-2/3*

ZOO LIGHTS FESTIVAL
At the Lincoln Park Zoo, more than 100,000 lights form the shapes of zoo animals, dinosaurs, and holiday decorations, from late November through early January. *312/742–2000.*

CHICAGO'S TALLEST BUILDINGS

The Sears Tower is in a knock-down, drag-out battle with Petronas Twin Towers in Kuala Lumpur, Malaysia, for the "world's tallest building" designation. Unfortunately, the 80-ft antennae can't lift the Sears beyond the Petronas in the all-important architectural-top height category. But here's how a few of Chicago's skyscrapers stack up against those in the rest of the world:

Sears Tower (Architecture)
    1,730 ft (3rd, after the two Petronas towers)

Amoco Building (Architecture)
    1,136 ft (11th)

John Hancock Center (Architecture)
    1,127 ft (12th)

DECEMBER

PRE-KWANZAA CELEBRATION
The city's largest pre-Kwanzaa event takes place at the South Shore Cultural Center and includes two days of performances, workshops, crafts, and food. The family-oriented celebration is held in advance of the African-American cultural holiday Kwanzaa, which runs from December 26 to January 1; other Kwanzaa-related events are held at the New Regal Theatre, DuSable Museum of African-American History, Chicago Cultural Center, Art Institute of Chicago, and other cultural institutions in the city. *312/747–2536.*

day trips out of town

THE WESTERN SUBURBS

In Chicago's western suburbs, gracious villages that date from the 1800s mingle with more modest developments from the postwar housing boom. An essential stop is Oak Park, one of the most interesting neighborhoods of residential architecture in the United States. Brookfield has one of the country's foremost zoos. Farther west in DuPage County is a string of pleasant destinations, including Old Naper Settlement, the best living history museum in the Chicago area, and Cantigny, a lavish estate.

A day trip to the western suburbs is best done by car; all towns are within 5 to 15 mi of each other. The main arteries serving the western suburbs are the Eisenhower Expressway (I–290), which goes west from the Loop and turns into I–88 at the border of DuPage County; the Tri-State Tollway (I–94/294), which semicircles the region from north to south; and I–355, which connects I–290 with I–55, the road from Chicago to St. Louis.

You can also take Metra commuter trains (312/836–7000) to individual attractions. The Metra Union Pacific West Line departs from the station at Citicorp Center (165 N. Canal St.) and stops in Oak Park and Wheaton. The Metra Burlington Northern Line departs from Union Station (210 S. Canal St.)

and stops at Brookfield, Lisle, Naperville, and Aurora.

The Chicago Office of Tourism (78 E. Washington St., 312/744–2400 or 800/406–6418) has some information on major attractions in the western suburbs, as does the Illinois Bureau of Tourism (100 W. Randolph St., 312/814–4732 or 800/226–6632). Also check with the Chicago Architecture Foundation (312/922–8687).

The Oak Park Visitors Center (158 N. Forest Ave., 708/848–1500) has useful detailed maps, tour information, and tickets for tours of other historic buildings in the River Forest–Oak Park area, including those by Prairie School architects E. E. Roberts and George Maher.

OAK PARK

Ten miles west of downtown Chicago, Oak Park is a living museum of American architectural trends and philosophies. Among familiar clapboard and Colonial-style houses are 25 houses designed or renovated by former resident Frank Lloyd Wright; architects who followed his Prairie School style designed many others here as well. Tour the Frank Lloyd Wright Home and Studio (951 Chicago Ave., 708/848–1976), stroll around the neighborhood, and gaze at the spectacular examples of early 20th-century architecture—from the outside, as all are privately owned. One of Wright's early public buildings, the stark concrete Unity Temple (875 W. Lake St., 708/383–8873) was erected in Oak Park in 1906 and still serves as a house of worship.

Oak Park, founded in the 1850s, also was the birthplace of Ernest Hemingway; fans can admire his boyhood home at 600 North Kenilworth Avenue, which is not open to the public, or stop in the Ernest Hemingway Birthplace (339 N. Oak Park Ave., 708/848–2222) or the small Ernest Hemingway Museum (200 N. Oak Park Ave., 708/848–2222) to learn about the writer's early life.

BROOKFIELD ZOO

The naturalistic settings of the 200-acre Brookfield Zoo, 15 mi southwest of downtown Chicago, give visitors the sense of being in the wild. Most noteworthy is the Tropic World exhibit, which simulates a tropical rain forest, complete with steam, waterfalls, rock cliffs, trees, shrubs, and even thunderstorms

at random intervals. Habitat Africa has a water hole and rock formations characteristic of the African savanna; the Swamp has a springy floor, push-button alligator bellows, and open habitats with low-flying birds; and the Living Coast allows visitors to venture into a totally dry underwater environment with sharks, rays, jellyfish, and turtles swimming through huge glassed-in passageways. Don't forget to buy a ticket for the daily dolphin shows, in a splendid building that accommodates 2,000 spectators. From late spring through early fall the "motorized safari" tram will carry you around the grounds for $2.50; in winter the free, heated Snowball Express does the job. 8400 W. 31st St., Brookfield, 708/485–0263. Zoo $7 Apr.–Sept., Mon., Wed., and Fri.–Sun.; $4 Tues. and Thurs.; free Oct.–Mar. Tues. and Thurs. Children's zoo $1 Mar.–Oct., free Nov.–Feb. Dolphin show $2.50; parking $4. Open weekdays 10–5, weekends 10–6.

LISLE

The old farm town of Lisle, 10 mi west of Brookfield, and 25 mi southwest of downtown Chicago, is being gentrified as the suburbs and new corporate centers sprawl west. The main attraction here is the Morton Arboretum, a ½-mi north after you exit I–88 at Route 53. Established by salt magnate Joy Morton in 1922, the Morton Arboretum offers 1,500 serene acres of plants, woodlands, and outdoor gardens. Spring is the best time to visit, when flowering trees are spectacular. Stroll along the arboretum's 13 mi of trails, or drive through some of its grounds. Tours and special programs are scheduled most Sunday afternoons. Rte. 53, 630/719–2400. $7 per car, walk-ins free; $3 per car Wed. Open Nov.–Mar., daily 7–5; Apr.–Oct., daily 7–7.

WHEATON

Cantigny, the 500-acre estate willed to the evangelical Wheaton College by legendary Chicago Tribune publisher Colonel Robert McCormick, has magnificent grounds and a museum. The estate, 30 mi west of downtown Chicago, contains splendid formal gardens, a restored 1870s mansion, and a tank park. 1 S. 151 Winfield Rd., 630/668–5161. Free, parking $5. Park open daily 9–6, mansion Tues.–Sun. 10–3:15, museum Tues.–Sun. 10–4; Memorial Day–Labor Day, sites open 1 hr later.

If you're with children, don't miss the excellent DuPage Children's Museum, where kids can play in a carpentry shop with real hand drills, hammers, and saws. Outside the museum, the municipally owned Rice Water Park offers water slides, children's play areas, and a sand volleyball pit. *Museum: 1777 S. Blanchard Rd., 630/260–9960. $4.50. Open Tues. and Thurs.–Sat. 9:30–5, Wed. 9:30–8, Sun. noon–5. Water Park: 630/690–4880. $13. Open mid-June–late Aug., Mon.–Sat. 11–9, Sun. noon–9.*

NAPERVILLE

A visit to Naperville, 25 mi southwest of the Loop, should include the Naper Settlement living history museum, lunch or afternoon tea downtown, and a leisurely stroll along the river walk. Naper Settlement contains several historically significant buildings that were moved to the grounds and restored by the local historic society. The impressive result is a bricks-and-sticks time-line of the evolution of a 19th-century prairie town. Many of Naper Settlement's buildings have hands-on activities and demonstrations. *Naper Settlement, 523 S. Webster St., 630/420–6010. $6.50. Open Apr.–June and Sept.–Oct., Tues.–Sat. 10–4, Sun. 1–4; July–Aug., daily 10–8; Nov.–Mar., holidays and special programs only (call for details).*

AURORA

Aurora, 33 mi southwest of downtown Chicago, offers a few noteworthy sights. First, there's Walter Payton's Roundhouse. The former football great bought a decaying railroad repair station and transformed it into this huge steak house and on-site microbrewery. Inside, there's the Payton Museum and, as one might expect, Super Bowl memorabilia. The next stop is the Blackberry Historical Farm-Village, where pioneer life is re-created in a prairie-town streetscape with a replica log cabin and an 1840s farmhouse. Then there's the Fermi National Accelerator Laboratory, where visitors can view self-guided exhibits on subatomic particles, nuclear reactions, and the history of atomic power in the United States. *Roundhouse: 205 N. Broadway, 630/264–2739. Free. Daily. Blackberry Historical Farm-Village: Galena Blvd. and Barnes Rd., 630/892–1550. $7.50. Late Apr.–Labor Day, daily 10–4:30. Fermi National Accelerator Laboratory: Batavia Rd. and Rte. 59, 630/840–3000. Free. Daily 6–8.*

SHERIDAN ROAD AND THE NORTH SHORE

All along the shore of Lake Michigan north of Chicago you'll find well-to-do old towns with gracious houses on lots ever larger and more heavily wooded the farther you travel north. The most southern of these towns is Evanston, which sits on the northern border of Chicago and is home to the lakefront campus of Northwestern University. Hollywood films have helped make the North Shore synonymous with the upper middle class through such hit films as *Home Alone* (filmed in Winnetka), *Ordinary People* (Lake Forest), and *Risky Business* (Glencoe).

This day trip is designed as a drive, although you can take a commuter train to individual attractions. The route follows Sheridan Road along the lakeshore, then turns west at Lake Forest to connect with Green Bay Road heading south. The other major artery serving the North Shore is the Edens Expressway (I–94).

The Metra Union Pacific North line (312/322–6777 or 312/836–7000) departs from the station at Citicorp Center (165 N. Canal St.) and stops in Evanston (Davis Street), Wilmette, Glencoe, Ravinia Park (special trains on concert nights), Highland Park, Highwood, Fort Sheridan, Lake Forest, Waukegan, and Zion.

The Chicago Transit Authority's Howard (Red) line (312/836–7000) and an extension will take you as far as Wilmette, with multiple stops in Evanston. Board it northbound along State Street in the Loop or at Chicago Avenue and State Street in the Near North area. Change at Howard for the Evanston (Purple line) shuttle. To reach the Northwestern campus, get off at Foster Avenue and walk east to Sheridan Road. The Howard line is not recommended after dark.

The Chicago Architectural Foundation (312/922–8687) has occasional walking, bicycle, and bus tours of parts of the North Shore. The Office of Undergraduate Admissions at Northwestern University (1801 Hinman Ave., 847/491–7271) organizes tours of the campus October–April, daily at 2, with additional tours Saturday at 12:30.

Call the Illinois Bureau of Tourism (100 W. Randolph St., 312/814–4732 or 800/226–6632) or the Lake County Illinois Convention and Visitors' Bureau (847/662–2700).

EVANSTON

Well-heeled Evanston, 14 mi north of downtown Chicago, is home to five institutions of higher learning, among them Northwestern University. The student population gives Evanston a college-town flavor, especially when purple N.U. flags grace many of Evanston's beautiful residences during football season. A variety of architectural styles converge on Evanston's elm-arched streets, including well-preserved or meticulously restored Victorians, Prairie-style houses, hip-roof bungalows, and turreted Queen Anne–style houses. Throughout the summer months Evanston's lakefront parks are the stage for diverse special events, from highbrow art fairs to rowdy ethnic music festivals. Even when things are quiet, the sandy beaches, sailboat launches, and playgrounds give this area a lasting appeal.

A visit to Evanston should include a stop at the Evanston Historical Society, which occupies a 28-room châteauesque mansion with spectacular 20-ft vaulted ceilings and stained-glass windows. If you're interested in exploring N.U.'s attractive lakefront campus, pick up a map at the visitor center, a Tudor Revival mansion at the corner of Sheridan Road and Clark Street. *Evanston Historical Society, 225 Greenwood St., 847/475–3410. $5. Open Wed.–Sun. 1–5.*

WILMETTE

You'll know the affluent village of Wilmette, which is 18 mi north of downtown Chicago, by the Baha'i House of Worship, an intriguing nine-sided building that incorporates architectural styles and symbols from many of the world's religions. The 191-ft building, surrounded by formal gardens, is the U.S. center of the Baha'i faith, which celebrates the unity of all religions. Nearby is the lakefront Gilson Park, with a rarely crowded public beach that's good for swimming. Even if you aren't traveling with kids, the Kohl Children's Museum is worth a visit. Its exhibit on Marc Chagall tells the French artist's life story with brilliantly simple demonstrations of his use of light, simplified form, paint, and glass in various works. The museum also has a child-size grocery store, a kid's version of King David's temple, and a re-created ancient sailing ship. *Baha'i House of Worship, 100 Linden Ave., Wilmette, 847/853–2300. Free. May–Sept., daily 10–10; Oct.–Apr., daily 10–5. Kohl Children's Museum, 165 Green Bay Rd., 847/256–6056. $3. Tues.–Sat. 10–4, Sun. noon–4.*

HIGHLAND PARK

Highland Park, 26 mi north of downtown Chicago, draws crowds for its stellar outdoor concerts at Ravinia Park. The summer home of the Chicago Symphony Orchestra, Ravinia also showcases superb jazz, chamber music, pop, and dance performances. Most concertgoers choose lawn seats so they can pack a picnic and enjoy music under the stars. The attractive homes of Highland Park are a year-round pleasure, especially the privately owned Willits House (1445 Sheridan Rd.). Designed by Frank Lloyd Wright in 1902, it's a successful early example of the Prairie style, with the influence of Japanese architecture in its overhanging eaves. *Ravinia Music Festival: Green Bay and Lake Cook Rds., 847/266–5100.*

LAKE FOREST

Lake Forest, 32 mi north of downtown Chicago, has long been recognized as the wealthiest and most exclusive of the city's suburbs. Its winding roads were specially designed to follow the course of ravines near the lake. There are palatial estates to admire, as well as the beautifully landscaped campuses of Lake Forest and Barat colleges. A wonderful place to shop is Market Square (Western Avenue and Sheridan Road), one of the nation's oldest planned shopping centers. Built in 1916, Market Square has intriguing shops and boutiques selling high-price, one-of-a-kind clothes, home accessories, and knickknacks.

CHICAGO BOTANIC GARDEN

The village of Glencoe, 24 mi from downtown Chicago, lays claim to the spectacular Chicago Botanic Garden. Its 15 gardens cover 300 acres and provide a feast for the senses, especially in the spring. Among the beautifully maintained horticulture are a rose garden, a three-island Japanese garden, an Illinois prairie, a waterfall garden, a sensory garden for people with visual impairments, an aquatic garden, a learning garden, and three big biodomes, which showcase a desert, a rain forest, and a formal topiary garden year-round. In winter, its 10 greenhouses are filled with blooms. Special event standouts include the spring daffodil show, the Japan Festival in May, an August bonsai show, and a winter orchid show. *Lake Cook Rd. and Rte. 41, 847/835–5440. $5 per car, tram tour $3.50. Daily 8–sunset; tours every ½ hr weekdays 10:30–3:30, weekends 10:30–4:30.*

chapter 5

ARTS, ENTERTAINMENT & NIGHTLIFE

Although the Lyric Opera, Chicago Symphony Orchestra, and Steppenwolf Theatre have internationally recognized names and reputations, it would be a mistake to overlook Chicago's small spots. Just as the city isn't just a bunch of skyscrapers and deep-dish pizza, it also isn't just bluesmen singing "Sweet Home, Chicago" or the next John Belushi or Chris Farley emerging from Second City. To find the best stuff, Chicagoans know to dig deep: into the 50-seat storefront theaters, South and West Side blues clubs, swing-specializing dance bars, and, yes, the suburbs.

Every few years, the arts-and-entertainment axis shifts to newer, hipper places. The downtown theater district, with ornate, old theaters, is being revived. Hot clubs continue to open in neighborhoods like Fulton Market, West Town, and Goose Island, in addition to the hip hangout of Wicker Park. The Smashing Pumpkins, Liz Phair, and other early '90s scenesters have grown into rock icons, leaving the independent-music nightclub wide open for new voices. And dance-club DJs continue to build on the house music their forefathers invented in the late '70s, developing cult followings all over town.

The Reader and New City—distributed Thursday and Wednesday, respectively, in bookstores, record stores, and bars and often gone before the end of the weekend—are your best guides to the entertainment scene. These free weeklies have comprehensive listings and reviews of performances and concerts. The monthly Chicago magazine, the free Illinois Entertainer, and the Friday and Sunday editions of the Chicago Tribune and Chicago Sun-Times are good sources of information on current shows and starting times.

performing arts

CONCERTS IN CHURCHES

7 e-5
FOURTH PRESBYTERIAN CHURCH OF CHICAGO
Across the street from the John Hancock Center, the church has a full professional concert series as well as noontime concerts every Friday at 12:10, a boon for office workers. Music includes choral groups, organ, jazz, gospel, harp, and piano. *Michigan Ave. at Delaware Pl., Near North, 312/787–4570.*

6 d-2
OLD ST. PATRICK'S CHURCH
Every year Old St. Pat's hosts several performances by Music of the Baroque, a concert by the Chicago Children's Choir, an evening of Celtic song and dance on St. Patrick's Day, a Deck the Halls Christmas concert, and the World's Largest Block Party, which includes a big-band stage and a rock stage. *700 W. Adams St., West Loop, 312/648–1021.*

4 d-8
OUR LADY OF MT. CARMEL CHURCH
Sunday liturgies feature a choir under the direction of Mt. Carmel music director William Ferris, who also heads the William Ferris Chorale. Organ recitals are held throughout the year. *690 W. Belmont Ave., Lakeview, 773/525–6264.*

2 e-7
ROCKEFELLER CHAPEL
The chapel hosts sacred music from Renaissance to contemporary compositions, an annual performance of the *Messiah,* and silent films accompanied by the chapel's regal organ. The 72-bell carillon, the second-largest in the world, is played weekdays at 6 PM and Sunday at noon. Get there half an hour early to climb the bell tower with the carillonneur; a 10-week summer carillon festival features international guest artists. *5850 S. Woodlawn Ave., Hyde Park, 773/702–2100.*

5 *d-2*

ST. PAUL'S UNITED CHURCH OF CHRIST

This large room with good acoustics and a beautiful organ is home to performances of the Chicago String Ensemble, Choral Ensemble of Chicago, Chicago Choral Artists, and Music of the Baroque. *2335 N. Orchard St., Lincoln Park, 773/348–3829.*

2 *h-7*

UNITED CHURCH OF HYDE PARK

This church hosts various choir performances and such chamber groups as Music of the Baroque. *1448 E. 53rd St., Hyde Park, 773/363–1620.*

DANCE

Several talented dance companies perform regularly throughout the year. Modern and jazz dance are strong here, and national companies make frequent touring stops. The **Chicago Dance Coalition Information Hot Line** (312/987–1123) lists upcoming dance performances.

4 *b-8*

ATHENAEUM THEATRE

This restored theater is a wonderful venue for the dance community. It hosts many innovative, small dance companies as well as the Spring Festival of Dance, Dance Chicago, and other dance showcases. *2936 N. Southport Ave., Lakeview, 773/935–6860.*

4 *c-3*

DANCE CENTER OF COLUMBIA COLLEGE

Modern dance companies frequently perform at the Dance Center, which hosts local, national, and international groups. The space has good sight lines and provoking fare. *4730 N. Sheridan Rd., Uptown, 773/989–3310.*

companies

8 *e-2*

BALLET CHICAGO

The professional arm of this company is no longer active, but the Ballet Chicago school has a preprofessional youth company for ages 3½ through adult, which performs classical ballet throughout the city. *185 N. Wabash Ave., Suite 2300, Loop, 312/251–8838.*

GUS GIORDANO JAZZ DANCE CHICAGO

Based in Evanston, Gus Giordano brings its brand of jazz dance on the road internationally, nationally, and locally, usually with a performance at the Athenaeum Theatre. *847/866–6779.*

8 *d-2*

HEDWIG DANCES

In residence at the Chicago Cultural Center, the company integrates dance with visual art, text, and music to create playful, highly theatrical pieces. Hedwig also runs a dance school, which gives some free performances and workshops. *78 E. Washington St., Loop, 773/ 871–0872.*

6 *c-2*

HUBBARD STREET DANCE CHICAGO

Hubbard Street's contemporary, jazzy vitality has made the group, formed in 1977, extremely popular. The company combines classical ballet techniques, theatrical jazz, and contemporary dance in a unique artistic style and can usually be seen at the Spring Festival of Dance and Ravinia. *1147 W. Jackson Blvd., Near West, 312/850–9744.*

JOFFREY BALLET OF CHICAGO

From classical to cutting edge, the Joffrey Ballet of Chicago is Chicago's premier classical dance company and has garnered acclaim for its energetic performances. It typically has a fall engagement at the Auditorium Theatre; holiday performances of its uniquely American production of *The Nutcracker*, also at the Auditorium; a spring engagement; and a summer show at Ravinia. *312/739–0120.*

4 *c-3*

MORDINE AND COMPANY

The longest-running dance company in the Midwest, Mordine and Company presents provocative works with highly theatrical, original choreography; technical sophistication; and subtle wit. The group is in residence at the Dance Center of Columbia College. *4730 N. Sheridan Rd., Uptown, 773/989–3310.*

MUNTU DANCE THEATRE OF CHICAGO

Muntu presents dynamic interpretations of contemporary and traditional African and African-American dance. The group performs around the city and across the country and sometimes has a spot at Dance Africa and the Spring Festival of Dance. 773/602–1135.

RIVER NORTH DANCE COMPANY

Rich in Chicago's strong jazz dance traditions, the company has attracted national attention with entertaining and accessible works set to some of the best music of this century. It usually performs in fall at the Athenaeum Theatre. 312/944–2888.

2 *c-1*

TRINITY IRISH DANCERS

Founded in 1990—long before the *Riverdance* craze—Trinity Irish Dancers shares the grace and explosive movement of traditional and progressive Irish dancing. The company also works in other dance forms and presents eclectic, multicultural programs. 6655 N. Avondale Ave., Edison Park, 773/774–5961.

festivals & special events

SPRING FESTIVAL OF DANCE

This festival, which runs from March through May annually, showcases renowned international, national, and local companies. For information call the co-presenter, Chicago Music and Dance Theater. 312/629–8696.

FILM

First-run movie houses downtown show standard blockbuster fare. For recorded movie previews and show times at area theaters—or to purchase tickets in advance—call 312/444–3456. Listed below are several outlets for independent films or art house fare. Others show second-run or late-night cult classics.

4 *b-8*

BREW AND VIEW

When the Vic Theatre is not being used for concerts, it turns into Brew and View and shows movies. Expect recent releases, cult films, midnight shows, and a rowdy crowd, which comes for the cheap movies and cheap beer. 3145 N. Sheffield Ave., Lakeview, 312/618–8439.

2 *h-7*

DOC FILMS

Film fanatics head to Hyde Park for DOC Films, the oldest continually running student film society in the country. Weeknights showcase classic, foreign, and independent films; weekends bring more popular second-run Hollywood fare. *Ida Noyes Hall, University of Chicago, 1212 E. 59th St., Hyde Park, 773/702–8575.*

5 *b-2*

FACETS MULTIMEDIA

Facets presents a variety of rare and exotic films in its cinema and video theater. If a particular day's fare doesn't strike your eclectic fancy, rent an art film from the well-stocked video store. *1517 W. Fullerton Ave., Lincoln Park, 773/281–4114.*

8 *f-4*

FILM CENTER AT THE SCHOOL OF THE ART INSTITUTE

The programming changes almost daily here. But one thing's certain: the films will be provoking. The Film Center shows retrospectives of major directors, revivals of rare classics, and new releases of unusual national and international films. Filmmakers and critics sometimes give lectures to accompany the films. *280 S. Columbus Dr., Loop, 312/443–3737.*

8 *e-5*

FINE ARTS THEATRE

The four screens of the Loews Fine Arts show a good selection of independent, foreign, and avant-garde films. *418 S. Michigan Ave., Loop, 312/939–3700.*

4 *b-6*

MUSIC BOX THEATRE

Great for people who love old theaters and old movies, this richly decorated 1920s movie palace shows a mix of foreign flicks, classics (like a 3-D version of Alfred Hitchcock's *Dial M for Murder*, complete with free glasses), and outstanding recent films (such as *Run Lola Run*), emphasizing independent filmmakers. *3733 N. Southport Ave., Lakeview, 773/871–6604.*

5 *d-2*

THREE PENNY

The theaters are small with lumpy seats, but the selection includes good second-run films, a sprinkling of art house films (for a long time, the only way to see the Oscar-winning *Boys Don't Cry* was at this theater), and midnight shows. *2424 N. Lincoln Ave., Lincoln Park, 773/935–5744.*

5 f-5
VILLAGE
Watch second-run films here, as well as some art films that you didn't catch the first time around. The Village shows four midnight films each Friday and Saturday night. *1548 N. Clark St., Gold Coast, 312/642–2403.*

festivals and special events
CHICAGO INTERNATIONAL FILM FESTIVAL
For two weeks in October, the festival presents more than 100 films, including premieres of Hollywood films, international releases, documentaries, short subjects, animation, videos, and student films. Stargazers can spot celebs at opening events. *312/332–3456.*

OPERA

8 e-3
AMERICAN CONSERVATORY OF MUSIC
Students and faculty of the conservatory present opera, classical, and jazz performances year-round. *36 S. Wabash Ave., Loop, 312/263–4161.*

CHICAGO OPERA THEATRE
The company offers innovative versions of traditional favorites, contemporary American pieces, and important lesser-known works, emphasizing theatrical as well as musical aspects of the shows. All performances are sung in English. *312/704–8420.*

1 e-3
LIGHT OPERA WORKS
From May to January, Light Opera Works stages Gilbert and Sullivan operettas, as well as Viennese, French, and other light operettas and American musicals. *Cahn Auditorium, Emerson St. and Sheridan Rd., Evanston, 847/869–6300.*

8 b-2
LYRIC OPERA OF CHICAGO
One of the top opera companies in America, the Lyric Opera presents elaborate, top-notch performances. Don't worry about understanding German or Italian; English translations are projected above the stage. Tickets are usually sold out, but if you call the day of performance, you may be able to buy a returned ticket. *20 N. Wacker Dr., Loop, 312/332–2244.*

ORCHESTRAS & ENSEMBLES

APOLLO CHORUS OF CHICAGO
One of the country's oldest oratorio societies, the Apollo Chorus performs Handel's *Messiah* every December, along with other choral classics throughout the year. *630/960–2251.*

CHICAGO BAROQUE ENSEMBLE
The ensemble plays throughout the city on such period instruments as the harpsichord, viola da gamba, and baroque cello. Its Monday evening rush-hour concerts, at the Union League Club (65 W. Jackson Blvd.), appeal to office workers who want to hear Bach and Vivaldi on period instruments. *773/761–7020.*

CHICAGO CHAMBER MUSICIANS
The group performs chamber music from the 17th to 20th century at Northwestern and DePaul universities from October to April. It also presents a free noontime concert the first Monday of each month at the Chicago Cultural Center. *312/225–5226.*

8 d-2
CHICAGO CHILDREN'S CHOIR
Children aged 4 to 18, from a broad spectrum of racial, ethnic, and economic groups, perform during the Christmas season, in early June, and at other times throughout the year. *Chicago Cultural Center, 78 E. Washington St., Loop, 312/849–8300.*

CHICAGO CHORAL ARTISTS
One of Chicago's finer choral groups, Chicago Choral Artists stands out from the crowd. Although high-quality classical music is the group's foundation, it broadly defines "classical," performing choral works from different ethnic traditions. *773/549–7751.*

2 c-4
CHICAGO SINFONIETTA
The Sinfonietta presents highly polished classical, romantic, and contemporary pieces exactly as they were written by the composer. The group performs about 15 times a year at various loca-

tions and is in residence at Dominican University in River Forest. *312/857–1062.*

8 *e-4*

CHICAGO SYMPHONY ORCHESTRA

One of the world's leading orchestras is led by music director Daniel Barenboim, with a strong line-up of guest conductors and soloists. The CSO performs in the recently renovated Orchestra Hall, with all-new acoustics. In summer you can see the CSO weekends at the outdoor Ravinia Festival. *220 S. Michigan Ave., Loop, 312/294–3000.*

CHORAL ENSEMBLE OF CHICAGO

The ensemble presents classical choral music and music of the British Isles in its performances at area churches. *773/935–3800.*

8 *e-4*

CIVIC ORCHESTRA OF CHICAGO

The Chicago Symphony Orchestra's training orchestra performs a repertoire

---

FREE ARTS SPOTS

For culture vultures on the cheap, these spots offer great entertainment at a great price—free!

American Conservatory of Music (Opera)
   Students and faculty present free opera, classical, and jazz concerts.

Civic Orchestra (Orchestras & Ensembles)
   The Chicago Symphony Orchestra's training orchestra gives free concerts.

Cultural Center (Performance Venues)
   A variety of free programming is offered, including the Dame Myra Hess Memorial Concert Series every Wednesday at 12:15.

Grant Park Symphony Orchestra (Orchestras & Ensembles)
   There are free concerts in the park from Wednesday through Sunday in the summer.

Rockefeller Chapel (Concerts in Churches)
   The 72-bell carillon at this Hyde Park chapel rings weeknights at 6, Sunday at noon.

Second City (Comedy)
   Free improv sets after mainstage shows every night but Friday.

---

similar to that of the parent organization and works with the same guest conductors. Performances are free, but advance tickets are required. *220 S. Michigan Ave., Loop, 312/294–3000.*

8 *d-2*

DAME MYRA HESS MEMORIAL CONCERT SERIES

A bonus for Loop workers, the Dame Myra Hess series, mostly classical in nature, presents a free concert with outstanding young musicians every Wednesday at 12:15 at the Chicago Cultural Center. *78 E. Washington St., Loop, 312/346–3278.*

8 *f-4*

GRANT PARK SYMPHONY ORCHESTRA

A program of the Chicago Park District, the Grant Park Symphony gives free concerts from Wednesday through Sunday during the summer at the James C. Petrillo Music Shell, in Grant Park. *Jackson Blvd. at Columbus Dr., Loop, 312/742–7638.*

HIS MAJESTIE'S CLERKES

The group, which takes its name from a Renaissance term for a professional chorister, performs mostly sacred and a cappella music in churches throughout the city from October through May. *312/461–0723.*

MUSIC OF THE BAROQUE

One of the Midwest's leading music ensembles specializing in Baroque and early classical music, the group organizes 17 performances of seven different programs a year from October through May in beautiful neighborhood churches. *312/551–1414.*

ORIANA SINGERS

The outstanding a cappella sextet presents intimate performances of classical and jazz year-round. No mikes, no props, no gimmicks. *773/262–4558.*

4 *d-8*

WILLIAM FERRIS CHORALE

This distinguished ensemble gives concerts throughout the year, focusing on 20th-century choral music with internationally famous guest artists. *690 W. Belmont Ave., Lakeview, 773/325–2000.*

WINDY CITY PERFORMING ARTS

Two groups, the Windy City Gay Chorus and the Unison Lesbian & Gay Singers, perform classical and contemporary pop and show tunes. Both groups have spring and holiday engagements, as well as a Pride Concert each year. 773/404–9242.

PERFORMANCE VENUES

1 c-3

ALLSTATE ARENA

The largest indoor "shed" in the Chicago area, the arena, formerly known as the Rosemont Horizon, is visible from the Northwest Tollway just after the toll-booth. Huge rock names, from Tina Turner to Fleetwood Mac, have appeared here in recent years. 6920 Mannheim Road, Rosemont, 847/635–6601.

ALPINE VALLEY MUSIC THEATRE

Though it's about two hours from town, the outdoor Alpine Valley occasionally snags big rock festivals that don't otherwise come to Chicagoland. 2699 Hwy. D, East Troy, Wisc., 262/642–4400.

8 d-2

CHICAGO CULTURAL CENTER

The Cultural Center's Preston Bradley Hall is home to a variety of music and dance performances, some free. Many concerts are timed to appeal to down-town office workers on lunch break or after work. 78 E. Washington St., Loop, 312/346–3278.

8 e-4

CURTISS HALL

This turn-of-the-20th-century recital hall in the Fine Arts Building has a lakefront view. Chamber music groups perform here, including vocal, string, and key-board ensembles. 410 S. Michigan Ave., Loop, 312/939–3380.

8 e-4

FULLERTON AUDITORIUM

Chamber ensembles occasionally perform at this auditorium in the Art Institute of Chicago. Programming also includes lectures. Michigan Ave. and Adams St., Loop, 312/443–3600.

8 d-4

HAROLD WASHINGTON LIBRARY CENTER

The 385-seat auditorium in the main branch of the Chicago Public Library is host to many dance and music perfor-mances throughout the year, some free. 400 S. State St., Loop, 312/747–4130.

2 g-7

MANDEL HALL

If you're in Hyde Park, Mandel Hall, on the University of Chicago campus, is a great spot for classical music, jazz, a folk festival, and opera performances. 1131 E. 57th St., Hyde Park, 773/702–7300.

7 f-6

MUSEUM OF CONTEMPORARY ART

The MCA's 300-person theater hosts cutting-edge events including readings, vocal, musical, dance, and jazz perfor-mances. The museum's First Friday events (the first Friday of each month) feature music, entertainment, and cul-ture, as well as hors d'oeuvres. 220 E. Chicago Ave., Streeterville, 312/280–2660.

7 d-5

THE NEWBERRY LIBRARY

The Newberry Consort, which performs music from the 13th to the 17th century, presents four concerts a year here. There are also a number of concerts related to events or exhibits at the library. 60 W. Walton St., Gold Coast, 312/943–9090.

1 d-7

NEW WORLD MUSIC AMPHITHEATRE

Though traffic and parking can be a nightmare, this huge outdoor rock venue showcases individual performers and sprawling, multistage events such as Lollapalooza and the Vans Warped Tour. I-80 and Harlem, Tinley Park, 708/614-1616.

1 d-2

RAVINIA

In summer you can picnic as you listen to the Chicago Symphony, as well as other performances from classical to jazz to pop groups, at Ravinia's large outdoor amphitheater and covered pavilion. Lawn seats are always available even when (rarely) those in the pavilion and the smaller Martin Theatre sell out.

Lake Cook and Green Bay Rds., Highland Park, 847/266–5100.

2 *g-5*

SOLDIER FIELD

When the Bears aren't playing football, rock bands such as the Rolling Stones open tours at this stately, open stadium. *425 E. McFetridge Dr., Near South Side, 312/747–1285.*

8 *e-4*

SYMPHONY CENTER

Symphony Center contains Orchestra Hall, which is best known as home of the Chicago Symphony, but the space also hosts a variety of concerts and recitals during the year. *220 S. Michigan Ave., Loop, 312/294–3000.*

7 *d-3*

THREE ARTS CLUB

In a landmark 1912 building modeled after a Tuscan palazzo, the Three Arts Club hosts a jazz series with five concerts a year as well as other events, including the NonSalon Series, which showcases women artists who work in different media. *1300 N. Dearborn Pkwy., Gold Coast, 312/944–6250.*

6 *a-1*

UNITED CENTER

A centrally located spot for gigantic shows—Bruce Springsteen and Ricky Martin are among the recent headliners—it has excellent sight lines no matter how far you sit from the stage. *1901 W. Madison St., Near West Side, 312/455–4500.*

TELEVISION SHOWS

8 *f-8*

THE JENNY JONES SHOW

The talk show tapes at the NBC Tower three days a week, usually Tuesday, Thursday, and Friday with tapings at 11 AM and 2:30 PM, although the schedule can vary. Call a week or two in advance to get free tickets. *454 N. Columbus Dr., Streeterville, 312/836–9485.*

8 *f-8*

JERRY SPRINGER SHOW

Call for tickets at least one month in advance. The show usually tapes at the NBC Tower Monday at 11 AM and 2 PM,

Tuesday at 6 PM, and Wednesday at 11 AM and 2 PM, but the schedule varies. You must be 18 or older. When you call, don't forget to mention the affair you had with your wife's boyfriend's sister without your wife knowing about it. They love that. *454 N. Columbus Dr., Streeterville, 312/321–5365.*

6 *c-1*

THE OPRAH WINFREY SHOW

Call no more than 30 days prior to the taping you want to attend. Tapings are usually held three days a week, but the studio is closed in summer. There are no tickets, but a seat reservation will be made in your name. You can make reservations for up to four seats, and you must provide the names of all guests in your party. You must be at least 16 years old and have valid ID; 16- and 17-year-olds must be accompanied by a parent and show a birth certificate. *1058 W. Washington Blvd., West Town, 312/591–9595 or 312/591–9222.*

THEATER

Touring productions of Broadway hits come through Chicago, but the real action is in the small off-Loop companies. The theater district in the Loop is currently undergoing a revival, and many grand old theaters have been redeveloped, including the Shubert and the Oriental; the Goodman has taken over the renovated Harris and Selwyn theaters. The *Reader* carries complete theater listings and reviews of the more avant-garde shows.

4 *d-7*

ABOUT FACE THEATRE

Once the home of the Famous Door Theatre, known for *Hellcab*, this 97-seat venue began housing About Face in 1998. About Face's material, such as 1996's *Dream Boy* and 1997's *The Boys in the Band Revival*, tends to deal with gay and lesbian issues. The theater is in the Jane Addams Hull House. *3212 N. Broadway, Lakeview, 773/549–7943.*

5 *c-2*

APOLLO THEATER

Light, upbeat musicals and comedies such as *Buddy*, the Buddy Holly story, find their home here. On Friday and Saturday nights, Apollo After Dark turns the space into a comedy shop with stand-up comedians and a house band. *2540 N. Lincoln Ave., Lincoln Park, 773/935–6100.*

4 *b-8*

THE ATHENAEUM THEATRE

Built in 1911, the restored theater has found its niche as a home to a variety of provoking music, opera, dance, and drama performances, some international in origin. *2936 N. Southport Ave., Lakeview, 773/935–6860.*

8 *e-5*

AUDITORIUM THEATRE

This architectural masterpiece, with excellent acoustics and sight lines, usually hosts touring Broadway hits or the latest Andrew Lloyd Webber musical. *50 E. Congress Pkwy., Loop, 312/922–2110.*

4 *c-8*

BAILIWICK ARTS CENTER

The Bailiwick presents new and classical material, including a summer Pride Performance series showcasing plays by gays and lesbians. *1229 W. Belmont Ave., Lakeview, 773/883–1090.*

4 *b-4*

BLACK ENSEMBLE THEATER

Expect musicals based on African-American composers and singers, such as *Wang Dang Doodle*, the story of local blues singer Koko Taylor, and *Chicago Golden Soul*, a musical chronicling Chicago's recording industry in the '60s and '70s. *Uptown Center Hull House, 4520 N. Beacon St., Uptown, 773/769–4451.*

6 *d-6*

BLUE RIDER THEATER

This multidisciplinary performance center presents only original work, including music, dance, theater, poetry, puppetry, video, and performance art. *1822 S. Halsted St., Pilsen, 773/486–7767.*

4 *d-8*

BRIAR STREET THEATRE

The modest space, which usually hosts local productions of hit Broadway plays, has been the home of the dynamic, edgy must-see Blue Man Group for several years. The group's specialty, in addition to deadpan comedy, fluorescent painting, Cap'n Crunch cereal-eating, and mouth-catching marshmallows, is elaborate, New Age–style drumming. *3133 N. Halsted St., Lakeview, 773/348–4000.*

6 *f-1*

CADILLAC PALACE THEATRE

Opened in 1926 as a vaudeville theater, the elaborate, elegant, chandelier-decorated Cadillac Palace recently underwent a $20 million renovation. It's part of the newly revived Randolph Street theater district, which includes the the Ford Center of Performing Arts, Oriental Theatre. *151 W. Randolph St., Loop, 312/384–1510.*

2 *f-1*

CENTER THEATER ENSEMBLE

Plays run the gamut from classic material to cutting-edge modern drama and comedies. *1346 W. Devon Ave., Rogers Park, 773/508–5422.*

2 *g-4*

CHICAGO SHAKESPEARE THEATRE

Having reopened in a large, round Navy Pier building with superb acoustics and broad sight lines in late 1999, the Chicago Shakespeare Repertory continues its decade-long run in the city. Its high-quality performances, from *King Lear* to Peter Whelan's play about Shakespeare's daughter, *The Herbal Bed*, keep the Bard's flame alive in the area. The theater has a sense of humor, too, putting on spoofs like *Hamlet: The Musical*, featuring former female impersonator Alexandra Billings in the campy Gertrude role. *Navy Pier, 600 E. Grand Ave., Near North, 312/595–5600 or 312/595–5656.*

8 *d-2*

CHICAGO THEATRE

A restored former movie palace and vaudeville house, the Chicago Theatre presents family musicals, such as *Victor/Victoria* and *Evita*, as well as concerts and special events. It's somewhat incongruous to see jeans–and–T-shirt rock concerts like Melissa Etheridge and the Indigo Girls at this beautifully designed, old-fashioned theater. *175 N. State St., Loop, 312/443–1130.*

2 *h-7*

COURT THEATRE

If you find yourself yearning for Chekhov, Ibsen, or Shaw, head to the University of Chicago campus. The Court revives classic plays, often presenting two plays in rotating repertory. *5535 S. Ellis Ave., Hyde Park, 773/753–4472.*

1 c-5

DRURY LANE OAK BROOK

Suburbanites come for the dinner-theater format here. Dinner is served two hours before the shows, which are often musicals such as *Me and My Girl* or *Crazy for You*. *Roosevelt Rd. and Rte. 83, Oak Brook Terrace, 630/530–8300.*

2 h-8

ETA CREATIVE ARTS FOUNDATION

In its 28th year, this performing arts center has a strong presence as an African-American theater. ETA presents six plays each year, has daytime shows for school groups, and gives classes in drama, music, and dance. *7558 S. South Chicago Ave., South Shore, 773/752–3955.*

CHICAGO TUNES

You can't escape hearing "Sweet Home, Chicago" or "My Kind of Town" in the Windy City, but we recommend some alternatives:

"Bad, Bad Leroy Brown," pop, Jim Croce.

"Blues for Mayor Daley," blues, Junior Wells.

"Chicago," pop, Frank Sinatra.

"Chicago Breakdown," blues, Big Maceo.

"Go Cubs Go," folk, Steve Goodman.

"In the Ghetto," rock, Elvis Presley.

"Is Chicago, Is Not Chicago," rock, Soul Coughing.

"Jesus Just Left Chicago," rock, ZZ Top.

"Lincoln Park Pirates," folk, Steve Goodman.

"The Night Chicago Died," pop, Paper Lace.

"Take Me Back to Chicago," pop, Chicago.

8 d-2

FORD CENTER OF PERFORMING ARTS, ORIENTAL THEATRE

The grand 1920s auditorium, with recently restored lavish finishes, makes modern theater magic with musicals such as *Ragtime*. *24 W. Randolph St., the Loop, 312/902–1400.*

2 g-4

GOODMAN THEATRE

The plays here are polished performances of classic and contemporary works. The Goodman, one of the oldest and best theater companies in Chicago, took over two historic theater buildings in the heart of the Loop in the fall of 2000. *170 N. Dearborn St., Loop, 312/443–3800.*

4 d-8

IVANHOE THEATER

Don't be discouraged by the building's nondescript exterior. The three theaters inside present an eclectic mix of musicals and other Broadway shows; some long-running standards have been *Hell Cab* and *Late Night Catechism*. *750 W. Wellington Ave., Lakeview, 773/975–7171.*

2 f-1

LIFELINE THEATRE

All plays here have been adapted from books. The company usually puts on a children's play and an adult play, such as *A Wrinkle in Time* and *Dr. Jekyll and Mr. Hyde*. *6912 N. Glenwood Ave., Rogers Park, 773/761–4477.*

4 b-6

MERCURY THEATER

The 300-seat Mercury Theater hosts off-Broadway plays, like *His Way*, a tribute to Frank Sinatra. *3745 N. Southport Ave., Lakeview, 773/325–1700.*

5 f-5

A RED ORCHID THEATRE

At the end of a long atrium mall, this intimate theater takes chances with dark, edgy plays such as *Born Guilty*, about the offspring of Nazis. Though it isn't on quite the same level as, say, Steppenwolf or Lookingglass, think of it as one of the best farm teams in the minor leagues. *1531 N. Wells St., Old Town, 312/943–8722.*

5 *d-4*

ROYAL GEORGE THEATRE CENTER

Performance spaces include a large, gracious mainstage theater with good sight lines; a black-box gallery theater; a "great room" theater; and a cabaret theater. *Forever Plaid*, a musical comedy, and *Flanagan's Wake*, an Irish wake with audience participation, are standards here. *1641 N. Halsted St., Old Town, 312/ 988–9000.*

5 *d-1*

SHATTERED GLOBE THEATRE

Storefront theaters like the Shattered Globe, which seats 50, are what the Chicago theater scene is all about. The company stresses ensemble acting and original work. *2856 N. Halsted St., Lincoln Park, 773/404–1237.*

8 *d-3*

SHUBERT THEATRE

Part of the downtown theater district, the Shubert, built in 1906, has been home to Broadway plays like *Rent* and *Chicago*, as well as some dance performances. *22 W. Monroe St., Loop, 312/ 977–1700.*

4 *c-7*

STAGE LEFT THEATRE

Left of center, the 50-seat storefront space offers some of the most thought-provoking theater in Chicago, focusing on social and political issues, such as tales of survival in Sarajevo. *3408 N. Sheffield Ave., Wrigleyville, 773/883–8830.*

4 *c-8*

THEATRE BUILDING

The three stages of this rehabbed warehouse host small and mid-sized groups, like Famous Door Theater and Lookingglass, with adventuresome fare. *1225 W. Belmont Ave., Lakeview, 773/327–5252.*

8 *e-6*

THEATRE SCHOOL, DEPAUL UNIVERSITY

The Theatre School produces a series of plays for adult audiences as well as one for families and young audiences. Performances are held in the grand and ornate Merle Reskin Theatre. *60 E. Balbo Dr., South Loop, 312/922–1999.*

companies

3 *h-5*

AMERICAN THEATER COMPANY

On the Waterfront was a typical worker-centric production from this company, which has gradually expanded beyond American plays. Not avant-garde in any tangible way, the company loves to showcase the sadness and heart of tough Midwesterners. *1909 W. Byron St., North Center, 773/929–1031.*

2 *f-3*

LOOKINGGLASS THEATRE COMPANY

The acrobatic style of performance utilizes theater, dance, music, and circus arts to present physically—and artistically—daring works. *Friends* star David Schwimmer is a Lookingglass alum. The company relocates with each production. *Offices at 2936 N. Southport Ave., Lakeview, 773/477–9257.*

4 *a-2*

NEO-FUTURISTS

The company presents several productions, including its late-night cult hit *Too Much Light Makes the Baby Go Blind*, a series of 30 ever-changing two-minute plays whose order is chosen by the audience. Randomness rules here. Admission costs $4 plus the roll of a die. *5153 N. Ashland Ave., Andersonville, 773/275–5255.*

1 *e-3*

ORGANIC TOUCHSTONE COMPANY

The company specializes in Midwest premieres of plays that have recently been successful in New York, London, and Los Angeles. *1420 Maple Ave., Evanston, 847/475–2800.*

4 *c-3*

PEGASUS PLAYERS

Each season brings at least one Stephen Sondheim musical, as well as other interesting and difficult works. Pegasus performs in the O'Rourke Performing Arts Center at Truman College. *1145 W. Wilson Ave., Uptown, 773/878–9761.*

PERFORMING ARTS CHICAGO

You can count on daring, cutting-edge pieces from this leading presenter of new directions in theater, music, and dance in various locations throughout the city. The series includes some of the world's most innovative performing artists. *312/663–1628.*

5 *d-4*

**STEPPENWOLF
THEATRE COMPANY**

Steppenwolf is often synonymous with Chicago theater, with many successful productions and a dark, Method-acting style. Alumni include John Malkovich, Gary Sinise, and Laurie Metcalf. *1650 N. Halsted St., Old Town, 312/335–1650.*

4 *d-3*

VICTORY GARDENS

The company, known for its workshops and Chicago premieres, stages works solely by local playwrights. Other stages in the building, though, are rented out to different companies. *2257 N. Lincoln Ave., Lincoln Park, 773/871–3000.*

festivals & special events

5 *f-2*

THEATRE ON THE LAKE

A large brick pavilion at the edge of the park presents plays during the summer in a screened-in setting. Local theater companies, such as Second City, Steppenwolf, and the Neo-Futurists, present revivals of their past productions here for a week at a time. *Fullerton Pkwy. at Lake Shore Dr., Lincoln Park, 312/742–7994.*

TICKETS

Some licensed services act as ticket brokers, buying and selling tickets to hard-to-get events and marking up the prices accordingly.

7 *h-7*

GOLD COAST TICKETS

Here you can get tickets to concerts, sports, and theater. *505 N. Lake Shore Dr., Streeterville, 800/889–9100. Closed Sun.*

8 *d-2*

HOT TIX

To save money on a theater ticket, stand in line at a Hot Tix booth. In addition to the three locations listed below, Hot Tix sells tickets at Chicago-area Tower Records stores. Unsold tickets are available, usually at half price (plus a service charge), on the day of performance only; you won't know what's available until that day. You must buy the tickets in per-

son, not over the phone; call for booth hours. Hot Tix also sells advance full-price tickets. *108 N. State St., Loop.*

7 *e-5*

Chicago Water Works Visitors Center, Michigan Ave. at Pearson St., Near North.

1 *e-3*

616 Sherman Ave., Evanston, 312/977–1755.

TICKETMASTER

Dominick's grocery stores and Tower Records stores act as Ticketmaster agents, accepting cash-only for ticket purchases. To charge tickets by phone, call 312/559–1212 for concerts and general events, and 312/902–1500 for the arts line.

8 *e-2*

**UNION TYSEN
ENTERTAINMENT
TICKET SERVICE**

Tickets for sports, theater, and concerts. *25 E. Washington St., Suite 1211, Loop, 312/726–3486. Closed Sun.*

nightlife

Shows usually begin between 9 PM and 10 PM; cover charges generally range from $3 to $15, depending on the day of the week. Most bars stay open until 2 AM Friday night and 3 AM Saturday, except for larger dance bars, which are often open until 4 AM Friday night and 5 AM Saturday.

BARS & LOUNGES

7 *c-6*

BAR LOUIE

Got the munchies? This small Italian taverna has eclectic music played by the bartenders and serves pub grub with an Italian twist—sandwiches, salads, pizza, and pastas—late into the night. *226 W. Chicago Ave., Near North, 312/337–3313.*

5 *a-8*

**BETTY'S BLUE
STAR LOUNGE**

A pool table made of blue felt anchors the large main room of this reasonably new club, which frequently has DJs and live bands in its dance area. *1600 W. Grand Ave., West Town, 312/243–1699.*

5 *b-6*

BIG WIG

Get wigged out at this hip bar, which has a beauty-salon-gone-bad theme. Have a drink while you sit in a barber's chair or at an old-fashioned dome hair dryer, or take a peek at the wigs behind the bar. DJs spin here weekends; though there's a cover charge, there's no dancing. *1551 W. Division St., West Town, 773/235–9100.*

2 *e-4*

BLACK BEETLE BAR & GRILLE

Despite the artiness (framed pictures on the walls and flowers on the tables), this is your basic bar, with T-shirted guys playing pool and the odd biker on the weekend. There's brunch on weekends. *2532 W. Chicago Ave., Ukee Village, 773/384–0701.*

5 *d-2*

THE BURWOOD

Though it's a bit of a meat market, especially on weekends, the Burwood is usually a nice, low-key neighborhood bar with the usual trimmings: weird oars on the ceiling, cheap Buds, pool tables, a popcorn machine, and a respectable rock jukebox. *724 W. Wrightwood Ave., Lincoln Park, 773/525–2593.*

5 *a-6*

CLUB FOOT

A club with a neighborhood tavern atmosphere, Club Foot offers the best of both worlds—a laid-back bar and a back room with DJs playing an eclectic mix of music. The best part: there's no cover charge. You'll also find pinball, pool, and a collection of rock memorabilia on the bar walls. *1824 W. Augusta Blvd., East Ukrainian Village, 773/489–0379.*

5 *c-1*

DELILAH'S

Behind the dark exterior is a bar with a bit of a punk attitude as well as a neighborhood feel. Musicians from local bands and indie labels, including Urge Overkill, Ministry, and Liz Phair, take turns being the DJ here. Delilah's assortment of offerings includes Punk Rock Mondays, Insurgent Country Wednesdays, pinball, pool, and some 120 whiskeys, 80 beers, and 400 bottles of booze on the wall. Its jukebox has the most thorough public hardcore collection in the city, if not everywhere. *2771 N. Lincoln Ave., Lincoln Park, 773/472–2771.*

4 *b-6*

GUTHRIE'S TAVERN

Just a ½ mi west of Wrigley Field, this somewhat quiet tavern attracts a more bookish clientele than that of the rocking ballpark bars: it has a collection of board games, from Clue to Stratego, for customer use. Another bonus: pretzels and mustard. *1300 W. Addison St., Wrigleyville, 773/477–2900.*

5 *a-5*

HOLIDAY CLUB

This is a swinger's mecca, Daddy-O. The '50s getup includes a well-stocked CD jukebox that ranges from Dean Martin and Frank Sinatra to early punk. On Sunday nights, the place turns into a bamboo lounge with Polynesian surf music. *1471 N. Milwaukee Ave., Wicker Park, 773/486–0686.*

5 *c-7*

IGGY'S

Iggy's is the dean of late-night dining, serving a full menu until 3:15 AM Friday, 4:15 AM Saturday, and 1:15 AM Sunday. The restaurant is downstairs, and upstairs is a lounge with outdoor deck and pool table. In summer, DJs spin tunes during the Sunday backyard barbecues. *700 N. Milwaukee Ave., East Ukrainian Village, 312/829–4449.*

4 *a-7*

IVAN'S

The vibe is retro, down to the vintage '50s wallpaper that was found hiding behind old paneling. The drinks fit the theme with sidecars, stingers, fog cutters, old-fashioneds, and, of course, martinis. Come here for cocktails and conversation, with a DJ every evening, although there is no dancing. *3358 N. Ashland Ave., Lakeview, 773/525–2140.*

2 *f-4*

LOTTIE'S

During Prohibition, Lottie used to run a speakeasy here with an illegal gambling operation. Now it's a more mainstream neighborhood hangout with sports on a big screen, two pool tables, 24 beers on tap, and an occasional bachelor party in the basement. *1925 W. Cortland St., Bucktown, 773/489–0738.*

4 b-5
JOY-BLUE
The three rooms here have different personalities, from microbrews to martinis and margaritas. A traditional tavern with 100 beers is in the front, a mahogany martini bar is in the middle, and a lounge with sofas and a pool table lies at the back. From Thursday through Saturday a DJ spins an eclectic mix from old school to new wave. *3998 N. Southport Ave., Lakeview, 773/477–3330.*

5 c-1
LUCKY STRIKE
Looking to bowl? Lucky Strike has eight vintage bowling lanes and six regulation-size pool tables in an Art Deco atmosphere. The wait for a lane can be long on the weekends, when it's full of twenty- and thirtysomethings who like to play games while swilling beer. *2747 N. Lincoln Ave., Lincoln Park, 773/549–2695.*

2 f-4
THE MAP ROOM
This friendly travelers' tavern, decorated with maps and travel books, has a worldly knowledge of beer, with more than 100 bottles and 26 varieties on tap.

LATE-NIGHT MUNCHIES

While most bars serve stale pretzels at midnight, these late-night dining and drinking spots prepare delectable comestibles until the wee hours of the morning.

Adagio (Jazz)
  The kitchen at this jazz club serves contemporary Italian cuisine until 11 PM.

Bar Louie (Bars & Lounges)
  Sandwiches, salads, pastas, and all things Italian until 1 AM weekdays, 3 AM weekends.

Iggy's (Bars & Lounges)
  The hip dean of late-night dining serves a full menu—not just pub grub—until 3:30 AM Friday, 4:30 AM Saturday.

Schubas Tavern (Pop/Rock)
  Harmony Grill, attached to Schubas, serves its late-night menu until 2 AM weekends.

Yvette (Piano Bar)
  The kitchen, with French-American fare, closes at 1 AM.

It hosts a monthly beer school, as well as international night on Tuesday, which includes a free buffet with food from different countries. *2100 W. Armitage Ave., Bucktown, 773/252–7636.*

5 a-3
MARIE'S RIPTIDE LOUNGE
It's a Bucktown late-night tradition; bar hoppers come here after other watering holes have closed. In the wee hours, people play trapshoot and dine on pickled eggs, sure to quell any alcohol-induced hunger pains. Ask Marie to play the videotape of when the Riptide was featured on *Late Night with Conan O'Brien*. *1745 W. Armitage Ave., Bucktown, 773/278–7317.*

7 b-6
MARTINI RANCH
This spot has been serving martinis since 1992, the beginning of the martini craze. Some 30 to 40 martinis are available, including a chocolate one; scotches, bourbons, beer, and cigars are also popular. There are occasional DJs, a pool table, and a small enclosed beer garden in the back. *311 W. Chicago Ave., Near North, 312/335–9500.*

5 c-5
NORTH BEACH CHICAGO
In the winter this is the closest you'll get to playing beach volleyball. Active types come here for volleyball leagues, court rental, and private parties. The reason: the three sand-filled indoor volleyball courts, a full-size basketball court, a nine-hole miniature golf course, four bowling lanes, and two large-screen TVs. *1551 N. Sheffield Ave., Near North, 312/266–7842.*

2 f-4
NORTHSIDE
Before Wicker Park became yuppie central, the Northside anchored the scene. Arty (and sometimes slightly yuppie) types come to drink, eat, shoot pool, and enjoy the enclosed beer garden. *1635 N. Damen Ave., Bucktown, 773/384–3555.*

4 c-8
SHEFFIELD'S
In the summer, come to this neighborhood spot after a Cubs game or just to enjoy the good weather in the beer garden. In winter, sit by the gas fireplace, play billiards, and pick from a selection of more than 50 beers, including

regional microbrews and a "bad beer of the month." *3258 N. Sheffield Ave., Lakeview, 773/281–4989.*

2 *f-4*
SUBTERRANEAN
Though its upstairs cabaret room is huge—two whole stories—this large bar in the heart of Wicker Park is mostly notable for its relaxed atmosphere. *2011 W. North Ave., Wicker Park, 773/278–6600.*

2 *f-3*
TEN CAT TAVERN
This ultra-relaxing bar rarely draws real, live cats, but its giant wall painting apparently hides 10 different felines. Otherwise, it's basically a neighborhood pool-and-beer joint. *3931 N. Ashland, Lakeview, 773/935–5377.*

2 *f-4*
TEN56
A former speakeasy, it's now a swanky cocktail spot for lounging. What a refreshing change—a martini bar without excessive attitude or a cover charge. *1056 N. Damen Ave., Ukrainian Village, 773/227–4906.*

7 *d-8*
WHAM BONGO BAR
With Jack Kerouac readings in the men's bathroom, this downtown bar moves to the Beat poet beat. There's live music Saturday as well as a Wednesday guitar jam and Thursday percussion jam; bring an instrument and play along, or grab one of the bongos or congas the staff passes out. *111 W. Hubbard St., River North, 312/396–9426. Closed Sun.*

BLUES

The searing, soulful strains of urban, electric blues are synonymous with sweet home Chicago. While baseball-capped college kids crowd the North Side bars, you can still find blues at the South Side clubs where it all began. The free **Chicago Blues Festival** (312/744–3370)—with a combination of old-old-school acoustic country-blues artists, more traditionally Chicago electric-blues guitarists, and occasional curveballs—is held in Grant Park each June.

1 *c-2*
BEALE STREET BLUES CAFE
Though it's a decent-size drive from the city's usual blues clubs, Palatine's growing Beale Street lures big names almost every night and is a key stop on the suburban blues circuit. Plus, Sam Cockrell and the Groove is the house band for a free Monday-night blues jam. *1550 N. Rand Rd., Palatine, 847/776–9850.*

7 *d-7*
BLUE CHICAGO
There are two Blue Chicago bars within two blocks of each other. Both have good sound systems and attract a diverse (sometimes touristy) crowd. The club at 536 North Clark is more intimate and has better sound, but if it's too crowded head to the larger club at 736 North Clark. One cover gets you into both bars. In addition to music, the bars are known for John Doyle's colorful paintings of 1920s-era blues singers; they're available in poster and T-shirt form at the 536 N. Clark venue. *536 N. Clark St., River North, 312/661–0100. Closed Mon.*

7 *d-6*
736 N. Clark St., River North, 312/642–6261. Closed Sun.

5 *d-2*
B.L.U.E.S.
Get close to the music at this narrow, intimate spot, which draws the best of Chicago's musicians, including Son Seals, Otis Rush, Big Time Sarah, and Magic Slim. (Seals, born in Osceola, Arkansas, once said he likes this club because "it reminds me of the jukejoints back home.") *2519 N. Halsted St., Lincoln Park, 773/528–1012.*

4 *c-8*
B.L.U.E.S. ETCETERA
A spacious spot with a dance floor, the bar offers a welcome change from other overcrowded clubs. Although it has less atmosphere, it attracts the same big-name talent as other blues bars. Be sure to stake out a spot early on the dance floor; when it fills up, it's almost impossible to see the stage from the comfortable barstools in back. *1124 W. Belmont Ave., Lakeview, 773/525–8989. Closed Sun.–Tues.*

8 *e-6*

BUDDY GUY'S LEGENDS

This spacious club is known for its superb sound and big-name artists, especially blues legend Buddy Guy himself, who sells out an entire month of shows every January. The kitchen serves Louisiana-style barbecue, which is surprisingly good for a club specializing in loud music. Even when he isn't performing, Guy sometimes sits in with the band. *754 S. Wabash Ave., South Loop, 312/427–0333.*

2 *g-7*

CHECKERBOARD LOUNGE

This joint is jumpin'! Top Chicago blues performers make music at this South Side survivor blues bar that opened in 1972. Although the neighborhood is rough, the live music is usually worth the trip. Be sure to check out the photos on the wall, including the Rolling Stones' performance here in the early '70s. *423 E. 43rd St., Kenwood, 773/624–3240.*

1 *b-6*

FRANKIE'S BLUE ROOM

For a while, during the new big-band craze of the late '90s, this Naperville nightclub was swing-dancing central. But while Liquid and a few other downtown clubs still fly the swing flag, Frankie's has returned to its live blues focus. *16 W. Chicago Ave., Naperville, 630/416–4898.*

7 *d-8*

HOUSE OF BLUES

You won't get much homegrown Chicago blues, but you will see top national performers from roots music to rock; all shows are standing room only. The elaborate decor includes an ornate stage, folk art from local artists on the walls, and secluded private balconies for the select set. Drop by during off-hours for lunch: the food is good and lesser-known locals provide the background music. The Sunday Gospel Brunch is a must-do. *329 N. Dearborn St., River North, 312/527–2583.*

5 *d-2*

KINGSTON MINES

The North Side's largest and oldest blues spot, it packs in rowdy blues fans for big-name continuous live entertainment on two stages weekends. It's a popular late-night blues stop where top-

flight musicians often jam after their own gigs. *2548 N. Halsted St., Lincoln Park, 773/477–4646.*

6 *g-4*

KOKO TAYLOR'S CELEBRITY

Just as singer Koko Taylor answered macho bluesman Bo Diddley's hit "I'm a Man" with her own "I'm a Woman," she answers macho bluesman Buddy Guy's nightclub with one of her own. Taylor, who's famous for her 1965 smash "Wang Dang Doodle" and a cameo in David Lynch's movie *Wild at Heart*, draws mid-range blues names such as soul man Otis Clay. The club sponsors a gospel buffet every Sunday. *1233 S. Wabash Ave., Near South, 312/360–1558.*

2 *g-8*

LEE'S UNLEADED BLUES

This small, triangle-shape club, with no cover charge, is for those who like their blues unadulterated and unleaded. Folding chairs fill the space, which has red-carpeted walls and tinsel dangling from the ceiling. It's one of those down-home blues clubs where the bassist, while performing on stage, actually has to step aside to let male customers use the rest room. *7401 S. South Chicago Ave., South Side, 773/493–3477.*

2 *e-4*

ROSA'S

Tony, the owner, came here from Italy out of love for the blues; his mother, Mama Rosa, is a fixture behind the bar in Chicago's friendliest blues club. Rosa's has nurtured several blues acts including guitarist Melvin Taylor, who plays Tuesday, and harmonica player Sugar Blue, who performs on Wednesday. The club also tends to lure more unusual blues and soul artists, such as underrecognized singer James Carr. *3420 W. Armitage Ave., Logan Square, 773/342–0452. Closed Sun.–Mon.*

5 *a-6*

SMOKE DADDY

The barbecue is as smoking as the music at this small bar, which holds about 80 people and has barbecue, blues, and jazz seven nights a week with no cover charge. There's no real stage here, so as you enter and exit you must walk past the band, which is usually crammed in a small space by the door. *1804 W. Division St., Wicker Park, 773/772–6656.*

BREWPUBS & MICROBREWERIES

5 *c-4*

GOOSE ISLAND BREWING CO.

Since 1988 Goose Island has brewed beers fresh daily. The flagship beers, such as Honker's Ale, are always available; specialty beers are offered seasonally. Come for good food and a free CD jukebox. A bonus: lots of free parking. *1800 N. Clybourn Ave., Near North, 312/915–0071.*

4 *c-7*

3535 N. Clark St., Wrigleyville, 773/832–9040.

5 *a-2*

HOPCATS BREWING CO.

A group of homebrewers opened Hopcats, which has a homebrew supply store in the basement. It offers six of its own beers on tap, as well as guest beers; there's always at least one Belgian beer. If you ask, they'll give you tours of the brewery in back of the kitchen. The spicy food goes beyond burgers and brats with items like panseared beernut-encrusted catfish. *2354 N. Clybourn Ave., Near North, 773/868–4461. Closed Mon.*

7 *d-7*

ROCK BOTTOM BREWERY

During the week, this spot is popular with an after-work crowd; on weekends it attracts suburbanites off the Ontario Street tourist corridor. The rooftop beer garden offers a brew with a view. All beers are made on the premises. *1 W. Grand Ave., River North, 312/755–9339.*

CABARET

4 *c-7*

FLY ME TO THE MOON

This spot converts from candlelit restaurant to cabaret and attracts Lincoln Parkers with its Italian food, cigars, martinis, and jazz. A jazz combo performs from Thursday through Sunday night. You're in no danger of missing the entertainment; no matter where you sit in the dining area or lounge, you can see the performers. *3400 N. Clark St., Lakeview, 773/528–4033.*

CIGAR BARS

1 *d-6*

KENDALL'S

Though the cigar-smoking renaissance has died down since Frank Sinatra died, the neo-swing movement ended and the hype from *Swingers* dissipated, Kendall's remains a fixture for diehards. Cigars range from $6 to $12, and the store also sells scotch and bourbon. *2263 N. Lincoln Ave., Lincoln Park, 773/348–7200.*

COFFEEHOUSES

2 *f-1*

NO EXIT

Find folk, jazz, poetry readings, theater, and comedy sketches in this comfortable coffeehouse setting reminiscent of the 1960s—not too surprising, since it opened in 1958. Backgammon and chess help you kick back. *6970 N. Glenwood Ave., Rogers Park, 773/743–3355. Closed Tues.*

2 *g-6*

JAZZ'N'JAVA

Though it lives up to its name by playing host to live jazz acts on Friday and Saturday night, this South Side coffeehouse is best known for its trash-talking chess matches. Players of all ages, who cheer for each other and mutter to themselves, retreat here when it's too cold to play at the outdoor Harper Court and North Avenue Beach. *3428 S. Martin Luther King Dr., Bronzeville, 312/791–1300.*

COMEDY

Improvisation is where the action is; stand-up comedy hasn't fared as well here. Most comedy clubs have a cover charge ($5–$16); many have a two-drink minimum on top of that.

ANNOYANCE THEATRE

The six-year-old improv-comedy theater closed at its original location, 3747 N. Clark St., in June 2000. So crude, offbeat, racy, long-running comedies such as *Coed Prison Sluts* and *God in a Box* have taken their final bows—for now. However, managing director Mark Sutton announced plans to reopen, in an unspecified location at an unspecified time. For more information, visit www.annoyanceproductions.com.

1 d-6

BARREL OF LAUGHS

Most people come here for the dinner package, which includes a performance by three comedians, a meal at the adjacent Senese's restaurant, and a reserved seat at the show. In the southwest suburbs, the club is a 30-minute drive from downtown. *10345 S. Central Ave., Oak Lawn, 708/499–2969. Closed Mon.–Tues.*

4 d-8

COMEDYSPORTZ

Comedy becomes a sporting event with "competitive improv," in which two teams vie for the favor of the audience. *3209 N. Halsted St., Lakeview, 773/296–1100. Closed Sun.–Thurs.*

4 c-7

IMPROV OLYMPIC

Monday nights, alumni night at this comedy club and school offer great improv, featuring some alums now at Second City. On other nights, team members present long-form comedic improvisations, which last about 40 minutes and draw on audience suggestions. The audience can participate in a free improv jam Saturday at midnight. *3541 N. Clark St., Wrigleyville, 773/880–0199. Closed Tues.*

5 f-4

SECOND CITY

Some of the hottest comedians in the country (John Belushi, Chevy Chase, Chris Farley) have come from Second City, an institution since 1959. Skit comedy is presented on two stages, the main stage and the second-floor ETC; call for reservations in advance. There's a free improvisation bonus every night but Friday. *1616 N. Wells St., Old Town, 312/337–3992.*

5 f-5

ZANIES

Chicago's best stand-up comedy spot, it books outstanding national talent; Jay Leno, Jerry Seinfeld, and Jackie Mason have all performed here. It has several suburban outposts. *1548 N. Wells St., Old Town, 312/337–4027. Closed Mon.*

1 c-1

230 Hawthorn Ct., Vernon Hills, 847/549–6030.

COUNTRY & WESTERN

5 a-5

BIG HORSE LOUNGE

Gina Black, singer for the twisted bluegrass band the Blacks, calls the Big Horse "a place where you can spill your drink on the ground and nobody's really going to notice." (She means that as a compliment.) The club plays host to mostly lesser-known local "twangcore" bands, such as Pistol Whipped and Yer Mother's Lovers. *1558 N. Milwaukee Ave., West Town, 773/384–0043.*

1 b-4

CADILLAC RANCH

In the western suburbs, this nightclub has line and couples' dancing, with live bands on the weekends. Dance lessons are offered Monday, Tuesday, Wednesday, and Friday. The pace changes on Thursday with retro Top 40 dance music. *1175 W. Lake St., Bartlett, 630/830–7200.*

4 b-3

CAROL'S PUB

There are many Southern folks in the crowd and on the staff at this neighborhood spot—a sign of authenticity. The house band plays country and country-rock tunes you can dance to. *4659 N. Clark St., Uptown, 773/334–2402.*

5 b-4

THE HIDEOUT

Thanks to the local Bloodshot Records and alternative-country transplants like the Mekons' Sally Timms and Jon Langford, Chicago has become an international capital for "y'allternative" music. The Hideout is one of several clubs, including Big Horse and the more established Schubas Tavern, to have picked up on the trend. *1354 W. Wabansia, between Bucktown and Lincoln Park, 773/227–4433.*

4 c-2

LAKEVIEW LOUNGE

This spot brings you back to when Uptown used to be the country. The neighborhood tavern has a small dance floor, plays country-and-western and oldies, and features a house band on weekends. *5110 N. Broadway, Uptown, 773/769–0994.*

DANCE CLUBS

Most dance clubs don't get crowded until late at night, and they remain open into the early morning hours. Cover charges range from $5 to $15. Some clubs have a dress code (which is usually enforced only with men) that bans gym shoes and baseball hats.

5 *d-5*

CIRCUS

Though it isn't technically a circus, this ringmaster's heaven occasionally showcases trapeze artists, fire eaters and other assorted freaks (including some-one named "The Amazing Dieter"). It also has a sense of humor, with tall clown puppets delivering messages to the customers. Celebrities such as David Schwimmer and Michael Jordan have organized private parties here. Oh, and there's excellent dance music. *901 W. Weed St., Old Town, 312/266–1200.*

5 *c-5*

CROBAR—THE NIGHTCLUB

Former Chicago Bulls rebounder Dennis Rodman used to hang out here before he left town to marry Carmen Electra and play with the Dallas Mavericks. Wednesday is "Lunacy" night; watch the cage girls and trapeze artists. Thursday is "Medusa" night, with grab-bag artists from hula to swing. Friday and Saturday feature house music; Sunday is gay night. The dress code (no gym shoes, sports attire, or hats) is strictly enforced. *1543 N. Kingsbury St., Near North, 312/413–7000. Closed Mon.–Tues.*

5 *d-5*

THE DRAGON ROOM

Dance, drink, and eat sushi at this three-level nightclub with a sushi and sake bar that serves sushi until 3:45 AM on Friday and Saturday. The crowded, claustro-phobic first floor has Euro dance music as well as dancehall and drum and bass; downstairs is a loungy bar lit by red Japanese paper lanterns. *809 W. Evergreen Ave., Near North, 312/751–2900. Closed Mon.–Tues.*

6 *d-1*

DRINK

This hot nightclub has a big dance floor, soaring ceilings, driving dance music, '70s psychedelia, and a good-looking crowd who talk and stalk. Thursday is salsa night. A low-ceilinged Moroccan room and a balcony ... dance floor provide ... writhing bodies in ... house space. *702 W. Fulton ... Market, 312/733–7800. Closed Sun.*

7 *d-7*

EXCALIBUR

On weekends, a large, young suburban crowd comes to this superdisco with multiple dance floors, bars, and a video-games room. The first floor plays dance music from the '70s through the '90s; upstairs, called Club X, spins techno and hip-hop. *632 N. Dearborn St., River North, 312/266–1944.*

5 *b-5*

EXIT

A dark punk playground, Exit has punk and alternative music, with dancing (some slamming). On "Bondage-A-Go-Go" night, the first and third Thursday of the month, chain yourself to the bar and submit to bondage beauties. Admission is free for women. *1315 W. North Ave., River West, 773/395–2700.*

5 *d-8*

FUNKY BUDDHA LOUNGE

Funky doesn't begin to describe this trendy spot with leopard-print pillows, red velvet drapes, a smell of incense, and a big metal Buddha guarding the front door. On the separate dance floor, hipsters dance to hip-hop, funk, Latin, and underground house. *728 W. Grand Ave., West Town, 312/666–1695.*

5 *f-7*

FUSE

Somewhat more manageable than rave parties at warehouses, this techno-heavy dance haven has the usual disco balls and bug-zapper lights. *738 N. Clark St., River North, 312/932–9289.*

7 *b-7*

KARMA

Clubbing reaches a higher level at this downtown dance club. In the second-floor Temple dance room, patrons moving to house music are obscured by thick smoke from the fog machine, cig-ars, and cigarettes. The third floor has another dance floor, booths offering privacy, and a few pool tables. *318 W. Grand Ave., River North, 312/321–1331. Closed Sun.–Wed.*

c-3

QUID

Swing's the thing at this open spot, which is ideal for dancing; there's swing dancing six nights a week. Live bands play from Thursday through Sunday, and swing lessons are held every night at 7:30 PM. Don't be intimidated; there's a mix of beginners and knowledgeable dancers, and the lessons get more difficult as the week progresses. Dress in swing gear and you'll get a discount. *1997 N. Clybourn Ave., Lincoln Park, 773/ 528–3400. Closed Mon.*

2 *f-4*

MAD BAR

Monday night, with DJs spinning drum and bass, is the popular night at this trendy joint. Live music three nights a week ranges from flamenco and samba to acid jazz and funk (particularly on "Oxygen Tuesdays"). Bodies crowd the small dance floor, but there's seating in the back for those who would rather observe. *1640 N. Damen Ave., Bucktown, 773/227–2277.*

5 *e-2*

NEO

This longtime, dimly lit Lincoln Park club is the spot for Gothic, industrial, and underground dance music. Tuesday nights are dedicated to Gothic music and culture. *2350 N. Clark St., Lincoln Park, 773/528–2622. Closed Sun. and Wed.–Thurs.*

7 *c-5*

POLLY ESTHER'S

Want to flash back to the '70s and '80s? Polly Esther's takes you back with its *Saturday Night Fever* dance floor and lava lamps upstairs and Michael Jackson tunes in the '80s Culture Club area downstairs. Don't forget your bell-bottoms. *213 W. Institute Pl., River North, 312/664–0777. Closed Sun.–Wed.*

2 *f-4*

RED DOG

This supreme funk parlor gets crowded in the wee hours of the morning with bodies dancing to funk and house in a no-holds-barred atmosphere (which is to say a large second-floor room with almost nothing on the walls and very few tables). Enter from the alley off Damen Avenue. *1958 W. North Ave., Wicker Park, 773/278–1009. Closed Sun. and Tues.*

4 *c-6*

SMART BAR

Downstairs from Metro, the low-ceiling Smart Bar attracts a funky, young crowd who dance to punk, ska, rock, techno, electronica, hip-hop, dancehall, and acid jazz. *3730 N. Clark St., Wrigleyville, 773/ 549–4140.*

7 *b-7*

SPY BAR

Image is everything at this subterranean bar, which attracts celebrities and posers with its contemporary design, custom-made metal work, brushed-stainless-steel bar, exposed-brick walls, secluded VIP area, and R&B, house, and DJ dance music. *646 N. Franklin St., River North, 312/587–8779. Closed Mon.*

ECLECTIC

8 *e-6*

HOTHOUSE

This nonprofit, multi-arts center is home to the progressive arts, jazz, world music, Afropop, new music, film, video, poetry, performance art, and all things political and socially conscious. It's also known for a diverse live-jazz roster, from Japanese boogie-woogie bandleader Yoko Noge to the Ethnic Heritage Ensemble. It feels more like a co-op than a nightclub. The two main performance rooms are filled with art. *31 E. Balbo Ave., South Loop, 312/362–9707.*

FOLK & ACOUSTIC

2 *d-7*

BABY DOLL POLKA CLUB

Going to Midway Airport? Lay over at the nearby Baby Doll, which has some of the best polka dancing in the city, with live music on Saturday and Sunday when the house band—Eddie Korosa and His Merry Makers Polka Band—is on hand. You'll see mostly regulars at this neighborhood institution. *6102 S. Central Ave., Midway, 773/582–9706. Closed Mon.*

2 *d-5*

FITZGERALD'S

It's worth driving to the suburbs for the top-notch mix of folk, jazz, blues, zydeco, and rock at this early 1900's roadhouse. Fitzgerald's has great sound and sight lines in addition to its wide range of roots music. The American Music Festival, every Fourth of July, delivers terrific "alternative country" bands for a reasonable admission charge; it's a good time to begin sampling the club's style. *6615 W. Roosevelt Rd., Berwyn, 708/788–2118. Closed Mon.*

3 *g-4*
OLD TOWN SCHOOL OF FOLK MUSIC
Chicago's first and oldest folk music school has served as folk central in the city since 1957. (Singer-songwriter Steve Goodman, who wrote "Lincoln Park Pirates" and "City of New Orleans," was a famous early student.) It has moved from its longtime home on Armitage Avenue (it still offers children's classes on Armitage, though). There's not a bad seat at the 425-seat space, with outstanding performances by top national and local acts, including country singer Steve Earle. *4544 N. Lincoln Ave., Lincoln Square, 773/525–7793.*

GAY & LESBIAN BARS & CLUBS

The *Windy City Times* (312/397–0025) and *Gay Chicago* magazine (773/327–7271) list nightspots, events, and gay and lesbian resources; both are free.

7 *d-8*
BATON SHOW LOUNGE
Boys will be girls in the glitzy lip-synching revues at this 30-year-old cabaret featuring female impersonators. Some of the regular performers, such as Chili Pepper and Mimi Marks, have become Chicago cult figures. The Baton is popular with a mixed crowd as well as with, inexplicably, some bachelorette parties. *436 N. Clark St., River North, 312/644–5269. Closed Mon.–Tues.*

4 *c-8*
BERLIN
You can't help but dance at Berlin, a multicultural, pansexual dance club where anything goes. The DJ spins progressive electronic dance music. Catch the fun theme nights, such as Prince night, disco Wednesday, and boys' night with male dancers. *954 W. Belmont Ave., Lakeview, 773/348–4975.*

4 *c-8*
BIG CHICKS
The bar sponsors several men's and women's sports teams, making it a favorite with alternative jocks. Despite the name, Big Chicks attracts both men and women with a great jukebox and fun-loving staff. *5024 N. Sheridan Rd., Edgewater, 773/728–5511.*

4 *d-6*
CHARLIE'S
You can dance nightly to achy-breaky tunes at this country-and-western dance club. It's mostly a boots-and-denim crowd on weekends; both suburbanites and city dwellers rate it high on their cruising lists. *3726 N. Broadway, Lakeview, 773/871–8887.*

4 *e-7*
THE CLOSET
Previously more oriented to women, this small, friendly joint attracts a mixed gay and lesbian crowd. Don't miss the infamous Bloody Sundays, for what are hailed as the best Bloody Marys in town. *3325 N. Broadway, Lakeview, 773/477–8533.*

BEER GARDENS

When the weather is good in Chicago, there's a mad rush outdoors. On warm summer nights, nothing beats sitting outside in a beer garden downing a drink or two. A selection of popular spots:

Cork & Kerry (Bars & Lounges)
Even the TVs move outside in this large Beverly beer garden.

John Barleycorn (Pubs & Taverns)
Plenty of tables ensures adequate seating, and a lighted waterfall provides good scenery.

Justin's (Pubs & Taverns)
Belly up to the 30-ft outdoor bar and have a beer in a bucket.

Moody's Pub (Pubs & Taverns)
The trilevel beer garden has ivy walls and a pond on each level.

Northside (Bars & Lounges)
A partially enclosed atrium patio protects you from the elements.

Sheffield's (Bars & Lounges)
This is the ideal shady stop after a day at the friendly confines of Wrigley Field.

One of the few gay bars downtown, Gentry (with a second location on Halstead Street) attracts businessmen to its upscale piano bar, where the staff wears tuxedos. A younger, more casual crowd hangs out at the video bar downstairs. *440 N. State St., River North, 312/836-0933.*

4 *d-7*

3240 N. Halsted St., Lakeview, 773/348-1053.

5 *d-1*

GIRLBAR

It caters to women who like women, except Wednesday, when the spot becomes Boybar. This is a suitably yuppie place with wood floors, track lighting, and intimate, mirrored dance floor. The upstairs has a pool table, dart board, and outdoor deck where the comfortable, clean-cut crowd can overlook Halsted Street. *2625 N. Halsted St., Lincoln Park, 773/871-4210. Closed Mon.*

4 *d-7*

LITTLE JIM'S

Video screens show films of varying repute at this neighborhood bar with a good mix of regulars. *3501 N. Halsted St., Lakeview, 773/871-6116.*

4 *d-7*

ROSCOE'S TAVERN

A crowded, friendly, upscale spot, Roscoe's has several rooms with a large open bar, great dance music, a pool room, fireplace, and outside café in the summer. *3356 N. Halsted St., Lakeview, 773/281-3355.*

4 *d-8*

SPIN

DJs spin dance, Latin, and industrial music at this spot. With three bars, two lounges, and a pool room, Spin attracts gay and straight crowds, but darkened street windows keep passersby guessing as to what's inside. *800 W. Belmont Ave., Lakeview, 773/327-7711.*

HOTEL BARS

7 *f-5*

THE BAR

Businesspeople looking for a quiet drink and a place to talk head to the Bar at the

Ritz-Carlton. Patrons watch sports or enjoy a cigar from the humidor here. Outside the bar is the Greenhouse, an atrium space where afternoon tea is served and where a piano player tickles the ivories every night. *Ritz-Carlton, 160 E. Pearson St., Near North, 312/266-1000.*

7 *f-5*

COQ D'OR

In the venerable Drake hotel, Coq d'Or serves executive cocktails—4-ounce drinks and then some—in a cigar-friendly atmosphere with two TVs and the music of piano player Buddy Charles (*see* Piano Bars, *below*). A harpist plays in the Drake's Palm Court, where afternoon tea is served. *Drake, 140 E. Walton Ave., Near North, 312/787-2200.*

7 *f-5*

SEASONS LOUNGE

In the Four Seasons Hotel, this lounge serves drinks and dessert to the sounds of jazz; it also has a martini menu and cigar bar. A trio performs Saturday night. *Four Seasons Hotel, 120 E. Delaware Pl., Near North, 312/280-8800.*

JAZZ

7 *d-8*

ANDY'S

Music lovers who work downtown head to Andy's for live jazz at noon weekdays, as well as for the after-work sets starting at 5 PM—a boon for music lovers who aren't night owls. This popular watering hole with a substantial bar menu has become one of Chicago's best spots for serious jazz. *11 E. Hubbard St., River North, 312/642-6805.*

6 *g-6*

COTTON CLUB

A favorite of upscale young black professionals, the elegant room draws big crowds and good bands. The Cab Calloway room, with jazz by candlelight, is modeled after the original Cotton Club in New York. The Great Room has disco and dancing, and an open mike is held every Monday. *1710 S. Michigan Ave., South Loop, 312/341-9787.*

5 *a-3*

GREEN DOLPHIN STREET

With the retro feel of a jazz supper club, this spot features smooth-voiced jazz divas and top ensembles with bossa, bebop, Latin, and world jazz. There's no cover charge for those who dine here. *2200 N. Ashland Ave., Bucktown, 773/395–0066.*

4 *c-3*
GREEN MILL
Opened in 1907, it is steeped in history. Deep leather banquettes and ornate wood paneling line the walls, and a photo of Al Capone occupies a place of honor behind the bar. The jazz entertainment is tops, along with the Uptown Poetry Slam on Sunday and the Big Swing on Tuesday. *4802 N. Broadway, Uptown, 773/878–5552.*

7 *d-7*
JAZZ SHOWCASE
The second-oldest jazz club in the country presents top national and international names in jazz. It's for serious listeners only; don't come here if you want background music. *59 W. Grand Ave., River North, 312/670–2473.*

7 *h-7*
JOE'S BE-BOP CAFE & JAZZ EMPORIUM
There are other places to go for serious jazz, but if you're at Navy Pier with out-of-town guests, stop here to listen to local veterans while you dine. Music starts at 6 PM weekdays at this spot owned by Joe Segal, who also owns Jazz Showcase. *700 E. Grand Ave., Navy Pier, 312/595–5299.*

8 *f-1*
THE METROPOLE
Fusion, bebop, and traditional jazz groups perform in an elegant art deco setting in the Fairmont Hotel. The intimate space has cabaret-style seating for 100 people. *Fairmont Hotel, 200 N. Columbus Blvd., Loop, 312/565–7444. Closed Sun.–Mon.*

2 *f-4*
THE NOTE
A youngish audience frequents this spot in the historic Flat Iron building. There's live music—Latin jazz, vintage jazz, and blues—several nights a week. A bonus: free pool after midnight. *1565 N. Milwaukee Ave., Wicker Park, 773/489–0011.*

4 *d-8*
POPS FOR CHAMPAGNE
Despite the incongruous name, Pops is a good spot for serious jazz fans, with instrumental and vocal ensembles. A champagne bar, with some 140 champagnes and a selection of tasty appetizers and desserts enhance the scene. *2934 N. Sheffield Ave., Lakeview, 773/472–1000.*

6 *g-6*
VELVET LOUNGE
Glorious music comes out of this weather-beaten storefront spot with rusted burglar bars in front. Owner Fred Anderson, who plays the saxophone, books traditional jazz ensembles. *2128½ S. Indiana Ave., Near South, 312/791–9050.*

PIANO BARS

7 *f-5*
COQ D'OR
Chicago legend Buddy Charles holds court here from Tuesday to Saturday. The dark room draws hotel guests as

---

BLUES HISTORY SPOTS

Although blues has passed its heyday in Chicago, you might want to check out these blues-history havens:

Blues Heaven Foundation (2120 S. Michigan Ave., Near South Side, 312/808–1286).
Once the home of famous blues label Chess Records, this building serves as headquarters for the late songwriter Willie Dixon's namesake charity.

Buddy Guy's Legends (Blues)
Since Chicago's primary blues ambassador, guitarist Buddy Guy, opened this club in 1989, he has collected a trove of memorabilia, including Koko Taylor's dress and Sunnyland Slim's shirt. All are on display.

Checkerboard Lounge (Blues)
Though many rock fans visit this joint to relive the Rolling Stones' fabled appearance in the '70s, it's more important for showcasing Buddy Guy and Junior Wells as the house band.

Kingston Mines (Blues)
More than 30 years old, this North Side fixture is a central gathering spot for blues musicians. Mines' regulars once formed the core of late guitarist Albert Collins' Icebreakers.

well as neighborhood regulars with its fine music and cocktails served in blown-glass goblets. *Drake hotel, 140 E. Walton Ave., Near North, 312/787–2200.*

5 *a-5*

DAVENPORT'S

With accomplished jazz, pop, and classical piano players every Wednesday through Sunday, this still-new bar sometimes attracts performers from nearby cabaret shows. *1383 N. Milwaukee Ave., West Town, 773/278–1830.*

7 *e-4*

JILLY'S BISTRO

Named for one of Sinatra's former bodyguards, the small room has live music daily. While patrons listen to swing and Sinatra, they drink, smoke cigars, and check out the scenery. Downstairs, by the way, is Jilly's Retro Club, with '70s and '80s retro dance music, and upstairs is Jilly's Singapore Inn, an American-Chinese restaurant. *1007 N. Rush St., Gold Coast, 312/664–1001.*

7 *d-3*

PUMP ROOM

A longtime celebrity hangout, the Pump Room has walls lined with photos of the rich and famous. Make yourself comfortable sitting around the padded piano in an elegant yet cozy setting. Jackets are required after 4:30 PM, and no jeans or sports attire is allowed at any time. *Omni Ambassador East, 1301 N. State Pkwy., Gold Coast, 312/266–0360.*

7 *d-7*

REDHEAD PIANO BAR

Sit around the piano at this spot, a piano bar in the truest sense of the phrase. Or if you'd rather talk than sing along, there are tables or seats at the main bar toward the back of the room. The upscale crowd consists largely of over-30 regulars. *16 W. Ontario St., River North, 312/640–1000.*

3 *g-4*

VILLA KULA

A low-key tearoom that serves delicious dessert and pastry, it has big wide tables and a relaxing decor. Veteran boogie-woogie pianist Erwin Helfer, frequently with just-as-veteran saxman John Brumbach, holds court on Saturday night. *4518 N. Lincoln Ave., Ravenswood, 773/728–3114.*

7 *d-3*

YVETTE

An elegant piano bar and restaurant, with French and American cuisine, Yvette has live music daily including pianists and jazz trios. Patrons pay attention to the entertainment here; it's not music to chat over. *1206 N. State St., Gold Coast, 312/280–1700.*

7 *d-3*

ZEBRA LOUNGE

An odd assortment of patrons hangs out here—both dressy and casual, sophisticated and sophomoric. Nonetheless, they all come to sing along with pianist Tommy Oman from Wednesday through Saturday. On Tuesday a magician performs card tricks and sleight of hand at your table. *1220 N. State St., Gold Coast, 312/642–5140.*

POP/ROCK

2 *f-3*

BEAT KITCHEN

With its good sound system and local pop, rock, jazz, country, and rockabilly acts, Beat Kitchen brings in the crowds. If you need a break from the music, head to the second floor, which is decorated like an old apartment, with easy chairs and board games. *2100 W. Belmont Ave., West Lakeview, 773/281–4444.*

2 *f-3*

BROTHER JIMMY'S

This club draws a steady stream of hard-drinking hippies and yuppies who like to watch guitarists jam for hours and hours and hours. Classic southern barbecue is on the menu. *2909 N. Sheffield Ave., Lincoln Park, 773/528–0888.*

2 *e-4*

CALIFORNIA CLIPPER

This atmosphere-oozing fixture near Wicker Park has big, beautiful booths and classic sailboat paintings. It showcases all varieties of pre–rock-and-roll music, from jazz to blues to rockabilly. Local boogie-woogie piano men Erwin Helfer and Barrelhouse Chuck have a regular engagement. *1002 N. California St., Humboldt Park, 773/384–2547.*

4 *c-6*

CUBBY BEAR

Across the street from Wrigley Field is this large sports bar and music venue. The emphasis is on rock, country-rock, and jazz. But sports fans are also catered to with some 50 TV sets, as well as pool tables, dart boards, video games, and pinball. During baseball season the Cubby Bear opens early to give Cubs fans another place to drown their sorrows. *1059 W. Addison St., Lakeview, 773/327–1662.*

5 *c-1*

DÉJÀ VU

Entertainment ranges from live bands, local band members taking a turn as DJ, and an eclectic jukebox at this Art Deco nightspot with its original 1891 bar. You can count on a couple of things at the Vu: turtle races the last Wednesday of each month and a packed bar after 2 AM, when other bars close. *2624 N. Lincoln Ave., Lincoln Park, 773/871–0205.*

2 *f-4*

DOUBLE DOOR

The space is large enough to attract some top-rate bands, from national groups to up-and-coming local and alternative ones, and yet it's small enough so you can enjoy the music, which ranges from rock to acid jazz. Since the Lounge Ax closed in early 2000, the Double Door and the Empty Bottle are really the only like-minded music clubs of this size. Enter on Damen, south of North Avenue. *1572 N. Milwaukee Ave., Wicker Park, 773/489–3160.*

5 *b-1*

ELBO ROOM

Bands perform downstairs in this multi-level space in an elbow-shape corner building. Live bands, seven days a week, play a strong dose of acid jazz, funk, pop, swing, and soul. All bands play original music; thankfully, you won't find cover tunes here. *2871 N. Lincoln Ave., Lakeview, 773/549–5549.*

2 *f-4*

EMPTY BOTTLE

With a smattering of toys and knick-knacks around the bar, the Empty Bottle is laid back and unpretentious. But when it comes to booking experimental rock, punk, and rockabilly bands from the indie scene, it's a serious place. The Festival of Improvised Music, a few nights every May, showcases the city's growing avant-garde jazz scene, including performers Ken Vandermark and Fred Lonberg-Holmes. *1035 N. Western Ave., Ukrainian Village, 773/276–3600.*

2 *f-3*

FIRESIDE BOWL

It used to be a bowling alley, and now it's a breeding ground for young bands. Although the lanes are still here, they're nothing but a prop. The real action is in the punk rock, indie, and ska bands. Avoid the filthy bathrooms as much as possible. *2648 W. Fullerton Ave., Logan Square, 773/486–2700.*

5 *c-5*

JOE'S SPORTS BAR

Joe's features live music (rock, blues, and disco) from Wednesday through Saturday and has a beer garden. When there's no music, it's a good place to watch football and basketball games. With three satellite dishes and 87 TV monitors, it's a good place to view just about any sporting event. *940 W. Weed St., Near North, 312/337–3486.*

3 *h-6*

MARTYRS'

A big shell of a space, with a 400-person capacity, Martyrs' has excellent sight lines and some good bookings. Monday features Irish music, on Tuesday the Dark Star Orchestra gives a Grateful Dead experience, and the rest of the week usually brings eclectic local and national rock groups. In recent years, the club has lured big names, such as singer-songwriting veteran Guy Clark, contemporary bluesman Chris Whitley, and country-soul chanteuse Shelby Lynne. *3855 N. Lincoln Ave., West Lakeview, 773/404–9494. Closed Sun.*

4 *c-6*

METRO

This former movie palace is an excellent place to see live music. The bands include progressive, nationally known artists—recent headliners include Bob Dylan, the Smashing Pumpkins, Iggy Pop, Steve Earle, and They Might Be Giants—and the cream of the local crop. The balcony gives a panoramic view of the space. *3730 N. Clark St., Wrigleyville, 773/549–0203.*

5 e-3

PARK WEST

The decor still smacks of the '80s, with black booths encircling the dance floor and stage; sometimes the performers do, too, like Elvis Costello, Joe Jackson, Boy George, and Run-D.M.C. It's a good place to see a glossily performed show in a pristine environment. Show up early to snag one of the many comfortable seats; otherwise, you're stuck fighting the dance-floor crowd for space. *322 W. Armitage Ave., Lincoln Park, 773/929–5959.*

5 a-6

PHYLLIS' MUSICAL INN

Wicker Park's first live music venue now has lots of competition, but it's still a good place to see low-budget shows by local bands. The narrow, worn rooms endure loud garage-type rock every day. *1800 W. Division St., Wicker Park, 773/486–9862.*

4 b-8

SCHUBAS TAVERN

With live music nightly, Schubas favors rock, rockabilly, country, and folk in a wood-paneled room with a laid-back atmosphere. When Chicagoans speak of their "alternative country" music scene, they're referring to homeboy band Wilco, Bloodshot Records, FitzGerald's in Berwyn, or this North Side fixture. Built in 1900 by the Schlitz Brewing Company, the building has a huge Schlitz logo carved into the exterior. Schlitz is still a bargain at $2. *3159 N. Southport Ave., Lakeview, 773/525–2508.*

5 e-2

TOWER RECORDS

Though it's not a concert venue, per se, this record store sponsors frequent in-store appearances by local and big-name musicians. The stage and sound quality are surprisingly professional for a retailer. Plus, for a corporate-run store, the CD selection is about as thorough as you'll find in the city. *2301 N. Clark St., Lincoln Park, 773/477–5994.*

4 c-7

WILD HARE

Calling itself the "reggae capital of America," the Wild Hare features infectious live reggae and world beat music, with a wide-open dance floor and Caribbean decor. Get here before the band starts at 9:30 PM to avoid the cover

charge. *3530 N. Clark St., Wrigleyville, 773/327–4273.*

PUBS & TAVERNS

3 e-6

ABBEY PUB

This busy, smoky Irish pub with Guinness and Harp on tap has a separate large concert hall that showcases Irish and Celtic music, with bands performing on the weekends. By day, the hall is used to show Irish, Scottish, and English soccer and rugby games. *3420 W. Grace St., North Center, 773/478–4408.*

5 g-8

BILLY GOAT TAVERN

Behind and one level down from the Wrigley Building, the Billy Goat Tavern was once a roost for home-grown comic John Belushi and the inspiration for *Saturday Night Live*'s classic "cheezborger, cheezborger" skit. It's also a longtime haunt of local journalists, most famously the late columnist Mike Royko. Grab a greasy hamburger (or cheeseburger) at this very casual grill, or just have a beer and absorb the atmosphere. (Note: Don't expect any healthy food whatsoever—not even chicken.) *430 N. Michigan Ave., Near North, 312/222–1525.*

4 b-6

CULLEN'S BAR AND GRILL

A superloud spot on weekend nights and a difficult place to find a table during sporting events, the old-fashioned-looking Cullen's is especially notable for its better-than-you'd-expect Irish bar fare. The mashed potatoes are delicious, and the meat loaf and shepherd's pie aren't bad, either. *3741 N. Southport Ave., Lakeview, 773/975–0600.*

4 d-8

DUKE OF PERTH

There's a fine selection of Scottish whiskey, beer, and hard cider from Great Britain at this comfortable-like-an-old-shoe Scottish bar. It's all you can eat fish-and-chips (for $6.95) on Wednesday and Friday night. *2913 N. Clark St., Lakeview, 773/477–1741.*

7 d-7

FADÓ IRISH PUB

Expect expertly drawn Guinness, a fine selection of Irish whiskeys, occasional live Irish music, and plenty of beer to go around. The pub is broken into six areas, which showcase different pub styles—a bit gimmicky, but it works. *100 W. Grand Ave., River North, 312/836–0066.*

4 *c-6*
GINGERMAN TAVERN
It's near Wrigley Field, but it's not a sports bar. The regulars here take their beer and billiards seriously, with more than 100 bottles and 15 brands on tap. *3740 N. Clark St., Wrigleyville, 773/549–2050.*

7 *b-6*
GREEN DOOR TAVERN
Don't be mistaken—this restaurant and tavern is not the Green Mill or Green Dolphin Street. It was originally a speakeasy during Prohibition and still has many of the old fixtures from those days. The building dates from 1872 and has housed a tavern since 1921. *678 N. Orleans St., River North, 312/664–5496. Closed Sun.*

2 *g-7*
HOUSE OF TIKI
With lounge singers on the jukebox (the good ones, like Ella Fitzgerald), alcohol-heavy fruit drinks, and a Polynesian cocktail theme, this South Side fixture still draws a mix of partying college students and more subdued regulars. *1612 E. 53rd St., Hyde Park, 773/684–1221.*

5 *d-2*
JOHN BARLEYCORN
This historic pub with a long wooden bar and separate darts area can get somewhat rowdy despite the classical music and art slides shown on video screens. There is a good selection of beers and a popular outdoor summer beer garden, plus a strange collection of paintings and sculpture. *658 W. Belden Ave., Lincoln Park, 773/348–8899.*

4 *b-7*
JUSTIN'S
Get a bucket of beer here—five long-neck Rolling Rock bottles served in a pail—for $10. Sit perched around tall round tables or in summer take the action outside to the beer garden, which is especially popular after a Cubs game. *3358 N. Southport Ave., Lakeview, 773/929–4844.*

8 *e-6*
KITTY O'SHEA'S
A handsome room in the Chicago Hilton and Towers, this pub comes complete with Irish music, food by Irish chefs, and, of course, Irish bartenders. There's music every night with no cover charge. *720 S. Michigan Ave., South Loop, 312/922–4400.*

4 *b-7*
LAUNDER BAR
What turns a sheepish conversation about shrunken sweaters into a smoldering love connection filled with eye contact and innuendo? Beer, of course. Though the Launder Bar isn't the only Chicago establishment to mix both kinds of suds, it smartly emphasizes "launder" over "bar" so clothes-washers don't feel the matchmaking pressure. There's very little to do while your clothes bob in the little round window, so crack a cold one and prepare to part with your secret bleach strategy. *3435 N. Southport Ave., Lakeview, 773/929–9274.*

5 *a-4*
LINCOLN TAVERN
The oldest watering hole in Bucktown and Wicker Park has been family owned and operated since 1950 and has featured Pabst on tap all of those years. The room is set up like a Wisconsin lodge and serves lunch during the week and a lodge-style dinner on Wednesday and Friday. Since family members put in a long day, the bar closes around 10 PM weeknights, 11 PM weekends. *1858 W. Wabansia Ave., Bucktown, 773/342–7778. Closed Sun.*

BEST MARTINIS

Though the lounge-music and swing-dancing crazes have died down since their mid-'90s peak, people still drink martinis. Here are two of the best spots:

Bar Louie (Bars & Lounges)
Velvet booths, cocktail tables, and a martini named "dreamsicle" are popular draws at this relaxing food-and-drink nightspot.

Martini Ranch (Bars & Lounges)
Famous for its chocolate martini, this something-for-everybody bar, open since 1992, also offers cigars, microbrews, and televised sporting events.

5 *e-4*

MARGE'S PUB

The oldest continuously running bar in Chicago has been in business for 112 years. Marge, who lives above the bar and has owned it for 43 years, stops in every now and then. Over the bar are black-and-white drawings of famous Chicagoans, including late *Chicago Tribune* columnist Mike Royko and Chicago Cubs broadcaster Harry Caray, Mayor Richard J. "Boss" Daley, and still-living (but departed to New Orleans) former Chicago Bears coach Mike Ditka. *1758 N. Sedgwick St., Old Town, 312/787–3900.*

2 *f-2*

MOODY'S PUB

The interior of Moody's is dark and woody, like a ski lodge. If you crave sunlight, head to the trilevel outdoor garden patio with ivy-covered walls, ponds, sun peeking through trees, and bland beer. *5910 N. Broadway, Edgewater, 773/275–2696.*

5 *f-5*

OLD TOWN ALE HOUSE

A mural at this pub painted in the '70s has immortalized some of the regulars here. You can still find some of those same customers and bartenders at the bar. A jukebox plays jazz, opera, rock, and classical music. *219 W. North Ave., Old Town, 312/944–7020.*

5 *d-2*

RED LION

This dark, authentic British pub is decked out with London Metro maps and serves up fish-and-chips, Guinness, and hard cider. A bookie joint in the 1930s, it's said to be one of America's most haunted places; ask the bartender to tell you some stories. *2446 N. Lincoln Ave., Lincoln Park, 773/348–2695.*

7 *f-5*

SHELLY'S BACK ROOM AMERICAN TAVERN

Although it has private cigar lockers available for yearly rental, as well as premium cigars, bourbons, and other spirits, Shelly's does not want to be labeled a cigar bar. The wood-paneled room has a good ventilation system that pushes in fresh air every 10 minutes. *192 E. Walton Pl., Streeterville, 312/255–9900.*

SPORTS BARS

8 *e-1*

ALUMNI CLUB

This straightforward Michigan Avenue sports bar is an anchor of the late-night Rush Street drinking scene. The Lincoln location has a Thursday-night acoustic jam session and weekend dance DJs. More importantly, television screens with sporting events blaze pretty much everywhere you look. *150 N. Michigan Ave., Near North, 312/345–1400.*

5 *f-6*

15 W. Division St., Gold Coast, 312/337–4349.

5 *d-3*

2251 N. Lincoln Ave., Lincoln Park, 773/348–5100.

1 *b-3*

871 E. Algonquin Rd., Schaumburg, 847/397–3100.

1 *e-6*

CORK & KERRY

This Beverly institution has a handsome old wood bar along with multiple televisions showing sports. In summer the action spills outside to the large beer garden, with bar stools, a sound system, and even TVs moved outside. *10614 S. Western Ave., Beverly, 773/445–2675.*

5 *e-3*

GAMEKEEPERS

Former frat boys and sports fans flock here. With more than 30 TVs and complete satellite sports coverage, there's barely a domestic or international event Gamekeepers doesn't get. *345 W. Armitage Ave., Lincoln Park, 773/549–0400.*

4 *c-7*

HI-TOPS CAFE

Within a ball's toss of Wrigley Field, this ultimate sports bar keeps fans coming with 12 satellites and 50 TV monitors. People come here to watch *South Park* on Wednesday or recent video releases from Blockbuster. A laid-back martini bar upstairs provides a respite from the crowd. *3551 N. Sheffield Ave., Wrigleyville, 773/348–0009.*

4 *c-7*

SLUGGERS

This sports spot, packed after games at nearby Wrigley Field, has fast- and slow-pitch batting cages on the second floor, as well as pool tables, air hockey tables, and an indoor golf range. In summer the air-conditioning is a plus after the ball game, and every once in a while the players make appearances. *3540 N. Clark St., Wrigleyville, 773/ 248–0055.*

WINE BARS

7 *d-7*
BIN 36
Offering 50 wines by the glass, this reasonably new, extremely spacious wine-lover's fantasy bar rents out wine lockers and regularly comes up with rare bottles. It's attached to the House of Blues hotel. *339 N. Dearborn St., Near North, 312/755–9463.*

7 *e-5*
CRU CAFÉ AND WINE BAR
As hoity-toity as its Gold Coast neighborhood, this recently opened European-style café has a snazzy, velvet-and-leather look and more than 400 wine bottles. *888 N. Wabash Ave., Gold Coast, 312/337–4078.*

5 *a-2*
RUDI'S WINE BAR AND CAFE
Some 70% of the wines (there are more than 100) are French, and 15 are served by the glass. This small spot, with 17 tables, has hearty French bistro cuisine and live jazz Monday night. *2424 N. Ashland Ave., Lincoln Park, 773/404–7834.*

4 *c-8*
STAR BAR
In the same building as Pops for Champagne, this upscale neighborhood spot offers fantastic spirits, including still and sparkling wines, beers from all over the world, scotches, cigars, and bourbons. *2934 N. Sheffield Ave., Lakeview, 773/472–7272.*

5 *b-3*
WEBSTER'S WINE BAR
More than 200 bottles of wine are available here, with at least 40 by the glass, in this storefront bar with a tin ceiling and plum-colored walls. You can also choose from ports, sherries, single malt scotches, and microbrews, as well as a light menu. *1480 W. Webster Ave., Lincoln Park, 773/868–0608.*

chapter 6

HOTELS

Chicago: The Windy City, The Third Coast, the City with Big Shoulders. Whatever moniker you use, it's a great tourist town and a great place to live. Chicago hotels range from the purely utilitarian to the utterly splendiferous, each with its own personal touch. Whether you're putting up the in-laws or looking for a vacation in your own hometown, there's a perfect Chicago hotel in your future.

When booking rooms there are a couple of things to remember. Be aware of the more than 1,000 conventions and trade shows scheduled in the city every year. Make every effort to avoid booking a room during the National Restaurant Association show in May, the hardware show in August, and the manufacturing technology show in September. Not only are rooms nonexistent, but so are tables at the city's popular restaurants.

When you make your reservation, be sure to get a confirmation number and keep it with you for reference. Notify the hotel if you anticipate arriving later than 5 PM; many hotels will guarantee your reservation with your credit card and have a room waiting for you even if you arrive at 2 AM. Inquire about the hotel's cancellation policy at the time of booking to avoid paying for a room you didn't occupy. Should you need to cancel your reservation, notify the hotel as soon as possible—and be sure to get a cancellation number. Otherwise, you may be responsible for at least one night's charge.

Hotel booking services book rooms in bulk at major hotels, often at a significant discount. A no-fee discount hotel-reservation service that specializes in Chicago is **Hot Rooms** (773/468–7666 or 800/468–3500); **Hotel Reservations Network** (800/964–6835) has inventory in Chicago.

This guide lists the facilities that are available but doesn't specify whether they cost extra: when pricing accommodations, always ask what's included. Most of the upscale hotels have business centers or at least the capability to assist with faxing, copying, and word processing; many also have meeting rooms of different sizes. Most offer room service, as well as laundry and dry cleaning. Cable TV is the standard in Chicago hotels and often comes with free or pay-per-view movie channels. Many hotels charge for using on-site health facilities. Guests at hotels that don't have their own health club may be allowed to use one nearby, usually for a daily fee in the $14 range. Ask for specifics if a particular facility is important to you.

Most Chicago hotels are found in and around the Loop and Lincoln Park and are easily accessible using trains, buses, and taxis.

Hotel price categories in this chapter are based on the standard weekday rate for one room, double occupancy. These are the rack rates—the highest price at which the rooms are rented. As noted above, discounts are often available. Many Chicago hotels quote rates based on single occupancy, with a second person adding $10–$20 to the nightly rate. Rates listed do not include the unpleasantly high 14.9% room tax.

price categories

CATEGORY	COST*
Very Expensive	over $260
Expensive	$180–$260
Moderate	$100–$179
Budget	under $100

VERY EXPENSIVE LODGING

5 *f5*

AMBASSADOR WEST

Faded tapestries, carved wood columns, and crystal chandeliers convey a sense of the 1924 origins of this boutique hotel. Room size varies greatly, and regular rooms don't have much in the way of amenities, though you do get free coffee in the lobby, the use of a small fitness room, and a newspaper. The neighboring Omni Ambassador East, still joined to its former sister by an underground passageway, maintains a more glamorous profile. *1300 N. State Pkwy., Old Town, 60610, 312/787–3700 or 800/300–9378, fax 312/640–2967. 160 rooms, 60 suites. Restaurant, lobby lounge, minibars, no-smoking floor, room service, barbershop, beauty salon, exercise room, dry cleaning, laundry service, concierge, concierge floor, meeting rooms, parking (fee). AE, D, DC, MC, V.*

5 *g-8*

CHICAGO MARRIOTT DOWNTOWN

This 46-story tower of white concrete stands as a city unto itself, with its own Kinko's business center, retail stores, and gourmet coffee counter in the lobby. Rooms are basic but full of amenities such as two-line phones, high-speed Internet access, coffeemakers, irons, and hair dryers. *540 N. Michigan Ave., Near North, 60611, 312/836–0100 or 800/228–9290, fax 312/836–6139. 1,151 rooms, 25 suites. 2 restaurants, bar, lobby lounge, in-room data ports, no-smoking floors, room service, indoor lap pool, beauty salon, hot tub, massage, sauna, steam room, basketball, exercise room, pro shop, video games, dry cleaning, laundry service, concierge, concierge floor, business services, meeting rooms, parking (fee). AE, D, DC, MC, V.*

5 *g-7*

DOUBLETREE GUEST SUITES

The ample-size rooms, view from the 30th-floor indoor pool and fitness room, and location just one block from Michigan Avenue make this all-suite hotel one of the nicest places to stay in Chicago. The homemade chocolate chip cookies guests receive at check-in are a nice touch; for something more substantial, try the signature pastrami salmon at Mrs. Park's Tavern. *198 E. Delaware Pl., Near North, 60611, 312/664–1100 or 800/ 222–8733, fax 312/664–9881. 345 suites. 2 restaurants, 2 bars, in-room data ports, minibars, no-smoking floors, room service, indoor lap pool, hot tub, massage, sauna, exercise room, video games, coin laundry, dry cleaning, laundry service, concierge, business services, meeting rooms, parking (fee). AE, D, DC, MC, V.*

5 *g-7*

THE DRAKE

Driving south on Lake Shore Drive, one is beckoned by the grande dame of Chicago hotels. Guests are surrounded by class and panache reminiscent of the hotel's 1920s beginnings. With all this and Michigan Avenue right outside the door, who could ask for more? *140 E. Walton Pl., Near North, 60611, 312/787–2200 or 800/553–7253, fax 312/787–1431. 474 rooms, 63 suites. 3 restaurants, 2 bars, lobby lounge, piano bar, in-room data ports, minibars, no-smoking floors, room service, barbershop, exercise room, dry cleaning, laundry service, concierge, concierge floor, business services, meeting rooms, parking (fee). AE, D, DC, MC, V.*

5 *f-8*

EMBASSY SUITES

This business hotel has suites with a microwave oven, minirefrigerator, coffeemaker, and sleeper sofa. A complimentary full breakfast each morning sends well-rested travelers energized to their meetings. *600 N. State St., Near North, 60610, 312/943–3800 or 800/362–2779, fax 312/943–7629. 358 suites. Restaurant, bar, in-room data ports, kitchenettes, minibars, no-smoking rooms, room service, indoor lap pool, hot tub, sauna, exercise room, dry cleaning, laundry service, concierge, concierge floor, business services, meeting rooms, car rental, parking (fee). AE, D, DC, MC, V.*

6 *g-2*

FAIRMONT HOTEL

Elegance and luxury afford guests a truly relaxing experience in a four-star hotel. Spacious guest rooms have extralong beds and oversize bathrooms with mini TVs and shower stalls separate from the bath. Bay windows offer great views of Grant Park and the lakefront. Singing waiters at Primavera, the hotel's Italian restaurant, create a festive atmosphere. *200 N. Columbus Dr., Loop, 60601, 312/ 565–8000 or 800/526–2008, fax 312/856– 1032. 626 rooms, 66 suites. 2 restaurants, 3 bars, lobby lounge, in-room data ports, in-room fax, minibars, no-smoking rooms, room service, golf privileges, cabaret, dry cleaning, laundry service, concierge, business services, meeting rooms, parking (fee). AE, D, DC, MC, V.*

5 *g-7*

FOUR SEASONS

Its location atop the 900 North Michigan Shops provides panoramic views, but it feels more like a grand English manor house than an urban skyscraper. Italian marble, handcrafted woodwork, and botanical prints personalize the guest rooms. A skylit pool, jogging track, spa services, and the notable Seasons restaurant make a stay at this fine hotel a vacation in itself. *120 E. Delaware Pl., Near North, 60611, 312/280–8800 or 800/332–3442, fax 312/280–1748. 174 rooms, 169 suites. 2 restaurants, bar, lobby lounge, in-room data ports, in-room safes, minibars, no-smoking floors, room service, indoor pool, hot tub, massage, sauna, steam room, exercise room, dry cleaning, laundry service, concierge, business services, meeting rooms, parking (fee). AE, D, DC, MC, V.*

5 *g-8*

HOTEL INTER-CONTINENTAL

Architectural delights abound in this hotel's public spaces, and guest rooms have neoclassical 1920s decor with inlaid woods and custom furnishings. The Olympic-size pool surrounded by majolica tile walls recalls the hotel's origins as the Medinah Athletic Club, which earned a nod from the National Register of Historic Places. The guest rooms are spacious. *505 N. Michigan Ave., Near North, 60611, 312/944–3882 or 800/628–2112, fax 312/944–3050. 819 rooms, 25 suites. Restaurant, bar, lobby lounge, in-room data ports, minibars, no-smoking floors, room service, indoor pool, massage, sauna, exercise room, dry cleaning, laundry service, concierge, business services, meeting rooms, parking (fee). AE, D, DC, MC, V.*

6 *g-1*

HOTEL MONACO

The French-deco inspired look, registration desk fashioned after a classic steamer trunk, and meeting rooms named for exotic destinations create a travel theme. Guests are treated to complimentary morning coffee and nightly wine receptions. The hotel is pet friendly and will even supply a pet goldfish-in-a-bowl on request. *225 N. Wabash Ave., 60601, 312/960–8500 or 800/397–7661, fax 312/960–1883. 170 rooms, 22 suites. Restaurant, bar, in-room data ports, minibars, no-smoking floors, room service, exercise room, dry cleaning, laundry service, concierge, business services, meeting rooms, parking (fee). AE, D, DC, MC, V.*

6 *f-3*

HYATT ON PRINTERS ROW

In the late 1800s Printers Row was a railway hub for the printing industry. By the 1970s the area was already in its second reincarnation as a location for the upwardly mobile. The hotel is small in scale, intimate, and close to the financial district and the Art Institute. The lobby and public areas show a distinctive Frank Lloyd Wright inspiration, with sober colors, dark woods, and Tiffany-style lamps. Black lacquer furniture lends an art deco look to the rooms, which all have a soothingly muted color scheme. *500 S. Dearborn St., Loop, 60605, 312/986–1234 or 800/233–1234, fax 312/939–2468. 158 rooms, 3 suites. Restaurant, bar, in-room data ports, minibars, no-smoking rooms, room service, exercise room, laundry service and dry cleaning, business services, meeting rooms, parking (fee). AE, D, DC, MC, V.*

6 *g-1*

HYATT REGENCY

Everything at this typical Hyatt is big: the rooms, the beds, the baths. A seemingly placid, two-story greenhouse belies the hustle and bustle underfoot in the very busy lobby. Large black-and-white photographs of Chicago landmarks add to the contemporary hotel decor. *151 E. Wacker Dr., Loop, 60601, 312/565–1234 or 800/233–1234, fax 312/565–2648. 2,019 rooms, 175 suites. 4 restaurants, bar, breakfast room, café, deli, sports bar, in-room data ports, minibars, no-smoking rooms, room service, beauty salon, massage, dry cleaning, laundry service, concierge, concierge floor, business services, convention center, meeting rooms, parking (fee). AE, D, DC, MC, V.*

5 *f-5*

OMNI AMBASSADOR EAST

The secluded setting makes it popular with movie stars and literary figures. Quiet, large rooms have a traditional feel. The lobby has an old-world elegance, with crystal chandeliers, marble floors, and curving banisters. For celebrity watching at its finest, check out the famous Pump Room. *1301 N. State Pkwy., Old Town, 60610, 312/787–7200 or 800/843–6664, fax 312/787–4760. 233 rooms, 52 suites. Restaurant, bar, lobby lounge, in-room data ports, minibars, no-smoking floors, room service, barbershop, beauty salon, exercise room, dry cleaning, laundry service, concierge, business services, parking (fee). AE, D, DC, MC, V.*

5 *g-8*

OMNI CHICAGO

Business travelers and vacationers alike get what they need at the Omni. Rooms are decorated in rich jewel tones; bookshelves stocked with reading material give the rooms a cozy feel, while personal faxes and computer printers appeal to the most harried businessperson. Its location on Michigan Avenue is a plus for shoppers. *676 N. Michigan Ave., Near North, 60611, 312/944–6664 or 800/843–6664, fax 312/266–3015. 347 suites. Restaurant, bar, in-room data ports, in-room safes, minibars, no-smoking floors, room service, indoor lap pool, hot tub, sauna, exercise room, dry cleaning, laundry service, concierge, business services, meeting rooms, parking (fee). AE, D, DC, MC, V.*

6 *f-2*

PALMER HOUSE HILTON

This distinguished landmark hotel is a tribute to Chicago's heyday. Now a link in the Hilton chain, the Palmer House has ornate and elegant public areas that include the opulent lobby with its elaborate ceiling murals. Rooms are less spectacular, with antique reproduction furniture. *17 E. Monroe St., Loop, 60603, 312/726–7500 or 800/445–8667, fax 312/263–2556. 1,551 rooms, 88 suites. 3 restaurants, bar, coffee shop, in-room data ports, minibars, no-smoking floor, room service, indoor pool, barbershop, hot tub, massage, sauna, steam room, exercise room, dry cleaning, laundry service, concierge, concierge floor, business services, meeting rooms, parking (fee). AE, D, DC, MC, V.*

5 *g-7*

PARK HYATT

If its key location in the heart of the Magnificent Mile doesn't draw you here, the superior service and luxurious accommodations will. Many rooms have window-seat views of Lake Michigan or the Chicago skyline. Amenities in the neutral-colored guest rooms include custom-designed furnishings, two-line phones, flat-screen televisions, and DVD and CD players. Two-person soaking tubs have sliding cherrywood doors that open into the bedroom. *800 N. Michigan Ave., Near North, 60611, 312/335–1234, fax 312/239–4000. 195 rooms, 8 suites. Restaurant, bar, in-room data ports, in-room safes, minibars, no-smoking rooms, room service, indoor pool, spa, health club, dry cleaning, laundry service, concierge, business services, meeting rooms, parking (fee). AE, D, DC, MC, V.*

5 *g-7*

REGAL KNICKERBOCKER HOTEL

This 1927 hotel is now up to speed with its Michigan Avenue competition. Rose moiré wallpaper lines the hallways, and exuberant floral bedspreads combined with gold- and cream-striped pillows create a rich European look. In keeping with its vintage heritage, bathrooms tend to be tiny, but closets are spacious. In the lobby there's a lounge serving 44 varieties of martinis. *163 E. Walton Pl., Near North, 60611, 312/751–8100 or 800/ 621–8140, fax 312/751–9205. 280 rooms, 25 suites. Restaurant, bar, coffee shop, lobby lounge, outdoor café, in-room data ports, minibars, no-smoking floor, room service, exercise room, dry cleaning, laundry service, concierge, concierge floor, business services, meeting rooms, parking (fee). AE, D, DC, MC, V.*

6 *f-1*

RENAISSANCE CHICAGO HOTEL

Behind the modern stone-and-glass exterior on the south bank of the Chicago River is a tidy '90s interpretation of early 20th-century splendor. Lavish floral carpets, tapestry upholstery, crystal-beaded chandeliers, and French Provincial furniture create rich-looking public areas. Rooms have sitting areas and rounded windows with spectacular river views. *1 W. Wacker Dr., Loop, 60601, 312/372–7200 or 800/468–3571, fax 312/372–0093. 513 rooms, 40 suites. 2 restaurants, café, lobby lounge, in-room data ports, minibars, no-smoking floor, room service, indoor pool, beauty salon, hot tub, sauna, exercise room, dry cleaning, laundry service, concierge, concierge floor, business services, meeting rooms, parking (fee). AE, D, DC, MC, V.*

5 *g-7*

RITZ-CARLTON

Owned by Four Seasons, the luxurious Ritz-Carlton has a shopper's dream location atop Water Tower Place. Rooms are wonderfully spacious and have 9-ft ceilings. Magnificent flower arrangements adorn the public areas. A wonderful afternoon tea is served. *160 E. Pearson St., Near North, 60611, 312/266– 1000 or 800/691–6906, fax 312/266– 1194. 344 rooms, 91 suites. 3 restaurants, bar, lobby lounge, in-room data ports, in-room safes, minibars, no-smoking floor, room service, indoor lap pool, spa, health* club, dry cleaning, laundry service, concierge, business services, meeting rooms, parking (fee), kennel. AE, D, DC, MC, V.

5 h-8

SHERATON CHICAGO HOTEL AND TOWERS

The Sheraton's guest rooms are large and nicely decorated, and its lighthouse-like location on the river guarantees unobstructed views. Weekend rates drop dramatically in winter to lure leisure travelers. Although the hotel is vast, with the largest ballroom in the Midwest, you won't feel in danger of getting lost. *301 E. North Water St., Near North, 60611, 312/464–1000 or 800/233–4100, fax 312/464–9140. 1,152 rooms, 52 suites. 3 restaurants, lobby lounge, snack bar, sports bar, in-room data ports, minibars, no-smoking rooms, room service, indoor lap pool, massage, sauna, exercise room, dry cleaning, laundry service, concierge, concierge floor, business services,*

GREAT HOTELS FOR CELEBRITY SPOTTING

The Drake
The grande dame of Chicago hotels has a guest list that once included Tony Bennett and Diana, Princess of Wales.

Four Seasons and Ritz-Carlton
These sister hotels are among the most plush and pampering in Chicago, a definite draw for the rich and famous.

Omni Ambassador East
The legendary Pump Room bar has long attracted celebrities from across the globe. Frank Sinatra was rumored to have a permanent seat at the bar.

Omni Chicago Hotel
If it's good enough for Oprah Winfrey's guests, it's sure to attract other celebrities as well.

Palmer House Hilton
Long known as one of Chicago's premier luxury hotels, old-school rich and famous still park themselves here for a taste of the good life.

Sheraton Chicago Hotel and Towers
Its location slightly off the beaten path makes this hotel perfect for celebrities who seek elegance and solitude. President Clinton was stationed here during one of his Chicago visits.

---

meeting rooms, parking (fee). AE, D, DC, MC, V.

5 g-6

SUTTON PLACE

Staying at the former Le Meridien is an unadulterated treat. An exceptionally friendly staff is at your beck and call, and the guest rooms meld modernism and tradition. Its location one block off of Michigan Avenue between the Rush Street nightlife district and the exclusive Oak Street shopping area is ideal. The luxurious bathrooms have a separate shower stall, soaking tub, terry-cloth robes, and hair dryers. *21 E. Bellevue Pl., Near North, 60611, 312/266–2100 or 800/606–8188, fax 312/266–2141. 206 rooms, 40 suites. Restaurant, bar, outdoor café, in-room data ports, minibars, no-smoking floor, room service, exercise room, dry cleaning, laundry service, concierge, business services, meeting rooms, parking (fee). AE, D, DC, MC, V.*

6 g-1

SWISSÔTEL

Modern design and extensive business services make the Swissôtel a favorite for those on the go. Its triangular Harry Weese design ensures panoramic lake or river vistas. The comfortable, contemporary-style guest rooms have two-line phones and marble bathrooms. Even those who hate to sweat may be inspired by the stunning 42nd-floor fitness center, pool, and spa with its remarkable views. *323 E. Wacker Dr., Loop, 60601, 312/565–0565 or 888/737–9477, fax 312/565–0540. 596 rooms, 36 suites. Restaurant, 2 bars, café, patisserie, in-room data ports, minibars, no-smoking floor, room service, indoor pool, hot tub, massage, sauna, spa, steam room, golf privileges, exercise room, dry cleaning, laundry service, concierge, business services, meeting rooms, parking (fee). AE, D, DC, MC, V.*

5 g-7

TALBOTT

There's a special satisfaction in finding a small, comfortable hotel just off the Magnificent Mile where the clerk is reading Nietzsche. The hunt-club atmosphere in the lobby's twin parlors is unusually personal and genuine; maybe it's because the owner chooses the antiques himself. The hotel's new bar, Basil's at the Talbott, serves light fare and has seasonal outdoor seating. Discounts often make the prices a bargain for the neighborhood. *20 E. Delaware Pl., Near North, 60611, 312/944–4970 or 800/825–2688, fax 312/944–7241. 94 rooms, 55 suites. Restaurant, bar, in-room data ports, in-room safes, minibars, no-smoking floor, room service, dry cleaning, laundry service, meeting rooms, parking (fee). AE, D, DC, MC, V.*

5 *g-7*
TREMONT HOTEL
Just off Michigan Avenue, this hotel has traditional old-world elegance and personal service. The Tudor-style lobby immediately sets the mood. Rooms are fitted with traditional Williamsburg-style decor and Baker furniture, with carefully mixed-and-matched florals, plaids, and stripes. Standard rooms can be quite cramped, with the desk placed in the narrow entry, so ask about size. *100 E. Chestnut St., Near North, 60611, 312/751–1900 or 800/621–8133, fax 312/751–8650. 120 rooms, 9 suites. Restaurant, 2 bars, in-room data ports, minibars, no-smoking floor, room service, in-room VCRs, dry cleaning, laundry service, meeting rooms, parking (fee). AE, D, DC, MC, V.*

5 *g-7*
WESTIN MICHIGAN AVENUE
Enormous icicle chandeliers reveal its '60s origins: you expect Doris Day to bound down the staircase at any moment. The location is perfect for shopping, especially in winter, as the major malls are steps from the door. A new restaurant, the Grill on the Abbey, opened in place of the lobby restaurant in 2000. *909 N. Michigan Ave., Near North, 60611, 312/943–7200 or 800/228–3000, fax 312/943–9347. 728 rooms, 23 suites. Restaurant, bar, in-room data ports, minibars, no-smoking floor, room service, beauty salon, massage, sauna, exercise room, dry cleaning, laundry service, concierge, business services, meeting rooms, parking (fee). AE, D, DC, MC, V.*

6 *f-1*
WESTIN RIVER NORTH
Rooms have stunning views of the Chicago River and nice extras such as a coffeemaker and Starbucks coffee. Skyline Rooms are geared to business travelers. If you forget your workout gear, the well-equipped fitness center will lend some to you. It's convenient to the Loop, the Merchandise Mart, and the House of Blues. *320 N. Dearborn St.,* *River North, 60610, 312/744–1900 or 800/937–8461, fax 312/527–2650. 400 rooms, 22 suites. Restaurant, lobby lounge, in-room data ports, minibars, no-smoking rooms, room service, massage, sauna, health club, dry cleaning, laundry service, concierge, business services, meeting rooms, parking (fee). AE, D, DC, MC, V.*

5 *g-7*
WHITEHALL HOTEL
A top-notch hotel since 1984, the Whitehall offers its guests peace and quiet as well as friendly, attentive service. Features such as video games, modem hookups, and voice mail bring modern touches to the intimate, old-world-style rooms. *105 E. Delaware Pl., Near North, 60611, 312/944–6300 or 800/948–4255, fax 312/944–8552. 213 rooms, 8 suites. Restaurant, bar, outdoor café, in-room data ports, in-room safes, minibars, no-smoking floor, room service, exercise room, dry cleaning, laundry service, concierge, concierge floor, meeting rooms, parking (fee). AE, D, DC, MC, V.*

EXPENSIVE LODGING

5 *f-6*
CLARIDGE HOTEL
On a tree-lined street in the Gold Coast, this vintage hotel is peaceful, quiet, and genteel. Standard rooms with one queen bed are on the small side; deluxe rooms are twice the size and contain either a king or two queen beds, a sitting area, and a coffeemaker. In-room amenities aren't lavish, but there is a decent Continental breakfast and free morning limousine service within a 2-mi radius. *1244 N. Dearborn Pkwy., Near North, 60610, 312/787–4980 or 800/245–1258, fax 312/266–0978. 161 rooms, 2 suites. Restaurant, lobby lounge, in-room data ports, minibars, no-smoking floor, room service, dry cleaning, laundry service, meeting rooms, parking (fee). AE, D, DC, MC, V.*

5 *g-8*
COURTYARD BY MARRIOTT
Business travelers get exactly what they want here: soothing, large rooms with desks; well-lighted work areas; and voice mail on every phone. It is just a few blocks north of the Chicago River, making it convenient to the Loop. Shaw's Crab House and Vong are good nearby

dining options, and the House of Blues is only a short walk away. *30 E. Hubbard St., Near North, 60611, 312/329–2500 or 800/321–2211, fax 312/329–0293. 302 rooms, 32 suites. Restaurant, bar, in-room data ports, no-smoking floor, room service, indoor lap pool, hot tub, exercise room, coin laundry, dry cleaning, laundry service, concierge, meeting rooms, parking (fee). AE, D, DC, MC, V.*

7 *e-3*

GOLD COAST GUEST HOUSE

This 1873 brick townhouse turned bed-and-breakfast in the middle of the Gold Coast is cozy and comfortable. Four guest rooms with private baths are decorated with both antiques and contemporary decor. The small living room has an 18-ft glass window that looks out onto a lush private garden. Room amenities include air-conditioning, ceiling fans, Egyptian cotton towels, and hospitality baskets with assorted toiletries. *113 W. Elm St., Gold Coast, 60610, 312/337–0361, fax 312/337–0362. 4 rooms. Breakfast room, no-smoking rooms, in-room VCRs, parking (fee). AE, D, MC, V.*

6 *g-3*

HILTON CHICAGO

Wonderfully situated across from Grant Park and near Chicago's great museums, this hotel has unmatched views of Lake Michigan. Each floor has its own lounge, and some suites have wood-burning fireplaces. The 28,000-square-ft health club includes an indoor track and swimming pool. It can be isolated at night. *720 S. Michigan Ave., Loop, 60605, 312/922–4400 or 800/445–8667, fax 312/ 922–5240. 1,476 rooms, 67 suites. 2 restaurants, 2 bars, deli, pub, in-room modem data ports, minibars, no-smoking floors, room service, indoor pool, beauty salon, hot tub, massage, sauna, health club, dry cleaning, laundry service, concierge, concierge floor, business services, meeting rooms, helipad, parking (fee). AE, D, DC, MC, V.*

6 *f-1*

HOTEL ALLEGRO

The Art Deco former Bismarck Hotel has been transformed into a haven for the hip. There are vibrant splashes of color throughout, and window treatments resemble the entrance to a sheik's tent. Rooms have irons and ironing boards and faxes. There's a wine

reception with live music Tuesday through Saturday in the lobby. The beautiful Palace Theatre is next door. *171 W. Randolph St., Loop, 60601, 312/236–0123 or 800/643–1500, fax 312/236–0197. 451 rooms, 32 suites. 2 restaurants, bar, in-room data ports, minibars, no-smoking floor, room service, massage, exercise room, shop, dry cleaning, laundry service, concierge, business services, meeting rooms, parking (fee). AE, D, DC, MC, V.*

5 *g-7*

RAPHAEL CHICAGO

Originally a dorm for nursing students, this charming hotel, just a block from Michigan Avenue, has comfortable, spacious rooms and pleasant, personal service. The rooms have a quirky style, with chaise longues, sitting areas, and arched entries. Obliging service, terry-cloth robes, and attractive weekend packages are among the features that draw a loyal following. *201 E. Delaware Pl., Near North, 60611, 312/943–5000 or 800/983–7870, fax 312/943–9483. 100 rooms, 72 suites. Restaurant, piano bar, in-room data ports, in-room safes, minibars, no-smoking floors, room service, library, dry cleaning, laundry service, meeting rooms, parking (fee). AE, D, DC, MC, V.*

5 *g-7*

SUMMERFIELD SUITES HOTEL

A small, intimate lobby paneled in cherrywood sets the tone for this traditional-looking all-suite hotel down the block from Neiman Marcus and other Michigan Avenue stores. Suites have microwaves, coffeemakers, refrigerators, VCRs, desks, and sofa beds. A rooftop pool keeps kids entertained in summer. The rate includes an extensive breakfast buffet. *166 E. Superior St., Near North, 60611, 312/787–6000 or 800/833–4353, fax 312/787–4331. 120 suites. Restaurant, bar, snack bar, in-room data ports, kitchenettes, no-smoking floor, in-room VCRs, pool, barbershop, exercise room, recreation room, coin laundry, dry cleaning, laundry service, meeting rooms, parking (fee). AE, D, DC, MC, V.*

6 *f-2*

W CHICAGO CITY CENTER

Built in 1929 as a private men's club in the heart of downtown Chicago, this hotel, slated to open by spring 2001, is perfect for business travelers and theatergoers. Rooms are hip, modern, and functional. For nearby entertainment, guests can head to the Art Institute or Lyric Opera. *172 W. Adams St., Loop, 60603, 312/332–1200 or 800/621–2360, fax 312/332–5909. 388 rooms, 2 suites. Restaurant, bar, café, in-room data ports, no-smoking floor, room service, spa, health club, dry cleaning, laundry service, concierge, business services, meeting rooms, parking (fee). AE, D, DC, MC, V.*

MODERATE LODGING

5 *e-3*

BELDEN-STRATFORD

A magnificent '20s facade draws guests to this relatively untrafficked area near Lincoln Park. The Belden-Stratford is primarily an upscale apartment building, but management keeps some attractively priced studios and suites for short-term stays. A complimentary bottle of wine awaits guests in the 9-ft-ceiling rooms, which all have some form of kitchenette. The elegant lobby houses two popular restaurants: Ambria and Mon Ami Gabi. *2300 N. Lincoln Park W, Lincoln Park, 60614, 773/281–2900 or 800/800–8301, fax 773/880–2039. 25 studios and suites. 2 restaurants, deli, kitchenettes, beauty salon, exercise room, coin laundry, dry cleaning, laundry service, business services, parking (fee). AE, D, DC, MC, V.*

5 *g-8*

BEST WESTERN INN OF CHICAGO

One block east of Michigan Avenue, this heavily trafficked 1927 hotel has bargain weekend rates for visitors who want to be near the Magnificent Mile. Rooms are basic and unremarkable but comfortable and clean. For a fee, guests can use the full health club across the street. *162 E. Ohio St., Near North, 60611, 312/787–3100 or 800/557–2378, fax 312/573–3136. 332 rooms, 25 suites. Restaurant, bar, no-smoking floor, room service, coin laundry, dry cleaning, laundry service, concierge, meeting rooms, parking (fee). AE, D, DC, MC, V.*

4 *d-8*

CITY SUITES

You might want to come here just for the famed cinnamon buns from nearby Ann Sather (*see* Chapter 1), or for the prime people-watching on nearby Clark Street. Two-thirds of this affordable hotel are suites, which have a separate sitting room, a pullout couch, and a refrigerator. The hotel is on a heavily trafficked street, so if noise is a concern, request a room on the east side of the building. *933 W. Belmont Ave., Lakeview, 60657, 773/404–3400 or 800/248–9108, fax 773/404–3405. 16 rooms, 29 suites. In-room data ports, refrigerators (some), room service, coin laundry, parking (fee). AE, D, DC, MC, V.*

5 *h-8*

DAYS INN LAKE SHORE DRIVE

This hotel has 33 stories right on Lake Michigan, and all of the smallish and basic rooms have views—half of them of Lake Michigan; the rest provide an expansive look at the city. Rooms are pleasant and sunny. Some nice extras, such as an outdoor pool on the seventh floor and Nintendo on the in-room TVs, make it popular with families, as does its proximity to the Children's Museum and the Ferris wheel at Navy Pier. *644 N. Lake Shore Dr., Near North, 60611, 312/943–9200 or 800/541–3223, fax 312/255–4411. 569 rooms, 9 suites. Restaurant, lounge, in-room data ports, in-room safes, no-smoking floors, room service, pool, exer-*

GREAT HOTELS FOR A DRINK

The Drake
With a jazz trio playing almost nightly in the Palm Court, there's no excuse for teetotaling.

The Fairmont
This great hotel bar serves 3-ft beer glasses that require a special stand on the table and practiced finesse to drink.

Palmer House Hilton
You can get myriad specialty drinks at the world famous Trader Vic's, a beach-theme bar nestled in the lower level.

Ritz-Carlton
For drinks of another sort, come for leisurely afternoon tea in the two-story greenhouse lobby.

Sutton Place
Sutton Hotel's Whiskey Bar, owned by Rande Gerber (Cindy Crawford's husband), is a hip, happening place to come for an after-work drink or a cocktail before heading out in the Gold Coast.

cise room, coin laundry, dry cleaning, laundry service, meeting rooms, parking (fee). AE, D, DC, MC, V.

⑤ g-7

HOLIDAY INN CHICAGO CITY CENTRE

This standout Holiday Inn draws rave reviews for its outdoor pool and health club down the hall at McClurg Court, and well-tended rooms. It's close to the lakefront and a beach, the Children's Museum at Navy Pier, and Michigan Avenue. 300 E. Ohio St., Near North, 60611, 312/787–6100 or 800/465–4329, fax 312/787–6259. 496 rooms, 4 suites. Restaurant, café, sports bar, in-room data ports, no-smoking floors, room service, outdoor pool, health club, coin laundry, dry cleaning, laundry service, concierge, meeting rooms, parking (fee). AE, D, DC, MC, V.

⑤ g-8

LENOX SUITES

The former Croyden caters to a business clientele. One block west of the Magnificent Mile, the all-suite hotel has executive studios with queen-size Murphy-style beds and one-bedroom suites, all with kitchen and wet bar and a sleeper sofa. Health-club facilities are nearby. Weekend rates are a good value. Juice and a muffin are delivered to your door every morning. 616 N. Rush St., Near North, 60611, 312/337–1000 or 800/445–3639, fax 312/337–7217. 324 suites. Restaurant, bar, coffee shop, in-room data ports, kitchenettes, minibars, no-smoking floors, room service, exercise room, coin laundry, dry cleaning, laundry service, concierge, business services, meeting rooms, parking (fee). AE, D, DC, MC, V.

④ e-7

THE MAJESTIC HOTEL

A welcoming fire burns in the library-style lobby, creating the atmosphere of an old English inn. Rooms are quaint and simple; suites have kitchenettes. The staff is helpful, and the reasonable price includes Continental breakfast featuring Ann Sather's (see Chapter 1) famous cinnamon buns. The Lakeview location puts you four blocks from Wrigley Field, close to the lakefront jogging path, restaurants, nightlife, and transportation downtown. 528 W. Brompton Ave., Lakeview, 60657, 773/404–3499 or 800/727–5108, fax 773/404–

3495. 31 rooms, 22 suites. In-room data ports, room service, coin laundry, meeting room, parking (fee). AE, D, DC, MC, V.

⑤ f-8

RIVER NORTH HOTEL

Look for this ice warehouse turned Best Western in the heart of the thriving River North entertainment district. The undistinguished exterior and outdated Deco-inspired lobby are more than offset by clean, large, and reasonably priced guest rooms with black-and-white tile bathrooms. Parking is free, a cost-saving rarity downtown. The sofa beds in the suites and the indoor pool make it a family favorite. 125 W. Ohio St., Near North, 60610, 312/467–0800 or 800/727–0800, fax 312/467–1665. 125 rooms, 25 suites. Bar, pizzeria, in-room modem lines, in-room safes, no-smoking floor, room service, indoor pool, sauna, exercise room, dry cleaning, meeting room, free parking. AE, D, DC, MC, V.

⑤ g-7

SENECA

Originally solely an apartment building, the Seneca is steadily increasing the number of rooms it rents out on a nightly basis. The majority are suites of varying sizes with either kitchenettes or full kitchens; even the smallest rooms have a refrigerator and a coffeemaker. The two restaurants and the popular deli in the building deliver. 200 E. Chestnut St., Near North, 60611, 312/787–8900 or 800/800–6261, fax 312/988–4438. 48 rooms, 82 suites. 2 restaurants, 2 bars, deli, in-room data ports, kitchenettes, no-smoking floors, refrigerators, beauty salon, exercise room, coin laundry, dry cleaning, laundry service, meeting rooms, parking (fee). AE, D, DC, MC, V.

BUDGET LODGING

⑤ g-7

CASS HOTEL

Built in 1927, the Cass is a favorite of bargain-conscious tourists and business travelers looking for cheap sleeps a short walk from Michigan Avenue shopping and River North nightlife. Rooms are clean, small, and functional; upgrades on furnishings, fixtures, and bathrooms were completed in 2000. Ask for one of the large rooms with two beds, all of which have a refrigerator and a wet bar. 640 N. Wabash Ave.,

Near North, 60611, 312/787–4030 or 800/227–7850, fax 312/787–8544. 150 rooms. Bar, coffee shop, in-room data ports, minibars (some), refrigerators (some), coin laundry, parking (fee). AE, D, DC, MC, V.

5 *e-1*
COMFORT INN LINCOLN PARK
This reasonably priced hotel, with half-timber Tudor exterior, is in a busy area of Lincoln Park and near plenty of nightlife; it's close to the lake and convenient to Wrigley Field. Unusual architectural features, such as wood trim in the shape of wagon wheels, add a quirky note to an otherwise clean, no-frills lodging. The three suites have hot tubs, and two have saunas. 601 W. Diversey Pkwy., Lincoln Park, 773/348–2810 or 800/228–5150, fax 773/348–1912. 71 rooms, 3 suites. In-room data ports, no-smoking rooms, meeting room, parking (fee). AE, D, DC, MC, V.

5 *e-1*
DAYS INN LINCOLN PARK
This well-kept-up Days Inn is a real find. A complimentary breakfast is served off the lobby in a pleasant room with a pressed-tin ceiling and brass chandeliers. Cheery floral bedspreads and light furniture brighten up the basic rooms, although bathrooms are on the small side. For about $15 extra a night, you can upgrade to a business suite. 644 W. Diversey Pkwy., Lincoln Park, 60614, 773/525–7010 or 800/576–3297, fax 773/525–6998. 126 rooms, 4 suites. Restaurant, bar, in-room safes, no-smoking rooms, coin laundry, meeting rooms, parking (fee). AE, D, DC, MC, V.

5 *f-7*
HOJO INN
On a main boulevard in downtown Chicago, this classic L-shape, two-story motor lodge stands as a campy vestige of the early 1970s. The rooms are well maintained, the staff is pleasant, parking is free, and the location is a short walk from such tourist favorites as the Rainforest Café and Sammy Sosa's Restaurant. 720 N. LaSalle St., Near North, 60610, 312/664–8100 or 800/446–4656, fax 312/664–2356. 7 rooms, 4 suites. Coffee shop, no-smoking rooms, free parking. AE, D, DC, MC, V.

5 *e-1*
THE WILLOWS
The formal French lobby of this boutique hotel opens onto a tree-lined street. The rooms are decorated with pleasant floral prints and Impressionist posters. The hotel, built in the 1920s, is in a lively neighborhood that's three blocks from the lake and a 10-minute walk to the Lincoln Park Zoo. Like the Majestic Hotel and City Suites Hotel, the Willows wins kudos for serving Ann Sather's (see Chapter 1) cinnamon buns as part of its complimentary Continental breakfast. 555 W. Surf St., Lakeview, 60657, 773/528–8400 or 800/787–3108, fax 773/528–8483. 51 rooms, 4 suites. In-room data ports, coin laundry, parking (fee). AE, D, DC, MC, V.

HOSTELS

2 *f-2*
CHICAGO INTERNATIONAL HOSTEL
European students flock to this well-maintained dormitory-style hostel. Linens are provided and a kitchen is available. One drawback—there's a curfew of midnight or 2 AM, depending on the day. The hostel is closed from 10 AM to 4 PM for cleaning. It's close to the Loyola stop on the Howard Street El line, making it easy to zip downtown. 6318 N. Winthrop Ave., near Loyola University, 60660, 773/262–1011, fax 773/262–3673. 85 dorm beds; 6 private rooms, 2 with bath. Coin laundry, free parking. No credit cards. Budget.

6 *g-3*
HOSTELLING INTERNATIONAL–CHICAGO
The historic loft building has dormitory-style rooms and some private rooms available. A dining hall with a self-service kitchen, a coffee shop, and a Mexican restaurant are on site, as well as a student center, a travel center, and a communication center with Internet kiosks and pay phones. A library room and multi-purpose room serve as meeting space for groups of 12 to 45 people. There is 24-hr access and security. 24 E. Congress Pkwy., South Loop, 60605, 312/360–0300, fax 312/360–0313. 500 dorm beds mid June–mid Sept., 250 dorm beds mid Sept.–mid June, 2–5 private rooms. Restaurant, dining room, exercise room, recreation room, coin laundry. MC, V. Budget.

HOTELS NEAR THE AIRPORTS

2 *a-2*

HOTEL SOFITEL

The murals in the lobby, fancy restaurant and brasserie serving French food, and upscale gift shop make for truly Continental accommodations. Large, comfortable rooms create a luxurious lodging experience, despite the hotel's proximity to the airport. Guests receive a rose and a bottle of Evian at turndown. *5550 N. River Rd., Rosemont 60018, 847/678–4488 or 800/233–5959, fax 847/678–4244. 288 rooms, 12 suites. 2 restaurants, bar, patisserie, in-room data ports, minibars, no-smoking floors, room service, indoor pool, massage, sauna, exercise room, dry cleaning, laundry service, concierge, business services, meeting rooms, airport shuttle, parking (fee). AE, D, DC, MC, V. Very Expensive.*

2 *a-2*

HYATT REGENCY O'HARE

This glittering Hyatt has an eight-story-high atrium with glass-enclosed elevators. Rooms, some with terraces, are elegantly appointed and are sound-proofed. Connected to the Rosemont Convention Center by a skyway, this Hyatt is geared toward the business traveler. *9300 W. Bryn Mawr Ave., Rosemont 60018, 847/696–1234 or 800/233–1234, fax 847/698–0139. 1,057 rooms, 42 suites. 4 restaurants, deli, sports bar, in-room data ports, in-room fax, no-smoking rooms, room service, indoor pool, massage, sauna, exercise room, shops, dry cleaning, laundry service, concierge, concierge floor, business services, meeting rooms, airport shuttle, parking (fee). AE, D, DC, MC, V. Very Expensive.*

2 *a-2*

O'HARE HILTON

The only hotel actually at the airport, the Hilton is connected to the terminals and is within easy access of public transportation to the city. Several Sleep Tight rooms have all manner of relaxation aids, from CD players to sound machines. Hilton Health-fit rooms—with exercise bikes, treadmills, and exercise tapes—and Stress-less rooms—with music machines, special dim lighting, and soundproofing—are also very popular. Day rates are available for travelers with short stopovers. *Box 66414, O'Hare International Airport,* 60666, 773/686–8000 or 800/445–8667, fax 773/601–1728. 822 rooms, 36 suites. Restaurant, sports bar, in-room data ports, minibars, no-smoking floor, room service, indoor lap pool, hot tub, massage, sauna, steam room, health club, dry cleaning, laundry service, concierge, business services, meeting rooms, airport shuttle, parking (fee). AE, D, DC, MC, V. Expensive.*

2 *8-2*

ROSEMONT SUITES

The guest rooms and public spaces of this handsome all-suite hotel directly across the street from the Rosemont Convention Center are decorated in the unmistakable style of Frank Lloyd Wright. A full breakfast and evening cocktails are complimentary. *5500 N. River Rd., Rosemont 60018, 847/678–4000 or 888/476–7366, fax 847/928–7659. 296 suites. Restaurant, bar, breakfast room, in-room data ports, kitchenettes, minibars, no-smoking floor, room service, indoor pool, hot tub, sauna, exercise room, video games, coin laundry, dry cleaning, laundry service, concierge, business services, meeting rooms, airport shuttle, free parking. AE, D, DC, MC, V. Very Expensive.*

2 *a-2*

TRAVELODGE O'HARE

The rooms in this two-story cinderblock motel are basic, but they're regularly redecorated, tidy, and incomparably cheap. *3003 Mannheim Rd., Des Plaines 60018, 847/296–5541 or 800/578–7878, fax 847/803–1984. 95 rooms. In-room data ports, no-smoking rooms, pool, dry cleaning, laundry service, meeting room, free parking. AE, D, DC, MC, V. Budget.*

B&B RESERVATION SERVICES

BED & BREAKFAST CHICAGO

This helpful service will set you up with a homey alternative to the traditional hotel stay. It has more than 70 options, from a guest room in a Victorian home to a furnished high-rise apartment. Accommodations are mostly in the Near North and Lincoln Park neighborhoods. Some are in Hyde Park, a good option for visitors who wish to stay close to the University of Chicago. *Box 14088, Chicago 60614, 773/248–0005 or 800/375–7084, fax 773/248–7090.*

chapter 7

CITY SOURCES

getting a handle on the city

basics of city life

Whether you're just visiting Chicago or making the Windy City your home, you need the essential information that makes our city tick. We've compiled an array of resources to get you there and back, with time to spare.

BANKS

Most banks are open from 9 AM until 6 PM during the business week. Some are open until 1 or 2 PM on Saturday. The main banks in Chicago, with a phone number to ask about branch locations, are as follows: **LaSalle Bank** (800/217–0963); **Harris Bank** (800/LION–101); **St. Paul Federal Bank** (773/622–5000); **Citibank** (312/263–6660); **TCF Bank** (847/ 678–6900); and **Bank One** (888/ 963–4000). Also, many Jewel supermarkets have bank offices inside (mostly St. Paul and TCF branches) with extended hours.

DRIVING

Thanks to the extensive network of mass transit services, a car is not a necessity in Chicago. Gas taxes, parking rates, and insurance premiums—plus the expense of wasting time in traffic snarls—can make auto ownership a pricey proposition.

ESSENTIAL NUMBERS

Chicago Botanic Garden (847/ 835–5440).

Chicago Cultural Center (312/346–3278).

Chicago Park District (312/747–2200).

Chicago Public Library (312/747–4300).

City Festivals/Special Events (312/ 744–3370).

CTA Customer Service (888/968–7282).

Highway Information (312/368–4636).

Moviefone (312/444–FILM).

Non-emergency Concerns (311).

Sports (312/976–1313).

Weather (312/976–1212).

If you do have a car, be aware that the speed limit is 55 mph on city expressways (especially enforced on holiday weekends), 45 mph on Lake Shore Drive (except in winter, when 35 mph is enforced).

Also watch out for accident-prone intersections, especially the notorious "six-corner" monstrosities involving diagonal streets. Hairpin turns can be frightening, so follow your traffic light, ignore the others, and watch for speed to pick up as the light turns red. On the north side, avoid Clark at Devon; Damen at Elston and Fullerton; and Broadway at Sheridan and Devon. On the south side, avoid 87th at Cottage Grove, and Stony Island at South Chicago and 75th. The O'Hare Airport area danger spot is at Higgins and Busse in Elk Grove Village. Around Midway, Cicero Avenue and the Stevenson Expressway can be messy.

Downtown, watch for preoccupied pedestrians and low-flying bike messengers.

Except when noted by signs, right turns at red traffic lights and right turns onto one-way streets are permitted. In fact, the driver behind you will insist.

licenses and state registration

Driver's licenses and license plates or renewal stickers are available from the Illinois Department of Motor Vehicles. New residents have 30 days after establishing a local residence to register a car for a license. At least three IDs including a photo, signature, and current address are required for initial registration and license. Annual license fee for passenger cars is $78. For a plate, proof of purchase and title is required. Title fee is $65. Renewal stickers may be purchased by mail, phone, or at local currency exchanges. All Illinois motor vehicles must be covered by liability insurance.

DEPARTMENT OF MOTOR VEHICLES

There are several DMV locations in the city: **Downtown** (100 W. Randolph St.); **North** (5401 N. Elston Ave.); **South** (9901 S. Dr. Martin Luther King Dr.); and **West** (5301 W. Lexington St.). All can be reached at the same phone number (312/793–1010).

city stickers

Besides a state driver's registration and license, city residents must purchase a sticker for their car by July 1 each year. Stickers are sold at the City Clerk's Office in City Hall or a Department of Revenue Substation: **Downtown** (401 W. Superior St.); **North** (2550 W. Addison St.); **West** (800 N. Kedzie Ave.); and **South** (2006 E. 95th St.); or at currency exchanges for $60. After July 15, the price goes up $30, and you will receive a ticket for not having the sticker on your car. For information, call 312/744–6861.

traffic

Why is it called "rush hour" when nobody's moving? That's something to ponder while stuck in traffic during traditional workday drive times: 6 to 10 AM and 3 to 7 PM. Streets are fairly clogged on Saturday afternoons and evenings as well. One-way streets have less traffic but more stop lights and stop signs. Any rain or snow can double travel times. And it's never a good idea to be driving anywhere near a sports venue after a game—especially if the home team lost, which could very well be the case in Chicago—or downtown during festivals, which are scheduled nearly every summer weekend.

Use Lower Wacker and Lower Michigan to avoid Loop congestion. Lower Wacker runs under Wacker Drive from Lake Shore Drive (east) to the Chicago River (north and west) and Eisenhower Expressway (south). This is the quickest westbound route from Columbus Drive in the Streeterville neighborhood to the Eisenhower Expressway in the Loop's southwest corner. Lower Michigan goes north from Lower Wacker under the Wrigley Building to Grand Avenue.

Generally speaking, Lake Shore Drive is the best north and south exit-entrance route for downtown, and Chicago Avenue is good for travel west. The diagonals to and from downtown—Ogden Avenue southwest and Milwaukee Avenue northwest—often work pretty well. Farther west of downtown, Ashland Avenue can provide a relatively swift north-south ride. Heading south to Indiana, many drivers exit the Dan Ryan Expressway for the Chicago Skyway Toll Bridge.

GAS STATIONS

Gas stations are plentiful in most areas of the city. The most prevalent brands are BP, Mobil, Shell, Citgo, and Marathon-Ashland. However, there's only one station in the Loop: at Congress and Dearborn. Stations close to the Loop are at Jackson and Morgan near Greektown, Roosevelt and Clinton near Soldier Field, and Ontario and LaSalle in River North.

GEOGRAPHY

Chicago addresses are easy to find. The city is laid out in a grid pattern, with streets running either north–south or east–west and radiating from a center point at State and Madison streets in the Loop. East and west street numbers ascend as you move away from State; north and south street numbers ascend as you move away from Madison. Each

NAMES AND NUMBERS

When speaking of highways, Chicagoans usually refer to names rather than numbers.

Bishop Ford Freeway
Interstate 94 south of Dan Ryan to Illinois route 394

Borman Expressway
I–80/I–94

Chicago Skyway
I–90 south of Dan Ryan into Indiana

Dan Ryan Expressway
I–90/I–94 from I–290 south

East–West Tollway
I–88

Edens Expressway
I–94 north of the Montrose Avenue split from the Kennedy

Eisenhower Expressway
I–290

Kennedy Expressway
I–90/I–94 to the junction and I–90 until it becomes the Northwest Tollway

Lake Shore Drive
U.S. 41

North–South Tollway
I–355

State Highway Information
312/368–4636

block is represented by a hundred number: eight blocks is about one mile. If you ever lose your sense of direction, remember that Lake Michigan is always east.

Chicago by law is divided into 50 wards, each comprising about 1/50th of the city's total population: about 2½ million people. Within the wards are about 3,000 voting precincts. Less formal divisions (though recognized on many official city maps) are called communities—77 areas mostly consisting of former suburbs and bits of unincorporated Cook County that the city annexed, a process that ended in the 1950s with the addition of O'Hare. Community borders are defined by streets, railroad lines, and branches of the Chicago River.

NEIGHBORHOODS

When Chicagoans talk about where they live, they talk about neighborhoods. Their neighborhood might also be one of the 77 mapped communities that are too well named to be anything else, such as **South Shore** around South Shore and 75th, or centered on a beautiful urban oasis, like **Jackson Park** around 63rd and Stony Island. But more likely, they live in a neighborhood with no strict borders.

Landmarks sometimes serve as popular labelers, such as Wrigley Park for **Wrigleyville** around Clark and Addison. Local commercial interests weigh in with the **Magnificent Mile** along North Michigan Avenue from Oak Street to the river. But defining a neighborhood can be tricky. **Little Italy** on the near west side is associated with Taylor Street. It's also a quality of food that restaurants elsewhere claim ("We serve Taylor Street pizza"). On the far north side, the neighborhood name of **West Rogers Park**, for the area around Ridge and Devon, seems to be overtaking the community name of **West Ridge**, an ethnic kaleidoscope best known for its Indian restaurants at Devon and Western. Some neighborhoods are too new for any map, such as **Central Station** just west of Soldier Field—the city's hottest new residential construction area—or seemingly too old, such as **Pullman**, at 111th Street and Cottage Grove on the far south side, the historic area where luxury train cars were built.

Considering all this confusion, it might be best simply to ask people what neighborhood they live in and let them explain it. You can also look for banners hanging from light posts or brown "honorary" street-name signs at intersections.

MEET THE NEIGHBORS

There are many ways for new residents to get to know their neighbors. Neighborhood museums provide interesting insights; park district programs are great for families; tours are informative; and even the Welcome Wagon serves Chicago.

Chicago Neighborhood Tours *(312/742–1190).*

Chicago Park District *(312/747–7187).*

Historic Pullman Visitor Center *(11141 S. Cottage Grove Ave., 773/785–8181).*

Hyde Park Historical Society *(5529 S. Lake Park Ave., 773/493–1893).*

Noble-Seymour-Crippen House *(5624 N. Newark Ave., Jefferson Park area, 773/631–4633).*

Ridge Historical Society *(10621 S. Seeley Ave., Beverly, 773/881–1675).*

Rogers Park/West Ridge Historic Museum *(6424 N. Western Ave., 773/764–4078).*

Welcome Wagon *(888/277–9295).*

HOLIDAYS

City offices are closed on the following holidays: New Year's Day; Martin Luther King Jr. Day, 3rd Monday in January; Lincoln's Birthday, February 12; Washington's Birthday, February 22; Pulaski Day, March 1; Memorial Day, last Monday in May; Independence Day, July 4th; Labor Day, 1st Monday in September; Veterans Day, November 11; Thanksgiving Day, 4th Thursday in November; Christmas Day.

LIQUOR LAWS

The drinking age in Illinois is 21. There are many different liquor licenses in the city, offering a range of restrictions and requirements; bars and restaurants vary as to the times liquor can be sold depending on their license. As a rule of

Chicago Neighborhoods

SAUGANASH

WEST ROGERS PARK

ROGERS PARK

Loyola U

NORTH PARK

EDGEWATER

Bryn Mawr Ave.

Western Ave.

Ravenswood Ave.

LINCOLN SQUARE

Foster Ave.

N. Branch Chicago R.

North Shore Channel

ALBANY PARK

Argyle St.

RAVENSWOOD

Elston Ave.

Montrose Ave.

Clark St.

UPTOWN

IRVING PARK

90

94

NORTH CENTER

Irving Park Rd.

Addison St.

AVONDALE

ROSCOE VILLAGE

Wrigley Field

LAKEVIEW

Diversey Ave.

Diversey Ave.

N. Branch Chicago R.

LOGAN SQUARE

DEPAUL

LINCOLN PARK

Lincoln Park Zoo

BUCK-TOWN

Halsted St.

HERMOSA

Bloomingdale Ave.

Lake Michigan

HUMBOLDT PARK

WEST TOWN

WICKER PARK

North Ave.

90

94

Leavitt St.

Ashland Ave.

NEAR NORTH

Water Tower

Chicago Ave.

Grand Ave.

UKRAINIAN VILLAGE

Kinzie St.

Navy Pier

Kinzie St.

Kinzie St.

WEST GARFIELD PARK

GARFIELD PARK

United Center

NEAR WEST SIDE

LOOP

Eisenhower Expwy.

290

TRI-TAYLOR

Ogden Ave.

Dan Ryan Expwy.

Roosevelt Rd.

Shedd Aquarium

Field Museum

LAWNDALE

UNIVERSITY VILLAGE

NEAR SOUTH SIDE

Soldier Field

Meigs Field

Cermak Rd.

Western Ave.

PILSEN

CHINA-TOWN

McCormick Place

LITTLE VILLAGE

S. Branch Chicago R.

55

BRIDGE-PORT

90

94

41

Chicago Sanitary and Ship Canal

55

McKINLEY PARK

Comiskey Park

DOUGLAS

ARCHER HEIGHTS

BRIGHTON PARK

Pershing Rd.

Pershing Rd.

OAKLAND

Central Park Ave.

Western Ave.

Stewart Ave.

43rd St.

GRAND BLVD.

KENWOOD

BACK OF THE YARDS

CANARY-VILLE

Cottage Grove Ave.

51st St.

Hyde Park Ave.

WEST ELSDON

GAGE PARK

Garfield St.

WASHINGTON PARK

HYDE PARK

Museum of Science and Industry

WEST LAWN

MARQUETTE PARK

WEST ENGLEWOOD

ENGLEWOOD

6th St.

Stony Island Ave.

WOODLAWN

67th St.

Pulaski Rd.

Leavitt St.

Aberdeen St.

90

South Chicago Ave.

SOUTH SHORE

ASHBURN

75th St.

GRESHAM

94

GRAND CROSSING

0   1 mile
0   1 km

N

275

thumb, most bars stop selling alcohol at around 2 AM; late-night bars stay open as late as 5 AM. Liquor stores customarily sell all types of alcohol, and restaurants serve what their particular license will allow.

NO SMOKING

Most offices and public areas are no-smoking or have no-smoking sections. Most restaurants set aside no-smoking tables; taverns generally don't.

PARKING

rules and enforcement

Parking is allowed on most Chicago streets, but there are many restrictions, particularly at night. Many neighborhoods enforce resident-only on-street parking with stickers identifying which cars belong to residents. Permit parking for a one-year period ending June 30 costs $25. Permits are available from the **Office of the City Clerk's Permit Sales Unit** (121 N. LaSalle St., Room 107, 312/744–5346). One-day guest passes may also be purchased in packs of 15 for $3.

Be sure to read all parking-restrictions signs carefully; your car may be ticketed and/or towed if illegally parked. The dreaded "Denver boot" is clamped onto wheels of illegally parked vehicles when the owner is found to hold five or more unpaid tickets. Retrieval requires payment of the outstanding tickets, a $60 boot fee, a $105 tow fee, plus a daily storage fee of $10.

Meters require a variety of amounts for a variety of times. Some meters in River North, Streeterville, the Gold Coast, and the Magnificent Mile need to be fed even at night. Specifics are posted on each meter.

There are no free spots in the Loop. Where there's no meter, there's no parking. Outside the Loop, side streets in commercial areas might be worth a scan if you're feeling lucky. But read all posted signs.

Beware of tow trucks: Never park in a residential or commercial lot, no matter how tempting. Towing is automatic along roads with red-and-white signs restricting parking between 3 and 7 AM from December 1 through April 1. And

signs posted along major streets warn of tows if more than two inches of snow accumulate on the pavement.

If your car was parked on a street or alley, it's been towed by the city, and will be at the nearest regional pound: **Central Auto Pound** (300 E. Randolph St., lower street level); **O'Hare** (5600 N. Mannheim Rd., next to Remote Lot F); **Pound #2** (10300 S. Doty Ave.); or **Pound #6** (701 N. Sacramento Ave.). To find out where your street-parked car was hauled, call 312/747–5513 or 312/747–8852 after 3 PM. And bring a wad of money (or major credit card).

If your car was parked in a lot not owned by the city, call the number posted on the sign you didn't see (or believe). Major private tow companies are **Lincoln Towing** (4882 N. Clark St., 773/561–4433; 4601 W. Armitage Ave., 773/237–0006); **Rendered Services** (3601 S. Iron St., 773/927–8888), and **Phillips Towing** (1168 N. Halsted St., 312/337–8330).

parking lots

Parking on the street is nearly impossible downtown and in popular neighborhoods like Lincoln Park and Rogers Park. Parking lots and garages, however, can be found within two blocks of just about any destination. Surface lots are a few dollars cheaper than self-park garages, which often charge $15 to $25 for over six-hour stays. (And take note whether the $1.50 to $2 city tax is included in a posted price.) Lower rates are offered early in the morning (before 8) or after work. City of Chicago offers the best deals at its 28 metered lots scattered throughout the city and its underground garage in Grant Park (312/294–4593). Major commercial lot operators are **System Parking** (312/819–5050), **InterParking** (773/436–7275), **CPS/Allright Parking** (312/578–1660), and **Standard Parking** (312/274–2000). Inquire about validated parking discounts at your destination.

PERSONAL SECURITY

Generally, Chicago is a safe city. But always use common sense. If a neighborhood strikes you as dangerous, it probably is. Wherever there are lights and people, there tends to be less crime. Stay away from undeveloped areas. Lock your car doors when you park and don't leave anything enticing visible through the windows. Pickpockets are a scourge on the Magnificent Mile and in the Loop. Other opportunists are likely to be on the prowl anywhere there are hiding places nearby, so it's not a good idea to walk casually around the city late at night.

PUBLIC TRANSPORTATION

Most of the city and the nearby suburbs are within blocks of a bus stop, subway station, or commuter train station. Public transit is provided by three main carriers: the **CTA** (Chicago Transit Authority) operates buses and elevated/subway trains in Chicago and 38 nearby suburbs; **Pace** runs buses in the suburbs throughout the region and connects with the CTA; and **Metra** (Metropolitan Rail) runs commuter trains between Chicago and surrounding suburban towns.

Rides on CTA buses and trains cost $1.50. You can either pay in exact change (coins only at the turnstile for trains; coins and bills at buses' fare boxes) or get a transit card that pays for both forms of transportation. Transit cards can be purchased at most stations, as well as at currency exchanges and grocery stores all over town. For every $10 you purchase on your card, an extra $1 in value is added, making the transit cards a must for regular riders. Add as much as you like to the card at an automated station and use the card until the money is used up. For 30¢ more you can transfer twice within two hours. Fares are automatically deducted at the turnstiles. Connections between all rail routes are free. Children under six ride free with adults.

Downtown weekday-morning and late-afternoon Rush Shuttle buses (clearly marked) are $1 cash. An Express surcharge of 25¢ is charged on downtown bus routes 2, 6, 14, and 147.

Door-to-door minibus service is available to qualified disabled riders. For information, call **CTA Paratransit** (312/432–7025 or TTY 312/432–7116).

Red Line trains and Blue Line (O'Hare/Forest Park) trains run all night; Orange Line (Midway) trains run till about 11:15 PM. Figure on 20-minute intervals between trains, except during peak weekday hours (12 minutes) and Blue Line overnight (60 minutes). Some buses run all night; some stop at 7 PM. Usually buses arrive every 20 to 30 minutes. Call **CTA** (888/968–7282) for information on specific routes.

cta buses

They can be slowed by traffic, but if you can't get there by train, you can by bus. Buses hit most places in the city, and most connect with at least one train station during their route. Express buses to the north side from the Loop cost an extra 25¢. Expect buses to be stuffed during rush hours. Information and directions to anywhere in the city or suburbs via rapid transit or bus is available any time from the **CTA Travel Information Line** (888/968–7282).

pace buses

If you're traveling to the suburbs, a Pace bus should be able to serve you. Regular fare is $1.25; transfer from a CTA bus or train is an extra 10¢. For more information on Pace hours and schedules, call **Pace Passenger Services** (847/364–PACE) weekdays.

cta trains

The rapid-transit train system is known as the El—short for elevated—even when the tracks are underground. Each of the seven lines has a color designation and a route name: Blue (O'Hare–Congress-Douglas), Brown (Ravenswood), Green (Lake Englewood–Jackson Park), Orange (Midway), Purple (Evanston), Red (Howard–Dan Ryan), and Yellow (Skokie Swift). Route names roughly indicate boundaries of the route; they were phased out by the CTA in 1999 but are still widely used by locals. Each stop and station entrance is open when the lines are in operation. So whenever and wherever trains are running, you can get on or off at all entries to each station. Information and directions to anywhere in the city or suburbs via rapid transit or bus are available any time from the **CTA Travel Information Line** (888/968–7282).

The CTA has a good safety record, but most trains do not have conductors. So if personal security is a concern at night, ride up front.

taxis

Except when it's raining or snowing, taxis are ubiquitous in popular Chicago neighborhoods and are a good alternative to driving. If you're flagging a cab, look for one with a lit sign—no light means the cab is already occupied. You can also call a cab; if you don't see your cab within 20 minutes after calling, call again. Or go to the closest hotel, where you'll always find a cab. The following are open 24 hours a day: **American-United Cab Association** (773/248–7600); **Checker Taxi** (312/243–2537); **Yellow Cab** (312/829–4222, 312/225–7456 lost & found); **Flash Cab** (773/561–1444).

If you have a complaint about a fare or a driver, call **City of Chicago, Department of Consumer Service, Public Vehicles Operations** (312/744–6227).

A water taxi service along the Chicago River—originating at Michigan Avenue Bridge (north bank–Wrigley Building) with stops at Madison Street and River East—**Wendella Riverbus** ($2 each way; 312/337–1446 for schedule) serves Metra commuters using Union Station and the Ogilvie Transportation Center.

commuter trains

Metra commuter trains run from three downtown terminals (LaSalle Street at LaSalle and Congress, Randolph Street under the Michigan Avenue Prudential Building, and Ogilvie Transportation Center, otherwise known as North Western Station, at Madison and Canal) to more than 230 city and suburban stations.

The Union Pacific North Line runs from the Ogilvie Transportation Center up the north shore to Ravinia Park and Wisconsin. The Union Pacific Northwest Line runs from the Ogilvie Transportation Center through the northwest suburbs including Schaumburg. The Union Pacific Line runs from the Ogilvie Transportation Center through Oak Park and the western suburbs. The Electric Main Line runs from Randolph Street through Beverly and the south suburbs. The Rock Island District Line runs from LaSalle Street to the far south side and on to Joliet. The South Shore Line runs from Randolph Street to McCormick Place and on to Michigan City and South Bend, Indiana.

Metra fares are separate from CTA and are based on distance traveled. Unlimited monthly passes offer a 30% discount. Occasional riders can save 15% if they buy a 10 ride packet, to be used within a year of purchase. A $5 weekend pass is good for unlimited rides on all lines except South Shore. Children under seven ride free with adults.

For route details, call the **Metra Travel Center** (312/322–6777 weekdays; 312/836–7000 evenings and weekends; 800/356–2079 for South Shore Line information).

PUBLICATIONS

daily

Chicago Tribune (312/222–3232). The area's dominant daily newspaper is known for its in-depth news reporting and has bureaus throughout the world. There's a strong roster of daily local columnists, with standouts Bob Greene and Mary Schmich on pop culture and lifestyles; Blair Kamin on architecture (a big deal in Chicago); John Kass on politics; Eric Zorn on local interests; Clarence Page on op-ed; and David Greising on business. Theme sections include technology on Monday, Kid-News on Tuesday, Food Guide on Wednesday, and local entertainment and real estate guides on Saturday and Sunday.

Chicago Sun-Times (312/321–3000). The light tabloid's main claims to fame are film critic Roger Ebert and an especially thorough sports section. Notable daily columnists include radio-TV maven Robert Feder, sportswriter Rick Telander, and local pop culture commentator Richard Roeper. Wednesday is Food section day, and Friday brings the local WeekendPlus entertainment and Home-life real estate guides.

Daily Southtown (708/633–6700). This newspaper focuses on the city's south side and adjacent suburbs.

Daily Herald (847/427–4300). It concentrates on the northwest and west suburbs and is widely available downtown.

Chicago Daily Defender (312/225–2400). This newspaper is geared toward the city's African-American community.

weekly

Chicago Reader (312/828–0350). The free weekly newspaper has Cecil Adams's quirkily informative "Straight Dope" column; Michael Miner's hot commentaries on local media; lengthy feature stories; and the city's most extensive entertainment listings. The classified ads are popular with apartment hunters and alternative-lifestyle consumers. It comes out on Thursday.

Crain's Chicago Business (312/649–5200). A glossy tabloid, it caters to large- and small-business owners with news and local stats. It comes out on Monday.

New City (312/243–8786). This free, slightly alternative entertainment guide is lighter than the *Reader*. It comes out on Thursday.

monthly

Chicago Magazine (312/222–8999). An upscale publication, it has news of the north side's cultural elite, extensive restaurant listings—led by Dennis Ray Wheaton's weighty reviews—and Terry Sullivan's meandering local column.

RADIO STATIONS

fm

WBEZ 91.5, National Public Radio, jazz

WXRT 93.1, alternative

WLIT 93.9, light rock

WXCD 94.7, classic rock

WNUA 95.5, smooth jazz

WNIB 97.1, classical

WLUP 97.9, rock

WFMT 98.7, classical

WUSN 99.5, country

WKQX 101.1, alternative

WTMX 101.9, pop rock

WVAZ 102.7, adult urban contemporary

WOJO 105.1, Spanish

WCKG 105.9, talk

WGCI 107.5, Top 40 soul

am

WSCR 670, sports talk

WGN 720, talk and sports (Cubs)

WBBM 780, news and sports (Bears)

WLS 890, talk and news

WMVP 1000, sports (White Sox, Bulls)

WTAQ 1300, Radio Disney

RECYCLING

You can put your clean paper (including newspaper, magazines, cardboard, and phone books), metals, glass, 1- and 2-grade plastics, and yard waste (grass clippings, weeds leaves, and twigs) into special WMI-brand blue bags for recycling. The blue bags are placed with other refuse for regular garbage pick-up and then hauled to sorting centers; from here the stuff is shipped to businesses that convert it into new paper and packaging materials. Blue bags cost about 11¢ each and are available at most grocery, drug, and hardware stores. Additionally, the city collects household chemical wastes such as paints, solvents, insecticides, weed killers, cleaning products, and batteries twice annually. Call 312/744–1614 for details.

TAXES AND TIPPING

sales tax and beyond

State, county, and city sales taxes total 8.75%. The hotel tax is 14.9% and the meal tax is 8.5%. The city's high gasoline and liquor taxes send many residents across the border into the suburbs or Indiana for fill-ups. Other pesky city taxes include 16¢ per pack of cigarettes.

tipping

If you enjoyed your meal, you should leave between 15% and 20% of the bill as a tip; 20% is becoming the standard. Many restaurants will automatically add a 15% or 18% gratuity to the bill for a large party. Cab drivers also expect about 15%. Just about any personal service providers, such as valet parkers, expect a buck.

TELEVISION

network

The local channels and their affiliates for network television in Chicago are as follows: CBS, Channel 2; NBC, Channel 5; ABC, Channel 7; WB, WGN, Channel 9; PBS, Channels 11 and 20; FOX, Channel 32; Univision, Channel 66; UPN, Channel 50.

cable

Local channel numbers depend on what cable system you're using and what region you're in. **AT&T** (773/434–8710), serves the north, near south, south, and southwest sides. **AT&T-Ameritech New Media** (800/848–2278) serves the south side. **Prime Cable** (773/736–1800) serves the west and northwest sides. **21st Century Telecom** (888/790–2121) serves downtown. Municipal information channels are 23 and 49. The city's cable TV information and complaint line is 312/744–4052.

VOTER REGISTRATION

Any U.S. citizen who is at least 18 and has lived in a city precinct for at least 30 days before the next election can vote in Chicago. Registration is at the **Board of Elections** (69 W. Washington St., Room 600, 312/269–7900) Monday through Friday from 9 AM to 5 PM. Bring two forms of ID, including one with your current address. You can also register at your neighborhood Chicago Public Library branch (312/747–4330 for locations).

WEATHER

Lake Michigan gives the city its own microclimate by moderating temperature extremes, making summer a bit cooler and winter a bit warmer than in the suburbs. Lake moisture creates occasional heavy "lake-effect" snow in the city, and when the wind whips off the lake late-November through mid-April, it can be brutal. In July, when the lake is warm, the city doesn't cool down much at night. For those who want to be ready for any extreme: the city's highest-ever temperature was 105°F and its lowest -27°F. The Weather Channel can be found on cable channel 30 or 62. Many Chicagoans are drawn to Tom Skilling's extensively detailed forecast weeknights at 9:30 on Channel 9.

resources for challenges & crises

BABY-SITTING SERVICES

American Registry for Nannies & Sitters (312/475–1515).

Nurture Network (2446 W. Winona St., 773/561–4610).

Treasured Offspring (8655 S. University Ave., 773/734–4111).

CATERING

general parties

All-American Picnics (704 Magna Dr., Round Lake, 800/974–2642) provides food and games.

Amazing Edibles (2603 W. Chicago Ave., 312/782–9800) caters for breakfast, lunch, and dinner meetings.

Fannie's Catering and Delicatessen (4718 W. Touhy Ave., Lincolnwood, 847/676–4000) specializes in party trays.

Fluky's (6821 N. Western Ave., 773/274–3652) is great for hot dogs as well as Italian beef and Polish sausage.

George Jewell (424 N. Wood St., 312/829–3663) is Chicago's top caterer, with a staff of 400.

Lee & Eddie's (261 Richert Rd., Wood Dale, 773/775–7377) covers corporate and social occasions.

Lem's Bar-B-Que House (5914 S. State St., 773/684–5007) provides ribs, chicken, and fish.

Lisi's (3220 N. Lincoln Ave., 773/348–6000) prepares hors d'oeuvres.

Lonnigan's (3403 W. 79th St., 773/434–9963) creates a homestyle buffet.

Planning Experts Ltd. (10732 S. Emerald Ave., 773/928–7200).

Polka Home Style Sausage (8753 S. Commercial Ave., 773/221–0395).

Sam's Wines & Liquors (1720 N. Marcey St., 312/664–4394) has the area's largest selection of wine, spirits, beer, and gourmet foods.

Wikstrom's Catering (5247 N. Clark St., 773/275–6100) prepares Scandinavian fare for everything from box lunches to weddings.

kids' parties
Amazing Party Productions (680 Broadview Ave., Highland Park, 847/432–8905).

Crafty Parties (1805 W. 95th St., 773/881–0121).

Nina's Party Planner (312/421–2633) serves the Loop area and specializes in popular cartoon theme parties.

Fantasy Headquarters (4065 N. Milwaukee Ave.; 773/777–0222) sells and rents costumes.

CHARITIES

Donate your old clothing, furniture, and computers to either of the following charities: **Salvation Army** (888/574–2587) or **Goodwill** (1001 W. Van Buren St., 312/491–2900).

CHILD ISSUES

Adoption Information Center of Illinois (800/572–2390).

Biracial Family Network (773/288–3644).

Bobby E. Wright Community Health Center (9 E. Kedzie Ave., 773/722–5260).

Family Resource Center on Disabilities (20 E. Jackson Blvd., Room 900, 312/939–3513, TDD 312/939–3519).

Friends of Battered Women & Their Children (2301 W. Howard St., 773/274–5232).

Foster Parent Information Services (800/624–5437).

State of Illinois Foster Care Recruitment (312/793–2160).

CITY GOVERNMENT

complaints
City Hall (121 N. LaSalle St., 311).

City of Chicago Department of Sewers (312/747–7000).

Inspector General Office (773/478–2127) for complaints against city employees, officials, or contractors.

other useful numbers
Aldermanic Info (312/744–3081).

Anti-Graffiti Hotline (312/744–1234).

City of Chicago Department of Streets and Sanitation (312/744–5000).

Mayor's Office (121 N. LaSalle St., 773/744–3300).

Mayor's Office for People with Disabilities (312/744–6673, TDD 312/744–7833).

COAST GUARD
Calumet Harbor Coast Guard (4001 E. 98th St., 773/768–4093).

CONSUMER PROTECTION
Better Business Bureau (312/832–0500).

City of Chicago Consumer Services Department (121 N. LaSalle St., Room 808, 312/744–4006).

Cook County States Attorney General–Consumer Fraud Division (312/603–8700).

COUNSELING & REFERRALS

aids
AIDS Foundation of Chicago (411 S. Wells St., 312/922–2322).

AIDS Hotline Chicago (312/855–0091).

AIDS Legal Council (1835 W. Harrison St., 312/733–8026).

alcoholism
Al-Anon Alateen Center (3859 W. 47th St., 773/890–1141).

Alcoholics Anonymous (200 N. Michigan Ave., 312/346–1475; 800/711–6375 for 24-hour help and referral).

crime
Crime Victims Division Office of the Attorney General (100 W. Randolph St., 312/814–2581).

States Attorney Victim-Witness Assistance Project (2600 S. California Ave., 773/869–7200).

drug abuse
Narcotics Anonymous (708/848–4884) is a 24-hour help line based in Oak Park.

A Safe Haven (2057 W. Jarvis Ave., 773/381–6249) offers sober living alternatives to drugs.

mental health
Illinois Psychiatric Society (20 N. Michigan Ave., 312/263–7391).

Institute for Psychoanalysis (122 S. Michigan Ave., 312/922–7474) gives both treatment and referrals.

Midwest Resources for Counseling and Psychotherapy (5443 S. Washtenaw Ave., 800/924–3488).

rape
Chicago Rape Crisis Hotline (888/293–2080) provides immediate help to victims as well as counseling and emotional assistance.

Resources for Sexual Violence Prevention (5737 S. University Ave., 773/702–7200) is a University of Chicago—based service that has supportive-interactive discussions, self-defense classes, and other relevant programs.

DOCTOR & DENTIST REFERRALS
Advocate Health Care Physician Referral Service (800/323–8622).

Chicago Dental Society Referral Service (312/836–7305).

Chicago Medical Society Referral Service (515 N. Dearborn St., 312/670–2550).

Children's Memorial Hospital (800/543–7362).

1-800-DOCTORS (800/362–8677).

Whole Health Response (773/761–7679) has information on alternative therapies (chiropractic, acupuncture, herbal medicine, nutrition, and massage).

EMERGENCIES

ambulance
Advanced Air Ambulance (312/201–0192) is available 24 hours a day and has a mobile intensive care unit (ICU).

Superior Ambulance Service (773/832–2000) has a mobile ICU as well as non-emergency transport.

Tower Ambulance (773/561–2308).

hospital emergency rooms
Augustana (2035 N. Lincoln Ave., 773/975–5128).

Cook County (1835 W. Harrison St., 312/633–6324).

Edgewater (5700 N. Ashland Ave., 773/878–6000).

Holy Cross (2701 W. 68th St., 773/471–8000).

Michael Reese Hospital (2929 S. Ellis Ave., 312/791–2882).

Northwestern Memorial (251 E. Huron St., 312/926–5188).

Our Lady of the Resurrection Medical Center (5645 W. Addison Ave., 773/794–7601).

Ravenswood (4550 N. Winchester Ave., 773/878–4300).

Rush Presbyterian–St. Luke's (1653 W. Congress Pkwy., 312/942–6428).

St. Mary of Nazareth (2233 W. Division St., 773/770–2418).

Swedish Covenant (5145 N. California Ave., 773/989–3800).

University of Chicago (5841 S. Maryland Ave., 773/702–6250).

poison control
Children's Memorial Hospital (773/880–3800).

Illinois Poison Center (800/942–5969).

suicide prevention
Northwestern Memorial Hospital (312/908–8100).

Ravenswood Hospital Medical Center (773/769–6200).

FAMILY PLANNING

Family Planning Associates Medical Group (773/725–0200 or 312/357–0045).

Planned Parenthood of Chicago (312/427–2275).

Winfield Moody Health Services (312/337–1037).

GAY & LESBIAN CONCERNS

Chicago Area Gay and Lesbian Chamber of Commerce (773/871–4190).

Gay and Lesbian Hotline (773/929–4357).

Gerber-Hart Gay and Lesbian Library and Archives (1127 W. Granville, 773/381–8030) hosts book clubs and other arts-related outlets, in addition to sharing informational materials.

Roommates Solutions (312/755–1887).

HOMEWORK HELP HOTLINES

Chicago Public Library (312/747–4300) fields questions.

Grandma, Please (773/271–0000) offers kids 7–14 help with homework (or just someone to talk with) from 3 to 6 PM schooldays. It's a program of the Jane Addams Hull House Senior Services Division.

HOUSE CLEANING HELP AGENCIES

Citywide Cleaning Service (773/581–5498).

McMaid (312/795–0267).

Mighty Maids–Mighty Men (773/472–7711).

INTERIOR DESIGN & ARCHITECT REFERRALS

American Institute of Architects Chicago (312/670–7770).

American Society of Interior Designers (312/467–5080).

LANDLORD/TENANT ASSISTANCE

Chicago Rents Right Hotline (312/742–7368) answers questions from tenants and landlords about rental relationships.

Illinois Tenants Union (773/478–1133) takes messages regarding landlord/tenant issues.

LEGAL SERVICES

American Civil Liberties Union (ACLU) Chicago (312/201–9740).

Chicago Bar Association (312/554–2001) provides a lawyer referral service to the general public.

Legal Assistance Foundation of Chicago (343 S. Dearborn St., 312/341–1070) is a by-appointment service of the Chicago Bar Association that offers free support in civil matters to Chicago residents who can't afford a lawyer.

West Law Information Center (312/641–3075) has training services for paralegals and law librarians and retrieves case information for center members.

LOST & FOUND

at airlines & airports
Property lost on a plane would be held by the airline; contact the airline directly at the numbers listed under Vacation & Travel information (see below). If your loss occurred on airport grounds, call **Meigs Field** (312/744–4787); **Midway** (773/838–3003); or **O'Hare International** (773/686–2385).

on other public transportation
TRAINS
Amtrak (312/655–2422).

Randolph Street Station (312/322–7819).

Union Station (312/322–4269) for all trains stopping here except Amtrak.

LONG-DISTANCE BUSES
Greyhound/Trailways (Loop: 312/408–5980; 95th St.: 312/408–5999; Cumberland: 773/693–2474).

BUSES & TRAINS
Chicago Transit Authority Buses & Trains (312/664–7200).

Pace Buses (847/364–7223).

Metra Trains (312/322–6777).

lost animals
If you lose your pet, call the **City Animal Care and Control Commission** (312/747–1406). It's easier to find your dog if it's wearing a license tag. In any case, all dogs must be current with rabies shots and be licensed ($2 fee). Licenses are available through the City Clerk Office (312/744–6861).

lost credit cards
American Express (800/528–4800).

Discover Card (800/347–2683).

MasterCard (800/307–7309).

Visa (800/336–8472).

PARKS FOR POOCHES

The Chicago Park District has established "pet-friendly" parks throughout the city. The parks are fenced in for off-leash frolicking. Hours are 7 AM–11 PM daily. Call 312/742-3647 for details:

- **Coliseum Park** *(14th St. and Wabash Ave.)*
- **Dog Beach** *(Belmont Harbor, 3200 N. Lake Shore Dr.)*
- **Hamlin Park** *(3035 N. Hoyne Ave.)*
- **Lots** *at Avondale and Wood, Noble and Blackhawk, and Orleans and Ohio*
- **Margate Park** *(4921 N. Marine Dr.)*
- **Promontory Point** *(5491-93 S. South Shore Dr.)*
- **Walsh Park** *(1722 N. Ashland Ave.)*
- **Wicker Park** *(1425 N. Damen Ave.)*
- **Wiggly Field** *(2645 N. Sheffield Ave.)*

---

lost traveler's checks
American Express Company Travel Service (800/221–7282).

Citibank (800/221–2426).

Thomas Cook (800/287–7362).

ON-LINE SERVICES
Ameritech.net (800/638–8775).

Cyberlink (888/758–4462).

Enteract (312/955–3000).

Interaccess (312/496–4500).

InterConnect DSL (888/551–4375).

SouthChicago.net (312/575–8722).

Suba Internet (773/929–8008).

Surfnet (773/283–9000).

Telocity DSL (888/808–3055).

PETS

adoptions
Anti-Cruelty Society (510 N. LaSalle St., 312/644–8338).

Tree House Animal Foundation (1212 W. Carmen Ave., 773/784–5488).

grooming
Animal Lovers' Pet Salon (2277 N. Clybourn Ave., 773/296–9343).

Betty & Wilma's Scrubbles and Such (912 S. Wabash Ave., 312/986–9797).

Pet Care Plus (811 W. Evergreen Ave., 312/397–9077).

Three Pups in a Tub (556 W. 37th St., 773/268–9274).

training
Chicago Canine Academy (4934 W. Belmont Ave., 773/685–3776).

Koven Dog Training (3927 N. Elston Ave., 773/463–4977).

K9 University (2225 W. North Ave., 773/384–4429).

veterinary hospitals

City Cat Doctor/Chicago Feline Medical Center (600 N. Wells St., 312/944–2287).

Emergency Night Weekend Holiday Vet Service (3123 N. Clybourn Ave., 773/281–7110).

Lakeview Animal Hospital (5009 N. Clark St., 773/561–4860).

VCA Animal Hospital (960 W. Chicago Ave., 312/738–3322).

veterinarian referrals

Friends of Animals (800/321–7387).

PHARMACIES OPEN 24 HOURS

Some Walgreens (800/925–4733) and Osco Drug (800/654–6726) stores are open all night. Call to find out which ones.

POLICE

For burglary, automobile theft, or anything that does not pose an imminent danger, call the Chicago Police by simply dialing 311. For an emergency, dial 911.

The Chicago Police Department recently initiated CAPS (Chicago Alternative Policing Strategy), a proactive partnership between police and community to identify and solve neighborhood crime problems. It involves the use of beat officers and community meetings.

district information

1st District: Central (11 E. 11th St., 312/747–6230).

2nd District: Wentworth (5101 S. Wentworth Ave., 312/747–8366).

3rd District: Grand Crossing (7040 S. Cottage Grove Ave., 312/747–8201).

4th District: South Chicago (2255 E. 103rd St., 312/747–8205).

5th District: Pullman (727 E. 111th St., 312/747–8210).

6th District: Gresham (819 W. 85th St., 312/747–8214).

7th District: Englewood (6120 S. Racine St., 312/747–8220).

8th District: Chicago Lawn (3515 W. 63rd St., 312/747–8224).

9th District: Deering (3501 S. Lowe St., 312/747–8227).

10th District: Marquette (2259 S. Damen Ave., 312/747–8246).

11th District: Harrison (3151 W. Harrison St., 312/746–8386).

12th District: Monroe (100 S. Racine Ave., 312/746–8396).

13th District: Wood (937 N. Wood St., 312/746–8350).

14th District: Shakespeare (2150 N. California Ave., 312/744–8290).

15th District: Austin (5327 W. Chicago Ave., 312/746–8300).

16th District: Jefferson Park (5430 W. Gale St., 312/744–8286).

17th District: Albany Park (4461 N. Pulaski Rd., 312/744–8347).

18th District: East Chicago (113 W. Chicago Ave., 312/744–8230).

19th District: Belmont (2452 W. Belmont Ave., 312/744–5983).

20th District: Foster (1940 W. Foster Ave., 312/744–8330).

21st District: Prairie (300 E. 29th St., 312/747–8340).

22nd District: Morgan Park (1830 W. Monterey St., 312/747–6381).

23rd District: Town Hall (3600 N. Halsted St., 312/744–8320).

24th District: Rogers Park (6464 N. Clark St., 312/744–5907).

25th District: Grand Central (5555 W. Grand Ave., 312/746—8605).

POSTAL SERVICES

General information (312/765–3210).

Zip Code information (312/654–3895).

Chicago Main Office (433 W. Van Buren St., 312/654–3895). Open weekdays 8 to 5, Saturday 7 to 3:30.

There are also post offices in virtually every neighborhood:

Ashburn 60652 (3639 W. 79th St., 773/767–0005).

Auburn Park 60620 (8345 S. Ashland Ave., 773/239–8593).

Austin 60644 (324 S. Laramie Ave., 773/378–4124).

Chicago Lawn 60629 (6037 S. Kedzie Ave., 773/925–3713).

Cicero Branch 60650 (2440 S. Laramie St., 708/652–1120).

Clearing 60638 (5645 S. Archer Ave., 773/767–7052).

Cragin 60639 (5100 W. Grand Ave., 773/237–5822).

Division Street 60651 (5001 W. Division St., 773/378–5348).

Dunning 60634 (6441 W. Irving Park Rd., 773/736–8876).

Edgebrook 60646 (6413 N. Kinzua St., 773/631–8055).

Elmwood Park 60635 (7300 W. Fullerton Ave., 708/453–9010).

Elsdon 60632 (3124 W. 47th St., 773/523–7142).

Englewood 60621 (611 W. 63rd St., 773/873–6972).

Evergreen Park 60642 (9359 S. Kedzie Ave., 708/422–7266).

Fort Dearborn 60610 and 60611 (540 N. Dearborn St., 312/644–7528).

Garfield Park 60624 (4222 W. Madison St., 773/722–4010).

Graceland Annex Station (3645 N. Lincoln Ave., 773/404–5877).

Grand Crossing 60619 (7748 S. Cottage Grove Ave., 773/483–0224).

Harwood Heights 60656 (7101 W. Gunnison St., 708/867–4878).

Hawthorne 60623 (2302 S. Pulaski Rd., 773/522–0466).

Hegewisch 60633 (13234 S. Baltimore Rd., 773/646–0266).

Hyde Park 60615 and 60653 (4601 S. Cottage Grove Ave., 773/924–9221).

Irving Park 60641 (3319 N. Cicero Ave., 773/725–2674).

Jackson Park 60637 (700 E. 61st St., 773/493–3124).

Jefferson Park 60630 (5401 W. Lawrence St., 773/736–1671).

Kedzie-Grace 60618 (3750 N. Kedzie Ave., 773/478–6714).

Lakeview 60613 (1343 W. Irving Park Rd., 773/327–2932).

Lincoln Park 60614 (2643 N. Clark St., 773/525–5959).

Logan Square 60647 (2339 N. California Ave., 773/489–1474).

Loop Station (211 S. Clark St., 312/427–4225).

Merchandise Mart (222 Merchandise Mart Plaza, 312/321–0386).

Midwest 60612 (2419 W. Monroe St., 312/243–1603).

Morgan Park 60643 (1805 W. Monterey St., 773/238–3441).

Mount Greenwood 60655 and 60658 (3349 W. 111th St., 773/238–1477).

Niles Branch 60714 (6977 W. Oakton St., 847/967–8848).

Northtown 60645 and 60659 (3401 W. Devon Ave., 773/463–2302).

Norwood Park 60631 (6300 N. Northwest Hwy., 773/776–0793).

Ogden Park 60636 (6559 S. Ashland Ave., 773/776–0793).

Pilsen 60608 (1859 S. Ashland Ave., 773/733–1156).

Ravenswood 60625 (2522 W. Lawrence Ave., 773/561–9294).

Riverdale Branch 60627 (419 W. 144th St., 708/849–7088).

Rogers Park 60626 and 60660 (1723 W. Devon St., 773/508–1200).

Roseland 60628 (11033 S. State St., 773/928–6611).

South Chicago 60617 (9308 S. South Chicago Ave., 773/221–4893).

South Shore 60649 (2207 E. 57th St., 773/375–4022).

Stockyards 60609 (4101 S. Halsted St., 773/247–6901).

Twenty-Second Street 60616 (2035 S. State St., 312/225–9110).

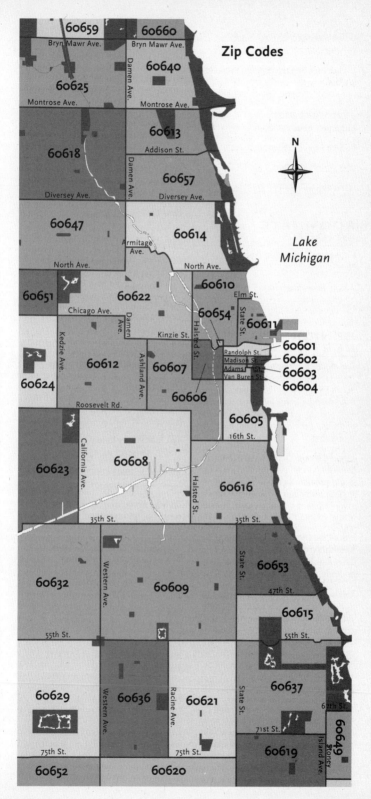

Zip Codes

60659
Bryn Mawr Ave.

60660
Bryn Mawr Ave.

60640

60625
Montrose Ave.

Damen Ave.

Montrose Ave.

60618

60613
Addison St.

60657

Diversey Ave.
Diversey Ave.

Damen Ave.

60647

60614

Armitage Ave.

North Ave.
North Ave.

Lake Michigan

N

60651

60622

60610
Elm St.

Chicago Ave.

60654

Damen Ave.

Kinzie St.

Halsted St.

State St.

60611

Randolph St.   60601
Madison St.   60602
Adams St.   60603
Van Buren St.   60604

60624

Kedzie Ave.

60612

Ashland Ave.

60607

60606

60605
16th St.

Roosevelt Rd.

60623

California Ave.

60608

Halsted St.

60616
35th St.

35th St.

60632

Western Ave.

60609

State St.

60653
47th St.

60615
55th St.

55th St.

60629

Western Ave.

60636

Racine Ave.

60621

State St.

60637

67th St.

Stoney Island Ave.

60649

71st St.

75th St.

75th St.

60619

60652

60620

Uptown 60640 (4850 N. Broadway, 773/561–8916).

Wicker Park 60622 (1635 W. Division St., 312/278–1919).

overnight mail
Airborne Express (800/974–7933).

Federal Express (800/463–3339).

UPS (800/742–5877).

USPS Express Mail (312/983–8450).

ROOMMATE FINDERS

Roommate Connection (160 E. Illinois St., 312/755–1887).

Simply Roommates (2438 N. Clark St., 773/755–4400).

SENIOR CITIZEN SERVICES

City of Chicago Department on Aging (general information: 121 N. LaSalle St., Room 100, 312/744–4016; ombudsman–nursing home information: 510 N. Peshtigo Ct., 312/744–5957; job training and placement: 510 N. Peshtigo Ct., 312/744–4407).

City of Chicago Department of Human Services (510 N. Peshtigo Ct., 312/744–5000) provides agency referrals, information, and other services to needy senior citizens on a short-term, on-site basis.

Elder Care Consulting Services (888/848–0700) offers protective services, case management, pre-screening, and referrals.

Metropolitan Family Services (312/986–4000), formerly United Charities, provides elder care at neighborhood-based centers throughout the city.

TELEVISION– CABLE COMPANIES

Ameritech/Americast (888/325–8090) serves a portion of the southwest side bordered roughly by 59th Street on the north to the city limits on the south and Ashland on the east to Central on the west, plus the neighborhood of Beverly.

AT&T Cable Services (773/434–8710) serves almost all of the city except part of the south side.

UTILITIES

gas
Peoples Gas (312/240–4000, 312/240–7000 for customer service, 312/240–7001 for emergencies).

electric
Com Ed (800/334–7661).

telephone
Ameritech (800/244–4444, 888/611–4466 for repairs).

water
City of Chicago Water Department (312/744–7038).

VOLUNTEERING

Donating time and skills to the work of local organizations is a great way to get acquainted with a neighborhood and meet people with similar interests.

Ada S. McKinley Community Services (725 S. Wells St., 312/554–0600).

Association House of Chicago (2150 W. North Ave., 773/772–7170).

Chicago Association for Retarded Citizens (8 S. Michigan Ave., 312/346–6230).

Chicago Lighthouse for the Blind (1850 W. Roosevelt Rd., 312/666–1331).

Chicago Urban League (4510 S. Michigan Ave., 773/285–5800).

Horizons Gay & Lesbian Community Services (961 W. Montana St., 773/472–6469).

Illinois Mentor (850 W. Jackson Blvd., 312/421–0703).

James Jordan Boys & Girls Club Family Center (2102 W. Monroe St., 312/226–2323).

Jane Addams Center Hull House Association (3212 N. Broadway, 773/549–1631).

Latin-American Youth Center (731 W. 17th St., 312/243–8508).

Lawyers Assistance Program (321 S. Plymouth Ct., 312/922–7332).

Little Brothers Friends of the Elderly (1603 S. Michigan Ave., 312/786–0501).

Volunteers of America (224 N. Desplaines Ave., 312/707–8707).

West Side Chicago Habitat for Humanity (3836 W. Lexington Ave., 773/826–9418).

ZONING & PLANNING

Building Permits (312/744–3450).

Commission on Landmarks (312/744–3200).

Department of Zoning (312/744–9042).

Electrical Permits (312/744–3464).

Mayor's Office for People with Disabilities (312/744–4441).

Plan Commission (312/744–4490).

learning

ACTING SCHOOLS

Act One Studio (640 N. LaSalle St., 312/787–9384) has adult and teen classes of all levels for stage, camera, and voice; the Meisner Technique is used.

Actors Gymnasium (929 Noyes St., Evanston, 847/328–2795) provides classes for children and adults that stress physicality, notably circus arts.

ETA Creative Arts Foundation (7558 S. South Chicago Ave., 773/752–3955) has African-American acting, dance, and music classes.

ImprovOlympic (3541 N. Clark St., 773/880–9993) has long-form (35-minute) improvisation training developed by Charna Halpern and the late Del Close.

Meyer Creativity (3540 N. Southport Ave., 773/281–1901) has Improv-skill training that helps people learn to accept and build upon unexpected situations in the workplace.

Player's Workshop (2936 N. Southport Ave., 773/929–6288) is the training school of Second City.

ART & PHOTOGRAPHY SCHOOLS

American Academy of Art (332 S. Michigan Ave., 312/461–0600) teaches a wide variety of visual arts, including graphic design, advertising design, painting, drawing, and computer art, but no photography.

Boulevard Arts Center (6011 S. Justin St., 773/476–4900) offers painting, drawing, theater, dance, music, and photography.

Columbia College (600 S. Michigan Ave., 312/663–1600; 773/989–3310 for Dance Center) specializes in performing, visual, media, and communication arts; degrees are offered.

Drawing Workshop (3 E. Ontario St., 312/944–5414) provides representational drawing at all levels; the skeletal structure is taught with clay.

Illinois Institute of Art (350 N. Orleans St., 800/351–3450) focuses on visual arts, fashion, interior design, and multimedia; degrees are offered.

Morning Glory Studio (1446 N. Wells St., 312/337–4422) has jewelry-making.

Palette & Chisel Academy of Fine Art (1012 N. Dearborn St., 312/642–4400) teaches life and still-life drawing, painting, and sculpting.

School of the Art Institute (37 S. Wabash Ave., 312/899–5100) has studio, performance, film, and video arts, plus history and theory. It's part of the Art Institute of Chicago; degrees are offered.

BALLROOM DANCING

Chicago Ballroom and Studio (3660 W. Irving Park Rd., 773/267–3411) gives swing, Latin, and waltz classes for singles or groups.

Eden Dance Services (4875 N. Magnolia St. and other locations, 773/769–1256) provides Latin classes for singles or groups.

Kasper Dance Studio (3201 N. Long Ave., 773/545–0222) has Latin and standard styles—such as English and Viennese waltzes, tango, slow fox trot, quick step—for all ages.

Kathy Brown Dance Studio (various locations throughout the city, 773/327–7645) teaches Latin, tango, and swing, plus stepping and country classes for singles or groups.

COLLEGES AND UNIVERSITIES

Chicago City Colleges (Daley College, 7500 S. Pulaski Rd., 773/838–7500; Harold Washington College, 30 E. Lake St., 312/553–5600; Malcolm X College, 1900 W. Van Buren Ave., 312/850–7000; Olive-Harvey College, 10001 S. Woodlawn Ave., 773/291–6100; Truman College, 1145 W. Wilson Ave., 773/878–1700; West Side Technical Institute, 2800 S. Western Ave., 773/843–4500; Wright College, 4300 N. Narragansett Ave., 773/777–7900, and 3400 N. Austin Ave., 773/481–8811.)

Chicago State University (9501 S. King Dr., 773/995–2402).

Columbia College (600 S. Michigan Ave., 312/663–1600).

DePaul University (1 E. Jackson Blvd., 312/362–8300; 2320 N. Kenmore Ave., 773/325–7000).

DeVry Institute of Technology (3300 N. Campbell Ave., 773/929–6550).

Illinois Institute of Technology (3300 S. Federal St., 312/567–3000).

MacCormac College (506 S. Wabash Ave., 312/922–1884).

North Park University (3225 W. Foster Ave., 773/244–6200).

Northeastern University (5500 N. St. Louis Ave., 773/583–4050).

Northwestern University, Chicago (710 N. Lake Shore Dr., 312/908–8649).

Robert Morris College (401 S. State St., 800/225–1520).

Roosevelt University (430 S. Michigan Ave., 312/341–3500).

University of Chicago (5801 S. Ellis Ave., 773/702–1234).

University of Illinois at Chicago (601 S. Morgan St., 312/996–7000).

COMPUTER TRAINING

Computer Learning Centers (200 S. Michigan Ave., 312/252–2946) teaches business systems, client-server, networks.

Computer Training Source (444 N. Wabash Ave., 312/923–2100, ext. 607) has home and office instruction, including one-day classes.

Mac University (1000 N. Halsted St., 312/943–9000) gives guidance to Apple computer users.

COOKING SCHOOLS

The **Chopping Block** (1324 W. Webster Ave., 773/472–6700) covers knife skills, sushi, and fish on the grill.

Cooking Academy of Chicago (2500 W. Bradley Pl., 773/478–9840) has hands-on evening classes teaching healthful cooking, bread-making, and more.

Cooking and Hospitality Institute of Chicago (361 W. Chestnut St., 312/944–2725) gives single classes and courses on knife skills, cake decorating, nutrition, baking, and pastry.

Culinary School of Kendall College (2408 Orrington Ave., Evanston, 847/866–1304) offers degree programs in culinary arts and management, as well as a one-year, part-time certificate in professional cookery or baking and pastry.

Oriental Market and Cooking School (2801 W. Howard St., 773/274–2826) provides single classes and courses in Chinese, Japanese, Korean, Indonesian, and Thai cooking.

CREATIVE WRITING

Chicago Dramatists Workshop (1105 W. Chicago Ave., 312/633–0630) teaches playwriting, screenwriting, and dramaturgy classes.

Newberry Library (60 W. Walton St., 312/255–3700) regularly schedules seminars and other classes on topics such as

poetry, memoirs, scripts, and murder
mysteries.

DANCE

Hedweg School of Dance (Chicago Cultural Center, 78 E. Washington St., 773/871–0872) gives classes for adults in modern, jazz, African, improv, flamenco, and swing, as well as yoga.

Joel Hall Dance Center (1511 W. Berwyn Ave., 773/293–0900) instructs ages three to adult in ballet, jazz, modern, African, and ballet.

Lou Conte Dance Studio (1147 W. Jackson St., 312/850–9766) caters to all abilities in jazz, ballet, hip-hop, modern. It also teaches dance fitness. It's affiliated with Hubbard Street Dance Chicago.

Ruth Page Foundation School of Dance (1016 N. Dearborn St., 312/337–6543) has classes for children and adults in ballet, jazz, and tap.

Sammy Dyer School (2411 S. Michigan Ave., 312/842–5934) provides instruction for all ages in ballet, tap, and jazz. It also has tumbling.

LANGUAGE SCHOOLS

esl
American English Academy (180 N. Michigan Ave., 312/853–0434).

English Language Education (310 S. Michigan Ave., 312/986–9798).

Feltre School (22 W. Erie St., 312/255–1133) specializes in English grammar for writing and public speaking.

french
Alliance Française de Chicago (810 N. Dearborn St., 312/337–1070).

Berlitz Language Center (875 N. Michigan Ave., 312/943–4262; 2 N. LaSalle St., 312/782–6820).

Inlingua School of Languages (200 W. Madison St., 312/641–0488).

german
Berlitz Language Center (875 N. Michigan Ave., 312/943–4262; 2 N. LaSalle St., 312/782–6820).

Goethe-Institute Chicago (150 N. Michigan Ave., 312/263–0472).

Inlingua School of Languages (200 W. Madison St., 312/641–0488).

italian
Berlitz Language Center (875 N. Michigan Ave., 312/943–4262; 2 N. LaSalle St., 312/782–6820).

Inlingua School of Languages (200 W. Madison St., 312/641–0488).

japanese
Berlitz Language Center (875 N. Michigan Ave., 312/943–4262; 2 N. LaSalle St., 312/782–6820).

Inlingua School of Languages (200 W. Madison St., 312/641–0488).

International Language Communications School (625 N. Michigan Ave., 773/549–6441).

spanish
Berlitz Language Center (875 N. Michigan Ave., 312/943–4262; 2 N. LaSalle St., 312/782–6820).

Inlingua School of Languages (200 W. Madison St., 312/641–0488).

Instituto Cervantes (875 N. Michigan Ave., 312/335–1996).

Spanish Studio (722 W. Diversey Pkwy.; 65 E. Wacker Dr.; 5650 S. Woodlawn Ave.; 773/348–2216) has Spanish Dinner Club conversation gatherings.

MUSIC SCHOOLS

Chicago Area Music Teachers Association (410 S. Michigan Ave., 312/427–0282) provides a referral service.

Bloom School of Jazz (520 N. Michigan Ave., 312/957–9300).

Jack Cecchini Guitar Studios (5344 N. Magnolia St., 773/275–4656) provides classical and modern guitar instruction.

Old Town School of Folk Music (909 W. Armitage Ave. and 4544 N. Lincoln Ave., 773/728–6000) teaches everything from violin to ukulele, plus other theater and movement classes for children ages six months through adults.

Sherwood Conservatory (1312 S. Michigan Ave., 312/427–6267) offers classical music training for all ages.

Suzuki-Orff School for Young Musicians (1148 W. Chicago Ave., 312/738–2646) specializes in classical violin and viola instruction.

WINE PROGRAMS

Chicago Wine School (2001 S. Halsted St., 312/266–9463), Patrick W. Fegan's independent school, presents five-week sessions at various levels.

House of Glunz (1206 N. Wells St., 312/642–3000) stages public tastings throughout the year, plus 60–80 private tastings for oenophiles from all over the Midwest.

Wine Tutors (474 N. Lake Shore Dr., 312/644–4858) will book classes for small groups.

vacation & travel information

AIRLINES

Aer Lingus (800/223–6537).

Aeroflot (888/340–6400).

Aeroméxico (800/237–6639).

Air Canada (800/776–3000).

Air France (800/237–2747).

Air India (800/621–8231).

Air Jamaica (800/523–5585).

Alaska Airlines (800/426–0333).

Alitalia (800/223–5730).

All Nippon Airways (800/235–9262).

America West (800/235–9292).

American Airlines/American Eagle (800/433–7300).

ATA/America Trans Air (800/435–9282).

Austrian Airlines (800/843–0002).

British Airways (800/247–9297).

Canadian Airlines (800/426–7000).

ComAir (800/354–9822).

Continental Airlines (800/525–0280 domestic, 800/231–0856 international).

Delta Airlines (800/221–1212).

El Al Israel (800/223–6700).

Frontier Airlines (800/432–1359).

Iberia Airlines (800/772–4642).

Japan Airlines (800/525–3663).

KLM Royal Dutch Airlines (800/374–7747).

Korean Air (800/438–5000).

Kuwait Airways (800/458–9248).

LOT Polish Airlines (800/223–0593).

Lufthansa (800/645–3880).

Mexicana (800/531–7921).

National Airlines (888/757–5387).

Northwest Airlines (800/225–2525 domestic, 800/447–4747 international).

Pro Air (800/477–6247).

Royal Jordanian (800/223–0470).

Sabena (800/955–2000).

SAS/Scandinavian Airlines (800/221–2350).

Southwest Airlines (800/435–9792).

Swissair (800/221–4750).

Tarom (773/601–2944).

Turkish Airlines (800/874–8875).

TWA (800/221–2000).

United Airlines (800/241–6522).

United Express/Great Lakes (800/241–6522).

US Airways (800/428–4322).

Vanguard Airlines (800/826–4827).

Virgin Atlantic (800/862–8621).

AIRPORTS

Chicago has two major airports. **O'Hare** (773/686–2200), if not technically the world's busiest airport, certainly feels like it. Its frumpy little sister, **Midway Airport** (773/767–0500), is undergoing a massive makeover to accommodate its growing lineup of value-priced domestic airlines. Construction is scheduled to last into 2004; meanwhile, allow an extra 30 minutes' travel time for traffic delays that may result. A 24-hour hot line, 773/643–9295, gives the latest construction lowdown. **Meigs Field** (312/922–5454), on the lakefront, primarily serves as a convenience for downtown corporate big guys and politicians commuting to and from the state capital. For lost and found, *see* At Airlines and Airports *in* Lost & Found, *above.*

getting there by public transportation

The Blue Line elevated train will take you from the Loop to right inside O'Hare's main terminal in less than an hour; the Orange Line gets you to Midway's main terminal in about 30 minutes. Each of these options costs a mere $1.50.

If you're traveling to O'Hare from the Loop by taxi, expect to pay nearly $40 with tip during rush hour and about $30 if there's no traffic. A ride to Midway from downtown will run around $30.

Some downtown hotels offer a shuttle to either airport for around $15; ask your concierge. Remember that taxis and shuttles are prone to the horrors of Chicago traffic.

Meigs Field is essentially in the Loop, so getting a cab into the city is easy.

getting there by car

Traffic is often backed up (no matter what the hour) to O'Hare. Take I–90 (Kennedy Expressway) directly to O'Hare. You can access I–90 west from I–94 (the Edens Expressway). If you are going to the airport in the evening (after 7 PM) or very early morning (before 6:45 AM), you can make good time on the highway.

O'HARE PARKING

Before starting out for O'Hare, call the parking hot line (800/547–5673). Within 2½ mi of the airport, parking availability updates are broadcast at 800 AM.

If time is tight and money isn't, the valet service near busy Terminal 1 is an option (Main Parking Garage, Level 1-A; $10 for the first hour, up to $30 a day). The pick-up/drop-off area is covered and there's a dedicated exit lane. For most folks, the Main Parking Garage serves as a centrally located sending-off and picking-up

point ($3 for the first hour, $20 for four hours, up to $50 a day).

Daily parking is available within short walks of domestic Terminals 1, 2, and 3 (Main Parking Garage, Levels 2C-6, and Outside Lots B and C; $3 for the first hour, up to $21 a day). The International Terminal 5 also has a lot for meeting and greeting (Lot D; $3 for the first hour, up to $29 a day).

Two options for long-term parking are just north of the airport. Economy Lot E ($2 for the first hour, up to $12 a day) is the closer of the two. Park and allow an extra 15 minutes to ride the ATS rail service to the terminals. Economy Lot F ($8 a day) is at Mannheim and Zemke Roads. Park and take a free shuttle bus to Lot E to connect with the ATS to the terminals; allow an extra 30 minutes.

Major credit cards are accepted at all lots. For more O'Hare parking details, call 773/686–2853.

Additionally, a lot is operated by **Park N Jet** (4005 N. Mannheim Rd., Schiller Park; 847/671–7275) just south of O'Hare. The cost is $8 a day, and there are free shuttle rides to all terminals.

MIDWAY PARKING

Close to the airport, drivers can tune their radios to 800 AM for traffic and parking information. The parking garage is off Cicero Avenue immediately behind the new main terminal and adjacent to the CTA Orange Line train station. To access the garage, take Cicero Avenue to Kilpatrick Avenue. For hourly parking, go to Level 3 ($3 for 30 minutes to one hour, up to $49 a day). Daily parking is on Levels 4, 5, and 6 (3 for 30 minutes to one hour, up to $20 a day).

Long-term lots are just north of the airport. The Blue Economy Lot is on 55th Street between Central and Cicero avenues. Park and take a free shuttle bus to the terminals; allow an extra 30 minutes. The Red Economy Lot is a bit closer to Cicero Avenue. The Yellow Economy Lot is closer still at 55th Street and Cicero Avenue. Enter off 55th Street at Kilpatrick Avenue; allow an extra 25 minutes for the shuttle ride ($4 for 1 to 2 hours, up to $8 a day).

There is also a lot operated by **Midway Park Saver** (4607 W. 59th St., 773/582–2233; $5.70 a day), adjacent to the CTA Orange Line station.

O'Hare International Airport

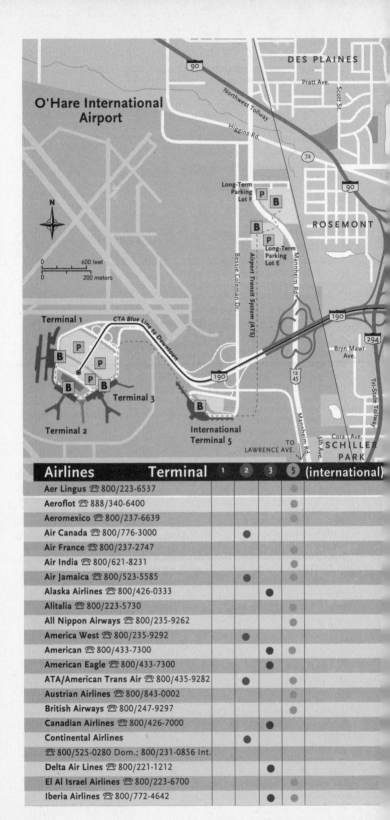

Airlines / Terminal	1	2	3	5 (international)
Aer Lingus ☎ 800/223-6537				●
Aeroflot ☎ 888/340-6400				●
Aeromexico ☎ 800/237-6639				●
Air Canada ☎ 800/776-3000		●		
Air France ☎ 800/237-2747				●
Air India ☎ 800/621-8231				●
Air Jamaica ☎ 800/523-5585		●		
Alaska Airlines ☎ 800/426-0333			●	
Alitalia ☎ 800/223-5730				●
All Nippon Airways ☎ 800/235-9262				●
America West ☎ 800/235-9292		●		
American ☎ 800/433-7300			●	●
American Eagle ☎ 800/433-7300			●	
ATA/American Trans Air ☎ 800/435-9282		●	●	
Austrian Airlines ☎ 800/843-0002				●
British Airways ☎ 800/247-9297				●
Canadian Airlines ☎ 800/426-7000			●	
Continental Airlines ☎ 800/525-0280 Dom.; 800/231-0856 Int.		●		
Delta Air Lines ☎ 800/221-1212			●	
El Al Israel Airlines ☎ 800/223-6700				●
Iberia Airlines ☎ 800/772-4642			●	●

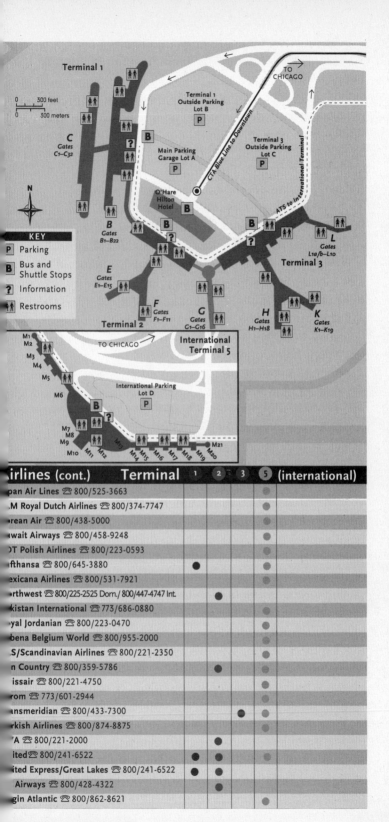

KEY

P	Parking
B	Bus and Shuttle Stops
?	Information
🚻	Restrooms

Terminal 1

0 — 300 feet
0 — 300 meters

C
Gates
C1–C32

N

Terminal 1
Outside Parking
Lot B
P

B

Main Parking
Garage Lot A
P

CTA Blue Line to Downtown

TO CHICAGO

Terminal 3
Outside Parking
Lot C
P

ATS to International Terminal

O'Hare
Hilton
Hotel
B

B
Gates
B1–B22

B

?

B

?

L
Gates
L1a/b–L10

Terminal 3

E
Gates
E1–E15

F
Gates
F1–F11

G
Gates
G1–G16

H
Gates
H1–H18

K
Gates
K1–K19

Terminal 2

M1
M2
M3
M4
M5
M6

TO CHICAGO

International
Terminal 5

International Parking
Lot D
P

B

?

M7
M8
M9
M10 M11 M12 M13 M14 M15 M16 M17 M18 M19 M20 M21

Airlines (cont.) Terminal	1	2	3	5 (international)
pan Air Lines ☎ 800/525-3663				●
M Royal Dutch Airlines ☎ 800/374-7747				●
rean Air ☎ 800/438-5000				●
wait Airways ☎ 800/458-9248				●
T Polish Airlines ☎ 800/223-0593				●
fthansa ☎ 800/645-3880	●			●
exicana Airlines ☎ 800/531-7921				●
rthwest ☎ 800/225-2525 Dom./ 800/447-4747 Int.		●		●
kistan International ☎ 773/686-0880				●
yal Jordanian ☎ 800/223-0470				●
bena Belgium World ☎ 800/955-2000				●
S/Scandinavian Airlines ☎ 800/221-2350				●
n Country ☎ 800/359-5786		●		●
issair ☎ 800/221-4750				●
rom ☎ 773/601-2944				●
ansmeridian ☎ 800/433-7300			●	●
rkish Airlines ☎ 800/874-8875				●
'A ☎ 800/221-2000		●		
ited ☎ 800/241-6522	●	●		●
ited Express/Great Lakes ☎ 800/241-6522	●	●		
Airways ☎ 800/428-4322		●		
gin Atlantic ☎ 800/862-8621				●

295

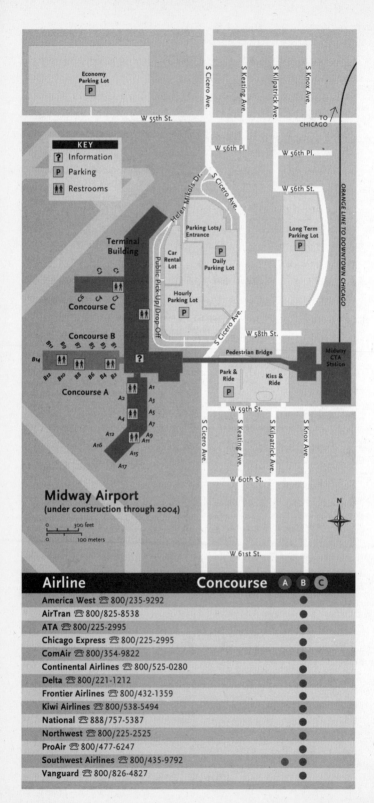

KEY

?	Information
P	Parking
🚻	Restrooms

Economy Parking Lot [P]

W 55th St.

S Cicero Ave.
S Keating Ave.
S Kilpatrick Ave.
S Knox Ave.

TO CHICAGO

W 56th Pl.
W 56th Pl.

W 56th St.

Helen Mikois Dr.
S Cicero Ave.

Parking Lots/ Entrance

Long Term Parking Lot [P]

ORANGE LINE TO DOWNTOWN CHICAGO

Terminal Building

Car Rental Lot

Daily Parking Lot [P]

Public Pick-Up/Drop-Off

Concourse C

Hourly Parking Lot [P]

Concourse B

S Cicero Ave.

W 58th St.

B14
B12 B10 B8 B6 B4 B2

Pedestrian Bridge

Midway CTA Station

Concourse A

A1
A2 A3
A4 A5
A7
A9
A12 A11
A16 A15
A17

Park & Ride [P]

Kiss & Ride

W 59th St.

S Cicero Ave.
S Keating Ave.
S Kilpatrick Ave.
S Knox Ave.

Midway Airport
(under construction through 2004)

0 ——— 300 feet
0 ——— 100 meters

W 60th St.

N

W 61st St.

Airline	Concourse (A)	(B)	(C)
America West ☎ 800/235-9292		●	
AirTran ☎ 800/825-8538		●	
ATA ☎ 800/225-2995		●	
Chicago Express ☎ 800/225-2995		●	
ComAir ☎ 800/354-9822		●	
Continental Airlines ☎ 800/525-0280		●	
Delta ☎ 800/221-1212		●	
Frontier Airlines ☎ 800/432-1359		●	
Kiwi Airlines ☎ 800/538-5494		●	
National ☎ 888/757-5387		●	
Northwest ☎ 800/225-2525		●	
ProAir ☎ 800/477-6247		●	
Southwest Airlines ☎ 800/435-9792	●	●	
Vanguard ☎ 800/826-4827		●	

CAR RENTAL

major agencies
Avis (800/831–2847; Loop, 312/782–6825).

Budget (773/686–6800).

Dollar (O'Hare, 773/686–2030; Midway, 773/735–7200).

Enterprise (800/736–8222).

Hertz (800/654–3131; O'Hare, 773/686–7272; Midway, 773/735–7272; Loop, 312/726–1476).

National (O'Hare, 800/227–7368; Midway, 773/471–3450; Loop, 312/236–2581).

Rent-a-Wreck (Midway, 773/585–7300; Lakeview, 773/281–1111).

local agencies
Lipin Rent-a-Car & Truck (1800 N. Ashland Ave., 773/278–7300).

Paragon Auto Leasing (2550 N. Cicero Ave., 773/622–7660).

Superior Auto Rental (12107 S. Halsted St., 773/821–7566).

CURRENCY EXCHANGE

Most Chicago banks do not exchange foreign currency, so it is best to arrive with some American dollars.

American Express Travel Agency (122 S. Michigan Ave., 312/435–2595; 625 N. Michigan Ave., 312/435–2570).

Foreign Currency Exchange (O'Hare International Airport, International Terminal 5, ground level, 773/686–7965).

Thomas Cook Currency Services, Inc. (100 E. Walton St., 312/649–0288).

World's Money Exchange (6 E. Randolph St., 312/641–2151).

EMBASSIES & CONSULATES

Austria (400 N. Michigan Ave., 312/222–1515).

Belgium (333 N. Michigan Ave., 312/263–6624).

Canada (180 N. Stetson St., 312/616–1860).

Chile (875 N. Michigan Ave., 312/654–8780).

Colombia (500 N. Michigan Ave., 312/923–1196).

Dominican Republic (4051 N. Kilbourn Ave., 773/427–8863).

Ecuador (500 N. Michigan Ave., 312/329–0266).

El Salvador (104 S. Michigan Ave., 312/332–1393).

England (400 N. Michigan Ave., 312/464–6120).

France (737 N. Michigan Ave., 312/787–5359).

Germany (676 N. Michigan Ave., 312/580–1199).

Ghana (19 S. LaSalle St., 312/236–0440).

Guatemala (200 N. Michigan Ave., 312/332–1587).

India (455 N. City Front Plaza, 312/595–0405).

Indonesia (72 E. Randolph St., 312/345–9300).

Ireland (400 N. Michigan Ave., 312/337–1868).

Israel (111 E. Wacker Dr., 312/297–4800).

Italy (500 N. Michigan Ave., 312/467–1550).

Korea (455 N. City Front Plaza, 312/822–9485).

Mexico (300 N. Michigan Ave., 312/332–7352).

Peru (180 N. Michigan Ave., 312/782–1599).

Philippines (30 N. Michigan Ave., 312/332–6458).

Poland (1530 N. Lake Shore Dr., 312/337–8166).

South Africa (200 S. Michigan Ave., 312/939–7929).

Spain (180 N. Michigan Ave., 312/782–4588).

Switzerland (737 N. Michigan Ave., 312/915–0061).

Thailand (700 N. Rush St., 312/664–3129).

Turkey (360 N. Michigan Ave., 312/263–0644).

Ukraine (10 E. Huron St., 312/642–4388).

Venezuela (20 N. Wacker Dr., 312/236–9655).

INOCULATIONS, VACCINATIONS & TRAVEL HEALTH

Travelers Medical Immunization Services (offices in Chicago, Oak Lawn, Crystal Lake, Gurnee, and Hinsdale; 888/220–6432).

Travel Immunization Service of Illinois Masonic Medical Center (938 W. Nelson St., 773/296–8414).

PASSPORTS

During peak travel times January through July, apply at least four weeks in advance of scheduled departure. Call before going, as certain information and documentation are necessary. The fee is $60. Some renewals can be done through the mail. Renewals cost $40. There are 30 designated post offices and outlying Clerk of Court offices that process passports. For information, contact **Chicago Passport Agency** (230 S. Dearborn St., Room 380, 312/341–6020), which is open weekdays 9–4. This office can accommodate late applications. Expedited service costs an extra $35.

passport photo agencies

Two identical photos are needed. These can be done by any photographer—even many Walgreens drug stores can take them—as long as they fit the required specifications.

Glenn's Custom Photo (951 W. Armitage Ave., 773/472–5050).

U.S. Passport Photo Service (27 W. Jackson Blvd., ground floor, 312/922–1234).

ROUTING SERVICES FOR U.S. TRIPS

AAA-Chicago Motor Club (100 W. Randolph St., Suite 213, Chicago 60601, 800/222–4357; $49.95 basic annual fee).

Allstate Motor Club (1500 Shure Dr., Arlington Heights 60004, 800/214–5132; $59.95 basic annual fee).

Amoco Motor Club (Box 4441, Carol Stream 60197, 800/732–9600; $68 basic annual fee).

Shell Motorist Club (Box 60199, Chicago 60660, 800/355–7263; $54 basic annual fee).

TOURIST INFORMATION

for local information

For general information and brochures, contact the city and state tourism offices below. The Chicago Office of Tourism will send out free information packets; call its toll-free phone number in advance (*see below*). You can also investigate its Web site, www.ci.chi.il.us/tourism. Visit one of Chicago's Welcome Centers for more city information.

CITYWIDE INFORMATION

Chicago Convention and Tourism Bureau, Inc. (McCormick Place-on-the-Lake, 2301 S. Lake Shore Dr., Chicago 60616, 312/567–8500 or 800/226–6632, 312/567–8533 for automated Fax Back Information Service) has guides, brochures, maps, and events listings oriented toward helping facilitate conventions, conferences, and groups.

Chicago Office of Tourism (Chicago Department of Cultural Affairs, 78 E. Washington St., Chicago 60602, 312/744–6630; to request an information packet call 312/744–2400 or 800/226–6632, TTY 312/744–2947 or 800/406–6418) is the source for brochures, maps, guides, and monthly events listings.

Mayor's Office of Special Events, General Information, and Activities (121 N. LaSalle St., Room 703, 60602, 312/744–3315, 312/744–3370 for 24-hour hot line).

Walk-In Welcome Centers: Water Works Pumping Station (163 E. Pearson St., daily 7:30–7); Chicago Cultural Center (77 E. Randolph St., weekdays 10–6, weekends 10–5); Illinois Market Place at Navy Pier (700 E. Grand Ave., Mon.– Thurs. 10–8, Fri.–Sat. 10–10, Sun. 10–8).

STATEWIDE INFORMATION

Illinois Bureau of Tourism (100 W. Randolph St., Suite 3-400, 60601, 312/814–4732, 800/226–6632 for brochures).

Illinois Tourist Information Center (100 W. Randolph St., Lobby) is open for walk-ins only, 8:30 AM–4:30 PM weekdays.

NEIGHBORING STATE INFORMATION

Indiana (statewide, 800/216–4612; Michigan City/LaPorte County, 800/634–2650).

Michigan (statewide, 888/784–7328; Harbor Country/New Buffalo, 800/362–7251).

Wisconsin (statewide, 800/432–8747; Door County, 800/527–3529).

for planning your travels

Considering a trip abroad? Tourist offices can send you brochures and answer travel questions.

British Tourist Authority (800/462–2748).

French Government Tourist Office (676 N. Michigan Ave., 312/751–7800).

Italian Government Travel Office (500 N. Michigan Ave., 312/644–0990).

Jamaica Tourist Board (500 N. Michigan Ave., 312/527–1295).

Japan National Tourist Organization (401 N. Michigan Ave., 312/222–0874).

Korea National Tourism Organization (737 N. Michigan Ave., 312/981–1717).

Mexican Government Tourism Office (300 N. Michigan Ave., 312/606–9252).

Netherlands Board of Tourism (312/819–1500).

Spain National Tourism Office (845 N. Michigan Ave., 312/642–1992).

U.S. Virgin Islands Tourist Office (500 N. Michigan Ave., 312/670–8784).

TRAVELER'S AID

Travelers & Immigrants Aid (773/686–7562 at O'Hare International Airport, or 773/489–7303).

U.S. CUSTOMS

U.S. Customs Service, Public Information (610 S. Canal St., 312/353–6100).

Immigration & Naturalization Service (219 S. Dearborn St., 312/353–7334).

visa information & travel advisories

Call the embassy, consulate, or tourist office of the country you plan to visit for up-to-date information on visa requirements, travel advisories, and service strikes. For U.S. State Department advisories on specific countries, call 877/394–8747 or 202/647–5225.

Ask Immigration (800/375–5283) answers questions on immigration, citizenship, visas, relatives abroad, and more.

U.S. Customs Service (312/886–5102) handles questions regarding the importation of goods.

DIRECTORIES

alphabetical listing of resources & topics

restaurants by neighborhood

shops by neighborhood

resources & topics

restaurants by neighborhood

shops by neighborhood

GRAND CROSSING

Part of the Solution, Inc. (fabrics), 100

GREEKTOWN

Athenian Candle Co. (candles), 81

HUMBOLDT PARK

Roeser's (food & drink, breads & pastries), 104

HYDE PARK

Gold Standard & Chalet Wine Shops (food & drink, wine & spirits), 109

Great Frame Up (framing), 110

O'Gara and Wilson, Booksellers Ltd. (books, antiquarian), 77

Powell's Bookstore (books, antiquarian), 77

Seminary Cooperative Bookstore, Inc. (books, general), 79

Sunflower Seed Health Foods (food & drink, health foods), 108

University of Chicago Bookstore (books, general), 79

JEFFERSON PARK

American Science & Surplus (miscellany), 122

Monk's Herb Center (food & drink, herbs & spices), 108

Napoleon's Tailor (clothing for men/general, unusual sizes), 87

Polonia Bookstore (ethnic items), 99

Sportiff Importer Ltd. (bicycles), 77

LAKEVIEW

Aardvark Eyewear (eyewear), 99

Aiko's Art Materials (art supplies), 72

Antique Resources (antiques, furniture), 70

Around the World Tobacco (tobacconist), 129

Babygap (clothing for children), 81–82

Barker & Meowsky (pets & pet supplies), 124

Barnes & Noble (books, general), 78

Billy Hork Framing (framing), 110

Bittersweet (food & drink, breads & pastries), 103

Boaters World CYN (sporting goods & clothing, boating), 126

Body Shop (beauty, fragrances & skin products), 73–74

Borders Books & Music (books, general), 78

Casa Compos (ethnic items), 98

CB2 (home furnishings), 112–113

Century Mall (mall and shopping center), 67

Chicago Antique Centre (antique center & flea market), 69

Chicago Music Exchange (music, musical instruments), 123

Coffee & Tea Exchange (food & drink, coffee & tea), 105

Contacts & Specs Unlimited (eyewear), 99

Cosmetic Center (beauty, fragrances & skin products), 74

Crest Lighting Studios (home furnishings, lamps & lighting), 118

Cupid's Treasures (erotica), 98

Danger City (antiques, furniture), 71

Daniels Antiques (antiques, furniture), 71

Elizabeth Marie (home furnishings, furniture & accessories), 116

Express (clothing for women/general, classic & casual), 87–88

Father Time Antiques (watches & clocks, antique), 132

Flashy Trash (clothing for women/general, vintage), 93

Flower Bucket (flowers & plants, florist), 101

Flower Cart (flowers & plants, florist), 101–102

Fly Paper (gifts & souvenirs), 111

Fourth World Artisans (ethnic items), 98

Frame Factory (framing), 110

Gap Kids (clothing for children), 82

Gold Standard & Chalet Wine Shops (food & drink, cheese, wine & spirits), 105, 109

Good Old Days (antiques, collectibles), 70

Great Frame Up (framing), 110

Hancock Fabrics (fabrics), 100

He Who Eats Mud (gifts & souvenirs), 112

Healing Earth Resources (gifts & souvenirs), 112

Hubba Hubba (clothing for women/general, vintage, jewelry, antique & collectible items), 93, 120

Intelligentsia Coffee Roasters and Tea Blenders (food & drink, coffee & tea), 105

J. Toguri Mercantile Company (ethnic items), 99

Johnny Sprocket's (bicycles), 76

Kozy's Bicycle Shop (bicycles), 76

Life Spring (food & drink, health foods), 108

Limited (clothing for women/general, classic & casual), 88

Lincoln Antique Mall (antique center & flea market), 69

Marshall's (clothing for women/general, discount & off-price), 92

Mothers Work Maternity Outlet (clothing for women/specialty, maternity), 95

National Rubber Stamp Company (stationery & office supplies), 127–128

Nuts on Clark (food & drink, nuts & seeds), 109

Office Depot (stationery & office supplies), 128

Office Max (stationery & office supplies), 128

P.O.S.H. (home furnishings, china, glassware, porcelain, pottery, silver), 116

Paper Boy (stationery & office supplies), 129

Pass the Salt & Pepper (linens), 122

MAGNIFICENT MILE

333

CITY NOTES

CITY NOTES

CITY NOTES

CITY NOTES

CITY NOTES